W9-CFR-898

American Casebook Series
Hornbook Series and Basic Legal Texts
Black Letter Series and Nutshell Series

of

WEST PUBLISHING COMPANY
P.O. Box 64526
St. Paul, Minnesota 55164–0526

Accounting

FARIS' ACCOUNTING AND LAW IN A NUTSHELL, 377 pages, 1984. Softcover. (Text)

FIFLIS, KRIPKE AND FOSTER'S TEACHING MATERIALS ON ACCOUNTING FOR BUSINESS LAWYERS, Third Edition, 838 pages, 1984. (Casebook)

SIEGEL AND SIEGEL'S ACCOUNTING AND FINANCIAL DISCLOSURE: A GUIDE TO BASIC CONCEPTS, 259 pages, 1983. Softcover. (Text)

Administrative Law

BONFIELD AND ASIMOW'S STATE AND FEDERAL ADMINISTRATIVE LAW, 826 pages, 1989. Teacher's Manual available. (Casebook)

GELLHORN AND BOYER'S ADMINISTRATIVE LAW AND PROCESS IN A NUTSHELL, Second Edition, 445 pages, 1981. Softcover. (Text)

MASHAW AND MERRILL'S CASES AND MATERIALS ON ADMINISTRATIVE LAW—THE AMERICAN PUBLIC LAW SYSTEM, Second Edition, 976 pages, 1985. (Casebook) 1989 Supplement.

ROBINSON, GELLHORN AND BRUFF'S THE ADMINISTRATIVE PROCESS, Third Edition, 978 pages, 1986. (Casebook)

Admiralty

HEALY AND SHARPE'S CASES AND MATERIALS ON ADMIRALTY, Second Edition, 876 pages, 1986. (Casebook)

MARAIST'S ADMIRALTY IN A NUTSHELL, Second Edition, 379 pages, 1988. Softcover. (Text)

SCHOENBAUM'S HORNBOOK ON ADMIRALTY AND MARITIME LAW, Student Edition, 692 pages, 1987 with 1989 pocket part. (Text)

Agency—Partnership

FESSLER'S ALTERNATIVES TO INCORPORATION FOR PERSONS IN QUEST OF PROFIT, Second Edition, 326 pages, 1986. Softcover. Teacher's Manual available. (Casebook)

HENN'S CASES AND MATERIALS ON AGENCY, PARTNERSHIP AND OTHER UNINCORPORATED BUSINESS ENTERPRISES, Second Edition, 733 pages, 1985. Teacher's Manual available. (Casebook)

REUSCHLEIN AND GREGORY'S HORNBOOK ON THE LAW OF AGENCY AND PARTNERSHIP, Second Edition, Approximately 650 pages, 1990. (Text)

SELECTED CORPORATION AND PARTNERSHIP STATUTES, RULES AND FORMS. Softcover. 727 pages, 1989.

STEFFEN AND KERR'S CASES ON AGENCY-PARTNERSHIP, Fourth Edition, 859 pages, 1980. (Casebook)

STEFFEN'S AGENCY-PARTNERSHIP IN A NUTSHELL, 364 pages, 1977. Softcover. (Text)

Agricultural Law

MEYER, PEDERSEN, THORSON AND DAVIDSON'S AGRICULTURAL LAW: CASES AND MATERIALS, 931 pages, 1985. Teacher's Manual available. (Casebook)

Alternative Dispute Resolution

KANOWITZ' CASES AND MATERIALS ON ALTER-

List current as of January, 1990

Alternative Dispute Resolution—Cont'd

NATIVE DISPUTE RESOLUTION, 1024 pages, 1986. Teacher's Manual available. (Casebook)

RISKIN AND WESTBROOK'S DISPUTE RESOLUTION AND LAWYERS, 468 pages, 1987. Teacher's Manual available. (Casebook)

RISKIN AND WESTBROOK'S DISPUTE RESOLUTION AND LAWYERS, Abridged Edition, 223 pages, 1987. Softcover. Teacher's Manual available. (Casebook)

TEPLE AND MOBERLY'S ARBITRATION AND CONFLICT RESOLUTION, (The Labor Law Group). 614 pages, 1979. (Casebook)

American Indian Law

CANBY'S AMERICAN INDIAN LAW IN A NUTSHELL, Second Edition, 336 pages, 1988. Softcover. (Text)

GETCHES AND WILKINSON'S CASES AND MATERIALS ON FEDERAL INDIAN LAW, Second Edition, 880 pages, 1986. (Casebook)

Antitrust—see also Regulated Industries, Trade Regulation

FOX AND SULLIVAN'S CASES AND MATERIALS ON ANTITRUST, 935 pages, 1989. Teacher's Manual available. (Casebook)

GELLHORN'S ANTITRUST LAW AND ECONOMICS IN A NUTSHELL, Third Edition, 472 pages, 1986. Softcover. (Text)

HOVENKAMP'S BLACK LETTER ON ANTITRUST, 323 pages, 1986. Softcover. (Review)

HOVENKAMP'S HORNBOOK ON ECONOMICS AND FEDERAL ANTITRUST LAW, Student Edition, 414 pages, 1985. (Text)

OPPENHEIM, WESTON AND MCCARTHY'S CASES AND COMMENTS ON FEDERAL ANTITRUST LAWS, Fourth Edition, 1168 pages, 1981. (Casebook) 1985 Supplement.

POSNER AND EASTERBROOK'S CASES AND ECONOMIC NOTES ON ANTITRUST, Second Edition, 1077 pages, 1981. (Casebook) 1984–85 Supplement.

SULLIVAN'S HORNBOOK OF THE LAW OF ANTITRUST, 886 pages, 1977. (Text)

Appellate Advocacy—see Trial and Appellate Advocacy

Architecture and Engineering Law

SWEET'S LEGAL ASPECTS OF ARCHITECTURE, ENGINEERING AND THE CONSTRUCTION PROCESS, Fourth Edition, 889 pages, 1989. Teacher's Manual available. (Casebook)

Art Law

DUBOFF'S ART LAW IN A NUTSHELL, 335 pages, 1984. Softcover. (Text)

Banking Law

LOVETT'S BANKING AND FINANCIAL INSTITUTIONS LAW IN A NUTSHELL, Second Edition, 464 pages, 1988. Softcover. (Text)

SYMONS AND WHITE'S TEACHING MATERIALS ON BANKING LAW, Second Edition, 993 pages, 1984. Teacher's Manual available. (Casebook) 1987 Supplement.

Business Planning—see also Corporate Finance

PAINTER'S PROBLEMS AND MATERIALS IN BUSINESS PLANNING, Second Edition, 1008 pages, 1984. (Casebook) 1987 Supplement.

Statutory Supplement. *See Selected Corporation and Partnership*

SELECTED CORPORATION AND PARTNERSHIP STATUTES, RULES AND FORMS. 727 pages, 1989. Softcover.

Civil Procedure—see also Federal Jurisdiction and Procedure

AMERICAN BAR ASSOCIATION SECTION OF LITIGATION—READINGS ON ADVERSARIAL JUSTICE: THE AMERICAN APPROACH TO ADJUDICATION, 217 pages, 1988. Softcover. (Coursebook)

CLERMONT'S BLACK LETTER ON CIVIL PROCEDURE, Second Edition, 332 pages, 1988. Softcover. (Review)

COUND, FRIEDENTHAL, MILLER AND SEXTON'S CASES AND MATERIALS ON CIVIL PROCEDURE, Fifth Edition, 1284 pages, 1989. Teacher's Manual available. (Casebook)

COUND, FRIEDENTHAL, MILLER AND SEXTON'S CIVIL PROCEDURE SUPPLEMENT. 419 pages, 1989. Softcover. (Casebook Supplement)

FEDERAL RULES OF CIVIL PROCEDURE—EDUCATIONAL EDITION. Softcover. 622 pages, 1989.

FRIEDENTHAL, KANE AND MILLER'S HORN-

Civil Procedure—Cont'd

BOOK ON CIVIL PROCEDURE, 876 pages, 1985. (Text)

KANE AND LEVINE'S CIVIL PROCEDURE IN CALIFORNIA: STATE AND FEDERAL 498 pages, 1989. Softcover. (Casebook Supplement)

KANE'S CIVIL PROCEDURE IN A NUTSHELL, Second Edition, 306 pages, 1986. Softcover. (Text)

KOFFLER AND REPPY'S HORNBOOK ON COMMON LAW PLEADING, 663 pages, 1969. (Text)

MARCUS, REDISH AND SHERMAN'S CIVIL PROCEDURE: A MODERN APPROACH, 1027 pages, 1989. Teacher's Manual available. (Casebook)

MARCUS AND SHERMAN'S COMPLEX LITIGATION–CASES AND MATERIALS ON ADVANCED CIVIL PROCEDURE, 846 pages, 1985. Teacher's Manual available. (Casebook) 1989 Supplement.

PARK'S COMPUTER-AIDED EXERCISES ON CIVIL PROCEDURE, Second Edition, 167 pages, 1983. Softcover. (Coursebook)

SIEGEL'S HORNBOOK ON NEW YORK PRACTICE, 1011 pages, 1978, with 1987 pocket part. (Text)

Commercial Law

BAILEY AND HAGEDORN'S SECURED TRANSACTIONS IN A NUTSHELL, Third Edition, 390 pages, 1988. Softcover. (Text)

EPSTEIN, MARTIN, HENNING AND NICKLES' BASIC UNIFORM COMMERCIAL CODE TEACHING MATERIALS, Third Edition, 704 pages, 1988. Teacher's Manual available. (Casebook)

HENSON'S HORNBOOK ON SECURED TRANSACTIONS UNDER THE U.C.C., Second Edition, 504 pages, 1979, with 1979 pocket part. (Text)

MURRAY'S COMMERCIAL LAW, PROBLEMS AND MATERIALS, 366 pages, 1975. Teacher's Manual available. Softcover. (Coursebook)

NICKLES' BLACK LETTER ON COMMERCIAL PAPER, 450 pages, 1988. Softcover. (Review)

NICKLES, MATHESON AND DOLAN'S MATERIALS FOR UNDERSTANDING CREDIT AND PAYMENT SYSTEMS, 923 pages, 1987. Teacher's Manual available. (Casebook)

NORDSTROM, MURRAY AND CLOVIS' PROBLEMS AND MATERIALS ON SALES, 515 pages, 1982. (Casebook)

NORDSTROM, MURRAY AND CLOVIS' PROBLEMS AND MATERIALS ON SECURED TRANSACTIONS, 594 pages, 1987. (Casebook)

RUBIN AND COOTER'S THE PAYMENT SYSTEM: CASES, MATERIALS AND ISSUES, 885 pages, 1989. (Casebook)

SELECTED COMMERCIAL STATUTES. Softcover. 1618 pages, 1989.

SPEIDEL'S BLACK LETTER ON SALES AND SALES FINANCING, 363 pages, 1984. Softcover. (Review)

SPEIDEL, SUMMERS AND WHITE'S COMMERCIAL LAW: TEACHING MATERIALS, Fourth Edition, 1448 pages, 1987. Teacher's Manual available. (Casebook)

SPEIDEL, SUMMERS AND WHITE'S COMMERCIAL PAPER: TEACHING MATERIALS, Fourth Edition, 578 pages, 1987. Reprint from Speidel et al., Commercial Law, Fourth Edition. Teacher's Manual available. (Casebook)

SPEIDEL, SUMMERS AND WHITE'S SALES: TEACHING MATERIALS, Fourth Edition, 804 pages, 1987. Reprint from Speidel et al., Commercial Law, Fourth Edition. Teacher's Manual available (Casebook)

SPEIDEL, SUMMERS AND WHITE'S SECURED TRANSACTIONS: TEACHING MATERIALS, Fourth Edition, 485 pages, 1987. Reprint from Speidel et al., Commercial Law, Fourth Edition. Teacher's Manual available. (Casebook)

STOCKTON'S SALES IN A NUTSHELL, Second Edition, 370 pages, 1981. Softcover. (Text)

STONE'S UNIFORM COMMERCIAL CODE IN A NUTSHELL, Third Edition, 580 pages, 1989. Softcover. (Text)

UNIFORM COMMERCIAL CODE, OFFICIAL TEXT WITH COMMENTS. Softcover. 1155 pages, 1987.

WEBER AND SPEIDEL'S COMMERCIAL PAPER IN A NUTSHELL, Third Edition, 404 pages, 1982. Softcover. (Text)

WHITE AND SUMMERS' HORNBOOK ON THE

Commercial Law—Cont'd

UNIFORM COMMERCIAL CODE, Third Edition, Student Edition, 1386 pages, 1988. (Text)

Community Property

MENNELL AND BOYKOFF'S COMMUNITY PROPERTY IN A NUTSHELL, Second Edition, 432 pages, 1988. Softcover. (Text)

VERRALL AND BIRD'S CASES AND MATERIALS ON CALIFORNIA COMMUNITY PROPERTY, Fifth Edition, 604 pages, 1988. (Casebook)

Comparative Law

BARTON, GIBBS, LI AND MERRYMAN'S LAW IN RADICALLY DIFFERENT CULTURES, 960 pages, 1983. (Casebook)

GLENDON, GORDON AND OSAKWE'S COMPARATIVE LEGAL TRADITIONS: TEXT, MATERIALS AND CASES ON THE CIVIL LAW, COMMON LAW AND SOCIALIST LAW TRADITIONS, 1091 pages, 1985. (Casebook)

GLENDON, GORDON AND OSAKWE'S COMPARATIVE LEGAL TRADITIONS IN A NUTSHELL. 402 pages, 1982. Softcover. (Text)

LANGBEIN'S COMPARATIVE CRIMINAL PROCEDURE: GERMANY, 172 pages, 1977. Softcover. (Casebook)

Computers and Law

MAGGS AND SPROWL'S COMPUTER APPLICATIONS IN THE LAW, 316 pages, 1987. (Coursebook)

MASON'S USING COMPUTERS IN THE LAW: AN INTRODUCTION AND PRACTICAL GUIDE, Second Edition, 288 pages, 1988. Softcover. (Coursebook)

Conflict of Laws

CRAMTON, CURRIE AND KAY'S CASES–COMMENTS–QUESTIONS ON CONFLICT OF LAWS, Fourth Edition, 876 pages, 1987. (Casebook)

HAY'S BLACK LETTER ON CONFLICT OF LAWS, 330 pages, 1989. Softcover. (Review)

SCOLES AND HAY'S HORNBOOK ON CONFLICT OF LAWS, Student Edition, 1085 pages, 1982, with 1988–89 pocket part. (Text)

SEIGEL'S CONFLICTS IN A NUTSHELL, 470 pages, 1982. Softcover. (Text)

Constitutional Law—Civil Rights—see also Foreign Relations and National Security Law

ABERNATHY'S CASES AND MATERIALS ON CIVIL RIGHTS, 660 pages, 1980. (Casebook)

BARRON AND DIENES' BLACK LETTER ON CONSTITUTIONAL LAW, Second Edition, 310 pages, 1987. Softcover. (Review)

BARRON AND DIENES' CONSTITUTIONAL LAW IN A NUTSHELL, 389 pages, 1986. Softcover. (Text)

ENGDAHL'S CONSTITUTIONAL FEDERALISM IN A NUTSHELL, Second Edition, 411 pages, 1987. Softcover. (Text)

FARBER AND SHERRY'S HISTORY OF THE AMERICAN CONSTITUTION, 458 pages, 1990. Softcover. (Text)

GARVEY AND ALEINIKOFF'S MODERN CONSTITUTIONAL THEORY: A READER, 494 pages, 1989. Softcover. (Reader)

LOCKHART, KAMISAR, CHOPER AND SHIFFRIN'S CONSTITUTIONAL LAW: CASES–COMMENTS–QUESTIONS, Sixth Edition, 1601 pages, 1986. (Casebook) 1989 Supplement.

LOCKHART, KAMISAR, CHOPER AND SHIFFRIN'S THE AMERICAN CONSTITUTION: CASES AND MATERIALS, Sixth Edition, 1260 pages, 1986. Abridged version of Lockhart, et al., Constitutional Law: Cases–Comments–Questions, Sixth Edition. (Casebook) 1989 Supplement.

LOCKHART, KAMISAR, CHOPER AND SHIFFRIN'S CONSTITUTIONAL RIGHTS AND LIBERTIES: CASES AND MATERIALS, Sixth Edition, 1266 pages, 1986. Reprint from Lockhart, et al., Constitutional Law: Cases–Comments–Questions, Sixth Edition. (Casebook) 1989 Supplement.

MARKS AND COOPER'S STATE CONSTITUTIONAL LAW IN A NUTSHELL, 329 pages, 1988. Softcover. (Text)

NOWAK, ROTUNDA AND YOUNG'S HORNBOOK ON CONSTITUTIONAL LAW, Third Edition, 1191 pages, 1986 with 1988 pocket part. (Text)

ROTUNDA'S MODERN CONSTITUTIONAL LAW: CASES AND NOTES, Third Edition, 1085 pages, 1989. (Casebook) 1989 Supplement.

VIEIRA'S CONSTITUTIONAL CIVIL RIGHTS IN A

Constitutional Law—Civil Rights—Cont'd

NUTSHELL, Second Edition, approximately 320 pages, 1990. Softcover. (Text)

WILLIAMS' CONSTITUTIONAL ANALYSIS IN A NUTSHELL, 388 pages, 1979. Softcover. (Text)

Consumer Law—see also Commercial Law

EPSTEIN AND NICKLES' CONSUMER LAW IN A NUTSHELL, Second Edition, 418 pages, 1981. Softcover. (Text)

SELECTED COMMERCIAL STATUTES. Softcover. 1618 pages, 1989.

SPANOGLE AND ROHNER'S CASES AND MATERIALS ON CONSUMER LAW, 693 pages, 1979. Teacher's Manual available. (Casebook) 1982 Supplement.

Contracts

CALAMARI, AND PERILLO'S BLACK LETTER ON CONTRACTS, 397 pages, 1983. Softcover. (Review)

CALAMARI AND PERILLO'S HORNBOOK ON CONTRACTS, Third Edition, 1049 pages, 1987. (Text)

CALAMARI, PERILLO AND BENDER'S CASES AND PROBLEMS ON CONTRACTS, Second Edition, 905 pages, 1989. Teacher's Manual Available. (Casebook)

CORBIN'S TEXT ON CONTRACTS, One Volume Student Edition, 1224 pages, 1952. (Text)

FESSLER AND LOISEAUX'S CASES AND MATERIALS ON CONTRACTS—MORALITY, ECONOMICS AND THE MARKET PLACE, 837 pages, 1982. Teacher's Manual available. (Casebook)

FRIEDMAN'S CONTRACT REMEDIES IN A NUTSHELL, 323 pages, 1981. Softcover. (Text)

FULLER AND EISENBERG'S CASES ON BASIC CONTRACT LAW, Fourth Edition, 1203 pages, 1981. (Casebook)

HAMILTON, RAU AND WEINTRAUB'S CASES AND MATERIALS ON CONTRACTS, 830 pages, 1984. (Casebook)

JACKSON AND BOLLINGER'S CASES ON CONTRACT LAW IN MODERN SOCIETY, Second Edition, 1329 pages, 1980. Teacher's Manual available. (Casebook)

KEYES' GOVERNMENT CONTRACTS IN A NUTSHELL, 423 pages, 1979. Softcover. (Text)

SCHABER AND ROHWER'S CONTRACTS IN A NUTSHELL, Second Edition, 425 pages, 1984. Softcover. (Text)

SUMMERS AND HILLMAN'S CONTRACT AND RELATED OBLIGATION: THEORY, DOCTRINE AND PRACTICE, 1074 pages, 1987. Teacher's Manual available. (Casebook)

Copyright—see Patent and Copyright Law

Corporate Finance

HAMILTON'S CASES AND MATERIALS ON CORPORATION FINANCE, Second Edition, 1221 pages, 1989. (Casebook)

Corporations

HAMILTON'S BLACK LETTER ON CORPORATIONS, Second Edition, 513 pages, 1986. Softcover. (Review)

HAMILTON'S CASES ON CORPORATIONS—INCLUDING PARTNERSHIPS AND LIMITED PARTNERSHIPS, Third Edition, 1213 pages, 1986. Teacher's Manual available. (Casebook) 1986 Statutory Supplement.

HAMILTON'S THE LAW OF CORPORATIONS IN A NUTSHELL, Second Edition, 515 pages, 1987. Softcover. (Text)

HENN'S TEACHING MATERIALS ON THE LAW OF CORPORATIONS, Second Edition, 1204 pages, 1986. Teacher's Manual available. (Casebook)

Statutory Supplement. *See Selected Corporation and Partnership*

HENN AND ALEXANDER'S HORNBOOK ON LAWS OF CORPORATIONS, Third Edition, Student Edition, 1371 pages, 1983, with 1986 pocket part. (Text)

SELECTED CORPORATION AND PARTNERSHIP STATUTES, RULES AND FORMS. Softcover. 727 pages, 1989.

SOLOMON, SCHWARTZ AND BAUMAN'S MATERIALS AND PROBLEMS ON CORPORATIONS: LAW AND POLICY, Second Edition, 1391 pages, 1988. Teacher's Manual available. (Casebook)

Statutory Supplement. *See Selected Corporation and Partnership*

Corrections

KRANTZ' CASES AND MATERIALS ON THE LAW OF CORRECTIONS AND PRISONERS' RIGHTS,

Corrections—Cont'd

Third Edition, 855 pages, 1986. (Casebook) 1988 Supplement.

KRANTZ' THE LAW OF CORRECTIONS AND PRISONERS' RIGHTS IN A NUTSHELL, Third Edition, 407 pages, 1988. Softcover. (Text)

POPPER'S POST-CONVICTION REMEDIES IN A NUTSHELL, 360 pages, 1978. Softcover. (Text)

ROBBINS' CASES AND MATERIALS ON POST-CONVICTION REMEDIES, 506 pages, 1982. (Casebook)

Creditors' Rights

BANKRUPTCY CODE, RULES AND FORMS, LAW SCHOOL EDITION. 828 pages, 1989. Softcover.

EPSTEIN'S DEBTOR-CREDITOR RELATIONS IN A NUTSHELL, Third Edition, 383 pages, 1986. Softcover. (Text)

EPSTEIN, LANDERS AND NICKLES' CASES AND MATERIALS ON DEBTORS AND CREDITORS, Third Edition, 1059 pages, 1987. Teacher's Manual available. (Casebook)

LOPUCKI'S PLAYER'S MANUAL FOR THE DEBTOR-CREDITOR GAME, 123 pages, 1985. Softcover. (Coursebook)

NICKLES AND EPSTEIN'S BLACK LETTER ON CREDITORS' RIGHTS AND BANKRUPTCY, 576 pages, 1989. (Review)

RIESENFELD'S CASES AND MATERIALS ON CREDITORS' REMEDIES AND DEBTORS' PROTECTION, Fourth Edition, 914 pages, 1987. (Casebook)

WHITE'S CASES AND MATERIALS ON BANKRUPTCY AND CREDITORS' RIGHTS, 812 pages, 1985. Teacher's Manual available. (Casebook) 1987 Supplement.

Criminal Law and Criminal Procedure—see also Corrections, Juvenile Justice

ABRAMS' FEDERAL CRIMINAL LAW AND ITS ENFORCEMENT, 866 pages, 1986. (Casebook) 1988 Supplement.

AMERICAN CRIMINAL JUSTICE PROCESS: SELECTED RULES, STATUTES AND GUIDELINES. 723 pages, 1989. Softcover.

CARLSON'S ADJUDICATION OF CRIMINAL JUSTICE: PROBLEMS AND REFERENCES, 130 pages, 1986. Softcover. (Casebook)

DIX AND SHARLOT'S CASES AND MATERIALS ON CRIMINAL LAW, Third Edition, 846 pages, 1987. (Casebook)

GRANO'S PROBLEMS IN CRIMINAL PROCEDURE, Second Edition, 176 pages, 1981. Teacher's Manual available. Softcover. (Coursebook)

HEYMANN AND KENETY'S THE MURDER TRIAL OF WILBUR JACKSON: A HOMICIDE IN THE FAMILY, Second Edition, 347 pages, 1985. (Coursebook)

ISRAEL, KAMISAR AND LAFAVE'S CRIMINAL PROCEDURE AND THE CONSTITUTION: LEADING SUPREME COURT CASES AND INTRODUCTORY TEXT, 728 pages, Revised 1989 Edition. Softcover. (Casebook)

ISRAEL AND LAFAVE'S CRIMINAL PROCEDURE—CONSTITUTIONAL LIMITATIONS IN A NUTSHELL, Fourth Edition, 461 pages, 1988. Softcover. (Text)

JOHNSON'S CASES, MATERIALS AND TEXT ON CRIMINAL LAW, Third Edition, 783 pages, 1985. Teacher's Manual available. (Casebook)

JOHNSON'S CASES AND MATERIALS ON CRIMINAL PROCEDURE, 859 pages, 1988. (Casebook) 1989 Supplement.

KAMISAR, LAFAVE AND ISRAEL'S MODERN CRIMINAL PROCEDURE: CASES, COMMENTS AND QUESTIONS, Seventh Edition, 1593 pages, 1990. (Casebook) Statutory Supplement.

KAMISAR, LAFAVE AND ISRAEL'S BASIC CRIMINAL PROCEDURE: CASES, COMMENTS AND QUESTIONS, Seventh Edition, 792 pages, 1990. Softcover reprint from Kamisar, et al., Modern Criminal Procedure: Cases, Comments and Questions, Seventh Edition. (Casebook) Statutory Supplement.

LAFAVE'S MODERN CRIMINAL LAW: CASES, COMMENTS AND QUESTIONS, Second Edition, 903 pages, 1988. (Casebook)

LAFAVE AND ISRAEL'S HORNBOOK ON CRIMINAL PROCEDURE, Student Edition, 1142 pages, 1985, with 1989 pocket part. (Text)

LAFAVE AND SCOTT'S HORNBOOK ON CRIMINAL LAW, Second Edition, 918 pages, 1986. (Text)

LANGBEIN'S COMPARATIVE CRIMINAL PROCE-

Criminal Law and Criminal Procedure—Cont'd

DURE: GERMANY, 172 pages, 1977. Softcover. (Casebook)

LOEWY'S CRIMINAL LAW IN A NUTSHELL, Second Edition, 321 pages, 1987. Softcover. (Text)

LOW'S BLACK LETTER ON CRIMINAL LAW, 433 pages, 1984. Softcover. (Review)

SALTZBURG'S CASES AND COMMENTARY ON AMERICAN CRIMINAL PROCEDURE, Third Edition, 1302 pages, 1988. Teacher's Manual available. (Casebook) 1989 Supplement.

UVILLER'S THE PROCESSES OF CRIMINAL JUSTICE: INVESTIGATION AND ADJUDICATION, Second Edition, 1384 pages, 1979. (Casebook) 1979 Statutory Supplement. 1986 Update.

VORENBERG'S CASES ON CRIMINAL LAW AND PROCEDURE, Second Edition, 1088 pages, 1981. Teacher's Manual available. (Casebook) 1987 Supplement.

Decedents' Estates—see Trusts and Estates

Domestic Relations

CLARK'S CASES AND PROBLEMS ON DOMESTIC RELATIONS, Third Edition, 1153 pages, 1980. Teacher's Manual available. (Casebook)

CLARK'S HORNBOOK ON DOMESTIC RELATIONS, Second Edition, Student Edition, 1050 pages, 1988. (Text)

KRAUSE'S BLACK LETTER ON FAMILY LAW, 314 pages, 1988. Softcover. (Review)

KRAUSE'S CASES, COMMENTS AND QUESTIONS ON FAMILY LAW, Third Edition, approximately 1425 pages, 1990. (Casebook)

KRAUSE'S FAMILY LAW IN A NUTSHELL, Second Edition, 444 pages, 1986. Softcover. (Text)

KRAUSKOPF'S CASES ON PROPERTY DIVISION AT MARRIAGE DISSOLUTION, 250 pages, 1984. Softcover. (Casebook)

Economics, Law and—see also Antitrust, Regulated Industries

GOETZ' CASES AND MATERIALS ON LAW AND ECONOMICS, 547 pages, 1984. (Casebook)

Education Law

ALEXANDER AND ALEXANDER'S THE LAW OF SCHOOLS, STUDENTS AND TEACHERS IN A NUTSHELL, 409 pages, 1984. Softcover. (Text)

Employment Discrimination—see also Women and the Law

ESTREICHER AND HARPER'S CASES AND MATERIALS ON THE LAW GOVERNING THE EMPLOYMENT RELATIONSHIP, Approximately 1000 pages, 1990. (Casebook) Statutory Supplement.

JONES, MURPHY AND BELTON'S CASES AND MATERIALS ON DISCRIMINATION IN EMPLOYMENT, (The Labor Law Group). Fifth Edition, 1116 pages, 1987. (Casebook) 1990 Supplement.

PLAYER'S CASES AND MATERIALS ON EMPLOYMENT DISCRIMINATION LAW, Second Edition, 782 pages, 1984. Teacher's Manual available. (Casebook)

PLAYER'S FEDERAL LAW OF EMPLOYMENT DISCRIMINATION IN A NUTSHELL, Second Edition, 402 pages, 1981. Softcover. (Text)

PLAYER'S HORNBOOK ON EMPLOYMENT DISCRIMINATION LAW, Student Edition, 708 pages, 1988. (Text)

Energy and Natural Resources Law—see also Oil and Gas

LAITOS' CASES AND MATERIALS ON NATURAL RESOURCES LAW, 938 pages, 1985. Teacher's Manual available. (Casebook)

SELECTED ENVIRONMENTAL LAW STATUTES—EDUCATIONAL EDITION. Softcover. 1031 pages, 1989.

Environmental Law—see also Energy and Natural Resources Law; Sea, Law of

BONINE AND MCGARITY'S THE LAW OF ENVIRONMENTAL PROTECTION: CASES—LEGISLATION—POLICIES, 1076 pages, 1984. Teacher's Manual available. (Casebook)

FINDLEY AND FARBER'S CASES AND MATERIALS ON ENVIRONMENTAL LAW, Second Edition, 813 pages, 1985. (Casebook) 1988 Supplement.

FINDLEY AND FARBER'S ENVIRONMENTAL LAW IN A NUTSHELL, Second Edition, 367 pages, 1988. Softcover. (Text)

RODGERS' HORNBOOK ON ENVIRONMENTAL

Environmental Law—Cont'd

LAW, 956 pages, 1977, with 1984 pocket part. (Text)

SELECTED ENVIRONMENTAL LAW STATUTES—EDUCATIONAL EDITION. Softcover. 1031 pages, 1989.

Equity—see Remedies

Estate Planning—see also Trusts and Estates; Taxation—Estate and Gift

LYNN'S AN INTRODUCTION TO ESTATE PLANNING IN A NUTSHELL, Third Edition, 370 pages, 1983. Softcover. (Text)

Evidence

BROUN AND BLAKEY'S BLACK LETTER ON EVIDENCE, 269 pages, 1984. Softcover. (Review)

BROUN, MEISENHOLDER, STRONG AND MOSTELLER'S PROBLEMS IN EVIDENCE, Third Edition, 238 pages, 1988. Teacher's Manual available. Softcover. (Coursebook)

CLEARY, STRONG, BROUN AND MOSTELLER'S CASES AND MATERIALS ON EVIDENCE, Fourth Edition, 1060 pages, 1988. (Casebook)

FEDERAL RULES OF EVIDENCE FOR UNITED STATES COURTS AND MAGISTRATES. Softcover. 378 pages, 1989.

GRAHAM'S FEDERAL RULES OF EVIDENCE IN A NUTSHELL, Second Edition, 473 pages, 1987. Softcover. (Text)

KIMBALL'S PROGRAMMED MATERIALS ON PROBLEMS IN EVIDENCE, 380 pages, 1978. Softcover. (Coursebook)

LEMPERT AND SALTZBURG'S A MODERN APPROACH TO EVIDENCE: TEXT, PROBLEMS, TRANSCRIPTS AND CASES, Second Edition, 1232 pages, 1983. Teacher's Manual available. (Casebook)

LILLY'S AN INTRODUCTION TO THE LAW OF EVIDENCE, Second Edition, 585 pages, 1987. (Text)

MCCORMICK, SUTTON AND WELLBORN'S CASES AND MATERIALS ON EVIDENCE, Sixth Edition, 1067 pages, 1987. (Casebook)

MCCORMICK'S HORNBOOK ON EVIDENCE, Third Edition, Student Edition, 1156 pages, 1984, with 1987 pocket part. (Text)

ROTHSTEIN'S EVIDENCE IN A NUTSHELL: STATE AND FEDERAL RULES, Second Edition, 514 pages, 1981. Softcover. (Text)

Federal Jurisdiction and Procedure

CURRIE'S CASES AND MATERIALS ON FEDERAL COURTS, Third Edition, 1042 pages, 1982. (Casebook) 1985 Supplement.

CURRIE'S FEDERAL JURISDICTION IN A NUTSHELL, Second Edition, 258 pages, 1981. Softcover. (Text)

FEDERAL RULES OF CIVIL PROCEDURE—EDUCATIONAL EDITION. Softcover. 622 pages, 1989.

REDISH'S BLACK LETTER ON FEDERAL JURISDICTION, 219 pages, 1985. Softcover. (Review)

REDISH'S CASES, COMMENTS AND QUESTIONS ON FEDERAL COURTS, Second Edition, 1122 pages, 1989. (Casebook)

VETRI AND MERRILL'S FEDERAL COURTS PROBLEMS AND MATERIALS, Second Edition, 232 pages, 1984. Softcover. (Coursebook)

WRIGHT'S HORNBOOK ON FEDERAL COURTS, Fourth Edition, Student Edition, 870 pages, 1983. (Text)

Foreign Relations and National Security Law

FRANCK AND GLENNON'S FOREIGN RELATIONS AND NATIONAL SECURITY LAW, 941 pages, 1987. (Casebook)

Future Interests—see Trusts and Estates

Health Law—see Medicine, Law and

Human Rights—see International Law

Immigration Law

ALEINIKOFF AND MARTIN'S IMMIGRATION PROCESS AND POLICY, 1042 pages, 1985. (Casebook) 1987 Supplement.

WEISSBRODT'S IMMIGRATION LAW AND PROCEDURE IN A NUTSHELL, (Second Edition, 438 pages, 1989, Softcover. (Text)

Indian Law—see American Indian Law

Insurance Law

DEVINE AND TERRY'S PROBLEMS IN INSURANCE LAW, 240 pages, 1989. Softcover. Teacher's Manual available. (Course book)

Insurance Law—Cont'd

DOBBYN'S INSURANCE LAW IN A NUTSHELL, Second Edition, 316 pages, 1989. Softcover. (Text)

KEETON'S CASES ON BASIC INSURANCE LAW, Second Edition, 1086 pages, 1977. Teacher's Manual available. (Casebook)

KEETON AND WIDISS' INSURANCE LAW, Student Edition, 1359 pages, 1988. (Text)

WIDISS AND KEETON'S COURSE SUPPLEMENT TO KEETON AND WIDISS' INSURANCE LAW, 502 pages, 1988. Softcover. (Casebook)

WIDISS' INSURANCE: MATERIALS ON FUNDAMENTAL PRINCIPLES, LEGAL DOCTRINES AND REGULATORY ACTS, 1186 pages, 1989. (Casebook)

YORK AND WHELAN'S CASES, MATERIALS AND PROBLEMS ON GENERAL PRACTICE INSURANCE LAW, Second Edition, 787 pages, 1988. Teacher's Manual available. (Casebook)

International Law—see also Sea, Law of

BUERGENTHAL'S INTERNATIONAL HUMAN RIGHTS IN A NUTSHELL, 283 pages, 1988. Softcover. (Text)

BUERGENTHAL AND MAIER'S PUBLIC INTERNATIONAL LAW IN A NUTSHELL, Second Edition, approximately 255 pages, 1990. Softcover. (Text)

FOLSOM, GORDON AND SPANOGLE'S INTERNATIONAL BUSINESS TRANSACTIONS—A PROBLEM-ORIENTED COURSEBOOK, 1160 pages, 1986. Teacher's Manual available. (Casebook) 1989 Documents Supplement.

FOLSOM, GORDON AND SPANOGLE'S INTERNATIONAL BUSINESS TRANSACTIONS IN A NUTSHELL, Third Edition, 509 pages, 1988. Softcover. (Text)

HENKIN, PUGH, SCHACHTER AND SMIT'S CASES AND MATERIALS ON INTERNATIONAL LAW, Second Edition, 1517 pages, 1987. (Casebook) Documents Supplement.

JACKSON AND DAVEY'S CASES, MATERIALS AND TEXT ON LEGAL PROBLEMS OF INTERNATIONAL ECONOMIC RELATIONS, Second Edition, 1269 pages, 1986. (Casebook) 1989 Documents Supplement.

KIRGIS' INTERNATIONAL ORGANIZATIONS IN THEIR LEGAL SETTING, 1016 pages, 1977. Teacher's Manual available. (Casebook) 1981 Supplement.

WESTON, FALK AND D'AMATO'S INTERNATIONAL LAW AND WORLD ORDER—A PROBLEM-ORIENTED COURSEBOOK, 1195 pages, 1980. Teacher's Manual available. (Casebook) Documents Supplement.

Interviewing and Counseling

BINDER AND PRICE'S LEGAL INTERVIEWING AND COUNSELING, 232 pages, 1977. Teacher's Manual available. Softcover. (Coursebook)

SHAFFER AND ELKINS' LEGAL INTERVIEWING AND COUNSELING IN A NUTSHELL, Second Edition, 487 pages, 1987. Softcover. (Text)

Introduction to Law—see Legal Method and Legal System

Introduction to Law Study

HEGLAND'S INTRODUCTION TO THE STUDY AND PRACTICE OF LAW IN A NUTSHELL, 418 pages, 1983. Softcover (Text)

KINYON'S INTRODUCTION TO LAW STUDY AND LAW EXAMINATIONS IN A NUTSHELL, 389 pages, 1971. Softcover. (Text)

Jurisprudence

CHRISTIE'S JURISPRUDENCE—TEXT AND READINGS ON THE PHILOSOPHY OF LAW, 1056 pages, 1973. (Casebook)

Juvenile Justice

FOX'S CASES AND MATERIALS ON MODERN JUVENILE JUSTICE, Second Edition, 960 pages, 1981. (Casebook)

FOX'S JUVENILE COURTS IN A NUTSHELL, Third Edition, 291 pages, 1984. Softcover. (Text)

Labor and Employment Law—see also Employment Discrimination, Social Legislation

FINKIN, GOLDMAN AND SUMMERS' LEGAL PROTECTION OF INDIVIDUAL EMPLOYEES, (The Labor Law Group). Approximately 1178 pages, 1990. (Casebook)

GORMAN'S BASIC TEXT ON LABOR LAW—UNIONIZATION AND COLLECTIVE BARGAINING, 914 pages, 1976. (Text)

GRODIN, WOLLETT AND ALLEYNE'S COLLEC-

Labor and Employment Law—Cont'd

TIVE BARGAINING IN PUBLIC EMPLOYMENT, (The Labor Law Group). Third Edition, 430 pages, 1979. (Casebook)

LESLIE'S LABOR LAW IN A NUTSHELL, Second Edition, 397 pages, 1986. Softcover. (Text)

NOLAN'S LABOR ARBITRATION LAW AND PRACTICE IN A NUTSHELL, 358 pages, 1979. Softcover. (Text)

OBERER, HANSLOWE, ANDERSEN AND HEINSZ' CASES AND MATERIALS ON LABOR LAW—COLLECTIVE BARGAINING IN A FREE SOCIETY, Third Edition, 1163 pages, 1986. (Casebook) Statutory Supplement.

RABIN, SILVERSTEIN AND SCHATZKI'S LABOR AND EMPLOYMENT LAW: PROBLEMS, CASES AND MATERIALS IN THE LAW OF WORK, (The Labor Law Group). 1014 pages, 1988. Teacher's Manual available. (Casebook) 1988 Statutory Supplement.

Land Finance—Property Security—see Real Estate Transactions

Land Use

CALLIES AND FREILICH'S CASES AND MATERIALS ON LAND USE, 1233 pages, 1986. (Casebook) 1988 Supplement.

HAGMAN AND JUERGENSMEYER'S HORNBOOK ON URBAN PLANNING AND LAND DEVELOPMENT CONTROL LAW, Second Edition, Student Edition, 680 pages, 1986. (Text)

WRIGHT AND GITELMAN'S CASES AND MATERIALS ON LAND USE, Third Edition, 1300 pages, 1982. Teacher's Manual available. (Casebook) 1987 Supplement.

WRIGHT AND WRIGHT'S LAND USE IN A NUTSHELL, Second Edition, 356 pages, 1985. Softcover. (Text)

Legal History—see also Legal Method and Legal System

PRESSER AND ZAINALDIN'S CASES AND MATERIALS ON LAW AND JURISPRUDENCE IN AMERICAN HISTORY, Second Edition, 1092 pages, 1989. Teacher's Manual available. (Casebook)

Legal Method and Legal System—see also Legal Research, Legal Writing

ALDISERT'S READINGS, MATERIALS AND CASES IN THE JUDICIAL PROCESS, 948 pages, 1976. (Casebook)

BERCH AND BERCH'S INTRODUCTION TO LEGAL METHOD AND PROCESS, 550 pages, 1985. Teacher's Manual available. (Casebook)

BODENHEIMER, OAKLEY AND LOVE'S READINGS AND CASES ON AN INTRODUCTION TO THE ANGLO-AMERICAN LEGAL SYSTEM, Second Edition, 166 pages, 1988. Softcover. (Casebook)

DAVIES AND LAWRY'S INSTITUTIONS AND METHODS OF THE LAW—INTRODUCTORY TEACHING MATERIALS, 547 pages, 1982. Teacher's Manual available. (Casebook)

DVORKIN, HIMMELSTEIN AND LESNICK'S BECOMING A LAWYER: A HUMANISTIC PERSPECTIVE ON LEGAL EDUCATION AND PROFESSIONALISM, 211 pages, 1981. Softcover. (Text)

KELSO AND KELSO'S STUDYING LAW: AN INTRODUCTION, 587 pages, 1984. (Coursebook)

KEMPIN'S HISTORICAL INTRODUCTION TO ANGLO-AMERICAN LAW IN A NUTSHELL, Second Edition, 280 pages, 1973. Softcover. (Text)

REYNOLDS' JUDICIAL PROCESS IN A NUTSHELL, 292 pages, 1980. Softcover. (Text)

Legal Research

COHEN'S LEGAL RESEARCH IN A NUTSHELL, Fourth Edition, 452 pages, 1985. Softcover. (Text)

COHEN, BERRING AND OLSON'S HOW TO FIND THE LAW, Ninth Edition, approximately 700 pages, 1989. (Coursebook)

Legal Research Exercises, 3rd Ed., for use with Cohen, Berring and Olson, 229 pages, 1989. Teacher's Manual available.

COHEN, BERRING AND OLSON'S FINDING THE LAW, 570 pages, 1989. Softcover reprint from Cohen, Berring and Olson's How to Find the Law, Ninth Edition. (Coursebook)

ROMBAUER'S LEGAL PROBLEM SOLVING—ANALYSIS, RESEARCH AND WRITING, Fourth Edition, 424 pages, 1983. Teacher's Manual with problems available. (Coursebook)

STATSKY'S LEGAL RESEARCH AND WRITING, Third Edition, 257 pages, 1986. Softcover. (Coursebook)

Legal Research—Cont'd

TEPLY'S LEGAL RESEARCH AND CITATION, Third Edition, 472 pages, 1989. Softcover. (Coursebook)

Student Library Exercises, 3rd ed., 391 pages, 1989. Answer Key available.

Legal Writing

CHILD'S DRAFTING LEGAL DOCUMENTS: MATERIALS AND PROBLEMS, 286 pages, 1988. Softcover. Teacher's Manual available. (Coursebook)

DICKERSON'S MATERIALS ON LEGAL DRAFTING, 425 pages, 1981. Teacher's Manual available. (Coursebook)

FELSENFELD AND SIEGEL'S WRITING CONTRACTS IN PLAIN ENGLISH, 290 pages, 1981. Softcover. (Text)

GOPEN'S WRITING FROM A LEGAL PERSPECTIVE, 225 pages, 1981. (Text)

MELLINKOFF'S LEGAL WRITING—SENSE AND NONSENSE, 242 pages, 1982. Softcover. Teacher's Manual available. (Text)

PRATT'S LEGAL WRITING: A SYSTEMATIC APPROACH, 422 pages, 1989. Teacher's Manual available. (Coursebook)

RAY AND RAMSFIELD'S LEGAL WRITING: GETTING IT RIGHT AND GETTING IT WRITTEN, 250 pages, 1987. Softcover. (Text)

SQUIRES AND ROMBAUER'S LEGAL WRITING IN A NUTSHELL, 294 pages, 1982. Softcover. (Text)

STATSKY AND WERNET'S CASE ANALYSIS AND FUNDAMENTALS OF LEGAL WRITING, Third Edition, 424 pages, 1989. (Text)

TEPLY'S LEGAL WRITING, ANALYSIS AND ORAL ARGUMENT, 576 pages, 1990. Softcover. (Coursebook)

WEIHOFEN'S LEGAL WRITING STYLE, Second Edition, 332 pages, 1980. (Text)

Legislation

DAVIES' LEGISLATIVE LAW AND PROCESS IN A NUTSHELL, Second Edition, 346 pages, 1986. Softcover. (Text)

ESKRIDGE AND FRICKEY'S CASES AND MATERIALS ON LEGISLATION: STATUTES AND THE CREATION OF PUBLIC POLICY, 937 pages, 1988. Teacher's Manual available. (Casebook)

NUTTING AND DICKERSON'S CASES AND MATERIALS ON LEGISLATION, Fifth Edition, 744 pages, 1978. (Casebook)

STATSKY'S LEGISLATIVE ANALYSIS AND DRAFTING, Second Edition, 217 pages, 1984. Teacher's Manual available. (Text)

Local Government

FRUG'S CASES AND MATERIALS ON LOCAL GOVERNMENT LAW, 1005 pages, 1988. (Casebook)

MCCARTHY'S LOCAL GOVERNMENT LAW IN A NUTSHELL, Second Edition, 404 pages, 1983. Softcover. (Text)

REYNOLDS' HORNBOOK ON LOCAL GOVERNMENT LAW, 860 pages, 1982, with 1987 pocket part. (Text)

VALENTE'S CASES AND MATERIALS ON LOCAL GOVERNMENT LAW, Third Edition, 1010 pages, 1987. Teacher's Manual available. (Casebook) 1989 Supplement.

Mass Communication Law

GILLMOR, BARRON, SIMON AND TERRY'S CASES AND COMMENT ON MASS COMMUNICATION LAW, Fifth Edition, 947 pages, 1990. (Casebook)

GINSBURG'S REGULATION OF BROADCASTING: LAW AND POLICY TOWARDS RADIO, TELEVISION AND CABLE COMMUNICATIONS, 741 pages, 1979 (Casebook) 1983 Supplement.

ZUCKMAN, GAYNES, CARTER AND DEE'S MASS COMMUNICATIONS LAW IN A NUTSHELL, Third Edition, 538 pages, 1988. Softcover. (Text)

Medicine, Law and

FURROW, JOHNSON, JOST AND SCHWARTZ' HEALTH LAW: CASES, MATERIALS AND PROBLEMS, 1005 pages, 1987. Teacher's Manual available. (Casebook) 1989 Supplement.

HALL AND ELLMAN'S HEALTH CARE LAW AND ETHICS IN A NUTSHELL, Approximately 389 pages, 1990. Softcover (Text)

KING'S THE LAW OF MEDICAL MALPRACTICE IN A NUTSHELL, Second Edition, 342 pages, 1986. Softcover. (Text)

SHAPIRO AND SPECE'S CASES, MATERIALS AND PROBLEMS ON BIOETHICS AND LAW, 892 pages, 1981. (Casebook)

Medicine, Law and—Cont'd

SHARPE, FISCINA AND HEAD'S CASES ON LAW AND MEDICINE, 882 pages, 1978. (Casebook)

Military Law

SHANOR AND TERRELL'S MILITARY LAW IN A NUTSHELL, 378 pages, 1980. Softcover. (Text)

Mortgages—see Real Estate Transactions

Natural Resources Law—see Energy and Natural Resources Law, Environmental Law

Negotiation

GIFFORD'S LEGAL NEGOTIATION: THEORY AND APPLICATIONS, 225 pages, 1989. Softcover. (Text)

PECK'S CASES AND MATERIALS ON NEGOTIATION, (The Labor Law Group). Second Edition, 280 pages, 1980. (Casebook)

WILLIAMS' LEGAL NEGOTIATION AND SETTLEMENT, 207 pages, 1983. Softcover. Teacher's Manual available. (Coursebook)

Office Practice—see also Computers and Law, Interviewing and Counseling, Negotiation

HEGLAND'S TRIAL AND PRACTICE SKILLS IN A NUTSHELL, 346 pages, 1978. Softcover (Text)

STRONG AND CLARK'S LAW OFFICE MANAGEMENT, 424 pages, 1974. (Casebook)

Oil and Gas—see also Energy and Natural Resources Law

HEMINGWAY'S HORNBOOK ON OIL AND GAS, Second Edition, Student Edition, 543 pages, 1983, with 1989 pocket part. (Text)

KUNTZ, LOWE, ANDERSON AND SMITH'S CASES AND MATERIALS ON OIL AND GAS LAW, 857 pages, 1986. Teacher's Manual available. (Casebook) Forms Manual. Revised.

LOWE'S OIL AND GAS LAW IN A NUTSHELL, Second Edition, 465 pages, 1988. Softcover. (Text)

Partnership—see Agency—Partnership

Patent and Copyright Law

CHOATE, FRANCIS AND COLLINS' CASES AND MATERIALS ON PATENT LAW, INCLUDING TRADE SECRETS, COPYRIGHTS, TRADEMARKS, Third Edition, 1009 pages, 1987. (Casebook)

MILLER AND DAVIS' INTELLECTUAL PROPERTY—PATENTS, TRADEMARKS AND COPYRIGHT IN A NUTSHELL, 428 pages, 1983. Softcover. (Text)

NIMMER'S CASES AND MATERIALS ON COPYRIGHT AND OTHER ASPECTS OF ENTERTAINMENT LITIGATION ILLUSTRATED—INCLUDING UNFAIR COMPETITION, DEFAMATION AND PRIVACY, Third Edition, 1025 pages, 1985. (Casebook) 1989 Supplement.

Products Liability

FISCHER AND POWERS' CASES AND MATERIALS ON PRODUCTS LIABILITY, 685 pages, 1988. Teacher's Manual available. (Casebook)

NOEL AND PHILLIPS' CASES ON PRODUCTS LIABILITY, Second Edition, 821 pages, 1982. (Casebook)

PHILLIPS' PRODUCTS LIABILITY IN A NUTSHELL, Third Edition, 307 pages, 1988. Softcover. (Text)

Professional Responsibility

ARONSON, DEVINE AND FISCH'S PROBLEMS, CASES AND MATERIALS IN PROFESSIONAL RESPONSIBILITY, 745 pages, 1985. Teacher's Manual available. (Casebook)

ARONSON AND WECKSTEIN'S PROFESSIONAL RESPONSIBILITY IN A NUTSHELL, 399 pages, 1980. Softcover. (Text)

MELLINKOFF'S THE CONSCIENCE OF A LAWYER, 304 pages, 1973. (Text)

PIRSIG AND KIRWIN'S CASES AND MATERIALS ON PROFESSIONAL RESPONSIBILITY, Fourth Edition, 603 pages, 1984. Teacher's Manual available. (Casebook)

ROTUNDA'S BLACK LETTER ON PROFESSIONAL RESPONSIBILITY, Second Edition, 414 pages, 1988. Softcover. (Review)

SCHWARTZ AND WYDICK'S PROBLEMS IN LEGAL ETHICS, Second Edition, 341 pages, 1988. (Coursebook)

SELECTED STATUTES, RULES AND STANDARDS ON THE LEGAL PROFESSION. Softcover. 549 pages, 1989.

SMITH AND MALLEN'S PREVENTING LEGAL

Professional Responsibility—Cont'd

MALPRACTICE, 264 pages, 1989. Reprint from Mallen and Smith's Legal Malpractice, Third Edition. (Text)

SUTTON AND DZIENKOWSKI'S CASES AND MATERIALS ON PROFESSIONAL RESPONSIBILITY FOR LAWYERS, 839 pages, 1989. (Casebook)

WOLFRAM'S HORNBOOK ON MODERN LEGAL ETHICS, Student Edition, 1120 pages, 1986. (Text)

Property—see also Real Estate Transactions, Land Use, Trusts and Estates

BERNHARDT'S BLACK LETTER ON PROPERTY, 318 pages, 1983. Softcover. (Review)

BERNHARDT'S REAL PROPERTY IN A NUTSHELL, Second Edition, 448 pages, 1981. Softcover. (Text)

BOYER'S SURVEY OF THE LAW OF PROPERTY, Third Edition, 766 pages, 1981. (Text)

BROWDER, CUNNINGHAM, NELSON, STOEBUCK AND WHITMAN'S CASES ON BASIC PROPERTY LAW, Fifth Edition, 1386 pages, 1989. Teacher's Manual available. (Casebook)

BRUCE, ELY AND BOSTICK'S CASES AND MATERIALS ON MODERN PROPERTY LAW, Second Edition, 953 pages, 1989. Teacher's Manual available. (Casebook)

BURKE'S PERSONAL PROPERTY IN A NUTSHELL, 322 pages, 1983. Softcover. (Text)

CUNNINGHAM, STOEBUCK AND WHITMAN'S HORNBOOK ON THE LAW OF PROPERTY, Student Edition, 916 pages, 1984, with 1987 pocket part. (Text)

DONAHUE, KAUPER AND MARTIN'S CASES ON PROPERTY, Second Edition, 1362 pages, 1983. Teacher's Manual available. (Casebook)

HILL'S LANDLORD AND TENANT LAW IN A NUTSHELL, Second Edition, 311 pages, 1986. Softcover. (Text)

KURTZ AND HOVENKAMP'S CASES AND MATERIALS ON AMERICAN PROPERTY LAW, 1296 pages, 1987. Teacher's Manual available. (Casebook) 1988 Supplement.

MOYNIHAN'S INTRODUCTION TO REAL PROPERTY, Second Edition, 239 pages, 1988. (Text)

UNIFORM LAND TRANSACTIONS ACT, UNIFORM SIMPLIFICATION OF LAND TRANSFERS ACT, UNIFORM CONDOMINIUM ACT, 1977 OFFICIAL TEXT WITH COMMENTS. Softcover. 462 pages, 1978.

Psychiatry, Law and

REISNER'S LAW AND THE MENTAL HEALTH SYSTEM, CIVIL AND CRIMINAL ASPECTS, 696 pages, 1985. (Casebook) 1987 Supplement.

Real Estate Transactions

BRUCE'S REAL ESTATE FINANCE IN A NUTSHELL, Second Edition, 262 pages, 1985. Softcover. (Text)

MAXWELL, RIESENFELD, HETLAND AND WARREN'S CASES ON CALIFORNIA SECURITY TRANSACTIONS IN LAND, Third Edition, 728 pages, 1984. (Casebook)

NELSON AND WHITMAN'S BLACK LETTER ON LAND TRANSACTIONS AND FINANCE, Second Edition, 466 pages, 1988. Softcover. (Review)

NELSON AND WHITMAN'S CASES ON REAL ESTATE TRANSFER, FINANCE AND DEVELOPMENT, Third Edition, 1184 pages, 1987. (Casebook)

NELSON AND WHITMAN'S HORNBOOK ON REAL ESTATE FINANCE LAW, Second Edition, 941 pages, 1985 with 1989 pocket part. (Text)

OSBORNE'S CASES AND MATERIALS ON SECURED TRANSACTIONS, 559 pages, 1967. (Casebook)

Regulated Industries—see also Mass Communication Law, Banking Law

GELLHORN AND PIERCE'S REGULATED INDUSTRIES IN A NUTSHELL, Second Edition, 389 pages, 1987. Softcover. (Text)

MORGAN, HARRISON AND VERKUIL'S CASES AND MATERIALS ON ECONOMIC REGULATION OF BUSINESS, Second Edition, 666 pages, 1985. (Casebook)

Remedies

DOBBS' HORNBOOK ON REMEDIES, 1067 pages, 1973. (Text)

DOBBS' PROBLEMS IN REMEDIES. 137 pages, 1974. Teacher's Manual available. Softcover. (Coursebook)

DOBBYN'S INJUNCTIONS IN A NUTSHELL, 264

Remedies—Cont'd

pages, 1974. Softcover. (Text)

FRIEDMAN'S CONTRACT REMEDIES IN A NUTSHELL, 323 pages, 1981. Softcover. (Text)

LEAVELL, LOVE AND NELSON'S CASES AND MATERIALS ON EQUITABLE REMEDIES, RESTITUTION AND DAMAGES, Fourth Edition, 1111 pages, 1986. Teacher's Manual available. (Casebook)

MCCORMICK'S HORNBOOK ON DAMAGES, 811 pages, 1935. (Text)

O'CONNELL'S REMEDIES IN A NUTSHELL, Second Edition, 320 pages, 1985. Softcover. (Text)

YORK, BAUMAN AND RENDLEMAN'S CASES AND MATERIALS ON REMEDIES, Fourth Edition, 1029 pages, 1985. Teacher's Manual available. (Casebook)

Sea, Law of

SOHN AND GUSTAFSON'S THE LAW OF THE SEA IN A NUTSHELL, 264 pages, 1984. Softcover. (Text)

Securities Regulation

HAZEN'S HORNBOOK ON THE LAW OF SECURITIES REGULATION, Student Edition, 739 pages, 1985, with 1988 pocket part. (Text)

RATNER'S MATERIALS ON SECURITIES REGULATION, Third Edition, 1000 pages, 1986. Teacher's Manual available. (Casebook) 1989 Supplement.

Statutory Supplement. *See Selected Securities Regulation*

RATNER'S SECURITIES REGULATION IN A NUTSHELL, Third Edition, 316 pages, 1988. Softcover. (Text)

SELECTED STATUTES, REGULATIONS, RULES, DOCUMENTS AND FORMS ON SECURITIES REGULATION. Softcover. Approximately 1250 pages, 1990.

Social Legislation

HOOD AND HARDY'S WORKERS' COMPENSATION AND EMPLOYEE PROTECTION IN A NUTSHELL, 274 pages, 1984. Softcover. (Text)

LAFRANCE'S WELFARE LAW: STRUCTURE AND ENTITLEMENT IN A NUTSHELL, 455 pages, 1979. Softcover. (Text)

MALONE, PLANT AND LITTLE'S CASES ON WORKERS' COMPENSATION AND EMPLOYMENT RIGHTS, Second Edition, 951 pages, 1980. Teacher's Manual available. (Casebook)

Sports Law

SCHUBERT, SMITH AND TRENTADUE'S SPORTS LAW, 395 pages, 1986. (Text)

Tax Practice and Procedure

GARBIS, STRUNTZ AND RUBIN'S CASES AND MATERIALS ON TAX PROCEDURE AND TAX FRAUD, Second Edition, 687 pages, 1987. (Casebook)

Taxation—Corporate

KAHN AND GANN'S CORPORATE TAXATION, Third Edition, 980 pages, 1989. Teacher's Manual available. (Casebook)

WEIDENBRUCH AND BURKE'S FEDERAL INCOME TAXATION OF CORPORATIONS AND STOCKHOLDERS IN A NUTSHELL, Third Edition, 309 pages, 1989. Softcover. (Text)

Taxation—Estate & Gift—see also Estate Planning, Trusts and Estates

MCNULTY'S FEDERAL ESTATE AND GIFT TAXATION IN A NUTSHELL, Fourth Edition, 496 pages, 1989. Softcover. (Text)

PENNELL'S CASES AND MATERIALS ON INCOME TAXATION OF TRUSTS, ESTATES, GRANTORS AND BENEFICIARIES, 460 pages, 1987. Teacher's Manual available. (Casebook)

Taxation—Individual

DODGE'S THE LOGIC OF TAX, 343 pages, 1989. Softcover. (Text)

GUNN AND WARD'S CASES, TEXT AND PROBLEMS ON FEDERAL INCOME TAXATION, Second Edition, 835 pages, 1988. Teacher's Manual available. (Casebook)

HUDSON AND LIND'S BLACK LETTER ON FEDERAL INCOME TAXATION, Second Edition, 396 pages, 1987. Softcover. (Review)

KRAGEN AND MCNULTY'S CASES AND MATERIALS ON FEDERAL INCOME TAXATION—INDIVIDUALS, CORPORATIONS, PARTNERSHIPS, Fourth Edition, 1287 pages, 1985. (Casebook)

MCNULTY'S FEDERAL INCOME TAXATION OF INDIVIDUALS IN A NUTSHELL, Fourth Edition, 503 pages, 1988. Softcover. (Text)

POSIN'S HORNBOOK ON FEDERAL INCOME TAXATION, Student Edition, 491 pages, 1983,

Taxation—Individual—Cont'd

with 1989 pocket part. (Text)

ROSE AND CHOMMIE'S HORNBOOK ON FEDERAL INCOME TAXATION, Third Edition, 923 pages, 1988, with 1989 pocket part. (Text)

SELECTED FEDERAL TAXATION STATUTES AND REGULATIONS. Softcover. 1618 pages, 1990.

SOLOMON AND HESCH'S PROBLEMS, CASES AND MATERIALS ON FEDERAL INCOME TAXATION OF INDIVIDUALS, 1068 pages, 1987. Teacher's Manual available. (Casebook)

Taxation—International

DOERNBERG'S INTERNATIONAL TAXATION IN A NUTSHELL, 325 pages, 1989. Softcover. (Text)

KAPLAN'S FEDERAL TAXATION OF INTERNATIONAL TRANSACTIONS: PRINCIPLES, PLANNING AND POLICY, 635 pages, 1988. (Casebook)

Taxation—Partnership

BERGER AND WIEDENBECK'S CASES AND MATERIALS ON PARTNERSHIP TAXATION, 788 pages, 1989. Teacher's Manual available. (Casebook)

Taxation—State & Local

GELFAND AND SALSICH'S STATE AND LOCAL TAXATION AND FINANCE IN A NUTSHELL, 309 pages, 1986. Softcover. (Text)

HELLERSTEIN AND HELLERSTEIN'S CASES AND MATERIALS ON STATE AND LOCAL TAXATION, Fifth Edition, 1071 pages, 1988. (Casebook)

Torts—see also Products Liability

CHRISTIE AND MEEKS' CASES AND MATERIALS ON THE LAW OF TORTS, Second Edition, approximately 1200 pages, March, 1990 Pub. (Casebook)

DOBBS' TORTS AND COMPENSATION—PERSONAL ACCOUNTABILITY AND SOCIAL RESPONSIBILITY FOR INJURY, 955 pages, 1985. Teacher's Manual available. (Casebook)

KEETON, KEETON, SARGENTICH AND STEINER'S CASES AND MATERIALS ON TORT AND ACCIDENT LAW, Second Edition, 1318 pages, 1989. (Casebook)

KIONKA'S BLACK LETTER ON TORTS, 339 pages, 1988. Softcover. (Review)

KIONKA'S TORTS IN A NUTSHELL: INJURIES TO PERSONS AND PROPERTY, 434 pages, 1977. Softcover. (Text)

MALONE'S TORTS IN A NUTSHELL: INJURIES TO FAMILY, SOCIAL AND TRADE RELATIONS, 358 pages, 1979. Softcover. (Text)

PROSSER AND KEETON'S HORNBOOK ON TORTS, Fifth Edition, Student Edition, 1286 pages, 1984 with 1988 pocket part. (Text)

ROBERTSON, POWERS AND ANDERSON'S CASES AND MATERIALS ON TORTS, 932 pages, 1989. Teacher's Manual available. (Casebook)

Trade Regulation—see also Antitrust, Regulated Industries

MCMANIS' UNFAIR TRADE PRACTICES IN A NUTSHELL, Second Edition, 464 pages, 1988. Softcover. (Text)

OPPENHEIM, WESTON, MAGGS AND SCHECHTER'S CASES AND MATERIALS ON UNFAIR TRADE PRACTICES AND CONSUMER PROTECTION, Fourth Edition, 1038 pages, 1983. Teacher's Manual available. (Casebook) 1986 Supplement.

SCHECHTER'S BLACK LETTER ON UNFAIR TRADE PRACTICES, 272 pages, 1986. Softcover. (Review)

Trial and Appellate Advocacy—see also Civil Procedure

APPELLATE ADVOCACY, HANDBOOK OF, Second Edition, 182 pages, 1986. Softcover. (Text)

BERGMAN'S TRIAL ADVOCACY IN A NUTSHELL, Second Edition, 354 pages, 1989. Softcover. (Text)

BINDER AND BERGMAN'S FACT INVESTIGATION: FROM HYPOTHESIS TO PROOF, 354 pages, 1984. Teacher's Manual available. (Coursebook)

CARLSON AND IMWINKELRIED'S DYNAMICS OF TRIAL PRACTICE: PROBLEMS AND MATERIALS, 414 pages, 1989. Teacher's Manual available. (Coursebook)

GOLDBERG'S THE FIRST TRIAL (WHERE DO I SIT? WHAT DO I SAY?) IN A NUTSHELL, 396 pages, 1982. Softcover. (Text)

HAYDOCK, HERR, AND STEMPEL'S FUNDAMENTALS OF PRE-TRIAL LITIGATION, 768 pages,

Trial and Appellate Advocacy—Cont'd

1985. Softcover. Teacher's Manual available. (Coursebook)

HEGLAND'S TRIAL AND PRACTICE SKILLS IN A NUTSHELL, 346 pages, 1978. Softcover. (Text)

HORNSTEIN'S APPELLATE ADVOCACY IN A NUTSHELL, 325 pages, 1984. Softcover. (Text)

JEANS' HANDBOOK ON TRIAL ADVOCACY, Student Edition, 473 pages, 1975. Softcover. (Text)

MARTINEAU'S CASES AND MATERIALS ON APPELLATE PRACTICE AND PROCEDURE, 565 pages, 1987. (Casebook)

NOLAN'S CASES AND MATERIALS ON TRIAL PRACTICE, 518 pages, 1981. (Casebook)

SONSTENG, HAYDOCK AND BOYD'S THE TRIALBOOK: A TOTAL SYSTEM FOR PREPARATION AND PRESENTATION OF A CASE, 404 pages, 1984. Softcover. (Coursebook)

Trusts and Estates

ATKINSON'S HORNBOOK ON WILLS, Second Edition, 975 pages, 1953. (Text)

AVERILL'S UNIFORM PROBATE CODE IN A NUTSHELL, Second Edition, 454 pages, 1987. Softcover. (Text)

BOGERT'S HORNBOOK ON TRUSTS, Sixth Edition, Student Edition, 794 pages, 1987. (Text)

CLARK, LUSKY AND MURPHY'S CASES AND MATERIALS ON GRATUITOUS TRANSFERS, Third Edition, 970 pages, 1985. (Casebook)

DODGE'S WILLS, TRUSTS AND ESTATE PLANNING–LAW AND TAXATION, CASES AND MATERIALS, 665 pages, 1988. (Casebook)

KURTZ' PROBLEMS, CASES AND OTHER MATERIALS ON FAMILY ESTATE PLANNING, 853 pages, 1983. Teacher's Manual available. (Casebook)

MCGOVERN'S CASES AND MATERIALS ON WILLS, TRUSTS AND FUTURE INTERESTS: AN INTRODUCTION TO ESTATE PLANNING, 750 pages, 1983. (Casebook)

MCGOVERN, KURTZ AND REIN'S HORNBOOK ON WILLS, TRUSTS AND ESTATES–INCLUDING TAXATION AND FUTURE INTERESTS, 996 pages, 1988. (Text)

MENNELL'S WILLS AND TRUSTS IN A NUTSHELL, 392 pages, 1979. Softcover. (Text)

SIMES' HORNBOOK ON FUTURE INTERESTS, Second Edition, 355 pages, 1966. (Text)

TURANO AND RADIGAN'S HORNBOOK ON NEW YORK ESTATE ADMINISTRATION, 676 pages, 1986. (Text)

UNIFORM PROBATE CODE, OFFICIAL TEXT WITH COMMENTS. 578 pages, 1987. Softcover.

WAGGONER'S FUTURE INTERESTS IN A NUTSHELL, 361 pages, 1981. Softcover. (Text)

WATERBURY'S MATERIALS ON TRUSTS AND ESTATES, 1039 pages, 1986. Teacher's Manual available. (Casebook)

Water Law—see also Energy and Natural Resources Law, Environmental Law

GETCHES' WATER LAW IN A NUTSHELL, 439 pages, 1984. Softcover. (Text)

SAX AND ABRAMS' LEGAL CONTROL OF WATER RESOURCES: CASES AND MATERIALS, 941 pages, 1986. (Casebook)

TRELEASE AND GOULD'S CASES AND MATERIALS ON WATER LAW, Fourth Edition, 816 pages, 1986. (Casebook)

Wills—see Trusts and Estates

Women and the Law—see also Employment Discrimination

KAY'S TEXT, CASES AND MATERIALS ON SEX-BASED DISCRIMINATION, Third Edition, 1001 pages, 1988. (Casebook)

THOMAS' SEX DISCRIMINATION IN A NUTSHELL, 399 pages, 1982. Softcover. (Text)

Workers' Compensation—see Social Legislation

WEST'S LAW SCHOOL ADVISORY BOARD

---

*

FINDING THE LAW

An Abridged Edition of "How to Find the Law, 9th ed."

by

Morris L. Cohen
Librarian and Professor of Law
Yale Law School

Robert C. Berring
Librarian and Professor of Law
School of Law (Boalt Hall)
University of California, Berkeley

Kent C. Olson
Head of Reference and Assistant Professor
University of Virginia Law Library

AMERICAN CASEBOOK SERIES®

WEST PUBLISHING CO.
ST. PAUL, MINN., 1989

50 West Kellogg Boulevard
P.O. Box 64526
St. Paul, MN 55164–0526

Printed in the United States of America

Library of Congress Cataloging-in-Publication Data

Cohen, Morris L., 1927—
Finding the law: an abridged edition of "How to find the law, 9th ed." / Morris L. Cohen, Robert C. Berring, Kent C. Olson.
p. cm. — (American casebook series)
Bibliography: p.
Includes indexes.
ISBN 0–314–54587–5
1. Legal research—United States. I. Berring, Robert C. II. Olson, Kent C. III. Cohen, Morris L., 1927— How to find the law. 9th ed. IV. Title. V. Series.
KF240.C5382 1989
340'.072073—dc20 89–32196
CIP

ISBN 0–314–54587–5

(C., B. & O.) Finding the law, 9th Ed. ACB
1st Reprint 1990

This book is dedicated
to the memory of
Frederick C. Hicks,
1875–1956

Bibliographer, librarian and teacher, he pioneered

in linking the bibliographic and functional aspects of teaching legal research;

in recognizing that the scope of legal research encompasses all fields which may be the subject of the law's concern;

in opposing the rigid distinction between primary and secondary research in law;

and in treating legal research as one of the most creative and challenging aspects of a lawyer's training and work.

*

To The Reader

As we enter the last decade of the twentieth century, the legal research process confirms the centrality of both change and tradition in legal literature. The law constantly changes but still reflects the traditions of its past. So it is with legal research. Its forms, theory and focus have changed remarkably since the last edition of this book, and yet they have retained most of their basic characteristics.

Those who research the law still seek rules in judicial decisions, statutes, and administrative documents, as the primary sources of authority. They also study the secondary materials which explain and analyze those rules. In this process, they use finding tools and research aids which make accessible both the primary sources and the secondary, explanatory literature. Yet the methods of legal research, and even the focuses of that research, continue to change. New technology has improved search techniques in a variety of ways and may gradually be affecting the substance of the literature it retrieves.

The forms of publication have expanded so that the bound book is now only one of several media in which law can be located and studied. Computer-based research services, microforms, online catalogs, optical and laser disks, and telefacsimile delivery are now part of the law's research apparatus. At the same time, new thinking about legal authority, sources of law, and legal process have led some to question the basic assumptions of legal research. Major changes in how research is done inevitably lead to questioning the purposes and uses of the products of that research. The successive impact of sociology, psychiatry and economics on law is now being followed by new scrutiny from the disciplines of literary theory, semantics, semiotics, heuristics and hermeneutics.

Revising a standard text for teaching legal research now requires more than simply updating references to sources and noting new publications. If the process of research is changing, the evidences of that change must be reflected and the student prepared for what is yet to come. Training today's law students must not only prepare them for current practices, but also offer some foreshadowing of changes to come. We have tried to meet that challenge by providing both the essentials of present bibliographic procedures and some sense of future developments. We have tried to describe the basic materials (an essential part of the enterprise, we believe), how they are used and how they interrelate, and what approaches and strategies are available to the researcher.

This edition is different from its predecessor in several ways. Discussion of computer-based research methods and resources has been integrated throughout the text, rather than tacked on at the end. *Shepard's Citations* and related tools are explained much earlier, since updating is among the simplest and most mechanical—yet most essential—of research procedures. *ALR* annotations, isolated in a separate chapter last time, are here treated with other case-finding tools such as digests. Several chapters and appendices now offer expanded coverage of practice materials and computer databases.

These are turbulent days for the teaching of legal research. Despite the vast increase in relevant sources and the multiplicity of research media and search procedures, American law schools still fail to give adequate curricular time and attention to this essential field. Despite the general acceptance of skills training for the lawyering process, *research* skills and their central role in the lawyer's craft are still not fully recognized. It is our hope that books like this will yet persuade the academic law community of the importance of such preparation as a valid component of a good legal education.

As we have noted in previous editions, reading alone is not sufficient for research training. Skill in research requires *practice* in the use of materials. For that purpose a new problem book has been developed by Lynn Foster and Nancy P. Johnson for use with this and other texts. The combination of theory and practice is essential here as elsewhere in legal education.

This edition of *Finding the Law* is an abridgment of the more comprehensive, new edition of *How to Find the Law.* It retains the full text and illustrations of those chapters of the larger work which focus on American law. For the more specialized coverage of international and foreign law, readers are referred to the bound 9th edition of *How to Find the Law.*

MORRIS L. COHEN
ROBERT C. BERRING
KENT C. OLSON

March 1989

Acknowledgments

The authors wish to thank the teachers of legal research and the users of the previous editions of *Finding the Law* and *How to Find the Law* for their comments and suggestions which helped us improve this edition. We also acknowledge the help and support of our library colleagues at the Yale Law School, the University of California at Berkeley School of Law, and the University of Virginia School of Law.

Morris Cohen extends further thanks to Ann J. Laeuchli and Margaret Durkin of the Yale Law Library for their assistance in the preparation of several chapters, and Ann Byler for her processing of the manuscript. Bob Berring acknowledges the help of Kathleen Vanden Heuvel in reading and criticizing early versions, and Jameelah Preston in preparing manuscripts. Kent Olson thanks Larry Wenger for supporting work of this type; Marsha Trimble for editorial troubleshooting and boundless patience; Lynn Foster for suggestions on several chapters; Pat Sparks (fellow native of East Bloomington) for a kinder, gentler production process; and the law students of U.Va. for explaining every day what questions need to be answered.

We also thank the following publishers for their permission to reproduce illustrative material from their publications: the American Association of Law Libraries; Information Access Co.; Martindale-Hubbell Co.; Oceana Publications, Inc.; the University of Washington Law Library; and the West Publishing Company.

Sample pages reprinted with permission from *Federal Rules Digest* (p. 604, 1954–1987) and *Michigan Digest* (Vol. 2, p. 620, 1920–1985), published by Callaghan and Company, 155 Pfingsten Rd., Deerfield, IL 60015.

Materials reprinted from the *Official Code of Georgia Annotated, New Mexico Statutes Annotated,* and the *Utah Code Annotated* with permission of The Michie Company.

Material reproduced with permission from *Congressional Index* and *Products Liability Reports,* published and copyrighted by Commerce Clearing House, Inc., 4025 W. Peterson Ave., Chicago, Illinois, 60646.

Sample entries from the *CIS/Index*, the *CIS Federal Register Index,* and the *American Statistics Index* are copyright 1979, 1984, 1986, 1989 by Congressional Information Service. All rights reserved.

Page from Bowker's *Code of Federal Regulations Index 1988* reprinted with permission of R.R. Bowker, New York, NY.

Sample page reprinted with permission from *Bender's Federal Practice Forms.* Copyright © 1988 by Matthew Bender & Co., Inc.

Index to Legal Periodicals, 1982–83, Copyright © 1982 by The H.W. Wilson Company. *Index to Legal Periodicals*, 1987–88, Copyright © 1987 by The H.W. Wilson Company. Material reproduced by permission of the publisher.

Material from the *Restatement (Second) of Contracts* copyright 1981, 1986 by The American Law Institute. Reprinted with the permission of The American Law Institute.

Page GG379 taken from *Guide to Reference Books,* 10th edition by Eugene Sheehy; copyright © 1986 by ALA. Reprinted with permission of the American Library Association.

Selections from *Encyclopedia of Associations: 1989.,* Karin E. Koek, Susan B. Martin, Annette Novallo, eds. Gale Research, 1989. Copyright © 1989, by Gale Research Inc. Reprinted by permission of the publisher.

Sample page from *A Guide to the United States Treaties in Force* reprinted with permission of William S. Hein & Co., Buffalo, New York.

Finally, we acknowledge our continuing debt to all teachers of legal research—those who taught us, those with whom we now teach, and those who will teach the readers of this book.

MORRIS L. COHEN
ROBERT C. BERRING
KENT C. OLSON

March 1989

Summary of Contents

*

Table of Contents

Appendices

FINDING THE LAW

An Abridged Edition of "How to Find the Law, 9th Ed."

*

Chapter 1

THE CONTEXT OF LEGAL RESEARCH

A. INTRODUCTION

Over one hundred years ago Dean C.C. Langdell told the members of the Harvard Law School Association:

> We have . . . constantly inculcated the idea that the library is the proper workshop of professors and students alike; that it is to us all that the laboratories of the university are to the chemists and physicists, the museum of natural history to the zoologists, the botanical garden to the botanists.[1]

1. Langdell, "The Harvard Law School", 3 *Law Q.Rev.* 123, 124 (1887).

Langdell's view of the library, as he explained to the alumni, was based on the assumption that "printed books are the ultimate source of all legal knowledge." [2]

Although the law library's resources are no longer limited to printed books, it remains the place where the records of "the law" are to be found. Legal education fosters the disciplined, pragmatic and critical intellectual process known as "thinking like a lawyer," but it could not possibly teach the whole body of legal doctrine of even one specialized area. Thus the law student must also learn the techniques of legal research, in order to use the library's resources to *find* the law as it has been defined by courts, legislatures and other governmental agencies.

B. CHARACTERISTICS OF LAW

American law has several readily discernible characteristics that shape the organizational structure of published legal materials. These characteristics thus determine the nature of legal research.

1. CASES AND STATUTES

The United States is a "common law" country. Briefly this means that the law of the land is viewed as an evolving body of doctrine determined by judges on the basis of cases which they must decide, rather than a group of principles expressly articulated and codified. The law grows as established principles are tested and adapted to meet new situations. The printed opinions are considered a *primary source* of the law, in that they are legally binding rather than merely descriptive or analytical. Publication of cases in this country has far exceeded anything ever seen in England, as over 100,000 judicial decisions are issued each year.[3] There have now been over three million cases published in this country, and most of those can be found in any law school library.

At the same time there is also a dramatic increase in the activity of both federal and state legislatures in enacting statutes, which have come to govern an ever greater variety of human activity. Statutes are authoritative and binding and are thus another *primary source.* An essential tension in the nature of legal research arises from the conflict and interplay between common and statutory law. The ruling principles in some areas are determined wholly by case law; other areas are governed partly by case law and partly by statute, or by statutes as construed and interpreted by the courts.

2. Id. Although the legal realists and, more recently, the critical legal studies movement have attacked Langdell's notion of law as a deductive science, his view of the centrality of the law library is still accurate.

3. The West Publishing Company's computerized WESTLAW system contains over 40,000 decisions issued in 1987 by federal courts and over 86,000 cases decided by state courts during the same year. Over 60,000 of these decisions are full opinions with West editorial summaries.

A third important primary source is administrative law. An administrative agency such as the Federal Trade Commission or a state's department of environmental protection promulgates regulations that determine a wide range of institutional and personal behavior within the agency's area of expertise. Agency regulations are similar in form to statutes but often much more detailed. Agencies also conduct hearings to address individual grievances or adjudicate particular disputes, and thus act in a "quasi-judicial" capacity. We will simplify our analysis for the remainder of this chapter by considering administrative regulations to be subsumed within the statutory category (like statutes, they are binding upon all people to whom they apply) and administrative adjudications within "judicial opinions" (both are binding upon the parties involved in the controversy and are the result of adversary proceedings).

2. PRECEDENT

A fundamental principle of our legal system which shapes the techniques of legal research is *stare decisis,* the doctrine that precedents should be followed. The doctrine embraces a basic concept of fairness, the sense that people similarly situated should be similarly dealt with, and that judgments should be consistent, rather than arbitrary, so that one may predict the consequences of contemplated conduct by reference to the treatment afforded similar conduct in the past.

This concept is the basis for the doctrine of *stare decisis,* and it explains the lawyer's need for access to the decided cases. A central function of appellate courts in both federal and state systems is to establish rules of conduct for society, as well as simply determining the rights of the parties appearing before them. A lower court in a jurisdiction is *bound* to follow a rule of law announced by a higher court in that jurisdiction in a similar case.

When you begin research into judicial opinions, therefore, you will be looking for a prior case, decided by the highest possible court in your jurisdiction and not overruled or modified, dealing with the issue presented by your own case, with material facts as similar as possible to the case now before you. If you find such a case, commonly called a "case in point," its rule will be binding on the lower court considering your own case.

Only decisions from the same jurisdiction are binding on a lower court, or *mandatory authority.* Decisions from courts in *other* jurisdictions are not binding, and need not be followed. A court in another state, though, may have considered a situation similar to that in issue. Its approach to the situation and its decision can be very useful for a court faced with similar questions. A decision which is not binding in a jurisdiction is called *persuasive authority.* A court may be persuaded to follow its lead and reach a similar conclusion, or may consider it poorly reasoned (or simply wrong) and arrive at a very different result.

The research process, of course, is usually complicated by the presence of several legal issues, rather than a single issue, and by the fact that no two cases are ever exactly the same on their material facts. It is often further complicated by the possibility that the passage of time has generated new social circumstances and interests, consideration of which might lead to a quite different result from that reached earlier.

Much of our law is embodied in statutes, which if applicable are even more binding than precedential decisions. Research into any legal problem will therefore include a search for an applicable statute. When you have found a statute which appears by its terms to cover your case, however, your research is far from finished. It is a peculiarity of American statutes that they are prolix and detailed, for the drafters of legislation usually attempt to enumerate in a statute all of the foreseeable situations to which they wish it to apply, in order that rights and obligations established by the legislation may be explicitly defined, and the consequences of contemplated conduct clearly perceived.

Perhaps because of this very specificity, or perhaps simply because language is an inadequate means for the communication of ideas or because lawyers often create ambiguity where ambiguity would not otherwise appear, it has usually been necessary for the courts to interpret, clarify and explain statutory language in the course of resolving legal controversies. Research, therefore, cannot be completed with only the text of a statute applicable to one's problem; it must include the judicial opinions which have interpreted and applied the statute, in order to ascertain the courts' understanding of the statute's terms. It is the judicial interpretation of the statute, rather than the naked statutory language, which is binding under the doctrine of *stare decisis.*

3. STABILITY AND CHANGE

A vital characteristic of our law is its manifestation of constant interplay between the desire to maintain certainty and stability (as exemplified by the reliance on precedent) and the need for flexibility in regulating the broad spectrum of activities in which human beings engage. Certainty and stability are basic requirements, for law is the most significant single means by which society is ordered and the rights and obligations of its members are defined. Without more, however, these qualities would be an inadequate foundation for the institutions of governing which make civilized life possible, for the law must also be capable of change if it is to satisfy the fresh aspirations and expectations which are constantly generated by a dynamic society. In short, the law must provide stability yet must not stagnate. It is the function of law to meet and satisfy changing and often conflicting societal needs without endangering the social order.

The need for the law to address new concerns is largely responsible for the ever-increasing number of cases and statutes mentioned above. As the law adapts to changing circumstances, the body of legal doctrine grows and becomes more detailed and specific. As courts and legislatures are confronted with areas of human behavior previously unconsidered, such as surrogate motherhood or catastrophic industrial accidents, they respond by developing new governing principles. Both the creation of doctrine in new areas and the further articulation of legal principles in existing fields make law a constantly changing body of knowledge. To respond to this constant change, the research tools of law must be regularly supplemented or replaced by current materials, and research methods must ensure that reliance on obsolete or superseded doctrine is avoided.

4. MULTIPLICITY OF SOURCES

Finally, it is characteristic of American law that it is derived from a multitude of sources. Our governmental organization includes a federal system consisting of a legislature, a hierarchy of courts, and an executive department, all having law-making functions. In addition, there are fifty states, each of which has its legislature, its hierarchy of courts, and its executive agencies, all of which make law. Within the state jurisdictions, moreover, there are lesser political subdivisions, cities, counties, and other entities, also having courts, ordinance-making bodies, and administrators.

The output of all of these various agencies of government results in the tremendous volume of judicial opinions and statutes published annually. Only a fraction of these primary sources will be mandatory authority for any given research issue, since most questions are governed by the law of a particular jurisdiction. Sources from other jurisdictions, though, may be relevant as persuasive authority or for comparative purposes.

C. CHARACTERISTICS OF THE PRIMARY SOURCES

Despite differences in their formats and functions, cases and statutes share basic features inherent in legal publication.

1. CHRONOLOGICAL PUBLICATION

It is characteristic of both primary sources that they are published chronologically, so that in any volume of reports, an opinion on a criminal appeal may be followed by an opinion in an antitrust matter, which in turn may be followed by an opinion in a civil rights controversy. Similarly, a legislature enacts statutes on a variety of subjects during any given legislative session. These, the *session laws,* are published in the order of their enactment, without regard to their substance. Any volume of session laws, like any volume of judicial opinions, consists of an undifferentiated mass of documents having no relationship to each other except that they appear in the volume in the order in which they were promulgated. The law library's shelves contain many series of several hundred sequentially numbered volumes consisting simply of chronologically published cases or statutes.

2. NEED FOR SUBJECT ACCESS

Cases and statutes arranged chronologically would be an impenetrable jungle to someone seeking information on a specific legal issue, without some means of *subject* access. There are, of course, means of finding those primary sources that deal with the legal subject or with the legally significant facts in which one is interested. To find relevant cases there are a variety of "finding tools," including digests, encyclopedias and indexes. Statutes, on the other hand, are generally recompiled into subject arrangements, which are then thoroughly indexed. The need for subject access has led to the development of various highly refined research systems, the mastery of which is essential to successfully finding relevant legal documents.

3. OFFICIAL AND UNOFFICIAL PUBLICATION

The primary sources are often published both officially and commercially. Decisions of the United States Supreme Court and Acts of Congress, for example, both appear in editions issued by the United States government and by private publishers. Similarly, primary sources in many states are published in more than one format. The government's edition is the *official* version of the opinion or statute, and is the one which must be cited in legal documents. The commercial versions, however, are far more popular among practitioners and scholars, for two reasons. They usually appear much more promptly than do the official texts, and they include a wide range of annotations, tables and other legal research aids that are rarely found in official publications.

4. COMPUTERIZED ACCESS

A final characteristic shared by primary sources is their increasingly prevalent inclusion in computer databases. In one sense computerization has little effect on legal sources, in that once an opinion or statute is issued it is not usually subject to revision or correction unless reconsidered by the court or legislature. Primary sources in a computer database are basically no different from the same sources in bound volumes. The inclusion of the full text of the sources in computers and their accessibility through online databases, however, has greatly reduced the difficulties created by chronological publication and the need for independently produced subject access.

Access to legal materials by computer is a development of the past two decades, but it is now one of the standard means of case research. Statutory research was slower to become computerized, but statutes from numerous states are now available on both WESTLAW and LEXIS, the two major computerized legal research systems.

D. ORGANIZATION OF THE FINDING TOOLS

The need for "finding tools" to provide access to the primary sources is readily apparent from our discussion of their chronological publication. This need is met by an array of digests, codes, indexes, encyclopedias, computers, and other materials, and the lawyer's research methods are determined by the structure of those tools. The use of each of the "finding tools" will be discussed in detail in subsequent chapters, but a short overview at the outset may be helpful.

1. CASE FINDERS

The need for subject access to judicial opinions is met primarily by the *digest,* a device which imposes on the reported cases an alphabetically arranged subject classification. The most comprehensive case digest system is the West Publishing Company's key number arrangement. *Annotations* on specific legal topics (typified by those in the *American Law Reports,* published by the Lawyers Co-operative Publishing Company and usually referred to as *ALR*), legal encyclopedias, and computer-based research systems are also important aids as case finders. Many lawyers and legal scholars begin their research by finding a relevant article in a legal periodical or a treatise. This approach may provide not only citations to relevant cases but also references to other textual treatments, which themselves will provide additional research leads.

It is important to remember that digests and annotations are merely tools which enable you to find primary authority. When you have found the cases which appear to be relevant to your problem, it then is necessary to read the cases themselves, exercising your own judgment in determining their applicability to your case. The lawyer who relies upon someone else's analysis of cases is acting unprofessionally and is courting disaster in the legal forum.

2. STATUTE FINDERS

Like opinions, statutes are published chronologically. The lawyer, however, is interested not in the day-by-day activities of the legislative body, but in sources for the solution of a specific problem.

Access to statutes is provided not by digests, but by codes. A code is a subject compilation of the current public, general statutes of a given jurisdiction, enabling one to find the statutory provisions affecting a particular legal problem, quickly and efficiently. Most statutory codes, particularly those published commercially, are very thoroughly indexed. The other attractions of these unofficial codes are the promptness with which they appear, the regularity with which they are supplemented, and the annotations they provide. An *annotated code* brings to the researcher not only the text of relevant statutes, as an official code would, but also abstracts of the judicial opinions which have interpreted, construed or applied each section of the code, together with citations to the texts of those opinions.

3. AUTHORITY FINDERS

When you have found the statute which governs your legal problem, and the cases which have interpreted and applied that statute, one further task remains before your research may be considered complete. You must now ascertain the *current authority* of your statute and cases. You must assure yourself that the statutory language upon which you propose to rely has not been amended by the legislature, and that the judicial interpretation you have found is consistent with the most recent court construction of its language. Whether or not a statute is involved, you must also be sure that the holdings of the cases upon which your legal argument will be based have not been modified or overruled by subsequent opinions, so that they no longer constitute authority for your legal position.

A tool called *Shepard's Citations* lists every case which has cited or in any way commented upon a prior case, and indicates the effect of each subsequent opinion upon the precedential authority of the cited case. Shepard's performs a similar function for statutes, indicating both modifications effected by the legislature and judicial opinions which have construed or applied an earlier statute.

"Shepardizing" is not the only way to update and verify the validity of primary sources. Annotated codes are regularly supplemented and updated so that the current authority of a statute can be determined. Other research tools provide various means of checking the validity of authorities. Among the most important are the online case-verification systems *Insta–Cite* and *Auto–Cite*, which provide references to any overruling or modifying subsequent opinions.

4. MULTIPURPOSE FINDERS

Finally a few words must be added about finding tools that combine all of the above functions, providing access to both cases and statutes as well as regular updating to assist in verification of current authority. These tools are the *looseleaf services*, which focus on specialized areas of law and monitor developments in both legislatures and courts, as well as in regulatory agencies. The services provide subscribers with frequent information about the latest developments in an area and usually reprint the texts of the subject's most important primary sources.

E. SECONDARY AND NONLEGAL SOURCES

Only statutes and judicial opinions are authoritative, in that they are binding within the jurisdictions in which they apply. Secondary sources, which include treatises, legal periodicals and other textual treatments of the law, may be said to have persuasive authority, however, to the extent that they provide well-reasoned statements of the law. The authority of a treatise or periodical article, moreover, may be buttressed by the scholarly reputation of its author; the continued citation by judges of such authors as Prosser, Wigmore and Williston indicates quite clearly that the force of their legal analyses has remained persuasive over the years. Even if not of the highest caliber, of course, secondary sources may help you analyze a problem and can provide fruitful research leads through references to both primary and other secondary sources.

In the 19th and the early 20th century, American judicial opinions typically cited only legal authorities in support of their conclusions. The traditional neglect of nonlegal sources of information was exacerbated by the establishment of separate schools for the study of law in the early 19th century. Prior to that separation, law had been only one of several university subjects the study of which was thought necessary to a broadly based education. Thereafter, however, the study of law developed independently, in relative isolation from the other academic disciplines. With increasing sophistication, we have come to see that the very nature of the lawyer's function includes the capacity to influence the direction of social change. That perception is reflected in judicial opinions which articulate quite clearly the social, economic, political and even psychological consequences with which they are concerned. Lawyers must increasingly do research in the literature of disciplines on the periphery of, or even remotely removed from law, for law has become in fact an interdisciplinary study. Research in materials considered "nonlegal" is thus an inherent part of legal research.

F. LEGAL EXPRESSION

A chapter of this kind should not end without a brief discussion of one of the lawyer's major tools, *words*. Professional facility in the use of language depends not only on superior skill in reading and writing the English language, but upon the development of special skill in the use of the language which is peculiar to the law. Much of current legal terminology is our heritage from days long past. Latin, law French, and the stylized language employed by early English lawyers have given us a mixed terminology which must be clearly understood if you are to read legal materials intelligently. You must understand a case in all its complexity; the unfamiliar terms must be looked up, and their meaning clearly understood, if your reading is to be purposeful. For that reason, a law dictionary should be readily available whenever you are reading legal materials.

At the same time lawyers bear a responsibility to express legal concepts in words readily understandable by more than just an inbred professional group. If the law is to play a role in shaping and governing society, it must be comprehensible to the members of society. An example of legal writing that *should* be (but often is not) clear to all is the language of statutory enactments. The words of a statute are the definitive expression of the legislature's will, and those words should define the reach of law with the utmost clarity and certainty. Every word in the statutory text, therefore, is important.[4]

Yet there is room for eloquence in legal writing. Unlike legislators, judges enjoy great freedom of expression in writing their opinions. Some of the most famous and influential judicial opinions achieved that status through the power expressed in their language. Jurists such as Holmes and Cardozo have a lasting impact in large part because they were articulate, forceful writers. Lawyers' writings, in court briefs or in letters to clients, can strive for the same standards.

Finally, on a more mundane level, the use of proper citation form is an essential skill of the legal researcher. Poor citations confuse, mislead and exasperate the reader of legal writing, and can be avoided with the exercise of care. Correct citations permit the reader to focus on the content of a legal argument rather than its stylistic errors or idiosyncracies. The most widely accepted guide to legal citation practice is *A Uniform System of Citation,* 14th ed. (Harvard Law Review Association, 1986), generally known as "the Bluebook" from its blue covers. That manual provides a thorough explanation of how to cite the law. While sometimes confusing, it is a necessary complement to a book such as this on finding legal sources.

G. SUMMARY

It has been the purpose of this chapter not only to introduce the kinds of resources and tools that will be discussed in detail in the later chapters of this book, but to attempt to show the relationship of the nature of law and the structure of legal literature to the methods employed in legal research. Some of these methods are cumbersome, largely because they must be adequate to deal meticulously with a growing mass of chronologically arranged materials, but they are usually effective. Practice will improve your facility in dealing with the complex situations which frequently surround legal controversies and will enable you quickly and efficiently to recognize relevant material. It is the creative function of legal research and legal reasoning to use recorded knowledge to evaluate competing interests critically and rigorously, in order to reach a reasoned decision and just result in view of all the facts and circumstances of a case.

H. ADDITIONAL READING

L.H. Carter, *Reason in Law,* 3d ed. (Scott, Foresman, 1987). A readable introductory text—chapters 1 to 4 are particularly useful here.

4. The view that there is no license to be taken with statutory language is not universally held. Former Judge Robert H. Bork of the U.S. Court of Appeals said of federal antitrust legislation: "In the Robinson–Patman Act, when Congress said it wanted to forbid price discrimination to protect competition, they said it with a wink. I don't think it's a judge's job to enforce winks." "Antitrust Ideas: 3 Problems," *N.Y. Times,* March 8, 1983, at D2.

E.H. Levi, *An Introduction to Legal Reasoning* (University of Chicago Press, 1948). Originally published at 15 *U.Chi.L.Rev.* 501 (1948). A brief but classic analysis of judicial decision-making.

K.N. Llewellyn, *The Bramble Bush: On Our Law and Its Study* (Oceana, 1951). A rewarding introduction to law study by an outstanding legal realist. Worth the effort, despite the sometimes heavy prose.

D. Mellinkoff, *The Language of the Law* (Little, Brown, 1963). A lively and witty study—historical, critical and prescriptive.

Chapter 2

COURT REPORTS

A. INTRODUCTION

American law, both in its popular manifestations and in the minds of many of its practitioners, focuses upon "case law." Law students are educated by the case method, lawyers portrayed in the media are almost always working on litigation, and the American legal system, along with the common law system generally, is most easily distinguished from other legal systems by its heavy reliance on the precedential value of judicial opinions. Traditionally, legal research courses and texts have given considerable attention to cases, their forms of publication, and their finding tools. This emphasis was perhaps justified by the idiosyncratic method of early case reporting and the complicated modern systems of case publication and digesting, but it was also a result of the commonly shared assumption that mastering case law research was the most important and the necessary first step in approaching legal research.

Today, most commentators acknowledge that statutory law plays a far more important role than case law in the day-to-day life of individuals in the United States, and the influence of administrative law is similarly pervasive. While the significance of case law in everyday life may be somewhat reduced, its vitality in legal thinking, and therefore in legal research, is unchallenged. It is impossible to conduct systematic research without a complete understanding of cases, their components, their systems of publication, and the means of access to them. The next three chapters will concentrate on these questions.

B. THE HIERARCHY OF COURT SYSTEMS

"Case law" generally refers to the written opinions of appellate courts on specific issues raised in litigated disputes. Only a tiny fraction of court cases result in such opinions. To understand this, one must have a sense of the basic structure of American judicial systems. In every jurisdiction, federal and state, there is a hierarchy of at least two and often three levels of courts.

The *trial court* level is the first level in the court system. In operation it may have numerous subdivisions and special branches (e.g., probate, family court, small claims court, etc.), but every jurisdiction has a trial court of general jurisdiction at which most disputes, both civil and criminal, are initially adjudicated. Here persons who wish to litigate a civil matter can bring before a trier of fact (a judge or jury) the issues in their case. Most criminal cases are brought to trial at this level.

It is in the trial court that issues of fact are determined. In an automobile accident case, for example, the trier of fact must decide such matters as the color of a traffic light or the relative speed of two vehicles. Either a jury or a judge will answer these factual questions, and those answers will be fixed for the balance of the litigation, unless some irregularity of procedure or bias can be shown in the fact-finding process. That is to say once the trial court determines the light was red for oncoming traffic, that fact is determined and cannot be appealed.

There is, however, another kind of issue that can arise at the trial court level—an issue of "law." The plaintiff, for example, might attempt to introduce testimony from a witness who claims to have heard the defendant's mother say that the defendant admitted he had been speeding at the time of the accident. Defense counsel might object that such testimony should not be admitted into evidence because of the *hearsay rule,* which governs what secondhand testimony is admissible at trial. A question concerning the admissibility of evidence is an issue of law and must be determined by the judge, even in a jury trial. If the trial judge issues a written opinion on the decision of that issue, it may be published and included within our notion of "case law."

The trial judge's ruling on an issue of law *can* be appealed to a higher court. The next level in most jurisdictions, including the federal court system, is the *intermediate appellate court.* If there was a valid evidentiary question posed, and if it was an issue that was appealable under the rules of the court system, then the appellate court would decide whether or not the trial court was correct in its ruling on the admission of evidence. If this occurs, the attorneys for each party file and exchange written briefs setting forth their respective positions, and an oral argument may be held. An appellate court usually consists of three or more judges, who confer and vote on the determination of the issue. One of the judges usually writes an opinion summarizing the question, stating the determination (or holding), and setting forth the reasoning behind it. The written resolution of such issues of law constitute the decision of the case. "Cases," as we will use the term in this text, represent those decisions, or the written determination of issues of law.

If the losing party in the appellate court continues to believe that his or her position is legally correct, the decision of that court can frequently be appealed to a *higher* court. The highest court in each jurisdiction, the *court of last resort,* is known as the Supreme Court in most states and in the federal system. (A few states have no intermediate appellate court, and appeals go directly from the trial court to the supreme court.) The court of last resort's pronouncements are binding on all trial and intermediate appellate courts in its jurisdiction.

Because judicial decisions resolve issues of law, most are generated from the upper two levels of the court systems. The United States District Courts (the trial courts of the federal system) do produce a substantial number of opinions, but very few states publish any decisions from their trial court level. Those that do, publish only a small fraction of the opinions written. Most trial court actions do not produce a written opinion at all. They do generate a record, as trial transcripts and pre-trial proceedings are filed with the clerk of the court, but such materials are rarely published. The absence of a written or published opinion often confuses novice researchers who expect to find a report of every "case." One may read in the newspaper about an important new case but find no published opinion, for the simple reason that no judicial opinion was written.[1]

Not all appellate decisions are published, since the sets of published cases for intermediate appellate courts are selective, like those for trial courts. On the other hand, virtually all decisions of the courts of last resort for every state and for the federal system are reported in full. Often, however, a court of last resort will simply reject an appeal from the lower court or affirm its holding by order without writing an opinion. When the Supreme Court of the United States refuses to hear a case, its action is known as *denying a petition for writ of certiorari,* or "cert. denied." A court of last resort may determine the outcome of a case by refusing to hear an appeal and thereby letting a lower court decision stand. Frequently newspapers carry articles about such "decisions" of a court, where no opinion was actually written and consequently no report of the case produced.

C. THE DISTINCTION BETWEEN HOLDING AND DICTUM

Under the doctrine of *stare decisis,* a case's holding will govern other cases in the same jurisdiction in which the facts and issues are substantially similar to those of the case which generated the rule of law. The holding, or *ratio decidendi,* of a case can usually be summed up in a single declaratory sentence. Everything else in the court's opinion is *dicta,* or *obiter dicta,* something "said by the way." Judges may comment in their opinions on any number of extraneous issues, or enlarge on their reasoning, or speculate about possibilities which are not material to the resolution of the immediate controversy.

The importance of the distinction between holding and dictum is that only the holding of the court is authoritative and binding in like cases under the doctrine of precedent. The reason for the distinction lies in the adversary system which is central to our legal process. That system assumes that both parties to a legal controversy will be represented by competent counsel, that counsel will each produce the best possible arguments for the resolution of disputed issues in his or her favor, that lapses in the legal reasoning espoused by either party will become apparent, and a right result will be reached. Whatever the validity of these assumptions, the consequence is that a court is considered competent to decide only those issues which were in dispute and which were therefore argued before it. The issues in dispute, of course,

1. Information on trial verdicts and damage awards, primarily for different types of tort litigation, is available in services known as *verdict reporters.* The best known of these publications is *Personal Injury Valuation Handbooks* (Jury Verdict Research, looseleaf); others include *Jury Verdicts Weekly* and *Verdicts, Settlements & Tactics* (Shepard's/McGraw–Hill, monthly).

are the issues the court is required to resolve in order to decide the controversy between the parties. The holding is limited to the decision and the significant or material facts upon which the court necessarily relied in arriving at its determination. Everything else is dicta and therefore not binding.

The language employed by the court in explaining and clarifying its decision helps one ascertain the court's intention regarding the narrowness or breadth of its decision, so no competent lawyer ever totally ignores dictum. A later court, however, is not bound by that dictum and may not be receptive to its rationale. While dictum cannot be ignored, then, it cannot be relied upon as precedent and cannot be cited as authority for a proposition, without explanation. It should be noted, however, that a court may clarify its views on an important legal question not necessarily before it in a case, in anticipation that the question will arise in the future. A well-reasoned dictum may be more persuasive—and therefore more significant—than an outworn holding.

D. PUBLICATION OF CASES

From its earliest beginnings in antiquity, the reporting of cases helped to achieve certainty in the law, by providing written records for later tribunals faced with similar issues and thereby reducing further disputes. The earliest evidence of recorded judicial decisions in England dates from the 11th century. Two hundred years later a series of case reports, known as the Year Books, began providing notes of debates between judges and counsel on the points in issue in cases. While not containing actual reports of decisions, the Year Books were used to guide pleaders in subsequent cases. Although manuscripts of reported cases exist from as early as the 13th century, the first printed versions appeared in about 1481 or 1482, and the Year Books continued until 1535.[2] The Year Books were replaced by *nominative* reporters, that is, reports named for the person who recorded or edited them. The first nominative reporter was prepared by Edmund Plowden and published in 1571. It was followed by numerous volumes by dozens of jurists and lawyers, of varying accuracy and authority.[3]

The decisions of American courts, on the other hand, were not published at all during the colonial period and the early years of independence. American lawyers and judges relied for precedent on the decisions of the English courts, even though only a limited number of those volumes were available here. The first volumes of American court decisions were not published until 1789, thirteen years after independence. Publication of domestic reports developed slowly, and

2. P.H. Winfield, *The Chief Sources of English Legal History* (Harvard University Press, 1925), chapter VII.

3. For an excellent history of early English reports after the Year Books, see L.W. Abbott, *Law Reporting in England 1485–1585* (Athlone Press, 1973). For a more extensive survey of the nominative reporters, see J.W. Wallace, *The Reporters, Arranged and Characterized with Incidental Remarks*, 4th ed. (Soule & Bugbee, 1882; reprinted by Dennis, 1959).

the courts of some states operated for decades without published decisions.

The movement for publication grew, however, spurred by several concerns. There was the patriotic feeling that it was important to construct an American system of jurisprudence. Now that the country had freed itself from English rule, it should no longer be subject to English case law.[4] Yet the doctrine of precedent created a need for the publication of decisions. If American judges rendered decisions which created new rights and responsibilities and changed the common law, those decisions should be recorded and made available to the public. Moreover, revolutionary times produced a general distrust of judges. Wary of unrepresentative authority, the citizens of the new republic felt that judges should be accountable for the decisions they made. Written decisions and their publication would facilitate that accountability.

Ephraim Kirby's *Reports of Cases Adjudged in the Superior Court of the State of Connecticut from the Year 1785 to May 1788* (Collier & Adam, 1789) is generally regarded as the first American reporter volume.[5] In a preface Kirby discusses the concerns which led to the publication of his reports, including the inapplicability of English law in the new country and the need to create a permanent body of American common law.

The early volumes of privately published court decisions differ markedly from the sophisticated case reporters of today. The individual reporter compiled the decisions (often from his own observation and notes, rather than from texts submitted by the judges), summarized the oral arguments, and often added his own analysis. Many of the early reports were quite unsystematic—they often contained decisions from several courts, and sometimes even from several jurisdictions. Alexander Dallas' first volume of the *United States Reports* contains only Pennsylvania decisions, and none from the U.S. Supreme Court. His second and third volumes contain cases from both Pennsylvania and the U.S. Supreme Court, and his fourth volume adds decisions from Delaware and New Hampshire.

Systematic official publication of judicial decisions was needed to bring order to reporting, but state appointment of reporters and officially sanctioned publication of decisions developed slowly. The first statute for this purpose was passed in Massachusetts in 1804,[6] and some

4. This is apparent from the "reception" statutes passed by many state legislatures, which accepted English common law but limited the "reception" to those cases which were not repugnant to the law of the newly independent state, and often further limited those to cases decided before the date of independence. *See, e.g.,* Act of January 28, 1777, §§ 2 to 3, 1 *Smith's Pa.Laws* 429 (current version at 1 Pa.Cons.Stat. § 1503).

5. Francis Hopkinson's *Judgements in the Admiralty of Pennsylvania* was also published in 1789, in Philadelphia by Dobson & Lang. Although some later reports include cases decided earlier than those in Kirby and Hopkinson, they were the first to be published.

6. Act of March 8, 1804, ch. 133, 1803 Mass.Acts 449.

other states soon followed. The Supreme Court of the United States had no official reporter until 1817,[7] and Pennsylvania had none until 1845.[8] Gradually the nominative reporters gave way to officially published sets of sequentially numbered reports. Some states subsequently renumbered their reports, incorporating the volumes of the nominative reporters as the first numbered volumes in the official set. Other states, particularly those which were among the early colonies, have many nominative volumes without an overall numbering sequence. To determine where particular citations can be found, researchers need to use tables of reports or dictionaries of legal abbreviations.

The development of official reports represented only the second phase of American case reporting. In the 19th century, as the population grew and the country expanded and became industrialized, the volume of litigation increased rapidly and the official reporting system became overburdened with the proliferation of judicial decisions. Furthermore, the reporter in many states became a political position and publication was subject to the uncertainties of legislative appropriation, so the reports were often inaccurate and frequently slow in appearing. In 1876, in response to the need for improved and more rapid publication, an entrepreneur in Minnesota, John B. West, started a private reporting system, beginning with selected decisions of the Minnesota Supreme Court in an eight-page weekly leaflet called the *Syllabi*.[9] Coverage gradually expanded, adding decisions from Minnesota federal and lower state courts, and abstracts of decisions from other states. The venture proved so successful that in 1879, West incorporated full decisions from five surrounding states in a new publication, the *North Western Reporter.*

By grouping states, the West Publishing Company was able to publish cases far more frequently than official reports could. Of more significance for legal research, West added to each case editorial material which allowed comprehensive and uniform subject access to the cases of different jurisdictions. Every decision was given numbered headnotes summarizing its points of law, and every headnote was

7. Act of March 3, 1817, ch. 63, 3 Stat. 376.

8. Act of April 11, 1845, ch. 250, 1845 Pa.Laws 374.

9. When West began his first publications, another commercial approach to reporting was already underway. This was the selective publication of a limited number of important decisions of general interest from the courts in many states, annotated with notes to reflect the state of the law throughout the country. Begun in 1871 by the Bancroft–Whitney Company, the first three of these reporters became known as the "Trinity Series": *American Decisions* (covering from the colonial period to 1868), *American Reports* (covering 1871 to 1887), and *American State Reports* (covering 1887 to 1911). In 1906 the Edward Thompson Company began the rival *American and English Annotated Cases,* which merged with Bancroft–Whitney's series to form *American Annotated Cases* in 1912. Meanwhile the Lawyers' Co-operative Publishing Company had since 1888 been publishing *Lawyers' Reports Annotated,* which entered its third series in 1914. All three publishers joined forces in 1918 to begin a new series, *American Law Reports Annotated.* This set, known as *ALR,* continues to this day as the modern successor to the annotated reports, but its annotations are far more important than the cases it still reprints. *ALR* and its federal counterpart, *ALR Federal,* will be discussed more fully in Chapter 4.

designated by its legal topic and a number indicating a particular subdivision of that topic. This scheme, known as the *key number system*, remains one of the most important means of finding cases and will be discussed at length in Chapter 4.

West's thriving business quickly drew competition from other publishers beginning their own series of regional reporters, with the result that some states were covered by two or three rival schemes.[10] West responded to the growing competition by establishing a national system, publishing all the states' decisions in seven regional reporters. Its comprehensive reporting and accuracy made it the dominant publisher of law reports within a few years. Some of the rival publications folded. Others were absorbed by West into its National Reporter System, which by 1887 covered every state and the federal system. West's unofficial publication of state court decisions has proven so effective that over one-third of the states have discontinued their official publications. In most states, however, cases appear in both official and unofficial editions.

Another unofficial version of some decisions may be published as part of the coverage of topical looseleaf services or specialized reporters. These research tools focus on specific areas of law such as antitrust or labor relations and often provide the full text of judicial decisions. Many cases in topical reporters also appear in official or West series, but some are not published elsewhere.

The most recent development in American case reporting is electronic storage and retrieval. The two major examples of this development are the competing commercial services LEXIS and WESTLAW[11]. The Ohio State Bar Association began work in 1966 on the system that became LEXIS and was introduced in 1973. A product of Mead Data Central, LEXIS was the first commercially successful computerized legal research system and contains the decisions of all fifty states and the federal system. The West Publishing Company's WESTLAW began in 1975, initially with only the headnotes to its published decisions. In 1979, it added full-text retrieval and now its coverage is similar to LEXIS. The major benefit of both databases is that they allow full-text searching of judicial decisions and a variety of databases containing other legal and law-related materials. The researcher can look for any combination of terms appearing in opinions, and access is no longer limited to publishers' indexes or digests.

Just as the West system has not supplanted official reports, however, the case databases have not eliminated the need for published reports with expert editorial treatment. Full-text searching will retrieve cases in which the court's language meets the specifications of the request. Some legal research can best be conducted in such a

10. "The New 'Reporters'," 19 *Am.L. Rev.* 930, 932 (1885).

11. For a survey of these developments, see Harrington, "A Brief History of Computer-Assisted Legal Research," 77 *Law Libr.J.* 543 (1985).

manner, while some topics will continue to be most fruitfully approached through use of an editorial index or another search tool. In most research situations the two methods complement each other. Moreover, the published versions of cases provide precise, standard citations allowing a reader convenient access to cited references, a feature not yet well developed in computer databases.

E. FORMS OF PUBLISHED DECISIONS

Judicial decisions are published successively in three different formats. The first appearance of most decisions is the official *slip opinion* issued by the court itself, usually a separate pamphlet publication of a single opinion (or opinions, if there are concurring or dissenting judges) in one case. It is individually paginated and contains the full text of the court's decision, sometimes with an official syllabus, or summary. Some slip opinions are simply copies of the original typescript decision, but in some jurisdictions they are printed and distributed on a subscription basis. Lawyers rarely subscribe to the slip opinions, however, because of their expense, their slow distribution, and the difficulty of organizing them for retrieval by subject.

The first form of publication that is distributed widely is the *advance sheet,* a pamphlet which contains the full text of a number of the court's decisions, arranged chronologically, and paginated in a continuous sequence. The advance sheet usually contains the syllabus, headnotes, digests, index and tables which appear in the permanent form of publication, the bound volume. However, advance sheets are preliminary in form, and judges may revise the text of their opinions between that publication and its final form in the bound volume. Most advance sheets contain the pagination that will appear in the bound volume, but occasionally there are minor variations. Advance sheets are published for most official reporters, for all West reporters, and for some other unofficial reporters.

The third stage of publication is the bound case reporter volume. The bound volumes consolidate several advance sheets and contain a large number of decisions arranged chronologically in the same sequence as they appeared in the advance sheets. They usually contain subject indexes, alphabetical lists of the cases reported therein, and often lists of words defined, statutes construed, and earlier cases cited. The volumes are numbered in a consecutive series. Some reporters have begun second or third series, starting at volume one again. This is done at an arbitrary time convenient for publication or sales purposes. A new series of a reporter does not replace the prior series, but merely continues it with a new numbering sequence. The notation that a series is other than the first must always be included in the citation to a case.

F. COMPONENTS OF A DECISION

The features of published decisions vary somewhat between publishers and series, but several components are standard and important for case research. References in this section are keyed to the pages that comprise Illustration A, the official report of a decision of the Supreme Court of the United States.

1. CAPTION

The *caption* (or *name* or *style*) of a case sets forth the names of the parties involved. The normal form is *X v. Y.* Note that the caption of the case beginning in Illustration A–1 is *Clark v. Community for Creative Non–Violence.* The party which appears first in the caption is usually the plaintiff, or the party bringing suit, and the second party the defendant. There are other names by which these parties can be designated. If it is a case on appeal, as is often the situation, the first party will often be the appellant or petitioner and the second party the appellee or respondent, no matter which was the original plaintiff. In some matters concerning the disposition of an estate or litigation over a particular piece of property, the caption *In re* may be used, followed by the name of the person or estate, or a description of the property which is the subject of the action. In a criminal prosecution, since the State brings the action, the first party will often be the jurisdiction itself, e.g., *United States,* or *Commonwealth of Massachusetts,* or *People of the State of New York.*

As a case goes through the levels of a court system, the parties may change places in the caption, and the defendant at the trial level becomes the petitioner at an appellate level. Thus it is important to check for a party's name in either position when searching for a case. Most digests have both a Table of Cases (listing cases under the first parties' names) and a Defendant–Plaintiff Table (providing cross-reference from the second parties' names) to facilitate searching for decisions by case name.

2. DOCKET NUMBER

The docket number, or record number, is assigned by the court clerk to the case when it is filed initially for the court's consideration. It is the number the court then uses to keep track of the documents and briefs filed in the case. In the case shown in Illustration A, the docket number is No. 82–1998.

The docket number is useful in following the case on the court's calendar before it is decided. Decisions which have not been published but are available in slip opinion form are usually filed and cited by docket number. Even long after the decision in a case has been published, its appeal record and briefs, increasingly valuable sources of information on important and complex decisions, are generally filed by docket number.

Illustration A–1

Opening page of a decision in the official *United States Reports*

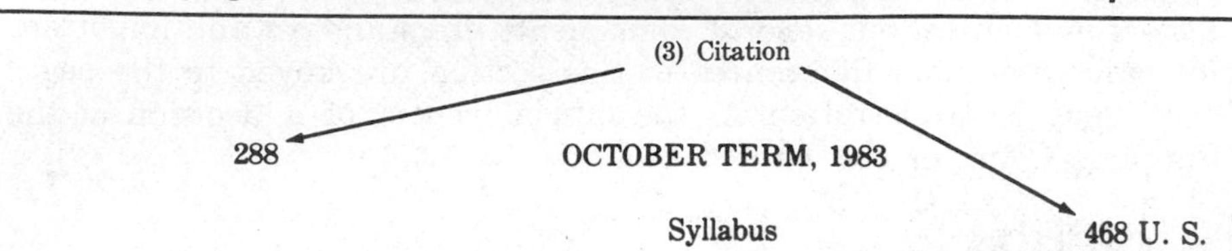

(1) Caption → CLARK, SECRETARY OF THE INTERIOR, ET AL. *v.* COMMUNITY FOR CREATIVE NON-VIOLENCE ET AL.

CERTIORARI TO THE UNITED STATES COURT OF APPEALS FOR THE DISTRICT OF COLUMBIA CIRCUIT

(2) Docket number → No. 82–1998. Argued March 21, 1984—Decided June 29, 1984

(4) Syllabus

In 1982, the National Park Service issued a permit to respondent Community for Creative Non-Violence (CCNV) to conduct a demonstration in Lafayette Park and the Mall, which are National Parks in the heart of Washington, D. C. The purpose of the demonstration was to call attention to the plight of the homeless, and the permit authorized the erection of two symbolic tent cities. However, the Park Service, relying on its regulations—particularly one that permits "camping" (defined as including sleeping activities) only in designated campgrounds, no campgrounds having ever been designated in Lafayette Park or the Mall—denied CCNV's request that demonstrators be permitted to sleep in the symbolic tents. CCNV and the individual respondents then filed an action in Federal District Court, alleging, *inter alia,* that application of the regulations to prevent sleeping in the tents violated the First Amendment. The District Court granted summary judgment for the Park Service, but the Court of Appeals reversed.

Held: The challenged application of the Park Service regulations does not violate the First Amendment. Pp. 293–299.

(a) Assuming that overnight sleeping in connection with the demonstration is expressive conduct protected to some extent by the First Amendment, the regulation forbidding sleeping meets the requirements for a reasonable time, place, or manner restriction of expression, whether oral, written, or symbolized by conduct. The regulation is neutral with regard to the message presented, and leaves open ample alternative methods of communicating the intended message concerning the plight of the homeless. Moreover, the regulation narrowly focuses on the Government's substantial interest in maintaining the parks in the heart of the Capital in an attractive and intact condition, readily available to the millions of people who wish to see and enjoy them by their presence. To permit camping would be totally inimical to these purposes. The validity of the regulation need not be judged solely by reference to the demonstration at hand, and none of its provisions are unrelated to the ends that it was designed to serve. Pp. 293–298.

(b) Similarly, the challenged regulation is also sustainable as meeting the standards for a valid regulation of expressive conduct. Aside from

Illustration A–2

Second page of the *United States Reports* decision

CLARK *v.* COMMUNITY FOR CREATIVE NON-VIOLENCE 289

288 Opinion of the Court

its impact on speech, a rule against camping or overnight sleeping in public parks is not beyond the constitutional power of the Government to enforce. And as noted above, there is a substantial Government interest, unrelated to suppression of expression, in conserving park property that is served by the proscription of sleeping. Pp. 298–299.

227 U. S. App. D. C. 19, 703 F. 2d 586, reversed.

WHITE, J., delivered the opinion of the Court, in which BURGER, C. J., and BLACKMUN, POWELL, REHNQUIST, STEVENS, and O'CONNOR, JJ., joined. BURGER, C. J., filed a concurring opinion, *post*, p. 300. MARSHALL, J., filed a dissenting opinion, in which BRENNAN, J., joined, *post*, p. 301.

(4) Syllabus

Deputy Solicitor General Bator argued the cause for petitioners. With him on the briefs were *Solicitor General Lee, Assistant Attorney General McGrath, Alan I. Horowitz, Leonard Schaitman*, and *Katherine S. Gruenheck*.

Burt Neuborne argued the cause for respondents. With him on the brief were *Charles S. Sims, Laura Macklin, Arthur B. Spitzer*, and *Elizabeth Symonds*.*

(5) Attorneys

JUSTICE WHITE delivered the opinion of the Court.

The issue in this case is whether a National Park Service regulation prohibiting camping in certain parks violates the First Amendment when applied to prohibit demonstrators from sleeping in Lafayette Park and the Mall in connection with a demonstration intended to call attention to the plight of the homeless. We hold that it does not and reverse the contrary judgment of the Court of Appeals.

I

The Interior Department, through the National Park Service, is charged with responsibility for the management and maintenance of the National Parks and is authorized to promulgate rules and regulations for the use of the parks in accordance with the purposes for which they were established.

(6) Opinion

**Ogden Northrop Lewis* filed a brief for the National Coalition for the Homeless as *amicus curiae* urging affirmance.

3. CITATION

While slip opinions are generally cited by docket number, published opinions are cited by the reporter volume in which they appear and the page number on which the caption appears. The citation does not always appear at the beginning of an opinion, but can readily be determined if the volume is in hand. In Illustration A, the volume number (468 U.S.) is indicated at the top right and the page number (288) at the top left. Citations normally include the year of decision, making the citation for this case 468 U.S. 288 (1984).

Reporters, particularly those published commercially, will often also include other citations of the case either above or below the caption. West's regional reporters provide the official citation if it is available when the West publication is issued. Reporters of Supreme Court cases published by West and Lawyers Co-op both provide citations to the official *United States Reports* and to the competition.

4. SYLLABUS AND HEADNOTES

Below the docket number in the illustration is the *syllabus,* a summary of the case's facts and the court's holding. In the official reports of some jurisdictions, the syllabus is prepared by the court itself. Many actions contain more than one question of law, and a court may dispose of two, three or more individual legal questions in a single opinion. It is also common for the reporter to prepare separate *headnotes* describing the various points decided by the court.

Although the official reporter is appointed by the court, the syllabus and headnotes are not an "official" part of the decision. The opinion itself gives the holding, although it is often not expressly designated as such. If the syllabus or headnotes are inconsistent with the court's opinion, the opinion governs.[12] The syllabus may still serve as a useful guide to what is discussed in the case. Many official reporters prepare only the briefest of summaries, however, and there may be none officially prepared in those states that have discontinued their official reports.[13]

The commercial publishers of case reports assign their editors to read and digest each decision which they print. These editors prepare their own headnotes, which are usually more extensive than those of the official reporter. They are specifically designed to aid the researcher in locating relevant material in the opinion, and are usually part of a larger system of digesting and case finding. In using unofficial reports, it is essential to remember that the headnotes are not prepared by the court or the official reporter, but by an editor working for a

12. Every U.S. Supreme Court slip opinion carries a warning that the syllabus "constitutes no part of the opinion of the Court and has been prepared by the Reporter of Decisions for the convenience of the reader," citing *United States v. Detroit Timber & Lumber Co.,* 200 U.S. 321, 337 (1906).

Ohio is unusual in providing that the syllabus be prepared by its Supreme Court as the official statement of the law of the case. Ohio Rev.Stat. § 2503.20. The syllabus governs if there is any inconsistency between it and the opinion.

13. Official reports are published for the Georgia Supreme Court and Court of Appeals, but no syllabi or headnotes accompany the cases. The statutory mandate requires only that the volumes contain the decisions and an index. Ga.Code Ann. § 50–18–26.

commercial publisher. The headnotes are thus merely finding aids and should not be cited or relied upon as authoritative.

5. ATTORNEYS

The names of the lawyers who represented the parties to an action usually appear after the syllabus and before the opinion of the court. Identifying the attorneys can be helpful because they may provide further information about the litigation or its outcome. They may be able to furnish copies of briefs they submitted. At one time reports regularly carried excerpts or summaries of the arguments of counsel, but this information is no longer provided in most reports.

6. OPINION

The name of the judge writing the opinion appears at the beginning of the opinion. At the appellate levels of a court system, it is likely that more than one judge will hear a case. In the court of last resort, there is usually a bench of five, seven or nine judges, while at the intermediate appellate level three or five judges are common. The decision thus may be the product of discussion and compromise among several judges. When it is impossible to achieve unanimity among them, more than one opinion may result. The opinion of the court, reflecting at least a majority of the vote, almost always appears first.[14] It can be assumed that all other judges subscribe to the first opinion, unless they have written or expressly joined in either a concurring or dissenting opinion.

A concurring opinion is written when one or more judges agree with the result reached by the majority of the court, but do not agree with the reasoning used to reach that result or with the opinion written for the majority. In some decisions, there is more than one concurring opinion.

Following the majority opinion and any concurrences, there may be one or more dissenting opinions. Dissenting opinions reflect the views of judges who do not agree with the result reached by the majority of the court. Sometimes judges will simply note their dissent, but often they set forth their reasons. Although dissenting opinions carry no force as precedent, they may have persuasive authority and can be cited if clearly labelled as dissents. Early dissents in some areas have led to changes in the law. Some opinions will feature a dizzying array of concurrences and dissents, and some judges may concur in part and dissent in part. This atomization of opinion is not uncommon among the justices of the Supreme Court of the United States.[15]

14. Occasionally there is no line of reasoning agreed upon by a majority, and a plurality opinion is printed first. Another type of opinion which should be noted is the *per curiam* opinion, which represents the court without authorship attributed to any individual judge. *Per curiam* opinions are generally short, and either cover points of law the court feels are too obvious to merit elaboration or represent sensitive issues the court does not want to treat at length. They do, however, carry the weight of precedent.

15. The Pentagon Papers case, *New York Times Co. v. United States,* 403 U.S.

G. SUPREME COURT OF THE UNITED STATES

The rest of this chapter describes the existing sets of reported decisions which the researcher will encounter in working with American case materials. Because of the preeminent role of the United States Supreme Court, in both practical and jurisprudential terms, its decisions will be discussed first and in some detail. Explanation of reporters covering lower federal courts and state courts will follow in subsequent sections.

The Supreme Court is the court of last resort in any federal dispute and has the final word on federal issues raised in state courts. In most situations, however, it has discretion to decline to review lower court decisions and disposes of most matters by denying petitions for *certiorari* or dismissing appeals. Only a small percentage of the cases appealed to the Supreme Court are accepted for consideration. There are some situations in which the Court *must* hear an appeal, and even cases in which the Court serves as the first forum for a dispute.[16] In the end, however, the Court typically writes opinions in fewer than 150 cases each year.

Today the decisions of the Supreme Court are available in a variety of formats, including three permanent, bound reporters, two looseleaf services, and two electronic databases. Its early cases were not so widely reported. The history of their publication corresponds to the brief history of American law reporting already described. The first reports were compiled by individuals and were known as "nominative" reporters. Even after the federal government began to officially sanction the reports, they were still private ventures of the individual reporters. Later sets, including current reprints, have incorporated the nominatives into the general numbering scheme of the *United States Reports* but retained the reporters' names. Thus the first ninety volumes of *U.S. Reports* are still cited by the name of the individual reporter.[17] The early reporters, their nominative and *U.S. Reports* citations, and dates of coverage are as follows:

713 (1971), had ten opinions: the Court's judgment announced in a brief *per curiam* opinion, plus six concurrences and three dissents.

16. Jurisdiction of the Supreme Court is determined by Congress pursuant to Article III, § 2 of the United States Constitution, and is prescribed in 28 U.S.C. §§ 1251 to 1259. The right to file an appeal rather than petition for discretionary review is generally limited to situations that threaten the balance of power between federal and state governments, such as when a state statute is found unconstitutional by a federal court (§ 1254) or a federal statute is held invalid by a state court (§ 1257). The Supreme Court has original jurisdiction in all controversies between two or more states (§ 1251).

17. Those working with older collections may find mixed into their sets some of the various recompilations that attempted to reprint earlier cases in smaller and less expensive editions. Perhaps the best known are those of Richard Peters (*Peters' Condensed Reports,* covering 1 to 25 U.S., 1790–1827, in four volumes) and Benjamin Curtis (*Curtis' Reports of Decisions,* covering 2 to 58 U.S., 1790–1854, in 22 volumes). These reprints are no longer used much, but are still found on the shelves of many law libraries and are occa-

Reporter	Nominative Citation	U.S. Reports Citation	Terms
A.J. Dallas	1–4 Dall.	1–4 U.S.	1790–1800
William Cranch	1–9 Cranch	5–13 U.S.	1801–1815
Henry Wheaton	1–12 Wheat.	14–25 U.S.	1816–1827
Richard Peters	1–16 Pet.	26–41 U.S.	1828–1842
Benjamin C. Howard	1–24 How.	42–65 U.S.	1843–1860
J.S. Black	1–2 Black	66–67 U.S.	1861–1862
John William Wallace	1–23 Wall.	68–90 U.S.	1863–1874

Thus the case in which the Supreme Court held that the reporter had no copyright in the text of the decisions is cited as *Wheaton v. Peters,* 33 U.S. (8 Pet.) 591 (1834), meaning that the case originally appeared in volume eight of *Peters' Reports* and is now in volume 33 of the renumbered set. The financial impact of that decision led ultimately to the demise of official reporting by private individuals and to the beginning of the modern series of officially published *U.S. Reports.*[18]

1. *UNITED STATES REPORTS*

The official reporter for the Supreme Court of the United States is the *United States Reports* (abbreviated in citations as U.S.). Although there are still individual reporters preparing the current volumes, they are now employees of the Court and their names are no longer used to designate their volumes.

The Supreme Court's annual term runs from October to July, and several volumes of *U.S. Reports* are added every year. Following the general pattern of publication, the decisions appear first in slip opinion form, followed by an official advance sheet (called the "preliminary print"), and finally appear in the bound *U.S. Reports* volume. Illustration A, earlier in this chapter, presents the beginning pages of a case in the *U.S. Reports.* Note that the official court reporter has prefaced the text of the decision with a *syllabus,* preliminary paragraphs summarizing the case and indicating what the Court has held.

The *U.S. Reports* is an accurate, well-indexed compilation of the full official text of all decisions of the Supreme Court of the United States. At first glance it might seem that it should provide quite adequately for the needs of researchers. Unfortunately, as with many official publications, the advance sheets and volumes of the *U.S. Reports* tend to appear quite slowly. Currently, almost two years pass between the announcement of a decision and its appearance in the advance sheet, and another year before its inclusion in a bound volume. Because of the importance of Supreme Court opinions, this slow pace of reporting is inadequate for practicing attorneys. In response to the need for more timely publication, commercial publishers produce a

sionally needed to trace citations to them in older works.

18. A history of the case and its impact on Supreme Court reporting can be found in Joyce, "Wheaton v. Peters: The Untold Story of the Early Reporters," 1985 *Sup.Ct. Hist.Soc'y Y.B.* 35.

variety of unofficial reporters which are distributed much more quickly than the official set.

2. *UNITED STATES SUPREME COURT REPORTS, LAWYERS' EDITION*

There are two commercial sets of Supreme Court decisions which not only publish cases sooner than the official reports but also provide special editorial features for the legal researcher. Both sets are very useful even after the appearance of a case in *U.S. Reports* and therefore are published in both advance sheets and permanent bound volumes. Both have been in existence since 1882.

United States Supreme Court Reports, Lawyers' Edition is published by the Lawyers Co-operative Publishing Company, or Lawyers Co-op. Popularly known as *Lawyers' Edition* (and cited as L.Ed.), the set began by reprinting all the earlier Supreme Court decisions in smaller type and fewer volumes than the official reports. Upon the completion of retrospective coverage, Lawyers Co-op continued publishing the Court's decisions as they were issued. After reaching one hundred volumes in 1956 (covering through volume 351 of *U.S. Reports*), it began a second series, known as *Lawyers' Edition 2d* (L.Ed.2d), which continues today.

Unlike the official set, *Lawyers' Edition* issues advance sheets which put decisions in researchers' hands in a matter of weeks rather than months. In addition to printing the official reporter's syllabus and the opinion, the editors at Lawyers Co-op prepare both a "summary" of each case and their own headnotes. They also provide cross-references to treatments of the case's subject in other Lawyers Co-op publications. These features are shown in Illustrations B–1 and B–2, the opening pages of the *Lawyers' Edition* version of *Clark v. Community for Creative Non–Violence,* the same case shown in its *U.S. Reports* version in Illustration A.

Each headnote in *Lawyers' Edition* is assigned a topic and section number by the editors. These headnotes are then reprinted, arranged by topic, in the companion set to the reports, *United States Supreme Court Digest, Lawyers' Edition.* The digest allows retrieval of other cases in the same subject area, and will be more fully described in Chapter 4, Case Finding. A table in each advance sheet and volume of *Lawyers' Edition* lists the digest topics and numbers appearing in that volume.

By the time a bound volume of *Lawyers' Edition* is ready for publication, the editors have added other useful features. First, they provide short summaries of the briefs of counsel. These permit study of the line of argument presented by each party and offer perspectives on the Court's decision. (Such summaries were a common feature of early reports, but now appear only in *Lawyers' Edition* and *New York Reports.*) Second, the editors prepare *annotations* on a few of the more important cases in each volume. These annotations analyze in considerable detail one or more of the points of law covered in the case and

Illustration B-1

The first page of a decision in *Lawyers' Edition*, showing publisher's summary and references to annotations and briefs

[468 US 288]

WILLIAM P. CLARK, Secretary of the Interior, et al., Petitioners

v

COMMUNITY FOR CREATIVE NON-VIOLENCE et al.

468 US 288, 82 L Ed 2d 221, 104 S Ct 3065

[No. 82-1998]

Argued March 21, 1984. Decided June 29, 1984.

Decision: National Park Service anti-camping regulation held constitutionally applied to Washington, D.C., demonstrators.

SUMMARY

The Community for Creative Non-Violence and several individuals brought suit in the United States District Court for the District of Columbia to prevent the application of a National Park Service regulation, prohibiting camping in national parks except in designated campgrounds, to a proposed demonstration in Lafayette Park and the Mall, in the heart of Washington, D.C., in which demonstrators would sleep in symbolic tents to demonstrate the plight of the homeless. The District Court granted summary judgment in favor of the Park Service. The United States Court of Appeals for the District of Columbia Circuit reversed on the ground that the application of the regulation so as to prevent sleeping in the tents would infringe the demonstrators' First Amendment right of free expression (703 F2d 586).

On certiorari, the United States Supreme Court reversed. In an opinion by WHITE, J., expressing the views of BURGER, Ch. J., and BLACKMUN, POWELL, REHNQUIST, STEVENS, and O'CONNOR, JJ., it was held that the Park Service regulation did not violate the First Amendment when applied to the demonstrators because the regulation was justified without reference to the content of the regulated speech, was narrowly tailored to serve a significant governmental interest, and left open ample alternative channels for communication of the information.

BURGER, Ch. J., while concurring fully in the court's opinion, filed a concurring opinion stating that the camping was conduct and not speech.

MARSHALL, J., joined by BRENNAN, J., dissented on the ground that the

SUBJECT OF ANNOTATION

Beginning on page 958, infra

Restriction of use of public parks as violating freedom of speech or press under First Amendment of Federal Constitution

Briefs of Counsel, p 956, infra.

Illustration B–2

The second page of a *Lawyers' Edition* decision, showing headnotes and cross-references

demonstrators' sleep was symbolic speech and that the regulation of it was not reasonable.

HEADNOTES

Classified to U.S. Supreme Court Digest, Lawyers' Edition

Constitutional Law § 960 — demonstration — camping

1a–1c. A National Park Service regulation prohibiting camping in national parks except in campgrounds designated for that purpose does not violate the First Amendment when applied to prohibit demonstrators from sleeping in Lafayette Park and the Mall, in the heart of Washington, D. C., in connection with a demonstration intended to call attention to the plight of the homeless. (Marshall and Brennan, JJ, dissented from this holding.)

[See annotation p 958, infra]

Parks, Squares, and Commons § 2 — camping

2a, 2b. Sleeping in tents for the purpose of expressing the plight of the homeless falls within the definition of "camping" in a National Park Service regulation defining camping as the use of park land for living accommodation purposes such as sleeping activities, or making preparations to sleep (including the laying down of bedding for the purpose of sleeping), or storing personal belongings, or making any fire, or using any tents or other structure for sleeping or doing any digging or earth breaking or carrying on cooking activities when it appears, in light of all the circumstances, that the participants, in conducting these activities, are in fact using the area as a living accommodation regardless of the intent of the participants or the nature of any other activities in which they may also be engaging.

Evidence § 102 — First Amendment — application

3a, 3b. Although it is common to place the burden on the government to justify impingements on First Amendment interests, it is the obligation of the person desiring to engage in assertedly expressive conduct to demonstrate that the First Amendment even applies.

Constitutional Law § 934 — expression — restriction

TOTAL CLIENT-SERVICE LIBRARY® REFERENCES

59 Am Jur 2d, Parks, Squares, and Playgrounds § 33
USCS, Constitution, 1st Amendment
US L Ed Digest, Constitutional Law §§ 934, 960
L Ed Index to Annos, Parks
ALR Quick Index, Parks and Playgrounds
Federal Quick Index, National Parks; Parks
Auto-Cite®: Any case citation herein can be checked for form, parallel references, later history and annotation references through the Auto-Cite computer research system.

ANNOTATION REFERENCE

Restriction of use of public parks as violating freedom of speech or press under First Amendment of Federal Constitution. 82 L Ed 2d 958.

present other primary authorities on the same topic. Since 1957 these annotations have been regularly supplemented, as will be explained in Chapter 4. References to briefs and annotations, both printed elsewhere in the volume, appear at the bottom of the page in Illustration B–1. Each volume also includes a table of cases reported, an index, a table of cross-references from official *U.S. Reports* citations, and a table of federal laws cited or construed in the volume.

Lawyers' Edition is part of the "Total Client–Service Library," a trademark name for the research system developed by the publisher to link its various publications. This "library" includes a wide range of primary and secondary sources such as statutory codes, annotations, and legal encyclopedias. Each Lawyers Co-op publication refers the researcher to other Co-op products that deal with the same issue.

3. WEST'S *SUPREME COURT REPORTER*

As part of its burgeoning National Reporter System, the West Publishing Company began coverage of the Supreme Court in the October 1882 term. Unlike Lawyers Co-op it did not attempt a retrospective recompilation, and the first volume of the *Supreme Court Reporter* contains cases reported in volumes 106 and 107 of the *U.S. Reports.* West has published one numbered volume of the *Supreme Court Reporter* (cited as S.Ct.) each year. The volumes grew larger with time, until two physical volumes were needed for the 1959 term's decisions. Since then West has published each year both the numbered volume and a supplement designated with an "A" (e.g., volumes 106 and 106A cover the October 1985 term).

Like *Lawyers' Edition,* the *Supreme Court Reporter* appears much more quickly than the official reports, reaching researchers in advance sheet form within weeks of decisions. It also includes tables of cases reported and of statutes construed in each advance sheet and volume, as well as a table of words and phrases judicially defined. Like Lawyers Co-op, West prepares its own summary, which it calls a *synopsis,* and headnotes for each case. These features are shown in Illustration C, the first page of the *Supreme Court Reporter* edition of *Clark v. Community for Creative Non–Violence.*

It is West's headnotes that make the *Supreme Court Reporter* an invaluable research tool. As in *Lawyers' Edition,* each headnote is assigned to a general topic and to a numbered subdivision within the topic. Subject access to the headnotes is provided in the *United States Supreme Court Digest,* a companion set to the reporter. Unlike the *Lawyers' Edition* classifications, however, West's "key number" classification system is used not only for Supreme Court decisions but for court decisions throughout its National Reporter System. Thus the same point of law discussed in a Supreme Court case can be researched in all reported federal and state court cases through West's comprehensive subject digest system, which will be discussed at length in Chapter 4, Case Finding.

Illustration C

The first page of a decision in West's *Supreme Court Reporter*, showing the synopsis and headnotes

CLARK v. COMMUNITY FOR CREATIVE NON-VIOLENCE 3065
468 U.S. 288 Cite as 104 S.Ct. 3065 (1984)

468 U.S. 288, 82 L.Ed.2d 221

$\lfloor_{288}$**William P. CLARK, Secretary of the Interior, et al., Petitioners**

v.

COMMUNITY FOR CREATIVE NON-VIOLENCE et al.

No. 82–1998.

Argued March 21, 1984.

Decided June 29, 1984.

Demonstrators permitted to participate in round-the-clock demonstration on the Mall and in Lafayette Park in Washington, D.C., brought action challenging the United States Park Service's denial of permission to sleep in temporary structures permitted to be erected as part of the demonstration. The United States District Court for the District of Columbia granted the government's motion for summary judgment, but the Court of Appeals, District of Columbia Circuit, reversed, 703 F.2d 586. Motion to vacate the order staying the mandate of the United States Court of Appeals for the District of Columbia Circuit was denied, 104 S.Ct. 478. Certiorari was granted, and the Supreme Court, Justice White, held that a National Park Service regulation prohibiting camping in certain parks did not violate the First Amendment though applied to prohibit demonstrators from sleeping in Lafayette Park and the Mall in connection with the demonstration, which was intended to call attention to the plight of the homeless.

Judgment of the Court of Appeals reversed.

Chief Justice Burger filed concurring opinion.

Justice Marshall dissented and filed opinion in which Justice Brennan joined.

1. United States ⇐57

Sleeping in tents for purpose of expressing plight of homeless falls within definition of "camping" in National Park Service regulation. U.S.C.A. Const.Amend. 1; 16 U.S.C.A. §§ 1, 1a–1, 3.

See publication Words and Phrases for other judicial constructions and definitions.

2. Constitutional Law ⇐90(1)

Although it is common to place burden upon government to justify impingements on First Amendment interests, it is obligation of person desiring to engage in assertedly expressive conduct to demonstrate that First Amendment even applies. U.S.C.A. Const.Amend. 1.

3. Constitutional Law ⇐90(3)

Expression, whether oral or written or symbolized by conduct, is subject to reasonable time, place and manner restrictions. U.S.C.A. Const.Amend. 1.

4. Constitutional Law ⇐90(3)

Message may be delivered by conduct that is intended to be communicative and that, in context, would reasonably be understood by viewer to be communicative, and symbolic expression of this kind may be forbidden or regulated if conduct itself may constitutionally be regulated, providing regulation is narrowly drawn to further substantial governmental interest and providing the interest is unrelated to suppression of free speech. U.S.C.A. Const. Amend. 1; 16 U.S.C.A. §§ 1, 1a–1, 3.

5. United States ⇐57

National Park Service regulation forbidding sleeping in certain areas was defensible either as time, place or manner restriction or as regulation of symbolic conduct. U.S.C.A. Const.Amend. 1; 16 U.S.C.A. §§ 1, 1a–1, 3.

6. United States ⇐57

Fact that sleeping, arguendo, may be expressive conduct, rather than oral or written expression, did not render prohibition against sleeping in certain areas of national parks any less an acceptable time, place or manner regulation. U.S.C.A. Const.Amend. 1; 16 U.S.C.A. §§ 1, 1a–1, 3.

In comparing the editorial treatments in Illustrations B and C, note that the publishers have assigned different topics to the same judicial text. The fact that the editors of the two commercial publications formulate different statements of the points of law in a case demonstrates the subjectivity of legal research. It also underscores the fact that headnotes are merely finding aids, guiding the reader to the actual words of the decision. In each reporter the numbers of the headnotes are inserted in brackets into the text of the majority opinion, so that the researcher can go directly to a particular point in the opinion.

Another useful feature of both commercial editions is the inclusion in the final, bound volumes of cross-references to the location of the same decision in the competing reporter and in the *United States Reports.* Moreover, each includes within the text of opinions a device known as *star paging,* indicating the beginnings of pages in the official edition. This enables the researcher to read the more useful commercial version but have available the precise official citations to the case and to any page within the case.

Star paging is not available until the final bound volumes of *Lawyers' Edition* and the *Supreme Court Reporter,* since the commercial publishers must wait for the government to issue the "preliminary print" pamphlets for the *U.S. Reports.* The long delay in publication means that the commercial advance sheets are heavily used, and in 1986 West began publishing an "interim edition" of the *Supreme Court Reporter.* The "interim edition" consists of two bound volumes, like the permanent edition, so that it can withstand wear and tear better than unbound pamphlets. It lacks parallel references to *U.S. Reports* and the official reports' final text corrections, however, and is printed on less expensive paper.

4. LOOSELEAF SERVICES

The three sources just described provide the full text of every opinion of the Supreme Court of the United States in a traditional case reporter format. There are other forms of legal publication in which decisions are available, usually long before any of the reporters are published.

Even the fastest advance sheet of *Lawyers' Edition* or the *Supreme Court Reporter* is not available until several weeks after a decision is announced, since the publishers' editors prepare their own summaries and headnotes for each case. Lawyers, and others interested in national policy or current affairs, need access to decisions much sooner. To answer this need, two services are published in looseleaf format to provide the text of each decision within a week of its issuance. Both services send subscribers reproductions of the slip opinions, with only short editorial summaries and no additional headnotes. The Bureau of National Affairs publishes *The United States Law Week,* and Commerce Clearing House publishes the *U.S. Supreme Court Bulletin.*

The United States Law Week is a two-volume looseleaf service updated weekly, with extra issues often published in busy weeks during the Supreme Court term. *U.S. Law Week* prints the slip opinion text, reduced slightly so that two columns fit on a page. All cases decided on one day make up one Supreme Court Opinions pamphlet. The pamphlets for an entire term are paginated consecutively and filed in a binder. *U.S. Law Week* is a very convenient way to monitor decisions of the Supreme Court and is one of the most popular of legal publications. Illustration D presents the beginning of the same case shown in the preceding illustrations, from the pamphlet "Opinions Announced June 29, 1984."

U.S. Law Week includes more than just Supreme Court decisions. A separate weekly section on Supreme Court Proceedings lists and summarizes new cases docketed, provides news of developments in cases on the calendar, and reports on oral arguments. An index to both Opinions and Proceedings sections provides access by subject, case name, and docket number. The other volume of *U.S. Law Week,* labeled "General Law Sections," contains news and abstracts of important opinions from other federal courts and state courts, and brief reports on legislative and administrative developments.

U.S. Supreme Court Bulletin, also published weekly, sends subscribers exact page-by-page photographic reproductions of slip opinions, printed on individual looseleaf sheets for filing in a binder. It also includes information on the Court's docket, with very brief summaries of pending cases and a table indicating the status of each case. It has separate indexes for opinions and docket, and includes a weekly report letter summarizing the latest developments. Its coverage is limited to the Supreme Court, so it has no general law sections like those in *U.S. Law Week.*

Both *U.S. Law Week* and the *Supreme Court Bulletin* are useful for locating the text of recently issued opinions, although neither has headnotes that are integrated into a larger research system. A citation to *U.S. Law Week* (abbreviated U.S.L.W.) is recognized as the standard means of identifying Supreme Court opinions until they appear in the standard reporters. A citation to the *Supreme Court Reporter* is preferred once a case is published in its advance sheets, and then after a long delay a case finally receives its official *U.S. Reports* citation.

Finding information on pending cases in *U.S. Law Week* can be a bit tricky for the uninitiated. At the back of the binder, a regularly updated pamphlet contains a table of cases by name. It indicates the page numbers of opinions, but for pending cases and other matters it contains only docket numbers. One next has to refer to a numerical Case Status Report following the case table, and look up the docket number to find page references for any actions taken. Another pamphlet contains an extensive topical index, which also provides references to docket numbers of all cases and to page numbers of opinions. In each list the entries for opinions are distinguished by heavy black typographical bullets, so that they are a bit easier to pick out from the mass of other cases.

Illustration D

The first page of an opinion in *U.S. Law Week*

52 LW 4986 *The United States* LAW WEEK 6–26–84

ment contention in this case is diminished because the "central purpose of the provision was not to empower States to favor local liquor industries by erecting barriers to competition." *Ante*, at 12. It follows, according to the Court, that "state laws that constitute mere economic protectionism are not entitled to the same deference as laws enacted to combat the perceived evils of an unrestricted traffic in liquor." *Ibid.* This is a totally novel approach to the Twenty-first Amendment.[15] The question is not one of "deference," nor one of "central purposes;"[16] the question is whether the provision in this case is an exercise of a power expressly conferred upon the States by the Constitution. It plainly is.

Accordingly, I respectfully dissent.

FRANK H. EASTERBROOK, Chicago, Ill. (W. REECE BADER, ROBERT E. FREITAS, JAMES A. HUGHES, ORRICK, HERRINGTON & SUTCLIFFE, and ALLAN S. HALEY, with him on the brief) for appellants; WILLIAM DAVID DEXTER, Special Assistant Attorney General of Hawaii, Renton, Wash. (TANY S. HONG, Atty. Gen., T. BRUCE HONDA, Dpty. Atty. Gen., and KEVIN T. WAKAYAMA, Spec. Asst. Atty. Gen., with him on the brief) for appellees.

No. 82–1998

WILLIAM P. CLARK, SECRETARY OF THE INTERIOR, ET AL., PETITIONERS *v.* COMMUNITY FOR CREATIVE NON-VIOLENCE ET AL.

ON WRIT OF CERTIORARI TO THE UNITED STATES COURT OF APPEALS FOR THE DISTRICT OF COLUMBIA CIRCUIT

Syllabus

No. 82–1998. Argued March 21, 1984—Decided June 29, 1984

In 1982, the National Park Service issued a permit to respondent Community for Creative Non-Violence (CCNV) to conduct a demonstration in Lafayette Park and the Mall, which are National Parks in the heart of Washington, D. C. The purpose of the demonstration was to call attention to the plight of the homeless, and the permit authorized the erection of two symbolic tent cities. However, the Park Service, relying on its regulations—particularly one that permits "camping" (defined as including sleeping activities) only in designated campgrounds, no campgrounds having ever been designated in Lafayette Park or the Mall—denied CCNV's request that demonstrators be permitted to sleep in the symbolic tents. CCNV and the individual respondents then filed an action in Federal District Court, alleging, *inter alia*, that application of the regulations to prevent sleeping in the tents violated the First Amendment. The District Court granted summary judgment for the Park Service, but the Court of Appeals reversed.

[15] It is an approach explicitly rejected in *Young's Market*, 299 U. S., at 63 (rejecting argument that the "State may not regulate importations except for the purpose of protecting the public health, safety or morals. . . ."), and in subsequent cases as well, see, *e. g.*, *Seagram & Sons* v. *Hostetter*, *supra*, 384 U. S., at 47 ("[N]othing in the Twenty-first Amendment . . . requires that state laws regulating the liquor business be motivated exclusively by a desire to promote temperance."). Because it makes the constitutionality of state legislation depend on a judicial evaluation of the motivation of the legislators, I regard it as an unsound approach to the adjudication of federal constitutional issues. Indeed, it is reminiscent of a long since repudiated era in which this Court struck down assertions of Congress's power to regulate commerce on the ground that the objective of Congress was not to regulate commerce, but rather to remedy some local problem. See generally, *Carter* v. *Carter Coal Co.*, 298 U. S. 238 (1936); *Schechter Poultry Corp.* v. *United States*, 295 U. S. 495 (1935); *Railroad Retirement Board* v. *Alton R. Co.*, 295 U. S. 330 (1935). In any event, the Court's analysis must fall of its own weight, for we do not know what the ultimate result of a regulation such as this may be. The immediate objective may be to encourage the growth of domestic distilleries, but the ultimate result—or indeed, objective—may be entirely to prohibit imported liquors for domestic consumption when the domestic industry has matured.

[16] I would suggest, however, that if vague balancing of "central purposes" is to govern the ultimate disposition of this litigation, a careful and thorough analysis of the actual economic effect of the tax exemption on the business of the taxpayers should be made before any serious consideration is given to their multi-million dollar refund claim.

Held: The challenged application of the Park Service regulations does not violate the First Amendment.

(a) Assuming that overnight sleeping in connection with the demonstration is expressive conduct protected to some extent by the First Amendment, the regulation forbidding sleeping meets the requirements for a reasonable time, place, and manner restriction of expression, whether oral, written, or symbolized by conduct. The regulation is neutral with regard to the message presented, and leaves open ample alternative methods of communicating the intended message concerning the plight of the homeless. Moreover, the regulation narrowly focuses on the Government's substantial interest in maintaining the parks in the heart of the Capital in an attractive and intact condition, readily available to the millions of people who wish to see and enjoy them by their presence. To permit camping would be totally inimical to these purposes. The validity of the regulation need not be judged solely by reference to the demonstration at hand, and none of its provisions are unrelated to the ends that it was designed to serve.

(b) Similarly, the challenged regulation is also sustainable as meeting the standards for a valid regulation of expressive conduct. Aside from its impact on speech, a rule against camping or overnight sleeping in public parks is not beyond the constitutional power of the Government to enforce. And as noted above, there is a substantial Government interest, unrelated to suppression of expression, in conserving park property that is served by the proscription of sleeping.

—— U. S. App. D. C. ——, 703 F. 2d 586, reversed.

WHITE, J., delivered the opinion of the Court, in which BURGER, C. J., and BLACKMUN, POWELL, REHNQUIST, STEVENS, and O'CONNOR, JJ., joined. BURGER, C. J., filed a concurring opinion. MARSHALL, J., filed a dissenting opinion, in which BRENNAN, J., joined.

JUSTICE WHITE delivered the opinion of the Court.

The issue in this case is whether a National Park Service regulation prohibiting camping in certain parks violates the First Amendment when applied to prohibit demonstrators from sleeping in Lafayette Park and the Mall in connection with a demonstration intended to call attention to the plight of the homeless. We hold that it does not and reverse the contrary judgment of the Court of Appeals.

I

The Interior Department, through the National Park Service, is charged with responsibility for the management and maintenance of the National Parks and is authorized to promulgate rules and regulations for the use of the parks in accordance with the purposes for which they were established. 16 U. S. C. §§ 1, 1a–1, 3.[1] The network of National Parks includes the National Memorial-core parks, Lafayette Park and the Mall, which are set in the heart of Washington, D. C., and which are unique resources that the Federal Government holds in trust for the American people. Lafayette Park is a roughly seven-acre square located across Pennsylvania Avenue from the White House. Although originally part of the White House grounds, President Jefferson set it aside as a park for the use of residents and visitors. It "functions as a formal garden park of meticulous landscaping with flowers, trees, fountains, walks and benches." National Park Service, U. S. Department of the Interior, *Resource Management Plan for President's Park* 4.3 (1983). The Mall is a stretch of land running westward from the Capitol to the Lincoln Memorial some two miles away. It includes the Washington Monument, a series of reflecting pools, trees, lawns, and other greenery. It is bordered by, *inter alia*, the Smithsonian Institution and the National Gallery of Art. Both the Park and the Mall were included in

[1] The Secretary is admonished to promote and regulate the use of the parks by such means as conform to the fundamental purpose of the parks, which is "to conserve the scenery and the natural and historic objects and the wild life therein . . . in such manner and by such means as will leave them unimpaired for the enjoyment of future generations." 16 U. S. C. § 1.

A number of other looseleaf services also print the text of selected Supreme Court decisions. When a case is decided in the subject area covered by a specialized looseleaf service, the service frequently publishes the full text of the case. A labor lawyer, for example, can read a recent Supreme Court decision on affirmative action in one of the labor looseleaf services. Looseleafs generally are combinations of primary sources and secondary material, as will be discussed in Chapter 10. Thus one can monitor the services in a particular field for quick access to the latest decisions as well as timely news and analysis.

5. WESTLAW AND LEXIS

Computerized access to the text of decisions of the Supreme Court is available through the online databases WESTLAW and LEXIS. The databases contain the text of opinions not only well before the publication of advance sheets but also sooner than either *U.S. Law Week* or the *Supreme Court Bulletin* can print and mail them. Although LEXIS was once the faster service, WESTLAW now allows access to most Supreme Court decisions the same day they are announced. As the first available source of United States Supreme Court opinions, the databases are widely consulted by lawyers needing immediate access to decisions. Most large research law libraries and many law firms have terminals for one or both of these computer systems. Illustrations E and F present printouts of screens from the WESTLAW and LEXIS displays of the case shown earlier in its printed forms.

In Illustration E, note that WESTLAW includes star paging similar to that found in *Lawyers' Edition* and the *Supreme Court Reporter.* This feature provides references to the exact pages in the *U.S. Reports* and the *Supreme Court Reporter* of material shown on the screen. It allows one to cite material directly from the database without going to the printed versions to find page references, and also makes it much easier to find particular passages upon turning to those versions for further reading. Until recently West and Mead Data Central were involved in litigation over the copyright status of star paging references, but the feature will undoubtedly become available on LEXIS now that their dispute has been settled.[19]

Both systems provide complete historical coverage of the Supreme Court since its first term in 1790.[20] Every case ever decided by the Supreme Court can be searched for particular terms or combinations of terms and concepts. The sophisticated retrieval capabilities of WESTLAW and LEXIS will be discussed in Chapter 4, Case Finding.

6. NEWSPAPER ACCOUNTS

Copies of decisions, as they are issued, are distributed to the press and any other interested persons at the Supreme Court in Washington, D.C. National newspapers, such as the *New York Times* and the *Washington Post,* assign reporters to the Supreme Court to follow and report on its activities. The day after most important decisions are

19. "West and Mead Data Settle Copyright Dispute," *Nat'l L.J.,* Aug. 1, 1988, at 6; *see West Publishing Co. v. Mead Data Central, Inc.,* 799 F.2d 1219 (8th Cir.1986), *cert. denied,* 479 U.S. 1070 (1987).

20. Coverage in both systems begins, as it does in the *United States Reports,* with a summary of a case before the Supreme Court of Pennsylvania in its September 1754 term. The case, *Anonymous,* 1 U.S. (1 Dall.) 1 (Pa.1754), held that the Statute of Frauds and Perjuries did not extend to the province.

Illustration E

Printout of three screens from the WESTLAW display of a case

```
                     COPR. (C) WEST 1989 NO CLAIM TO ORIG. U.S. GOVT. WORKS
Citation                   Rank(R)          Page(P)        Database   Mode
104 S.Ct. 3065             R 1 OF 1         P 1 OF 57      SCT        T
 468 U.S. 288, 82 L.Ed.2d 221

     William P. CLARK, Secretary of the Interior, et al., Petitioners
                                  v.
              COMMUNITY FOR CREATIVE NON-VIOLENCE et al.
                             No. 82-1998.
                         Argued March 21, 1984.
                         Decided June 29, 1984.
 Demonstrators permitted to participate in round-the-clock demonstration on the
 Mall and in Lafayette Park in Washington, D.C., brought action challenging the
 United States Park Service's denial of permission to sleep in temporary
 structures permitted to be erected as part of the demonstration.  The United
 States District Court for the District of Columbia granted the government's
 motion for summary judgment, but the Court of Appeals, District of Columbia
 Circuit, reversed, 703 F.2d 586.  Motion to vacate the order staying the
 mandate of the United States Court of Appeals for the District of Columbia
 Circuit was denied, 104 S.Ct. 478.  Certiorari was granted, and the Supreme
 Court, Justice White, held that a National Park Service regulation prohibiting
 camping in certain parks did not violate the First Amendment though applied to
 prohibit demonstrators from sleeping in Lafayette Park and the Mall in
 connection with the demonstration, which was intended to call attention to the
```

Synopsis

```
                     COPR. (C) WEST 1989 NO CLAIM TO ORIG. U.S. GOVT. WORKS
104 S.Ct. 3065             R 1 OF 1         P 4 OF 57      SCT        P
 (2)
 92k90(1)
 CONSTITUTIONAL LAW
 k. In general.
 U.S.Dist.Col. 1984.
 Although it is common to place burden upon government to justify impingements
 on First Amendment interests, it is obligation of person desiring to engage in
 assertedly expressive conduct to demonstrate that First Amendment even
 applies.  U.S.C.A. Const.Amend. 1.
 Clark v. Community for Creative Non-Violence
 104 S.Ct. 3065, 468 U.S. 288, 82 L.Ed.2d 221
```

Headnote

```
                     COPR. (C) WEST 1989 NO CLAIM TO ORIG. U.S. GOVT. WORKS
104 S.Ct. 3065             R 1 OF 1         P 15 OF 57     SCT        P
 suppression of expression, in conserving park property that is served by the
 proscription of sleeping.  Pp. 3071-3072.
  227 U.S.App.D.C. 19, 703 F.2d 586 (1983), reversed.
  Paul M. Bator, Cambridge, Mass., for petitioners.
  Burt Neuborne, New York City, for respondents.

  Justice WHITE delivered the opinion of the Court.

  The issue in this case is whether a National Park Service regulation
```

Opinion

rendered, articles in these and other papers discuss the decisions, and a side bar on an inside page summarizes actions of the Court. While newspapers rarely provide any material that would be cited in a legal brief, they inform lawyers and researchers of major developments. On occasion newspaper accounts even include docket numbers, a valuable aid in finding the opinions in the more traditional legal sources. Many newspapers, including those mentioned above, feature excerpts from the opinions themselves in cases of major national impact.

Illustration F

Printout of two screens from the LEXIS display of a case

LEVEL 1 - 1 OF 1 CASE

CLARK, SECRETARY OF THE INTERIOR, ET AL. v. COMMUNITY FOR CREATIVE NON-VIOLENCE ET AL.

No. 82-1998.

SUPREME COURT OF THE UNITED STATES

468 U.S. 288; 82 L. Ed. 2d. 221; 52 U.S.L.W. 4986; 104 S. Ct. 3065

Argued March 21, 1984

June 29, 1984

SYLLABUS:

In 1982, the National Park Service issued a permit to respondent Community for Creative Non-Violence (CCNV) to conduct a demonstration in Lafayette Park and the Mall, which are National Parks in the heart of Washington, D.C. The purpose of the demonstration was to call attention to the plight of the homeless, and the permit authorized the erection of two symbolic tent cities. However, the Park Service, relying on its regulations -- particularly one that permiys "camping" (defined as including sleeping activities) only in

---

468 U.S. 288; 82 L. Ed. 2d. 221; 52 U.S.L.W. 4986; 104 S. Ct. 3065

JUSTICE WHITE delivered the opinion of the Court.

The issue in this case is whether a National Park Service regulation prohibiting camping in certain parks violates the First Amendment when applied to prohibit demonstrators from sleeping in Lafayette Park and the Mall in connection with a demonstration intended to call attention to the plight of the homeless. We hold that it does not and reverse the contrary judgment of the Court of Appeals.

I

The Interior Department, through the National Park Service, is charged with responsibility for the management and maintenance of the National Parks and is authorized to promulgate rules and regulations for the use of the parks in accordance with the purposes for which they were established. 16 U.S.C. §§ 1, 1a-1, 3. n1 The network of National Parks includes the National Memorial-core parks, Lafayette Park and the Mall, which are set in the heart of Washington, D.C., and which are unique resources that the Federal Government holds in trust for the American people. Lafayette Park is a roughly 7-acre square located across Pennsylvania Avenue from the White House. Although originally part of the White House grounds, President Jefferson set it aside as a park for the use of residents and visitors. It is a "garden park with a . . . formal landscaping o

H. LOWER FEDERAL COURTS

Below the Supreme Court in the federal court system are both intermediate appellate courts and trial courts. Congress was given the power to create the lower federal courts by Article III of the Constitution, which vests the judicial power of the United States "in one supreme Court, and in such inferior Courts as the Congress may from time to time ordain and establish." The Judiciary Act of 1789, which established the federal court system, created thirteen District Courts, one for each of the eleven states that had ratified the Constitution as well as for the Districts of Kentucky and Maine, and three Circuit Courts.[21] Both District and Circuit Courts served as trial courts, with the Circuit Courts having appellate jurisdiction in limited areas. Over the next hundred years, the structure of the federal court system changed several times. In 1891 Congress created the Circuit Courts of Appeals to serve as intermediate appellate courts,[22] and twenty years later it abolished the old Circuit Courts.[23] The Circuit Courts of Appeals were renamed the United States Courts of Appeals in 1948.[24]

There are now thirteen United States Courts of Appeals, consisting of the First through Eleventh Circuits, each covering three or more states; the District of Columbia Circuit; and the Federal Circuit.[25] Each Court of Appeals hears cases from the trial courts within its circuit, and its decisions have binding authority over those trial courts. The map in Illustration G shows the geographic jurisdiction of the numbered circuits.

The trial courts in the federal system are the United States District Courts. The geographic jurisdiction of the district courts is generally based on state boundaries, with each state having one or more districts. California, New York and Texas are each divided into four districts, while twenty-six of the states have just one district apiece.

It is a surprising fact that no official case reporter publishes the decisions of these lower federal courts. Although records for each case are kept on file with the clerk of the individual court, there are no official publications of the decisions of these courts other than their slip opinions.[26] The slip opinions are not widely distributed, and the decisions can be obtained effectively only through unofficial reporters or online through WESTLAW or LEXIS.

Until the advent of computerized research, however, the only comprehensive source of decisions of the lower federal courts was in the

21. Judiciary Act of 1789, ch. 20, §§ 2 to 4, 1 Stat. 73.

22. Act of March 3, 1891, ch. 517, 26 Stat. 826.

23. Act of March 3, 1911, ch. 231, § 289, 36 Stat. 1087, 1167.

24. Act of June 25, 1948, ch. 646, § 2(b), 62 Stat. 869, 985.

25. The Courts of Appeals for the District of Columbia Circuit and the Federal Circuit are both in Washington. The D.C. Circuit has a general appellate jurisdiction like the other circuits, but is kept busy by the presence in Washington of federal agencies. The Federal Circuit was created in 1982 with a specialized subject jurisdiction, and hears appeals from throughout the country on such matters as customs, patents and public contracts. See 28 U.S.C. § 1295 for an account of the Federal Circuit's jurisdiction.

26. The Court of Appeals for the Federal Circuit does have an official reporter for the customs cases it decides, continuing the official reports of the former U.S. Court of Customs and Patent Appeals. Official reports are also published for specialized federal tribunals such as the U.S. Court of International Trade and the U.S. Tax Court.

Illustration G

Map from *Federal Reporter* volume, showing jurisdiction of U.S. Courts of Appeal

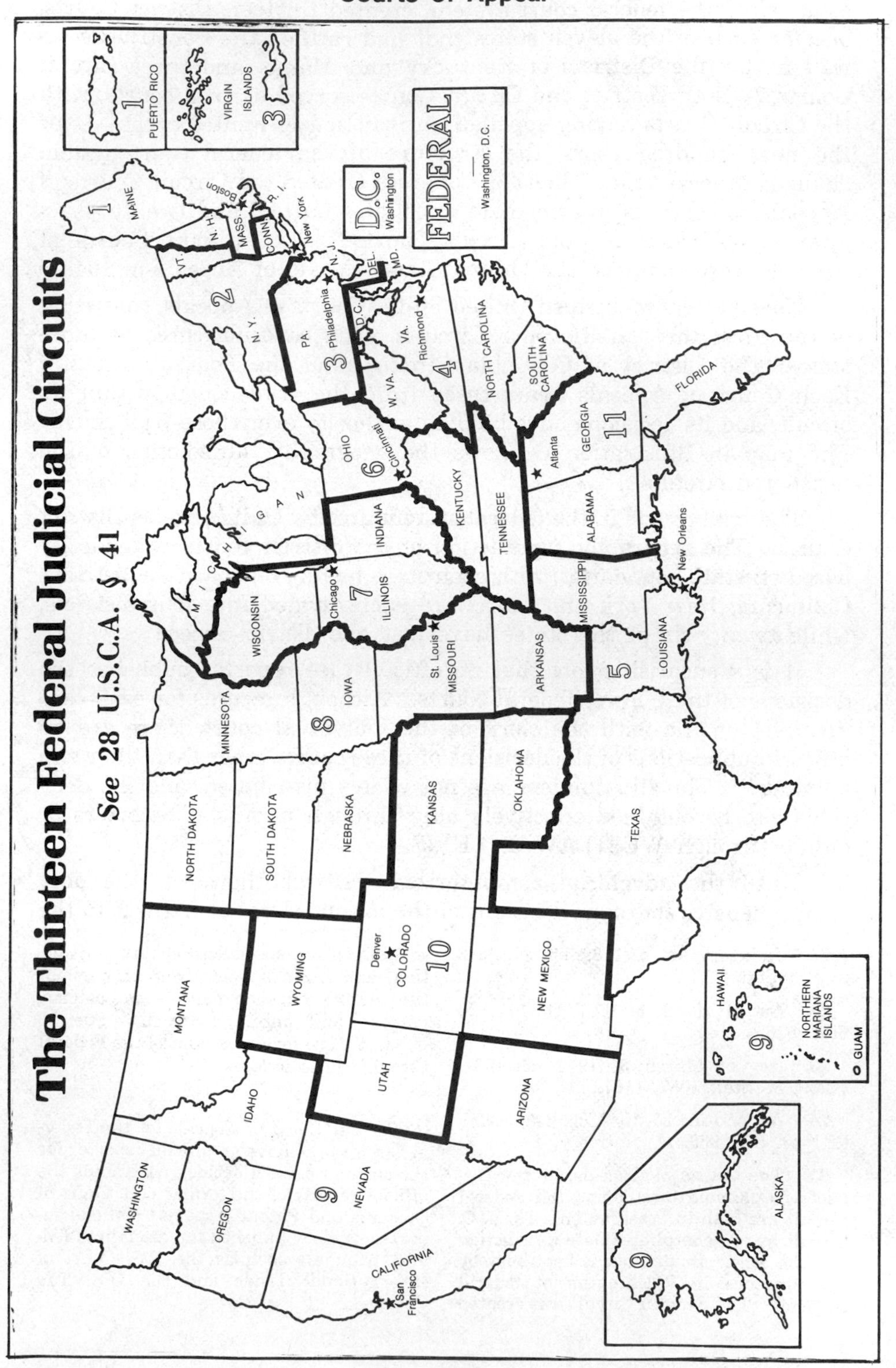

publications of the West Publishing Company. These publications continue to be essential but selective reporters of lower federal court decisions.

1. *FEDERAL CASES*

During the 19th century a number of individual "nominative" reporters published decisions of the many lower federal courts. Over sixty separate reporters, most covering but a single court, published cases of the circuit and district courts, and scattered decisions appeared in more than a hundred other publications.[27] Chaos attended any attempt to retrieve federal cases, and in a few instances different reporters presented varying texts of the same decision. Only a few libraries throughout the country could have a comprehensive collection of federal case law.

This troublesome situation was resolved by the West Publishing Company, which collected the decisions from all of the various reporters and compiled them into a single closed set entitled *Federal Cases* (and cited as F.Cas.). West arranged the more than 20,000 cases in alphabetical order by case name and assigned a number to each. The resulting thirty-volume set, published from 1894 to 1897, contains all available lower federal court case law up to 1880. If the only available citation is from one of the original nominative reporters, the researcher can consult the digest volume accompanying the set, which includes a table with cross-references from the various reporters to the case's location in *Federal Cases.* The alphabetical arrangement, however, means that the name of a case usually provides quick and easy access. Any published lower federal court case decided before 1880 can thus be found in *Federal Cases* by (1) names of the parties, (2) nominative reporter citation through the conversion table, or (3) the case number assigned by the West Publishing Company.

2. *FEDERAL REPORTER* AND *FEDERAL SUPPLEMENT*

Well before it compiled the historical *Federal Cases,* the West Publishing Company began in 1880 a set called the *Federal Reporter* to cover current decisions of the lower federal courts. *Federal Reporter* (cited as F., or in some older cases as Fed.) systematically published decisions from both Circuit and District Courts, as well as the new Circuit Courts of Appeals following the reorganization of the federal judiciary system in 1891.[28] The dramatic increase in federal litigation

27. Lists of the nominative reporters, by circuits and districts, and of all the various publications printing cases appear in the first volume of West's *Federal Cases,* at pages xxxvii and xxxix. The prefaces and biographical notes written by the nominative reporters are reprinted in volume thirty, beginning at page 1261.

28. The creation of the Circuit Courts of Appeals prompted the publication of two commercial reporters limited, unlike the *Federal Reporter,* to the appellate decisions. Banks & Brothers published *Blatchford's United States Courts of Appeals Reports* (U.S.App.) from 1893 to 1899; each of the first 54 volumes contained only one circuit's decisions, but this method was abandoned in 1898 for the final nine volumes of the set. The West Publishing Company launched *United States Circuit Courts of Appeals Reports* (C.C.A.) in 1892 as an annotated reporter to compete with its own *Federal Reporter.* Publication of the series was taken over by Lawyers Co-op in 1899 and returned to West in 1910. The annotations disappeared in 1916, and the

in the early part of this century caused the series to grow quickly. When the set reached 300 volumes in 1924, the publisher introduced a larger, double-column format and began the *Federal Reporter, Second Series* (cited F.2d). This series is still being published, and now consists of more than eight hundred volumes.

The scope of the *Federal Reporter* was gradually expanded to include decisions of various specialized federal courts created by Congress. Opinions of the U.S. Commerce Court appeared during its short life from 1910 to 1913; the Court of Customs and Patent Appeals was added in 1929 and the Court of Claims in 1930. In 1932 West divided the *Federal Reporter* into two parts and began publishing a new reporter, *Federal Supplement* (F.Supp.), for the decisions of the United States District Courts and the Court of Claims. The *Federal Reporter* continued to publish the decisions of the appellate courts, adding the Emergency Court of Appeals from 1942 to 1961 and the Temporary Emergency Court of Appeals since 1972. Coverage of the Court of Claims returned to the *Federal Reporter* from 1960 until that court and the Court of Customs and Patent Appeals were abolished in 1982. *Federal Supplement* included decisions beginning in 1956 of the United States Customs Court, which was replaced by the United States Court of International Trade in 1980. Current *Federal Supplement* coverage consists of the District Courts, the Court of International Trade, the Special Court under the Regional Rail Reorganization Act of 1973, and the Judicial Panel on Multidistrict Litigation.

Many researchers labor under the mistaken assumption that *all* cases considered by the federal courts are represented by decisions published in one of the reporter series. In fact, only a small percentage of the matters that come before the courts even result in written opinions. Initially, all opinions issued by the U.S. Circuit Courts of Appeals appeared in the *Federal Reporter,* but even from the beginning only a selection of U.S. District Court opinions were published.

The explosive growth in the number of cases being decided by the federal courts in the 1960's caused increasing concern that *too many* cases were being published. The cost of maintaining the reporters and the burden of researching innumerable routine and repetitive decisions led the Judicial Conference of the United States in 1972 to request that each circuit determine criteria to limit publication. An advisory council created by the Federal Judicial Center drafted recommendations that publication be limited to opinions (1) laying down a new rule of law or altering an existing rule, (2) involving a legal issue of continuing public interest, (3) criticizing existing law, or (4) resolving an apparent conflict of authority.[29] Each of the U.S. Court of Appeals established publication rules, and fewer than half of federal appellate decisions are

series itself ceased in 1920 after 171 volumes.

29. Advisory Council on Appellate Justice, *Standards for Publication of Judicial Opinions* 15–17 (Federal Judicial Center and National Center for State Courts, 1973).

now published.[30] Despite efforts to stem the tide of published cases, however, both the *Federal Reporter* and *Federal Supplement* continue to grow at staggering rates. In 1987 a total of 57 volumes were added to the two reporter series.[31]

3. SPECIALIZED WEST REPORTERS

One solution attempted by West to slow the growth of the *Federal Reporter* and *Federal Supplement* has been the creation of topical reporters offering decisions in certain specialized fields separately to researchers primarily interested in those subjects. The first and most important of this breed is *Federal Rules Decisions* (cited F.R.D.), which began in 1940. It contains selected opinions of the United States District Courts on matters related to the Federal Rules of Civil Procedure and the Federal Rules of Criminal Procedure. In addition to the text of decisions, the reporter includes proceedings of judicial conferences, speeches, and articles on federal procedural law. *Federal Rules Decisions* does not contain *all* District Court procedural decisions; many cases involving interpretation of court rules continue to appear in *Federal Supplement,* and opinions in one reporter are generally not reprinted in the other.

In recent years West has responded to congressional restructuring of the specialized federal judiciary by creating new topical reporters rather than adding courts to *Federal Reporter* or *Federal Supplement.* In 1980 *West's Bankruptcy Reporter* began publication to cover proceedings under the bankruptcy reforms enacted in 1978.[32] Most of each *Bankruptcy Reporter* consists of Bankruptcy Court decisions, but some District Court opinions appear here instead of in *Federal Supplement.* The reporter also includes bankruptcy opinions from the Supreme Court and Courts of Appeals, but these are simply reprinted from the *Supreme Court Reporter* and *Federal Reporter* with their original page numbers.

Similarly, when Congress abolished the Court of Claims in 1982 and established the United States Claims Court to assume its trial jurisdiction,[33] West created the *United States Claims Court Reporter.* The new reporter includes the trial court decisions of the Claims Court and appellate decisions from the Court of Appeals for the Federal

30. The history of this process is explained and analyzed in Reynolds & Richman, "The Non–Precedential Precedent—Limited Publication and No–Citation Rules in the United States Courts of Appeals," 78 *Colum.L.Rev.* 1167 (1978), and Reynolds & Richman, "An Evaluation of Limited Publication in the United States Courts of Appeals: The Price of Reform," 48 *U.Chi.L.Rev.* 573 (1981). For a more critical view of limited publication, see Hoffman, "Nonpublication of Federal Appellate Court Opinions," 6 *Just.Sys.J.* 405 (1981).

31. In a recent article Federal Circuit Judge Philip Nichols, Jr. wrote of "[t]he bloating of the current volumes of *Federal Reporter* and their rabbit-like multiplication on library shelves." Nichols, "Selective Publication of Opinions: One Judge's View," 35 *Am.U.L.Rev.* 909 (1986).

32. Bankruptcy Reform Act of 1978, Pub.L. No. 95–598, 92 Stat. 2549.

33. Federal Courts Improvement Act of 1982, Pub.L. No. 97–164, 96 Stat. 25.

Circuit and the Supreme Court. The appellate decisions, however, are merely reprints like those in the *Bankruptcy Reporter.*

Since 1978 West has also published the decisions of the United States Court of Military Appeals, and selected decisions of the Courts of Military Review, in *West's Military Justice Reporter.* This series has not affected the volume of other West reporters, since it simply replaced *Court–Martial Reports,* published from 1951 to 1975 by Lawyers Co-op. Also worth noting are two subject reporters consisting of cases reprinted from West's federal and state reporter series: *West's Education Law Reporter,* begun in 1982, and *West's Social Security Reporting Service,* begun in 1983. Both reproduce cases as they originally appear, without new page numbers, but each contains articles and other materials of interest to practitioners in the field.

Each of these subject-oriented reporters contains the standard West research aids, including the key-number digesting system, and represents a response to the flood of case law and the need of specialists to have affordable access to primary materials in their fields. If they are successful, more West topical reporters are likely.

4. LOOSELEAF SERVICES AND TOPICAL REPORTERS

Looseleaf services typically bring together all of the major types of legal publications on one subject, frequently with weekly supplementation, several indexing approaches, and explanatory text material. A very comprehensive looseleaf service may include federal and state court decisions, federal and state statutes, and federal and state administrative regulations and rulings, all in the particular subject field of the service. Sometimes the decisions appear only as abstracts, but most of the major services provide the full text of decisions, including many lower federal court cases which do not appear in the West reporters described above.

The three largest publishers of looseleaf services, Commerce Clearing House, Prentice Hall, and Bureau of National Affairs, also issue bound volume series of the full text of court decisions in their selected subject areas. These topical reporters give a more permanent form to decisions which have already appeared in the looseleaf service and which may not be included in *Federal Reporter* or *Federal Supplement.*

The series that focus specifically on *federal* court decisions include those in the areas of copyright (*Copyright Law Decisions,* published by CCH); international trade (*International Trade Reporter Decisions,* BNA); patents (*United States Patents Quarterly,* BNA); securities (*Federal Securities Law Reports,* CCH); and taxation (*American Federal Tax Reports, Second Series,* Prentice Hall, and *U.S. Tax Cases,* CCH). Series in the fields of environmental law (*Environment Reporter Cases,* BNA) and labor relations (such as *Labor Cases* and *Employment Practices Decisions,* CCH, or *Labor Relations Reference Manual* and *Fair Employment Practice Cases,* BNA) also consist predominantly of federal decisions. Most of these series also include reports of agency adjudications as well as state court decisions.

Other reporters, not issued in conjunction with the major looseleaf services, also specialize in the publication of federal court decisions. Since 1939 Callaghan & Company has published *Federal Rules Service,* which is now in its third series. The Callaghan service prints decisions from all levels of the federal court system concerning the Federal Rules of Civil Procedure and the Federal Rules of Appellate Procedure. Most but not all of its decisions also appear in West reporters. In 1979 Callaghan began a new series, called the *Federal Rules of Evidence Service,* to cover cases construing the Federal Rules of Evidence. Both Callaghan services are accompanied by digests which arrange the case headnotes by rule number. The Lawyers Co-operative Publishing Company has since 1969 been publishing *ALR Federal* as a component of its annotated reporter system, with about two dozen decisions printed in each volume. *ALR Federal* will be discussed further in Chapter 4.

Finally, federal court decisions also appear in other, specialized topical reporters. Those in the fields of admiralty (*American Maritime Cases,* published by American Maritime Cases, Inc.) and bankruptcy (*Bankruptcy Court Decisions,* CRR Publishing, and *Collier Bankruptcy Cases 2d,* Matthew Bender) deal with distinctly federal issues. Several other reporters print both federal and state cases, often including administrative agency decisions as well.

5. WESTLAW AND LEXIS

Another important source of federal decisions are the two computerized legal research services, WESTLAW and LEXIS. They provide full-text coverage of all federal court cases that appear in print in the various West reporters, back to the earliest decisions in *Federal Cases.* Access to the decisions is provided through databases of varying size, scope and cost; one can search all federal cases of the past several decades or limit oneself to a particular court.

New decisions are usually available via the computer terminals before they appear in advance sheets. The West Publishing Company, for example, adds a new case to its WESTLAW system as soon as it receives the slip opinion from the court. It inserts its headnotes, any necessary typographical or editorial changes, and star paging references to the *Federal Reporter* later when the case is ready to be published. LEXIS does not make editorial corrections or additions, so it too can add decisions immediately upon receipt. As with current Supreme Court decisions, the fastest way for someone not at the courthouse to see an important new opinion is by computer, online.

Both systems include decisions which appear in the looseleaf or topical reporters but which may not be published in a West reporter. Both WESTLAW and LEXIS also include the text of many slip opinions that are never published at all. Although most court rules limiting the number of published decisions provide that "unreported" decisions cannot be cited as precedent, some courts permit citations to such decisions if a copy is served on all parties and the court.

The availability of computerized databases creates a disadvantage for the practitioner who does not have access to computerized research tools, and who must compete with government agencies and law firms that have such terminals at their disposal. This inequity is not being alleviated by the limited number of public or shared terminals available. The situation is not essentially different than the problem of inequality in access to research facilities between large firms and single practitioners or between urban and rural practitioners, and the differences in representation for the rich and poor generally in our society, but the computer is certainly increasing these inequities. This problem in legal research must be faced by the courts, the legal profession, and society as a whole.

I. STATE COURTS

The decisions of the courts of the fifty states have traditionally been published in both official and unofficial reporters, but West's unofficial publication of state court decisions has proven so effective that over one-third of the states have discontinued their own official series.[34] For the states which still publish their own reporters, that publication is the authoritative text of decisions and must be cited in briefs, arguments and memoranda to the courts. Most professional research, however, is actually conducted in an unofficial reporter covering decisions of that state—usually one of the reporters in West's comprehensive National Reporter System. There are several other unofficial sources for state decisions, including the two computer research systems (WESTLAW and LEXIS), the looseleaf services in some subject fields, and specialized topical reporters issued by a number of different publishers.

1. OFFICIAL REPORTS

The most striking features of the official reports today are almost all negative—the trend of discontinuance; the long delays in publication; the relative lack of auxiliary research aids in most of them (as compared to their commercial counterparts); and the failure of many to provide preliminary access to decisions by advance sheets. Their positive aspects should in fairness be stated: many are still well prepared and a few offer useful research features like headnotes, summaries, tables, extensive indexing, and texts of new court rules. Some official reports are exemplary, useful research tools, and a few publish decisions as quickly as West does. It is sad to note, however,

34. Appendix B at the end of this book lists the available reports, including designation of those with official status, for all of the states.

that the long and often distinguished history of official reporting, which succeeded the early nominative reporting, is now waning.[35]

Most of the surviving official state reports include *only* the decisions of the highest court in the state, usually called the Supreme Court. More than a dozen of the more populous (and hence more litigious) states publish more than one official report, the second set usually reporting decisions from the intermediate appellate court. New York is one of the few states to issue three official reporters (*New York Reports* for its highest court, the Court of Appeals; *Appellate Division Reports* for the Appellate Division of its Supreme Court; and *Miscellaneous Reports,* containing a selection of lower court decisions.)

Slip opinions in individual cases are issued by at least the highest court in most states, but these are usually not widely distributed. Advance sheets, although not always as prompt as their West counterparts, are available in well over half of the states that publish official reports.

In several states West is now publisher of the official reports, continuing the state's numbered report series but adding its own editorial headnotes. Several other states, such as California and Wisconsin, have official reports prepared by other commercial publishers and accompanied by state-specific case-finding digests. Illustration H shows the first page of a case from *California Official Reports,* the advance sheet service for both *California Reports* and *California Appellate Reports,* which are published by the Bancroft–Whitney Company.

Most of the states which have discontinued their official reports have designated a West reporter as the official reporter for the state. This is either the regional reporter covering the state, or an "offprint" reporter which reproduces the state's decisions from the West regional reporter in separate volumes but maintains the same regional page numbers.

In states with official reports, those reports are the authoritative source for the decisions and must be cited in briefs and other court papers. It is customary in most legal writing to add the unofficial regional reporter citation of the text, so that readers can easily find a case no matter which version they have available. Many reporter series, including West's regional reporters, indicate the other citation at the beginning of a case, *if* another citation exists when the case is printed. Due to the slower publication of most official reports, however, the unofficial citation is frequently the only one available for recent cases. A researcher with a citation to one source for a state decision can find its *parallel citation* through various tables and other resources to be described in the next chapter.

35. It is just as sad to see the physical deterioration of the books themselves due to the high acid content of book paper since the industrial revolution. An increasing number of these early reports, however, have been filmed and are available in microform.

Illustration H

Advance sheet opinion in *California Official Reports*

NELSON v. BOARD OF SUPERVISORS 25
190 Cal.App.3d 25; — Cal.Rptr. — [Mar. 1987]

[No. D004711. Fourth Dist., Div. One. Mar. 10, 1987.]

JOYCE NELSON et al., Plaintiffs and Appellants, v.
BOARD OF SUPERVISORS OF SAN DIEGO COUNTY et al.,
Defendants and Respondents.

SUMMARY

The superior court, in an action for mandate, injunction, and declaratory relief brought against a county by homeless indigent county residents to challenge the statutory and constitutional validity of certain county regulations, entered a judgment of dismissal after sustaining the county's general demurrer to the complaint without leave to amend. The residents brought the action after they were denied general assistance benefits pursuant to county regulations which authorized termination of such benefits to recipients who failed to establish a "valid address" within 60 days. The residents alleged that the regulations violated the county's mandatory duty, pursuant to Welf. & Inst. Code, § 17000, to provide general relief to indigent county residents. In addition, they alleged that the regulations created a classification which unconstitutionally discriminated against indigent county residents without "valid addresses." (Superior Court of San Diego County, No. 552669, Mack P. Lovett, Judge.)

The Court of Appeal reversed. It held that the residents' allegations were sufficient to proceed on both the statutory and the constitutional claims. (Opinion by Kremer, P. J., with Wiener and Lewis, JJ., concurring.)

HEADNOTES

Classified to California Digest of Official Reports, 3d Series

(1) **Public Aid and Welfare § 4—County Assistance—General Relief.**— Welf. & Inst. Code, § 17000, imposes a mandatory duty on counties and cities to provide general relief to indigent residents. The term "general relief" refers to the residual funds by which indigents who

[E7377]

2. WEST'S NATIONAL REPORTER SYSTEM

The West Publishing Company's development of the National Reporter System in the 1880's was a turning point in access to legal information. Its nationwide coverage and distribution allowed researchers to read cases from every state, and its systematic editorial treatment allowed them to find relevant cases from any jurisdiction.

The National Reporter System began with the publication of the *North Western Reporter* (cited as N.W.) in 1879. The years 1884 to 1887 saw cases from the appellate courts of every other state added to West's system in five additional reporters named after regions of the country: *Atlantic* (A.), *North Eastern* (N.E.), *Pacific* (P.), *South Eastern* (S.E.), *South Western* (S.W.), and *Southern* (So.). The grouping of states in each reporter remains unchanged (except for the addition of newly admitted states to the *Pacific Reporter*), and is shown in map form in Illustration I. The naming of the regions and the allocation of the states reflect the perspective of a 19th century Minnesota publisher (Kansas is in the *Pacific Reporter,* Kentucky in the *South Western*), but the regions are simply convenient groupings so that decisions of several states can be published promptly and conveniently.

In 1928 the *South Western Reporter* reached 300 volumes and, like the *Federal Reporter* before it, began a second series. By 1942, after either 200 or 300 volumes, the other reporters followed suit. Each continues today in its second series, adding a "2d" to each citation: A.2d, N.E.2d, N.W.2d, P.2d, S.E.2d, S.W.2d, and So.2d. The reporters include the opinions of both courts of last resort and intermediate appellate courts, where such exist.

Even in the 1880's New York was a heavily populated, litigious state with an extensive court system. Its intermediate appellate decisions would have swamped the *North Eastern Reporter,* so in 1888 West established a separate reporter for the state, the *New York Supplement* (N.Y.S.). The decisions of the New York Court of Appeals appear in both the *North Eastern Reporter* and the *New York Supplement.* Lower court decisions are only in the *Supplement,* which is in its second series and cited as N.Y.S.2d.

As the population and court system of California grew in this century, its reported decisions occupied more and more space in the *Pacific Reporter.* In 1960 West launched a new *California Reporter* (Cal.Rptr.) for its cases. The decisions of the court of last resort, the California Supreme Court, are printed in both the regional and the state reporter, while intermediate appellate decisions are only in *West's California Reporter.*

Because the New York and California reporters contain appellate decisions that do not appear in a multistate regional reporter, they are considered integral parts of the National Reporter System. West also publishes reporter series that are limited to the decisions of other states, but the cases also appear in the regional reporter that covers the state. One of these reporters, *West's Illinois Decisions,* gives cases its

Illustration I

Map of West's regional reporters and their coverage

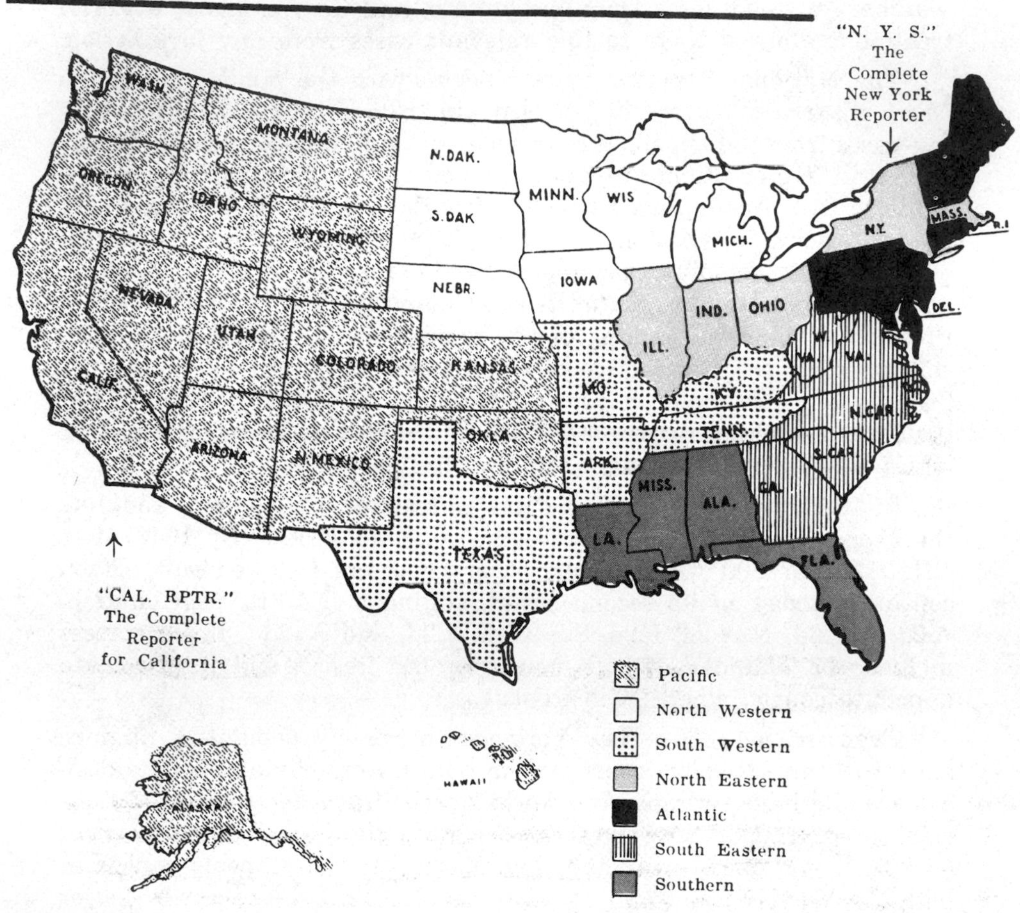

own page numbers, but all the others merely reprint selected contents from one of the regional reporters. There are over thirty of these "offprint" reporters, published for practitioners in the state who wish to purchase their state's decisions but rarely need cases from other states.

All these reporters are linked by West's systematic editorial control. Every case has a synopsis and headnotes prepared by a West editor, similar to those shown in Illustration C from the *Supreme Court Reporter*. These headnotes are arranged by subject in *digests*, tools for finding cases which will be discussed in Chapter 4. West publishes digests that cover all fifty states and the federal court system, digests just for the states within some of the regional reporters, and digests limited to the cases of individual states.

Each reporter volume and advance sheet contains other helpful features, including a digest of its contents and tables of cases reported, of statutes and rules considered, and of words and phrases defined. Regional reporter advance sheets also carry other material for current awareness, such as summaries of recent developments and texts of newly promulgated court rules.

3. LOOSELEAF SERVICES AND TOPICAL REPORTERS

Almost all of the looseleaf services and topical reporters described in the "Lower Federal Courts" section contain state court decisions. Even legal issues that are distinctly federal can arise in state court, so some state cases appear even in patent or federal tax services. Other series, such as *Media Law Reporter* (published by BNA) and *Trade Cases* (CCH), include a representative selection of state cases.

Public Utilities Reports (published by Public Utilities Reports, Inc., and in its fourth series) and *Uniform Commercial Code Reporting Service* (published by Callaghan & Co., and in its second series) are worth noting not only because they focus on issues commonly litigated in state courts, but because each series is accompanied by its own digesting system. Both sets have tables of cases as part of their digests, although neither lists cases separately by jurisdiction.

There are also the new topical reporters published by West and already mentioned for their inclusion of federal court decisions: *West's Education Law Reporter,* which includes a great number of state cases reprinted from the regional reporters; and *West's Social Security Reporting Service,* which is limited mostly to federal cases but does contain a few reprinted state cases.

Finally, a few of the legal newspapers published in large cities report lower court decisions which do not appear in the standard state court reports or the regional reporters. These elusive opinions are generally accessible only through the indexes included periodically in some of the newspapers. New York, however, has a digest specifically designed for this purpose: the *New York Journal Digest-Annotator,* covering decisions published in the *New York Law Journal.*

4. WESTLAW AND LEXIS

The online database systems WESTLAW and LEXIS are important and increasingly comprehensive sources for state court decisions. New decisions from all state appellate courts are added to the databases, usually before they are available in published form, and retrospective coverage of case law is an ongoing project for both systems. Decisions of every state are available online from at least 1965, and each system has cases dating back to the 19th century for a growing number of states. WESTLAW also provides star paging references to West's regional reporters.

In both systems, state cases are available either in databases for the individual states or in multistate databases. Using comprehensive databases covering all fifty states and the District of Columbia, lawyers can search for specific legal concepts or particular words in the appellate opinions of the entire country. In addition, WESTLAW offers topical databases for each state in areas such as corporations or family law, allowing specialists to limit their research to cases in their fields.

J. SUMMARY

This chapter has described the publication of court decisions, one of the central sources of American law and one of the most important and interesting forms of legal publication. Although often criticized as an overused and outdated method of learning, the analysis of cases continues to play an essential role in legal education. Case law also has a key role in legal research, not as a pedagogical device but as a vital resource. The central role of court reports in legal research may become increasingly apparent as the discussion returns to them again and again throughout this book.

The variety and overwhelming detail of the published reports should not obscure the literary quality and the multifaceted significance of the decisions they contain. The style of judicial opinions ranges from mundane prose and legalese to the clear, sharp texts of masters like Learned Hand and Oliver Wendell Holmes and the sometimes poetic humanism of Benjamin Nathan Cardozo. One can be moved by the human drama reflected in opinions which struggle to resolve the disputes arising between ordinary people, which reveal the tensions and conflicts besetting groups in society, or which judge the individual who has broken the law. The published cases also reflect the social, economic and political changes which have affected our world. We usually confront these movements as impersonal, abstract forces, but in the microcosm of the law reports they can be seen more vividly. One can trace in decisions on the law of property, for example, the evolution from feudalism to mercantilism to capitalism, and then through the industrial revolution, the welfare state, and the modern post-industrial society. There are more than headnotes, citations, and holdings in these volumes.

K. ADDITIONAL READING

M.A. Franklin, *The Biography of a Legal Dispute* (Foundation Press, 1968). An introductory description of American civil procedure, by tracing the progress of a single case.

R.A. Leflar, *Appellate Judicial Opinions* (West, 1974). An anthology of short writings on various aspects of judicial opinions.

K.N. Llewellyn, *The Common Law Tradition: Deciding Appeals* (Little, Brown, 1960). A classic jurisprudential study of appellate law.

E.C. Surrency, "Law Reports in the United States," 25 *Am.J.Legal Hist.* 48 (1981). An historical survey.

A. Vestal, "Reported Opinions of the Federal District Courts: Analysis and Suggestions," 52 *Iowa L.Rev.* 379 (1966); "Publishing District Court Opinions in the 1970's," 17 *Loyola L.Rev.* 673 (1971). Critiques of modern reporting of federal cases.

T.A. Woxland, " 'Forever Associated with the Practice of Law': The Early Years of the West Publishing Company," *Legal Reference Services Q.*, Spring 1985, at 115.

T.J. Young, Jr., "A Look at American Law Reporting in the 19th Century," 68 *Law Libr.J.* 294 (1975). Another historical view.

Chapter 3

CASE VERIFICATION AND UPDATING

A. INTRODUCTION

Under the doctrine of precedent, the holdings of governing cases determine the resolution of issues in subsequent controversies. Authoritative decisions continue to have binding effect regardless of their age. Yet the mere fact that a case once held something does not make that the law for all time. The standing and authority of a case are always subject to either sudden change or gradual erosion. A decision may be reversed on appeal to a higher court or may be overruled years later by a decision of the same court. Later courts may also criticize or question the reasoning of a decision, or may limit its holding to a specific factual situation. Any of these circumstances may diminish or negate the authority of the case so as to render its citation useless or even counter-productive. Because constant change is a basic characteristic of the legal system, the researcher must always determine the *current* status of any case which appears to be relevant to an issue at hand.

This function is usually performed by an ingenious series of research tools called *Shepard's Citations,* which consist of lists of citations indicating every time a published decision is cited or affected by a subsequent decision. In 1873 Frank Shepard began printing lists of citations to Illinois Supreme Court cases on gummed paper for attorneys to stick in the margins of their bound reporters. Before long he began publishing his citation lists in book form, and coverage expanded gradually to include every state and the federal courts. Shepard's case citators are now available both in published volumes with regular supplements, and online through the WESTLAW and LEXIS computerized research systems.

The scope of *Shepard's Citations* extends beyond cases to include treatment of statutes, administrative documents, and some secondary material, as will be revealed in relevant sections of this book. Shepard's/McGraw–Hill, Inc. also publishes a variety of other legal research materials, but its case citators are its great innovation and are among the most essential tools in legal research. *Shepard's Citations* are such basic tools that the process of searching the history of a decision is commonly called *Shepardizing* a case.

Before a case can be relied upon in court as authoritative, its continuing validity must be determined. A lawyer who neglects this step in the research process may base arguments on cases subsequently reversed or limited in scope, thereby risking embarrassment *and* practicing law incompetently. In a recent federal case, defense counsel failed to inform the court that a case on which it relied had been specifically overruled and was "admonished that diligent research, which includes Shepardizing cases, is a professional responsibility." [1]

B. THE FUNCTIONS OF SHEPARD'S CITATIONS

Shepard's citators facilitate the verification of authority through a system of concise abbreviations consisting almost exclusively of page citations and one- or two-letter symbols. A Shepard's entry may look strange and impenetrable at first, but once the format is understood Shepard's is really a fairly simple tool to use. Under the citation of a published decision, a list of citations indicates every subsequent time that decision is mentioned. If the court in the subsequent decision took some specific action with regard to the earlier case (e.g., affirmed or overruled it) or indicated some specific attitude (e.g., followed it or

1. *Cimino v. Yale University,* 638 F.Supp. 952, 959 n. 7 (D.Conn.1986).

distinguished its facts), that action or attitude is noted by an alphabetical symbol preceding the volume number of the citing case.

Since determining current status is the purpose of using Shepard's, it is important that a search be as up-to-date as possible. Shepard's editorial staff comprehensively monitors new court decisions and updates its bound volumes through paperback supplements. Depending on the age of a decision, a search for citing references will often require the use of more than one volume or pamphlet.

One aspect of Shepard's which often confuses researchers at first is its idiosyncratic abbreviations. To fit citations in limited spaces Shepard's uses very concise abbreviations, many of which appear in no other publications. *West's California Reporter,* for example, is uniformly cited elsewhere as "Cal.Rptr.," but appears in Shepard's listings as "CaR." At the beginning of each Shepard's volume, however, there is a table of the reporter abbreviations used, so it is easy to dispel alarm caused by an unfamiliar abbreviation.

In any Shepard's listing, the volume number of the cited source is indicated in the top margin, and the beginnings of new volumes in large bold type. In Illustration A, a page from *Shepard's Kansas Citations,* the coverage includes cases in volume 198 and volume 199 of *Kansas Reports.* The smaller bold numbers between dashes are the page numbers of cited cases. Finally, the citations below each bold number are the *citing* references.

Although their primary purpose is to indicate the current status and treatment of primary sources, entries in *Shepard's Citations* provide a variety of other important information. The various features are indicated in Illustration A with numbers corresponding to the following sections.

1. PARALLEL CITATIONS

Many cases are published in more than one report series. Decisions of the Supreme Court of the United States appear in the *United States Reports, Lawyers' Edition,* and *Supreme Court Reporter,* and most state cases are printed in both official reports and one of the regional reporters of West's National Reporter System. Often researchers have one citation to a case and need to find a different report of that case. A lawyer who has read the unofficial edition of a case may need its official citation to cite in a brief, while a researcher may know only the official citation but wish to use the editorial headnotes available in a commercial version. Different citations to the same judicial decision are referred to as *parallel citations.*

Shepard's Citations provide one of the easiest ways to find parallel citations. The first entry for most cited cases, in parentheses, is the parallel citation to another series of reports. Illustration A shows that the parallel *Pacific Reporter* citation for the case printed at 199 Kan. 1 is 427 P.2d 67.

Illustration A

Shepard's Kansas Citations, 1986 case edition part one, showing (1) parallel citation, (2) case history, (3) treatment and related cases, and (4) secondary material and annotations

KANSAS REPORTS

Vol. 198

cc395F2d755
cc425F2d305
199Kan[2]152
199Kan[1]476
199Kan[2]799
199Kan[3]803
200Kan[3]160
200Kan[4]160
200Kan[3]419
201Kan[3]96
201Kan[2]794
202Kan[3]206
202Kan[4]206
203Kan[3]97
203Kan[4]307
203Kan[4]363
205Kan[4]833
209Kan[4]496
210Kan[3]810
f212Kan[2]815
214Kan[4]372
215Kan[3]371
217Kan[3]190
217Kan[3]721
220Kan[3]150
2KA2d[4]594
4KA2d[2]237
16KLR127
20KLR708
10A31054s

-479-
(426P2d267)
US cert den
389US933
cc206Kan304
199Kan343
199Kan450
200Kan168
200Kan629
201Kan129
201Kan791
202Kan[1]199
202Kan205
202Kan[1]300
202Kan402
203Kan[1]611
203Kan[1]648
204Kan54
204Kan683
204Kan827
205Kan760
206Kan390
207Kan837
208Kan44
208Kan948
209Kan704
210Kan425
210Kan506
212Kan466
214Kan640
216Kan434
221Kan723
222Kan147
223Kan384
f223Kan721
224Kan729
226Kan[1]509
227Kan345
d228Kan122
231Kan660
233Kan610
9KA2d406
16KLR128
396NE456
53A21102s

73A2769s
9A3858s
73A3913n
73A3922n
27A41197n
27A41253n

-507-
(426P2d42)
206Kan[1]542

-509-
(426P2d143)
98A3712n

-517-
(426P2d98)
s199Kan16
cc204Kan836
206Kan[1]601
208Kan58
215Kan[1]373
221Kan407
100A2177s
34A399n
97A3118n

-520-
(426P2d157)
210Kan756
211Kan183
218Kan725
9Wsb189

-523-
(426P2d178)
198Kan[5]690
199Kan[5]150
199Kan[4]452
200Kan[2]24
200Kan[4]24
200Kan[4]189
200Kan[1]465
201Kan[1]792
203Kan[5]210
203Kan[5]655
204Kan[2]638
206Kan[1]150
206Kan[4]261
206Kan[1]517
208Kan[5]649
210Kan[2]577
210Kan[4]577
220Kan[4]222
220Kan[5]222
231Kan[3]145
d3KA2d[4]581
d3KA2d[5]581
21KLR325

-527-
(426P2d49)
cc193Kan654
cc399F2d311
199Kan[1]191
200Kan[1]203
200Kan428
200Kan[1]463
f204Kan[1]362
204Kan434
204Kan[1]818
204Kan[1]840
21KLR302

-532-
(426P2d288)
199Kan[5]476
200Kan[2]28
210Kan[6]514
214Kan[6]570
215Kan[2]487
217Kan[1]676
57A2302s
89A31212n
89A31221n

-543-
(426P2d95)
199Kan74
199Kan[1]485
200Kan[2]466
200Kan[3]467
202Kan[3]758
230Kan[3]359
16KLR125
21KLR324

-547-
(426P2d67)
201Kan[3]764
201Kan[4]765
213Kan[2]707
j224Kan[4]50
45JBK33
16KLR143
17KLR491
28A2116s
71A2942s
78A21060s
43A3763n

-556-
(426P2d60)
217Kan[1]95
224Kan[1]327
233Kan[6]377
8KA2d[1]457
16KLR137

-564-
(426P2d55)
202Kan[2]717
207Kan[2]328
d210Kan[3]146
222Kan[3]388
39A2153s

-571-
(426P2d82)
d199Kan647
200Kan359
201Kan[1]488
212Kan67
216Kan[2]343
217Kan[1]109
220Kan[2]65
220Kan235
233Kan1054
234Kan[5]746
q234Kan[5]749
5KA2d308
6KA2d[2]919
352FS[1]692
546FS541
37JBK294
39JBK259
42JBK192
46JBK149
16KLR133
16KLR144

16KLR215
18KLR389
18KLR469
23KLR599
27KLR351
28KLR27
21Wsb198
22StnL743
60VaL1192
81A2138s

-585-
(426P2d251)
s199Kan615
214Kan[4]607
491F2d[3]183
17KLR341
11Wsb363
10A2833s
35A21011s
60A3376n

-605-
(426P2d238)
cc198Kan706
199Kan[1]267
202Kan[1]417
203Kan[5]127
205Kan[5]109
206Kan[5]78
f220Kan[5]397
222Kan[5]200
2KA2d[1]615
18KLR452

-613-
(426P2d106)
218Kan600 (2)

-623-
(426P2d134)
199Kan[1]295
214Kan165
215Kan[1]445
36JBK102
21KLR302
18A31095n

-629-
(426P2d100)
f1KA2d304
20KLR664
9Wsb21
75McL322
34A31153n

-637-
(426P2d153)
203Kan161
215Kan[1]713
216Kan304
47JBK31
28KLR44

-642-
(426P2d114)
f202Kan[3]195
203Kan[1]860
204Kan[3]350
f206Kan[2]404
f206Kan[3]404
208Kan239
208Kan[1]863

-648-
(426P2d159)
s198Kan290
201Kan[1]76
204Kan[1]606
207Kan733
213Kan254
9A3462s

-650-
(426P2d39)
s196Kan228
203Kan[1]636
205Kan222
f205Kan[2]441

-655-
(426P2d92)
199Kan35

-659-
(426P2d151)
204Kan[1]829
q208Kan[1]191
229Kan[1]129
397US[1]391
25LE[1]438
90SC[1]1187
452F2d[2]790
9Wsb186 (1)

-662-
(426P2d52)
cc190Kan771
cc190Kan775
cc190Kan777
199Kan364
200Kan426

-666-
(426P2d26)
203Kan[3]476
203Kan[3]896
207Kan[3]212
208Kan[3]43
217Kan[3]317 (3)

-671-
(426P2d138)
200Kan[3]653
18KLR436
27A3588n

-678-
(426P2d118)
201Kan[2]773
d206Kan[2]398
51JBK93
16KLR125
16KLR414 (4)

-685-
(426P2d74)

-691-
(426P2d149)
203Kan[1]482
203Kan[2]482
204Kan[1]33

-695-
(426P2d30)
cc192Kan91
cc204Kan305
201Kan[1]651
203Kan[1]167

228Kan611
16KLR143
17KLR467
18KLR401

-706-
(426P2d244)
cc198Kan605
j208Kan[1]715
209Kan172
218Kan97
226Kan459
235Kan790
1KA2d284

-715-
(426P2d44)
202Kan[1]429
202Kan[2]429
203Kan[2]527
j208Kan[3]424
214Kan[3]404
214Kan[3]462
215Kan[3]229
215Kan[2]242
18KLR437

-723-
(426P2d21)

Vol. 199

-1-
(427P2d67)
202Kan110
205Kan468
209Kan255
210Kan[2]413
218Kan[5]84
221Kan527
j224Kan612
233Kan[3]366
o233Kan369
1KA2d[7]690
1KA2d[5]692
1KA2d[6]692
441F2d[4]35
e446F2d[3]931
481F2d[5]714
720F2d[7]17
37JBK183
17KLR496
27KLR373
19Wsb226
23Wsb503
20A2235s
39A2477s
27A3815n
27A3822n
39A31341n
39A31356n
42A31131n
42A31139n
42A31149n
25A4800n
25A4826n

-16-
(427P2d500)
s198Kan517
204Kan201
o209Kan[1]234
57A2302s
100A2177s
34A399n

97A3118n

-17-
(427P2d627)
199Kan120
202Kan[1]307
206Kan372
211Kan[1]602
220Kan548
16KLR126
19LE1315n
1A31251s

-23-
(427P2d586)
202Kan[1]300
206Kan[1]34
16KLR128
9A3858s
10A3314s

-26-
(427P2d484)
209Kan606
210Kan[1]223
7KA2d[1]183
16KLR147
17KLR359

-33-
(427P2d606)
203Kan[3]648
203Kan[1]878
203Kan[2]878
203Kan[7]882
205Kan17
208Kan198
216Kan281
d225Kan[3]262

-40-
(427P2d591)
s193Kan201
200Kan[5]570
201Kan[2]458
201Kan[2]612
202Kan237
204Kan[2]157
204Kan158
204Kan472
f207Kan[2]732
208Kan[2]74
209Kan428
210Kan[6]47
62A26s

-48-
(427P2d465)
203Kan[4]572
203Kan[6]574
205Kan[4]631
205Kan[5]631
205Kan[6]635
206Kan[3]743
f208Kan[2]148
f208Kan[3]149
e209Kan[2]90
209Kan630
f209Kan[1]631
f209Kan[2]631
f209Kan[3]631
d210Kan157
214Kan[4]345
214Kan[2]346
214Kan[3]346
217Kan[6]321

217Kan[1]681
f218Kan[1]716
d221Kan292
225Kan[1]488
j225Kan493
227Kan[1]793
d1KA2d[2]700
d1KA2d[3]700
3KA2d[1]396
4KA2d[1]20
e4KA2d[2]304
e6KA2d[5]289
17KLR367
27KLR318
20Wsb498
48A2270s
1A3382s
99A3344n
27A4913n

-59-
(427P2d461)
220Kan[2]71
233Kan409
2KA2d[1]57
7KA2d[1]451
7KA2d[2]451
55A2673s

-64-
(427P2d621)
199Kan[1]646
200Kan359
204Kan[1]27
204Kan[1]170
208Kan83
217Kan109
218Kan701
219Kan[1]690
f5KA2d[1]734
18KLR470
23KLR599
52MnL628
96A370n
96A396n
99A3187n

-69-
(427P2d490)

-73-
(427P2d492)
199Kan152
199Kan594
200Kan379
200Kan426
220Kan474

-77-
(427P2d481)
213Kan[1]430
214Kan[2]707
215Kan[2]833
218Kan[2]601
219Kan[2]676
3KA2d[2]333
3KA2d335
18KLR458
3A3180s

-82-
(427P2d473)
204Kan[1]190
217Kan[2]349

Continued

Shepard's has citators for both official state reports and regional reporters, so it is possible to find an official citation listed under a regional reporter citation and to find a regional reporter citation using an official citation. Similarly, Shepard's has lists for all three editions of U.S. Supreme Court opinions, each with parallel citations to the other two. If a state has discontinued its official reports, the only source of its recent decisions is the National Reporter System and no parallel citation is listed. On the other hand, if a case is reprinted in one of the annotated or topical reporters as well as in official and regional reporters, there may be more than one parallel citation listed.

Parallel citations are usually included the first time a case appears in a Shepard's volume or pamphlet, and are not repeated in later supplements. Sometimes a parallel citation is not available at the time the case is initially listed in Shepard's, as when a *Supreme Court Reporter* case is cited by other courts long before the official *U.S. Reports* version appears. In such cases the parallel citation is provided in the first volume published after it becomes available.

Other resources to be discussed later in this chapter also can be used to find parallel citations, but are often not as convenient as Shepard's. Some are only updated annually, far less frequently than *Shepard's Citations.* Others are not published at all, and are available only through online computer systems.

2. CASE HISTORY

After the parallel citation are *case history* citations, those indicating prior or subsequent proceedings in the same case. The most significant history citations for determining a case's validity are subsequent decisions by a higher appellate court. If a decision is affirmed, modified or reversed on appeal, the citation for the higher court's decision appears preceded by a letter indicating its effect. History citations are always preceded by identifying abbreviations assigned by Shepard's editors. A table explaining these abbreviations is found in the front of each Shepard's volume. The table in *Shepard's Kansas Citations* is reproduced here in the top portion of Illustration B, under the "History of Case" heading. These same abbreviations are used in the citator for every jurisdiction, although some state Shepard's include additional abbreviations for other actions of their courts.

In Illustration A the case at 199 Kan. 1 has no history citations listed, but the entry under 198 Kan. 479 indicates that the U.S. Supreme Court denied *certiorari* at 389 U.S. 933 and that a connected case appears in volume 206 of *Kansas Reports.*

The use of the notations preceding the listed citations is the first step in determining whether or not the case being Shepardized is still good authority. If a case was reversed on appeal, it cannot be cited *as authority.* Even a reversed case, of course, may contain passages worth reading or reasoning worth considering. Such a case *can* be cited in a brief, as long as it is clearly noted that it is not binding precedent.

Illustration B

Shepard's Kansas Citations, history and treatment abbreviations

ABBREVIATIONS—ANALYSIS

History of Case

a (affirmed)	Same case affirmed on appeal.
cc (connected case)	Different case from case cited but arising out of same subject matter or intimately connected therewith.
D (dismissed)	Appeal from same case dismissed.
m (modified)	Same case modified on appeal.
r (reversed)	Same case reversed on appeal.
s (same case)	Same case as case cited.
S (superseded)	Substitution for former opinion.
v (vacated)	Same case vacated.
US cert den	Certiorari denied by U. S. Supreme Court.
US cert dis	Certiorari dismissed by U. S. Supreme Court.
US reh den	Rehearing denied by U. S. Supreme Court.
US reh dis	Rehearing dismissed by U. S. Supreme Court.

Treatment of Case

c (criticised)	Soundness of decision or reasoning in cited case criticised for reasons given.
d (distinguished)	Case at bar different either in law or fact from case cited for reasons given.
e (explained)	Statement of import of decision in cited case. Not merely a restatement of the facts.
f (followed)	Cited as controlling.
h (harmonized)	Apparent inconsistency explained and shown not to exist.
j (dissenting opinion)	Citation in dissenting opinion.
L (limited)	Refusal to extend decision of cited case beyond precise issues involved.
o (overruled)	Ruling in cited case expressly overruled.
p (parallel)	Citing case substantially alike or on all fours with cited case in its law or facts.
q (questioned)	Soundness of decision or reasoning in cited case questioned.

It is even possible that a higher court decision listed with an "r" in Shepard's did not reverse the judgment on the specific issue being researched. Only by reading and analyzing the citing decision can a researcher determine its precise effect. The abbreviations in *Shepard's Citations* assist in case analysis but are no substitute for reading the decisions themselves.

Only decisions which directly affect the result in the case being Shepardized are considered part of its "case history." A decision need not be reversed or modified by a higher court, however, to have its status as authority diminished or erased. Subsequent unrelated decisions, by overruling the case or limiting its holding, may yet have an important impact on its status as precedent.

3. TREATMENT AND RELATED CASES

Following any parallel citations and history citations in a Shepard's display are references to other cases which have mentioned the cited case. Shepardizing almost any case will yield a list of later cases which have in any way cited it. Shepard's provides several ways of indicating what attitudes toward the case are expressed by later courts or what aspects of the cited case are discussed. The *treatment* of a case by later decisions may have just as important an effect on its precedential value as a direct reversal or affirmance. For example, courts may refuse to follow a case under very similar circumstances, limiting its holding to the specific situation under which it arose.

In the parallel citation and case history sections of a Shepard's listing, the references are to the beginning page (or *citation*) of the relevant case. In the treatment section, on the other hand, each reference is to the exact page within a decision on which the Shepardized case is cited. The researcher can immediately turn to the citing reference, and from the reporter volume discern the proper citation of the citing case. Some of the citations in the "treatment" section of a Shepard's listing are assigned abbreviation symbols to indicate the attitude or effect stated by the citing court. These symbols are shown in the *bottom* portion of Illustration B, under the heading "Treatment of Case." It is important to note that in assigning these notational symbols, the Shepard's editors rely largely upon the specific language of the citing court. Hence they will not indicate, for example, that a case has been overruled if such effect is not expressly stated in the later decision, no matter how contrary the holding.[2] Other symbols, such as "d" for "distinguished" or "q" for "questioned," may be just as important as an overruling in determining the precedential value of a decision.[3] The citations in the treatment section of a Shepard's listing are arranged by court. Decisions of that jurisdiction's

2. For over thirty years, *Shepard's United States Citations* indicated that the separate-but-equal doctrine of *Plessy v. Ferguson,* 163 U.S. 537 (1896), was questioned in *Brown v. Board of Education,* 347 U.S. 483 (1954), rather than overruled by *Brown.* Only when Judge John R. Brown noted this fact in a recent opinion, *United States v. Holmes,* 822 F.2d 481, 503 n. 2 (5th Cir.1987) (Brown, J., concurring and dissenting), did Shepard's add a belated "overruled" notation in its *Plessy* entry. Although Shepard's follows the express words of opinions, it can occasionally be swayed by later criticism.

3. In *Glassalum Engineering Corp. v. 392208 Ontario Ltd.,* 487 So.2d 87 (Fla.App. 1986), the appellee relied on a case, *Gonzalez v. Ryder Systems, Inc.,* 327 So.2d 826 (Fla.App.1976), the holding of which had been abrogated by an amendment to the Florida Rules of Civil Procedure. As the court noted:

By shepardizing the *Gonzalez* case, one would have been alerted that its soundness or reasoning had been questioned in a later case; and by reading that later case, *Rivera v. A.M.I.F., Inc.,* 417 So.2d 304, one would have discovered that *Gonzalez* is no longer the law. . . .

If counsel did not observe Shepard's "questioned" signal (designated by a "q") and read *Rivera,* then they, at the least, performed inadequately: appellant's counsel (now the beneficiary of this court's own research) lost the opportunity to argue the controlling *Rivera* case; appellee's counsel, the opportunity to attempt to convince this court why we should not, as we do, find *Rivera* dispositive. Without belaboring the point, we remind the bar that, as this case so dramatically shows, cases must be shepardized and that when shepardizing, counsel must mind the "p's" and "q's." 487 So.2d at 88 (footnotes omitted).

courts are listed first. If cases from the court of last resort and from an intermediate appellate court are published in separate reporters, the high court's decisions precede those of the appellate court. Within the listing for each reporter, however, citations are listed chronologically. There is no ranking by importance or effect on the cited case. A citation to an overruling case may appear towards the end of a long list of other cases. Citations to cases from other jurisdictions generally follow the cases of the home jurisdiction, although some Shepard's units limit this section to *federal* cases. Although the scope of coverage in the various Shepard's units will be discussed more fully later in this chapter, generally cases from other states appear only in the Shepard's for regional reporters and not those for state reports.

Shepard's employs another notational system to aid researchers interested in particular points of law in the cited case. Small raised numbers to the left of the page numbers of the citing cases indicate the headnote number of the cited case corresponding to the specific issue being discussed. If a case addresses several issues but only one aspect is relevant to a particular research problem, one simply determines which headnote or syllabus paragraph addresses the issue and scans the Shepard's listing for that number.

In Illustration A the case at 199 Kan. 1 was cited in several subsequent cases in *Kansas Reports* before being *overruled* at 233 Kan. 366. The three entries immediately after the overruling citation are all references to a case in volume one of *Kansas Court of Appeals Reports.* The point of law abstracted in headnote seven is discussed on page 690, and the points in headnotes five and six on page 692. Note that these are all references to the same citing case, but covering different headnote points. Following the Kansas appellate court citations are four references to citations in federal court cases.

The later cases listed in Shepard's presumably touch upon some or all of the legal issues involved in the original case, so that Shepard's can function as a tool for finding related cases. Many of the later cases that are found, however, may prove to make only passing reference to the cited case, particularly if there is no raised number indicating a particular point under discussion. Moreover, later cases which deal with similar issues but do not expressly cite the original case will not be found through Shepardizing. For these reasons Shepard's is just one of several tools used for finding cases on a particular topic.

For some cases there are few or no citing references in Shepard's. Note in Illustration A that the only reference to 198 Kan. 723 is its parallel *Pacific Reporter* citation. In such situations Shepard's is of little help in a search for related cases. The fact that no citations can be found, however, may itself have some meaning. Several court decisions have mentioned the lack of citations in Shepard's as an indication that earlier decisions are of limited merit or scope.[4]

4. In *Meadow Brook National Bank v. Recile,* 302 F.Supp. 62, 82 (E.D.La.1969), the federal district court in applying Louisiana law noted that an 1865 Louisiana Supreme Court case relied upon by the plaintiff was "clearly a maverick decision

4. SECONDARY MATERIAL AND ANNOTATIONS

Finally, after the references to citing cases, Shepard's listings include citations indicating when a decision has been mentioned in secondary sources and annotations. Shepard's state citators include citing references in the *American Bar Association Journal,* nineteen major national law reviews, and bar journals and law reviews published in the particular state. Note in Illustration A that the case at 199 Kan. 1 has been cited in the *Journal of the Kansas Bar Association* (JBK), *University of Kansas Law Review* (KLR), and *Washburn Law Journal* (Wsb). As with citing cases, these references are to the exact page on which the cited case is mentioned. Every state Shepard's, except those for Delaware, Hawaii and Rhode Island, includes at least one law review or bar journal from that state, allowing lawyers in a state to find references to cases in those periodicals which most closely monitor developments in that state's courts.

For federal court cases, the procedure for finding law review articles is a bit different. Except for references to the *American Bar Association Journal,* periodical citations are not generally included with cases in the regular Shepard's listing.[5] Instead a separate publication, *Shepard's Federal Law Citations in Selected Law Reviews,* is used for locating references in the nineteen law reviews covered in each of the state citators.

Over a dozen state Shepard's units, including those for the three largest states, also include references to attorney general opinions which discuss a cited case.

Annotations in *American Law Reports* (*ALR*) or *Lawyers' Edition* are also included among citing sources in both state and federal Shepard's units. The case at 199 Kan. 1 in Illustration A, for example, has been cited almost a dozen times in six *ALR* annotations. All annotation references in Shepard's include a suffix symbol indicating the nature of the source. The first two citations are followed by the letter "s," indicating that the reference appears in a supplement to an annotation, while the others are followed by an "n," which means simply that the citing source is an annotation.

Last and least, a Shepard's listing may also include reference to one or more of the many legal treatises published by Shepard's/ McGraw–Hill, Inc. The abbreviations used for these works are included in the list at the front of each volume. Obviously, they are included not for their scholarly or practical value but merely because they are issued by the same publisher.

. . . totally ignored by every subsequent decision on the subject."

The courts in *Jeffres v. Countryside Homes of Lincoln, Inc.,* 214 Neb. 104, 123, 333 N.W.2d 754, 764 (1983), and *Amalgamated Casualty Insurance Co. v. Helms,* 239 Md. 529, 540, 212 A.2d 311, 319 (1965), used the absence of citations to denigrate decisions from other states which they did not care to follow.

5. Law review citations to Supreme Court decisions were added to *Shepard's U.S. Citations* in 1986–88 supplementary volumes. See discussion of this citator in section C.1, below.

C. THE COVERAGE OF SHEPARD'S CASE CITATORS

The process of Shepardizing is essentially a simple one: using the proper unit of Shepard's, the researcher locates the citation for a particular case and finds a list of references to parallel citations, earlier or later proceedings in the same case, decisions in other cases, and various other documents. Determining the proper Shepard's unit to use is a necessary first step. Shepard's not only publishes citators for the cases of every jurisdiction, but publishes citators for every set of official reports and every unit of the National Reporter System. If a case has more than one citation, it can be Shepardized in more than one citator. While the coverage of Shepard's units overlaps considerably, it is important to know what information is available in each.

1. *UNITED STATES CITATIONS*

Decisions of the Supreme Court of the United States are covered in the "Cases" volumes of *Shepard's United States Citations.* Because many Supreme Court decisions are frequently cited in subsequent opinions from federal and state courts, this massive set consists of seventeen bound volumes, numbered from 1A to 12, supplemented at times by several pamphlets.

A Supreme Court case may be Shepardized in these volumes under its official *United States Reports* citation or its citation in either of the permanent unofficial reporters. The list of citing sources obtained will vary, however, according to which citation is used. Citations in subsequent Supreme Court decisions and lower federal court cases are provided under all three citations, but the *U.S. Reports* section also includes citations from several federal administrative agency reports and from state court decisions, as well as opinions of the United States Attorney General and articles in the *American Bar Association Journal.* If a state court decision is published in both official and regional reporters, both citations are included in the Shepard's listing.

Law review citations to Supreme Court cases appear in the separate *Shepard's Federal Law Citations in Selected Law Reviews,* and until 1988 were not included in *U.S. Citations.* Five supplementary volumes published in late 1988, however, included lists of law review citations under all three citations for Supreme Court decisions. These volumes are labelled "Supplement 1986–1988," but include law review citations since 1973. This editorial change is not explained in the volumes' prefaces, and it is yet to be seen whether it will extend to supplementary pamphlets or to citations of other federal law sources.

A recent innovation in Shepard's coverage is the inclusion in the supplements of *slip opinion* references to published cases. Shepard's editors examine slip opinions from the Supreme Court and from a majority of the United States Courts of Appeals, and include citations in those opinions in their listings. Because a slip opinion by definition has no citation, the reference Shepard's provides is a docket number, such as 86–881 or 87–4048. The docket number is preceded by an abbreviation indicating the deciding court, such as "USDk" for the Supreme Court or "DkDC" for the District of Columbia Circuit. The inclusion of docket numbers in Shepard's makes its coverage more current, although in most libraries the citing opinions are rarely available except through an online database.

A Shepard's listing under a case's *Lawyers' Edition* or *Supreme Court Reporter* citation includes any citing federal court cases and annotations in *ALR* or *Lawyers' Edition.* In the permanent bound volumes of *U.S. Citations,* however, other citing materials, such as state cases, appear *only* under the official citation. Supplements covering the years since 1984, on the other hand, do include state court citations to Supreme Court cases under each of the three citations. This exception proves essential for finding references to recent Supreme Court decisions, since the official *U.S. Reports* citation is not available for up to two years after the date of decision. If Shepard's did not list state court references to Supreme Court opinions under the unofficial citations, there would be no way of using a citator to find them for two years.

It is important to understand that the different Shepard's listings for an opinion cover the same judicial decision but that each is keyed to the particular editorial treatment in the version it covers. This means that the small raised numbers indicating which headnote issue is being discussed refer to the headnote numbers in that particular version of the case. The three versions of Supreme Court opinions will often have a different number of headnotes, or will assign headnotes to different parts of the opinion. A subsequent citing case may appear in all three listings, with a different raised number in each. A frequent mistake researchers make is to look for headnote numbers from one edition while scanning the Shepard's listing under a different version. You cannot use a *Supreme Court Reporter* headnote number to limit a search for cases listed under the *U.S. Reports* citation, but must examine the official version of the case to determine which of *its* syllabus paragraphs summarizes the point of law in issue.

Illustration C shows the listings under the three versions of a little-cited Supreme Court decision, *Estate of Keller v. Commissioner,* 312 U.S. 543 (1941). Note that each provides a parallel reference to the other two, and to citations of related Supreme Court decisions. All three contain citations from federal court decisions, although the same point of law has been assigned headnote number three in the *U.S. Reports,* number one in *Lawyers' Edition,* and numbers four and five in the *Supreme Court Reporter.* Only the *U.S. Reports* listing contains references to citing federal administrative decisions and state court decisions, and only the two commercial listings include references to citing annotations in *Lawyers' Edition* and *ALR.*

Illustration C

Comparison of three listings for same case in *Shepard's United States Citations*

UNITED STATES REPORTS
Vol. 312

—543—
(85LE1032)
(61SC651)
s311US630
s85LE400
s61SC50
s113F2d833
cc311US625
cc85LE397
cc61SC32
p312US531
Cir. 2
156F2d[3]871
183F2d[3]291
Cir. 5
e148F2d[3]78
j148F2d[3]78
Cir. 6
139F2d[3]258
f193F2d[3]967
Cir. 7
j199F2d[3]495
Cir. 9
122F2d1001
Cir. 10
62FS[3]238
45BTA896
13TCt164
13TCt167
20TCt757
56TCt495
Calif
104CA2d509
231P2d878
Conn
132Ct8
42A2d368
La
207La647
21So2d861
Mass
315Mas709
54NE172
N J
43NJ294
135NJE420
135NJE438
38A2d901
39A2d388
204A2d135
N Y
197NYM234
94NYS2d408
Pa
465Pa67
348A2d120
Wash
35Wsh2d868
216P2d215

LAWYERS' EDITION
Vol. 85

—1032—
(312US543)
(61SC651)
s85LE400
cc85LE397
cc85LE996
Cir. 2
156F2d[1]871
183F2d[1]291
Cir. 5
e148F2d[1]78
j148F2d[1]78
Cir. 6
139F2d[1]258
f193F2d[1]967
Cir. 7
j199F2d[1]495
Cir. 9
122F2d[1]1001
Cir. 10
62FS[1]238
14LE833n
150AR1270n
159AR1338n

SUPREME COURT REPORTER
Vol. 61

—651—
(312US543)
(85LE1032)
s61SC50
cc61SC32
cc61SC646
Cir. 2
156F2d[4]871
183F2d[4]291
Cir. 5
e148F2d[4]78
j148F2d[4]78
Cir. 6
139F2d[4]258
f193F2d[4]967
Cir. 7
j199F2d[4]495
Cir. 9
122F2d[5]1001
Cir. 10
62FS[4]238
14LE833n
150AR1270n
159AR1338n

Coverage of Supreme Court decisions is just one part of *Shepard's United States Citations.* For each jurisdiction Shepard's provides citations to both cases *and* statutes. The treatment of statutes and related materials such as constitutions and court rules is not discussed in this chapter but is an important part of each jurisdictional Shepard's unit. Part 2 of *Shepard's United States Citations* is used to find citations to either legislative or judicial treatments of federal statutes, and includes coverage of other material such as the United States Constitution, treaties, and federal court rules.

To confuse the uninitiated researcher, there are also two other Shepard's units bearing the label *Shepard's United States Citations* on the spines of their volumes. *Shepard's United States Administrative Citations* provides citations to the decisions and orders of various federal administrative agencies, commissions and courts, and will be discussed in Chapter 8. *Shepard's United States Citations: Patents and Trademarks* provides citations to patents (listed numerically) and to copyrights and trademarks (listed alphabetically) as well as to relevant decisions of the courts and the Commissioner of Patents.

2. *FEDERAL CITATIONS*

Citations to the decisions of the lower federal courts can be found in *Shepard's Federal Citations,* a voluminous set divided into two parts. Generally Part 1 covers the United States Courts of Appeals and Part 2 the United States District Courts and the United States Claims Court. The publications which can be Shepardized in Part 1 are the *Federal Reporter* and *Federal Cases,* and those covered in Part 2 are the *Federal Supplement, Federal Rules Decisions, Court of Claims Reports,* and *United States Claims Court Reporter.* Citing sources are the same in both parts, with coverage similar to that in *U.S. Citations.* Coverage incorporates all levels of the federal system, including slip opinions from the Supreme Court and several of the Courts of Appeals, as well as state cases in both official and National Reporter System citations. As with the Supreme Court, the only periodical included is the *American Bar Association Journal,* with treatment in the law reviews relegated to *Shepard's Federal Law Citations in Selected Law Reviews.*

3. STATE AND REGIONAL SHEPARD'S UNITS

A separate unit of Shepard's Citations is published for each of the fifty states, for the District of Columbia, and for Puerto Rico. In addition to cases, each of these units typically covers citations to the state's statutes, attorney general opinions, and municipal charters and ordinances. The scope of coverage varies somewhat between states, so it is wise for a lawyer to be familiar with the contents of the particular Shepard's for the state in which he or she practices.

The "Cases" portion of a state Shepard's unit contains sections listing citations to the official reports of the jurisdiction, and to the regional reporter covering that state. The official reports section of *Shepard's Kansas Citations* has already been shown, in Illustration A, and its features discussed. The listing provides case history citations, followed by subsequent citing cases in the state's official *Kansas Reports* and *Kansas Court of Appeals Reports.* After the Kansas cases, the listing includes citations in federal cases, law review articles, and annotations. It does *not* include any citations from courts in other states.

The regional reporter section of a state Shepard's has far fewer citing sources. Illustration D shows the *Pacific Reporter* section of *Shepard's Kansas Citations.* Parallel citations to *Kansas Reports* are provided, but the only other citations listed are subsequent Kansas cases (as published in the *Pacific Reporter*) and federal cases. Cases which have a precedential impact on the decision being Shepardized *would* thus appear here. Note that the case at 427 P.2d 67, the same case examined earlier in its *Kansas Reports* form, was overruled at 662 P.2d 1272. While the regional section of a state Shepard's has fewer citing sources, it may be a convenient tool if the volumes for Shepard's regional citator are unavailable and if the regional reporter is the only version of the state's cases at hand. Moreover, if the official reports are published more slowly than the regional reporter, as is usually the case, new citations will appear in the official reports section only when page numbers have been assigned. They will be listed under the regional citations much earlier, so a recent important case could be listed *only* here for several months or longer. To be up to date, therefore, it is important to check under both citations.

If official reports are no longer published for a state, then there are no parallel citations and the regional reporter version of a case is the only one available. Its citation is also then the only one used in the state Shepard's unit, and citations in law reviews and *ALR* annotations are listed under the regional reporter citation.

Shepardizing a case in the state unit, under either official or regional citation, will yield references to any home state case or federal case that has affected its authority in any way. As these are the only cases that can be presented to the court as binding authority, some researchers stop Shepardizing when they have completed their search in the appropriate state unit. One can expand a search by tracing the treatment of a state decision in the courts of every other state, however, by using the Shepard's unit for the regional reporter. A separate unit of Shepard's is published for each series in the National Reporter System, including the *New York Supplement* and *California Reporter.* Illustration E shows the same Kansas case, at 427 P.2d 67, as listed in *Shepard's Pacific Reporter Citations.* Note that the same Kansas and federal cases appear first, followed by citing cases from other states, listed by their regional reporter citations. Although decisions from other state courts are not binding on the courts of the home state, they are often useful as persuasive authority, particularly if no relevant decisions within the home state can be found.

The citing cases from other states are listed separately by state, in two sequences. First are cases from states in the same regional reporter as the case being Shepardized, arranged alphabetically by state. Then in a second alphabetical arrangement are cases from states covered in the other regional reporters. Note that annotations are

Illustration D

Shepard's Kansas Citations, 1986 case edition part two

PACIFIC REPORTER, 2d SERIES (Kansas Cases)

Vol. 427

642P2d[4]982
699P2d[1]35

-82-
(198Kan571)
d433P2d388
437P2d[3]227
441P2d[8]860
510P2d[11]201
532P2d[3]1055
535P2d[5]933
551P2d[6]893
552P2d[3]942
615P2d[4]820
636P2d[4]223
668P2d[11]147
675P2d[14]891
q675P2d[14]894
352FS[5]692
546FS[12]541

-92-
(198Kan655)
427P2d[4]608

-95-
(198Kan543)
430P2d[1]242
436P2d[3]859
436P2d[4]859
451P2d[4]232
634P2d[4]1122

-98-
(198Kan517)
s427P2d500
cc465P2d925
481P2d[4]1019
490P2d[3]637
524P2d[4]1124
559P2d[3]809

-100-
(198Kan629)
f564P2d[6]555

-106-
(198Kan613)
545P2d[8]337

-114-
(198Kan642)
f448P2d[1]19
457P2d[6]105
461P2d[2]787
f479P2d[8]841
f479P2d[9]841
491P2d[7]903
494P2d[5]1080
494P2d[6]1080

-118-
(198Kan678)
443P2d[7]318
443P2d[9]318
d479P2d[12]866

-124-
(198Kan460)
s424P2d864
440P2d[1]607
446P2d[1]784
498P2d[1]59
499P2d[1]1089
q504P2d[3]189
504P2d[4]189

504P2d[1]201
e512P2d[2]362
f515P2d[1]801
518P2d[1]433
d531P2d[2]444
600P2d155
q634P2d[2]1092
646P2d[2]1146

-129-
(198Kan473)
cc395F2d755
cc425F2d305
427P2d[4]602
430P2d[5]255
433P2d[7]453
433P2d[4]472
434P2d[7]1006
434P2d[9]1006
436P2d[7]976
439P2d[7]390
443P2d[4]260
447P2d[6]810
447P2d[7]810
453P2d[7]10
454P2d[8]504
454P2d[9]530
473P2d[9]70
496P2d[10]1399
504P2d[7]175
f512P2d[4]331
520P2d[10]1262
524P2d[7]1123
535P2d[7]927
538P2d[7]1388
551P2d[7]900
585P2d[9]620
604P2d[4]286

-134-
(198Kan623)
429P2d[3]106
519P2d[2]627
524P2d[1]707

-138-
(198Kan671)
438P2d[3]55

-143-
(198Kan509)

-149-
(198Kan691)
454P2d[1]540
454P2d[2]540
460P2d[1]106

-151-
(198Kan659)
465P2d[1]932
q490P2d[1]383
q490P2d[2]383
622P2d[2]663
397US[1]391
25LE[1]438
90SC[1]1187
452F2d[1]790

-153-
(198Kan637)
453P2d[1]13
527P2d[2]1352
527P2d[3]1352
532P2d[1]1307

-157-
(198Kan520)
504P2d[1]204
505P2d[1]1117
545P2d[6]328

-159-
(198Kan648)
s424P2d612
439P2d[2]76
464P2d[2]223
486P2d[2]849
515P2d[2]1209

-238-
(198Kan605)
cc426P2d244
428P2d[2]840
449P2d[2]481
449P2d[1]487
452P2d[9]855
468P2d[9]183
476P2d[9]699
f552P2d[9]878
563P2d[9]470
586P2d[1]60

-244-
(198Kan706)
cc426P2d238
j494P2d[8]1061
495P2d[11]980
542P2d[11]661
563P2d[11]537
563P2d[8]537
602P2d[11]84
684P2d[11]423

-251-
(198Kan585)
s433P2d414
522P2d[8]1306
491F2d[5]183

-267-
(198Kan479)
US cert den
389US933
cc477P2d971
429P2d[1]929
430P2d[24]278
430P2d[4]281
434P2d[18]803
438P2d[7]115
439P2d[16]90
443P2d[1]262
447P2d[1]804
447P2d[5]809
448P2d[14]33
449P2d[24]548
455P2d[24]515
455P2d[6]572
460P2d[16]614
465P2d[7]930
466P2d[7]298
473P2d[7]52
480P2d[16]52
486P2d[2]853
490P2d[16]422
495P2d[1]89
498P2d[6]91
502P2d[24]733
502P2d781
513P2d[16]253
522P2d[24]368
532P2d[11]1318

562P2d[2]192
563P2d[2]1445
573P2d[24]1043
f576P2d[11]656
585P2d[11]1056
601P2d[7]1140
606P2d1034
d612P2d[24]169
647P2d[11]1304
664P2d[24]1358
682P2d125

-288-
(198Kan532)
430P2d[7]255
434P2d[1]827
502P2d[12]658
521P2d[14]280
524P2d[2]760
538P2d[1]1396

Vol. 427

-67-
(199Kan1)
446P2d[2]727
470P2d[3]832
497P2d[2]147
497P2d[3]147
502P2d[18]653
542P2d[14]351
561P2d[1]795
574P2d[19]231
574P2d[17]232
574P2d[14]233
574P2d[15]233
j584P2d[18]145
662P2d[13]1271
o662P2d1272
441F2d[7]35
e446F2d[12]931
e446F2d[13]931
481F2d[14]714
720F2d[16]17

-443-
(199Kan89)
440P2d[9]629
e441P2d[2]838
e441P2d[3]839
446P2d[4]729
446P2d[9]729
452P2d[7]291
452P2d[4]295
452P2d[9]296
454P2d[7]444
454P2d[7]478
468P2d[9]240
479P2d[7]374
479P2d[9]874
493P2d[6]563
493P2d[5]564
493P2d[4]565
f494P2d[4]1098
f494P2d[7]1098
f494P2d[3]1099
f494P2d[5]1099
f494P2d[9]1099
497P2d[9]299
d497P2d[7]301
498P2d[3]273
d522P2d[3]418
524P2d[9]1131
524P2d[7]1133
524P2d[8]1133

542P2d[4]350
545P2d[9]309
567P2d[4]875
590P2d[7]1041
636P2d[6]229
404F2d[9]54
d271FS[9]240
339FS[7]233

-448-
(199Kan156)
433P2d[2]402

-453-
(199Kan123)
s381P2d356
436P2d[1]363
439P2d[6]130
442P2d[2]11
466P2d[1]310
481P2d[3]997
515P2d[1]809
d515P2d1035
520P2d[6]1224
542P2d[7]693
607P2d[6]497
672P2d[7]604
686P2d[7]147
686P2d[8]147

-457-
(199Kan162)
428P2d[2]836
433P2d[4]402
436P2d[7]387
436P2d[3]414
449P2d[6]523
460P2d[1]619
460P2d[2]620
460P2d[4]620
460P2d[8]620
460P2d[6]621
481P2d[3]979
j524P2d[2]765
552P2d[2]1362
558P2d[2]149
579P2d[3]728
579P2d[4]728

-461-
(199Kan59)
551P2d[2]864
574P2d[1]567
643P2d[1]1142
643P2d[2]1142
661P2d[4]1245

-465-
(199Kan48)
455P2d[7]545
455P2d[11]546
470P2d[7]789
470P2d[9]789
470P2d[11]791
482P2d[6]21
f490P2d[5]629
f490P2d[6]629
e495P2d[3]998
e495P2d[5]998
498P2d82
f498P2d[2]83
f498P2d[5]83
f498P2d[6]83
d499P2d547
520P2d[7]1222
520P2d[4]1223

520P2d[5]1223
520P2d[6]1223
537P2d[10]173
538P2d[2]727
f545P2d[1]349
d559P2d331
d573P2d[3]1052
d573P2d[5]1104
d573P2d[6]1104
592P2d[1]869
592P2d[9]869
j592P2d872
595P2d[1]1143
601P2d[2]1177
e605P2d[5]164
610P2d[2]591
e628P2d[9]236

-473-
(199Kan82)
460P2d[4]540
d536P2d[5]1390
j536P2d[5]1391
298FS[1]913

-478-
(199Kan96)
427P2d[1]447
468P2d[1]240
476P2d[1]638
494P2d[1]1099

-481-
(199Kan77)
516P2d[2]938
516P2d[3]938
522P2d[7]183
529P2d[7]169
545P2d[7]337
549P2d[7]572
594P2d[7]1113
594P2d[2]1114

-484-
(199Kan26)
498P2d[1]85
500P2d[1]62
638P2d[4]984

-490-
(199Kan69)

-492-
(199Kan73)
427P2d[5]602
433P2d[6]553
436P2d[3]362
436P2d[4]362
436P2d[4]876
552P2d[6]954

-495-
(199Kan154)
427P2d[2]601
427P2d[3]601
439P2d[2]107
439P2d[3]107
453P2d[1]46
453P2d[3]46
564P2d[1]457

-497-
(199Kan128)
s199P2d792
cc332F2d849
454P2d[3]493

-500-
Case 1
(199Kan16)
s426P2d98
460P2d[2]616
o495P2d[1]1026
495P2d[2]1026

-500-
Case 2
(199Kan142)
cc422F2d852
433P2d[1]425
440P2d[3]660
486P2d[2]506

-586-
(199Kan23)
448P2d[1]33
476P2d[4]240

-588-
(199Kan112)

-591-
(199Kan40)
s392P2d942
438P2d[1]119
441P2d[5]826
443P2d[5]303
447P2d[1]836
460P2d445
460P2d446
464P2d[1]188
f486P2d[5]849
490P2d[5]363
497P2d[7]306
499P2d[7]204

-598-
(199Kan147)
429P2d[4]929
429P2d[5]929
429P2d[2]930
433P2d[2]346
433P2d[4]453
433P2d[5]453
f436P2d[10]361
f436P2d[8]361
f436P2d[9]361
438P2d[12]86
440P2d[4]633
443P2d[2]260
453P2d[2]46
453P2d[4]46
460P2d[2]502
464P2d[5]165
478P2d[2]215
479P2d[4]851
491P2d[10]904
497P2d[3]290
502P2d[4]852
524P2d739

-603-
(199Kan108)
s454P2d550
427P2d[2]609
427P2d[3]609
430P2d[3]297

434P2d[3]800
434P2d[3]814
f438P2d[3]466
440P2d[3]658
441P2d[2]858
441P2d[3]858
449P2d[3]566
449P2d568
451P2d[3]238
461P2d[3]803
479P2d[2]839
483P2d[2]1045
483P2d[3]1045
495P2d[3]910
557P2d[3]1248
558P2d[4]1090
558P2d[3]1095

-606-
(199Kan33)
455P2d[8]572
457P2d[1]126
457P2d[2]126
457P2d[7]129
468P2d[10]262
491P2d[10]945
531P2d18
531P2d[5]20
d589P2d[8]619

-611-
(199Kan136)
cc398P2d339
448P2d[7]22
461P2d[13]814
531P2d[5]449

-616-
(199Kan116)
US reh den
in393US902
v392US308
v20LE1115
v88SC2065
cc481P2d1015
448P2d[3]33
454P2d[11]552
f456P2d[5]2
f456P2d[7]2
486P2d[4]853
524P2d[11]774
524P2d[11]1125
578P2d[10]1112
412US[5]231
36LE[5]865
93SC[5]2050
380F2d[2]164
419F2d[5]819
f468F2d[5]25
496F2d[5]674
280FS[5]636
299FS[4]323

-621-
(199Kan64)
433P2d[1]387
437P2d[1]227
459P2d180
460P2d[3]573
490P2d[1]398
535P2d[1]933
545P2d1107
549P2d[3]1034
f624P2d[3]988

included, but that the references to law review articles found in the state unit are not supplied in the regional citator. Because of the difference in coverage, it is always important when using Shepard's for finding related material to examine both state and regional units.

Illustration E

Shepard's Pacific Reporter Citations, 1987 volume

Vol. 427 PACIFIC REPORTER, 2d SERIES

– 67 –
(199Kan1)
446P2d[2]727
470P2d[3]832
497P2d[2]147
497P2d[3]147
502P2d[18]653
542P2d[14]351
561P2d[1]795
574P2d[19]231
574P2d[17]232
574P2d[14]233
574P2d[15]233
j584P2d[18]145
662P2d
[[13]1271
o662P2d1272
Cir. 5
441F2d[7]35
Cir. 8
720F2d[16]17
Cir. 10
e446F2d[12]931
e446F2d[13]931
481F2d[14]714
Calif
65CaR[4]145
Ore
641P2d614
Ill
385NE82
395NE581
Mass
282NE414
Va
269SE792
W Va
275SE13
20A2235s
39A2477s
27A3815n
27A3822n
39A31341n
39A31356n
42A31131n
42A31139n
42A31149n
25A4800n
25A4826n

– 79 –
(49Haw675)
US cert den
in396US822
s448P2d337
543P2d[3]1361
543P2d[4]1361
543P2d[6]1362
647P2d[5]703
649P2d[1]1147
649P2d[2]1147
653P2d[2]1155
655P2d876
712P2d1143
Colo
613P2d[10]323
NM
444P2d[11]970
572P2d[7]1261
603P2d[6]1107
Okla
569P2d[5]973
586P2d[7]1098
19A31366n
20A3993n

RLPB§1.51

– 86 –
(49Haw688)
462P2d[2]198
462P2d[2]909

– 94 –
(49Haw672)
s395P2d273
588P2d[2]445
615P2d[2]97
f706P2d[3]1313

– 96 –
(247Or13)
464P2d[4]318
584P2d[4]767
616P2d[2]1177
616P2d[3]1177
636P2d[1]928
688P2d[4]822

– 97 –
(247Or1)
467P2d[7]659
467P2d[10]659
473P2d[2]146
o475P2d[2]80
548P2d[2]190
585P2d[5]16
585P2d[6]16
h585P2d[4]17
588P2d1284
d597P2d[10]808
Haw
652P2d[8]1133
Ill
364NE545
445NE406

– 102 –
(246Or621)
cc426P2d878

– 105 –
(247Or33)
456P2d[2]484
473P2d[5]134
17A21388s

– 107 –
(246Or617)
427P2d415
433P2d[2]618
484P2d1124
NM
563P2d1178

– 108 –
432P2d[8]474

– 109 –
(247Or38)
543P2d[6]1089
559P2d[6]874

– 112 –
515P2d[1]1168
572P2d[1]294
572P2d[1]591
646P2d[1]1295

– 115 –
433P2d[2]854
443P2d[1]767

451P2d[1]398

– 116 –
e542P2d[2]1325

– 124 –
434P2d[1]492
77A3235n

– 125 –
(102Az174)
430P2d[2]143
431P2d[1]685
433P2d[2]75
453P2d[2]507
459P2d[3]347
d476P2d[1]678
478P2d[1]519
478P2d[2]519
481P2d[2]849
d484P2d[2]219
498P2d212
499P2d[2]103
508P2d[2]333
514P2d1002
515P2d[1]906
554P2d[1]924
d554P2d[2]924
559P2d[1]198
559P2d[2]198
687P2d[1]1212
687P2d[2]1212
Idaho
f679P2d[2]678
Okla
481P2d[1]165
La
379So2d1091

– 126 –
(102Az175)
22A2939s

– 129 –
(102Az178)
cc493P2d125
496P2d[3]587

– 131 –
(102Az180)
452P2d[2]105
464P2d[3]607
464P2d[1]657
464P2d[2]676
466P2d[1]754
472P2d[1]71
477P2d[1]757
516P2d[1]331

– 135 –
(102Az184)
cc427P2d137
456P2d[4]933
504P2d496
519P2d[4]1147
583P2d[3]1382

– 137 –
(102Az186)
cc427P2d135

– 138 –
(102Az187)
442P2d[8]112
457P2d[6]737
480P2d[1]385

– 142 –
(102Az191)
cc389P2d263
70A2268s
39A4570n

– 143 –
(102Az192)
436P2d[1]909
489P2d[6]849
494P2d[6]387
505P2d[1]576
538P2d[1]410
663P2d[2]999
667P2d[2]205
680P2d[3]1248
683P2d[3]334
709P2d[3]528
d709P2d[7]528
709P2d[2]1341
f710P2d[1]1093
Alk
457P2d[1]250
Kan
657P2d[7]42
Ohio
276NE252

– 146 –
(5AzA342)
463P2d[14]116
464P2d[3]677
464P2d[3]817
464P2d[5]817
528P2d[8]190
723P2d673
Ala
363So2d765
Fla
283So2d402
416So2d1224
32A2184s
77A314n
77A331n

– 154 –
(5AzA350)
5A41091n

– 156 –
(5AzA352)
569P2d[6]249
Okla
591P2d298
Utah
j462P2d[1]174

– 161 –
(66C2d685)
(58CaR561)
s54CaR481
442P2d[3]373
442P2d[6]374
j451P2d[5]439
561P2d[4]1147
f591P2d[3]68
59CaR[4]657
59CaR[5]657
61CaR[6]403
69CaR[3]317
69CaR[6]318
73CaR[5]293
j75CaR[5]799
83CaR[4]249
83CaR[5]252
83CaR[7]252

d85CaR[4]722
d85CaR[5]722
d85CaR[3]723
d85CaR[7]723
89CaR[6]108
e89CaR[4]383
e89CaR[6]383
94CaR[5]754
104CaR532
109CaR[5]280
133CaR[3]336
134CaR[5]366
137CaR[4]459
f153CaR[3]45
f187CaR[4]290
f200CaR491
212CaR[8]349
220CaR[5]180
220CaR[8]705

– 164 –
(66C2d680)
(58CaR564)
cc405P2d553
cc46CaR513
432P2d[4]234
443P2d[4]574
470P2d[2]358
470P2d[4]358
475P2d[2]655
475P2d[3]655
488P2d[3]394
488P2d[4]394
493P2d[1]111
493P2d[2]111
493P2d[3]111
505P2d[4]1374
516P2d[2]866
521P2d868
544P2d[2]939
547P2d[2]449
547P2d[3]1391
551P2d[4]22
551P2d[2]843
555P2d[1]1108
561P2d[4]288
573P2d[3]854
575P2d[3]758
575P2d[1]759
611P2d[1]463
611P2d[3]463
653P2d328
672P2d[3]434
672P2d[1]435
f673P2d[1]239
685P2d[2]1191
686P2d1186
689P2d[4]120
704P2d[4]1337
62CaR[4]618
70CaR[4]110
87CaR[2]374
87CaR[4]374
90CaR[2]423
90CaR[3]423
97CaR[3]202
97CaR[4]202
99CaR[1]879
99CaR[2]879
99CaR[3]879
106CaR[4]318
111CaR[2]162
113CaR612
126CaR[2]803
128CaR[2]673
129CaR[3]111

130CaR[4]718
131CaR[2]227
133CaR[1]868
137CaR[4]198
143CaR[3]410
144CaR[3]215
144CaR[1]216
165CaR[1]122
165CaR[3]122
187CaR37
196CaR[3]844
196CaR[1]845
f197CaR[1]569
205CaR[2]840
206CaR382
207CaR[4]548
217CaR[4]846
Ariz
596P2d[4]30
Kan
646P2d[2]463
Nev
575P2d[1]932
j575P2d[1]934
Md
347A2d562
ND
326NW882
80A31244n
26A41010n
26A41019n

– 167 –
(66C2d601)
(58CaR567)
s50CaR24
s53CaR842
s58CaR567
62CaR[2]462
149CaR[3]514
150CaR[2]836
201CaR[3]251

– 171 –
(66C2d633)
(58CaR571)
s54CaR360
f568P2d[9]393
590P2d[1]848
590P2d[9]848
72CaR[9]68
76CaR[3]707
113CaR[9]744
128CaR[2]289
f140CaR[9]668
151CaR[9]739
152CaR[1]721
152CaR[9]721
167CaR[1]646
187CaR343
193CaR[9]788

– 179 –
(66C2d606)
(58CaR579)
432P2d[11]961
434P2d[25]611
441P2d[22]940
446P2d[11]152
446P2d[18]528
446P2d[31]528
447P2d[11]652
449P2d[27]181
460P2d[1]482
471P2d[1]4
471P2d[1]37

474P2d[2]995
483P2d[1]1213
f498P2d[21]442
515P2d[1]115
515P2d[22]16
515P2d[10]282
519P2d[11]570
521P2d[7]101
j521P2d[31]466
525P2d[10]78
551P2d[6]381
577P2d[11]688
587P2d[10]230
598P2d[26]835
j613P2d232
e623P2d[6]233
e623P2d[7]233
668P2d[16]783
687P2d[23]913
61CaR[33]492
61CaR[26]493
61CaR[29]749
62CaR[21]862
63CaR[11]273
63CaR[28]305
h63CaR[30]305
63CaR[29]307
64CaR[25]315
65CaR[22]241
65CaR565
67CaR[4]686
68CaR[21]122
69CaR[22]100
71CaR[11]174
72CaR[32]35
72CaR[10]36
72CaR[11]344
72CaR[18]648
72CaR[31]648
73CaR[10]293
73CaR[11]412
73CaR[16]680
73CaR[23]680
74CaR[27]245
75CaR604
76CaR[10]524
76CaR[11]524
76CaR[18]524
76CaR[24]525
81CaR[1]610
81CaR[27]844
81CaR[28]844
83CaR[1]79
83CaR[2]79
84CaR[10]690
84CaR[25]690
84CaR[10]695
84CaR[11]695
87CaR[1]684
87CaR[13]687
90CaR[2]27
90CaR[26]298
90CaR[27]298
90CaR[28]298
91CaR[35]317
92CaR[27]416
92CaR[11]528
e93CaR[13]102
94CaR[4]122
94CaR[3]123
94CaR225
94CaR[1]261
d95CaR[30]426
d95CaR[31]426
j95CaR[33]426
j95CaR[34]427

97CaR[11]214
98CaR[13]180
98CaR[21]180
99CaR[10]101
102CaR[26]48
102CaR[1]150
f102CaR[21]602
103CaR[23]229
105CaR[27]438
108CaR[10]923
110CaR[11]215
110CaR[22]216
110CaR[10]338
112CaR[11]522
113CaR[7]365
j113CaR[31]474
115CaR[10]638
119CaR[34]185
119CaR[35]185
d119CaR
[[11]607
121CaR[22]567
123CaR818
126CaR66
127CaR93
127CaR[22]301
131CaR[6]61
140CaR[30]105
140CaR[10]276
141CaR[23]591
144CaR[2]114
144CaR[10]272
144CaR[11]272
144CaR544
144CaR[2]605
144CaR[6]605
144CaR[9]605
145CaR[11]553
145CaR[14]640
150CaR[10]788
d150CaR
[[21]826
d150CaR
[[25]826
154CaR[1]575
157CaR[14]565
157CaR[26]675
158CaR[10]277
e159CaR
[[15]489
e159CaR
[[16]489
j159CaR492
f160CaR[15]658
164CaR141
164CaR[1]555
j166CaR171
166CaR326
e171CaR[6]672
e171CaR[7]672
174CaR[7]434
j174CaR435
175CaR590
d176CaR
[[15]326
d176CaR
[[17]327
177CaR[7]245
178CaR[20]142
181CaR[9]403
182CaR[15]120
f188CaR[1]47
f188CaR[1]57
189CaR[35]890
192CaR[15]120
Continued

Illustration F reproduces for comparison the three listings already shown in Illustrations A, D and E for *United Trust Co. v. Pyke,* 199 Kan. 1, 427 P.2d 67 (1967). Do not forget that the small raised numbers included in listings under official and regional reporter citations correspond to the headnotes in that particular version. Headnote numbers from one source have no relevance in the listing under the other citation, and citing cases are assigned different numbers for each place they are listed. Note that the F.2d cases citing 199 Kan. 1 are assigned numbers 4, 3, 5 and 7, while the same F.2d cases citing 427 P.2d 67 (the same opinion) have the numbers 7, 12, 13, 14 and 16. The designation "e," assigned to the reference at 446 F.2d 931 and indicating that the holding of the Kansas case is explained there, is used for one reference in the *Kansas Reports* listing and two in the *Pacific Reporter* listings. This means that the federal case addresses issues summarized in only one official Kansas headnote but spanning two different West headnotes.

For cited cases published since the inception of the National Reporter System in the late 19th century, the regional Shepard's unit is the only place to find citing cases from other states. Since earlier cases do not have regional reporter citations, however, they cannot be Shepardized in those units. Shepard's coverage under the official citations of the earliest cases, therefore, includes citations from the courts of other states as published in the regional reporters. The only citing cases not included are decisions from other states published before the National Reporter System began.[6] The scope of Shepard's coverage is vast but not universal.

4. TOPICAL SHEPARD'S UNITS

Shepard's also publishes a variety of specialized topical citators, most of which include citations to cases in their subject area. While the topical units are less comprehensive than the standard jurisdictional Shepard's units, their advantage is that they include citing material not covered in the regular units. *Shepard's Federal Energy Law Citations,* for example, includes citations to federal court cases by Federal Energy Regulatory Commission decisions. Many of the specialized units also feature as *cited* material administrative decisions and regulations in the area, and they will be discussed further in Chapter 8.

The following topical citators include coverage of court cases in their fields:

Shepard's Bankruptcy Citations
Shepard's Corporation Law Citations
Shepard's Federal Energy Law Citations
Shepard's Federal Labor Law Citations
Shepard's Federal Occupational Safety and Health Citations

6. "One problem for legal historians is that ante-bellum cases cannot be shepardized between states. Thus, the only way to determine if a case has been cited by other courts is to read the decisions of the other courts." Finkelman, "Exploring Southern Legal History," 64 *N.C.L.Rev.* 77, 95 n. 105 (1985).

Illustration F

Comparison of three listings for same case in *Shepard's Kansas Citations* and *Shepard's Pacific Reporter Citations*

SHEPARD'S KANSAS CITATIONS, PART ONE

199 Kan.

-1-
(427P2d67)
202Kan110
205Kan468
209Kan255
210Kan[2]413
218Kan[5]84
221Kan527
j224Kan612
233Kan[3]366
o233Kan369
1KA2d[7]690
1KA2d[5]692
1KA2d[6]692
441F2d[4]35
e446F2d[3]931
481F2d[5]714
720F2d[7]17
37JBK183
17KLR496
27KLR373
19Wsb226
23Wsb503
20ALR2d235s
39ALR2d477s
27ALR3d815n
27ALR3d822n
39ALR3d1341n
39ALR3d1356n
42ALR3d1131n
42ALR3d1139n
42ALR3d1149n
25ALR4th800n
25ALR4th826n

SHEPARD'S KANSAS CITATIONS, PART TWO

427 P.2d

-67-
(199Kan1)
446P2d[2]727
470P2d[3]832
497P2d[2]147
497P2d[3]147
502P2d[18]653
542P2d[14]351
561P2d[1]795
574P2d[19]231
574P2d[17]232
574P2d[14]233
574P2d[18]233
j584P2d[18]145
662P2d[13]1271
o662P2d1272
441F2d[7]35
e446F2d[12]931
e446F2d[13]931
481F2d[14]714
720F2d[16]17

SHEPARD'S PACIFIC REPORTER CITATIONS

427 P.2d

– 67 –
(199Kan1)
446P2d[2]727
470P2d[3]832
497P2d[2]147
497P2d[3]147
502P2d[18]653
542P2d[14]351
561P2d[1]795
574P2d[19]231
574P2d[17]232
574P2d[14]233
574P2d[18]233
j584P2d[18]145
662P2d
[[13]1271
o662P2d1272
Cir. 5
441F2d[7]35
Cir. 8
720F2d[16]17
Cir. 10
e446F2d[12]931
e446F2d[13]931
481F2d[14]714
Calif
65CaR[4]145
Ore
641P2d614
Ill
385NE82
395NE581
Mass
282NE414
Va
269SE792
W Va
275SE13
20ALR2d235s
39ALR2d477s
27ALR3d815n
27ALR3d822n
39ALR3d1341n
39ALR3d1356n
42ALR3d1131n
42ALR3d1139n
42ALR3d1149n
25ALR4th800n
25ALR4th826n

Shepard's Federal Tax Citations
Shepard's Immigration and Naturalization Citations

Shepard's Insurance Law Citations
Shepard's Medical Malpractice Citations
Shepard's Military Justice Citations
Shepard's Partnership Law Citations
Shepard's Products Liability Citations
Shepard's Uniform Commercial Code Case Citations

The publisher has in recent years continued to add new specialized citators, so others may soon exist. This list does not include those specialized citators (such as *Shepard's Law Review Citations*) for which the coverage does not include citations to court cases.

D. THE FORMATS OF SHEPARD'S CITATIONS

A common error made by novice researchers attempting to use Shepard's is the failure to look in a volume or supplement that may have essential citing cases listed. A single volume or pamphlet rarely contains all of the citations to a particular case. Instead a researcher may have to consult more than one volume, each covering a different span of years, and up to three supplementary pamphlets. In an effort to simplify access to its material Shepard's has recently recompiled and reissued many of its citator units, reducing the number of volumes in which a researcher must look. For each citator, however, there is usually one or more bound volume and one or more paperbound supplement. The largest jurisdictions have gold-covered annual or semi-annual supplements, while every Shepard's unit includes red-covered supplement pamphlets. Many units are further supplemented between publication of these pamphlets by newsprint advance sheets. To insure that the researcher has at hand all the necessary parts, Shepard's prints a list on the cover of each pamphlet, "What Your Library Should Contain," indicating which issues are current and may be needed for a complete search in that citator. Checking the list on the cover of the most recent supplement will ensure that no essential components are missing or have been overlooked. The cover of a *Shepard's Kansas Citations* advance sheet, with its "What Your Library Should Contain" feature, appears in Illustration G.

To provide the latest information on the status of cases, Shepard's citators need to be supplemented promptly and frequently. *Shepard's United States Citations, Shepard's Federal Citations,* and *Shepard's Federal Labor Law Citations* are supplemented every month. State citators for twenty states are supplemented eight times a year, while those for the less populous states are only published every two or three months. *Shepard's Wyoming Citations* is the least frequently supplemented state unit, appearing twice each year.

The tables of abbreviations for reporters and for Shepard's treatment symbols, provided in the front of each bound volume, are also included at the beginning of each gold or red paperbound supplement, but do not appear in the uncovered interim advance sheets. It cannot

Illustration G

***Shepard's Kansas Citations*, advance sheet cover**

VOL. 60 FEBRUARY, 1989 NO. 6

Shepard's Kansas Citations

ADVANCE SHEET EDITION
CASES AND STATUTES

(USPS 656430)

WHAT YOUR LIBRARY SHOULD CONTAIN:

- 1986 Bound Volume, Cases (Parts 1 and 2)*
- 1986 Bound Volume, Statutes*

**Supplemented with January, 1989 Cumulative Supplement Vol. 60 No. 5 and February, 1989 Advance Sheet Vol. 60 No. 6*

DESTROY ALL OTHER ISSUES

SEE TABLE OF CONTENTS ON PAGE THREE

SEE "THIS ISSUE INCLUDES" ON PAGE FOUR

be overemphasized that these convenient tables are essential for turning Shepard's from an indecipherable jumble into a simple and effective research tool.

As mentioned at the outset of the chapter, Shepard's case citators are also available online through the WESTLAW and LEXIS database systems. One great advantage of the online versions of Shepard's is that all citing entries are cumulated in one listing, eliminating the need to search through several volumes and pamphlets. Moreover, the systems allow the researcher to go directly to a Shepard's display for any case being viewed, and then from Shepard's to the text of a citing case. This allows Shepardizing to be a more integral part of the process of finding and reading cases, rather than an afterthought that might be neglected.

Perhaps the most important advantage offered by online Shepard's retrieval, however, is that the computer can scan the listing and limit a display to particular requests. A researcher interested only in a particular point of law, as indicated in Shepard's by a certain headnote number, need not read carefully through several columns of irrelevant cases but can automatically retrieve only those citing cases on point. A display can also be limited to those cases with particular history or treatment symbols, so that one can retrieve, for example, only those cases that distinguish or limit the holding of the cited decision.

Unfortunately the online versions of Shepard's are no more current than the printed supplements. Shepard's adds material to its databases only after the same material appears in print form, so that at times the published version is actually available in libraries first. The publisher may have valid commercial reasons for delaying online access to its product, but its protectionist approach negates the vast improvement in retrieval time possible through computerized access.

For most jurisdictions Shepard's online coverage is retrospective, duplicating everything in the "Cases" sections of its published volumes. In over a dozen states and for the federal courts, however, online coverage does not yet include material published in early volumes, beginning as late as 1969 for some reporters. When Shepardizing an early case, therefore, the researcher must be aware that a Shepard's database may be lacking important citations. For example, if online coverage for a state Shepard's unit begins in 1958, a Shepard's display will not indicate that a case was overruled or questioned in 1907 or 1957. LEXIS Shepard's displays do indicate the scope of coverage at the top of the first screen, but WESTLAW users must enter a "scope" command to determine any limitations in the database in use.

Illustration H shows a LEXIS Shepard's display for 427 P.2d 67, restricted to those cases referring to the point of law summarized in headnote 14. Note the scope of coverage explained at the top of the screen and the numbers in the lefthand column, which can be used to view the citing cases.

Illustration H

A LEXIS Shepard's printout, restricted to headnote 14

```
              (c) 1989 McGraw-Hill, Inc. - DOCUMENT 1 (OF 2)

CITATIONS TO: 427 P.2d 67
SERIES: SHEPARD'S PACIFIC REPORTER CITATIONS
DIVISION: PACIFIC REPORTER, 2d SERIES
COVERAGE: Shepard's 1987 Volume & Supplements Through 03/89 Supplement.

RESTRICTIONS: 14

NUMBER  ANALYSIS                  CITING REFERENCE                PARA   NOTES
------ ---------------- ------------------------------------ ---- ----------
  1    parallel citation       (199 Kan. 1)
  7                              542 P.2d 351                     14
 11                              574 P.2d 233                     14
                                   Cir. 10
 20                              481 F.2d 714                     14

-----------------------------------------------------------------------------
To see the text of a citing case, press the citing reference NUMBER and then
the TRANSMIT key.
For further explanation, press the H key (for HELP) and then the TRANSMIT key.
```

E. OTHER VERIFICATION AND UPDATING TOOLS

Shepard's Citations is the preeminent resource in the field of case verification, an essential component of American legal research for over a century. No publication or service attempts to duplicate Shepard's work of listing every subsequent citation to every published decision. Some specialized looseleaf services, such as Commerce Clearing House's *Standard Federal Tax Reports* and Prentice Hall's *Federal Taxes,* publish sets of citator volumes for cases in their subject area. For general purposes, there are materials which serve *some* of the same purposes as *Shepard's Citations.* There are volumes which simply provide parallel citations, and computer databases that focus specifically on the validity and authority of cited cases.

1. PARALLEL CITATION TABLES

The *National Reporter Blue Book,* published by West and supplemented annually, consists of lists of case citations for every volume of official reports, with cross-references to National Reporter System citations. In Illustration I, the listing for volume 199 of *Kansas Reports* shows that the first case in that volume is also published at 427 P.2d 67.

For approximately half of the states, West publishes a *Blue and White Book,* which also has parallel citation tables from regional reporter locations to official reports. The blue pages in one of these volumes duplicate the information provided in the *National Reporter Blue Book,* with parallel citations from the official reports to the regional reporter; and the white pages provide the opposite references,

Illustration I

Page from *National Reporter Blue Book*, 1970 supplement

197 KANSAS REPORTS

Kan.		P.2d	Kan.		P.2d	Kan.		P.2d	Kan.		P.2d	Kan.		P.2d	Kan.		P.2d
Pg.	Vol.	Pg.	Pg.	Vol.	Pg.	Pg.	Vol.	Pg.	Pg.	Vol.	Pg.	Pg.	Vol.	Pg.	Pg.	Vol.	Pg.
1	414	67	157	415	373	321	416	791	456	419	870	602	419	865	693	421	32
13	415	411	163	415	377	323	416	777	463	419	927	610	419	882	694	421	170
18	415	257	171	415	289	327	416	302	468	419	834	622	419	828	704	421	45
23	415	261	174	415	283	334	416	788	471	419	836	627	419	937	708	421	194
38	415	384	180	415	226	338	416	736	486	419	860	630	419	891	712	421	40
58	415	217	186	415	250	345	416	297	492	419	935	636	419	639	718	421	197
67	415	287	188	416	67	351	416	711	495	419	817	638	419	640	728	420	1016
70	415	421	199	416	61	360	416	255	502	419	812	639	418	141	731	421	213
74	415	236	207	416	281	363	416	717	509	419	822	641	418	138	740	421	190
80	415	234	212	416	259	371	416	285	517	419	912	643	418	137	747	421	51
83	415	251	241	416	729	374	417	137	524	419	931	645	418	140	756	421	1
91	415	406	251	417	261	377	416	754	529	419	922	647	418	139	766	420	1012
98	415	415	267	416	760	385	416	780	536	419	847	649	418	136	772	421	8
106	415	278	275	416	783	389	416	766	554	419	902	651	421	33	777	421	181
113	415	223	279	416	290	395	416	741	567	419	896	660	421	16	788	420	1019
118	415	272	289	416	750	407	416	786	576	419	832	668	421	58	793	421	205
126	415	398	296	416	724	410	416	771	580	419	876	676	421	24	804	421	11
136	415	241	302	416	257	417	417	139	589	419	918	687	421	48	810	421	177
146	415	231	306	416	703	427	417	273	594	419	1017	691	421	22	816	420	1012
150	415	291	317	416	287	448	417	255									

198 KANSAS REPORTS

Kan.		P.2d	Kan.		P.2d	Kan.		P.2d	Kan.		P.2d	Kan.		P.2d	Kan.		P.2d
Pg.	Vol.	Pg.	Pg.	Vol.	Pg.	Pg.	Vol.	Pg.	Pg.	Vol.	Pg.	Pg.	Vol.	Pg.	Pg.	Vol.	Pg.
1	422	959	93	422	560	222	424	571	359	424	620	507	426	42	637	426	153
4	422	898	100	422	976	228	424	871	365	424	581	509	426	143	642	426	114
14	422	565	111	422	871	239	424	552	371	424	513	517	426	98	648	426	159
16	422	868	115	422	874	242	424	535	390	424	488	520	426	157	650	426	39
21	422	894	127	422	914	250	424	498	403	424	276	523	426	78	655	426	92
26	422	567	135	422	1009	271	424	471	413	424	265	527	426	49	659	426	151
30	422	888	139	422	943	275	424	478	421	424	586	532	426	288	662	426	52
39	422	955	147	422	920	282	424	865	431	424	624	543	426	95	666	426	26
44	422	573	161	422	884	290	424	612	436	424	593	547	426	67	671	426	138
48	422	1012	166	422	971	301	424	261	447	424	561	556	426	60	678	426	118
52	422	964	173	422	949	307	424	256	452	424	473	564	426	55	685	426	74
61	422	961	181	422	932	313	424	528	458	424	276	571	426	82	691	426	149
66	422	557	192	422	941	321	424	271	459	424	864	585	426	251	695	426	30
70	422	906	195	422	559	325	424	483	460	426	124	605	426	238	706	426	244
79	422	564	196	424	601	331	424	541	467	426	21	613	426	106	715	426	44
80	422	570	211	424	565	345	424	576	473	426	129	623	426	134	723	426	21
84	422	862	219	424	274	351	424	555	479	426	267	629	426	100			

199 KANSAS REPORTS

Kan.		P.2d	Kan.		P.2d	Kan.		P.2d	Kan.		P.2d	Kan.		P.2d	Kan.		P.2d
Pg.	Vol.	Pg.	Pg.	Vol.	Pg.	Pg.	Vol.	Pg.	Pg.	Vol.	Pg.	Pg.	Vol.	Pg.	Pg.	Vol.	Pg.
1	427	67	123	427	453	238	428	799	373	429	931	508	430	246	669	433	373
16	427	500	128	427	497	245	428	774	387	430	204	514	431	879	679	433	367
17	427	627	132	427	625	251	428	783	394	430	228	538	431	518	686	433	389
23	427	586	136	427	611	259	428	789	403	430	304	554	431	532	696	433	558
26	427	484	142	427	500	265	428	838	417	430	298	572	431	531	707	433	407
33	427	606	147	427	598	272	428	779	425	429	821	574	431	676	716	433	459
40	427	591	154	427	495	277	428	809	431	429	925	576	433	538	720	433	585
48	427	465	156	427	448	284	428	833	434	430	235	591	433	550	728	433	344
59	427	461	162	427	457	290	428	758	443	430	294	598	433	418	732	433	555
64	427	621	167	428	768	293	429	103	449	429	928	607	433	462	736	433	572
69	427	490	175	428	814	299	428	825	453	430	259	610	433	347	752	434	316
73	427	492	189	428	760	309	429	101	459	430	268	615	433	414	757	433	356
77	427	481	192	428	847	312	430	188	469	430	210	621	433	351	767	433	425
82	427	473	194	428	762	335	430	264	472	430	251	628	433	437	783	433	363
89	427	443	203	428	458	340	430	275	483	430	241	638	433	380	787	433	567
96	427	478	208	428	794	354	429	942	487	430	212	649	433	464	793	433	467
100	427	632	215	428	843	357	430	285	501	430	293	652	433	454	797	433	470
108	427	603	220	429	95	362	429	923	503	430	243	659	433	444	800	433	450
112	427	588	228	428	804	366	430	222	507	430	315	666	433	397	806	433	399
116	427	616	235	428	456												

from the regional reporter to the official reports. A state's *Blue and White Book* is only available in that state.

Parallel citations, of course, can often be found without use of either Shepard's or a book of conversion tables. If an official citation is available at the time the regional reporter goes to press, it is provided at the beginning of the decision. Most of the official reports indicate the National Reporter System locations of their cases, although several follow the lead of the *United States Reports* and do not supply this useful piece of information.

2. AUTO–CITE AND INSTA–CITE

Both LEXIS and WESTLAW have online databases designed specifically for the purpose of verifying the accuracy and validity of citations. These databases do not provide the breadth of information available in Shepard's, but focus specifically on developments in the same litigation and cases which have a precedential impact on the decision being verified. Called *Auto–Cite* on LEXIS and *Insta–Cite* on WESTLAW, these systems operate similarly to Shepard's in that the researcher simply types in the citation to a case. The resulting display includes the name of the case, any parallel citations, and the names and citations of relevant cases, with the effect of each subsequent decision noted. Even if there are no subsequent developments in a case or later decisions affecting its authority, Auto–Cite and Insta–Cite are simple and trustworthy means of verifying the accuracy of citations and of finding parallel citations.

Auto–Cite is a citation verification service of VERACORP and its affiliated companies, Lawyers Co-operative Publishing Company, Bancroft–Whitney Company, and the Research Institute of America. Its display lists first the case for which information is sought, followed by any subsequent decisions in the same case and any later cases which have affected its validity. In a second paragraph, any published prior decisions are listed. Finally, Auto–Cite also lists any annotations in the *ALR* series or in *Lawyers' Edition* that have cited any of the cases in its display. The first screen of the Auto–Cite display for 199 Kan. 1 is shown in Illustration J; the list of annotations continues onto additional screens.

Insta–Cite is a citation verification and case history service of the West Publishing Company. Unlike Auto–Cite, it lists decisions in chronological order, with an arrow marking the citation transmitted by the researcher. Like Auto–Cite, it verifies citations, provides case names and parallel citations, and lists cases in the direct and precedential history of a case. Cases in the "direct history" are those rendered in the course of the same litigation, while "precedential history" involves subsequent decisions with a significant impact on the authority of the case. Direct history and citation verification are available for any federal case on WESTLAW. Direct history is provided for state cases published since 1938 and citation verification for state cases is available from 1920, but precedential history is only included for cases affected by decisions published since 1972.

Illustration J

The first screen of an Auto–Cite display

```
Auto-Cite Service, Copyright (c) 1989, VERALEX INC.:

199 KAN 1:

United Trust Co. v Pyke*1 (1967) 199 Kan 1, 427 P2d 67 (superseded by statute
as stated in Re Estate of Shields*2 (1977) 1 Kan App 2d 688, 574 P2d 229, affd
Re Estate of Shields*3 (1978) 224 Kan 604, 584 P2d 139) and (ovrld by Harper v
Prudential Ins. Co.*4 (1983) 233 Kan 358, 662 P2d 1264)
  NO PRIOR HISTORY CITED

Annotations citing the case(s) indicated above with asterisk(s):

*1  Homicide as precluding taking under will or by intestacy, 25 ALR4th 787,
    secs. 3, 14.

    Felonious killing of one cotenant or tenant by the entireties by the other
    as affecting the latter's right in the property, 42 ALR3d 1116, secs. 6, 9,
    14.
 AUTO-CITE information continues, press the NEXT PAGE key.
To return to LEXIS, press the EXIT SERV key.  To resume prior citation research,
transmit RESUME followed by the service name (SHEPARDS).

For further explanation, press the H key (for HELP) and then the TRANSMIT key.
```

Insta–Cite also includes references to the cited case in *Corpus Juris Secundum,* West's legal encyclopedia. The Insta–Cite display for 199 Kan. 1, indicating succinctly that the case was overruled in 1983, is shown in Illustration K.

A strong advantage the two systems have over *Shepard's Citations* is speed of updating. New developments are added to the databases as they become available, rather than on a monthly or bimonthly publication basis. For recent cases it would be wise to check Auto–Cite or Insta–Cite, if available, for developments since the latest Shepard's supplement.[7]

Illustration K

An Insta–Cite display

```
CITATION: 199 KAN. 1                  INSTA-CITE                        ONLY PAGE
 =>    1  UNITED TRUST CO. V. PYKE, 199 KAN. 1, 427 P.2D 67 (KAN., APR 25, 1967)
              (NO. 44651)
            OVERRULED BY
       2  HARPER V. PRUDENTIAL INS. CO. OF AMERICA, 233 KAN. 358, 662 P.2D 1264
              (KAN., APR 29, 1983) (NO. 54,707)

          (NOTE: DIRECT HISTORY: COVERAGE BEGINS - FEDERAL 1754, STATE 1938.
                 PRECEDENTIAL HISTORY: COVERAGE BEGINS - 1972.
                 TO VIEW EARLIER CASE HISTORY, TYPE SH AND PRESS ENTER.)
(C) COPYRIGHT WEST PUBLISHING COMPANY 1989
```

7. The marketing materials of each system claim that it is the faster and more reliable of the two. A more objective viewpoint, with descriptions of the editorial processes involved in creating the databases, appears in Bintliff, "Auto–Cite and Insta–Cite: The Race to Update Case Histories," 15 *Colo.Law.* 1675 (1986).

Using either Auto–Cite or Insta–Cite, the researcher does not even need to know the beginning page of an opinion to find its proper citation and determine its precedential validity. Both systems respond to an internal page citation by providing the correct citation and its accompanying display. A researcher using *Shepard's Citations* in either print or online formats, on the other hand, can retrieve nothing without a case's correct citation.

As legal research becomes increasingly automated, the Auto–Cite and Insta–Cite systems may take over the verification functions traditionally deemed to be Shepard's primary function. *Shepard's Citations* will remain, however, as the basic means of finding all later cases citing a decision.

3. WESTLAW AND LEXIS

Finally, the full-text databases of WESTLAW and LEXIS can be used to find subsequent references to a decided case. One can search the case databases for the names of parties or a case citation and retrieve every document in which those terms appear. A search for *all* subsequent cases would merely duplicate the results found in Shepard's, without the aid of editorial information on the citing cases. A search limited to decisions within the past year, however, will often retrieve new cases that have not yet been covered in Shepard's print or online citators. In an area of law that is rapidly developing, it may well be worth the expense to obtain the up-to-the-minute citations available through full-text retrieval.

F. SUMMARY

Shepard's Citations will rear its head throughout this volume, not only as a means of checking the status of cases but as a basic tool for finding and analyzing case law. It may appear a strange and uninviting system of notation at first. As with many new things, experience will show not only its value but its simplicity in use.

The current status of primary sources other than cases also needs to be verified. Statutes may be repealed or amended by the legislature, or declared unconstitutional by a court; regulations may be superseded and treaties abrogated. As these primary sources are introduced in later chapters, means for determining their status, including *Shepard's Citations,* will be explained.

G. ADDITIONAL READING

Frank Shepard Company, *A Record of Fifty Years of Specializing in a Field that is of First Importance to the Bench and Bar of the United States: An Insight into an Establishment that has Grown from Small Beginnings to the First Rank in the Law Publishing Field* (Frank Shepard Co., 1923). Of interest only to bibliographic types, but full of laudatory prose and early photographs of Shepard's staffers at work.

How to Use Shepard's Citations: A Presentation of the Scope and Functions of Shepard's Citation Books and Services with Methods and Techniques to Enhance their Value in Legal Research (Shepard's/McGraw–Hill, 1986). A helpful manual, and proof that the publisher still can wield an imposing book title.

Chapter 4

CASE FINDING

A. INTRODUCTION

Having described court reports and the ways to determine whether a judicial decision can be cited as precedent, we turn now to the several research methods and tools employed in locating decisions, a process generally called *case finding.* It is the purpose of this chapter to show the researcher how to locate a specific case or to identify decisions relevant to a particular legal issue. Since much of legal research involves the search for relevant judicial precedents, case finding is an essential legal research skill.

Otto Preminger's classic movie "Anatomy of a Murder" features a scene in which one of the defense attorneys, who is hoping to bolster an insanity defense in a murder trial, paces excitedly around a law library, then spins on his heel and snatches a book from a shelf, seemingly guided only by instinct. Opening it, he finds a case in point and exclaims in joy. Real-life lawyers, unfortunately, cannot rely on such good fortune. When one considers that there are over three million reported decisions available for perusal, to which are added an annual increment of 100,000 new decisions, the need for more systematic search techniques is clear.

The research apparatus of American law includes a finely developed, wide-ranging infrastructure of tools specifically designed for case finding, and a variety of other more general resources which can be used for this purpose. There are at least three major approaches for locating decisions. *Digests* consist of headnotes from cases arranged by topic and used for finding decisions on specific subjects; they also include tables listing cases by name and providing reporter citations. *Annotations* are articles on specific legal topics, discussing and explaining relevant cases from all jurisdictions. *Computerized legal research systems* are capable of finding cases involving particular fact situations, using specific legal terminology, involving specified litigants or attorneys, or decided by particular judges or courts. A number of other resources can also be very useful as means of finding relevant case law. They will be mentioned in this chapter, but explained more fully in later parts of the book.

It must be emphasized at the outset that there are a great variety of case-finding methods and that no *one* approach can be recommended for *all* situations. A skillful researcher is familiar with the various tools available and can analyze a problem to determine what sort of approach would be most fruitful. Particular methods are clearly preferable for certain types of searches, while in most situations one can reasonably choose from a number of alternative approaches or use a combination of tools and methods.

B. WEST KEY-NUMBER DIGESTS

Although computerized research services are becoming the primary case-finder for many researchers, the most well-developed and probably still the most widely used method of case location is the *digest*, a tool which reprints in a subject arrangement the headnote summaries of each case's points of law. The summaries are usually grouped under alphabetically arranged topics and then organized by subject within that topic. A digest functions in a manner similar to an index; instead of simple one-line entries, however, it consists of paragraphs describing the legal principles decided.

English precursors to modern American digests began with *Statham's Abridgment,* published about 1490, which consisted of summaries of case law grouped under alphabetically arranged subject headings. This, and its many successors, employed relatively few subjects, broad in scope and lacking the detailed subdivisions of modern digests. The first comprehensive American digest, covering both law and equity and both state and federal courts, began publication in 1848 as the *United States Digest.* That digest was published annually for over fifty years, with a retrospective compilation covering 1790–1869 issued in the 1870's.[1] In 1887 the West Publishing Company acquired the property rights to the *United States Digest,* including its classification scheme, and began publication of a new annual *American Digest.* This series has developed since into the set of West digests known as the American Digest System.

1. OVERVIEW

The West Publishing Company's National Reporter System, as described in Chapter 2, is a comprehensive scheme of publication of appellate court decisions from all jurisdictions. The West system, however, does not end simply with the systematic reporting of deci-

1. B.V. Abbott, *United States Digest, First Series* (Little, Brown, 14 vols., 1874–76).

sions. In order to facilitate access to all of these reported decisions, West editors provide each case with headnotes abstracting the legal and factual issues which the decision addresses. Each headnote is assigned to a legal topic and a numbered subdivision of that topic. West's digests are basically compiled subject arrangements of these headnotes.

The West system divides all foreseeable legal situations into seven major categories: Persons, Property, Contracts, Torts, Crimes, Remedies, and Government. These seven areas are subdivided into more than four hundred individual topics, which are then arranged in one alphabetical sequence. Each of the topics is further subdivided in an increasingly narrow refinement, and each of the resulting subtopics is then assigned a classification number, which West calls a "key number." A separate numbering sequence is used for each of the topics, so a particular point of law is known by its topic name and its key number within that topic. Some of the larger and more complex topics have thousands of key numbers, while smaller topics have only a few. This subject framework seeks to provide a particular topic and key number subdivision to cover *every* conceivable legal situation that could be treated in a case. This effort may represent an oversimplification and potential distortion of the legal universe, but it remains an impressive achievement which has had an enormous intellectual impact on American jurisprudence.[2]

Illustration A shows the beginning of the list of 410 topics now in use; the full list is printed in the front of most digest volumes. The topics vary widely in scope (e.g., from the very broad "Criminal Law" to the relatively narrow "Bounties") and in current importance (from "Blasphemy" to "Civil Rights"). The subject structure created by West around the turn of the century not only survives, but is still relatively effective and widely used today. West periodically adds new subdivisions within a topic, and occasionally adds new topics as needed, but for the most part West's original divisions have been maintained.[3]

The digest system is most easily understood by examining how it is constructed. Every decision West publishes is read by its editorial staff. *Each* of the legal issues treated by a decision is identified, summarized, and assigned a topic and subtopic key number from the West classification scheme. These summaries or abstracts, with their topic names and key numbers, are then placed in separate headnotes at the beginning of the published opinions. Some headnotes which cannot be so neatly pigeonholed are assigned more than one key number. A short decision may have just one headnote, while some long opinions

2. For a discussion of the impact of West's digest system on legal thinking, see Berring, "Legal Research and Legal Concepts: Where Form Molds Substance," 75 *Calif.L.Rev.* 15, 24–25 (1987).

3. West continues to adapt its scheme to the changing law, although its changes are slow and cautious. Obviously changes cannot be made casually or too frequently in a system so large and complex. Nonetheless in the past decade West has added several new topics, such as "Condominium" and "Commodity Futures Trading Regulation," and eliminated over twenty topics through new combinations and reorganizations. Five separate topics, for example, were compiled into the new "Implied and Constructive Contracts."

Illustration A

List of digest topics in the *Ninth Decennial Digest, Part 2*

LIST OF DIGEST TOPICS

The digest topics used in this digest conform to the American Digest System

Abandoned and Lost Property
Abatement and Revival
Abduction
Abortion and Birth Control
Absentees
Abstracts of Title
Accession
Accord and Satisfaction
Account
Account, Action on
Account Stated
Accountants
Acknowledgment
Action
Action on the Case
Adjoining Landowners
Administrative Law and Procedure
Admiralty
Adoption
Adulteration
Adultery
Adverse Possession
Affidavits
Affray
Agriculture
Aliens
Alteration of Instruments
Ambassadors and Consuls
Amicus Curiae
Animals
Annuities
Appeal and Error
Appearance
Arbitration
Armed Services
Arrest
Arson
Assault and Battery
Assignments
Assistance, Writ of
Associations
Assumpsit, Action of
Asylums
Attachment
Attorney and Client
Attorney General
Auctions and Auctioneers
Audita Querela
Automobiles
Aviation
Bail
Bailment
Bankruptcy
Banks and Banking
Beneficial Associations
Bigamy
Bills and Notes
Blasphemy
Bonds
Boundaries
Bounties
Breach of Marriage Promise
Breach of the Peace
Bribery
Bridges
Brokers
Building and Loan Associations
Burglary
Canals
Cancellation of Instruments
Carriers
Cemeteries
Census
Certiorari
Champerty and Maintenance
Charities
Chattel Mortgages
Chemical Dependents
Children Out-of-Wedlock
Citizens
Civil Rights
Clerks of Courts
Clubs
Colleges and Universities
Collision
Commerce
Commodity Futures Trading Regulation
Common Lands
Common Law
Common Scold
Compounding Offenses
Compromise and Settlement
Condominium
Confusion of Goods
Conspiracy
Constitutional Law
Consumer Credit
Consumer Protection
Contempt
Contracts
Contribution
Conversion
Convicts
Copyrights and Intellectual Property
Coroners
Corporations
Costs
Counterfeiting
Counties
Court Commissioners
Courts
Covenant, Action of
Covenants
Credit Reporting Agencies
Criminal Law
Crops
Customs and Usages
Customs Duties
Damages
Dead Bodies
Death
Debt, Action of
Debtor and Creditor
Declaratory Judgment
Dedication
Deeds
Deposits and Escrows
Deposits in Court
Descent and Distribution
Detectives
Detinue
Disorderly Conduct
Disorderly House

have several dozen or more. Illustration B shows an opinion from the Michigan Court of Appeals, including two headnotes written by West's editors for its *North Western Reporter.* Note that each headnote has a topic and key number assigned to it.

West first publishes its reported decisions in advance sheets for each reporter series. Each advance sheet contains a section entitled "Key Number Digest," which reprints the headnote abstracts of each of the cases included, arranged by the topics and key numbers assigned to them in the West report. Each West advance sheet thus contains a mini-digest in which one can find, by topic and key number, the cases published therein covering a particular point of law. The advance sheets are later compiled into bound volume reporters, each of which carries a similar digest section. Of course, many topics and key numbers do not appear in any individual advance sheet or volume. Illustration C shows a typical page from the Key Number Digest of a bound volume of the *North Western Reporter 2d,* including the first headnote abstract from the decision in Illustration B.

If digesting extended no further than each individual advance sheet or volume, it would simply function as an index to the cases immediately at hand and would be of limited research value. West, however, takes the same headnotes and publishes them in separate sets covering many volumes of reporters. As will be explained in the following pages, there are digest sets covering individual states, sets covering separate multistate units of the National Reporter System, and a comprehensive set spanning the decisions of each and every jurisdiction.

Illustration D shows the page from *West's Michigan Digest* containing the first headnote from the case in Illustration B. This set covers all published decisions of Michigan appellate courts from 1838 to date in one alphabetical series of volumes. Each volume is updated annually by means of a *pocket part.*

Pocket parts are a common method of updating legal publications, first used in 1916 in *McKinney's Consolidated Laws of New York Annotated.* Changes and new information are printed in a supplement which fits into a pocket flap inside the back cover of the volume. The volume stays up to date without having to be republished. By looking in one *Michigan Digest* volume and its pocket part, a researcher can see headnotes to all the Michigan cases on a topic for over 150 years.

The set is brought further up to date by supplementary pamphlets published between annual pocket parts. Each supplement, whether annual pocket part or interim pamphlet, indicates its scope by listing the most recent reporter volumes it covers. A search can then be brought even more up to date by searching in the Key Number Digests in volumes and advance sheets published since the latest digest supplement.

West in effect publishes two interlocking, comprehensive services: a system of case reporting which contains the full text of appellate

Illustration B

A decision, with headnotes, in the *North Western Reporter*

122 Mich.App. 418

William L. FISHER, Plaintiff-Appellant,

v.

Karen LOWE, Larry Moffet and State Farm Mutual Automobile Insurance Company, Defendants-Appellees.

Docket No. 60732.

Court of Appeals of Michigan.

Submitted Nov. 3, 1982.

Decided Jan. 10, 1983.

Released for Publications May 6, 1983.

A wayward Chevy struck a tree
Whose owner sued defendants three.
He sued car's owner, driver too,
And insurer for what was due
For his oak tree that now may bear
A lasting need for tender care.

The Oakland County Circuit Court,
John N. O'Brien, J., set forth
The judgment that defendants sought
And quickly an appeal was brought.

Court of Appeals, J.H. Gillis, J.,
Gave thought and then had this to say:
1) There is no liability
Since No-Fault grants immunity;
2) No jurisdiction can be found
Where process service is unsound;
And thus the judgment, as it's termed,
Is due to be, and is,
Affirmed.

1. Automobiles ⚷251.13

Defendant's Chevy struck a tree—
There was no liability;
The No-Fault Act comes into play
As owner and the driver say;
Barred by the Act's immunity,
No suit in tort will aid the tree;
Although the oak's in disarray,
No court can make defendants pay.
M.C.L.A. § 500.3135.

2. Process ⚷4

No jurisdiction could be found
Where process service was unsound;
In personam jurisdiction
Was not even legal fiction
Where plaintiff failed to well comply
With rules of court that did apply.
GCR 1963, 105.4.

William L. Fisher, Troy, in pro. per.

Romain, Donofrio & Kuck, P.C. by Ernst W. Kuck, Southfield, for defendants-appellees.

Before BRONSON, P.J., and V.J. BRENNAN and J.H. GILLIS, JJ.

J.H. GILLIS, Judge.

[1, 2] We thought that we would never see
A suit to compensate a tree.

A suit whose claim in tort is prest
Upon a mangled tree's behest;

A tree whose battered trunk was prest
Against a Chevy's crumpled crest;

A tree that faces each new day
With bark and limb in disarray;

A tree that may forever bear
A lasting need for tender care.

Flora lovers though we three,
We must uphold the court's decree.

Affirmed.[1]

1. Plaintiff commenced this action in tort against defendants Lowe and Moffet for damage to his "beautiful oak tree" caused when defendant Lowe struck it while operating defendant Moffet's automobile. The trial court granted summary judgment in favor of defendants pursuant to GCR 1963, 117.2(1). In addition, the trial court denied plaintiff's request to enter a default judgment against the insurer of the automobile, defendant State Farm Mutual Automobile Insurance Company. Plaintiff appeals as of right.

The trial court did not err in granting summary judgment in favor of defendants Lowe and Moffet. Defendants were immune from tort liability for damage to the tree pursuant to § 3135 of the no-fault insurance act. M.C.L. § 500.3135; M.S.A. § 24.13135.

The trial court did not err in refusing to enter a default judgment against State Farm. Since it is undisputed that plaintiff did not serve process upon State Farm in accordance with the court rules, the court did not obtain personal jurisdiction over the insurer. GCR 1963, 105.4.

Illustration C

Key Number Digest in 333 N.W.2d, showing the first headnote in Illustration B

AUTOMOBILES ⚷297

McKenzie v. Ladd Trucking Co., 333 N.W.2d 402, 214 Neb. 209.

⚷153. Law of road.

Iowa 1983. Driving on the left side of the road in situations other than the exceptions set forth in statute is negligence per se in rural as well as urban areas. I.C.A. § 321.297.—Bannon v. Pfiffner, 333 N.W.2d 464.

⚷159. Acts in emergencies.

Iowa 1983. A driver is excused from violating a statutory rule of the road if he is confronted by an emergency not of his own making and by reason thereof fails to obey the statute.—Bannon v. Pfiffner, 333 N.W.2d 464.

If ice has not formed on the highway so far as the driver reasonably observes, although the weather may be inclement, and driver proceeds in accordance with conditions as they appear, but suddenly encounters an unanticipated patch of ice and slides, the driver may rightly claim an emergency, with the decision of whether the ice was reasonably foreseeable being for the jury to make.—Id.

If a person tortiously brings about an emergency, he cannot rely on it as an excuse for resulting harm under § 296 of the Restatement (Second) of Torts although he conducts himself property in the emergency itself.—Id.

A motorist who is confronted with an emergency which is not of his own making may not be completely absolved from exercise of care under § 296 of the Restatement (Second) of Torts unless motorist conducts himself as a reasonably prudent person in a similar emergency.—Id.

⚷168(3). Nature of highway.

Iowa 1983. If the icy condition of a highway is general, the driver must be taken as being aware of it and, if he proceeds in normal fashion notwithstanding the ice and eventually slides on a patch of it, he cannot set up the icy condition as an emergency, which requires an unforeseen combination of circumstances, including the element of unforeseeability.—Bannon v. Pfiffner, 333 N.W.2d 464.

⚷168(9). Obstruction of view.

Neb. 1983. Conditions blocking visibility impose upon a driver the duty to exercise a degree of care commensurate with the existing conditions, including waiting to proceed until it can be done in safety.—McKenzie v. Ladd Trucking Co., 333 N.W.2d 402, 214 Neb. 209.

⚷208. —— Vehicles crossing.

Neb. 1983. When a motorist, being in a place of safety, sees, or by the exercise of reasonable care could have seen, the approach of moving vehicle and moves from the place of safety into the path of that vehicle and is struck, the motorist's own conduct constitutes negligence more than slight, as a matter of law, and precludes recovery.—McKenzie v. Ladd Trucking Co., 333 N.W.2d 402, 214 Neb. 209.

Where each truck driver was aware of the presence and location of the other's vehicle, where each knew the general custom of usage of the premises on which the vehicles were located, and where each driver proceeded to move into the path of the other at a time when each admitted that his visibility in that direction was blocked, each driver was guilty of contributory negligence which was more than slight, and neither owner could recover.—Id.

(B) ACTIONS.

⚷245(49). Acts in emergencies.

Iowa 1983. If ice has not formed on the highway so far as the driver reasonably observes, although the weather may be inclement, and driver proceeds in accordance with conditions as they appear, but suddenly encounters an unanticipated patch of ice and slides, the driver may rightly claim an emergency, with the decision of whether the ice was reasonably foreseeable being for the jury to make.—Bannon v. Pfiffner, 333 N.W.2d 464.

Whether defendant's decedent, the eastbound motorist, was confronted with a sudden emergency because, although the weather was inclement, ice had not formed so far as she reasonably observed, she proceeded in accordance with conditions as they appeared, and suddenly encountered an unanticipated patch of ice, which caused her vehicle to slide into westbound lane where it collided head-on with vehicle driven by plaintiff's decedent, was a question for jury.—Id.

Question whether defendant's decedent, the eastbound motorist, negligently produced the emergency under § 296 of the Restatement (Second) of Torts when her vehicle encountered an unanticipated patch of ice, causing vehicle to slide into westbound lane and head-on into vehicle of plaintiff's decedent, was question of fact for jury.—Id.

Whether evidence showing that brake lights on eastbound vehicle of defendant's decedent flashed on prior to time vehicle encountered unanticipated ice and slid over into westbound lane and head-on into vehicle of plaintiff's decedent was evidence which showed lack of reasonable care under § 296 of the Restatement (Second) of Torts was question for jury.—Id.

Whether conduct of defendant's decedent in sudden emergency prior to time of fatal collision with vehicle driven by plaintiff's decedent was reasonable under evidence indicating that defendant's decedent had an estimated distance of 100 feet in which to adjust for a newly encountered condition, that her vehicle was traveling 66 feet each second, and that time it took to cover 100 feet was approximately one and one-half seconds was question for jury.—Id.

(D) EFFECT OF NO FAULT STATUTES.

⚷251.13. —— Vehicles, persons, occurrences within restrictions.

Mich.App. 1983.
Defendant's Chevy struck a tree—
There was no liability;
The No-Fault Act comes into play
As owner and the driver say;

Barred by the Act's immunity,
No suit in tort will aid the tree;
Although the oak's in disarray,
No court can make defendants pay,
M.C.L.A. § 500.3135.—Fisher v. Lowe, 333 N.W.2d 67.

VI. INJURIES FROM DEFECTS OR OBSTRUCTIONS IN HIGHWAYS AND OTHER PUBLIC PLACES.

(B) ACTIONS.

⚷297. Parties.

Mich.App. 1983. In view of state's statutory jurisdiction over all state trunkline highways,

(11)

Illustration D

A page from *West's Michigan Digest*, covering part of one key number

⚷251.13 AUTOMOBILES

3 Mich D—118

Mich.App. 1983. Injury to eye, which occurred when pedestrian was splashed by city bus with water, slush, ice, and lye while he was standing at bus stop, was foreseeable injury which arose out of city's use of bus as motor vehicle for purposes of no-fault personal protection benefits, since it was eminently foreseeable that bus, upon encountering pool of water while being operated in normal fashion as motor vehicle, would propel puddle of water containing caustic chemical in direction of nearby pedestrian. M.C.L.A. § 500.-3105.—Jones v. Tronex Chemical Corp., 341 N.W.2d 469, 129 Mich.App. 188.

Mich.App. 1983. For purposes of section of no-fault statute precluding recovery of personal protection insurance benefits if a person is the owner of an uninsured motor vehicle "involved" in an accident, a parked uninsured vehicle is not "involved" in the accident unless one of the exceptions to the parked vehicle provision is applicable. M.C.L.A. §§ 500.3106, 500.3113.—Braun v. Citizens Ins. Co., 335 N.W.2d 701, 124 Mich.App. 822.

For purposes of section of no-fault statute precluding recovery of personal protection insurance benefits if the person is the owner of an uninsured motor vehicle "involved" in an accident, a parked vehicle can be "involved" in the accident when the vehicle is parked in such a way as to cause unreasonable risk of the bodily injury which occurred. M.C.L.A. §§ 500.3106, 500.3113.—Id.

In action brought by plaintiff who was injured when he was pinned between an automobile and the tow truck which had pulled his uninsured automobile out of a snow drift, evidence sustained finding that plaintiff's automobile was "involved" in the collision, because the vehicle was parked in such a way as to cause an unreasonable risk of bodily injury which occurred, and therefore, plaintiff's recovery was barred by statute precluding recovery of personal protection insurance benefits if a person is the owner of an uninsured motor vehicle "involved" in an accident. M.C.L.A. § 500.3113.—Id.

Mich.App. 1983. Damage to loader which contractor was transporting on his tractor, caused by striking underside of an overpass, arose out of contractor's use of its tractor as motor vehicle, and thus, under No-Fault Act, contractor was not liable in tort to owner of loader for damage thereto. M.C.L.A. §§ 500.3123(1), 500.3135.—National Ben Franklin Ins. Co. v. Bakhaus Contractors, Inc., 335 N.W.2d 70, 124 Mich.App. 510.

Mich.App. 1983. Uninsured motorist is outside the basic no-fault system of allocating the costs of accidents and remains subject to tort liability. M.C.L.A. § 500.3135(1, 2).—Jones v. Detroit Auto. Inter-Ins. Exchange, 335 N.W.2d 39, 124 Mich. App. 363.

Mich.App. 1983.
Defendant's Chevy struck a tree—
There was no liability;
The No-Fault Act comes into play
As owner and the driver say;

Barred by the Act's immunity,
No suit in tort will aid the tree;
Although the oak's in disarray,
No court can make defendants pay,
M.C.L.A. § 500.3135.—Fisher v. Lowe, 333 N.W.2d 67, 122 Mich.App. 418.

Mich.App. 1982. Statute requires compliance with security requirements of no-fault insurance after 30-day period, 30-day period being intended to protect tourists and other transient nonresidents from criminal sanctions imposed by the Act. M.C.L.A. §§ 500.3102, 500.3135(2).—Berrien County Road Com'n v. Jones, 326 N.W.2d 495, 119 Mich.App. 315.

Defendants, having paid their dues in risk-spreading system by voluntarily acquiring insurance, and being owners or registrants of motor vehicle as defined in statute, though neither plaintiff's nor defendants' vehicle was required to be registered as vehicle within the state and therefore neither was required to be covered by no-fault insurance, were entitled to immunity provided by the no-fault act. M.C.L.A. §§ 500.3101(1, 3, 4), 500.3102, 500.3135(2).—Id.

Mich.App. 1981. Damages awarded to plaintiff for personal injuries sustained as result of negligence of state in failing to maintain roads were not subject to no-fault motor vehicle act since act applied only to accidents caused by motor vehicles and not to those caused by negligent highway maintenance. M.C.L.A. § 500.3135.—Longworth v. Michigan Dept. of Highways and Transp., 315 N.W.2d 135, 110 Mich.App. 771.

Mich.App. 1981. A motorcycle owner may not recover no-fault benefits for damage to his motorcycle unless it was properly parked at time of the accident; like an automobile owner, a motorcycle owner has option of purchasing collision coverage if he wishes to insure his motorcycle against damage resulting from accidents other than those in which the motorcycle is properly parked, notwithstanding definition of "motor vehicle" as a vehicle which has more than two wheels. M.C.L.A. §§ 500.3101 et seq., 500.3101(2), 500.3121, 500.3123; GCR 1963, 515.2.—Burk v. Warren, 307 N.W.2d 89, 105 Mich.App. 556, modified 360 N.W.2d 585, 417 Mich. 959, appeal after remand 359 N.W.2d 541, 137 Mich.App. 715, affirmed DiFranco v. Pickard, 398 N.W.2d 896, 427 Mich. 32.

No-fault law has abolished tort liability with respect to unintentionally occasioned property damage arising from the use, ownership or maintenance of motor vehicles within the state and automobile owner, including a motorcycle owner, who has not obtained his own collision insurance has no recourse to tort when his vehicle is damaged by another insured vehicle. M.C.L.A. § 500.-3123(1)(a).—Id.

Mich.App. 1981. In automobile accident case in which owner and manager of shopping center and contractor in charge of parking lot snow removal were named defendants on basis of their alleged failure to remove pile of snow obscuring stop sign, No-Fault Act did not apply to plaintiff's claims against shopping center defendants and she could therefore seek recovery for economic damages caused by alleged failure to maintain safe parking area. M.C.L.A. § 500.3135.—Pustay v. Gentelia, 304 N.W.2d 539, 104 Mich.App. 250.

Mich.App. 1981. While installation of auxiliary gas tank might arguably fall outside strict definition of "maintenance" where truck equipment company was correcting carburetor flooding problem when accident occurred, acts of truck equipment company constituted "maintenance" of vehicle for purposes of determining applicability of no-fault insurance statute. M.C.L.A. §§ 500.-3101 et seq., 500.3121.—Liberty Mut. Ins. Co. v. Allied Truck Equipment Co., 302 N.W.2d 588, 103 Mich.App. 33.

Accident must arise out of maintenance of vehicle for No-Fault Insurance Act to apply, and causal connection to be established between the injuries and maintenance of vehicle need not approach proximate cause. M.C.L.A. §§ 500.3101 et seq., 500.3121.—Id.

Where vehicle, at time of fire, was in care and custody of bailee and fire occurred as result of negligent act of bailee in placing exposed light bulb in position where gasoline could fall on it, accident arose out of bailment-for-hire, not out of maintenance of motor vehicle within meaning of No-Fault Insurance Act, and, therefore, Garage Keepers' Liability Act, and not No-Fault Insurance Act, applied. M.C.L.A. §§ 256.541 et seq., 500.3101 et seq.—Id.

decisions from state and federal courts, and a digest structure providing for the classification and retrieval, by subject, of the points of law determined in all judicial decisions reported by West. By providing uniform editorial treatment for each jurisdiction's opinions and having the points of law in each published decision classified into the same subject scheme, a highly effective case finding mechanism is created. When a researcher locates a case in which a relevant point of law is discussed, the West headnotes can be scanned to identify the topic and key numbers assigned to that point of law. These topics and key numbers can then be used as locators in the West digests to find other decisions from all West reporters on the same issues. The system theoretically allows a researcher to find decisions from any time period in any American jurisdiction on any specific topic.

It should be emphasized that these digests do not constitute legal authority and contain no substantive narrative text. They are effective for identifying and locating relevant decisions, but those decisions must be read and evaluated (and then Shepardized and evaluated again) before being cited in a brief, argument, or memorandum. Each case is decided on its own facts. Its listing under a particular digest topic and key number may be appropriate and helpful, but its relevance and authority for the researcher's purpose must be determined from the opinion itself.

2. DIGESTS OF FEDERAL COURT OPINIONS

The digests published by West are numerous, but parallel the format of the publisher's case reporters outlined in Chapter 2. Just as the discussion in that chapter began with the federal court system, here we will first discuss the digests covering the decisions of the Supreme Court of the United States and the lower federal courts.

a. United States Supreme Court Digest

West's *United States Supreme Court Digest* provides access to decisions of the Supreme Court of the United States, by subject and by case name. Its format is similar to that used in all other West digests: headnote abstracts (in this case from West's *Supreme Court Reporter*) arranged by West topics and key numbers. Each of the more than 400 topics is included, with an explanation of its scope and an outline of its arrangement of key numbers, even though there have been no Supreme Court headnotes classified under more than thirty of the topics.[4] The topics are arranged in alphabetical order in about two dozen volumes, each supplemented with an annual pocket part. The set has grown gradually as the publisher periodically recompiles the contents of an overcrowded volume and reissues its contents in two separate books, designated with numbers such as "2" and "2A."

4. Three topics, "Arson," "Notaries," and "Sodomy," have been in the West system since it began, but did not receive their first Supreme Court headnotes until the 1980's.

The *United States Supreme Court Digest* is totally cumulative, back to the Court's beginning in 1790.[5] Once a researcher has identified a proper topic and key number, all Supreme Court cases on that specific legal issue may be located by looking in one bound volume and its pocket part. A key number search for Supreme Court cases may be further updated by consulting the "Cumulative Key Number Digest" in the advance sheets of West's *Supreme Court Reporter.* Unlike other West reporter advance sheets, the digest in the latest issue of the *Supreme Court Reporter* cumulates all headnote references for the entire Supreme Court term. The headnotes themselves are printed only for cases printed in that one advance sheet, but names and citations are provided for all earlier cases in the term.

Accompanying the digest volumes containing the alphabetically arranged topics are several additional finding aids. A two-volume "Table of Cases" lists each Supreme Court decision under the name of the plaintiff or first party named (in cases before the Supreme Court, usually the petitioner or appellant), and provides citations to the case in all three reporters as well as the key numbers under which its headnotes are classified. A "Defendant–Plaintiff Table" volume lists the cases under defendants' (respondents' or appellees') names, providing citations but not key numbers. A four-volume "Descriptive–Word Index" includes entries for legal and factual issues addressed in the headnotes, and provides references to topics and key numbers. Finally, a "Words and Phrases" volume lists all terms judicially defined by the Supreme Court, with references to case names and citations. The use of the case tables and the subject index will be explained in section B.5, "Finding Cases in the West Digests," and the use of "Words and Phrases" will be discussed later in the chapter.

b. Federal Digests

West also publishes a series of digests covering the decisions of the several levels of the federal court system. These digests cover in one sequence the U.S. Supreme Court (duplicating coverage of the *United States Supreme Court Digest*), the U.S. Courts of Appeals, the U.S. District Courts, and various specialized federal courts. Under each key number, headnotes from Supreme Court cases are listed first and Court of Appeals cases second, followed by the District Courts and other lower federal courts. Within each hierarchical level, digest entries are alphabetized by the state from which the case originated.

There are four separate digests, but they are simply successive series, each covering a different time period. The unfortunate use of different names for the four digests confuses some researchers. The original set was sensibly called the *Federal Digest,* and covers cases through 1939. When its supplementation grew too unwieldy, West published *Modern Federal Practice Digest* (now covering cases from

5. Coverage actually begins in 1754, with the first case in volume one of *United States Reports.* The only case digested under the topic "Embracery" is a Pennsylvania Supreme Court decision, *Morris's Lessee v. Vanderen,* 1 U.S. 64 (1782).

1940 to 1960). When this second series also became difficult to use efficiently, *West's Federal Practice Digest 2d* (now covering cases from 1961 to 1975) was published. Because the third series was called "2d," it follows that the fourth series, recently completed in 120 volumes and covering all cases reported since November 1975, is called *West's Federal Practice Digest 3d.* The current volumes of the *Federal Practice Digest 3d* are updated by annual pocket parts, which are further supplemented several times each year by pamphlets.

For many searches of current interest, it may be necessary only to consult the most recent digest set and its supplements. For comprehensive research of all federal case law, however, all four series must be used. The same classification system is used in all West digests, so the same topic and key number can be searched in all four series. Each series also contains one or more volumes for each of the basic finding aids described above: Tables of Cases, Defendant–Plaintiff Tables, Descriptive–Word Indexes, and Words and Phrases. The series can be distinguished from each other by the colors of their bindings: *Federal Digest,* red; *Modern Federal Practice Digest,* green; *Federal Practice Digest 2d,* blue; and *Federal Practice Digest 3d,* red.

c. *Specialized Digests*

Just as West publishes reporters covering the decisions of specialized federal tribunals, it publishes digests for the headnotes from those reporters. The same material appears as well in the *Federal Practice Digest 3d* and its predecessors, but for some research the specialized digests may be a more convenient research tool. Each follows on a smaller scale the pattern of the larger federal digests, with accompanying tables and indexes.

West's Bankruptcy Digest covers all cases reported in *West's Bankruptcy Reporter,* which began publication in 1979. *West's Military Justice Digest* covers the decisions in *West's Military Justice Reporter* of the United States Court of Military Appeals and the Courts of Military Review for the various service branches. The *United States Claims Court Digest* indexes all cases reported in the *United States Claims Court Reporter,* and decisions of the former United States Court of Claims (published in the *Federal Reporter* or *Federal Supplement*) are covered in the *United States Court of Claims Digest.*

In addition, both *West's Education Law Reporter* and *West's Social Security Reporting Service* include digests for the decisions they reprint. In both sets, however, the digest provides only the National Reporter System citations and does not indicate where in the topical reporter the cases appear. A researcher with access only to the topical set must then look up the cases' names in an accompanying Table of Cases to find their locations.

3. DIGESTS OF STATE COURT OPINIONS

Just as the opinions of most state appellate courts are published in both official reports and in West regional reporters, for most states there are two West key number digests covering those decisions: a state digest and a regional digest. It is the scope of coverage and not the digest entries that distinguishes state from regional digests, since the abstracts in both are taken from the headnotes in West's National Reporter System.

a. *State Digests*

Forty-six state digests are published by West, including one for the District of Columbia. All but two of the digests cover a single jurisdiction, while the *Dakota Digest* and *Virginia and West Virginia Digest* each cover two states. Only Delaware, Nevada and Utah do not have individual West digests; Delaware decisions, however, are covered in the *Atlantic Digest,* and Nevada and Utah in the *Pacific Digest.*

Most of the state digests are cumulated in one series like the *United States Supreme Court Digest,* so that a researcher need only look in one volume and one pocket part for all of the decisions since the beginning of a state's appellate court system. Volumes are occasionally recompiled and split into two, as required by the quantity of headnotes. More than ten states now have *two* series, with the original set used only for research in older case law. Coverage in the second series begins usually in the 1930's and is updated by pocket parts. New York has *three* series, with the coverage in the latest beginning in 1961. Every state digest is updated between annual pocket parts by one or more interim pamphlets. (These are published several months after pocket parts are issued, however, so there is not always one available.)

In addition to state court cases, West state digests cover the decisions of federal courts sitting in that state, and decisions of the U.S. Court of Appeals and U.S. Supreme Court in cases arising in the state. This sometimes useful feature is often overlooked by researchers. For New York digests, coverage of federal decisions begins only with the current third series.

In addition to the alphabetical arrangement of topics, each of the state digests includes the finding tools and indexing features described above in the discussion of the *United States Supreme Court Digest:* Tables of Cases, Defendant–Plaintiff Tables, Descriptive–Word Indexes, and Words and Phrases.

b. *Regional Digests*

Although West publishes seven regional reporters, it only publishes five current regional digests. There is no current regional digest for the cases appearing in the *North Eastern* or *South Western Reporter,* although coverage of the ten states in those reporters is provided by state digests. The *Southern Digest* is complete in one series. The *Atlantic, North Western,* and *South Eastern Digests* are each in a second series beginning in the 1930's. The *Pacific Digest* is in four series, with the current set designated *West's Pacific Digest, Beginning 367 P.2d.* As with the federal digests the divisions are chronological, and a researcher attempting comprehensive coverage must search all components (including the pocket part to the current series, and interim supplementary pamphlet, if any). The regional digests include Tables of Cases (by plaintiff only) and Descriptive–Word Indexes. They do *not* contain Defendant–Plaintiff Tables or Words and Phrases.

The *Pacific, South Eastern,* and *Southern Digests* include indexing of cases published in the region's state reports before the beginning of West's National Reporter System. Coverage is retrospective to the earliest published cases, starting with California cases from 1850 in the *Pacific Digest,* with Virginia cases from 1729 in the *South Eastern Digest,* and with Louisiana cases from 1809 in the *Southern Digest.*

For most states, then, one can search for decisions in either a state digest or a regional digest. If a choice between the two is available, the decision may depend on the time permitted for the research, the number of cases decided in a particular area, or whether authority from other jurisdictions might be persuasive or would simply be irrelevant. Regional digests are of diminishing importance, but remain handy tools if material from other jurisdictions would be useful. State digests, uncluttered by decisions from other jurisdictions or by the commentary found in most other sources, are among the quickest and most convenient ways to determine one state's judgments in a specific area of law.

4. THE COMPREHENSIVE AMERICAN DIGEST SYSTEM

There remains the colossus of West's digesting system, one series including all of the material mentioned to this point. In one massive set appear the headnotes for the courts of every state and federal jurisdiction. The American Digest System is the appropriate tool either if one seeks to find cases from throughout the country or if a specific state's digest is unavailable.

a. Century Digest *and* Decennial Digests

Although digests covering all federal and state courts were published in the nineteenth century, the first truly comprehensive digest was not completed until 1904. Seven years earlier, in 1897, the West Publishing Company began publication of the *Century Edition of the American Digest,* or *Century Digest.* In fifty volumes, this digest contains abstracts of all reported cases decided between 1658 and 1896. Its classification system is similar to that used in current digests, but its section numbers are *not* the same as the "key numbers" used in all subsequent West digests. The *Century Digest* includes an index in its final volume and extensive cross-references throughout all fifty volumes.

By the time of West's next major digest publication, the *1906 Decennial Edition of the American Digest,* its classification scheme had been "so thoroughly tested that it is possible to designate each of its 44,000 black-letter sections by a permanent section number."[6] This set, now known as the *First Decennial Digest,* covers cases from 1897 to 1906 and uses basically the same classification system still in use today. Although classifications have gradually been refined or changed with developments in the law, one can frequently trace a key number back to the turn of the century. Because the numbers in the *Century Digest* are different from those in later digests, the *First Decennial Digest* includes cross-references providing the *Century* counterparts of modern topics and key numbers. A researcher can thus find abstracts of all published American decisions on a specific point of law since the 1600's. Those few researchers who begin their work in the *Century* can use a table in volume 21 of the *First Decennial* to find the modern equivalent of the old classification.

The *First Decennial Digest* was followed by succeeding *Decennials,* each providing comprehensive coverage of a ten-year period, through the *Eighth Decennial Digest* covering 1966 to 1976. The number of cases digested had become so large that the *Eighth Decennial* spanned fifty volumes, the same number of volumes in which the *Century Digest* covered 238 years. To make subsequent digest units slightly more manageable, West began issuing them in five-year cumulations. The *Ninth Decennial Digest, Part 1* covers cases published from 1976 to 1981, and the *Ninth Decennial Digest, Part 2* covers 1981 to 1986.

Within a *Decennial Digest* it is likely that almost every topic and most key numbers will be represented by at least one headnote, and some of the more common key numbers may include thousands of digested cases. Each of the over four hundred topics in a *Decennial Digest* begins with a scope note and an outline of its classification, even if there are no cases assigned to it.[7] Under each key number, cases are listed in the following order: first federal decisions in hierarchical order (Supreme Court first), then the courts of each state in alphabetical order. Only very common key numbers, however, will have entries from *every* jurisdiction. Each decision is represented, as it was in the smaller digest units, beginning with the digest section of the reporter advance sheet where the decision appeared, by a reprinting of the original headnote abstract. The headnote is followed by the citation to the decision, so that one may easily locate and read the full text of the case. Illustration E shows the same abstract from the Michigan case seen earlier, this time as it appears with abstracts from six other states on a page in the *Ninth Decennial Digest, Part 2.*

6. Preface, 1 *First Decennial Digest* v, v-vi (West, 1908). On page vii, the publisher's preface went on to explain the value of this permanence:

> As a consequence, the old chaotic conditions which existed when every digester used an individual classification of his own is fast disappearing. The lawyer who is familiar with the American Digest classification does not have to study the mental peculiarities and idiosyncracies of the compiler of each new digest which he takes up.

7. The topic "Dueling," for example, carried no cases between 1925 and 1977. The topic "Criminal Law," on the other hand, has occupied six or more volumes in each *Decennial* unit since 1966.

Illustration E

A page from the *Ninth Decennial Digest, Part 2*

⚷251.13 AUTOMOBILES 4 9th D Pt 2—246

Vehicle Reparations Act applicable to motor vehicle "user," which is defined in the Act to mean person who resides in household in which any person owns or maintains motor vehicle, which category did not include subject passenger. KRS 304.39-020(15), 304.39-060(1), (2)(c).—Id.

Ky.App. 1983. Automobile accident victim who failed to file rejection of no fault insurance with Department of Insurance presented no proof of rejection, and thus was subject to "no fault" threshold requirements. KRS 304.39-010 et seq, 304.39-060(1), (2)(b), (5)(a).—Thompson v. Piasta, 662 S.W.2d 223.

Md.App. 1985. Under proper circumstances, passengers in taxicabs may seek recovery for injuries caused by uninsured motorists from the Maryland Automobile Insurance Fund. Code 1957, Art. 48A, § 541(c).—Pope v. Sun Cab Co., Inc., 488 A.2d 1009, 62 Md.App. 218, certiorari granted Maryland Auto. Ins. Fund v. Sun Cab Co., 497 A.2d 484, 304 Md. 47, affirmed 506 A.2d 641, 305 Md. 807.

Mich. 1982. Neither motorist nor his no-fault insurer is subject to liability for damage to a moving vehicle, but no-fault insurer is subject to liability for damage to a parked vehicle. M.C.L.A. §§ 500.3121, 500.3123(1)(a), 500.-3135(2)(d).—Heard v. State Farm Mut. Auto. Ins. Co., 324 N.W.2d 1, 414 Mich. 139, 27 A.L.R.4th 163.

Mich. 1981. Tort liability abolished by no-fault act is only such liability as arises out of ownership, maintenance or use of motor vehicle, not liability which arises out of other conduct, such as negligent keeping of cattle. M.C.L.A. § 500.3101 et seq.—Citizens Ins. Co. of America v. Tuttle, 309 N.W.2d 174, 411 Mich. 536.

In context of no-fault act, abolition of tort liability "arising from" ownership, maintenance or use of motor vehicle carries implicit sense of tort liability for injuries or damages caused by ownership, maintenance or use of motor vehicle. M.C.L.A. § 500.3135(2).—Id.

Only persons who own, maintain or use motor vehicles can be subject to tort liability for injuries or damage caused by ownership, maintenance or use of motor vehicle; nonmotorist tort-feasor cannot be subject to tort liability for injuries or damage caused by ownership, maintenance or use of motor vehicle. M.C.L.A. § 500.3135(2).—Id.

Abolition of tort liability for injuries or damage caused by ownership, maintenance or use of motor vehicle does not abolish tort liability of nonmotorist tort-feasor. M.C.L.A. § 500.-3135(2).—Id.

Person is to be relieved of tort liability arising from ownership, maintenance or use of motor vehicle only upon participating, through payment of premiums, in system for spreading costs of compensating vehicular injuries without regard to fault. M.C.L.A. §§ 500.3101 et seq., 500.-3135(2).—Id.

Both nonmotorist tort-feasor and uninsured motorist are outside basic no-fault system of allocating costs of accidents and both remain subject to tort liability. M.C.L.A. § 500.3101 et seq.—Id.

Mich.App. 1986. There is no right to sue for motorcycle damage under the minitort provision of the No-Fault Act. M.C.L.A. §§ 500.-3101(2)(c), 500.3135(2), (2)(d).—Nerat v. Swacker, 388 N.W.2d 305.

Mich.App. 1985. Estate of passenger who was killed when pickup she was riding in collided with uninsured motor vehicle may have common-law cause of action in tort, as the No-Fault Act, M.C.L.A. § 500.3101 et seq., did not abolish the tort liability of uninsured motorists.—Aetna Cas. & Sur. Co. v. Collins, 373 N.W.2d 177, 143 Mich.App. 661.

Mich.App. 1985. Tort liability of an uninsured motorist or liability which does not arise from tort-feasor's ownership or operation of a motor vehicle is not abrogated by No-Fault Act. M.C.L.A. § 500.3116(2).—Ryan v. Ford Motor Co., 368 N.W.2d 266, 141 Mich.App. 762.

Mich.App. 1985. Though garage mechanic was actually working on insured's automobile at the time of the alleged negligence which resulted in insured's being sprayed with radiator fluid and suffering personal injuries, mechanic was, in fact, a nonmotorist tort-feasor, against whom tort action could be maintained; that is, the suit was not one for damages for personal injuries arising out of ownership, maintenance, or use of motor vehicle so as to be barred by the No-Fault Insurance Act. M.C.L.A. § 500.3135.—Coleman v. Franzon, 366 N.W.2d 86, 141 Mich.App. 99.

Mich.App. 1983. Injury to eye, which occurred when pedestrian was splashed by city bus with water, slush, ice, and lye while he was standing at bus stop, was foreseeable injury which arose out of city's use of bus as motor vehicle for purposes of no-fault personal protection benefits, since it was eminently foreseeable that bus, upon encountering pool of water while being operated in normal fashion as motor vehicle, would propel puddle of water containing caustic chemical in direction of nearby pedestrian. M.C.L.A. § 500.3105.—Jones v. Tronex Chemical Corp., 341 N.W.2d 469, 129 Mich.App. 188.

Mich.App. 1983. For purposes of section of no-fault statute precluding recovery of personal protection insurance benefits if a person is the owner of an uninsured motor vehicle "involved" in an accident, a parked uninsured vehicle is not "involved" in the accident unless one of the exceptions to the parked vehicle provision is applicable. M.C.L.A. §§ 500.3106, 500.3113.—Braun v. Citizens Ins. Co., 335 N.W.2d 701, 124 Mich.App. 822.

For purposes of section of no-fault statute precluding recovery of personal protection insurance benefits if the person is the owner of an uninsured motor vehicle "involved" in an accident, a parked vehicle can be "involved" in the accident when the vehicle is parked in such a way as to cause unreasonable risk of the bodily injury which occurred. M.C.L.A. §§ 500.3106, 500.3113.—Id.

In action brought by plaintiff who was injured when he was pinned between an automobile and the tow truck which had pulled his uninsured automobile out of a snow drift, evidence sustained finding that plaintiff's automobile was "involved" in the collision, because the vehicle was parked in such a way as to cause an unreasonable risk of bodily injury which occurred, and therefore, plaintiff's recovery was barred by statute precluding recovery of personal protection insurance benefits if a person is the owner of an uninsured motor vehicle "involved" in an accident. M.C.L.A. § 500.3113.—Id.

Mich.App. 1983. Damage to loader which contractor was transporting on his tractor, caused by striking underside of an overpass, arose out of contractor's use of its tractor as motor vehicle, and thus, under No-Fault Act, contractor was not liable in tort to owner of loader for damage thereto. M.C.L.A. §§ 500.-3123(1), 500.3135.—National Ben Franklin Ins. Co. v. Bakhaus Contractors, Inc., 335 N.W.2d 70, 124 Mich.App. 510.

Mich.App. 1983. Uninsured motorist is outside the basic no-fault system of allocating the costs of accidents and remains subject to tort liability. M.C.L.A. § 500.3135(1, 2).—Jones v. Detroit Auto. Inter-Ins. Exchange, 335 N.W.2d 39, 124 Mich.App. 363.

Mich.App. 1983.
Defendant's Chevy struck a tree—
There was no liability;
The No-Fault Act comes into play
As owner and the driver say;

Barred by the Act's immunity,
No suit in tort will aid the tree;
Although the oak's in disarray,
No court can make defendants pay,
M.C.L.A. § 500.3135.—Fisher v. Lowe, 333 N.W.2d 67, 122 Mich.App. 418.

Mich.App. 1982. Statute requires compliance with security requirements of no-fault insurance after 30-day period, 30-day period being intended to protect tourists and other transient nonresidents from criminal sanctions imposed by the Act. M.C.L.A. §§ 500.3102, 500.3135(2).—Berrien County Road Com'n v. Jones, 326 N.W.2d 495, 119 Mich.App. 315.

Defendants, having paid their dues in risk-spreading system by voluntarily acquiring insurance, and being owners or registrants of motor vehicle as defined in statute, though neither plaintiff's nor defendants' vehicle was required to be registered as vehicle within the state and therefore neither was required to be covered by no-fault insurance, were entitled to immunity provided by the no-fault act. M.C.L.A. §§ 500.-3101(1, 3, 4), 500.3102, 500.3135(2).—Id.

Mich.App. 1981. Damages awarded to plaintiff for personal injuries sustained as result of negligence of state in failing to maintain roads were not subject to no-fault motor vehicle act since act applied only to accidents caused by motor vehicles and not to those caused by negligent highway maintenance. M.C.L.A. § 500.3135.—Longworth v. Michigan Dept. of Highways and Transp., 315 N.W.2d 135, 110 Mich.App. 771.

Minn.App. 1986. No-Fault Act did not bar a governmental agency established under the laws of Quebec, Canada to administer automobile insurance plan covering Quebec citizens from maintaining a subrogation action against driver of automobile involved in Minnesota collision in which Quebec resident met her death; agency paid benefits to surviving husband as result of wife's death and took assignment from heirs and next-of kin of their claims against the other motorist. M.S.A. § 65B.53, subds. 2, 3.—Regie de l'assurance Auto. du Quebec v. Jensen, 389 N.W.2d 537.

N.H. 1983. Tractor with backhoe attachment is "motor vehicle" for purposes of Financial Responsibility Act. RSA 259:61.—Royal Globe Ins. Companies v. Fletcher, 459 A.2d 255, 123 N.H. 189.

N.J.Super.A.D. 1984. Fact that automobile was object of robbery during which plaintiff's decedent was killed did not transform incident into "accident involving an automobile" within meaning of State Automobile Reparation Reform Act. N.J.S.A. 39:6A-1 et seq., 39:6A-4.—Uzcategui-Gaymon v. New Jersey Mfrs. Ins. Co., 472 A.2d 163, 193 N.J.Super. 71.

N.Y.A.D. 1 Dept. 1983. New York resident who registered vehicle in Connecticut and whose automobile was uninsured in either New York or Connecticut and thus could not qualify as a covered person under New York no-fault law was liable for basic economic loss for damages to himself and could not recover those amounts from third-party tort-feasor. McKinney's Insurance Law § 671, subd. 1.—Wilson v. E. & J. Trucking Corp., 462 N.Y.S.2d 660, 94 A.D.2d 666.

For references to other topics, see Descriptive-Word Index

~~Each *Decennial Digest* unit contains two finding aids: a Table of Cases, listing alphabetically the name of every case appearing in the unit, and a Descriptive-Word Index, which serves as the basic subject~~

finding tool for all West digests.[8] Until 1976 the *Decennials* included no Defendant–Plaintiff Tables, but beginning with the *Ninth Decennial Digest, Part 1,* there are tables listing cases under both parties' names.

The *Decennial Digests* are massive tools offering subject access to all American jurisdictions for five- or ten-year periods. In one place, headnotes and citations are available from all cases published during the years of coverage and dealing with any specific point of law.

b. General Digest

Unlike the digests for individual jurisdictions or regions, the *Decennial Digests* are not supplemented by pocket parts, and once they are published they are not updated and recompiled. They are published every five or ten years to provide comprehensive coverage of a specific period. A search in the most recent *Decennial* can, however, be updated by using a series of bound volumes known as the *General Digest.* Each new *General Digest* volume contains the latest headnotes in all West reporters, arranged by topic. The entire digest spectrum, from "Abandoned and Lost Property" to "Zoning and Planning," is covered in each *General Digest* volume. In effect, these volumes are "advance sheets" for the next *Decennial Digest,* and once publication of the *Decennial* is completed they are no longer needed.

In recent years twelve volumes of the *General Digest* have been published annually. These abstracts are not cumulated again until the publication of the next edition of the *Decennial Digest.* Depending on the date of the most recent *Decennial,* a researcher may need to examine fifty or more *General Digest* volumes to find recent cases. Most key numbers do not appear in every *General Digest* volume, so examining each volume would be fruitless and time-wasting. One can determine which volumes contain a particular key number, however, by consulting a "Table of Key Numbers" included in each volume of the *General Digest.* This table is cumulative in every tenth volume, indicating in one location which of the previous ten volumes contain abstracts for each topic/key number combination. In addition, the most recent table includes references to all volumes published since the latest ten-volume cumulative table. If, for example, there have been sixteen volumes in the current *General Digest* series, one would have to consult tables in volume 10 (for references in volumes 1 through 10) and volume 16 (for references in volumes 11 through 16). Illustration F shows a sample page from a Table of Key Numbers.

In addition to abstracts arranged by topic and key number and the Table of Key Numbers, each *General Digest* volume contains a Descriptive–Word Index, a Table of Cases listing decisions abstracted in that volume, and a "Table of Cases Affirmed, Reversed, etc.," which lists earlier cases affected by that volume's decisions. These indexes and

8. The *Century Digest* and the *First Decennial Digest* share a combined Table of Cases, located in volumes 21 to 25 of the *First Decennial;* and combined Descriptive–Word Indexes cover both the *First* and *Second Decennials,* and the *Third* and *Fourth Decennials,* respectively.

Illustration F

The first page of a *General Digest* Table of Key Numbers

TABLE OF KEY NUMBERS

GENERAL DIGEST, VOLUMES 1–8, 7th SERIES

A Time Saver for Locating The Latest Cases

Example: Having found a proposition of law under the topic Drains ⇐57, refer to the same topic and Key in this table which will show that other cases appear in the General Digest, Seventh Series, Volume 1. Search is therefore unnecessary in Volume 2–8 of the General Digest, Seventh Series.

ABANDONED AND LOST PROPERTY
⇐
1—4, 5, 8
2—4
3—2, 4, 8
4—2, 4
5—6
10—4
11—4
12—4

ABATEMENT AND REVIVAL
⇐
4—3, 5, 6, 7
5—4
7—2, 4, 5, 8
8(1)—6, 7
8(2)—3, 4, 5, 6, 7, 8
8(4)—3, 8
9—2, 4, 6, 7, 8
11—5, 6
12—1, 4, 8
13—6
17—3
30—8
41—3, 6
42—4
43—3
52—3, 6
53—3
54—2, 5
55(1)—6
57—6, 8
58—6
58(1)—4, 5
63—6, 7
71—5
77—7
81—4

ABDUCTION
⇐
1—8
12—2

ABORTION AND BIRTH CONTROL
⇐
.50—2, 4, 6
1.30—1, 6
15—7

ABSENTEES
⇐
5—6
7—3

ABSTRACTS OF TITLE
⇐
3—3

ACCESSION
⇐
1—3
2—3

ACCORD AND SATISFACTION
⇐
1—1, 2, 3, 4, 5, 6, 7, 8
2—8
2(1)—1, 2
2(2)—1
3(2)—5
4—1, 3, 5, 8
5—1, 6, 7
7(1)—7, 8
8(1)—5
9—4, 5, 7, 8
10(1)—2; 3, 4, 6, 7, 8
11(1)—6
11(2)—2, 5, 6, 8
11(3)—2, 7
15—2
17—5
18—6, 8
19—4, 5
20—7, 8
23—2, 7
24—5, 8
25(1)—4
25(2)—3
26(1)—1, 8
26(3)—1, 5, 6, 7, 8
27—2, 4, 8

ACCOUNT
⇐
1—7
4—4, 5
9—3
14—8

ACCOUNT—Cont'd
⇐
15—3
17(1)—5, 7
22—8

ACCOUNT, ACTION ON
⇐
2—3, 4
3—1, 2, 4
4—1
6(1)—3
6(2)—2
6(3)—3
6(5)—6
7—1, 2, 3, 4, 5, 6
8—3, 4, 5, 6
10—3
12—3
13—2, 3, 5

ACCOUNT STATED
⇐
1—2, 7, 8
3—4, 5
4—2
5—2, 3, 5, 6
6(1)—2, 7
6(2)—2, 3, 5
6(4)—8
7—1
16—4
19(3)—1, 2, 5, 8
20(1)—1

ACCOUNTANTS
⇐
5—5, 6
8—1, 2, 3, 4
9—3, 4, 8
10—2, 3, 4, 5
11—2

ACKNOWLEDGMENT
⇐
1—2
11—2
29—1, 7
33—7
36(1)—2

ACKNOWLEDGMENT—Cont'd
⇐
45—7
48—4, 6, 8
62(1)—3
62(2)—2

ACTION
⇐
1—2
2—2, 5, 6
3—1, 3, 5, 6, 7, 8
5—1, 5, 6, 7, 8
6—1, 2, 3, 4, 5, 6, 7, 8
8—1
9—1
10—4, 5
12—1, 2, 4, 7
13—1, 2, 3, 4, 5, 6, 7, 8
14—1, 2
17—1, 3, 4, 5, 6, 8
18—6, 8
20—4
22—1, 4, 5
23—5
27(1)—1, 2, 3, 4, 5, 6, 7
27(2)—4, 5, 6, 8
27(5)—6
35—3, 5
36—2, 3, 4, 6, 8
38(1)—1, 2, 4, 5, 6
38(3)—3, 4, 5, 6
38(4)—2, 3
38(6)—3, 4, 5, 6, 7
43—6
45(1)—1, 5, 6, 8
47—3, 6, 7
48(1)—1, 4
48(2)—4
50(1)—7
50(2)—4
50(3)—4
50(4)—2
50(9)—2
53(1)—1, 3, 4, 5, 7
53(2)—3
57(1)—1, 6
57(2)—6
57(3)—2
57(4)—3, 8
57(6)—2, 4

1267

tables cumulate in every tenth volume, like the Table of Key Numbers, but they do *not* cumulate in volumes between the ten-volume cumulations. The latest volumes, therefore, must be searched individually or not at all. Even in the ten-volume cumulations there is no Defendant–

Plaintiff Table, so recent cases can be found only under the plaintiffs' names.

The *General Digest* is currently in its seventh series, which began in 1986. If West's format of *Decennial* publication does not change, this series will continue until 1991, at which point it will be entirely superseded by the *Tenth Decennial Digest, Part One.*

The following table traces in chronological order the present components of the American Digest System:

Years Covered	Digest Unit	Number of Volumes
1658–1896	*Century Digest*	50
1897–1906	*First Decennial Digest*	25
1907–1916	*Second Decennial Digest*	24
1916–1926	*Third Decennial Digest*	29
1926–1936	*Fourth Decennial Digest*	34
1936–1946	*Fifth Decennial Digest*	52
1946–1956	*Sixth Decennial Digest*	36
1956–1966	*Seventh Decennial Digest*	38
1966–1976	*Eighth Decennial Digest*	50
1976–1981	*Ninth Decennial Digest, Part 1*	38
1981–1986	*Ninth Decennial Digest, Part 2*	48
1986–date	*General Digest, Seventh Series*	In progress

With the increasing use of computer services and the availability of more convenient federal and state digests, one may well question the continued utility of this comprehensive and unwieldy set. While older *Decennial* volumes do little but gather dust, however, recently published *Decennials* can be useful compendia of contemporary case law from throughout the country.

5. FINDING CASES IN THE WEST DIGESTS

Having described the structure and forms of publication of the various West digests, we turn now to the actual search procedures employed in their use. How does one find cases in the digests? There are three basic approaches: working from a case, by subject searching in indexes, or by analyzing the classification outline of a particular topic.

a. Starting With a Case

The simplest and often the most successful means of approaching a digest is with a case already in hand. Half the battle of legal research is won by having "one good case" to serve as a basis for finding other cases and resources. As seen in the last chapter, for example, the Shepard's listing for one case can serve as a springboard to numerous later decisions on the same issues.

When using a digest, starting with a case means that there is no need to search through indexes or figure out the digest's classification system. The appropriate topics and key numbers are already available in the headnotes of the decision in hand. If a headnote has been written for that part of the opinion addressing the issue being researched, the topic and key number assigned to the headnote can be searched in the digests for other relevant cases. Occasionally the key number assigned covers a very broad area, so that the digest includes abstracts of many irrelevant cases, but more often it's an ideal lead and a shortcut through the indexes and finding aids.

To read a decision and examine its headnotes, of course, one must know its citation. Often a researcher has heard of a relevant case but does not know where to find it. A case name may come up in conversation or may be mentioned in nonlegal literature with no reference to its citation. Using the tables in West's digests, however, one can easily use a case name to find its citation. As noted in the discussion of the different digests, every digest has a Table of Cases, an alphabetical listing of all cases covered in the publication. Each jurisdictional digest has a complete listing of published cases from that jurisdiction, updated by pocket parts and further updated by interim pamphlets. For digests in more than one series, each component has a table of the cases for its period. There are, for example, four separate case tables in federal digests, with the most recent (in *West's Federal Practice Digest 3d*) covering cases since 1975.

The decisions known most often by name only are those of the Supreme Court of the United States. One can easily find all three citations to famous cases such as *Brown v. Board of Education* or *Roe v. Wade* by using the Table of Cases in the *United States Supreme Court Digest.* This table is cumulative from the beginning of the Court, and was updated and republished in 1986 as volumes 14 and 14A of the set.

Illustration G shows the page of the *Michigan Digest* table of cases listing *Fisher v. Lowe,* the case in Illustration B. Note that following the name of each case are its citations in both official and regional reporters. If a case has been affirmed, reversed or modified on appeal or rehearing, that information is included as well, with a citation to the later decision. (The decision immediately following *Fisher v. Lowe* in the illustration was *reversed* by the Michigan Supreme Court.) Finally the listing includes the topics and key numbers under which the headnote abstracts can be found in the digest. One can go directly to those key numbers from the Table of Cases. If one has not yet read the case, however, it is usually better to go first to the opinion to determine which headnotes, if any, are indeed relevant to a particular search.

The topics and key numbers provided in the Tables of Cases are of most value for cases decided before the National Reporter System volumes began including key number classifications for each headnote, in about 1909. A person seeking cases on issues related to those in such a case cannot go directly from the reporter to the digest classification. One can, however, use a Table of Cases to find the appropriate digest entries for the decision's points of law.

Illustration G

A page from the Table of Cases in *West's Michigan Digest*

References are to Digest Topics and Key Numbers

Fisher v. Johnson Milk Co 383 Mich 158, 174 NW2d 752—Neglig 25, 27; Sales 441(3).
Fisher v. Johnson Milk Co 163 NW2d 652, 13 MichApp 10, rev 383 Mich 158, 174 NW2d 752—Judgm 181(29, 33), 185.3(21); Prod Liab 41.
Fisher v. Kavanagh 100 FSupp 248—Int Rev 764.3.
Fisher v. Lowe, MichApp, 333 NW2d 67, 122 MichApp 418.—Autos 251.13; Proc 4.
Fisher v. Michigan Dept. of Mental Health, MichApp, 339 NW2d 692, 128 MichApp 72, rev 368 NW2d 229, 422 Mich 884, reconsideration den 374 NW2d 418—App & E 175; Judgm 181(11), 185(2), 186, 829(3); Offic 114; Phys 18.40; States 79, 191(2).
Fisher v. Muller 53 MichApp 110, 218 NW2d 821—Const Law 284(2), 285, 309(2); Decl Judgm 345; Estop 62.1, 62.3; Evid 65, 86; Statut 245; Tax 360, 363, 431, 491, 505, 619, 689(2), 818.
Fisher v. Provin 25 Mich 347—Hus & W 14.2(6), 14.4.
Fisher v. Stolaruk Corp., EDMich, 648 FSupp 486.—Labor 1570, 1572.
Fisher v. Stolaruk Corp., EDMich, 110 FRD 74.—Contracts 19, 93(1); Fed Civ Proc 2725.
Fisher v. Sunfield Tp., MichApp, 415 NW2d 297, 163 MichApp 735.—Tax 348(6), 485(3), 493.8, 498.9.
Fisher v. Travelers Indem Co 13 MichApp 208, 163 NW2d 822—Insurance 508.
Fisher v. Volkswagenwerk Aktiengesellschaft, MichApp, 321 NW2d 814, 115 MichApp 781.—Death 11, 39; Ex & Ad 509(1).
Fisher-New Center Co, Appeal of 375 Mich 559, 134 NW2d 753—Tax 493.9.
Fisher-New Center Co v. City of Detroit 38 MichApp 750, 197 NW2d 272—Tax 490, 493.1, 535, 537, 543(1).
Fisher-New Center Co v. Michigan State Tax Commission 381 Mich 713, 167 NW2d 263—Admin Law 462, 788; Tax 452, 485(3), 493.8, 493.9.
Fisher-New Center Co v. Michigan State Tax Commission 380 Mich 380, 157 NW2d 271, reh 381 Mich 713, 167 NW2d 263.
Fisher-New Center Co v. Wayne County 38 MichApp 750, 197 NW2d 272. See Fisher-New Center Co v. City of Detroit.
Fisher Provision Co v. LoPatin 65 MichApp 568, 237 NW2d 562—Corp 340(3).
Fisher's Estate, In re 70 MichApp 117, 245 NW2d 427. See Gruskin v. Fisher.
Fishleigh v. Detroit United Ry, Mich, 171 NW 549, 205 Mich 145.—App & E 1004.1(4).
Fisk, In re, BkrtcyMich, 36 BR 924.—Bankr 2233(1), 2559, 2784; Judgm 828(3.53).
Fisk v. Allis Chalmers Credit Corp., BkrtcyMich, 36 BR 924. See Fisk, In re.
Fisk v. Fisk, Mich, 53 NW2d 356, 333 Mich 513.—App & E 1056.1(4).
Fisk v. Powell 349 Mich 604, 84 NW2d 736—App & E 1008.1(1).
Fister v. Henschel 7 MichApp 590, 152 NW2d 555—App & E 1010.1(7); Brok 9, 11; Damag 22, 40(2), 190.
Fister Realty Co v. Henschel 7 MichApp 590, 152 NW2d 555. See Fister v. Henschel.
Fiszer v. White Pine Copper Co 405 Mich 105, 274 NW2d 411. See Kostamo v. Marquette Iron Mining Co.
Fitch v. Constantine Hydraulic Co, Mich, 6 NW 91, 44 Mich 74.—Arbit 3.2.
Fitch v. Crime Victims' Compensation Bd 99 MichApp 363, 297 NW2d 667—Crim Law 1220.
Fithian v. Papalini, Mich, 378 NW2d 467, 424 Mich 77. See Leggett, Matter of Estates of.
Fittante v. Schultz 383 Mich 722, 179 NW2d 20. See Albert, In re.
Fittante v. Schultz 20 MichApp 259, 174 NW2d 29—Contempt 20, 24.
Fitterer Engineering Associates, Inc., Matter of, BkrtcyMich, 27 BR 878.—Atty & C 175, 182(1); Bankr 2573, 2603; Fed Cts 407.
Fitz v. Board of Educ. of Port Huron Area Schools, EDMich, 662 FSupp 1011, aff 802 F2d 457.—Armed S 114(1), 118(7), 119; Schools 133.9; States 18.15.
Fitzcharles v. Mayer 284 Mich 122, 278 NW 788—Trial 139.3.
Fitzgerald v. Challenge Cook Bros, Inc 80 MichApp 524, 264 NW2d 348—Work Comp 2251.
Fitzgerald v. Detroit United Ry 206 Mich 273, 172 NW 608—App & E 1060.1(1), 1064.1(4); Trial 133.1.
Fitzgerald v. Hubert Herman, Inc 23 MichApp 716, 179 NW2d 252—Contracts 816(1); Trial 139.1(17).
Fitzgerald v. Lozier Motor Co 187 Mich 660, 154 NW 67—Trial 139.1(3).
Fitzke v. Shappell 468 F2d 1072—Civil R 13.12(1, 6); Const Law 272(2); Fed Civ Proc 654, 1788.5, 2539, 2543, 2544.
Fitzpatrick, In re Estate of, MichApp, 406 NW2d 483.—Courts 202(5); Wills 435, 523, 552(1), 552(3).
Fitzpatrick v. Wolfe, MichApp, 406 NW2d 483. See Fitzpatrick, In re Estate of.
Fitzwater v. Fitzwater 97 MichApp 92, 294 NW2d 249—Const Law 305(5); Courts 12(2.35); Divorce 403(7); Parent & C 3.4(2).
511 Detroit Street, Inc. v. Kelley, CA6 (Mich), 807 F2d 1293, cert den 107 SCt 3211, 96 LEd2d 698—Const Law 46(1), 90.1(1), 90.4(1); Crim Law 13.1(1), 986.-2(1); Obscen 2.5.
Fizer v. Onekama Consol Schools 83 MichApp 584, 269 NW2d 234—Mun Corp 869, 907; Schools 97(4).
Fjerstad's Estate, In re 47 MichApp 100, 209 NW2d 302. See Besemer v. Fjerstad's Estate.
F J Siller & Co v. City of Hart 400 Mich 578, 255 NW2d 347—Arbit 2.1, 7.9, 9, 82(1).
F J Siller & Co v. City of Hart 68 MichApp 265, 242 NW2d 547, rev 400 Mich 578, 255 NW2d 347—Arbit 2.1, 7, 82(1).
Flack v. Waite 18 MichApp 339, 170 NW2d 922—Dismissal 81(3, 6).
Flager v. Associated Truck Lines, Inc 52 MichApp 280, 216 NW2d 922—Neglig 93(5, 10).
Flaherty v. Smith 87 MichApp 561, 274 NW2d 72—Parent & C 2(14).
Flaig v. Bendix Corp 488 FSupp 336, aff 701 F2d 177—Civil R 38, 44(1).
Flamini, Matter of, BkrtcyMich, 23 BR 668.—Bankr 3361.
Flamini, Matter of, BkrtcyMich, 19 BR 303, on reh 23 BR 668.—Bankr 2023, 3350; Statut 263, 268, 270.
Flamm v. Scherer 40 MichApp 1, 198 NW2d 702—Contracts 321(1); Evid 442(6); Sales 98, 174, 405, 417.
Flamm Pickle & Packing Co v. Scherer 40 MichApp 1, 198 NW2d 702. See Flamm v. Scherer.
Flanagan v. General Motors Corp 95 MichApp 677, 291 NW2d 166—Costs 105, 172; Judges 49(2); Judgm 181(1, 33).
Flanders Co v. Canners' Exchange Subscribers at Warner Inter-Insurance Bureau 235 Mich 157, 209 NW 113—Insurance 579.1.
Flat Hots Co v. Peschke Packing Co, Mich, 8 NW2d 295, 301 Mich 331.—App & E 1011.1(1), 1012.1(3).
Fleckenstein v. Citizens' Mut Auto Ins Co 326 Mich 591, 40 NW2d 733—Insurance 435.2(4).
Fleischer v. Bucilli 13 MichApp 135, 163 NW2d 637—Costs 173(1); Damag 71, 91(1), 184; Spec Perf 114(1), 129; Ven & Pur 350.
Fleisher v. U S 91 F2d 404—Crim Law 1144.3.
Fleming v. Chrysler Corp 575 F2d 1187—Labor 136, 416.3.
Fleming v. Chrysler Corp., EDMich, 659 FSupp 392.—States 18.45, 18.49.
Fleming v. Chrysler Corp, DCMich, 416 FSupp 1258, aff 575 F2d 1187—Labor 136, 219, 221, 416.3, 759, 777.
Fleming v. Mohawk Wrecking & Lumber Co 67 SCt 1129—Statut 219(6).
Fleming v. Rex Oil & Gas Co 43 FSupp 950—Commerce 62.56.
Flemings v. Jenkins, MichApp, 360 NW2d 298, 138 MichApp 788.—Autos 251.15, 251.19.
Fletcher v. Advo Systems, Inc., DCMich, 616 FSupp 1511.—Fed Civ Proc 202, 203; Fed Cts 286, 289, 303, 306; Rem of C 31.
Fletcher v. Aetna Cas & Sur Co 409 Mich 1, 294 NW2d 141. See Bradley v. Mid-Century Ins Co.
Fletcher v. Aetna Cas & Sur Co 80 MichApp 439, 264 NW2d 19, aff Bradley v. Mid-Century Ins Co, 409 Mich 1, 294 NW2d 141, 20 ALR4th 1069—Damag 89(2); Insurance 4.4, 531.3(2), 602.2(1); Interest 39(1); Statut 263.
Fletcher v. Flynn 368 Mich 328, 118 NW2d 229—App & E 1003(4).
Fletcher v. Ford Motor Co., MichApp, 342 NW2d 285, 128 MichApp 823, appeal den—Evid 363; Prod Liab 96, 98.
Fletcher v. Grinnell Bros 62 FSupp 258—Commerce 62.60.
Fletcher v. Harafajee 100 MichApp 440, 299 NW2d 53—Work Comp 1087, 2168, 2253.
Fletcher v. Kentucky Inns, Inc 88 MichApp 456, 276 NW2d 619—Corp 113.
Fletcher v. State Treasurer 384 Mich 289, 181 NW2d 909—Costs 221; Insurance 72.9.
Fletcher v. State Treasurer 16 MichApp 87, 167 NW2d 594, aff 384 Mich 289, 181 NW2d 909—Costs 221; Insurance 8, 72.9; Statut 181(1).
Fletcher v. Stratton 20 MichApp 540, 174 NW2d 307—Autos 246(9, 38).
Fletcher, Baby Girl, Matter of 79 MichApp 219, 256 NW2d 444. See Baby Girl Fletcher, Matter of.
Flexitype & Douglas Offset Co v. Department of Treasury, Revenue Division 52 MichApp 153, 216 NW2d 609—Tax 1237, 1336.
Flick v. Larue, DCMich, 608 FSupp 1281, aff 821 F2d 649—Civil R 13.1, 13.4(5), 13.8(1), 13.13(1).
Flinn v. Sun Oil Co 96 MichApp 59, 292 NW2d 484—App & E 969; New Tr 29; Sales 427; Trial 295(5); Witn 379(10).
Flint Bd of Ed v. Williams 88 MichApp 8, 276 NW2d 499—Schools 160; Statut 181(1, 2), 223.1, 223.4.
Flint, City of. See City of Flint.

All digest units have tables listing cases by plaintiffs' names. The state and federal digests, but not the regional digests, also have Defendant–Plaintiff Tables providing cross references from the second party's name to the first party's. If only one party to a case is known and nothing is found under the name in the Table of Cases, often a search in the Defendant–Plaintiff Table will turn up the case. This is particularly true in fields such as criminal law, where the name of the defendant is often the most common means of identifying a case. The Defendant–Plaintiff Tables do not include the case history information or the topics and key numbers that are part of the Tables of Cases listings, but they do contain both official and National Reporter System citations. Defendant–Plaintiff Tables are updated in pocket parts, but not in interim supplementary pamphlets.

If a case is too recent to be included in the latest supplement to the digest, a search for its name can be brought up to date by looking in the "Cases Reported" tables in reporter bound volumes and advance sheets. National Reporter System bound volumes generally contain two Cases Reported tables. One consists of a single alphabetical list of all cases in the volume, listed under both plaintiffs' and defendants' names. The other, in reporters covering more than one jurisdiction, lists cases separately under each jurisdiction, by plaintiff only. Advance sheets, on the other hand, include only the latter table, listing cases only by plaintiff and separately for each jurisdiction. The tables in advance sheets do, however, cumulate for the contents of each bound volume; instead of looking in every single advance sheet, a person searching for the name of a recent case needs only to look in the last advance sheet for each bound volume number. Since the Cumulative Cases Reported tables in advance sheets cover more than one pamphlet, the names of cases appearing in the issue being examined instead of earlier issues are printed in bold type. In the regional reporters the table also indicates on what pages of the pamphlet cases from each state are printed, so that an attorney wishing to scan a state's latest decisions each week can easily do so. Illustration H is a page of the Cumulative Cases Reported table from an advance sheet for the *North Western Reporter.*

If one knows the name of a case but not its jurisdiction, the Tables of Cases in the *Decennial* and *General Digests* may be used to find its citation. All cases published before 1907 are contained in one table in volumes 21 to 25 of the *First Decennial Digest,* and each subsequent *Decennial* includes a table of cases for its time period. (The first *Decennial* Defendant–Plaintiff Table, unfortunately, was not published until the *Ninth Decennial, Part 1,* covering 1976 to 1981.) For the period since the most recent *Decennial,* each *General Digest* volume contains a listing of the cases it covers. Starting with the *General Digest, Seventh Series,* which began in 1986, these listings cumulate in every tenth volume. Searching the *Decennial* or *General Digests* for a case by name is not such an onerous task if the date of decision is

Illustration H

Cumulative Cases Reported table in a *North Western Reporter* advance sheet

CUMULATIVE CASES REPORTED

429 N.W.2d

(Cases in bold type appear in this issue)

IOWA

(Cases in this issue, pp. 558–571)

MICHIGAN

(Cases in this issue, pp. 573–667)

known or can be estimated. Otherwise it may be necessary to look in over a dozen tables, covering from the 17th century to the current year.

Occasionally a judicial decision is referred to by a "popular name," or a term other than the names of its parties. For example, *Youngstown Sheet & Tube Co. v. Sawyer,* 343 U.S. 579 (1952), is often referred to as the "Steel Seizure Case." The closing pages of *Shepard's Acts and Cases by Popular Names: Federal and State* list many of these names, and provide reporter citations (but neither dates nor parties' names). A few of the designations included are very well-known, but many are quite obscure, "popular" only in the broadest sense of the term. In recent years the use of "popular names" has declined precipitously, and very few new cases are being added to the list.[9]

b. *Descriptive-Word Indexes*

Each West digest includes a minutely constructed index referring to the specific topics and key numbers under which decisions on that subject have been abstracted in the digest. These "Descriptive-Word Indexes" are simply detailed subject indexes to the contents of the digests. The indexes are usually quite large, occupying three or more volumes in most jurisdictional digests.

There are generally two types of entries in a Descriptive-Word Index. Each West key number is represented in every jurisdictional and regional digest's index, even if no cases are represented, so the Descriptive-Word Index functions in part as a subject index to the key number classifications. Descriptive-Word Indexes for different jurisdictions or regions are quite similar, in that a particular entry will refer in any digest to the same key number. In addition, however, there are entries for specific fact situations represented by individual cases covered in the digest. The Descriptive-Word Index for each jurisdiction therefore contains some entries unique to its jurisprudence.

The *Decennial* and *General Digests* also contain Descriptive-Word Indexes, but these lists no longer attempt to be comprehensive finding tools. The index in the *Ninth Decennial Digest, Part 1,* for example, is less than a quarter of the size of the index for the *Eighth Decennial,* although the digest itself is almost as large. The indexes in *General Digest* volumes are usually only seven or eight pages long. (If they *did* index every case digested, of course, the Descriptive-Word Indexes would be nearly as massive as the digests themselves.) If a jurisdictional or regional digest is available, its comprehensive Descriptive-Word Index is usually a better first place to look for general coverage of a subject. The indexes in recent *Decennial* or *General Digest* volumes,

9. Similar popular name tables were published in some older West digests, including the first *Federal Digest* and the *Second* through *Sixth Decennials.* These tables have long since been discontinued, but may occasionally be useful for older cases, since the Shepard's and West tables do not duplicate coverage entirely.

Shepard's Acts and Cases by Popular Names serves a far more important function as a finding tool for legislative acts, as will be discussed in Chapter 5.

however, can be useful resources for searches concerning currently developing areas of legal doctrine.

West suggests that before consulting a Descriptive–Word Index, the researcher analyze the problem to be searched, and determine very specific words or phrases to be used by breaking the problem down into the following elements common to every case:

(1) the *parties* involved;

(2) the *places* where the facts arose, and the *objects* or *things* involved;

(3) the *acts* or *omissions* which form the *basis of action* or *issue*;

(4) the *defense* to the action or issue; and

(5) the *relief* sought.

In the case of *Fisher v. Lowe,* shown in Illustration B earlier in the chapter, the plaintiff is suing to recover for damage to an oak tree struck by an automobile. The defendants asserted that no-fault insurance granted them immunity from tort liability. The attorneys for the parties could have found relevant case law by looking in a Descriptive–Word Index under such terms as "trees" or "no fault insurance." As a general rule, one should use search terms that are both *specific* and *material.* General terms such as "automobiles" or "negligence" are likely to have too many references covering an enormous number of irrelevant issues and cases. A search term such as "oak" would be very specific, but has no legal importance and does not even appear in the index.

Illustrations I and J reproduce pages from the Descriptive–Word Index in *West's North Western Digest 2d* showing entries under "Trees—automobile collision" and "No fault insurance—limitation of tort remedy." Note that under "Trees" one is directed to a variety of topics and key numbers that might arise in such a case, but not the topic and key number used in *Fisher v. Lowe.* Under "No fault insurance," on the other hand, one is directed to the digest location where the West editors classified the first *Fisher* headnote.

A misleading byproduct of many law school legal research problems is that they encourage the belief that for every hypothetical problem there is a perfectly-designed case abstract waiting to be found. In practice one seldom finds a precedent in which an identical fact situation raises the exact legal issues with which one is confronted. What one realistically hopes to find is a precedent that involves *similar* facts and the same legal issues. One must usually draw analogies from similar situations. Descriptive–Word Indexes can be quite effective in finding precedential cases, if used with an understanding that they may not always contain the precise factual terms one would wish to find.

c. *Topical Analysis*

One can also find cases by examining the topic outlines, printed at the beginning of each digest topic in any of the jurisdictional or

Illustration I

Entries under "Trees" in a Descriptive–Word Index

36 N W D 2d—411 **TREES**

References are to Digest Topics and Key Numbers

Illustration J

A Descriptive–Word Index entry for the classification used in *Fisher v. Lowe*

NO 35 N W D 2d—36

References are to Digest Topics and Key Numbers

Decennial digests. A researcher who knows which topic is most relevant to an issue, or who can determine which is most appropriate by scanning the list of topics at the beginning of the digest, can focus on that one topic for searching. The topic outlines begin with a general summary of major subdivisions, followed by a detailed outline of all individual key numbers. The researcher finds relevant key numbers and then examines the abstracts listed under those numbers for cases on point. Illustration K shows the page including the key number classification for the first *Fisher v. Lowe* headnote in the "Automobiles" outline, from the *Ninth Decennial Digest, Part 2.* The page shown is part of an eleven-page outline for the topic "Automobiles."

If one knows an area of law well and is able to place a particular problem in its logical location within that area, this approach may not only lead to relevant cases but may clarify one's thinking about the issue by placing it in context. Without a thorough understanding of a body of law, however, this is usually an ineffective means of research. The process of scanning the subdivisions for the relevant key numbers may be very time-consuming and the chances of choosing the appropriate key number limited. Moreover, a researcher unfamiliar with the classification system may not even choose the correct topic. Many contractual issues are found, for example, under "Sales" or "Vendor and Purchaser" rather than under the topic "Contracts." A more prudent use of topic outlines is to refer to them *after* using the Descriptive–Word Index to find the correct topic, if a precise key number in the index is not located.

6. SUMMARY

The comprehensive scope of West digests makes them one of the most important case-finding tools. The key number system spans all federal and state jurisdictions, and *every* point of law treated in a published case fits somewhere and somehow into the classification scheme.

There are, however, several dangers and disadvantages inherent in the use of digests, and these should be recognized by the researcher. Instead of narrative text or explanatory comments, digests frequently consist only of long, undifferentiated series of abstracts which the researcher must plow through and attempt to synthesize. Because digests contain summaries of the points of law in court decisions, there may be the temptation to treat those summaries as primary source material. As noted before, however, a case should *never* be cited merely on the basis of a digest abstract. The point digested may be dictum, or the opinion may clarify it in ways not shown in the headnote. The decision itself must be read and evaluated, and for that reason every digest abstract includes a case citation.

The universal nature of the key number system allows it to be used in all jurisdictions, but does so sometimes at the expense of recognizing significant differences between states in approaches to jurisprudential

Illustration K

Part of a topical outline in the *Ninth Decennial Digest, Part 2*

4 9th D Pt 2—9 **AUTOMOBILES**

V. INJURIES FROM OPERATION, OR USE OF HIGHWAY.—Cont'd

(B) ACTIONS.—Cont'd

⇐246. Instructions.—Cont'd
(19). Lookout, signals, and warnings.
(20). Speed and control.
(21). Acts in emergencies.
(22). Proximate cause of injury.
(23). Contributory negligence.
(24). —— Reliance on care of person causing injury.
(25). —— Vehicles meeting or crossing.
(26). —— Vehicles following, overtaking, or passing.
(27). —— Vehicles at rest or unattended.
(28). —— Collision with bicycle or motorcycle.
(29). —— Owners, riders, or drivers of animals.
(30). —— Persons on foot in general.
(31). —— Persons crossing or walking along highway.
(32). —— Persons moving to or from street cars.
(33). —— Persons standing or sitting in highway or street.
(34). —— Persons under disability in general.
(35). —— Children.
(36). —— Passenger, guest or occupant.
(37). —— Acts in emergencies.
(38). —— Injury avoidable notwithstanding contributory negligence.
(39). Applicability to pleadings and evidence.
(40). —— Violation of statute or ordinance in general.
(41). —— Equipment and lights on vehicles.
(42). —— Identity, status and competency of operator.
(43). —— Signals and warnings.
(44). —— Defects in vehicles.
(45). —— Willful, wanton, or reckless acts or conduct.
(46). —— Vehicles stopping, backing, or turning.
(47). —— Vehicles meeting or crossing.
(48). —— Vehicles following, overtaking, or passing.
(49). —— Persons on foot in general.
(50). —— Persons crossing or walking along highway or street.
(51). —— Children.
(52). —— Persons moving to or from street cars.
(53). —— Persons standing or sitting in highway or street.
(54). —— Passenger, guest or occupant.
(55). —— Vehicles at rest or unattended.
(56). —— Speed and control.
(57). —— Proximate cause of injury.
(58). —— Contributory negligence.
(59). —— Injuring or frightening animals.
(60). Presumptions and burden of proof.
247. Verdict and findings.
248. Judgment and review.
249. Damages.
250. Lien on vehicle for injuries.
251. Costs.

(C) ACCIDENT INDEMNITY FUNDS.

⇐251.1. Uninsured or unknown motorists indemnity funds in general.
251.2. Statutory provisions.
251.3. Persons protected.
251.4. Limitation of liability.
251.5. Proceedings for compensation.
251.6. —— Notice.
251.7. —— Arbitration.
251.8. —— Evidence.

(D) EFFECT OF NO FAULT STATUTES.

⇐251.11. Abolition of tort liability in general.
251.12. —— Constitutional and statutory provisions.
251.13. —— Vehicles, persons, occurrences within restrictions.
251.14. —— "Threshold" requirement in general.
251.15. —— Nature of injury; serious or permanent injury.
251.16. —— Expenses included in threshold computation.
251.17. —— Elements of recovery; economic or non-economic loss.
251.18. —— Procedure peculiar to no fault cases; jurisdiction.
251.19. —— Evidence and fact questions.

VI. INJURIES FROM DEFECTS OR OBSTRUCTIONS IN HIGHWAYS AND OTHER PUBLIC PLACES.

(A) NATURE AND GROUNDS OF LIABILITY.

⇐252. In general.
253. Requirements of statutes and ordinances.
254. Places to which liability extends.
255. Cause of or responsibility for defects, obstructions, or dangerous conditions.
256. Care required as to condition of way in general.
257. Sufficiency and safety of way in general.
258. Nature of defects.
259. Defective plan of construction.
260. Oil or tar on highway.
261. Embankments, excavations, and openings.
262. Water, snow, or ice.
263. Obstructions.
264. —— In general.
265. —— Poles and wires.
266. Failure to prevent or remove defects or obstructions.
267. Smoke or steam obstructing view.
268. Falling objects.
269. Property adjacent to highway.
270. Bridges.
271. Culverts.
272. Notice of defects or obstructions.
273. —— In general.
274. —— Hidden or latent defects.
275. —— To public officers, agents, or private citizens.
276. —— Constructive notice.
277. Precautions against injuries.

issues. Digest classifications are choices made at the West Publishing Company, not in the courts, and may be misleading or have an unwarranted impact on subsequent interpretation of a holding.[10] The

10. "'If they do a headnote wrong,' says Robert Hursh of Lawyers Co-op, 'it's as though a case has been overruled. Any-

West system of topics and key numbers, however, is not the only way to classify legal situations, and other digesting and indexing systems exist that divide legal subjects in very different ways. An unsuccessful search in the digests does not preclude more favorable results in other systems.[11] Often a textual discussion of an area of law, such as in a legal encyclopedia or a law review article, offers a clearer and more selective introduction to relevant case law.

Several other case finding methods will be described in this chapter, but the West key number digest remains an ingenious and essential part of the research apparatus. While a digest may not always be the best place to *begin* a search for relevant decisions, it is often a very effective tool for enlarging a search from the topics and key numbers of a known relevant decision.

C. OTHER DIGESTS

Because the West Publishing Company publishes digests spanning the entire field of American state and federal jurisprudence, its key number classification system is more widely used and better known than any other digesting system. West is not the only publisher of digests, however, and key numbers are not the only means of classification. West is the only publisher of *comprehensive* digests. Other digests are available for specific jurisdictions and specialized areas of research. These digests may prove as useful as West's in particular research situations and may lead to different cases than would be found using the key number system.

1. *UNITED STATES SUPREME COURT DIGEST, LAWYERS' EDITION*

In Chapter 2 we discussed the two commercial reporters for the opinions of the Supreme Court of the United States, West's *Supreme Court Reporter* and Lawyers Co-operative Publishing Co.'s *United States Supreme Court Reports, Lawyers' Edition.* For both editions the publishers' editorial staffs prepare headnotes to accompany the opinions. Like the headnotes in the *Supreme Court Reporter,* each headnote in *Lawyers' Edition* is assigned to a legal topic and a numbered subdivi-

thing they omit is not the law.' " M. Mayer, *The Lawyers* 431 (Harper & Row, 1967).

11. The holding in a recent New York case was based on an appellate court precedent that neither party had cited. To determine the statute of limitations for bail jumping, the court had to determine whether bail jumping was a "continuous offense." The appellate court had clearly made such a determination in another context, not involving the statute of limitations. The court noted that the controlling case was

so difficult to find because the editors at West Publishing Co. indexed it solely as a "habitual offender case" (Criminal Law, West's New York Digest 3d, vol 13, key No. 1202[7]). Its import as a dispositive limitations case for the crime of bail jumping was completely overlooked. The question arises: how can a case which is clearly controlling on a particular issue properly serve as precedent when it is virtually unknown and undiscoverable? This dilemma evokes the age-old query—is there a sound if a tree falls in the forest but nobody hears it?

People v. Barnes, 130 Misc.2d 1058, 1063, 499 N.Y.S.2d 343, 346 (1986).

sion of that topic. The Lawyers Co-op classification scheme, like West's, divides the legal issues covered by the decisions of the Supreme Court into some 400 topics and numerous numbered sections of those topics. The two publishers' lists of topics are not the same, however, nor are the subject arrangements of the sections within each topic identical. The two systems may assign the same point of law to two different topics.[12]

The headnotes in *Lawyers' Edition* are compiled and published in a set of volumes entitled *United States Supreme Court Digest, Lawyers' Edition.* The digest is cumulative from the Court's earliest decisions. It is organized like the West digest, in that each topic begins with an outline of its contents and consists of the text of headnotes arranged by section number. Each headnote's topic and section number are indicated in the reporter, so a researcher reading a *Lawyers' Edition* decision can go straight from the opinion to the relevant headnote and then to the digest for other cases on the same topic. In addition to case headnotes, digest entries include references to other Lawyers Co-op research aids such as annotations, in *Lawyers' Edition* itself and in *ALR,* and the publisher's legal encyclopedia, *American Jurisprudence 2d.*

Some claim that the *Lawyers' Edition* digest, designed specifically for Supreme Court decisions, is better adapted to the issues in those decisions than the West system, which has to be general enough to cover *all* jurisdictions. Because the *Lawyers' Edition* classifications are limited to one court, however, they cannot be used to find relevant cases from lower federal courts and from state jurisdictions. Even lawyers arguing before the Supreme Court cannot ignore precedent from lower courts.

The *Lawyers' Edition* digest can be accessed through a Word Index and by topical analysis, as well as from the cases' headnotes, the same three basic approaches applicable to West digests. The two-volume Word Index functions in a manner similar to West's Descriptive–Word Indexes, providing references to topics and sections numbers. A four-volume Table of Cases contains entries under both plaintiffs' and defendants' names in one alphabetical listing, as well as some "popular name" listings. Plaintiff entries include all three reporter citations and the digest classifications assigned to the headnotes, but those under defendants are mere cross-references to plaintiff listings and do not even contain citations. The set also includes several volumes containing the text of federal court rules and rules of evidence.[13]

12. Compare the editorial treatments in Illustrations B–2 and C in Chapter 2, on pages 30 and 32. The second headnote in *L.Ed.2d* and the first headnote in *S.Ct.* cover the same issue, whether sleeping in tents for the purpose of expressing the plight of the homeless falls within the National Park Service definition of "camping." Yet Lawyers Co-op editors have assigned the headnote to the topic "Parks, Squares, and Commons," while West editors assigned it to the topic "United States."

13. *Lawyers' Edition* also has a *Desk Book,* a handy volume with several useful features such as an "Index to Cases and Annotations" and a "Table of Federal

Each volume of the digest is updated by an annual pocket part. *Lawyers' Edition* advance sheets contain several tools for finding more recent cases, including a Table of Cases and a subject index containing short summaries of holdings. A Table of Classifications lists any topics and key numbers to which headnotes have been assigned. It indicates the beginning page numbers of relevant cases, but does not include abstracts or headnotes. These finding aids cumulate for each volume of *L.Ed.2d,* but not for the entire term. Since the opinions of one term often span five volumes, it may be necessary to examine up to five separate pamphlets to find a case or topic.

2. STATE DIGESTS

Although West publishes digests for 47 states, digests from other publishers are available in a few states. Lawyers in states where competing digests are published usually develop a preference for one or the other, but they should be aware of both systems. No single approach to legal classification is perfectly designed for analysis of all legal problems. There are situations where one approach appears ill-suited but a different system may produce results.

Bancroft–Whitney, publisher of the official *California Reports* and *California Appellate Reports,* also publishes digests using headnotes from its reports. Older cases are covered in *McKinney's New California Digest,* and recent cases are digested in *California Digest of Official Reports, 3d Series.* The third series contains notes from *Cal.3d* and *Cal.App.3d,* as well as coverage of California federal court cases and references to the legal encyclopedias *American Jurisprudence 2d* and *California Jurisprudence 3d.*

Callaghan & Co. publishes digests for the cases of three midwestern states. *Callaghan's Illinois Digest 3d, Callaghan's Michigan Digest* and *Callaghan's Wisconsin Digest* cover state supreme and appellate court cases, as well as federal cases construing and applying state law. They also include references to treatises, law review articles, and annotations, as well as indexes and case tables. Illustration L shows a page from *Callaghan's Michigan Digest,* including an entry for the same point of law in *Fisher v. Lowe* digested by West in Illustrations C through E.

Nevada is one of the three states for which West does not publish a digest, although its cases are covered in the *Pacific Digest* and the American Digest System. An attorney researching Nevada law can use the *Nevada Digest,* published by the Legislative Counsel of the State of Nevada. This set of about fifty looseleaf volumes contains abstracts of

Laws, Rules, and Regulations Cited or Construed." Coverage begins with the October 1956 term, reported in 1 L.Ed.2d. The book also contains a Table of Cases with entries for "all *full* decisions (those reported with opinions)" since the October 1956 term. Its format is the same as the full Table of Cases in the digest. Because it omits the Court's first 150 years and the multitude of orders and memoranda in the larger case table, however, it is a quicker and easier place to find recent opinions.

Illustration L

A page from *Callaghan's Michigan Digest*

§ 175 AUTOMOBILES AND MOTOR VEHICLES

(MSA § 24.13106; MCL § 500.3106). Shinabarger v. Citizens Mut. Ins. Co., 90 Mich App 307, 282 NW2d 301.

1979 Under no-fault insurance act providing for recovery of personal protection benefits for injury arising out of ownership, operation, maintenance, or use of parked motor vehicle as motor vehicle, establishment of causal connection between injury and use of motor vehicle is sufficient to entitle insured to recovery even though such connection does not amount to proximate cause and even though independent cause exists as well, provided that injury is not result of independent cause in no way related to use of vehicle even though vehicle is sight of injury (MSA § 24.13106; MCL § 500.3106). Shinabarger v. Citizens Mut. Ins. Co., 90 Mich App 307, 282 NW2d 301.

1980 Since there was no specific exception of two-wheeled vehicles from definition of "vehicle" in property protection insurance benefits exclusion statute, definition of vehicle in statute clearly includes motorcycle (MSA § 24.13123; MCL § 500.3123). Degrandchamp v. Michigan Mut. Ins. Co., 99 Mich App 664, 299 NW2d 18.

1981 A person who seeks no-fault insurance benefits from his insurer must establish a causal connection between the use of a motor vehicle and the injury which is more than incidental and fortuitous and which is foreseeably identifiable with the normal use of the vehicle; an assault by an armed assailant upon the driver of a vehicle is not the type of conduct which is so foreseeably identifiable, and the fact that a vehicle is commercially rather than privately insured is inconsequential to the issue. Ciaramitaro v. State Farm Ins. Co., 107 Mich App 68, 308 NW2d 661.

1981 A plaintiff's injuries arose out of the operation and use of a motor vehicle as a motor vehicle, as a matter of law, where the plaintiff, a service station attendant engaged in fueling an automobile, was struck by another automobile (MSA § 24.13105; MCL § 500.3105). Gutierrez v. Dairyland Ins. Co., 110 Mich App 126, 312 NW2d 181.

1981 The term "physical contact" in the hit-and-run provision of the Motor Vehicle Accident Claims Act has been given a wider meaning than a strict interpretation would require because of the remedial nature of the act and because the possiblity of fraud is minimal; "physical contact" has been construed to include situations where no direct contact occurs, the most common circumstances where recovery is permitted being (1) where the hit-and-run vehicle strikes a second or intervening vehicle which in turn is propelled into plaintiff's vehicle, and (2) where an object is propelled into the plaintiff's vehicle by another vehicle which does not stop (MSA § 9.2812; MCL § 257.1112). Adams v. Zajac, 110 Mich App 522, 313 NW2d 347.

1981 A no-fault insurer is liable to pay benefits for accidental bodily injury arising out of and which is foreseeably identifiable with the normal ownership, operation, maintenance, or use of a motor vehicle where the injured person establishes a causal connection which is more than incidental, fortuitous, or "but for" between the use of a motor vehicle and the injury. Gajewski v. Auto-owners Ins. Co., 112 Mich App 59, 314 NW2d 799.

1983 No tort liability arises for damage to a tree caused by an automobile insured under the no-fault insurance act. Fisher v. Lowe, 122 Mich App 418, 333 NW2d 67.

1983 A plaintiff alleges a sufficient causal connection between his bodily injury and the use of a vehicle for him to maintain an action for such injury under the no-fault insurance provision pertaining to injuries arising from parked vehicles where the plaintiff alleges that he was injured while attempting to open the vehicle door with the intention of unloading the contents of the vehicle. Teman v. Transamerica Ins. Co. of Michigan, 123 Mich App 262, 333 NW2d 244.

1959 Excess clause which was contained in liability policy issued to lessor of truck, and which was in conflict with other insurance and pro rata clauses in policy issued to leasee of truck, was controlling, and would be given its full effect, to render lessor's insurer liable to full extent of policy limits for payment of claims against lessor and lessee arising from accident involving insured truck. Citizens Mut. Automobile Ins. Co. v. Liberty Mut. Ins. Co., 273 F2d 189.

1964 Operation of a crane for moving concrete from ready-mix concrete truck and pouring it into foundation of building being constructed, was an insured use under insurance policy insuring truck owner against liability for injury arising out of use of vehicle, including loading and unloading, so that policy covered injuries resulting when boom upon crane fell and injured an employee of general contractor. St. Paul Mercury Ins. Co. v. Huitt, 336 F2d 37.

Nevada state and federal cases and of Nevada attorney general opinions.

All of these digests are organized by alphabetically arranged topics divided into numbered sections. Cases published in *California Reports, California Appellate Reports, Illinois Appellate Court Reports,* and *Wisconsin Reports* indicate the digest classification assigned to each headnote, so researchers can go directly from a case to related material in the digest. Headnotes in *Illinois Reports, Michigan Reports, Michigan Appeals Reports,* and *Nevada Reports* do not include digest classifications.

To find state cases *by name,* one can use the Tables of Cases published as part of any of West's digests or as part of the other digest discussed above. An alternative approach is to use one of *Shepard's Case Names Citators,* which are published for over forty states. These citators are simply alphabetical listings of cases, with coverage ranging from state to state. Most cover decisions from the last thirty to sixty years. These tools are not "digests," but they perform one of the functions of a digest.

Legal research is not a uniform matter in all states. Because each state has slightly different ways of disseminating and indexing its decisions, a person practicing law or doing research in a particular state would do well to become familiar with the distinct characteristics of its publications.[14]

3. SPECIALIZED DIGESTS

Any series of case reports needs some means of providing subject access to the decisions it contains, or it will be of very little use to researchers. Access to cases in the National Reporter System is provided through West's American Digest System and its jurisdictional and regional digests. Other publishers of judicial opinions use a variety of methods to provide access, but digest systems are widely used. The main advantage a classified digest has over a simply alphabetical index is its rigorous analytical framework. In theory all cases on a particular issue will receive the same classification, even if the descriptive terms used in the opinions differ widely.

Almost all of the specialized looseleaf and topical reporters mentioned in Chapter 2 provide subject access to their cases through digests of some sort. Some digests appear only in each volume of opinions as a guide to its contents, but employ a consistent classification framework so that one can find relevant cases by looking under the same classifica-

14. Guides to legal research in individual states are listed in Appendix A, at the end of this volume. Other tools digesting cases from particular states include the *Florida Digestive Index* and *Georgia Digestive Index,* both published by the Harrison Company. The latter set is in two units, separately covering decisions of the Georgia Supreme Court and Court of Appeals. Lawyers Co-op publishes *Florida Supplement 2d Digest* to accompany its reporter of Florida trial court and administrative decisions. Butterworth's *Dunnell Minnesota Digest* includes textual summaries of Minnesota law, making it more of a legal encyclopedia than a digest.

tion number in every volume. Other digests are published separately, to cover cases appearing in five or ten years' worth of reporter volumes, and some are published as cumulative sets for all reported cases.

These topical digests are of three basic types. Some are organized on an alphabetical basis similar to West's system, but with topics designed for a specialized area of law. Digests for *American Maritime Cases, Public Utilities Reports,* or the *United States Patents Quarterly* work in this way.

Instead of alphabetized digest topics, a second group of specialized reporters have one classified numerical framework for the entire body of legal doctrine. Headnotes are assigned to classified subdivisions within topics, but those topics are arranged by subject rather than alphabetically. The Bureau of National Affairs uses this approach in its digests covering cases in the *Environment Reporter* and *Labor Relations Reference Manual.* Labor law topics such as "Picketing," "Boycotts," and "Other Methods of Publicizing Disputes," for example, are grouped within the division "Economic Weapons of Labor."

The third group of specialized reporters are those which focus on specific laws or court rules and use digest arrangements based on those subject materials. Digest paragraphs are grouped by code or rule section, each of which is then divided into numbered subject subsections. The major tax looseleafs, CCH's *Standard Federal Tax Reports* and Prentice Hall's *Federal Taxes,* consist largely of digest paragraphs from cases organized in this manner. To accompany the *UCC Reporting Service,* Callaghan & Co. publishes the *Uniform Commercial Code Case Digest,* organized by U.C.C. section. Callaghan also publishes digests arranged by rule for federal procedural and evidence rules. The *Federal Rules Digest, 3d Ed.* provides access to the *Federal Rules Service,* and the *Federal Rules of Evidence Digest* accompanies the *Federal Rules of Evidence Service.*

Finally, digests are published to accompany *American Law Reports,* the annotated reporters commonly known as *ALR.* These digests contain both headnote paragraphs from the cases printed in *ALR* and citations of relevant annotations. The purpose and scope of *ALR,* and the use of its digests, will be discussed in the next section.

D. ANNOTATIONS

As mentioned in Chapter 2, at the same time that West's National Reporter System was being developed in the late 19th century, other publishers were attempting a different approach to commercial case reporting. These publishers selected "leading cases" for full-text publication, and provided commentaries, or *annotations,* describing other cases with similar facts or procedures. Competition between the two approaches continued for several years, with West's system of comprehensive reporting eventually winning the day.[15]

Although selective publication of cases was unsuccessful, the accompanying annotations proved to be useful research tools. Originally the cases were the primary feature of the reporters and the annotations a secondary research benefit, but with time this focus changed. Annotated reporting has survived as a means of providing extensive commentaries on specific points of law, by summarizing and analyzing cases from all jurisdictions. The Lawyers Co-operative Publishing Company and Bancroft-Whitney, publishers of several earlier series of annotated reporters, in 1919 began publication of *American Law Reports*. *ALR* has been published in several successive series, including two series currently being issued: *ALR4th* for general and state legal issues, and *ALR Federal* for issues of federal law. The earlier series of *ALR* are still used, and will also be discussed in this section. Lawyers Co-op is also the publisher of *United States Supreme Court Reports, Lawyers' Edition,* which includes editorial annotations in addition to Supreme Court opinions.

An *ALR* volume consists of about twenty cases, each followed by an exhaustive analysis of decisions from throughout the country on issues closely related to one addressed in the printed case. Initially the cases printed in *ALR* were important in their own right and often of national significance, but today they are chosen for their convenience as springboards for the extensive accompanying annotations. The cases are often unread by the researcher. The annotations, on the other hand, are valuable research aids and case-finding tools. Each annotation is a thoroughly researched survey of a particular legal issue, tracing its development and its judicial treatment in all jurisdictions. The holdings of all published cases on the particular issue are abstracted, and the discussion organized so that the cases are arranged to form a cohesive picture of the law. While it is rarely possible to reconcile all conflicting decisions, an annotation presents the decisions in a manner that permits a lawyer to compare their fact situations with his or her own. The annotations range in length, depending on the complexity of the issues covered and the frequency with which they arise in published cases, from short articles of a few pages to extensive treatments of several hundred pages. Each annotation is updated annually by the publisher by references to new decisions on the topic, so that even older annotations continue to be current and useful resources.

Digests and annotations are the preeminent research tools designed specifically for finding cases. A digest system is a comprehensive

15. Early annotated reporters are listed in Chapter 2, at page 18 fn. 9. One of the rare occasions on which early law publishers articulated their opposing viewpoints was a symposium published in 1889. In response to a request to comment on the most effective system of publishing cases, John B. West of the West Publishing Company presented the argument for comprehensive publication, and James Briggs of Lawyers Co-op advocated selective publication. "A Symposium of Law Publishers," 23 *Am.L.Rev.* 396 (1889).

analytical framework in which every point of law has its theoretical place. The classification and arrangement of case abstracts in a digest are determined by a pre-existing scheme. Annotations, on the other hand, do not form a comprehensive body of material, since each is written on a specific legal issue. Because each annotation is individually written, its organization is determined by the nature of the cases published on that specific issue. For some legal problems there are no relevant annotations to be found. An annotation directly on point, however, can be enormously helpful. Being able to find an annotation on an issue with which one is confronted is an immense time-saver, since it means someone else has already read and synthesized the relevant case law.

1. COMPONENTS OF THE ANNOTATED REPORTING SYSTEM

The Lawyers Co-op system of annotated reports includes *United States Supreme Court Reports, Lawyers' Edition* and several series of *ALR*. *Lawyers' Edition* is one of the main sources of United States Supreme Court decisions, but each volume also includes about four annotations on specific legal issues addressed in some of that volume's opinions. *ALR* volumes, on the other hand, consist primarily of annotations but also contain the texts of several opinions.

American Law Reports has begun new series several times since its inception in 1919. The publisher made changes in *ALR*'s format and provided improved methods of updating annotations in 1948 and again in 1965, and started new series to implement and note the changes. In 1969, four years after the third series began, the publisher began a separate series focusing on issues arising in the federal courts. (Until 1980 the start of each new *ALR* series was more than a matter of marketing or numbering convenience; the hundredth volume of the third series, however, was followed by 1 *ALR4th* without any significant changes or improvements.) The series and their dates of publication are:

ALR (First Series)	1919 to 1948	175 volumes
ALR2d (Second Series)	1948 to 1965	100 volumes
ALR3d (Third Series)	1965 to 1980	100 volumes
ALR4th (Fourth Series)	1980 to date	Current
ALR Federal	1969 to date	Current

Annotations in the modern series (*ALR3d, ALR4th,* and *ALR Federal*) have a relatively uniform format, are updated in the same manner, and share common systems of access through indexes and digests. Annotations in *ALR2d* are similar to more recent annotations, but lack some of their features and have a different updating method. Annotations in the first series of *ALR* are generally less extensive in coverage and less sophisticated in their research aids. Many of the older annotations have not been replaced, however, so some familiarity with them is necessary.

2. THE STRUCTURE OF AN ANNOTATED REPORT

An annotated report is a hybrid creature, containing elements of a case report, a law review article, and an encyclopedia treatment. This section describes the component parts of an *ALR* annotation, using one from *ALR3d* as an example. The annotation, at 95 A.L.R.3d 508, deals with an issue which might have arisen in the *Fisher v. Lowe* case, "Measure of Damages for Injury to or Destruction of Shade or Ornamental Tree or Shrub."

a. *The Case Report*

Each annotation is preceded by the report of a selected court decision, the subject of which is used as the theme of the annotation which follows the decision. Preceding the annotation at 95 A.L.R.3d 508 is *Williams v. Hanover Insurance Co. of New York,* a 1977 decision of the Court of Appeal of Louisiana. This printing of the case, at 95 A.L.R.3d 504, contains the same text as that published in the *Southern Reporter,* but with different introductory editorial matter. Instead of West headnotes, the opinion has a summary and headnotes prepared by Lawyers Co-op editors. Even points of law not covered by the annotation have headnotes, which are assigned topics and section numbers from a digesting scheme developed for *ALR.* Illustration M–1 shows the page containing the headnotes and the beginning of the court's opinion.

b. *Cross-References and Finding Aids*

The opinion is followed by an annotation on a specific point of law addressed in the case. On the annotation's title page there is a box containing cross-references to other publications in the Total Client-Service Library, Lawyers Co-op's name for the research system which links its publications. These cross-references appear only in *ALR3d, ALR4th,* and *ALR Federal,* and enable a researcher who has found a relevant annotation to go directly to applicable sections of encyclopedias, formbooks, digests, and other research tools. The Total Client-Service Library References are shown at the bottom of Illustration M–2.

A series of finding aids preceding the text of almost every annotation helps the reader identify and locate its most relevant sections for the problems being researched.[16] These finding aids are shown in Illustrations M–2 and M–3. They include the annotation's outline, or table of contents (the beginning of which appears in Illustration M–2), a detailed subject index (the last part of which is at the top of Illustration M–3) and a Table of Jurisdictions Represented in the cases discussed in the annotation (in the bottom half of Illustration M–3). Both the index and the table of jurisdictions give specific references to the sections and subsections in which relevant material for the researcher's problem can

16. These aids, and the Total Client-Service Library box, are omitted from very brief annotations. Short annotations on new areas of law discuss only a handful of cases and may not even be divided into sections. Some annotations on matters of first impression discuss only the one case *ALR* prints in full.

Illustration M–1

Headnotes and the beginning of an opinion in *ALR3d*

95 ALR3d WILLIAMS v HANOVER INS. CO.
(La App) 351 So 2d 858, 95 ALR3d 504

HEADNOTES

Classified to ALR Digests

Accord and Satisfaction § 2 — by part payment

1. When one party delivers a draft or check for less than the amount of a disputed claim with a notation thereon that acceptance constitutes full payment and it is subsequently endorsed by the payee, this acceptance constitutes an accord and satisfaction and bars recovery for the unpaid portion of the claim. Where there is no evidence or indication that a check is given as payment in full of a disputed claim and there is no mutual understanding that if the check is accepted the claim will be deemed to have been paid in full, then accord and satisfaction does not result and the creditor is not estopped from claiming the balance.

Interest § 28 — when recoverable — as damages — for injury to property

2. Property owners were not entitled to recover legal interest on the amount of a partial payment draft by an insurance company for damages to shrubbery caused by the automobile of defendant's insured where the partial payment draft was given to the property owners prior to their suit for damages to an oak tree caused by the same collision, where the property owners could have collected the draft without prejudicing their claim for other damages, and where the draft would have been paid promptly upon presentation.

Damages § 266 — measure of compensation — injury to real property — trees

3. Property owners were entitled to recover from defendant insurance company for the loss of the esthetic value of a tree due to its injury resulting from a collision involving the defendant's insured where for some seven to eight years following the accident the esthetic value of the tree had been and would be affected. Since the extensive damage done to the ornamental tree required seven or eight years to heal, an award of $350, or an average of from $45 to $50 per year, was insufficient and would be increased to $700.

[Annotated]

APPEARANCES OF COUNSEL

Naff, Kennedy, Goodman, Donovan & Parnell by **Frank S. Kennedy**, Shreveport, for plaintiffs-appellants.

Blanchard, Walker, O'Quin & Roberts by **Jerald L. Perlman**, Shreveport, for defendants-appellees.

Before **Price, Marvin** and **Jones,** JJ.

OPINION OF THE COURT

Jones, Judge.

Plaintiffs appeal seeking to increase a judgment for damages to a live oak tree caused when the automobile of defendant's insured collided with the tree some five years before trial. The trial judge did not award legal interest on $130, which was allowed as damages to shrubbery, because defendant delivered to plaintiffs a partial payment draft for this amount prior to suit. Plaintiffs seek legal interest on the partial payment. We increase the award for damages and otherwise affirm.

THE LEGAL INTEREST CLAIM

Shortly after the accident, plaintiffs' expert witness estimated the cost

505

be found. The most relevant index entry for *Fisher v. Lowe* research, on a page not included in the illustrations, might be: "Automobile

Illustration M-2

The first page of an *ALR3d* annotation

ANNOTATION

MEASURE OF DAMAGES FOR INJURY TO OR DESTRUCTION OF SHADE OR ORNAMENTAL TREE OR SHRUB

by

Kristine Cordier Karnezis, J.D.

TOTAL CLIENT-SERVICE LIBRARY® REFERENCES

1 Am Jur 2d, Adjoining Landowners § 24; 22 Am Jur 2d, Damages § 143

8 Am Jur Pl & Pr Forms (Rev Ed), Damages, Forms 71–76

7 Am Jur Legal Forms 2d, Damages § 83:4

3 Am Jur Proof of Facts 491, Damages, Proof No. 1, 5

US L Ed Digest, Damages § 116

ALR Digests, Damages § 266

L Ed Index to Annos, Damages; Eminent Domain; Trees

ALR Quick Index, Eminent Domain; Trees and Shrubbery; Value n Valuation

Federal Quick Index, Damages; Eminent Domain; Trees

Consult POCKET PART in this volume for later cases

508

colliding into tree, loss of aesthetic value caused by, § 6[a]." The jurisdictional table is an alphabetical list of states, indicating all sections of the annotation citing cases from its courts. A researcher

Illustration M-3

Index, table of jurisdictions, and beginning of text in an *ALR* annotation

§ 1[a] DAMAGES—TREES AND SHRUBS 95 ALR3d
95 ALR3d 508

TABLE OF JURISDICTIONS REPRESENTED

Consult POCKET PART in this volume for later cases

US: §§ 3[a, e], 4[a], 5[a]
Ala: §§ 3[a, b, f, h]
Ark: §§ 3[a–e, h]
Cal: §§ 3[a, g], 4[a]
Colo: §§ 3[a, c], 4[c]
Conn: §§ 3[a, b, d], 4[b, c], 5[a]
Del: §§ 3[a, f], 4[a]
Fla: §§ 3[a, b, h], 4[a–c], 5[a], 6[a]
Ga: §§ 3[a, d, g]
Idaho: §§ 3[a], 4[b], 5[a]
Ill: §§ 3[a], 4[a, b], 5[a, c]
Ind: §§ 3[a, f]
Iowa: §§ 3[a, d, f], 4[b], 5[a]
Kan: §§ 3[a, c–e], 4[b], 5[a, b]
Ky: §§ 3[a, g]
La: §§ 3[a, c, d], 4[a–c], 5[b], 6[a, b]
Me: §§ 3[a–d], 5[a, b]
Md: §§ 3[a, c, f, g], 4[a], 5[a]
Mass: §§ 3[a, c, g], 5[c]
Mich: §§ 3[a–c, g], 4[c]
Minn: §§ 3[a], 4[a, c], 5[a], 6[a]
Miss: §§ 3[a]
Mo: §§ 3[a, c, d, g, h], 5[c]
Neb: §§ 5[b]
NH: §§ 3[a, c], 4[a], 5[a, b]
NJ: §§ 4[a]
NY: §§ 3[a, c, e, f, g, h], 4[a], 5[a, c]
ND: §§ 3[a, c]
Ohio: §§ 3[a, c, f], 4[a]
Okla: §§ 3[a, e]
Or: §§ 3[a, f], 4[a]
Pa: §§ 3[a, c, f, g, h]
SC: §§ 3[a, b, f, h]
SD: §§ 3[a], 5[a, b]
Tenn: §§ 3[a, d, f, h]
Tex: §§ 3[a, b, e-h], 4[a, c], 5[a-c]
Utah: §§ 3[a, h], 4[a, c]
Vt: §§ 3[a, c, h]
Va: §§ 3[a]
Wash: §§ 3[a, f], 4[a, b]
Wis: §§ 3[a, f], 5[a, b], 6[a]

§ 1. Introduction

[a] Scope

This annotation[1] collects and analyzes the cases which have determined

1. It supersedes §§ 15–17 of the annotation in 69 ALR2d 1335. And as to the matters covered herein, it is no longer necessary to consult an earlier annotation at 161 ALR 549.

510

interested only in the material of a specific jurisdiction can thus immediately locate all relevant references. Instead of a Table of

Jurisdictions Represented, *ALR Federal* annotations have a Table of Courts and Circuits, which lists sections citing cases from the Supreme Court and from each of the thirteen circuits (including District Court decisions), as well as occasional other courts.

c. *Body of the Annotation*

The text of the annotation shown begins at the very bottom of Illustration M–3 and continues on Illustration M–4. The first two sections of most recent *ALR* annotations follow the same format. Section 1[a] describes the scope of the annotation, setting out in detail what is and is not covered. Section 1[b], "Related matters," lists other *ALR* annotations on similar or related topics, and sometimes includes references to treatises and law review articles. Section 2, "Summary and comment," begins with a general overview of the law of the area, summarizing the annotation's contents in an encyclopedic manner. The overview is usually followed by a subsection called "Practice Pointers," which describes practical and procedural aspects of litigation involving the annotation topic.

The remaining sections of the annotation are organized according to the facts and holdings of the cases discussed. In the annotation illustrated, for example, Section 6 is "Loss of aesthetic value or of comfort and convenience." This is divided into subsections a, "Held to be proper measure," and b, "Held not to be proper measure." Within each subsection the facts and holdings of the relevant cases are summarized. If the same conclusion has been reached by numerous courts, as is often the case, the annotation states the general principle and lists the case citations arranged by jurisdiction. Those cases which confront new issues or differ from the majority rule are then discussed in full.

ALR annotations are distinguished from other treatments of particular legal issues, such as law review articles, in that they continue to be updated and kept current after their initial publication. Even though the illustrative annotation was published in 1979, it can provide access to cases decided in the 1980's. For annotations in its different series, *ALR* uses three distinct methods of updating and supplementation. These methods will be discussed next.

3. UPDATING ANNOTATIONS

Just like other legal publications, as soon as an annotation is written and published it is potentially out of date. New cases are decided, old cases are overruled, and the law summarized in the text may change. Because judicial opinions are not changed or supplemented once they are issued, the researcher must use updating tools such as *Shepard's Citations* to determine their current status. Once an *ALR* annotation is published, on the other hand, Lawyers Co–op editors continue to search for relevant cases to update it. The supplementation is an integral part of an annotation, and gives all *ALR* volumes continuing value as current case-finding tools.

Illustration M-4

Continuation of text in *ALR* annotation

95 ALR3d DAMAGES—TREES AND SHRUBS § 2
95 ALR3d 508

the measure of compensations damages to be used when growing ornamental or shade trees[2] are injured or destroyed.[3] The terms "destruction" and "injury" include all wrongful cutting and removing, as well as destruction and injury due to such things as blows, fire, gases, chemicals, and other noxious agents.

Since the annotation does not purport to represent the statutory law of any jurisdiction except insofar as it is reflected in the reported cases within the scope of the annotation, the reader is reminded to consult the latest relevant enactments.[4]

[b] Related matters

Liability for damages to adjacent land or building caused by dredging. 62 ALR3d 526.

Liability for injury caused by spraying or dusting of crops. 37 ALR3d 833.

Rights and liabilities of adjoining landowners as to trees, shrubbery, or similar plants growing on boundary line. 26 ALR3d 1372.

Construction of insurance coverage as to loss of or injury to trees, lawns, and shrubbery. 14 ALR3d 1056.

Measure of damages for wrongful removal of earth, sand, or gravel from land. 1 ALR3d 801.

Measure of damages for destruction of or injury to trees and shrubbery. 69 ALR2d 1335.

Venue of action for the cutting, destruction, or damage of standing timber or trees. 65 ALR2d 1268.

Liability of public utility to abutting owner for destruction or injury of trees in or near highway or street. 64 ALR2d 866.

Liability for injury or damage by tree or limb overhanging street or highway. 54 ALR2d 1195.

Landowner's or occupant's liability in damages for escape, without negligence, of harmful gases or fumes from premises. 54 ALR2d 764.

Measure and elements of damages for pollution of a stream. 49 ALR2d 253.

Expense incurred by injured party in remedying temporary nuisance or in preventing injury as element of damages recoverable. 41 ALR2d 1064.

Interest on damages for period before judgment for injury, or detention, loss, or destruction of, property. 36 ALR2d 337.

Measure of damages for conversion or loss of, or damage to, personal property having no market value. 12 ALR2d 902.

§ 2. Summary and comment

Where damages have been sought for the destruction of or injury to shade or ornamental trees or shrubs,

2. As to the measure of damages for injury to or destruction of ornamental or shade trees as nursery stock, see the annotation at 69 ALR2d 1335.

3. An injurious effect, rather than a beneficial one (perhaps entitling the landowner to nominal damages, only), is assumed to have taken place.

Insofar as eminent domain proceedings involve compensation for a taking prior to an actual physical injury to or destruction of property, such cases are not within the scope of the annotation. However, a case involving injury to or destruction of trees or shrubbery which the owner did not receive prior compensation for is within its scope.

4. Although the question of punitive damages is not covered herein, counsel for a party seeking damages for injury to or destruction of shade or ornamental trees or shrubbery should check the relevant statutes to see if double or treble damages may be sought for willful or malicious injury to or destruction of such trees.

511

It has been seventy years since *ALR* began publication, and the publishers have twice introduced more convenient and effective ways to update annotations. For *ALR* annotations written since 1965, supplementation is achieved through *pocket parts.* Information on later cases is provided in a supplement inserted in the back of each volume. Because annotations written before 1965 are frequently consulted, however, some familiarity with the two formats previously employed is necessary.

Particularly when using older *ALR* volumes, it is important to check the supplementation *before* reading an annotation. The annotation may well have been *superseded* by a more recent treatment of the same subject, incorporating later developments. If there is a superseding annotation, the supplementation provides a reference to it.[17]

a. The Modern Era: Pocket Parts

Every *ALR* volume since the beginning of *ALR3d* in 1965 is published with a pocket in the inside back cover. Each year a new pocket part supplement is inserted in each volume, updating the annotations with references to new cases, more recent annotations, and other new research tools. New cases are assigned to the particular sections of annotations to which they relate, and their facts and holdings are briefly summarized. A researcher examining any volume of *ALR3d, ALR4th,* or *ALR Federal* thus has both the main annotation and a current annual supplement at hand at the same time. Illustration N shows a page from the pocket part for 95 *A.L.R.3d.* Under the heading "95 ALR3d 508–534," summaries of new cases on injury to or destruction of shade trees are arranged by annotation section number.

If there are new developments in the law, new annotation sections may be added in the supplement. In the pocket part for 95 *A.L.R.3d,* for example, an annotation on discriminatory prosecution has a new subsection for cases discussing prosecutorial treatment of illegal aliens. If, after several years, changes in the law make an annotation obsolete or cause its supplement to be unwieldy or confusing, a new annotation on the topic will be written. As noted above, either a particular section or an entire annotation may be *superseded* by a later annotation. If so, the older section or annotation is no longer kept current and should not even be used. At times a *supplementary* annotation is written to cover new developments not discussed in the original annotation, and both annotations should be consulted. In either case, the pocket part will provide this information. Under the listing for an annotation (or a particular section), instead of new cases there will be a reference to the newer annotation. For this reason, it is always wise to check the pocket part supplement briefly before spending much time reading the original annotation.

Beginning with 32 L.Ed.2d, published in 1973, each volume of *Lawyers' Edition* also has a pocket part providing supplementary mate-

17. Another way to determine whether an annotation has been superseded is through an "Annotation History Table," published in the *Index to Annotations* and *Index to Annotations (L.Ed. and ALR Fed.).* Use of these tables will be discussed at the end of this section.

Illustration N

Pocket part update for *ALR3d* annotations

ployee to her old position and wage upon completion of renovation, hours reduction did not have detrimental effect on her retirement, she had no other work prospects when she quit, and employee was given new position because her former position had been temporarily eliminated. Rodeen v Department of Employment Secur. (1987) 47 **Wash** App 60, 733 P2d 544.

95 ALR3d 484–503

95 ALR3d 484 § 1[b] [p. 486]

What constitutes a transaction, a contract for sale, or a sale within scope of UCC Article 2. 4 ALR4th 85.

What constitutes "goods" within scope of UCC Article 2. 4 ALR4th 912.

Applicability of UCC Article 2 to mixed contracts for sale of goods and services. 5 ALR4th 501.

Risk of loss—damage to or destruction of goods. 25 Am Jur Proof of Facts 2d 99.

Misrepresentation in sale of animal. 35 Am Jur Proof of Facts 2d 607.

VERALEX®: Cases and annotations referred to herein can be further researched through the VERALEX electronic retrieval system's two services, **Auto-Cite®** and **SHOWME®**. Use Auto-Cite to check citations for form, parallel references, prior and later history, and annotation references. Use SHOWME to display the full text of cases and annotations.

95 ALR3d 484 § 4[a] [p. 501]

Seller of feeder pigs who had been in business for over 30 years, and who by his occupation held himself out as having knowledge or skill peculiar to such goods, was "merchant" under UCC § 2-104(1). Musil v Hendrich (1981) 6 **Kan** App 2d 196, 627 P2d 367, 31 UCCRS 432.

In breach-of-warranty and strict liability action by buyer of certified bean seed against seller, in which seller filed third-party claims against both seed processor and seed supplier, court held (1) that processor's claim that mere economic loss could be recovered on express or implied warranty theory under Uniform Commercial Code (see UCC §§ 2-313(1), 2-314(1), 2-315), but not on theory of strict liability in tort, would be sustained; (2) that added expenses and lesser crop yield can be recovered on claim based on warranty theory; (3) that attaching tag labeled "certified seed" constituted express warranty; and (4) that farmers can be considered to be "merchants" for purposes of sale provisions of Article 2. Hagert v Hatton Commodities, Inc. (1984, **ND**) 350 NW2d 591, 39 UCCRS 102 (citing annotation).

95 ALR3d 484 § 5 [p. 502]

In action by farmers and farming corporation against seller of seed potatoes for breach of express and implied warranties in which defendant crossclaimed against wholesaler and grower, wholesaler's warranty disclaimer was ineffective under UCC § 2-316 where sale was on oral contract and where invoice containing disclaimer was received after sale was completed so that it was not part of bargain between parties; disclaimer was ineffective under UCC § 2-207 where Code does not imply disclaimers and where construction of that section under which buyer who accepts goods becomes bound by additional terms set by seller even if they materially alter terms agreed to by both parties, was specifically rejected by court; wholesaler's disclaimer was also ineffective where its language did not make clear that buyer was assuming risks as to quality of goods; disclaimer was inconspicuous where it was set in smallest type on entire invoice; implied warranty of merchantability was not disclaimed by course of dealing or trade usage under UCC § 1-205 where evidence did not prove either prior assent between parties or dominant pattern in industry. Hartwig Farms, Inc. v Pacific Gamble Robinson Co. (1981) 28 **Wash** App 539, 625 P2d 171, 30 UCCRS 1552.

95 ALR3d 508–534

95 ALR3d 508 § 1[b] [p. 511]

Tree or limb falls onto adjoining private property: personal injury and property damage liability. 54 ALR4th 530.

Damages for injury to real property. 42 Am Jur Proof of Facts 2d 247.

VERALEX®: Cases and annotations referred to herein can be further researched through the VERALEX electronic retrieval system's two services, **Auto-Cite®** and **SHOWME®**. Use Auto-Cite to check citations for form, parallel references, prior and later history, and annotation references. Use SHOWME to display the full text of cases and annotations.

95 ALR3d 508 § 3[a] [p. 513]

Also holding or recognizing that ordinarily measure of damages for destruction of or injury to ornamental or shade trees or shrubbery is difference in value of land just before and just after destruction or injury;

Colo—Kroulik v Knuppel (1981) 634 P2d 1027.

Fla—Clark v J.W. Conner & Sons, Inc. (1983, Fla App D2) 441 So 2d 674, review den (Fla) 449 So 2d 264 (recognizing rule).

Ga—Millholland v Stewart (1983) 166 Ga

rial for its annotations. *Lawyers' Edition* pocket parts also contain two other sections: corrections in opinions made after the volume was published, and a "Citator Service." This service consists of brief summaries of the holdings of later Supreme Court opinions "making significant references" to decisions in that volume. Each summary is preceded by a phrase such as "Followed in," "Distinguished in," or "Cited in," similar in function to the one-letter signals used by Shepard's.

A researcher using an annotation can even find citations to cases decided since publication of the latest pocket part supplement, by calling a toll-free number printed on the cover of each pocket part. This "Latest Case Service" is available without charge for all annotations in *ALR2d, ALR3d, ALR4th, ALR Federal,* and *Lawyers' Edition 2d.*

b. Later Case Service *Volumes*

Supplementation for *ALR2d* is very similar to that for the later series of *ALR,* with one major difference. *ALR2d* volumes have no pocket parts. Instead the updating information appears in a separate set of *Later Case Service* volumes. Each of these blue volumes supplements from one to six *ALR2d* volumes.[18] Just as in the pocket parts for *ALR3d, ALR4th,* and *ALR Federal,* later material is assigned to specific subdivisions of each annotation and the holdings of new cases are summarized. Each *Later Case Service* volume is supplemented by an annual pocket part, and replacement volumes are issued occasionally when the pocket parts get too cumbersome to be used effectively.

The *Later Case Service* method of supplementation is also used for the first thirty-one volumes of *Lawyers' Edition, Second Series.* Annotations in these volumes are updated by two *Later Case Service and Citator Service* volumes, which are in turn updated by pocket parts. The "Citator Service" feature is the same as that described in the pocket parts for volumes of *Lawyers' Edition* since 32 L.Ed.2d.

Later Case Service volumes are an effective means of supplementing annotations, but require the researcher to consult two separate volumes and to integrate three separate texts: the original annotation, the update in the *Later Case Service* volume, and the update's update in the pocket part. For these reasons the supplementation method was changed for *ALR3d* to the current system of pocket parts in each annotations volume. Any time an *ALR2d* annotation is used, however, remember that its companion *Later Case Service* volume should also be consulted.

18. To date the only *Later Case Service* volume supplementing just one *ALR2d* volume is that for 78 *A.L.R.2d,* which contains several products liability annotations. The annotations "Liability of manufacturer or seller for injury caused by automobile or other vehicle, aircraft, boat, or their parts, supplies, or equipment" and "Liability of manufacturer or seller for injury caused by industrial, business, or farm machinery, tools, equipment, or materials" are each supplemented by over 150 pages of later cases, even though individual sections have been superseded by twelve later annotations.

c. ALR Blue Book of Supplemental Decisions

For its first series of 175 volumes, *ALR* employs a truly primitive method of providing updates to its annotations. The *ALR Blue Book of Supplemental Decisions* simply lists for each annotation the citations of relevant later cases. There is no textual discussion and no indication of which section of the annotation the cases concern. Instead all case citations are in one list arranged by state, in a format similar to that used in *Shepard's Citations.* Six successive permanent volumes of the *Blue Book* have been issued, each listing cases from a different time period. The first covers the period 1919 to 1946, for example, and the sixth 1976 to 1983. An annual paperback pamphlet lists supplemental decisions since the most recent permanent volume. To search comprehensively for all later cases, one must examine *seven* different lists.

The latest *Blue Book* pamphlet also includes the citations of any annotations superseding or supplementing those in volumes 1 to 175 of *ALR.* Because this information is cumulated in the most recent pamphlet, the researcher does not have to look through numerous *Blue Book* volumes to determine whether an annotation has been superseded. Checking the latest pamphlet is an essential first step in using the first series of *ALR,* since the annotations are at least forty years old and a great number of them have been superseded.

To update an annotation through the *Blue Books* requires the use of several volumes, which provide no indication of the holdings or relevance of the new decisions. Although this cumbersome method continues to be used for annotations from the first series of *ALR,* researchers are fortunate that it was abandoned with the first volume of *ALR2d.*[19]

d. *Annotation History Tables*

As noted earlier, the latest supplement to an annotation, whether in a pocket part, *Later Case Service* volume, or *Blue Book* volume, will indicate if the annotation has been superseded and is no longer being kept current. The *ALR* system also includes another way to determine the validity of annotations, an "Annotation History Table." This table allows a researcher to check rapidly for the citation of an older annotation and then go immediately to the more current annotation, instead of finding and examining the supplementary material for the obsolete annotation. This method can save considerable time when one has a reference to an older annotation but has not yet retrieved its volume.

The main Annotation History Table appears at the end of the five-volume *Index to Annotations,* the primary tool for finding annotations, and lists all annotations which have been supplemented or superseded

19. The toll-free "Latest Case Service" is *not* available for annotations in the first series of either *ALR* or *L.Ed.* There is in fact no supplementation at all for annotations in the first series of *Lawyers' Edition,* unless a separate later annotation was written on the same topic.

by annotations in *ALR2d, ALR3d, ALR4th, ALR Federal,* or either series of *Lawyers' Edition*.[20] While the table includes references to annotations in the first series of *ALR* which have been supplemented or superseded in *later* series, it unfortunately does *not* indicate if an annotation was superseded in a later first series volume. For this reason, the latest *Blue Book* supplement should be checked instead of the Annotation History Table to check the status of early annotations.

A supplementary Annotation History Table appears in the pocket part for volume five of the *Index to Annotations.* Before looking at an older *ALR* annotation, it is well worthwhile to check both tables to be certain that there is not a later annotation one should be reading instead. Illustration O shows a page from the Table of Annotations indicating superseded *ALR2d* annotations.

4. FINDING ANNOTATIONS

There are several ways to find annotations. Both an *Index to Annotations* and a series of digests are published as part of the *ALR* system. The full text of annotations can be electronically searched for key terms on LEXIS. The citation verification systems *Auto–Cite* and *Shepard's* include references to all annotations in which a particular case is cited. Finally, references to relevant annotations appear in many other publications, including treatises and statutory compilations.

a. Index to Annotations

The basic tool for subject access to annotations is *Index to Annotations,* a five-volume set published in 1986. The index consists of an alphabetical list of both factual and legal terms, each thoroughly subdivided by subject. The language used is more straightforward than many legal indexes, and there are extensive cross-references. Even if an annotation is not listed under the first place one looks, there will usually be a cross-reference to the appropriate location. Illustration P shows a page of entries under the heading "Trees and shrubbery." Under the subdivision "Damages" is a reference to the annotation shown in Illustration M. Where only part of an annotation addresses an indexed topic, the index entry provides the applicable section numbers. *Index to Annotations* is updated quarterly by pocket parts located in the *front* of each volume.

The fifth volume of *Index to Annotations* also contains a Table of Laws, Rules, and Regulations, indicating where federal and state acts are cited in annotations, and the Annotation History Table, shown in Illustration O.

Index to Annotations provides coverage of annotations in *ALR2d, ALR3d, ALR4th, ALR Federal,* and *Lawyers' Edition 2d.* The annota-

20. A shorter Annotation History Table appearing in *Index to Annotations (L.Ed. and ALR Fed.)* covers annotations in both series of *Lawyers' Edition* and in *ALR Federal.*

Illustration O

An "Annotation History Table" page from *Index to Annotations*

ANNOTATION HISTORY TABLE

§ 6 Superseded 2 ALR4th 807
§ 11 Superseded 34 ALR3d 470, 18 ALR4th 360, and 53 ALR Fed 140
§ 15 Superseded 13 ALR4th 533 and 15 ALR4th 582

75 ALR2d 717–734
Superseded 67 ALR Fed 463

75 ALR2d 778–788
Superseded 58 ALR3d 148

75 ALR2d 833–843
Superseded 97 ALR3d 528

75 ALR2d 1085–1105
Superseded 5 ALR4th 1153

76 ALR2d 9–78
§ 21.6 superseded 53 ALR3d 239

76 ALR2d 91–120
Superseded 96 ALR3d 22

76 ALR2d 805–870
Superseded 41 ALR4th 131

76 ALR2d 874–888
Superseded 10 ALR4th 246

76 ALR2d 1087–1113
§ 5 superseded 75 ALR3d 505

76 ALR2d 1301–1304
Superseded 31 ALR4th 329

77 ALR2d 504–533
Superseded 34 ALR4th 1054 and 43 ALR4th 189

77 ALR2d 841–908
§§ 15, 16 Superseded 2 ALR4th 330

77 ALR2d 917–934
Superseded 32 ALR4th 56

77 ALR2d 1233–1248
Superseded 98 ALR3d 13

77 ALR2d 1307–1314
Superseded 26 ALR4th 455

77 ALR2d 1355–1366
Superseded 18 ALR4th 542 & 22 ALR4th 863

78 ALR2d 309–312
Superseded 86 ALR3d 571

78 ALR2d 412–420
Superseded 69 ALR Fed 600

78 ALR2d 446–448
Superseded 25 ALR3d 383

78 ALR2d 460–588
§§ 25[e], 26[e], 28[f], 30[c], and 44 Superseded 3 ALR4th 489
§§ 34.5, 34.6 superseded 81 ALR3d 394
§ 35 Superseded 1 ALR4th 411
§§ 36 & 37 Superseded 97 ALR3d 627
§§ 48, 49, 60, and 61 superseded 81 ALR3d 318
§§ 50 and 51.5 Superseded 16 ALR4th 137

78 ALR2d 594–692
§ 50 Superseded 2 ALR4th 262
§§ 62–66 Superseded 7 ALR4th 852
§§ 88–90 Superseded 8 ALR4th 70
§ 61 Superseded 10 ALR4th 854
§§ 51 and 64 Superseded 13 ALR4th 476
§ 70 Superseded 19 ALR4th 326

78 ALR2d 696–733
§ 25[d] Superseded 84 ALR3d 877
§ 20 Superseded 11 ALR4th 1118
§ 14 Superseded 15 ALR4th 1186
§ 23 Superseded 33 ALR4th 1189

78 ALR2d 738–755
§§ 3–5 Superseded 95 ALR3d 390

78 ALR2d 905–907
Superseded 45 ALR4th 11

78 ALR2d 1404–1410
Superseded 93 ALR3d 420

79 ALR2d 431–475
§§ 29, 36 Superseded 46 ALR4th 1197

79 ALR2d 990–999
Superseded 20 ALR3d 1127 and 38 ALR4th 200

80 ALR2d 488–590
§§ 30,31,32 and 40 [s] Superseded 94 ALR3d 291 and 15 ALR4th 909
§§ 33 & 34 Superseded 18 ALR4th 206

80 ALR2d 598–674
§ 39[n] Superseded 89 ALR3d 210
§ 32 Superseded 93 ALR3d 99
§§ 19–26 Superseded 1 ALR4th 748
§§ 30, 34, 38, 39(f), *(1)*, and *(o)* Superseded 34 ALR4th 95
§§ 31, 37, 39[b, g, i, m] Superseded 35 ALR4th 663
§§ 27, 28, 29, and 39[d] Superseded 36 ALR4th 170

81 ALR2d 138–221
Superseded 12 ALR4th 462 & 29 ALR4th 1045

81 ALR2d 229–332
§§ 18–21 Superseded 36 ALR4th 419

81 ALR2d 350–376
§ 3 Superseded 36 ALR4th 419

81 ALR2d 927–939
§ 6 Superseded 94 ALR3d 990

81 ALR2d 1240–1270
Superseded 78 ALR Fed 23 and 45 ALR4th 602

82 ALR2d 1429–1468
Superseded 44 ALR4th 271

83 ALR2d 7–297
§ 10 Superseded 11 ALR4th 748

83 ALR2d 497–526
§ 3 superseded 56 ALR3d 641

83 ALR2d 926–930
§ 5 Superseded 8 ALR4th 387

83 ALR2d 955–971
Superseded 18 ALR4th 858

83 ALR2d 1051–1060
Superseded 9 ALR4th 1189

83 ALR2d 1117–1121
Superseded 45 ALR4th 1021

83 ALR2d 1169–1171
Superseded 9 ALR4th 1121

83 ALR2d 1368–1402
§§ 6, 11, & 16 Superseded 15 ALR4th 1043

84 ALR2d 348–367
Superseded 25 ALR4th 671

84 ALR2d 906–917
Superseded 68 ALR Fed 360

84 ALR2d 1017–1026
Superseded 24 ALR4th 105

84 ALR2d 1059–1072
§ 3 Superseded 43 ALR Fed 424

84 ALR2d 1288–1320
§ 11 [b] Superseded 15 ALR4th 1127

85 ALR2d 838–841
Superseded 99 ALR3d 628

85 ALR2d 1105–1106
Superseded 26 ALR4th 639

85 ALR2d 1111–1123
§ 5 Superseded 23 ALR4th 955

86 ALR2d 138–194
§§ 3-10 Superseded 33 ALR Fed 403

86 ALR2d 277–285
Superseded 7 ALR4th 1016

86 ALR2d 384–415
Superseded 46 ALR Fed 24

86 ALR2d 435–437
Superseded 47 ALR3d 998

86 ALR2d 489–601
Superseded 33 ALR3d 703

86 ALR2d 937–961
§§ 6–8 Superseded 8 ALR4th 387

86 ALR2d 1132–1147
Superseded 25 ALR4th 934

1126 **Consult POCKET PART for Later Entries**

tions in the first series of *ALR* are indexed in a separate *ALR First Series Quick Index.* Although many annotations in the first series have

Illustration P

A page from *Index to Annotations*

INDEX TO ANNOTATIONS

486 **Consult POCKET PART for Later Annotations**

been superseded by annotations in later series or address topics that seldom arise in modern litigation, the *ALR First Series Quick Index* may be helpful if one is researching a legal field that has changed little in recent decades and the *Index to Annotations* provides no leads.[21]

b. ALR *Digests*

An older means of access to *ALR* annotations, still maintained by the publisher, is the digest system. *ALR* digests are organized in a fashion similar to that used in West and other digests. The entire body of legal doctrine is divided into some 400 topics, which are then subdivided into numerical sections. Each topic begins with an explanation of its scope and an outline of its contents. Digest sections contain cross-references to treatments of the subject in the Total Client–Service Library's encyclopedias and formbooks, citations of relevant annotations, and headnotes from cases printed in *ALR*. All *ALR* headnotes are reprinted in the digest, including those summarizing points of law not addressed in the annotation following the case. Digest headnote entries on annotated issues are followed by "[Annotated]" in bold type.

There are three separate digests for the various series of *ALR*. *ALR Digest to 3d, 4th, Federal* was published in 1985 and consists of nine volumes updated by pocket parts. There is no index to the digest, so one must either examine the outline of a particular topic to find relevant sections or have a section number already in hand. *ALR Digest* section references appear in *American Jurisprudence 2d* and other Lawyers Co–op publications, including the *United States Supreme Court Digest, Lawyers' Edition.* Because the *ALR* and *Lawyers' Edition* digests do not use the same classification system, each includes cross-references to comparable sections in the other. One could also approach the digest from a case headnote in *ALR,* to find related cases or annotations. If the headnote covers an *annotated* topic, however, it is much quicker to turn to the annotation itself, where related annotations are listed in section 1[b], "Related matters."

Illustration Q shows a page from the *ALR Digest to 3d, 4th, Federal* containing a headnote from *Williams v. Hanover Ins. Co.* already seen in Illustration M–1. This issue, whether interest can be recovered on damages awarded for damages to shrubbery, was *not* annotated in 95 *ALR3d.* The digest section includes another headnote on an annotated topic, however, as well as references to several other annotations, *Am. Jur.2d,* and practice materials.

Older cases and annotations can be found in two earlier *ALR* digests, the twelve-volume *Permanent ALR Digest* for the first series and the seven-volume *ALR2d Digest.* The same classification system is used in all three digests, so one can find earlier cases and annotations under the same section number examined in *ALR Digest to 3d, 4th,*

21. Annotations in the first series of *Lawyers' Edition* are also excluded from *Index to Annotations* coverage. They are included, however, in *Index to Annotations* *(L.Ed. & ALR Fed.),* an adjunct to *United States Supreme Court Reports, Lawyers' Edition.*

Illustration Q

A page from *ALR Digest to 3d, 4th, Federal*

§ 24 INTEREST

Consult other ALR Digests for earlier cases

attorneys' estimate of that figure as stated to their clients when the work was about two-thirds complete, and where, on appeal, a new basis of the award was used, and the amount, under quantum meruit, was raised to $5,000, legal interest to which the attorneys were entitled on their claim commenced on the date of final judgment in the court below. *Pittman & Matheny v Davidge (1966, La App 1st Cir) 189 So 2d 706, 29 ALR3d 815, cert den 249 La 768, 191 So 2d 143 and cert den 249 La 771, 191 So 2d 144.*

[Annotated]

On a judgment in favor of an attorney for services rendered, interest is properly awarded from the date the statement for services rendered was delivered to the client. *Nugent v Downs (1970, La App) 230 So 2d 597, 57 ALR3d 575.*

The award of pre-judgment interest is largely discretionary with a trial court and the trial court does not abuse its discretion where it does not award pre-judgment interest from the date of a real estate broker's demand for payment of a commission due him for the sellers' failure to deliver good title. *Smithwick v Young (1981, Tenn App) 623 SW2d 284, 28 ALR4th 994.*

§ 25 For detention of debt or property

Text References:

18 Am Jur 2d, Conversion §§ 99, 100

§ 26 For carrier's delay or negligence in delivery

Text References:

14 Am Jur 2d, Carriers §§ 647, 1322

§ 27 For wrongful seizure or attachment

Text References:

6 Am Jur 2d, Attachment and Garnishment § 628

In an action wherein a judgment in a prior action obtained by the defendants against the plaintiff was set aside, and wherein the plaintiff sought damages for the malicious prosecution of the earlier action, the plaintiff is entitled to compensatory damages not only for the amount of money taken from his bank account by levy under a writ of execution issued on the judgment in the earlier action, but also for the loss of use of such money from the date it was taken, and under such circumstances, interest from such date is a proper measure of the loss of the use thereof. *Munson v Linnick (1967, 4th Dist) 255 Cal App 2d 589, 63 Cal Rptr 340, 27 ALR3d 1104 (disapproved Babb v Superior Court of Sonoma County, 3 Cal 3d 841, 92 Cal Rptr 179, 479 P2d 379).*

§ 28 For injuries to, or destruction of, property

Text References:

2 Am Jur 2d, Admiralty § 213; 22 Am Jur 2d, Damages §§ 192-194; 70 Am Jur 2d, Shipping §§ 344, 612; 77 Am Jur 2d, United States § 92

Practice References:

Federal Procedural Forms L Ed (Ch 47), Maritime Law and Procedure

1 Am Jur Pl & Pr Forms (Rev), Admiralty, Forms 51-61

17 Am Jur Trials 501, Preparing a Ship Collision Case for Trial

28 USCS § 1961; 46 USCS §§ 743, 745, 762, 782

US L Ed Digest, Interest §§ 20, 30

Annotations:

Comment Note.—Allowance of prejudgment interest on builder's recovery in action for breach of construction contract, 60 ALR3d 487

Comment Note.—Measure of damages for conversion of corporate stock or certificate, 31 ALR3d 1286

Right to interest in admiralty cases, pending appeal, of judgment creditor appealing unsuccessfully on ground of inadequacy, 15 ALR3d 434

Award of prejudgment interest in admiralty suits, 34 ALR Fed 126

When damages will be assessed against negligent salvor, 28 ALR Fed 223

Measure and elements of damages in action for wrongful death under general maritime law, 18 ALR Fed 184

Determination of amount of award or damages under Death on the High Seas Act (46 USCS §§ 761-768), 16 ALR Fed 679

Property owners were not entitled to recover legal interest on the amount of a partial payment draft by an insurance company for damages to shrubbery caused by the automobile of defendant's insured where the partial payment draft was given to the property owners prior to their suit for damages to an oak tree caused by the same collision, where the property owners could have collected the draft without prejudicing their claim for other damages, and where the draft would have been paid promptly upon presentation. *Williams v Hanover Ins. Co. (1977, La App) 351 So 2d 858, 95 ALR3d 504.*

In an action to recover against a stockbroking company for negligently but innocently assisting in the conversion, by the owner's husband, of stock certificates that left the company's possession or control after it had guaranteed the signatures forged by the husband, the owner, apart from her right to recover the value of the stocks, is entitled to consequential damages limited to interest thereon, and it is reversible error to allow, in lieu of such interest, the equivalent of after-accrued dividends including stock splits. *Amlung v Bankers Bond Co. (1967, Ky) 411 SW2d 689, 31 ALR3d 1277.*

[Annotated]

Federal.[22]

While *Index to Annotations* is more commonly used than the digests and provides more direct access to annotations, there are situations in which the digest approach may be helpful. The digest's systematic classification may be useful if a word search in the index is unsuccessful. Examining the digest outline for a topic may place a legal issue in context or provide a survey of related matters. Finally, if a relevant case is printed in *ALR* but the issue being researched is not annotated, one can read the headnotes to determine the appropriate digest classification and then find related annotations and headnotes.

c. *Online Access Through LEXIS and Auto-Cite*

All *ALR* annotations except those in the first series are available online through LEXIS. One can thus search the full text of all *ALR2d, ALR3d, ALR4th,* and *ALR Federal* annotations for particular terms or phrases. A more effective search in many instances is to look for keywords only in the *titles* of annotations. Many title terms too specific to be included in an index listing may nonetheless be relevant in particular circumstances. Because the titles of *ALR* annotations are generally lengthy and descriptive, a title keyword search usually retrieves annotations on point. A full-text search, on the other hand, may turn up several annotations which focus on unrelated issues but include the keywords in describing the facts and holdings of the cases discussed.

Even LEXIS users who do not choose to search in *ALR* do so, if they use the files containing either all federal cases or all state cases. A search in these files automatically retrieves all annotations meeting the specifications of the search. The user can then examine the annotations, and may discover useful research leads. It should be noted, however, that an additional access charge is usually levied for the pleasure of seeing the annotations. LEXIS is in effect dangling *ALR* in front of searchers' noses and forcing a choice between incurring more expense and ignoring potentially significant information.[23]

Any time a case citation is verified on Auto-Cite, the automated system described in Chapter 3, the case history is followed by a display of all annotations citing the case or any other case listed in the history. The first page of an Auto-Cite display is shown in Illustration J in Chapter 3, on page 78. In that illustration, each of four cases listed is marked with an asterisk, noting that it has been cited in one or more annotations. The full titles and citations of the annotations are provid-

22. The first two digests include tables of cases, a feature discontinued in the *ALR Digest to 3d, 4th, Federal.* One can easily determine if a case is printed in *ALR,* however, by looking in *Shepard's* for an *ALR* parallel citation.

The first two series also included another means of locating annotations, *Word Indexes.* These detailed indexes are similar to West "Descriptive-Word Indexes." The *Word Index* approach was not continued in *ALR3d,* and is little used today.

23. In 1988, LEXIS began providing access to files containing all federal or all state cases but *not* annotations, for the same charge as the files *with* annotations.

ed in Auto–Cite, including the sections in which the case is discussed. *Shepard's Citations* also provides the citations of citing annotations, but the inclusion of an annotation's title in Auto–Cite allows the researcher to determine more readily its relevance to a particular research issue.

Auto–Cite lists citing annotations not only as part of its case verification function. One can also enter the citation of an annotation and retrieve a list of other annotations which cite it, or "collateral annotations." This same listing appears in the annotation itself, under section 1[b], "Related matters," although the Auto–Cite list is updated more frequently than *ALR* 's annual pocket parts.

d. Shepard's Citations *and Other Publications*

Shepard's case citators, discussed in Chapter 3, indicate any time a case is either printed in *ALR* or mentioned in an *ALR* annotation. If the case is printed in full, the *ALR* citation is listed in parentheses as one of its parallel citations. If the case is cited or discussed in an annotation, the exact page in *ALR* is listed as citing reference. In either situation, a researcher Shepardizing a case and seeing an *ALR* citation has a good chance of finding several more related cases by examining the annotation. Occasionally, of course, the citing annotation may turn out to be on a different point of law in the case than the one being researched.

Finally, references to *ALR* annotations abound in a variety of other legal publications, including judicial opinions, treatises, and some state codes. *ALR* annotations are frequently cited by judges and other writers because they provide impartial and extensive surveys of legal doctrine from all jurisdictions. The works with the most prominent cross-references to relevant annotations are those published by Lawyers Co-op as part of its Total Client–Service Library, including the legal encyclopedia *American Jurisprudence 2d.*

5. SUMMARY

Annotations can be very useful research tools for many legal problems. If an annotation has been written on a point being researched, that means someone has already examined the issue and collected every relevant case. The annotation's analysis may be informative and helpful; even if it is not, the assembly of case citations will be a valuable time-saver. Because each annotation is written about a specific topic, however, coverage in the series is not comprehensive or encyclopedic. There are many issues for which no annotation can be found. Because *ALR* cannot be used for every research problem, the skilled researcher is able both to take advantage of an annotation's help and to press on alone with other case-finding resources.

Remember that annotations are only case finders, and are not law. They can be cited as useful gathering points for related decisions, but are not generally regarded as persuasive authority. Scholarly law review articles differ from annotations in that they often *are* considered persuasive. (Unlike annotations, however, they are not updated after publication.) The purpose of annotations is not to persuade. It is to gather and synthesize the cases from every jurisdiction, and to provide a comprehensive survey of court decisions on a particular point of law.

E. COMPUTERIZED RESEARCH SYSTEMS

The two major computerized legal research systems, West Publishing Company's WESTLAW and Mead Data Central's LEXIS, have revolutionized the ways in which case research is conducted. Both services allow access to the full texts of judicial opinions, and permit researchers to retrieve all cases with any specified terms or combinations of terms. One can also search for opinions by a particular judge or cases involving specified parties, to mention only two of numerous possibilities.

Although both systems offer far more than just cases, with extensive databases of statutes, administrative materials, and secondary sources, court decisions remain their primary focus. Both WESTLAW and LEXIS contain full texts of opinions from the federal courts and from all fifty states. Cases available online include not only those published in official reports and commercial reporters such as West's National Reporter System, but "slip opinions" obtained from the courts and inaccessible through traditional printed resources.

Some aspects of computerized research have already been discussed in this and earlier chapters. In Chapter 2, we discussed the extensive scope of online case databases and emphasized the speed with which new decisions are available electronically. In Chapter 3, we explained the case verification systems Insta–Cite (a component of WESTLAW) and Auto–Cite (available on LEXIS), as well as online access to *Shepard's Citations* through either system.

In this section we briefly discuss WESTLAW and LEXIS capabilities for case-finding. While the systems differ in coverage and in search techniques, they are quite similar in concept and design. The specific methods of searching in each system can best be learned through the extensive training programs and tutorial materials developed expressly for that purpose.[24] Instead of teaching computerized legal research, this section surveys its possibilities and limitations.

1. CASE DATABASES

The first decision an online researcher must make is the choice of database in which to search. In both WESTLAW and LEXIS, one can

24. The basic instructional materials for the two systems are *WESTLAW Introductory Guide to Legal Research* (West, 1988) and *Learning LEXIS* (Mead Data Central, 1989). The first five chapters of W. Harrington, *The Dow Jones–Irwin Lawyer's Guide to Online Data Bases* (Dow Jones–Irwin, 1987), provide an interesting and readable introduction to online research and a comparative explanation of searching procedures on both systems. St. Martin's has recently published F.R. Shapiro, *LEXIS: The Complete User's Guide* (1989).

search the decisions of a particular state or a particular court, or can use databases which combine the decisions either of all fifty states or of all federal courts. Whether to limit research to a particular jurisdiction depends on a variety of factors, such as the nature and purpose of the research, the amount of available time and money, and the value of precedent from other jurisdictions.

The decisions available for any particular state are basically the same in either WESTLAW or LEXIS, although one system may have more extensive retrospective coverage and one may have quicker access to recent opinions. The major difference in the cases appearing in the two systems is that LEXIS documents consist simply of opinions as received from the courts, while WESTLAW includes (for cases published in West reporters) the West synopses and headnotes.

As part of their display of a case, both systems provide citations to any published versions, whether in official reports, West reporters, and other topical reporters. One can retrieve the citation from the computer and then go to one of these printed resources for further examination, or simply use the computer but cite to the published source. Until recently, a case that was available online but was not otherwise published was referred to as a "slip opinion" (the same term used to designate the original document issued by the court). In 1988, however, both WESTLAW and LEXIS instituted systems by which cases found only online can be cited. Each case is assigned a unique citation, which is used until a published citation is available. Before a United States Court of Appeals case is printed in the *Federal Reporter,* for example, it can be cited as "1989 WL 4339 (D.C.Cir.)" or "1989 U.S.App. LEXIS 973."

2. SEARCH STRATEGIES

Both WESTLAW and LEXIS enable the user to search the full text of opinions for any words or phrases he or she believes may appear in relevant cases. This alone would be an immense aid in situations where digests and other printed indexes are not specific enough or are not organized in a way to meet particular research needs. More importantly, the systems permit the use of Boolean searching techniques, which make it possible to retrieve documents containing two or more words or phrases in specified combinations. For example, one can retrieve all cases containing the words "damages" and "shrubbery," or all cases where those two words appear within five or ten words of each other. Instead of functioning as a simple concordance to every word in every opinion, the systems thus allow a unique and complex set of search criteria to be created for any research issue.

This ability to combine two search terms means that one can automatically limit retrieval to cases containing each of several essential elements, instead of scanning several columns or pages of a digest or an annotation for cases with particular facts. It also means that one can combine two concerns in a way not possible in most printed resources. An attorney working on the *Fisher v. Lowe* litigation, for example, might have to choose whether to research issues of tree damages or issues of no-fault insurance, since even a case directly on point would be indexed under one but not the other. Online, however, both issues can be combined in one search to retrieve any cases directly on point.

When searching opinions for a relevant fact or issue, one must try to frame a search request to include any words or phrases that judges would use to express the concept. For printed indexes and digests, an editor ensures that all references to a particular subject can be found in one place. All cases on attorneys, for example, would be listed under "attorneys." Because a full-text database has no intervening editor, however, the user must search not just for "attorney," but also for other terms a judge might use instead, such as "counsel," "lawyer," or "pettifogger." The art of framing successful search requests can be learned only through a familiarity both with the legal terminology of the subject area and the potentials of the computer system. Preliminary planning of a search by analysis of the problem and careful selection of search words and connectors is essential.

The inclusion in WESTLAW's databases of West synopses and headnotes lends some standardization, since these editorial additions may contain descriptive terms which are normally used but which may not be employed by a particular judge. In addition, West digest topics and key numbers can be used in WESTLAW searches, either alone or in combination with words or phrases in opinions. The researcher can thus use a topic or key number to limit retrieval to a particular subject matter and keywords to specify fact situations within that subject. This is particularly valuable in areas such as constitutional law or securities regulation where all cases would be classified similarly but the descriptive language used by the courts may vary widely.

An aspect of online searching that can be extremely valuable is the use of document *fields* (in WESTLAW) or *segments* (in LEXIS). Fields or segments are specific parts of a case, such as the names of the parties, or the judge writing the opinion, or the date of decision. A search request limited to a particular field or segment can retrieve, for example, all cases involving a specific corporation or decided after a certain date. It would be a lengthy and tedious process manually to find all opinions written by a particular judge. Online databases can easily retrieve a complete list of a judge's opinions, and allow the researcher to combine that request with other search terms to find a judge's opinions on particular issues. In WESTLAW, one can use the "synopsis" field to search only for words appearing in the paragraphs added by West to summarize each case's facts and holding, and can thus retrieve a smaller body of cases more precisely on point.

3. INTEGRATING MANUAL AND COMPUTERIZED RESEARCH

Although many law library resources, such as reporters and digests, are expensive to acquire, they do not cost more money each time they are used by a researcher. Under most circumstances, on the other hand, the cost of WESTLAW or LEXIS is based on the amount of use. While almost all law schools have arrangements that allow use of the systems at a flat, discounted rate, other users incur a fee each time they go online. The key to efficient use of the databases is to remember that they are generally case-finding tools and not case reporters. The terminal should be used to frame searches, skim highlights, and obtain citations. Unless a case is not available in print, the efficient researcher then looks for decisions in the standard reporters. Carelessness in searching or reading whole cases online can become very expensive.

There are important reasons other than financial constraints for not relying exclusively on computerized research. There are many research situations where the benefit of a publisher's editorial work in organizing and analyzing cases is indispensable. A digest or annotation can arrange cases by precise issue addressed and disregard the occasional discursive aside, while the computer cannot distinguish between holding and incidental dictum. The computer has no way of distinguishing the most important and influential cases in an area of law, but a treatise or law review article will focus its discussion on such cases. Finally, although both WESTLAW and LEXIS are expanding the scope of their databases and adding older cases, there are many opinions which are not online and which can be found only through manual research techniques.

WESTLAW and LEXIS can undoubtedly achieve results impossible through manual research. They add great flexibility and incredible speed to the process of case finding. They are not foolproof, however, and may miss essential cases simply because the courts' vocabulary or phrasing does not precisely match the search request. The computerized systems are most effective when used as part of a carefully developed research strategy integrating a number of different approaches. Computers can never eliminate one of the most important research steps, *reading* relevant cases retrieved by either manual or electronic methods. One must read a case to analyze its reasoning and to determine on what precedent it relies.

F. OTHER CASE-FINDING TOOLS

This chapter has concentrated on materials such as digests and annotations which are designed expressly for the purpose of case finding. Because finding judicial decisions is a central part of most legal research, however, almost every research tool to be discussed in this book can serve as a case-finding tool to some extent. Other primary sources such as statutes include notes of relevant cases, to aid in interpreting and applying the terms of the primary source. Virtually every secondary source in law provides citations to cases, either to support the positions taken and the statements made in its text or to provide primary source references as part of its informational function.

These other research tools are discussed more fully in other chapters, but their importance as case finders should not be overlooked. For some research issues, digests, annotations, and computerized research are the most effective and valuable tools. For other problems, however, beginning with one of these other resources may save considerable time or may be the proper approach. To find United States Court of Appeals cases interpreting a Supreme Court holding, for example, one would use Shepard's instead of a digest or annotation. To find cases construing a legislative provision, one would turn first to an annotated code. Unfortunately, there is no simple, cut-and-dried case-finding technique that can be applied to every problem.

1. *SHEPARD'S CITATIONS*

As already discussed in Chapter 3, Shepard's case citators are used to verify the authority of a decision and to trace its subsequent judicial history and treatment. A Shepard's listing for a case also includes every subsequent published decision citing the case. Armed with one case on an issue, a researcher can usually use Shepard's to find numerous more recent decisions on related matters. Whether a decision is cited by later courts depends on such factors as its weight as authority and the strength of its reasoning, and some published decisions may never be cited at all. Shepardizing most cases, however, provides a list of later decisions. These cases can then be examined for other authorities on which they rely, and Shepardized themselves to find still more recent cases.

As will be seen in subsequent chapters, Shepard's also publishes citators for various other legal materials, including statutes, court rules, and law review articles. Each of these citators includes references to cases discussing or mentioning the subject material. To find cases in *Shepard's Citations,* one thus does not even need to start with a case. A wide variety of primary and secondary legal authorities will do almost as well.

2. ANNOTATED STATUTES

Since many cases and many research problems involve the application or interpretation of statutes, the use of annotated statutory codes (to be discussed in the next chapter) is frequently the best initial case-finding approach for such problems. Following the text of each statutory section, an annotated code provides annotations containing headnote paragraphs from decisions which have applied or interpreted the section. These abstracts are composed like headnotes in West reporters; in the *United States Code Annotated* and the many state codes published by West, they are in fact identical to West's headnotes and digest entries. The annotations, like the statutes themselves, are updated regularly, usually in annual pocket parts and interim pamphlets.

Using an annotated code to find cases has the major advantage of saving research steps. In one resource are located the statutory text needed for the problem and the case abstracts in the annotations, as well as the other notes and cross-references which are usually provided in the codes.

3. *WORDS AND PHRASES*

Many cases turn on the definition or interpretation of a particular word or phrase, in a statute, a contract, or some other legal document. Case finding often involves the search for decisions containing such interpretations. To meet this need, West publishes *Words and Phrases,* a specialized digest of judicial definitions of legally significant words and phrases. *Words and Phrases* consists of ninety volumes of headnote abstracts drawn from West reporters and identical to the abstracts appearing in West digests and annotated codes. Here the abstracts are presented under the alphabetically arranged words and phrases which they define, interpret or construe. *Words and Phrases* covers all federal and state jurisdictions.

West also publishes, as part of each of its federal and state digests, a "Words and Phrases" table. These tables provide citations to cases but do not reprint headnotes. If the construction applied by a particular court is important, as it often is, the digest "Words and Phrases" may be the best place to look first. The encyclopedic *Words and Phrases* set is available for comprehensive research in all jurisdictions. In either event, the "words and phrases" approach is faster and more efficient than other tools if research concerns the judicial interpretation of a particular term.

Both *Words and Phrases* and the tables in jurisdictional digests are supplemented by annual pocket parts and by tables appearing in the advance sheets and bound volumes of all West reporters. *Words and Phrases* will be discussed more fully and illustrated in Chapter 13, Other Legal Research Sources.

4. ENCYCLOPEDIAS AND TREATISES

The two national legal encyclopedias, *Corpus Juris Secundum* and *American Jurisprudence 2d,* and the several state encyclopedias often serve as excellent and easily accessible case finders. Legal encyclopedias have two major functions: they explain and summarize basic legal doctrines, and they provide footnote citations to supporting primary authority. Even a researcher who does not need the overview provided by the text can use the footnotes to find relevant cases. Because encyclopedias are generally well-indexed and clearly written, appropriate sections are often easier to locate than they are in digests, and case citations thus easier to find.

Legal treatises perform functions similar to encyclopedias, but limit their focus to relatively specialized areas of legal doctrine. Their texts may be more interesting and opinionated than the impartial approaches taken in the encyclopedias, but like encyclopedias they use extensive footnotes to cases to support their propositions. A good treatise combines an informative text with convenient access to primary authorities. Legal encyclopedias, treatises, and the Restatements of the Law (which can also be used for finding cases) are discussed in Chapter 12.

5. PERIODICAL ARTICLES

Articles in legal periodicals, particularly those in academic law reviews, are often the single best place to begin researching a legal issue. A recent article on a specific topic will articulate the current status of legal doctrine, without requiring the reader to examine a pocket part or other supplement. In addition, most law review articles are packed with footnotes citing cases, statutes, regulations, other articles, and numerous other secondary sources. References to cases are usually, but not always, an important component of these footnotes. A law review article may distinguish relevant cases in far greater detail than a treatise would, with extensive quotations reprinted in the footnotes.

Even law review articles that are barely readable are useful as research tools, since the footnotes should have been checked extensively for accuracy and relevance by long-suffering but ambitious law students working on the law review staff. Various aspects of legal periodicals, including procedures for finding relevant articles, will be discussed in Chapter 11.

6. LOOSELEAF SERVICES

One of the great research values of topical looseleaf services is their effectiveness in bringing together several forms of authority in one set of volumes, with prompt supplementation and integrated indexing approaches. For the subject it covers, a typical looseleaf provides the texts of statutes; judicial and administrative decisions, either full text or abstracted; administrative rules and regulations; and an explanatory discussion of legal developments. Many services also include a series of topical case reporter volumes, with its own set of finding aids. These finding aids, both in the looseleaf service and the reporter volumes, invariably include tables of cases and subject indexing, and sometimes also include case digests and citators. Because these finding tools are usually designed specifically for the subject field, they often provide the most efficient access to the subject covered. Looseleafs will be discussed further in Chapter 10.

G. SUMMARY

The enormous body of published decisions in American law is accessible through the varied research tools described in this chapter. Case digests, represented by the many units of the West Key–Number Digest system, can be used to find cases from any period or jurisdiction. Annotations gather cases on specific legal or factual issues. WESTLAW and LEXIS provide vast opportunities for creative and effective case research. Citators permit one to go straight from a single relevant case to other, more recent decisions. Annotated statutory codes are most useful for problems involving a statutory provision. *Words and Phrases* can be used when the search focuses on legally significant terminology. Encyclopedias and treatises provide case citations while summarizing and explaining the law. Periodical articles provide useful analyses as well as extensive references to various resources. Looseleafs focus on specific subjects and include information on any relevant developments, including cases.

The wise researcher learns all of these approaches, tests them, uses them, and develops individual preferences for particular types of problems. Flexibility, rather than rote application of a single procedure, is required for fully effective case research, since the creative use of several resources will often lead to the best and most thorough result.

Chapter 5

STATUTES

A. Introduction.
B. Pattern of Statutory Publication.
   1. Slip Laws.
   2. Session Laws.
   3. Statutory Compilations or Codes.
   4. Annotated Codes.
C. Federal Statutes.
   1. Slip Laws.
   2. Advance Session Law Services.
   3. *U.S. Statutes at Large.*
   4. Codification of Federal Statutes.
      a. *Revised Statutes.*
      b. *U.S. Code.*
      c. *U.S. Code Annotated.*
      d. *U.S. Code Service.*
      e. WESTLAW and LEXIS U.S. Code Databases.
D. Federal Statutory Research.
   1. Finding Statutes.
      a. Indexes.
      b. Tables.
   2. Updating Statutes.
      a. *USCA* and *USCS.*
      b. Shepard's Statutory Citators.
   3. Interpreting Statutes.
      a. Judicial Decisions.
      b. Legislative History.
      c. Other Resources.
E. Other Forms of Federal Legislation.
   1. U.S. Constitution.
   2. Treaties.
   3. Interstate Compacts.
   4. Reorganization Plans.
F. State Statutory Research.
   1. Slip Laws and Session Laws.
   2. State Codes.
      a. Annotated Codes.
      b. WESTLAW and LEXIS Code Databases.

A. INTRODUCTION

Statutes and other legislative forms constitute the second category of primary legal sources. Because of the focus on appellate decisions in American legal education, and on cases in the popular conception of the lawyer's work, the role of statutory law in legal research tends to be underemphasized. In practice, however, statutory law is central to many legal issues, and the initial step in approaching most research problems is to ascertain whether there is a governing statute, rather than immediately searching for judicial precedents. Indeed, the vast majority of appellate decisions today involve the application or interpretation of statutes, rather than merely consideration of common law principles.[1]

The term "legislation" can be broadly construed to include constitutions, statutes, treaties, municipal charters and ordinances, interstate compacts, and reorganization plans. In this chapter we will focus on federal and state statute publications, although there will be briefer discussions of the other types of legislation. Administrative regulations and court rules are considered "delegated legislation," but are treated separately in Chapters 8 and 9, respectively.

As in the previous consideration of case law, the federal nature of our government and legal system is important in understanding legislation. The U.S. Congress and the legislatures of the fifty states each have their own structures and procedures for the initiation and passage of legislation. Similarly, the forms of publication of statutory materials vary from jurisdiction to jurisdiction, although they share similar features.

B. PATTERN OF STATUTORY PUBLICATION

The texts of enacted legislation for the various jurisdictions of the United States are issued successively in a series of forms which constitute a common pattern. The names of each form may differ among the

1. An interesting study of the impact on the courts of this growth of legislation is to be found in Professor Guido Calabresi's Oliver Wendell Holmes lectures, published as *A Common Law for the Age of Statutes* (Harvard University Press, 1982).

jurisdictions, but the generic equivalent always exists. The pattern of statutory publication is as follows:

Slip Law
Session Laws
Code
Annotated Code

Although statutory research generally begins in an annotated code, an understanding of the earlier forms of the statute provides an essential background.

1. SLIP LAWS

"Slip laws" are separately issued pamphlets, each of which contains the text of a single act. Typically, they are individually paginated, designated by a chapter or law number, and issued officially by the government. Slip laws for most states are not widely distributed and are received only in larger research law libraries. Many lawyers rarely see statutes in this initial form, but slip laws are usually the first official text of laws to be published.

2. SESSION LAWS

The term "session laws" refers to the permanent publication, in chronological sequence, of the slip laws enacted during a legislative session. The federal government and each of the fifty states publish some form of session laws, usually in bound volumes issued after considerable delay, following the end of each legislative session. Most jurisdictions also have commercial legislative publication services which provide more prompt access to new laws as they are enacted. These services, providing the texts of new laws in pamphlet form, are known as "advance session law services."

In most states, the session laws constitute the *positive law* form of legislation, *i.e.*, the authoritative, binding text of the laws, and the determinative version if questions arise from textual variations in subsequent printed versions. Other forms (such as codes) are only *prima facie* evidence of the statutory language, unless they have been designated as positive law by the legislature.

Session law publications for the various states have several common characteristics, including noncumulative subject indexes for each volume and, frequently, tables indicating which existing laws have been modified or repealed by newly enacted legislation.

3. STATUTORY COMPILATIONS OR CODES

As used in this chapter, the term "code" refers to a publication of the public, general and permanent statutes of a jurisdiction in a fixed subject or topical arrangement. Statutory codes preserve the original language of the session laws more or less intact, and merely rearrange and group them under broad subject categories in order to enhance access to the text. In this process of rearranging the individual statutes, amendments are incorporated, repealed laws are deleted, and minor technical adjustments are sometimes made in the text of the laws to fit them into a functional and coherent compilation.

Statutory codes may appear in either official or unofficial editions. Official statutory codes are published or sanctioned by the state. They normally include the text of the law and brief editorial notes as to the authority and historical development of the law.

Despite their convenience in providing subject access, official codes have certain shortcomings. Like other official publications such as court reports, they are usually issued more slowly than commercial versions. More important, their limited editorial notes are simply not adequate for most statutory research. They do not provide citations to judicial interpretations of a statute, which are important extrinsic aids in determining its meaning or extent. The researcher must turn to the unofficial, annotated codes for access to this type of material.

4. ANNOTATED CODES

An annotated code reproduces the text and arrangement of the official code. It also incorporates new legislation, revisions and amendments within that structure, and deletes repealed laws. Its unique contribution to legal research is the inclusion of *annotations* after each statutory section. These include references to relevant judicial or administrative decisions, administrative code sections, encyclopedias, attorney general opinions, legislative history materials, law reviews, and treatises.

The annotated code provides more than just case citations, because the references to decisions usually take the same form as the headnotes found in reporter volumes. These brief editorial descriptions of the points of law involved allow researchers to browse the annotations to find relevant cases. This can be an enormous time-saver, since some statutory sections have been construed in thousands of court cases. Other sections which have not yet been considered in published court decisions may have no annotations, despite the common misperception that annotations follow *every* section in an annotated code.

Another advantage of the unofficial codes is their more frequent supplementation by means of pocket parts and pamphlet supplements. These features of the commercial editions of the annotated codes make them the most effective research sources for statutory material.

C. FEDERAL STATUTES

The various steps in the enactment of a federal law are outlined and documented below in Chapter 7, Legislative History. The process is often long and complicated, beginning formally with the introduction of a bill and ending with passage by both houses of Congress of either an act or a joint resolution, and its approval by the President (or repassage over a Presidential veto).[2] Under the Constitution and subsequent judicial interpretations, there are only three forms of federal legislation: acts, joint resolutions, and treaties. Simple and concurrent resolutions do not result directly in laws.

Each enactment is designated either as a "public law" or a "private law." Generally private laws are passed for the specific benefit of an individual or a small group of individuals, whereas public laws are intended to be of general application.[3] The two categories are numbered, as enacted, in separate series. Although private laws are issued in a slip law form and appear in the federal session law publication (the *Statutes at Large*), most of the other publications discussed in this chapter contain only public laws.

The distinction between acts and joint resolutions is no longer of great significance. Over ninety percent of federal laws are passed as acts, with joint resolutions used primarily for fiscal measures. Prior to the 77th Congress in 1941, acts and joint resolutions were numbered in separate chronological series, but now they are issued in one chronological sequence of "Public Laws," without any distinction other than the preliminary designation: "Act" or "Joint Resolution," and the clause of intent: "Be it enacted" or "Resolved."

1. SLIP LAWS

The first official form of publication of a federal law is the *slip law,* a separately paginated pamphlet text of each law, with no internal indexing. Each law is designated by a public law number, *e.g.,* Public Law 92–195. The first part of the number represents the number of the Congress which enacted the law (in this case, the 92d Congress) and the second part of the number indicates the chronological sequence of its enactment (the 195th public law enacted by that Congress).

The form of the printing is almost identical to that which appears in the *Statutes at Large,* and in recent years both the slip law and *Statutes at Large* publication include a brief summary of the legislative history of each law after the text. Illustration A shows the beginning of a typical federal law, in either its slip law or *Statutes at Large* form.

The slip law is the first authoritative official text of the statute and is rebuttable as evidence of the law only by reference to the enrolled Act. When the *Statutes at Large* are published, they supersede the slip law as authority. Slip laws are generally distributed rather slowly, however, and most researchers rely for the text of recently enacted federal statutes on one of the commercial services to be described next.

2. ADVANCE SESSION LAW SERVICES

The two general advance session law services for federal statutes are West Publishing Company's *United States Code Congressional and*

2. U.S. Const., Art. I, § 7.

3. In this century most private laws concern special relief for individuals under the immigration laws. For more on this distinction, see Note, "Private Bills in Congress," 79 *Harv.L.Rev.* 1684 (1966).

Illustration A

The first page of a law in the *U.S. Statutes at Large*, in a format similar to the slip law

Public Law 92-195

AN ACT

December 15, 1971
[S. 1116]

To require the protection, management, and control of wild free-roaming horses and burros on public lands.

Be it enacted by the Senate and House of Representatives of the United States of America in Congress assembled, That Congress finds and declares that wild free-roaming horses and burros are living symbols of the historic and pioneer spirit of the West; that they contribute to the diversity of life forms within the Nation and enrich the lives of the American people; and that these horses and burros are fast disappearing from the American scene. It is the policy of Congress that wild free-roaming horses and burros shall be protected from capture, branding, harassment, or death; and to accomplish this they are to be considered in the area where presently found, as an integral part of the natural system of the public lands.

Wild horses and burros. Protection.

SEC. 2. As used in this Act—

Definitions.

(a) "Secretary" means the Secretary of the Interior when used in connection with public lands administered by him through the Bureau of Land Management and the Secretary of Agriculture in connection with public lands administered by him through the Forest Service;

(b) "wild free-roaming horses and burros" means all unbranded and unclaimed horses and burros on public lands of the United States;

(c) "range" means the amount of land necessary to sustain an existing herd or herds of wild free-roaming horses and burros, which does not exceed their known territorial limits, and which is devoted principally but not necessarily exclusively to their welfare in keeping with the multiple-use management concept for the public lands;

(d) "herd" means one or more stallions and his mares; and

(e) "public lands" means any lands administered by the Secretary of the Interior through the Bureau of Land Management or by the Secretary of Agriculture through the Forest Service.

SEC. 3. (a) All wild free-roaming horses and burros are hereby declared to be under the jurisdiction of the Secretary for the purpose of management and protection in accordance with the provisions of this Act. The Secretary is authorized and directed to protect and manage wild free-roaming horses and burros as components of the public lands, and he may designate and maintain specific ranges on public lands as sanctuaries for their protection and preservation, where the Secretary after consultation with the wildlife agency of the State wherein any such range is proposed and with the Advisory Board established in section 7 of this Act deems such action desirable. The Secretary shall manage wild free-roaming horses and burros in a manner that is designed to achieve and maintain a thriving natural ecological balance on the public lands. He shall consider the recommendations of qualified scientists in the field of biology and ecology, some of whom shall be independent of both Federal and State agencies and may include members of the Advisory Board established in section 7 of this Act. All management activities shall be at the minimal feasible level and shall be carried out in consultation with the wildlife agency of the State wherein such lands are located in order to protect the natural ecological balance of all wildlife species which inhabit such lands, particularly endangered wildlife species. Any adjustments in forage allocations on any such lands shall take into consideration the needs of other wildlife species which inhabit such lands.

Jurisdiction; management.

Administrative News (known as *USCCAN* or, in Bluebook form, *U.S. Code Cong. & Admin.News*) and Lawyers Co-operative Publishing Company's *Advance* pamphlets to the *United States Code Service* (*USCS*). Both services issue monthly pamphlets, generally publishing new federal statutes within a month or two of enactment. In both *USCCAN* and *USCS Advance,* each page of statutory text indicates the location at which it will eventually appear upon publication in the official *Statutes at Large.*

In addition to the text of newly enacted public laws, each service publishes Presidential proclamations, executive orders, amendments to court rules, and selected administrative regulations. Each service pamphlet includes a cumulative index and various tables which aid in locating the sections of the Code that have been affected by recent legislative, executive or administrative action.

There are two major differences between the two services. *USCCAN* publishes not only the text of statutes but selective legislative history materials leading to their enactment, such as House and Senate Reports, whereas *USCS Advance* pamphlets provide legislative history references but do not reprint the documents themselves.

The other difference is that *Advance* pamphlets are designed only for temporary use, until the new material has been incorporated into *USCS,* but *USCCAN* pamphlets are cumulated at the end of each year into bound volumes. *USCCAN* thus forms a permanent commercial version of the official *Statutes at Large.* It can be used to find the text of statutes since it began publication (as *United States Code Congressional Service*) in 1941, although its pagination has been the same as that in the *Statutes at Large* only since 1975.

73. *U.S. STATUTES AT LARGE*

The official, permanent session law publication for federal laws is the *United States Statutes at Large* (cited as Stat.). At the end of each annual session of Congress, the public and private laws enacted are cumulated and published in chronological order as the *Statutes at Large* for that session, along with concurrent resolutions, Presidential proclamations, and reorganization plans. In recent years, each session's compilation has comprised one, two or three volumes, with overall indexes by subject and individuals' names at the end of each volume. The several volumes for each session bear one volume number. A federal session law is cited by its Public Law number and the volume and page in which it appears in *Statutes at Large.*[4]

The *Statutes at Large* were inaugurated in 1846, published by Little, Brown & Co. under Congressional authorization.[5] Beginning

4. Session laws before 1957 are designated by chapter numbers, not Public Law numbers. Public Law numbers have been assigned to Acts of Congress since 1901, but chapter numbers remained the traditional and primary means of identification until they were discontinued at the end of the 1956 session.

5. By Joint Resolution of March 3, 1845, 5 Stat. 798. Two earlier chronological publications of federal laws preceded the Little, Brown *Statutes at Large,* both also issued by private publishers with official authorization, and both under the title *Laws of the United States.* The first was the Folwell edition in twelve volumes cov-

with volume 18 (1873–75), the *Statutes at Large* have been published by the U.S. Government Printing Office.

The first eight volumes of the *Statutes at Large* covered legislation retrospectively to 1789 and treaties to 1778 as follows:

Vols. 1–5: Public Laws of the 1st to 28th Congresses (1789–1845);

Vol. 6: Private Laws of the 1st to 28th Congresses (1789–1845);

Vol. 7: Treaties with Indian tribes (1778–1845); and

Vol. 8: Treaties with foreign countries (1778–1845).

Volume 9 then covered three Congresses, volumes 10 to 12 covered two each, and volumes 13 to 49 one each. With volume 50 (1936), the present pattern of one numbered volume for each *session* began. (Prior to 1936, in addition to the *Statutes at Large* for each Congress, pamphlet or session laws were also published for each individual session.) Through volume 64 (1950–51), the full texts of newly approved treaties were also included in each volume, but that practice was discontinued when a separate series, *U.S. Treaties and Other International Agreements,* was begun in 1950.

Although the publication of current volumes of the *Statutes at Large* has been slow, lagging three or four years behind the end of the session covered, they are the authoritative text of federal statutes, superseding the slip laws. The *Statutes at Large* is the positive law form of statutes, and "legal evidence of laws . . . in all the Courts of the United States."[6] The *United States Code* is only *prima facie* evidence of the laws, except for those of its titles which have been reenacted by Congress as positive law.[7]

Each *Statutes at Large* volume includes an index to its contents.[8] These indexes facilitate access to each volume, but access to individual volumes is inadequate for most research. One cannot effectively search each session laws volume for statutes on a specific issue, and then analyze successive amendments and repeals in order to determine what laws are currently in force.

4. CODIFICATION OF FEDERAL STATUTES

The most useful publications of federal laws are not those published chronologically, but those that are arranged by subject. The most important of these is the current United States Code in its various editions, but one earlier codification which remains a source of positive law must first be discussed.

ering the first thirteen Congresses (1789–1815), published pursuant to the Act of March 3, 1795, 1 Stat. 443. The second was the Bioren and Duane edition in ten volumes covering the first twenty-eight Congresses (1789–1845), published pursuant to the Act of April 18, 1814, 3 Stat. 129.

6. 1 U.S.C. § 112 (1982).

7. 1 U.S.C. § 204 (1982).

8. Volumes 71 (1957) to 90 (1976) also included tables indicating which existing laws had been modified or repealed by laws published in each volume. This feature, useful for current awareness but of limited historical value, was discontinued in 1977.

a. Revised Statutes

Because of the difficulty of research in the numerous volumes of the *Statutes at Large* with their noncumulating separate indexes, it became apparent by the middle of the 19th century that some form of codification or subject arrangement was needed. After much drafting and redrafting and great legislative effort (and after a few private efforts at publication of subject arrangements), the only *complete* revision of federal laws was enacted on June 22, 1874, and published as 18 Stat. Part 1 under the title, *Revised Statutes of the United States, Passed at the First Session of the Forty-Third Congress, 1873–'74; Embracing the Statutes of the United States, General and Permanent in Their Nature, in Force on [December 1, 1873] . . .* It did not contain private or temporary acts, or laws otherwise not conceived to be of general, permanent interest.

This first edition of the *Revised Statutes* is variously and confusingly called the "Revised Statutes of 1873" (for the cut-off date of the laws included therein), or "of 1874" (for the date of its enactment) or "of 1875" (for the date of its publication). In any case, the publication was more than just a topical arrangement of laws into seventy-four subject titles.[9] It was a reenactment as *positive law* of all the laws included in it, and expressly repealed their original *Statutes at Large* texts. Therefore, the *Revised Statutes* is *the* authoritative text for any law predating its publication which remains in force, unless it has since become part of one of the reenacted positive law titles of the U.S. Code.

Errors in the first edition and some dissatisfaction with it led to the publication of a second edition of the *Revised Statutes* in 1878 (under the Act of March 2, 1877, 19 Stat. 268). The second edition, although more frequently used today than the first, was not a reenactment as positive law of the laws it contained, and thus it does not have the same status as the earlier version.[10]

Almost fifty more years of publication of the *Statutes at Large* then ensued before another effort at an official codification of federal laws was undertaken. The chaos and inconvenience in statutory research were somewhat alleviated by privately published subject arrangements, but the need for a new official code was apparent.

b. U.S. Code

After much legislative travail, a new codification effort was approved on June 30, 1926, and published as 44 Stat. Part 1 under the title: *The Code of the Laws of the United States of America of a General*

9. Although the *Revised Statutes* is divided into 74 titles, the section numbering is continuous through the work, as distinguished from its successor, the United States Code, which begins each title with a new sequence of section numbers.

10. Two supplements to the *Revised Statutes* were subsequently issued for the periods 1874–91 and 1892–1901, but these also did not have the status of positive law. They were chronological arrangements rather than title-by-title supplements to the *Revised Statutes,* although they did contain lists of *Revised Statutes* sections affected by the subsequent legislation.

and Permanent Nature, in Force December 7, 1925 . . . It has since been known as the *United States Code.*

Unlike the *Revised Statutes,* the new Code was not a positive law reenactment and did not repeal the prior *Statutes at Large.* It was *prima facie* evidence of the law, rebuttable by reference to the *Statutes at Large.* However, Congress subsequently began revising the titles of the Code and reenacting each into positive law as the revision is completed. So far, over forty per cent of the titles have been so reenacted, and are now legal evidence; for the rest the *Statutes at Large* remains legal evidence and the Code is *prima facie* evidence. A list of titles at the beginning of each *U.S. Code* volume indicates which have been reenacted as positive law.[11] A copy of that list is shown in Illustration B.

The U.S. Code is arranged in fifty subject titles, generally in alphabetical order. Titles are divided into chapters and then into sections, with a continuous sequence of section numbers for each title. Citations to the Code indicate the title and section numbers, and the year of publication, e.g., 16 U.S.C. § 1311 (1982).

Following each statutory section in the *U.S. Code,* there is a parenthetical reference to its source in the *Statutes at Large,* including sources for any amendments. This reference enables one to locate the original text, which may be the positive law form, and from there to find legislative history documents relating to the law's enactment. The *Code* also includes historical notes and cross-references to related sections. Illustration C shows the *U.S. Code* page on which the codified form of the session law in Illustration A begins.

The *U.S. Code* is reissued in a new edition every six years, and updated between editions by annual bound supplements. Each year's supplement incorporates material in preceding supplements, so that only the latest one need be consulted for changes since the last revision. Both *Code* and supplement are multivolume works. The 1982 edition consists of twenty-five volumes, and its *Supplement IV* fills eight volumes.

The *U.S. Code* features a number of useful research aids, including an extensive general index and several tables. The index for the 1982 *Code* fills five volumes. In the table of "Acts Cited by Popular Name," printed in the final text volume, laws are listed alphabetically under either short titles assigned by Congress or popular names by which they have become known. A person knowing only the name of an act can

11. The distinction between titles which are positive law and titles which are *prima facie* evidence is only rarely a matter of concern, since the code text is taken from the original language of the enactment. Certain changes in form or numbering may occur in order to fit the text into the existing code framework, but these variations are not substantive. Occasional errors have been made, however, so the distinction is of potential legal effect. *See, e.g., American Bank & Trust Co. v. Dallas County,* 463 U.S. 855, 864 n. 8 (1983); *Stephan v. United States,* 319 U.S. 423 (1943); *Royer's, Inc. v. United States,* 265 F.2d 615 (3d Cir.1959).

Illustration B

List of titles from *United States Code*, 1982 edition, with notice of reenactment

TITLES OF UNITED STATES CODE

*1. General Provisions.
2. The Congress.
*3. The President.
*4. Flag and Seal, Seat of Government, and the States.
*5. Government Organization and Employees; and Appendix.
†6. [Surety Bonds.]
7. Agriculture.
8. Aliens and Nationality.
*9. Arbitration.
*10. Armed Forces; and Appendix.
*11. Bankruptcy; and Appendix.
12. Banks and Banking.
*13. Census.
*14. Coast Guard.
15. Commerce and Trade.
16. Conservation.
*17. Copyrights.
*18. Crimes and Criminal Procedure; and Appendix.
19. Customs Duties.
20. Education.
21. Food and Drugs.
22. Foreign Relations and Intercourse.
*23. Highways.
24. Hospitals and Asylums.
25. Indians.
26. Internal Revenue Code.
27. Intoxicating Liquors.
*28. Judiciary and Judicial Procedure; and Appendix.
29. Labor.
30. Mineral Lands and Mining.
*31. Money and Finance.
*32. National Guard.
33. Navigation and Navigable Waters.
‡34. [Navy.]
*35. Patents.
36. Patriotic Societies and Observances.
*37. Pay and Allowances of the Uniformed Services.
*38. Veterans' Benefits.
*39. Postal Service.
40. Public Buildings, Property, and Works.
41. Public Contracts.
42. The Public Health and Welfare.
43. Public Lands.
*44. Public Printing and Documents.
45. Railroads.
46. Shipping.
47. Telegraphs, Telephones, and Radiotelegraphs.
48. Territories and Insular Possessions.
*49. Transportation; and Appendix.
50. War and National Defense; and Appendix.

*This title has been enacted as law. However, any Appendix to this title has not been enacted as law.
†This title was enacted as law and has been repealed by the enactment of Title 31.
‡This title has been eliminated by the enactment of Title 10.

Page III

use this table to find its citation in both the *Statutes at Large* and the *Code.*

A Tables volume contains various parallel conversion tables which provide references between earlier revisions and later texts, and between different forms of statutory publication. Table I covers U.S. Code titles that have been revised and renumbered since the adoption

Illustration C

A page from the *United States Code*, 1982 edition

§ 1311 TITLE 16—CONSERVATION Page 1074

year ending September 30, 1980, the Secretary shall not enter into agreements with owners and operators which would require payments to owners or operators in any calendar year under such agreements in excess of $10,000,000. In carrying out the program, in each fiscal year after the fiscal year ending September 30, 1980, the Secretary shall not enter into agreements with owners and operators which would require payments to owners or operators in any calendar year under such agreements in excess of $30,000,000. Not more than 15 percent of the funds authorized to be appropriated in any fiscal year after the fiscal year ending September 30, 1980, may be used for agreements entered into with owners or operators in any one State.

(Pub. L. 91-559, § 11, Dec. 19, 1970, 84 Stat. 1471; Pub. L. 96-182, § 4, Jan. 2, 1980, 93 Stat. 1317.)

AMENDMENTS

1980—Pub. L. 96-182 limited the restrictions on the Secretary's authority to enter into agreements in excess of $10,000,000 to each fiscal year through the fiscal year ending Sept. 30, 1980, and added restrictions relating to agreements in excess of $30,000,000 for each fiscal year after fiscal year ending Sept. 30, 1980, and that not more than 15 percent of the funds authorized to be appropriated in any fiscal year after the fiscal year ending Sept. 30, 1980, may be used for agreements entered into with owners or operators in any one State.

LIMITATIONS ON AUTHORIZATION OF APPROPRIATIONS FOR WATER BANK PROGRAMS FOR FISCAL YEARS 1982, 1983, AND 1984

Pub. L. 97-35, title I, § 120, Aug. 13, 1981, 95 Stat. 368, provided in part that, notwithstanding any other provision of law, there was authorized to be appropriated for necessary expenses to carry into effect the provisions of the Water Bank Act (16 U.S.C. 1301-1311) not to exceed $10,876,000 for fiscal year 1982, $10,854,000 for fiscal year 1983, and $10,813,000 for fiscal year 1984.

§ 1311. Rules and regulations

The Secretary shall prescribe such regulations as he determines necessary and desirable to carry out the provisions of this chapter.

(Pub. L. 91-559, § 12, Dec. 19, 1970, 84 Stat. 1471.)

CHAPTER 30—WILD HORSES AND BURROS: PROTECTION, MANAGEMENT, AND CONTROL

Sec.
1331. Congressional findings and declaration of policy.
1332. Definitions.
1333. Powers and duties of Secretary.
(a) Jurisdiction; management; ranges; ecological balance objectives; scientific recommendations; forage allocation adjustments.
(b) Inventory and determinations; consultation; overpopulation; research study: submittal to Congress.
(c) Title of transferee to limited number of excess animals adopted for requisite period.
(d) Loss of status as wild free-roaming horses and burros; exclusion from coverage.

Sec.
1334. Private maintenance; numerical approximation; strays on private lands: removal; destruction by agents.
1335. Recovery rights.
1336. Cooperative agreements; regulations.
1337. Joint advisory board; appointment; membership; functions; qualifications; reimbursement limitations.
1338. Criminal provisions.
(a) Violations; penalties; trial.
(b) Arrest; appearance for examination or trial; warrants: issuance and execution.
1338a. Transportation of captured animals; procedures and prohibitions applicable.
1339. Limitation of authority.
1340. Joint report to Congress; consultation and coordination of implementation, enforcement, and departmental activities; studies.

CHAPTER REFERRED TO IN OTHER SECTIONS

This chapter is referred to in title 43 section 1901.

§ 1331. Congressional findings and declaration of policy

Congress finds and declares that wild free-roaming horses and burros are living symbols of the historic and pioneer spirit of the West; that they contribute to the diversity of life forms within the Nation and enrich the lives of the American people; and that these horses and burros are fast disappearing from the American scene. It is the policy of Congress that wild free-roaming horses and burros shall be protected from capture, branding, harassment, or death; and to accomplish this they are to be considered in the area where presently found, as an integral part of the natural system of the public lands.

(Pub. L. 92-195, § 1, Dec. 15, 1971, 85 Stat. 649.)

SHORT TITLE

Pub. L. 92-195, Dec. 15, 1971, 85 Stat. 649, [enacting this chapter] is popularly known as the Wild Free-Roaming Horses and Burros Act.

§ 1332. Definitions

As used in this chapter—

(a) "Secretary" means the Secretary of the Interior when used in connection with public lands administered by him through the Bureau of Land Management and the Secretary of Agriculture in connection with public lands administered by him through the Forest Service;

(b) "wild free-roaming horses and burros" means all unbranded and unclaimed horses and burros on public lands of the United States;

(c) "range" means the amount of land necessary to sustain an existing herd or herds of wild free-roaming horses and burros, which does not exceed their known territorial limits, and which is devoted principally but not necessarily exclusively to their welfare in keeping with the multiple-use management concept for the public lands;

(d) "herd" means one or more stallions and his mares; and

(e) "public lands" means any lands administered by the Secretary of the Interior

of the Code in 1926, showing where former sections of the title are incorporated into the latest edition. Table II indicates the status of sections of the *Revised Statutes of 1878* within the Code, and Table III lists the *Statutes at Large* in chronological order and indicates where each section is incorporated into the Code. Other tables cover executive orders, proclamations, reorganization plans, and internal cross-references within the Code.

Although statutory provisions are often affected by judicial decisions, there is no indication or reflection in the *U.S. Code* of such interpretations, even if a statute has been declared unconstitutional. Sections of the Code are changed only by subsequent legislation, and an unconstitutional provision remains in the text with no warning of its status until it is actually repealed or amended. Before relying on a Code provision, it is therefore necessary to use other resources (such as the annotated editions of the Code or *Shepard's Citations*) to ascertain what judicial treatment may have occurred.

Despite this shortcoming, the *U.S. Code* is a well-prepared and effective research tool, accompanied by thorough indexing and helpful tables. Its publication is not as tardy as some other government publications such as the *Statutes at Large,* but its latest volumes still are generally eight months to two years out of date. For more current coverage, it is necessary to use one of the commercial annotated editions of the Code.

c. U.S. Code Annotated

In 1927 the West Publishing Company began publication of an unofficial, annotated edition of the U.S. Code, entitled *United States Code Annotated* (cited as U.S.C.A.). This edition retains the text and organization of the official version, employing identical title and section numbers. It provides the same research aids found in the official *Code,* such as authority references, historical notes, cross references, tables, and index. It has two major advantages for researchers: it also includes abstracts of decisions and references to secondary sources to aid in the interpretation of Code sections, and it is updated on a more frequent basis and in a variety of ways.

USCA includes several editorial features after each section of the Code, in addition to simply citing the *Statutes at Large* origin of the text. Where relevant, it also provides references to such sources as the *Code of Federal Regulations* and legislative history materials in *U.S. Code Congressional and Administrative News* (*USCCAN*). An annotation section labeled "Library References" contains citations to West's American Digest System topics and key numbers, to the legal encyclopedia *Corpus Juris Secundum,* and to West treatises on the statutory subject.

Following each Code section which has been interpreted or applied judicially, *USCA* provides "Notes of Decisions," consisting of abstracts of judicial decisions that have interpreted the particular section. These annotations are usually preceded by an alphabetical subject index, which assists in locating those on particular aspects or parts of the statutory section. Because judicial interpretations are a vital part of reading and understanding statutes, these case abstracts are the most important aspect of an annotated code. They also take a great deal of space, causing the *USCA* version of the Code to occupy well over 200 volumes. Illustrations D–1 and D–2 show a code section as printed in *USCA,* followed by various research aids and notes of decisions. Note in Illustration D–2 that the chapter was held unconstitutional in a U.S. District Court decision, which was reversed by the Supreme Court.

USCA provides extensive annotations of judicial decisions not only for the fifty titles of the U.S. Code, but for the provisions of the U.S. Constitution and for several major sets of court rules, such as the Federal Rules of Civil Procedure (in several volumes following Title 28) and the Federal Rules of Criminal Procedure (in several volumes following Title 18). These aspects of *USCA* will be discussed separately in the chapters on constitutional law (Chapter 6) and court rules (Chapter 9).

Access to *USCA* is provided by a multivolume general index for the entire set and individual indexes for each title. Indexes to individual titles are not updated until a volume is revised and replaced, but a new edition of the general index is issued each year in softcover volumes. The set also contains many of the same parallel conversion tables published in the *U.S. Code,* as well as a popular name table, which is located in the final general index volume.

USCA is far more current than the official edition, and is kept up to date by several forms of supplementation. The most basic of these is the annual pocket part, which is inserted in the back of each volume and indicates any changes in the statutory text, additional annotations to judicial decisions, and later notes and references to other sources. A list in the front of each pocket part indicates the cut-off point for coverage of decisions from the various reporter series. Illustration D–3 shows a page from a *USCA* pocket part, providing updated coverage of cases on wild horses and burros as well as the text of amendments to statutes on the protection of wild and scenic rivers.

Unlike official *U.S. Code* volumes, which are replaced every six years, *USCA* volumes are generally replaced when the supplement becomes unwieldy. Several new volumes are published each year, but parts of the set are several decades old. Every volume is up to date, though, since new statutes and annotations are printed in its current pocket part. Every time a *USCA* volume is used, its pocket part *must* be checked for more recent developments.

Between annual pocket parts, other forms of supplementation are used. Legislative and judicial developments are noted in quarterly noncumulative pamphlets supplementing the entire set. Each pamphlet is arranged by Code section, and contains the text of new laws and notes of recent decisions. The public laws printed in each pamphlet are listed on its front cover and spine, and the reporter volumes covered are listed in a table at the front of the pamphlet.

Illustration D-1

The first page of a chapter in *United States Code Annotated*

CHAPTER 30—WILD HORSES AND BURROS: PROTECTION, MANAGEMENT, AND CONTROL

Cross References

Necessity of amendments to this chapter to facilitate humane adoption or disposal of wild horses and burros, see section 1901 of Title 43, Public Lands.

§ 1331. Congressional findings and declaration of policy

Congress finds and declares that wild free-roaming horses and burros are living symbols of the historic and pioneer spirit of the West; that they contribute to the diversity of life forms within the Nation and enrich the lives of the American people; and that these horses and burros are fast disappearing from the American scene. It is the policy of Congress that wild free-roaming horses and burros shall be protected from capture, branding, harassment, or death; and to accomplish this they are to be considered in the area where presently found, as an integral part of the natural system of the public lands.

(Pub.L. 92–195, § 1, Dec. 15, 1971, 85 Stat. 649.)

136

Illustration D-2

Annotations for 16 U.S.C.A. § 1331 (West 1985)

Historical Note

Short Title. Pub.L. 92–195, Dec. 15, 1971, 85 Stat. 649 [enacting this chapter] is popularly known as the Wild Free-Roaming Horses and Burros Act.

Legislative History. For legislative history and purpose of Pub.L. 92–195, see 1971 U.S. Code Cong. and Adm.News, p. 2149.

Code of Federal Regulations

Purpose and objectives, see 43 CFR 4700.0–1 et seq.

Library References

Animals ⇐2.
Game ⇐3½, 7 et seq.
Public Lands ⇐7.

C.J.S. Animals §§ 4 to 9.
C.J.S. Game §§ 7, 10 et seq.
C.J.S. Public Lands §§ 3 to 5, 41.

Notes of Decisions

Common law 1
Constitutionality 2
Jurisdiction 4
State regulation or control 3

---

1. Common law

Under common law, wild animals are owned by state in its sovereign capacity, in trust for benefit of people, and this sovereign ownership vested in colonial government and was passed to states. State of N.M. v. Morton, D.C.N.M.1975, 406 F.Supp. 1237, reversed on other grounds 96 S.Ct. 2285, 426 U.S. 529, 49 L.Ed.2d 34, rehearing denied 97 S.Ct. 189, 429 U.S. 873, 50 L.Ed.2d 154.

2. Constitutionality

This chapter was constitutional exercise of congressional power under property clause, U.S.C.A. Const. Art. 4, § 3, cl. 2, at least insofar as it was applied to prohibit New Mexico Livestock Board from entering upon public lands of United States and removing wild burros under New Mexico Estray Law, 1953 Comp.N.M. § 47–14–1 et seq. Kleppe v. New Mexico, N.M.1976, 96 S.Ct. 2285, 426 U.S. 529, 49 L.Ed.2d 34, rehearing denied 97 S.Ct. 189, 429 U.S. 873, 50 L.Ed.2d 154.

In absence of any evidence to support theory and in absence of any congressional findings to indicate it was in any way based on U.S.C.A. Const. Art. 1, § 8, cl. 3, this chapter could not be sustained as exercise of power granted in commerce clause. State of N.M. v. Morton, D.C.N.M.1975, 406 F.Supp. 1237, reversed on other grounds 96 S.Ct. 2285, 426 U.S. 529, 49 L.Ed.2d 34, rehearing denied 97 S.Ct. 189, 429 U.S. 873, 50 L.Ed.2d 154.

3. State regulation or control

This chapter overrides New Mexico Estray Law, 1953 Comp.N.M. § 47–14–1 et seq., insofar as it attempts to regulate federally protected animals. Kleppe v. New Mexico, N.M.1976, 96 S.Ct. 2285, 426 U.S. 529, 49 L.Ed.2d 34, rehearing denied 97 S.Ct. 189, 429 U.S. 873, 50 L.Ed.2d 154.

4. Jurisdiction

This chapter does not establish exclusive federal jurisdiction over public lands in New Mexico. Kleppe v. New Mexico, N.M.1976, 96 S.Ct. 2285, 426 U.S. 529, 49 L.Ed.2d 34, rehearing denied 97 S.Ct. 189, 429 U.S. 873, 50 L.Ed.2d 154.

§ 1332. Definitions

As used in this chapter—

(a) "Secretary" means the Secretary of the Interior when used in connection with public lands administered by him through the Bureau of Land Management and the Secretary of Agriculture in connection with public lands administered by him through the Forest Service;

(b) "wild free-roaming horses and burros" means all unbranded and unclaimed horses and burros on public lands of the United States;

(c) "range" means the amount of land necessary to sustain an existing herd or herds of wild free-roaming horses and burros, which

Illustration D-3

Pocket part supplementation for *USCA*

§ 1283. Management policies

[See main volume for text of (a) and (b)]

(c) Water pollution

The head of any agency administering a component of the national wild and scenic rivers system shall cooperate with the Administrator, Environmental Protection Agency and with the appropriate State water pollution control agencies for the purpose of eliminating or diminishing the pollution of waters of the river.

(As amended Pub.L. 99-590, Title V, § 509, Oct. 30, 1986, 100 Stat. 3337.)

1986 Amendment. Subsec. (c). Pub.L. 99-590 substituted "Administrator, Environmental Protection Agency" for "Secretary of the Interior".

§ 1286. Definitions

As used in this chapter, the term—

[See main volume for text of (a) and (b)]

(c) "Scenic easement" means the right to control the use of land (including the air space above such land) within the authorized boundaries of a component of the wild and scenic rivers system, for the purpose of protecting the natural qualities of a designated wild, scenic or recreational river area, but such control shall not affect, without the owner's consent, any regular use exercised prior to the acquisition of the easement. For any designated wild and scenic river, the appropriate Secretary shall treat the acquisition of fee title with the reservation of regular existing uses to the owner as a scenic easement for purposes of this chapter. Such an acquisition shall not constitute fee title ownership for purposes of section 1277(b) of this title.

(As amended Pub.L. 99-590, Title V, § 510, Oct. 30, 1986, 100 Stat. 3337.)

1986 Amendment. Subsec. (c). Pub.L. 99-590 added provisions relating to function of appropriate Secretary for any designated wild and scenic river with respect to acquisition of fee title.

Law Review Commentaries

Governmentally created erosion on the seashore: The Fifth Amendment washed away. Leslie M. MacRae, 89 Dick.L.Rev. 101 (1984).

§ 1287. Authorization of appropriations

Code of Federal Regulations

Land uses, see 36 CFR 251.9 et seq.

CHAPTER 30—WILD HORSES AND BURROS: PROTECTION, MANAGEMENT AND CONTROL

§ 1332. Definitions

Notes of Decisions

Takings 2
Wild free-roaming horses and burros 1

2. Takings

Damage to private lands caused by wild horses and burros protected by the Wild Free-Roaming Horses and Burros Act did not constitute a "taking," entitling private owners to compensation from the government; although grazing habits of the animals diminished value of the property in question, such reduction in value did not constitute a taking, where property owners were not deprived of all "economically viable use" of their lands. Mountain States Legal Foundation v. Hodel, C.A.10 (Wyo.) 1986, 799 F.2d 1423, certiorari denied 107 S.Ct. 1616, 94 L.Ed.2d 800.

§ 1333. Powers and duties of Secretary

Notes of Decisions

Adoption of horses and burros 9

5. Population of horses

Secretary of Interior is not required to maintain wild horse population levels on public lands at levels existing at time of enactment of Wild Free-Roaming Horses and Burros Act and holders of

These quarterly pamphlets are further updated in two ways. During each legislative session, the monthly advance pamphlets of *USCCAN* contain the text of newly enacted statutes in chronological order, and provide parallel tables indicating the Code sections affected by the new laws. Recent judicial decisions can be found by using "Tables of Statutes Construed" in the front of all National Reporter System bound volumes and advance sheets. After checking to see when coverage in the latest pocket part or quarterly supplement ends, one can find recent federal cases by scanning these tables in the front of recent issues of the *Supreme Court Reporter* and lower federal court reporters.

d. U.S. Code Service

The second unofficial annotated federal code publication is the *United States Code Service* (cited as U.S.C.S.), published by Lawyers Co-operative Publishing Company. It was preceded by a similar compilation entitled *Federal Code Annotated,*[12] which contained some of the same features as its much improved successor.

USCS maintains the original title and section numbering of the *U.S. Code,* but there is some variation in the text. *USCS* preserves more closely the context and language of the original *Statutes at Large* text and uses parentheticals and notes for clarification. Illustrations E–1 and E–2 show two pages from *USCS.* Note in the section beginning at the bottom of Illustration E–2 that the text follows that in the *Statutes at Large* (Illustration A), unlike that in the *U.S. Code* and *USCA* (Illustrations C and D–2).

Like *USCA, USCS* expands on many of the research aids published in the *U.S. Code* (authority references, historical notes, cross-references, etc.), in a section titled "History; Ancillary Laws and Directives." It then provides references to the *Code of Federal Regulations,* and a "Research Guide," with references to *American Law Reports* (*ALR*) annotations, the Lawyers Co-op encyclopedia *American Jurisprudence 2d* (*Am.Jur.2d*), other Lawyers Co-op practice publications, and law review articles.

The case annotations following Code sections are located under the title "Interpretive Notes and Decisions." They are usually preceded by a detailed topical outline and include both judicial and administrative decisions. Illustration E–2 includes these various features following 16 U.S.C.S. § 1331.

Like *USCA, USCS* has a multivolume general index and individual title indexes. The *USCS* general index consists of several bound volumes which are updated in a single looseleaf volume. There are also several volumes of tables providing parallel references and citations from popular names.

USCS is updated in much the same way as *USCA.* Cumulative annual pocket parts show changes in statutory text and provide addi-

12. Published by Bobbs–Merrill, 1936–71, then acquired by Lawyers Co-op and replaced by volumes under the present title.

Illustration E-1

The first page of a chapter in *United States Code Service*

CHAPTER 30. WILD HORSES AND BURROS: PROTECTION, MANAGEMENT, AND CONTROL

CROSS REFERENCES

This chapter is referred to in 43 USCS § 1901.

Auto-Cite®: Any case citation herein can be checked for form, parallel references, later history, and annotation references through the Auto-Cite computer research system.

---

§ 1331. Congressional findings and declaration of policy

Congress finds and declares that wild free-roaming horses and burros are living symbols of the historic and pioneer spirit of the West; that they contribute to the diversity of life forms within the Nation and enrich the lives of the American people; and that these horses and burros are fast disappearing from the American scene. It is the policy of Congress that

551

tional annotations. Quarterly cumulative supplements entitled *Later Case and Statutory Service* function as interim supplementation be-

Illustration E–2

Continuation of text and annotations for 16 U.S.C.S. § 1331 (Law. Co-op. 1984)

wild free-roaming horses and burros shall be protected from capture, branding, harassment, or death; and to accomplish this they are to be considered in the area where presently found, as an integral part of the natural system of the public lands.

(Dec. 15, 1971, P. L. 92-195, § 1, 85 Stat. 649.)

HISTORY; ANCILLARY LAWS AND DIRECTIVES

Short titles:

Act Dec. 15, 1971, P. L. 92-195, 85 Stat. 649 [enacting 16 USCS §§ 1331 et seq.] is popularly known as the Wild Free-Roaming Horses and Burros Act.

CODE OF FEDERAL REGULATIONS

Range management, 36 CFR Part 222.
Prohibitions—Forest Service, Department of Agriculture, 36 CFR Part 261.
Wild free-roaming horse and burro protection, management, and control, 43 CFR Part 4700.
Law enforcement—criminal, 43 CFR Part 9260.

RESEARCH GUIDE

Am Jur:

63 Am Jur 2d, Public Lands § 30.

INTERPRETIVE NOTES AND DECISIONS

Wild Free-Roaming Horses and Burros Act (16 USCS §§ 1331 et seq.), enacted to protect all unbranded and unclaimed horses and burros on public lands of United States, is constitutional exercise of congressional power under property clause. Kleppe v New Mexico (1976) 426 US 529, 49 L Ed 2d 34, 96 S Ct 2285, reh den 429 US 873, 50 L Ed 2d 154, 97 S Ct 189.

In 1971, Congress enacted Wild Free-Roaming Horses and Burros Act (16 USCS §§ 1331–1340) to preserve primeval status of "all unbranded and unclaimed horses and burros on public lands of United States." American Horse Protection Asso. v United States Dept. of Interior (1977) 179 App DC 246, 551 F2d 432.

§ 1332. Definitions

As used in this Act [16 USCS §§ 1331 et seq.]—

(a) "Secretary" means the Secretary of the Interior when used in connection with public lands administered by him through the Bureau of Land Management and the Secretary of Agriculture in connection with public lands administered by him through the Forest Service;

(b) "wild free-roaming horses and burros" means all unbranded and unclaimed horses and burros on public lands of the United States;

(c) "range" means the amount of land necessary to sustain an existing herd or herds of wild free-roaming horses and burros, which does not exceed their known territorial limits, and which is devoted principally but not necessarily exclusively to their welfare in keeping with the multiple-use management concept for the public lands;

tween the annual pocket parts, and a monthly *Advance* pamphlet contains the text of newly enacted statutes, executive documents, court rules and selected regulations, with tables for determining which Code sections have been affected by recent legislative or administrative action.

Also like *USCA, USCS* devotes several heavily annotated volumes to the U.S. Constitution and to major sets of court rules. The rules volumes, however, are all shelved at the end of the set, rather than after particular titles to which they relate.

There are other differences between these two versions of federal statutes. *USCS,* for example, publishes the frequently amended Internal Revenue Code in a looseleaf format, with separate binder sections for Code text and annotations. It also includes a volume of annotations on *uncodified* laws, arranged by *Statutes at Large* citation. Generally, *USCA* tends to be more comprehensive, including notes of decisions that *USCS* editors exclude as obsolete or repetitive. (In Illustration E–2, *USCS* notes the Supreme Court decision upholding the chapter but omits the reversed lower court decision.) In another respect *USCS* is more comprehensive, because it provides notes of administrative decisions, which are not found in *USCA.* For many provisions, each edition will note some cases the other omits. At any given time, one of the competitors may also be a bit more up to date than the other.

Many researchers work in libraries that subscribe to only one annotated edition of the U.S. Code. For them there is no dilemma choosing which to use. A person with access to both *USCA* and *USCS* should become somewhat familiar with each, and will probably develop a personal preference for one or the other. One edition can be used on a regular basis for most research needs, but the other may occasionally be needed for its editorial features or to ensure comprehensive coverage.

e. *WESTLAW and LEXIS U.S. Code Databases*

The text of the U.S. Code is also available online for computerized research, in either WESTLAW or LEXIS. WESTLAW's database, USC, contains the statutory text and *Statutes at Large* references in the *United States Code Annotated,* but does not include any of *USCA* 's annotations or other research aids. LEXIS contains the Code as published in *USCS,* including the history notes and references to other Lawyers Co-op publications, but it too omits the notes of decisions.

The online Code databases are generally up to date within a few months or less. The currency of the Code or of particular titles is indicated on scope or directory screens, and should be checked before relying on an online search for current information.

The online researcher can retrieve a known statutory provision by searching for a particular citation, or can find statutes on a particular subject by searching for a combination of descriptive words. Because each of the three published versions of the Code is extensively indexed, the WESTLAW and LEXIS databases are most useful in situations where an issue is not adequately covered in indexes or where a combination of particular terms is important. If the interpretation of a statutory word or phrase is in issue, an online search can be used to quickly and efficiently retrieve all Code provisions using that word or phrase. A statute that would appear unrelated in an index may provide guidance on Congressional use of a particular term. Because the annotations in *USCA* and *USCS* are usually more descriptive than the formal statutory language, incorporating the annotations into the databases would enhance the ability to retrieve sections relevant to particular legal problems.

A search of the Code online retrieves only those *sections* which match the particular query. The systems treat each Code section as a separate document, so that there are over 40,000 sections or documents in a Code database. The online display of a section includes a heading indicating the title and chapter in which it belongs, but there is otherwise little perspective of its place in the subject scheme. A searcher can enter commands to display other sections classified before or after a section which matches the search query, and gain some sense of its context. Thus far, however, neither system allows users to view an index or table of contents, in order to see relationships between various code provisions.

D. FEDERAL STATUTORY RESEARCH

Because of the different forms of publication, research in statutory law varies considerably from that in case law. Although some of the approaches are similar, there are generally fewer finding tools other than subject indexes and tables. The emphasis is instead on regularly updated, heavily annotated primary sources. The need for extrinsic aids to statutory interpretation, such as judicial decisions and legislative history, gives an added dimension to statutory research. As with judicial decisions, the research process must include Shepard's citators to verify the current status and authority of a statute and to trace the history of its judicial and legislative treatment.

This section discusses general resources in federal statutory research. For specific areas other tools providing more editorial assistance may be available. Topical looseleaf services, for example, often print the text of relevant federal laws, provide notes of judicial and administrative decisions, and update texts promptly. A researcher in a subject area covered by a thorough looseleaf service may not need to use the broad finding and updating tools to be described here.[13] Other useful resources, particularly in areas *not* covered by looseleaf services, are compilations of statutes in particular subject fields, published on occasion by Congressional committees and government agencies with

13. The availability of additional legal texts (such as court decisions and administrative rulings and regulations), plus weekly supplementation, explanatory discussion, and varied indexing, make looseleaf services particularly useful sources for statutory research in specialized subject fields. They are more fully described in Chapter 10, and a selected list by subject appears in Appendix E.

responsibilities in those fields; by trade associations, public interest groups and labor unions; and by commercial publishers. These collections are rarely supplemented with adequate regularity, however, so it is usually necessary to update the search elsewhere.

1. FINDING STATUTES

Statutory research typically begins with a search to determine whether there are statutes applicable to the particular problem or topic under consideration, and then locating the relevant statutory provisions. Sometimes, however, one has a reference to a particular law by number or popular name, and merely needs a table to locate that statute in its code form. There are various indexes and tables for these purposes.

a. Indexes

Although statutory codes, like case digests, can be approached through a broad topical approach, this method involves the same disadvantages for statutory research as it does for cases. To select conceptually, from the fifty titles of the U.S. Code, the particular title most likely to deal with the problem under study, and then to scan its outline to identify relevant sections is far too uncertain and circuitous. Therefore, unless some identification of a particular statute is available, one generally analyzes the problem into its component issues, reduces those issues to specific catchwords or phrases, and then uses those search words in the subject index to one of the Code editions (if, as is usually the case, one is seeking all of the applicable statutory law, currently in force) or to a *Statutes at Large* volume (if one is seeking a law enacted in a particular session).

The index to the official *U.S. Code* is quite thorough and extensive, and is updated in the cumulative annual supplement. It forms the basis, in fact, for the indexes in both *USCA* and *USCS,* which make only slight modifications in its entries. The major advantage offered by the indexes in the annotated codes is that they are more frequently updated. The *USCA* index volumes are revised and reissued annually, and the *USCS* index is supplemented by the looseleaf "General Index Update Service." Material in the quarterly pamphlets updating both annotated codes is also indexed, for *USCA* in the back of each pamphlet and for *USCS* in an additional "Index to Cumulative Later Case and Statutory Service" in the looseleaf index update binder. Illustration F shows a page from the general index in the *U.S. Code.*

Every volume of the *Statutes at Large* has its own index, and there are also indexes for the annual volumes of *U.S. Code Congressional and Administrative News,* and cumulative indexes in each monthly issue of *USCCAN* and *USCS Advance.* The older indexes in bound volumes can be used to find laws from particular years, and the pamphlet indexes to find the latest laws passed by Congress.

Illustration F

A typical page from the General Index to the *United States Code*, 1982 edition

Most of these indexes include plenty of cross-references, which are of two basic types. Cross-references between subject headings provide notice of related statutes covered elsewhere in the index. Entries for terms which are *not* used as subject headings indicate the synonymous or related terms which are used instead. A researcher who looks in the index under "Cattle" finds references to "Animals," "Beef Research and Information," and "Dairies," rather than no entry at all. Since indexers cannot foresee all possible terms a researcher might use, of course, it may sometimes be necessary to reformulate a query before finding any information. If an issue turns out not to be covered by federal statutory law, there may be no index entry to be found.

For access to early federal laws, one can consult the indexes to earlier editions of the *U.S. Code,* the *Revised Statutes,* or individual *Statutes at Large* volumes. Two retrospective indexes to federal law prepared by the Library of Congress are also of occasional use in historical research. These indexes cover the periods indicated in their respective titles: M.G. Beaman & A.K. McNamara, *Index Analysis of the Federal Statutes, 1789–1873* (U.S. Government Printing Office, 1911), and W.H. McClenon & W.C. Gilbert, *Index to the Federal Statutes, 1874–1931* (U.S. Government Printing Office, 1933).[14] These include only general, public and permanent laws.

b. Tables

A researcher often has reference to a particular statute, and does not need to use a subject index. If the reference provides a current U.S. Code citation, access to the statute is no problem. Frequently, however, the reference gives only the name of a statute or provides an outdated or *Statutes at Large* citation. Two types of tables provide assistance in these situations.

Popular name tables consist of alphabetical lists of statutes, providing citations to their session law and codified locations. For an older statute, "popular name" often means a name with which it has come to be associated over time, such as "Mann Acts" or "White–Slave Laws." Most modern statutes, on the other hand, specify short titles by which they may be cited. These names, such as "Marine Plastic Pollution Research and Control Act of 1987," are also listed in popular name tables.

As noted above, all three editions of the U.S. Code include these tables. All three provide references to Public Law numbers, to *Statutes at Large* citation, and to Code location. Most codified acts are not printed all in one place, so the table usually lists scattered sections of the Code where provisions appear. The popular name table in the *U.S. Code* is quite thorough, but not as current as those in *USCA* and *USCS.* The *USCA* table is printed in the last index volume, which is reissued every year; the *USCS* table is in a bound volume with other tables,

14. The McClenon & Gilbert index superseded G.W. Scott & M.G. Beaman, *Index Analysis of the Federal Statutes, 1873–1907* (U.S. Govt. Printing Office, 1908).

updated by an annual pocket part. The *USCA* table is further updated by an "Alphabetical Table of Laws" in the front of each quarterly pamphlet, and a table near the back of each issue of *USCCAN,* which cumulates each month for the entire session of Congress. The *USCS* table is updated in the back of every quarterly *Cumulative Later Case and Statutory Service* and monthly *Advance* pamphlet. Illustration G shows a page from the *USCA* popular name table.

Another popular name table covering federal laws is most useful to the researcher who has only the name of an act and does not know whether it came from Congress or a state legislature: *Shepard's Acts and Cases by Popular Names: Federal and State.* This work will be discussed with tools of state statutory research on page 182 below.

The other tables that allow access to statutes are *parallel reference tables.* These tables list one citation for a statute, typically its session law location, and provide a cross-reference to another citation where it may be found, usually as codified. The most extensive and useful parallel reference tables in federal statutory research are from Public Law number or *Statutes at Large* citation to the U.S. Code. All three versions of the Code have such tables, and the *USCA* and *USCS* tables are updated in the accompanying quarterly and monthly pamphlets. The newer tables add citations for new statutes and update information on older statutes that have been repealed or moved. Illustration H shows a page from the *Statutes at Large* parallel reference table in *USCS.*

Other parallel reference tables in all three Code editions provide access from *Revised Statutes* sections to U.S. Code sections, and explain the disposition of sections of Code titles which have been revised. The latter tables can be very handy if one has a reference to a Code section from an older case or article, but upon trying to locate the text finds either nothing at all or an unrelated provision.

2. UPDATING STATUTES

Just as finding decisions is not all there is to case research, finding statutes through indexes, tables, or other means is just the first step of statutory research. Before relying on a statute as authority, one must verify that it is still in force and ascertain how it has been affected by subsequent legislation and by judicial decisions.

a. USCA *and* USCS

One reason that annotated codes are such powerful research tools is that they serve two essential functions: they print the text of a primary authority and they provide regularly updated information on its validity and treatment. The frequent and varied supplementation for *USCA* and *USCS* has already been described. These updating materials provide the text of amendments to a statutory provision and include carefully edited, topically arranged annotations of interpretive judicial decisions. A case researcher must do a good deal of work to

Illustration G

A page from the Popular Name Table in *USCA*

POPULAR NAME TABLE 1332

White Cane Safety Day Act
Pub. L. 88–628, Oct. 6, 1964, 78 Stat. 1003 (Title 36, § 169d)

White Charger Act
Pub. L. 86–616, § 10, July 12, 1960, 74 Stat. 395 (Title 10, § 3297 note)

White Earth Reservation Land Settlement Act of 1985
Pub.L. 99–264, Mar. 24, 1986, 100 Stat. 61 (Title 25, § 331 note)
Pub. L. 100–153, § 6(a), (b), Nov. 5, 1987, 101 Stat. 887 (Title 25, § 331 notes)
Pub.L. 100–212, § 4, Dec. 24, 1987, 101 Stat. 212 (Title 25, § 331 note)

White House Conference for a Drug Free America
Pub.L. 99–570, Title I, §§ 1931 to 1938, Oct. 27, 1986, 100 Stat. 3207–56 (Title 20, § 4601 note)
Pub. L. 100–138, §§ 1 to 3, Oct. 23, 1987, 101 Stat. 820, 821 (Title 20, § 4601 notes)

White House Conference on Handicapped Individuals Act
Pub. L. 93–516, title III, Dec. 7, 1974, 88 Stat. 1631 (Title 29, § 701 note)
Pub. L. 93–651, title III, Nov. 21, 1974, 89 Stat. 2–16 (Title 29, § 701 note)
Pub. L. 94–224, §§ 1, 2, Feb. 27, 1976, 90 Stat. 201 (Title 29, § 701 note)

White House Conference on Productivity Act
Pub. L. 97–367, Oct. 25, 1982, 96 Stat. 1761 (Title 15, § 2401 note)

White House Conference on Small Business Authorization Act
Pub.L. 98–276, May 8, 1984, 98 Stat. 169 (Title 15, § 631 note)

White House Police Act
Apr. 22, 1940, ch. 133, 54 Stat. 156 (See Title 3, § 203)

White Phosphorous Matches Act
Apr. 9, 1912, ch. 75, 37 Stat. 81

White Pine Blister Rust Protection Act
Apr. 26, 1940, ch. 159, 54 Stat. 168 (Title 16, § 594a)
July 1, 1978, Pub. L. 95–313, § 13(a)(2), 92 Stat. 374 (Title 16, § 594a)

White Russian Act
June 8, 1934, ch. 429, 48 Stat. 926

White-Slave Laws
Mar. 26, 1910, ch. 128, 36 Stat. 263
June 25, 1910, ch. 395, 36 Stat. 825 (See Title 18, §§ 2421–2424)

White-Slave Traffic Act
See White-Slave Laws

Whitman Mission National Historic Site
Pub. L. 87–471, May 31, 1962, 76 Stat. 90 (Title 16, § 433n)

Wholesome Meat Act
Pub. L. 90–201, Dec. 15, 1967, 81 Stat. 584 (Title 19, § 1306; Title 21, §§ 601–623, 641–645, 661, 671–680, 691)

Wholesome Poultry Products Act
Pub. L. 90–492, Aug. 18, 1968, 82 Stat. 791 (Title 21, §§ 451–461, 463–465, 467, 467a–467f, 470)

Widows' Pension Act
Apr. 19, 1908, ch. 147, 35 Stat. 64

Wilcox Air Base Act
Aug. 12, 1935, ch. 511, § 4, 49 Stat. 610 (See Title 10, § 9774)

Wild and Scenic Rivers Act
Pub. L. 90–542, Oct. 2, 1968, 82 Stat. 906 (Title 16, §§ 1271–1287)
Pub. L. 92–560, § 2, Oct. 25, 1972, 86 Stat. 1174 (Title 16, § 1274)
Pub. L. 93–279, § 1, May 10, 1974, 88 Stat. 122 (Title 16, §§ 1274, 1275, 1276, 1278, 1286, 1287)
Pub. L. 93–621, § 1, Jan. 3, 1975, 88 Stat. 2094 (Title 16, §§ 1275, 1276, 1278)
Pub. L. 94–199, §§ 3(a), 5(a), Dec. 31, 1975, 89 Stat. 1117, 1118 (Title 16, §§ 1274, 1276)
Pub. L. 94–273, § 2(11), Apr. 21, 1976, 90 Stat. 375 (Title 16, § 1287)

Illustration H

A typical parallel reference table in *USCS*

85 Stat STATUTES AT LARGE 92d Cong

Pub. L	Section	Stat. Page	USCS Title	USCS Section	Status
		1971 Dec—Cont'd			
92-184—Cont'd					
		638-642	Appn.		Un-class.
92-185	1	642	38	765	
	2	643	38	765 nt	
92-186	1-3	643	Spec.		Un-class.
92-187	1	644	5	2108	
	2	644	5	5924	
	3	644	5	7152	
92-188	1	645	38	703, 741	
	2	645	38	707	
	3	645	38	prec 701	
	4	645	38	707 nt	
92-189	1	646	25	640a nt	
	2	646	25	640a	
	3	646	25	640b	
	4	646	25	640c	
	5		25	640c-1	Added
	6		25	640c-2	Added
92-190		646	31	52b	
92-191	1	647	18	1716	
	2	647	39	3001	
	3	647	18	1716 nt	
92-192		647	Spec.		Un-class.
92-193		648	38	704	
92-194		648	5	5542	
92-195	1	649	16	1331	
	2	649	16	1332	
	3	649	16	1333	
	4	650	16	1334	
	5	650	16	1335	
	6	650	16	1336	
	7	650	16	1337	
	8	650	16	1338	
	9		16	1338a	Added
	10[9]	651	16	1339	Redes.
	11[10]	651	16	1340	Redes.
92-196		651-660	Local		Un-class.
92-197	1	660	38	411	
	2	660	38	413	
	3	661	38	414	
	4	661	38	415	
	5	662	38	417	
	6	662	38	321, 341	
	7	662	38	724	
	8	662	38	417 nt	
	9	662	38	322	
	10	662	38	411 nt	
92-198	1(a), (b)	663	38	521	
	• 1(c), (d), (e)	663	38	541	
	1(f)	664	38	542	
	2	664	38	503	
	3	664	38	3012	
	4	664	38	521 nt	
	5	664	38	101	

Pub. L.	Section	Stat. Page	USCS Title	USCS Section	Status
		1971 Dec—Cont'd			
92-198—Cont'd					
	6	664	38	521 nt	
92-199		664	Spec.		Un-class.
		1971 Dec. 17			
92-200	1-10	665-680	Local		Un-class.
		1971 Dec. 18			
92-201		681	Appn.		Un-class.
92-202		682-685	Appn.		Un-class.
	1-18	686, 687	Appn.		Un-class.
92-203	1	688	43	1601 nt	
	2	688	43	1601	
	3	689	43	1602	
	4	689	43	1603	
	5	690	43	1604	
	6	690	43	1605	
	7	691	43	1606	
	8	694	43	1607	
	9	694	43	1608	
	10	696	43	1609	
	11	696	43	1610	
	12	701	43	1611	
	13	702	43	1612	
	14	702	43	1613	
	15	705	43	1614	
	16	705	43	1615	
	17	706	43	1616	
	18	710	43	1617	
	19	710	43	1618	
	20	710	43	1619	
	21	713	43	1620	
	22	713	43	1621	
	23	715	43	1622	
	24	715	43	1623	
	25	715	43	1624	
	26, 27	715, 716	43	1601 nts	
	28		43	1625	Added
	29		43	1626	Added
	30		43	1627	Added
	31		43	1628	Added
92-204		716-720	Appn.		Un-class.
	301	720	10	4308 nt	
		721-726	Appn.		Un-class.
	701, 702	726	Appn.		Un-class.
	703	726	31	700	
	704	726	Appn.		Un-class.
	705	727	31	649a	
	706, 707	727	Appn.		Un-class.

182

update a decision, but a statutory researcher finds much of the work already done by the annotated code.

b. Shepard's Statutory Citators

For the most thorough and up-to-date information on the status of a particular statutory provision, its citation should be Shepardized in the statutory unit of *Shepard's United States Citations.* For federal statutes, Shepard's indicates any subsequent legislation or federal court decision citing a provision. Much of what appears in a Shepard's listing will also be noted in *USCA* and *USCS,* but Shepardizing can retrieve cases which were not included in annotations as well as recent legislative developments that may not yet be incorporated into the Code.

One advantage Shepard's has over the annotated codes is that it is arranged by the *exact* provision which has been cited. A researcher trying to interpret a specific subsection can use Shepard's to find cases citing that subsection. A case citing a range of sections, on the other hand, is listed under an entry indicating the entire range, so one must check not only the listing for a specific section but any listings for relevant ranges of sections. Illustration I shows a sample page from *Shepard's U.S. Citations.* Note the entries under "§ 1331 et seq.," "§§ 1331 to 1340," and the various subsections of § 1332.

A statute may be cited in a variety of ways—by its *Statutes at Large* citation, under a former classification in the U.S. Code, or by its present Code citation. For statutes currently in force, Shepard's lists all citing references under the current Code citation. If citations appeared in a Shepard's volume published *before* a provision was codified or moved, however, one would have to search under the citation by which the statute was known at the time of publication to find these older references.

As it does for cases, Shepard's uses signals to indicate significant judicial and legislative actions affecting a cited statute. These signals precede citing references, and indicate, for example, whether a provision has been amended or repealed by subsequent legislation or declared unconstitutional or invalid in a court decision. These abbreviations are explained at the beginning of each Shepard's statutory volume. Illustration J shows the signals used in *Shepard's U.S. Citations.* Note in Illustration I that § 1331 was held unconstitutional (U) by the District Court and constitutional (C) by the Supreme Court.

Shepard's U.S. Citations plays a particularly important role for statutory provisions not included in the current *U.S. Code.* There are separate sections for provisions in older editions of the *Code* and for provisions printed only in the *Statutes at Large* (including the *Revised Statutes*). This is usually the easiest way to find cases citing statutes no longer in effect or published only as session laws. (While *USCS* does include a volume of annotations on uncodified laws and treaties, it

Illustration I

A page from *Shepard's United States Citations*, statute edition

UNITED STATES CODE '82 Ed.

T. 16 § 1244

Subsec. f
A94St68
Subd. 1
A97St45
Subd. 3
Ad97St45
Subd. 4
Ad97St45
§ 1245
A92St3515
A97St45
§ 1246
Subsec. a
A92St3515
A97St45
A97St46
Subsec. b
A92St3515
A97St46
Subsec. c
A92St3516
A97St46
Subsec. d
A92St160
A92St3516
Subsec. e
A92St3516
A97St45
Subsec. f
A97St46
ClCt
8ClC177
Subsec. g
A92St160
A92St3516
A97St47
Subsec. h
A92St3516
A97St47
448US36
65LE579
100SC2520
Subsec. i
A92St3516
A97St47
Subsec. j
Ad97St47
Subsec. k
Ad97St48
§ 1247
Subsec. a
A92St3516
Subsec. d
RnSubsec e
[97St48
Subsec. d
(97St48)
Ad97St48
§ 1249
A92St160
Subsec. a
A92St3517
A97St48
Subsec. c
Ad92St3517
A94St1360
A94St68
A97St49
Subd. 2
Ad97St49
§ 1250
Ad97St49

§ 1251
Ad97St50
§ 1271
et seq.
Cir. DC
533F2d705
750F2d1086
Cir. 3
536FS46
Cir. 4
393FS1116
Cir. 5
470F2d1124
489F2d569
Cir. 6
497F2d1238
410FS760
Cir. 8
470F2d297
325FS728
342FS1211
564FS1092
Cir. 9
532F2d670
701F2d830
393FS624
405FS13
500FS189
539FS699
589FS1141
Cir. 10
570F2d1366
725F2d560
ClCt
5ClC414
CtCl
607F2d936
EP§ 6.33
11ARF574n
§§ 1271 to
1287
Cir. 1
711F2d474
544FS514
Cir. 8
524FS321
524FS689
Cir. 9
716F2d716
732F2d1464
737F2d785
Cir. 10
568FS587
ClCt
5ClC413
§ 1271
Cir. 4
393FS1118
Cir. 8
524FS322
524FS691
564FS1090
Cir. 9
595F2d6
ClCt
5ClC414
CtCl
607F2d940
§ 1272
Cir. 4
393FS1116
Cir. 8
564FS1090
CtCl
607F2d940

§ 1273
A90St1238
429US891
50LE174
97SC250
CtCl
607F2d938
Subsec. a
A92St3533
Cir. 1
544FS514
Cir. 4
393FS1118
Cir. 8
564FS1094
Subd. 1
Cir. DC
533F2d704
Subd. 2
Cir. DC
533F2d704
Cir. 4
393FS1116
Cir. 9
732F2d1467
Subsec. b
Cir. 4
393FS1116
EP§ 6.33
§ 1274
Cir. DC
533F2d704
Cir. 4
393FS1118
Cir. 9
754F2d1509
ClCt
5ClC414
Subsec. a
Subd. 1
Cir. 9
716F2d716
Subd. 2
Cir. 8
636F2d238
Subd. 3
A90St2330
Subd. 6
A94St3370
ClCt
5ClC414
Subd. 9
Ad86St1174
Subd. 10
Ad88St122
A92St3533
Subd. 11
Ad89St1117
Subd. 12
Ad89St1117
Cir. 9
660F2d737
Subd. 13
Ad90St2327
Subd. 14
Ad90St2327
Subd. 15
Ad90St2329
Subd. 16
Ad92St3521
A98St1714

Subd. 17
Ad92St3522
Subd. 18
Ad92St3522
Subd. 19
Ad92St3523
A93St666
Subd. 20
Ad92St3527
Subd. 21
Ad92St3528
Subd. 22
Ad92St3528
A94St1137
Subd. 23
Ad92St3529
Cir. Fed.
740F2d934
Subd. 24
Ad94St952
Subds. 25 to
50
Ad94St2412
Subd. 51
Ad98St1491
Ad98St1714
Subd. 52
(98St1632)
Ad98St1632
Subd. 52
(98St2274)
Ad98St2274
Subd. 53
Ad98St2274
Subsec. b
A92St3533
§ 1275
Cir. DC
533F2d704
Subsec. a
Rs88St122
A88St2094
Subsec. b
A90St2330
Cir. 8
564FS1094
§ 1276
A88St122
A88St2094
A92St3530
Cir. DC
533F2d709
Cir. 4
393FS1116
Subsec. a
Cir. DC
533F2d704
Subd. 22
Cir. Fed.
740F2d934
Subd. 24
Cir. DC
627F2d504
Subd. 47
A90St2330
Subd. 57
Ad89St1118
Subd. 58
Ad90St2330
Subd. 76
Ad94St68

Subds. 77 to
88
Ad94St2415
Subd. 89
Ad98St261
Subd. 90
(98St2259)
Ad98St2259
Subd. 90
(98St2274)
Ad98St2274
Subsec. b
A94St68
A98St2260
Cir. 8
564FS1094
Subd. 3
A93St667
A98St2259
Subd. 4
A93St667
Ad94St2415
Subd. 5
Ad94St2415
§ 1277
ClCt
5ClC414
EP§ 6.33
Subsec. a
Cir. 8
524FS690
564FS1090
Cir. 9
500FS189
Subsec. b
Cir. 8
524FS690
Cir. 9
500FS189
Subsec. c
Cir. 8
564FS1091
Subsec. d
ClCt
8ClC177
Subsec. e
Cir. 8
636F2d237
Subsec. g
Subd. 3
A92St3533
§ 1278
429US891
50LE174
97SC250
Cir. DC
627F2d504
Cir. 1
544FS514
Cir. 4
393FS1119
CtCl
607F2d935
EP§ 6.34
Subsec. a
A90St1238
Cir. DC
533F2d709
627F2d507
Cir. 1
711F2d474
CtCl
607F2d941

Subsec. b
Cir. DC
533F2d708
627F2d504
Cir. 4
393FS1116
Subd. 1
Rs88St122
A88St2094
Cir. DC
533F2d709
Cir. 4
393FS1116
Subd. 2
A88St122
Cir. DC
533F2d709
Cir. 4
393FS1123
§ 1279
CtCl
607F2d941
Subsec. b
A94St2417
§ 1280
CtCl
607F2d941
EP§ 6.34
Subsec. a
Subd. 3
Cir. 9
529FS996
Cir. Fed.
740F2d934
Subsec. b
A94St2416
Cir. Fed.
740F2d934
EP§ 6.34
§ 1281
ClCt
5ClC414
CtCl
607F2d941
Subsec. a
Cir. 8
564FS1094
Cir. 9
660F2d737
ClCt
5ClC414
Subsec. b
ClCt
5ClC414
Subsec. c
Cir. 9
543FS791
ClCt
5ClC414
Subsec. d
Cir. 8
636F2d237
Cir. 9
660F2d737
Subsec. e
Cir. 8
564FS1091
§ 1283
Subsec. a
A92St3533
Cir. 9
589FS1151

§ 1284
Subsec. a
Cir. DC
627F2d1248
Subsec. b
Cir. 1
544FS515
Subsec. d
Cir. 9
709F2d1256
§ 1285a
Ad92St3534
§ 1285b
Ad94St2416
§ 1286
Subsec. c
A88St122
Cir. 8
524FS690
564FS1091
Cir. 9
500FS189
§ 1287
Rs88St122
A92St3532
§ 1301
et seq.
Cir. 8
477F2d1034
348FS338
§§ 1301 to
1311
Cir. 8
473F2d347
§ 1301
ClCt
8ClC178
§ 1302
A93St1317
464US316
78LE501
104SC658
§ 1304
A93St1317
ClCt
8ClC178
§ 1310
A93St1317
§ 1311
et seq.
Cir. 9
529FS985
§ 1311
464US316
78LE501
104SC658
§ 1331
et seq.
C426US531
C49LE34
C96SC2286
Cir. 5
742F2d174
Cir. 8
552F2d822
499FS1260
Cir. 9
608F2d815
679F2d151
C685F2d338
403FS1206
460FS881
471FS524
471FS992
504FS365
Cir. 10

740F2d793
EP§ 6.13
49LE1246n
49LE1268n
§§ 1331 to
1340
448US35
65LE579
100SC2520
Cir. DC
551F2d433
694F2d1311
Cir. 9
601F2d1083
626F2d620
590FS1372
Cir. 10
740F2d795
465FS662
574FS1532
§ 1331
C426US531
C49LE38
C96SC2288
Cir. DC
551F2d433
694F2d1311
Cir. 9
608F2d811
626F2d620
C685F2d339
403FS1207
600FS587
Cir. 10
740F2d795
U406FS1237
§ 1332
Cir. 10
740F2d795
U406FS1237
Subsec. a
Cir. DC
551F2d433
Subsec. b
C426US531
C49LE38
C96SC2288
Cir. DC
551F2d433
Cir. 9
626F2d621
C685F2d339
403FS1208
C504FS366
Cir. 10
740F2d796
U406FS1238
Subsec. c
Cir. DC
694F2d1317
Subsec. f
Ad92St1810
Cir. DC
694F2d1317
Cir. 9
600FS588
§ 1333
Cir. 9
403FS1217
Cir. 10
740F2d795
U406FS1237
574FS1535

covers only a fraction of the many court citations to the *Statutes at Large.*)

Illustration J

Table of abbreviations used in *Shepard's United States Citations*, statute edition

ABBREVIATIONS—ANALYSIS

Form of Statute

Amend.	Amendment	Proc.	Proclamation
App.	Appendix	Pt.	Part
Art.	Article	Res.	Resolution
Ch.	Chapter	§	Section
Cl.	Clause	St.	Statutes at Large
Ex. Ord.	Executive Order	Subch.	Subchapter
H.C.R.	House Concurrent Resolution	Subcl.	Subclause
No.	Number	Subd.	Subdivision
¶	Paragraph	Sub ¶	Subparagraph
P.L.	Public Law	Subsec.	Subsection
Pr.L.	Private Law	Vet. Reg.	Veterans' Regulations

Operation of Statute

Legislative

A	(amended)	Statute amended.
Ad	(added)	New section added.
E	(extended)	Provisions of an existing statute extended in their application to a later statute, or allowance of additional time for performance of duties required by a statute within a limited time.
L	(limited)	Provisions of an existing statute declared not to be extended in their application to a later statute.
R	(repealed)	Abrogation of an existing statute.
Re-en	(re-enacted)	Statute re-enacted.
Rn	(renumbered)	Renumbering of existing sections.
Rp	(repealed in part)	Abrogation of part of an existing statute.
Rs	(repealed and superseded)	Abrogation of an existing statute and substitution of new legislation therefor.
Rv	(revised)	Statute revised.
S	(superseded)	Substitution of new legislation for an existing statute not expressly abrogated.
Sd	(suspended)	Statute suspended.
Sdp	(suspended in part)	Statute suspended in part.
Sg	(supplementing)	New matter added to an existing statute.
Sp	(superseded in part)	Substitution of new legislation for part of an existing statute not expressly abrogated.
Va	(validated)	

Judicial

C	Constitutional.	V	Void or invalid.
U	Unconstitutional.	Va	Valid.
Up	Unconstitutional in part.	Vp	Void or invalid in part.

ABBREVIATIONS—COURTS

Cir. DC–U.S. Court of Appeals, District of Columbia Circuit
Cir. (number)–U.S. Court of Appeals Circuit (number)
Cir. Fed.–U.S. Court of Appeals, Federal Circuit
CCPA–Court of Customs and Patent Appeals

The scope of citing references in the statute sections of *Shepard's U.S. Citations* is limited to subsequent statutes and treaties, federal court decisions, *ALR* or *Lawyers' Edition* annotations, and the *American Bar Association Journal.* Citations in state cases and acts or in law reviews are *not* included. To find state court decisions or legislative acts citing a federal statute, one must turn to Shepard's citators for each individual state. Articles citing federal statutes in nineteen leading law reviews are listed in *Shepard's Federal Law Citations in Selected Law Reviews.* Like *Shepard's U.S. Citations,* these citators list statutes in force under their current Code citation and other provisions under earlier *Code* or *Statutes at Large* citations.

As discussed in Chapter 3, Shepard's case citators can be used either in print or online through WESTLAW or LEXIS. Electronic access is *not* available for Shepard's statutory citators, however, so the only way to Shepardize a federal statute is through the books and pamphlets of *Shepard's United States Citations,* Shepard's state citators, and *Shepard's Federal Law Citations in Selected Law Reviews.* Citations to statutes in decisions and articles can be found using the online systems, but only by searching in full-text case or periodical databases. Such a search, using either the title or citation of a statute, will often find very recent references that have yet to be covered by either an annotated code or Shepard's.

3. INTERPRETING STATUTES

The procedures for finding and updating statutes just described constitute the basic methods of statutory research. An essential purpose of such research is to determine what Congress meant by a particular enactment. To do so, one must use resources discussed more fully in other chapters of this book. Because they are treated elsewhere, the following materials are only noted here.

a. Judicial Decisions

Judicial interpretations and constructions of ambiguous or controverted statutory language are often used to establish the meaning of a statute. Such interpretations may have been made in earlier cases dealing with the specific statute, or in cases involving other statutes containing similar provisions or language. Relevant decisions can be located through several methods, including: (1) reading the annotations in *USCA* or *USCS;* (2) Shepardizing a statutory provision; or (3) searching WESTLAW or LEXIS full-text case databases for references to a statute by citation or name. The publication of judicial decisions and procedures of case research have been discussed in Chapters 2 through 4.

b. Legislative History

To determine the meaning of a statutory provision, one can investigate the legislative documents that led to its enactment. Various versions of a bill, reports of Senate and House Committees that considered the proposed legislation, transcripts of floor debates, and other Congressional materials may all be of use in interpreting the text of a statute. These legislative history documents, and the finding aids and research procedures for their investigation, are treated in detail in Chapter 7.

c. *Other Resources*

Statutes are often discussed in looseleaf services, periodical articles, and treatises. Such discussions may be quite helpful in statutory research and interpretation, and often include references to cases, other statutes, legislative history materials, and regulations. Specialized finding aids of varying quality exist for each of these types of secondary material. Looseleaf services will be discussed in Chapter 10; legal periodicals in Chapter 11; and treatises in Chapter 12.

Attorney general opinions are an important source of persuasive statutory interpretation on the *state* level, but U.S. Attorney General opinions are not prepared or consulted on such a regular basis. They may be of occasional use, however, and are discussed in Chapter 8.

E. OTHER FORMS OF FEDERAL LEGISLATION

Statutes are not the only form of federal legislation. Most of the following additional legislative materials are discussed elsewhere, but they should be noted in this context.

1. U.S. CONSTITUTION

The federal Constitution is the basic, organic legislation of the United States, and appears in a variety of published sources. These publications, and research in constitutional law generally, are discussed in Chapter 6.

2. TREATIES

Treaties are international agreements negotiated between sovereign powers. Article VI of the Constitution provides that treaties made under the authority of the United States have the same legal authority and force as statutes. They are a special kind of federal legislation because they do not follow the usual enactment process through Congress. Under Article II, § 2, the President "shall have Power, by and with the Advice and Consent of the Senate to make treaties, provided two thirds of the Senators present concur." Treaty legislation thus arises in the executive branch but requires legislative approval to become law. The publication and research sources for treaties are discussed in detail in Chapter 15.

3. INTERSTATE COMPACTS

The Constitution, as interpreted by the courts, authorizes agreements between the states, provided they are first approved by Congress.[15] After the compact is agreed upon the states, it goes to Congress for authorizing legislation. When enacted, each compact thus appears in the *U.S. Statutes at Large* and in the session laws of the states which are parties to it. The Council of State Governments publishes a description of such compacts in *Interstate Compacts & Agencies,* which is revised from time to time and updated between revisions in the Council's biennial publication, the *Book of the States.*

Most interstate compacts also appear in the annotated statutory codes of the states enacting them, and are listed as cited material (by their statutory enactment) in Shepard's statutory citators. One can use either of those publications to locate cases which have applied or interpreted interstate compacts.

4. REORGANIZATION PLANS

Reorganization plans are an unusual hybrid form of legislation. They consist of Presidential proposals to reorganize executive agencies below the departmental level, submitted to Congress for approval pursuant to a general authorizing statute. Reorganization plans are treated with other Presidential lawmaking materials in Chapter 8.

F. STATE STATUTORY RESEARCH

Statutory research approaches on the state level are quite similar to the federal paradigm already discussed at length. This section will be more brief, and assumes familiarity with principles outlined in the preceding sections on statutory publication generally and federal statutory research.

1. SLIP LAWS AND SESSION LAWS

State statutes are enacted and published in a manner similar to the federal pattern. Most states publish their statutes initially in a slip law form, but some do not.[16] All states publish bound session law volumes. The titles of these publications vary from state to state (*e.g., Alaska Session Laws, California Statutes, Acts and Resolves of Massachusetts, Laws of New York*); they are listed with other state primary sources in Appendix B at the back of this volume. Like the *U.S. Statutes at Large,* they all print acts chronologically and include noncumulative subject indexes and tables. Illustrations K–1 and K–2 show pages from a state session law publication.

Official state session laws are usually not published until well after the end of a legislative session. In over half of the states, commercially

15. Article I, § 10 provides: "No state shall, without the Consent of Congress, . . . enter into any Agreement or Compact with another State. . . ." For further information, see F.L. Zimmerman & M. Wendell, *The Law and Use of Interstate Compacts* (Council of State Governments, 1976).

16. For information on the availability of state slip laws and on state legislative activity generally, see M.L. Fisher, *Guide to State Legislative and Administrative Materials,* 4th ed. (Rothman, 1988) and L. Hellebust, *State Legislative Sourcebook* (Government Research Service, annual).

Illustration K-1

Title page of 1980 *Oklahoma Session Laws*

OKLAHOMA
SESSION LAWS
1980

THIRTY-SEVENTH LEGISLATURE

SECOND REGULAR SESSION
Convened January 8, 1980
Adjourned Sine Die June 16, 1980

FIRST EXTRAORDINARY SESSION
Convened July 7, 1980
Adjourned Sine Die July 11, 1980

GEORGE NIGH, GOVERNOR
GENE C. HOWARD, President Pro Tempore of the Senate
DANIEL D. DRAPER, JR., Speaker of the House of Representatives

published advance session law services, sometimes known as "legislative services," provide quicker access to current acts. These monthly or bimonthly pamphlets are generally issued by the publisher of a state's annotated code, as a form of supplementation to the code. They are similar to West's *USCCAN* (but without the legislative history component) and to the *USCS Advance* pamphlets. These services are listed in Appendix B for those states for which they are available.

Those services published by the West Publishing Company are available electronically through WESTLAW, and online access for

Illustration K-2

Sample page in 1980 *Oklahoma Session Laws*

Ch. 74 LAWS THIRTY-SEVENTH LEGISLATURE

SECTION 2. 70 O.S.1971, Section 2-106, is amended to read as follows:

§ 2-106. Withdrawal of candidate

A person who has filed a notification and declaration as a candidate for membership on a board of education may withdraw his name as a candidate upon a sworn affidavit presented to the office of the county election board before ballot printing begins for any election in which his name will appear as a candidate.

Section 3. **Poll watchers** 38a

Any candidate for office of a member of the board of education of a school district or area vocational-technical school district, shall be entitled to have a watcher present at any place where an official count is being conducted as prescribed in Section 7-130 of Title 26 of Oklahoma Statutes.

SECTION 4. **Repealer**

70 O.S.1971, Section 2-103, is hereby repealed.

SECTION 5. **Effective date**

This act shall become effective January 1, 1981.

Approved April 14, 1980. Emergency.

ANIMALS—DOG BITES—LIABILITY

CHAPTER 75

H.B.No.1736

AN ACT RELATING TO ANIMALS; AMENDING 4 O.S.1971, SECTION 42.1; ESTABLISHING LIABILITY FOR DOG BITES OR INJURIES UNDER CERTAIN CIRCUMSTANCES; MAKING LOCATION WHERE INJURIES OCCURRED MORE GENERALIZED; AND PROVIDING AN EFFECTIVE DATE.

Be it enacted by the People of the State of Oklahoma:

SECTION 1. 4 O.S.1971, Section 42.1, is amended to read as follows:

§ 42.1 Personal injury by dog—Liability of owner

The owner or owners of any dog shall be liable for damages to the full amount of any damages sustained when his dog, without provocation, bites or injures any person while such person is in or on a place where he has a lawful right to be.

other services is probably not far off. Other electronic services, such as Electronic Legislative Search System (ELSS) from CCH and STATE NET from Public Affairs, Inc., can be used to find recent and pending legislation in the states, although they do not provide the texts of bills or acts. STATE NET is available through a WESTLAW gateway.

2. STATE CODES

State statutory compilations are published in a wide variety of forms and with a wide array of "official" status. Code provisions in some states are reenacted as positive law, but in most states they are only *prima facie* evidence of the authoritative session laws. Some states have an official, unannotated code, regularly revised and published by the state on an annual or biennial basis. A few small states prepare their own annotated codes. Others have arrangements with commercial publishers to prepare annotated codes, which are legislatively or administratively sanctioned as "official." Many states, however, rarely revise their official codification, so they become obsolete and only of historical interest.[17] In such states, the subject arrangement of an earlier official code is usually retained and updated by a commercial publisher. In most state codes, a certificate or prefatory note in the front of each volume indicates its status as authority.

a. Annotated Codes

At least one annotated code is published for every state, and several larger states have two annotated codes issued by competing publishers. While codes vary from state to state in frequency of updating and in editorial quality, they are the most useful and most frequently consulted versions of state statutes.

Most state codes are published in bound volumes with pocket part supplements, although several are published in pamphlets filed in looseleaf binders. In either form, both statutory provisions and annotations are updated at least once a year. Many codes are further updated by pamphlets issued between annual supplements, containing the latest amendments and case notes. Every code is accompanied by an index, and most include parallel reference tables.

In addition to noting state and federal cases applying or interpreting statutory provisions, the state codes provide various research aids. West publishes codes for twenty states, and provides references to relevant key numbers and *C.J.S.* sections. Lawyers Co-op publishes a few codes, which include references to *ALR* annotations and *Am.Jur.2d.* Codes from other publishers include a wider variety of research references. The Michie Company, which publishes codes for nearly two dozen states, frequently includes references to *both Am.Jur.2d* and *C.J.S.* Illustrations L and M show pages from annotated codes for Oklahoma (published by West) and Georgia (published by Michie).

Several of the commercial annotated codes still have the proprietary names of former editors or publishers (*e.g., McKinney's Consolidated Laws of New York* and *Vernon's Annotated Missouri Statutes,* both actually published by West), which have been retained for their local familiarity and good will. Appendix B, at the back of this volume,

17. For example, the *Consolidated Laws of New York* have not been officially reissued since 1909.

Illustration L

Okla.Stat.Ann., tit. 4, § 42.1 (West Supp.1988), statutory section as it appears in 1988 pocket part

CHAPTER 3.—DOGS

§ 42.1. Personal injury by dog—Liability of owner

The owner or owners of any dog shall be liable for damages to the full amount of any damages sustained when his dog, without provocation, bites or injures any person while such person is in or on a place where he has a lawful right to be.

Amended by Laws 1980, c. 75, § 1, eff. Oct. 1, 1980.

Historical Note

Section 2 of Laws 1980, c. 75, provides that this act shall become effective October 1, 1980.

Law Review Commentaries

Annual Survey of Oklahoma Law:
Torts—
Animal bites. 3 Okl. City U.L.Rev. 405 (1978).
Dog bite. 6 Okl. City U.L.Rev. 289 (1981).

Notes of Decisions

Evidence 2.5
Jury questions 2.7
Other animals 4
Owner 5
Presumptions and burden of proof 2.3

---

1. Liability for injuries by dog in general

Dog owner's liability for damages under statute exists where injured party proves ownership, lack of provocation, injury, and lawful presence of injured party on dog owner's premises at time of attack. Hampton By and Through Hampton v. Hammons, Okl., 743 P.2d 1053 (1987).

Even though victim's hair, which may have had scent of cats on it, may have touched face of dog, act of turning head causing hair to brush on dog did not constitute "provocation" within meaning of this section governing liability of dog owners and dog owners were liable for injuries sustained when dog bit top of victim's head. Hunt v. Scheer, Okl.App., 576 P.2d 1190 (1978).

2.3. Presumptions and burden of proof

To establish liability under dog bite statute, plaintiff had burden of proving ownership of dog or dogs by defendant, lack of provocation, bite or injury to plaintiff from the dog involved, and plaintiff's lawful presence on premises at time of attack. Hood v. Hagler, Okl., 606 P.2d 548 (1979).

Where each dog owner allegedly allowed his or her dog and that of other defendant to roam freely back and forth between their lands, and both dogs were allegedly involved in attack on plaintiff, who had her back to dogs when she was bitten, burden shifted to dog owners to exonerate themselves by showing that bite was made by other party's dog, and plaintiff was not required to point to which of two dogs actually bit her. Id.

2.5. Evidence

In action for dog bite, in view of some evidence of dogs having bitten subsequent to attack on

plaintiff and of plaintiff's testimony as to what took place on day of attack, testimony of owner of one of the dogs that it was his opinion that neither of the dogs would have attacked unless provoked was admissible, despite its nature of such evidence as character evidence, and it was proper to submit issue of lack of provocation to jury. Hood v. Hagler, Okl., 606 P.2d 548 (1979).

2.7. Jury questions

In view of slight inconsistencies in plaintiff's description of the dogs which attacked her, and of evidence introduced to show that dogs of similar breed frequently roamed neighborhood, there was fact question as to ownership of dogs which attacked plaintiff, and it was proper for trial court to submit question of liability to jury. Hood v. Hagler, Okl., 606 P.2d 548 (1979).

In dog bite case, wherein there was admitted evidence that dogs were large and at least part German shepherd and barked at those going to and from area involved and while barking often got close enough to bite, that dogs were primarily kept for protection and were trained as guard dogs and that one of the dogs had bitten since incident in question, combination of facts justified submission to jury on basis of common-law negligence. Id.

4. Other animals

Rule that owner of livestock has common-law duty to prevent his animals from trespassing without reference to § 98 of this title and that if owner either intentionally or negligently permits his livestock to run loose then he is responsible for all damages proximately caused by the animal's trespass is limited to trespassing domestic animals not covered by § 98 and not known to be vicious. Carver v. Ford, Okl., 591 P.2d 305 (1979).

Evidence in action to recover for injuries sustained by six-year-old child who was allegedly bitten by neighbor's pet woolly monkey presented jury questions whether the child was actually bitten by the monkey and, if she was bitten, whether the child provoked the bite. Whitefield v. Stewart, Okl., 577 P.2d 1295 (1978).

Owner who chooses to harbor a monkey on his premises is responsible for the acts of the animal to the same extent as provided in this section imposing modified absolute liability on dog owners. Id.

In suit to recover for injuries sustained by six-year-old child who was allegedly bitten by neighbor's woolly monkey, the trial court properly admitted evidence that the child had on previous occasions teased the monkey; such evidence was probative in determining whether there was provocation. Id.

5. Owner

Definition of animal owner within meaning of municipal ordinance was broader than meaning found in this section, and where legislation did not conflict, definition of "owner" within municipal ordinance operates to extend definition to include person who harbors or maintains dog. Hampton By and Through Hampton v. Hammons, Okl., 743 P.2d 1053 (1987).

Illustration M

Ga.Code Ann. § 51-2-6 (1982), statutory section as it appears in 1982 bound volume

51-2-6. Liability of owner or keeper of dog for damage done to livestock while off his premises.

If any dog, while not on the premises of its owner or the person having charge of it, kills or injures any livestock, the owner or person having charge of the dog shall be liable for damages sustained by the killing or maiming of the livestock and for the full costs of action. (Ga. L. 1865-66, p. 76, § 1; Code 1868, § 2914; Code 1873, § 2965; Code 1882, § 2965; Civil Code 1895, § 3822; Civil Code 1910, § 4418; Code 1933, § 105-111.)

Cross references. — For further provisions regarding liability of owner of dog which kills or injures livestock or poultry, see § 4-8-4.

JUDICIAL DECISIONS

Under this section, owner is liable for certain acts of his dog, thus recognizing that the dog is property. Graham v. Smith, 100 Ga. 434, 28 S.E. 225, 62 Am. St. R. 323, 40 L.R.A. 503 (1897); Columbus R.R. v. Woolfolk, 128 Ga. 631, 58 S.E. 152, 119 Am. St. R. 404, 10 L.R.A. (n.s.) 1136 (1907).

RESEARCH REFERENCES

Am. Jur. 2d. — 4 Am. Jur. 2d, Animals, § 94 et seq.

C.J.S. — 3A C.J.S., Animals, § 194 et seq.

ALR. — Validity, construction, and effect of statute eliminating scienter as condition of liability for injury by dog or other animal, 1 ALR 1113; 142 ALR 436.

Character and extent of claims for which lien on animal damage feasant attaches, 26 ALR 1047.

Owner or keeper of trespassing dog as subject to injunction or damages, 107 ALR 1323.

Contributory negligence, assumption of risk, or intentional provocation as defense to action for injury by dog, 66 ALR2d 916.

Liability for injury inflicted by horse, dog, or other domestic animal exhibited at show, 80 ALR2d 886.

51-2-7. Liability of owner or keeper of vicious or dangerous animal for injuries caused by animal.

A person who owns or keeps a vicious or dangerous animal of any kind and who, by careless management or by allowing the animal to go at liberty, causes injury to another person who does not provoke the injury by his own act shall be liable in damages to the person so injured. (Orig. Code 1863, § 2907; Code 1868, § 2913; Code 1873, § 2964; Code 1882, § 2964; Civil Code 1895, § 3821; Civil Code 1910, § 4417; Code 1933, § 105-110.)

History of section. — The language of this section is derived in part from the decision in Conway v. Grant, 88 Ga. 40, 13 S.E. 803 (1891).

Cross references. — As to care, confinement, etc., of wild animals, see Ch. 5, T. 27.

indicates the available codes and their specific designations for each state.

b. WESTLAW and LEXIS Code Databases

After a slow start, WESTLAW and LEXIS are now actively adding statutes of the various states to their systems. As of this writing, WESTLAW and LEXIS each offers access to codes for at least half of the states. Their coverage differs so that most states are now available on at least one system. It is likely that both systems will be offering the statutes of all states before long. The databases for many of the states include case annotations and references to secondary materials, and these features will probably be added for the others in the near future.

In addition to databases for specific codes, both systems offer the ability to search at once in all available state codes. Statutory language differs from state to state, but this is nonetheless a powerful capability for someone doing comparative statutory research or interested in finding how a particular word or phrase has been applied in other states.

The frequency of updating varies from state to state. Before relying on an online code as current, a prudent researcher would verify its status by consulting the online database directories or scope screens.

3. FINDING STATE STATUTES

Almost all annotated codes include parallel reference tables comparable to those in the three versions of the U.S. Code, and every code has an extensive index. These indexes frequently occupy several volumes, and are either supplemented or reissued each year. Illustrations N and O show pages from the indexes for Oklahoma and Georgia, providing access to the code provisions seen in the preceding illustrations.

Only a few state codes include tables of acts by name, but comprehensive coverage of state popular name acts is provided in two forms by Shepard's Citations. The Shepard's citator for each state includes a "Table of Acts by Popular Names or Short Titles." These tables, which are updated in the supplementary pamphlets, generally provide citations only to codes, not session laws. In addition, *Shepard's Acts and Cases by Popular Names: Federal and State,* two volumes published in 1986 with a quarterly pamphlet supplement, provides one alphabetical listing of statutes from throughout the country. The nationwide *Acts and Cases by Popular Names* sometimes has more current information than the list in a state citator.[18] It is most useful in situations where the title of an act, but not the state of enactment, is known, or when

18. For both the state listings and the general *Acts and Cases,* paperback supplements list new acts but take no notice of the recodification or moving of older acts. Such changes are only recognized when a volume is recompiled and reissued. The more current source for a particular state, then, depends on whether the state citator was published before or after the most recent revision of *Shepard's Acts and Cases by Popular Names.*

Illustration N

Page from *Oklahoma Statutes Annotated* General Index D to L volume (West 1982)

DOCUMENTS

76

Illustration O

Page from *Official Code of Georgia Annotated* General Index A to H volume (Michie 1988)

similar acts from several states are sought. Its listings can provide citations of acts from numerous states on related topics. Illustration P shows a typical page from the 1986 edition of *Shepard's Acts and Cases by Popular Names: Federal and State.*

Multistate statutory searches are not frequently required by practitioners, but they are quite common in scholarly research. Searching fifty state codes is very time-consuming, particularly since different indexes often treat similar subjects in very different ways.[19] Rather than expecting a single search procedure to work for every state, one must approach each index as its own system of classifications and cross-references.

There are several resources which may help in multistate statutory searches. As more state codes become searchable on WESTLAW and LEXIS, an online keyword search may retrieve most relevant documents if terminology is fairly standard. The last volume of the *Martindale–Hubbell Law Directory* contains digests of state laws on a variety of standardized subjects, and provides references to statutory primary sources. Topical looseleaf services in some subject areas reprint state laws; the *Environment Reporter,* for example, contains state laws and regulations on such issues as air pollution, mining, and waste disposal.

State laws on particular subjects are also collected or surveyed in a variety of other sources, such as treatises, law review articles, and government publications. Some of these sources provide the texts of laws, but even those that only list code citations can save a considerable amount of research time. Extensive guides to these collections and surveys of state laws have been published in recent years. L. Foster & C. Boast, *Subject Compilations of State Laws: Research Guide and Annotated Bibliography* (Greenwood Press, 1981) is arranged by subject, with descriptive annotations and indexes by author and publisher. It is updated by supplements by C. Nyberg & C. Boast for 1979–83 (Greenwood Press, 1984), and by C.R. Nyberg for 1983–85 and 1985–88 (Boast & Nyberg, 1986, 1989). Another guide to subject compilations is J.S. Schultz, *Comparative Statutory Sources: U.S., Canadian, Multinational,* 3d ed. (Hein, 1987).

4. UPDATING AND INTERPRETING STATE STATUTES

Each state has an annotated code providing notice of statutory amendments and judicial interpretations, but updating coverage is also

19. There have been attempts to index all state laws upon enactment, but these have lapsed and are now rarely used except for study of the periods they cover. From 1925 to 1948, the Legislative Research Service of the Library of Congress prepared a biennial *State Law Index,* covering the session laws of all the states. Entries were listed under broad subject headings and then alphabetically by state. In 1963 the American Bar Foundation and Bobbs–Merrill undertook a similar project, and produced a computer-generated keyword index of federal and state statutes. This index was issued commercially under several names (*Current State Legislation Index, Automated Statutory Reporter, Aspen Computerized Law Index,* and then *Monthly Digest of Current Legislation*) by several publishers, but then discontinued in 1972.

Illustration P

A page from *Shepard's Acts and Cases by Popular Names: Federal and State*

Dockery Act (Accounting)
U.S. Code 1982 Title 22, §4211
U. S. Code 1982 Title 28, §604
U.S. Code 1982 Title 31, §§3301, 3323, 3324, 3521, 3522, 3529, 3541, 3702
U.S. Code 1982 Title 41, §§20, 21
U.S. Code 1982 Title 43, §14
July 31, 1894, c. 174, 28 Stat. 162, §§3 to 25
Sept. 13, 1982, P.L. 97-258, 96 Stat. 877

Doctors' and Dentists' Draft Law
U.S. Code 1982 Title 50, Appendix, §454 et seq.
June 29, 1953, c. 158, 67 Stat. 86

Doctors Draft Act
U.S. Code 1982 Title 50, Appendix, §454 et seq.
Sept. 9, 1950, c. 939, 64 Stat. 826
June 29, 1953, c. 158, 67 Stat. 86

Doctors Immunity Act
Conn. Gen. Stat. 1983, §52-557b

Dr. King's Birthday Act
D.C. Code 1981, §§1-504, 28-2701

Doctors Lien Act
Ill. Rev. Stat. 1981, Ch. 82, §101.1 et seq.

Doctor's Title Act
Okla. Stat. 1981, Title 59, §725.1 et seq.

Documentary Letters of Credit Act
Pa. Cons. Stat., Title 13, §5101 et seq.

Documentary Stamp Act (Minerals)
Mis. Code 1972, §27-31-71 et seq.

Documentary Stamp Tax Act
U.S. Code 1970 Title 26, §4301 et seq.
July 12, 1876, c. 181, 19 Stat. 88
Feb. 10, 1939, c. 2, 53 Stat. 1
Cal. Revenue and Taxation Code §11901 et seq.
Fla. Stat. 1983, 201.01 et seq.
Haw. Session Laws 1876, Ch. 55
Mich. Comp. Laws 1979, 207.501 et seq.
N.Y. Tax Law (Consol. Laws Ch. 60) §270 et seq.
Pa. 1935 Pamph. Laws 203, No. 90
S.C. Code of Laws 1976, §12-21-310 et seq.

Documentary Transfer Tax Act
Cal. Revenue and Taxation Code §11901 et seq.

Documents Act
D.C. Code 1981, §§1-1531 et seq., 1-1611, 1-1612
Md. Anno. Code 1974, SG, §7-201 et seq.

Documents Act (Government)
Ga. Official Code Anno. 50-18-50 et seq.

Documents Inspection Act
Cal. Code of Civil Procedure §2031

Documents of Title (Commercial Laws)
La. Rev. Stat. Anno., 10:7-101 et seq.

Documents of Title (Uniform Commercial Code)
See Uniform Commercial Code—Documents of Title

Documents of Title Act
Pa. Cons. Stat., Title 13, §7101 et seq.

Dodd Act (Taxation)
Ohio Laws Vol. 112, p. 501

Dodge Act (Settlement of Estates)
Mich. Comp. Laws 1979, 701.1 et seq.

Dog Act
Cal. Food and Agricultural Code §30501 et seq.
Conn. Gen. Stat. 1983, §22-327 et seq.
Mas. Gen. Laws 1984, 140:136A et seq.
Mich. Comp. Laws 1979, 287.261 et seq.
Ohio Rev. Code 1953, 955.01 et seq.
Pa. Purdons Stat., Title 3, §459-101 et seq.
R.I. Gen. Laws 1956, 4-13-1 et seq.
Va. Code 1950, §29-213.5 et seq.

Dog Act (Personal Injuries)
Ill. Rev. Stat. 1981, Ch. 8, §366

Dog Act (Rabies Control)
W.Va. Code 1966, §19-21A-1 et seq.

Dog Act (Research Laboratories)
Ill. Rev. Stat. 1981, Ch. 111½, §128 et seq.

Dog and Cat Humane Death Act
Ten. Code Anno., 44-17-301 et seq.

Dog and Horse Lien Act
S.C. Code of Laws 1976, §29-15-60

Dog and Horse Racing Act
Fla. Stat. 1983, 550.011 et seq.

Dog Bite Act (Liability)
Az. Rev. Stat., §24-521 et seq.
Cal. Civil Code §3342
Ky. Rev. Stat. 1971, 258.275
Mas. Gen. Laws 1984, 140:155
N.J. Stat. Anno, 4:19-16

Dog Collar and Tag Act
N.C. Gen. Stat. 1943, §67-6

Dog, Game and Inland Fish Act
Va. Code 1950, §29-1 et seq.

provided by Shepard's Citations for each state. Because Shepard's lists every citing case from the state, its entry for a provision may well be more thorough than that found in an annotated code. The frequency of code supplementation varies, and Shepard's coverage may also be considerably more current. If a code is only supplemented annually, it is vital to check Shepard's for later developments.

The mechanics of Shepardizing state statutes is similar to that described earlier for federal statutes, except that statutes are generally listed *as cited.* The entries in *Shepard's U.S. Citations* are updated so that all citations to acts in force are listed under the current provision. Such extensive editorial work is not performed for all state statutes, and cases citing sections in session laws or earlier statutory revisions are listed only in those places. Also, while coverage in *Shepard's U.S. Citations* is limited to citations in later statutes, cases, and *ALR* annotations, state Shepard's units include citations in legal periodicals published in the state and in selected national periodicals as well. Illustration Q shows a typical page from a Shepard's state statutory citator.

In several states, Shepard's also provides references to citations of statutes in attorney general opinions. The state attorneys general are often called upon to render opinions on statutory language of uncertain effect. These opinions can be very useful and influential in statutory interpretation, particularly because there is far less legislative history information available on the state level than in federal research. Publication and indexing of attorney general opinions are notoriously poor, so the principal means of access are through references in Shepard's or in notes following code sections in annotated codes. Many state Shepard's units and several state codes do not provide such references, but both WESTLAW and LEXIS have databases providing access to attorney general opinions from almost every state.

5. UNIFORM LAWS AND MODEL ACTS

For many years, one of the major aspects of the law reform movement in this country has been a drive for the enactment of uniform laws by the several states, in those fields in which uniformity would be beneficial. To this end, the National Conference of Commissioners on Uniform State Laws was formed in 1892. The Conference, consisting of representatives of each state, meets annually to draft, promulgate and promote uniform laws, which the states can then adopt as proposed, or modify, or reject, as they see fit. Over two hundred uniform laws have been approved by the Conference, of which over a hundred have been adopted by at least one state. The Uniform Commercial Code, jointly sponsored by the Conference and the American Law Institute, has been enacted by every state.[20]

20. Louisiana has adopted only Articles 1, 3, 4, 5, 7 and 8.

Illustration Q

Citations to *Okla.Stat.Ann.* tit. 4, § 42.1, in *Shepard's Oklahoma Citations,* statute edition

OKLAHOMA STATUTES—OKLAHOMA STATUTES ANNOTATED

1981 T. 3A § 204

§ 204
A
[1983HB1022
A1985SB260
§§ 204.1 to 204.3
Ad
[1983HB1022
§ 204.1
A
[1983HB1296
A1984SB415
A1985SB62
Rs1986SB511
§ 204.1A
Ad1986SB511
§ 204.2
A1985SB260
A1986SB511
§ 205
A
[1983HB1022
§§ 205.1 to 205.7
Ad
[1983HB1022
§ 205.2
A1984SB415
A1985SB260
A1986SB511
Subd. B
716P2d668
Subd. C
716P2d668
¶ 1
716P2d668
§ 205.2a
Ad1985SB260
§ 205.5
A1985SB260
§ 205.6
A
[1985HB1065
A1986SB511
§ 207
A
[1983HB1022
A
[1983HB1296
A1986SB511
727P2d106
§ 208
A
[1983HB1022
§§ 208.1 to 208.9
Ad
[1983HB1022
§ 208.3
A
[1985HB1065
A1985SB260
§ 208.10
Ad1985SB260
TITLE 4
§ 41
381P2d906
§ 42.1
A
[1980HB1736
501P2d814
576P2d1191
577P2d1295
591P2d306
606P2d548
§ 42.2
501P2d814
606P2d548
§ 85.1
et seq.
633P2d748
§ 85.1
A1974SB500
§ 85.2
633P2d749
§ 85.3
A1974SB500
A
[1980HB1757
633P2d749
§ 85.4
A
[1980HB1757
633P2d749
§ 85.5
A1974SB500
633P2d750
§ 85.6
A1974SB500
633P2d750
§ 85.10
633P2d750
§ 85.11
A1974SB500
633P2d750
§ 98
494P2d307
512P2d251
555P2d1280
591P2d306
§ 132
et seq.
387P2d619
51A2397n
§ 135
A1968SB605
378P2d333
387P2d619
512P2d251
21OkLR383
§ 136
A1968SB605
378P2d333
387P2d620
512P2d251
21OkLR383
§ 141
A1968SB605
21OkLR383
§ 144
460P2d933
§ 149
11StnL467
§ 150
11StnL467
§ 161
318P2d623
§ 191
378P2d847
563P2d136
§ 192
376P2d265
563P2d133
764F2d755
§ 193
378P2d847
§ 268
A1963C110
§ 270.2
A
[1968HB1003
§§ 499 to 499.10
Ad
[1986HB1190
§§ 501 to 508
Ad
[1981HB1277
TITLE 5
§ 1
et seq.
504P2d413
§ 2
356P2d734
385P2d876
436P2d44
629P2d1270
§ 3
629P2d1270
31OkLR514
Subd. 3
586P2d1108
§ 4
316P2d139
§ 5
A1965C483
379P2d851
614P2d49
§ 6
et seq.
393P2d854
§§ 6 to 9
571P2d451
§ 6
364P2d83
388P2d872
393P2d852
394P2d509
442P2d317
571P2d449
599P2d1104
609P2d1276
614P2d49
619P2d622
645P2d1002
650P2d861
713P2d570
725P2d1238
352F2d139
50BRW310
7ClC375
48OBJ2603
49OBJ706
56OBJ2964
§ 7
360P2d941
380P2d961
388P2d872
394P2d506
452P2d150
571P2d450
599P2d1104
614P2d49
282F2d382
295F2d535
352F2d138
228FS128
31OkLR342
§ 8
388P2d872
571P2d450
91A2626n
§ 9
521P2d793
571P2d450
§ 11
1965p307
A1965C440
§ 12
et seq.
431P2d426
37OBJ878
§ 12
341P2d247
504P2d413
31OkLR536
§ 13
356P2d734
385P2d876
504P2d413
37OBJ878
31OkLR528
69Geo707
§ 14
21OkLR387
§ 15
431P2d429
§ 17
et seq.
532P2d844
§ 17
532P2d847
§ 17.1
532P2d844
§ 17.2
532P2d844
TITLE 6
§ 101
et seq.
1965p1231
1965C244
353P2d135
382P2d445
391P2d889
401P2d482
412P2d130
430P2d794
434P2d211
512P2d167
520P2d675
579P2d1268
618P2d936
735P2d352
361FS143
651FS475
59BRW610
§§ 101 to 1415
54OBJ2042
§ 102
A1976SB590
A1982SB552
A1983SB77
A1986SB502
Subd. A
A1968SB491
59BRW612
Subd. J
59BRW612
§ 103
A1971SB304
A1982SB552
Subd. H
394FS1070
§ 104
A1980SB556
A1984SB521
§ 201
et seq.
59BRW612
§ 201
A
[1970HB1648
A1971SB304
A1975SB159
A1976SB554
A
[1977HB1155
A1979SB254
A1980SB556
A1980SB634
A
[1981HB1074
A1982SB552
A1985SB43
52OBJ2105
Subd. B
52OBJ2109
Subd. C
A1967C52
Subd. D
A1967C365
§ 201.1
Ad1985SB43
§ 202
A1975SB159
A
[1977HB1311
A1984SB521
A
[1985HB1164
412P2d130
Subd. A
52OBJ2109
Subd. B
52OBJ2109
Subd. C
52OBJ2109
Subd. E
56OBJ2561
§ 203
A
[1982HB1761
A
[1985HB1339
441P2d376
§ 203
(1982C60)
766F2d1449
Subd. 3
59BRW615
Subd. 5
59BRW615
§ 204
A1971SB304
A
[1985HB1339
441P2d376
§ 206
441P2d376
21OkLR387
§ 207
A1970SB581
A1978SB500
A1980SB556
A1982SB583
430P2d795
434P2d211
476P2d324
483P2d732
503P2d550
503P2d552
512P2d170
524P2d14
627P2d424
642P2d1142
662P2d320
700P2d1012
708P2d1090
735P2d353
52OBJ2107
Subd. A
708P2d1091
735P2d353
Subd. D
735P2d353
§ 208
A1986SB502
§ 209
A
[1970HB1648
A
[1977HB1311
A1979SB254
Subd. D
350P2d335
§ 210
A1982SB552
A
[1985HB1339
§ 211
A
[1970HB1648
A1971SB304
A1975SB159
A
[1977HB1311
A1979SB254
A
[1984HB1522
A
[1986HB1619
§ 212
A1967C267
A
[1970HB1648
A1971SB304
A
[1975HB1256
A1975SB159
A1982SB552
§ 213
A1967C54
A1986SB502
§ 219
A1968SB491
§ 220
A1984SB521
§ 222
A1974SB455
A
[1979HB1020
A1983SB40
§ 224
Ad1980SB416
§ 294
476P2d323
§ 295
476P2d323
§§ 301 to 313
704P2d492
§ 301
A1982SB583
483P2d731
682P2d234
C704P2d492
708P2d1092
735P2d354
Subd. A
C704P2d492
735P2d354
Subd. B
C704P2d493
§ 302
A
[1970HB1648
A&Rn§303.1
[1982SB583
§ 303
A1967C258
A
[1970HB1648
A1971SB304
A1982SB583
52OBJ2109
§ 304
A1982SB583
§ 305
A1975SB159
A1982SB583
704P2d494
52OBJ2109
Subd. A
A1967C258
¶ 3
30OkLR524
Subd. B
A1968SB491
Subd. C
A1967C258
Subd. D
A1967C258
§ 306
A1975SB159
A
[1977HB1311
A1978SB499
A1980SB556
Rs1982SB583
412P2d129
452P2d777
476P2d325
524P2d14
642P2d1142
735P2d353
Subd. A
642P2d1142
52OBJ2109
Subd. B
A1967C258
52OBJ2109
Subd. C
1965C244
A1967C258
569P2d996
627P2d425
52OBJ2109
Subd. D
1965C244
A1968SB491
483P2d732
52OBJ2109
Subd. E
1965C244
52OBJ2109
Subd. F
A1967C258
483P2d732
503P2d550
524P2d14
52OBJ2109
¶ 1
483P2d731
512P2d167
524P2d14
579P2d1268
627P2d426
¶ 2
476P2d323
512P2d168
579P2d1271
627P2d426
¶ 7
30OkLR524
Subd. G
A1967C258
§§ 306.1 to 313
Ad1982SB583
§ 306.1
A1983SB77
A1984SB521
A
[1985HB1339
§ 307
A1975SB159
A1980SB556
Rs1982SB583
704P2d493
735P2d353
Subd. B
A1968SB491
§§ 307.1 to 313
735P2d353
§ 307.1
704P2d496
§ 308
704P2d494
735P2d353
§ 309
A1983SB77
704P2d494
735P2d354
Subd. D
735P2d353
Subd. E
735P2d353
§ 310
A1983SB77
704P2d495
735P2d354
Subd. A
735P2d353
§ 311
704P2d495
735P2d354
§ 312
A1983SB77

All of the uniform laws which have been adopted by at least one state are compiled in an annotated set called *Uniform Laws Annotated,* master ed. (West, 1968–date), with annual pocket part supplementation and periodic additions. *U.L.A.* includes the Commissioners' notes on each law, explains variations in individual states' enactments, and provides references to law review commentaries and court decisions from all adopting states. The notes of decisions are in the usual West format of headnote abstracts. These annotations, reflecting the interpretations of a uniform law in states which have enacted it, are particularly important for research in states which are considering adopting a law or have recently done so.

Tables in each volume and pocket part list states which have adopted each uniform law. In addition, an annual pamphlet accompanying the set provides a directory of uniform acts, lists for each state of enacted uniform legislation, and a brief index covering all acts. Each individual act is indexed in full in the back of its volume.

Another important publication on uniform laws is the annual *Handbook of the National Conference of Commissioners on Uniform State Laws.* The *Handbook* contains current information about pending laws under consideration by the Conference and discussions of new and proposed legislation. It is one of the few sources of the texts of uniform laws which have not yet been adopted by any state.

"Model acts" are drafted for fields where individual states are likely to modify a proposed law to meet their needs, rather than adopt it *in toto.* The National Conference has drafted some model acts, but two of the more influential model acts were developed by the American Law Institute: the Model Penal Code and the Model Business Corporation Act. Research tools for these acts include *Model Penal Code and Commentaries* (American Law Institute, 6 vols., 1980–85), and *Model Business Corporation Act Annotated,* 3d ed. (Prentice Hall Law & Business, 4 vols., 1985–date).

It should be noted that neither uniform laws nor model acts have any legal effect in a state unless actually adopted by its legislature. When adopted, they appear in the session laws and annotated code. These sources are, of course, invaluable for research purposes, since only they contain the actual text *as enacted,* with whatever changes and variations were made in the form proposed by the National Conference.

G. LOCAL LAW SOURCES

Legal problems and issues are governed not only by federal and state law, but also by the laws of counties, cities, villages, and other local units. Local laws are a form of delegated legislation, based on law-making powers granted by the state legislatures, or, in the case of Washington, D.C. and other federally controlled areas, by the U.S. Congress.

Despite the trend toward greater centralization of governmental authority over the last fifty years, local laws remain important in many areas of daily life and economic activity. Housing, transportation, social welfare, education, municipal services, zoning, and environmental conditions are all heavily regulated at this level of government. Local taxation is an ever-increasing area of legal activity. Consequently, local law is a frequent subject of research. This research is often very frustrating, since local law sources in general are poorly published, inadequately indexed, and infrequently supplemented.

1. MUNICIPAL CHARTERS AND ORDINANCES

A city's *charter* is its organic law, similar in purpose to a federal or state constitution. An *ordinance* is a measure passed by its council or governing body to regulate municipal matters, and is the local equivalent of a federal or state statute. Most of the larger cities in the United States publish collections of their charter and ordinances in codes of varying quality. Very few municipal codes include annotations to case law. There has been a movement by several small private publishers to prepare codes for smaller cities and towns, and these have greatly improved access to local law in the communities served.

In general, however, individual ordinances (if their existence is known and they can be identified) must be obtained from the Clerk's Office of the county, city or town. In larger cities, municipal reference libraries can be very helpful, and some public libraries are useful sources of information on local law.

State digests, state legal encyclopedias and local practice sets include references to court decisions on particular local law problems and may discuss local ordinances in point. General legal treatises on municipal law may be helpful for their discussion of broader issues, but are less likely to provide local references.

2. SHEPARDIZING ORDINANCES

Each of Shepard's state statutory citators include coverage of local ordinances of the state's counties, cities, and towns, providing references to judicial decisions applying or interpreting the ordinances. The ordinances are listed under the name of the local government unit and then alphabetically by subject. In addition, a subject index indicates which localities have ordinances listed under each subject, so that ordinances on related topics can be found and Shepardized. These two approaches can be seen in Illustrations R–1 and R–2.

3. *ORDINANCE LAW ANNOTATIONS*

Besides covering ordinances in its state citators, Shepard's also publishes a digest of national scope on judicial decisions involving local ordinances, entitled *Ordinance Law Annotations* (13 vols., 1969–date). This service provides brief abstracts of decisions under broad subject headings, which are arranged alphabetically and subdivided into more

Illustration R-1

Ordinance citations in *Shepard's Georgia Citations*, arranged by local government unit

ORDINANCES De Kalb County

CRAWFORD

Traffic
Speed-Regulation
200Ga198
36SE2d356

DACULA

Disorderly Conduct
Public Drunkenness-Penalty
103GaA600
120SE2d311

DALLAS

Loitering
Public Places-Impeding Traffic-Prohibitions
248Ga166
281SE2d615
34Mer62
—Prohibition
U248Ga164
253Ga251
U281SE2d613
319SE2d850

Traffic
Speed-Regulation
96GaA659
101SE2d169
10Mer177

DALTON

Air Rifles
Discharge-Prohibition
104GaA349
121SE2d657
Minors-Possession-Prohibition
104GaA349
121SE2d657

Buildings
Awnings-Porticos-Regulation
72GaA114
33SE2d119
—Porticos-Signs-Construction
72GaA114
33SE2d119
Inspector-Appointment-Duties
70GaA559
72GaA113
83GaA219
29SE2d113
33SE2d116
63SE2d291
Signs-Regulation
72GaA114
33SE2d119

Disorderly Conduct
Prohibition
C69GaA438
C25SE2d726
Public Quarreling-Prohibition
C69GaA438
C25SE2d726

Dogs
Registration-Regulation
8GSB205

Intoxicating Liquors
Beer-Wholesale Dealers-License Tax
184Ga277
186Ga601
57GaA845
191SE130
197SE57
198SE677
Licenses-Revocation-Provisions
246Ga300
252Ga77
271SE2d356
311SE2d176
33Mer193
Sales-Presence of Minors-Prohibition
246Ga299
271SE2d355

Railroads
Crossings-Bell
51GaA150
179SE852
—Signals
131GaA179
205SE2d471
Speed
63GaA172
10SE2d457

Streets
Paving-Assessment
94GaA196
94SE2d90
Sidewalks-Obstructions-Removal
201Ga754
41SE2d145

Taxation
Beauticians-Licenses
191Ga46
11SE2d193

Taxicabs
Stands-Prohibition
201Ga755
41SE2d145

Traffic
Speed-Regulation
63GaA173
80GaA252
10SE2d459
55SE2d908

Utilities
Bills-Payment-Delinquency-Provisions
161GaA713
288SE2d747
Management and Control-Provisions
161GaA713
288SE2d746

Vaccination
Requirement
8GaL342

Zoning
Districts-Residential
201Ga690
211Ga98
40SE2d751
84SE2d39
5GaL39
Public Service Buildings-Location
Va201Ga690
Va211Ga98
Va40SE2d751
Va84SE2d39

DAWSON

Taxation
Traveling Salesmen-Licenses
188Ga450
4SE2d165

DECATUR

Buildings
Permit-Plans-Specifications
214Ga226
104SE2d117
8GaL629

City Employees
Retirement System-Minimum Benefit
Ad1985p5205

Railroads
Station-Location
414FS106

Signs
Regulations
614F2d54

Streets
Closing-Vacation
189Ga732
7SE2d730
Railways-Paving-Assessment
179Ga471
176SE494
295US167
297US625
79LE1368
80LE928
55SC703
56SC607

Zoning
Districts-Amendment
79GaA671
54SE2d723
—Business
214Ga226
104SE2d117

DE KALB COUNTY

Alcoholic Beverages
Licensed Establishments-Employees-Permit-Requirement
C253Ga713
C324SE2d451
Open Container-Prohibition
349SE2d800
Sales-Minors-Identification-Requirement
255Ga441
339SE2d258

Animal Control
129GaA383
133GaA597
199SE2d556
211SE2d639

Bookstores
Adult-Regulations
U231Ga609
U203SE2d154
—Regulation-Violations-Penalty
U231Ga609
U203SE2d154

Businesses
Wholesale Dealers-Audit Fee
229Ga483
192SE2d343

City Employees
Discipline-Hearing-Provisions
648F2d412
Hearings-Decision-Finality
648F2d412
Position Classification-Provisions
648F2d412
Transfer-Provisions
648F2d412

Definitions
County
254Ga21
326SE2d215

Dogs
Running at Large-Prohibition
120GaA537
122GaA511
146GaA221
171SE2d572
177SE2d836
246SE2d130

Fire Code
Violations-Liability-Individuals
256Ga757
353SE2d32

(Continued)

Illustration R-2

Subject index to ordinances in *Shepard's Georgia Citations*

INDEX TO ORDINANCES C-D

specific subtopics. The set is kept up to date by annual pocket parts, and includes a two-volume table of cases arranged by state and city or county. Unlike the state citators, which provide access to decisions involving ordinances of specific localities, *Ordinance Law Annotations* allows one to survey municipal lawmaking throughout the country. Illustrations S–1 and S–2 show sample pages from this publication.

H. SUMMARY

Statutory law plays a pivotal role in the modern legal system and in legal research. Most appellate decisions involve the application or interpretation of statutes. Administrative regulations, court rules, and local laws all derive from delegations of power created by statute. The scope of judicial jurisdiction or executive authority is largely determined by legislative enactments. All legal research must therefore include the question: Is there a statute on point?

This chapter can perhaps best be summarized by the following questions applicable to every statutory research problem:

1. What statutory materials are available for the jurisdiction and what is their authority?

2. What statutory research approaches are best suited to this issue in this jurisdiction?

3. Have I found all possible sources of statutory law on this issue?

4. Is what I have found current, reflecting the latest enactments and the most recent judicial interpretations?

5. What other extrinsic aids to statutory interpretation are available on this problem?

I. ADDITIONAL READING

J. Davies, *Legislative Law and Process in a Nutshell* (West, 1975).

C.S. Diver, "Statutory Interpretation in the Administrative State," 133 *U.Pa.L.Rev.* 549 (1985).

J.W. Hurst, *Dealing with Statutes* (Columbia University Press, 1982).

"Special Issue on Legislation: Statutory and Constitutional Interpretation," 48 *U.Pitt.L.Rev.* 619 (1987).

W.P. Statsky, *Legislative Analysis and Drafting*, 2d ed. (West, 1984).

U.S. Office of the Federal Register, *How to Find U.S. Statutes and U.S. Code Citations,* 3d rev. ed. (U.S. Govt. Printing Office, 1977).

Illustration S–1

A sample page from Shepard's *Ordinance Law Annotations*, showing the scope of the topic "Animals, Domestic"

ANIMALS, DOMESTIC

EDITORIAL COMMENT. Animals of various kinds have been domesticated by human beings for thousands of years. Most such animals are used for the production of food or work, but a substantial number are purely for companionship or amusement. In any event, the animal world gets a lot of attention from lawmakers and judges. Some of the finest examples of judicial humor are found in the "dog bite" cases. We do not have space, in a work of this kind, to reproduce such examples, but some very interesting cases are digested here. To cite just one such case, a Tennessee court in 1899 found that a policeman was justified in arresting a disorderly mule found loitering about the streets, with no apparent business and no evidence of ownership. Whether or not the mule was advised of his legal rights does not appear (§39).

Several of the cases digested below arose a good many years ago, but we have included them because they have a certain historical value, and may shed light on modern day traffic and parking problems. Moreover, the horse was once thought to be almost completely replaced by automobiles and tractors, but now we have more horses than ever before. So the horse cases may have some current value.

In this topic we have included only animals having some domestic use. The hunting of animals is covered in HUNTING AND FISHING. And the production from animals kept for food is treated in FOOD, except that dairy product cases will be found in MILK; DAIRIES; DAIRY PRODUCTS. Slaughtering, and related activities, are dealt with in SLAUGHTERHOUSES; RENDERING PLANTS; TANNERIES.

286

Illustration S–2

Continuation of *Ordinance Law Annotations* topic, including abstracts of two decisions on local ordinances

I. RUNNING AT LARGE

§1. Dogs

For the purpose of imposing civil liability under a city leash ordinance making it unlawful for a person owning or possessing a dog to allow it to be at large upon the streets, a motorcyclist riding on a public street is a member of the group sought to be protected and the harm he suffered when the dog caused his motorcycle to flip over is the kind of harm that the ordinance was designed to prevent. Whether the dog owners' violation of the ordinance was the proximate cause of the injuries is a question for the jury.

Wyo Endresen v Allen (1978) 574 P2d 1219.

Violation of a prohibition against allowing dogs to be at large does not create strict liability. There must be evidence of some degree of knowledge, either actual or constructive. To recover for civil liability it must be established that a person comes within the scope of the ordinance and intentionally or negligently allows the dog to run at large.

Ariz Santanello v Cooper (1970) 106 Ariz 262, 475 P2d 246.

Chapter 6

CONSTITUTIONAL LAW

A. INTRODUCTION

The constitution is the organic document of a political entity and of its legal system. Constitutions set the parameters for governmental action; they allocate power and responsibility among the branches of government and between the central government and its political subdivisions. In addition, they describe the fundamental rules by which the system functions, and, in some jurisdictions, they also define the basic rights of individuals. Constitutions can take any number of forms, ranging from relatively brief and general statements (the United States Constitution can be easily printed in ten pages) to quite lengthy documents of considerable specificity (the Texas constitution covers 160 pages [1]).

The Constitution of the United States defines its own primacy in our legal system. Article VI of the Constitution states: "This Constitution, and the Laws of the United States which shall be made in Pursuance thereof; . . . shall be the supreme Law of the Land; . . . ." Research in constitutional law in the United States is shaped by our concept of judicial review, which was derived in part from that clause of Article VI. This doctrine, established by Chief Justice Marshall's opinion in *Marbury v. Madison,* 5 U.S. (1 Cranch) 137 (1803), established the power of the judicial branch to review actions of the executive and legislature and to rule on their constitutionality. The power has, of course, been extensively used during various periods in our history at both the federal and state levels, and has greatly increased litigation over constitutional issues. Occasionally, it has also created political crises.

Because of the frequent judicial interpretation and application of constitutional provisions, and the vast secondary literature which has been and undoubtedly will be written on the Constitution, only a small part of constitutional law research relates to locating relevant constitutional provisions. The related historical background, judicial interpretations, legislative actions, and scholarly commentaries are a major focus of most research problems. The relationship of federal and state constitutional issues, and the conflict between federal and state jurisdiction and prerogatives introduce further complications in constitutional research. In any event, the constitutional documents of the United States and of the fifty states represent a separate and distinct literature with their own research procedures and tools.

B. THE UNITED STATES CONSTITUTION

The Constitution of the United States is usually considered the oldest constitutional document in continuous force in the world today. It provides the authority for all federal legislation (*i.e.,* treaties, acts, joint resolutions, and interstate compacts).

The text of the Constitution can be found in a variety of sources. It appears in many pamphlet editions, in standard reference works such as *Black's Law Dictionary,* and in almost all state and federal statutory compilations. Because its text is infrequently amended, obtaining a current version is not difficult. Perhaps the most easily accessible version is the one included in the *United States Code.*

Most research into problems of constitutional law requires extrinsic aids, beyond the text of the Constitution. The researcher therefore also needs access to interpretive judicial decisions and the scholarly analysis

1. "Constitution of Texas 1876, Unannotated," in 1 *Vernon's Annotated Constitution of the State of Texas* 1 (1984).

of commentators. The following sections describe the research tools available for such access—annotated editions of the Constitution, citators, digests, indexes, databases, and secondary sources.

1. ANNOTATED TEXTS

An annotated edition of the U.S. Constitution is one that provides notes of judicial decisions which have applied or interpreted its provisions. Three such "annotated" texts of the Constitution are in common use throughout the country, and many state codes include the Constitution annotated specifically with the decisions of that state's courts.

Two of the most important versions of the Constitution are part of the unofficial, annotated editions of the U.S. Code: the "Constitution" volumes of the *United States Code Annotated* (West) and of the *United States Code Service* (Lawyers Co-operative). The format and use of these sets are similar and have been described in Chapter 5, Statutes. They provide multivolume printings of the U.S. Constitution containing brief abstracts of the relevant cases decided under each clause, section, or amendment.

a. USCA

United States Code Annotated, following the traditional West approach, provides extensive coverage by including annotations to both federal *and* state decisions that concern each article or amendment of the U.S. Constitution. As a result, the text of the Constitution, when annotated in *USCA,* requires ten volumes.[2] The annotations to the due process clause of the Fourteenth Amendment alone fill two volumes. The volumes are kept up to date with annual pocket parts and by the intervening supplementary pamphlets covering all of *USCA.* As part of the West research system, the annotations for each clause include relevant key numbers, providing access to digests covering the Supreme Court, lower federal courts, and all state courts covered by the National Reporter System; cross-references to other West publications; and citations to periodical articles, Attorneys General opinions, and Executive Orders. The case annotations are arranged by subject, and an alphabetical index of the subjects annotated under each section is provided just before the annotations themselves. An index to the Constitution is printed at the end of the final volume, containing Amendments 14 to End. Illustration A shows the page from the bound volume of the *USCA* containing Article II, Section 4, concerning impeachment of the President and other federal officers.

b. USCS

The "Constitution" volumes of the *United States Code Service* serve many of the same functions as those of the *USCA.* The text of each

2. The *USCA* Constitution volumes were published as a "Bicentennial Edition" in 1987, after a thorough revision which eliminated annotations to many redundant and obsolete cases. The ten new volumes reduced the number of pages almost by half, replacing seventeen volumes and eleven pamphlets or pocket parts.

Illustration A

Article II, § 4 as printed in *United States Code Annotated*

Section 4. Impeachment

Section 4. The President, Vice President and all civil Officers of the United States, shall be removed from Office on Impeachment for, and Conviction of, Treason, Bribery, or other high Crimes and Misdemeanors.

CROSS REFERENCES

Effect of judgment of impeachment, see section 3, clause 7, of Art. 1.

"Former President" for purposes of retirement benefits as one whose service terminated other than by removal pursuant to this section, see 3 USCA § 102 note.

Power of impeachment by House of Representatives, see section 2, clause 5, of Art. 1.

Power of Senate to try impeachments, see section 3, clause 6, of Art. 1.

Treason, see section 3 of Art. 3.

LIBRARY REFERENCES

Encyclopedias

Impeachment as method of removal of officers, see C.J.S. United States § 62.

Law Reviews

Presidential immunity from criminal prosecution. George E. Danielson, 63 Geo.L.J. 1065 (1975).

Removal of the President: Resignation and the procedural law of impeachment. Edwin Brown Firmage and R. Collin Mangrum, 1974 Duke L.J. 1023.

Treason, bribery, or other high crimes and misdemeanors- -A study of impeachment. Jerome S. Sloan and Ira E. Garr, 47 Temple L.Q. 413 (1974).

Texts and Treatises

Judicial, legislative and executive immunities, discussed generally, see Criminal Law Defenses § 204.

Sec. 4 **THE PRESIDENT Art. 2**

Texts and Treatises—Cont'd

Ultimate remedy: impeachment for high crimes and misdemeanors, see Tribe, American Constitutional Law § 4–16.

WESTLAW ELECTRONIC RESEARCH

See WESTLAW guide following the Explanation pages of this volume.

NOTES OF DECISIONS

Immunity 2
Officers of United States 1

---

1. Officers of United States

A member of Congress is not an officer of the United States in the constitutional meaning of the term as in the case of Blount, on an impeachment before the Senate in 1799, the question arose whether a senator was a civil officer of the United States within the purview of the Constitution, and the Senate decided that he was not. Member of Congress, 1882, 17 Op.Atty.Gen. 420.

2. Immunity

This clause does not imply immunity of the President from routine court process. Nixon v. Sirica, 1973, 487 F.2d 700, 159 U.S.App.D.C. 58.

section is printed, followed by annotations of court decisions arranged by subject. The *USCS* volumes also provide cross-references to *Lawyers' Edition* and *ALR* annotations, to other Lawyers Co-op publications such as *American Jurisprudence 2d* and *Federal Procedure, Lawyers Edition,* and to law review articles. *USCS* includes fewer annotations than *USCA,* so that the Constitution and its amendments, with annotations, are contained in only four volumes. There is an index at the end of the final volume. The four volumes are supplemented annually by pocket parts, and between pocket parts by *USCS*'s "Later Case and Statutory Service" pamphlets. Illustration B shows the impeachment clause as printed in the *USCS* version of the Constitution.

c. *The Library of Congress Edition*

Despite their usefulness as case finders for decisions under particular clauses of the Constitution, the *USCA* and *USCS* editions of the U.S. Constitution contain no descriptive or explanatory text. Many researchers find them too massive and cumbersome for achieving an understanding of constitutional doctrines, and turn instead to a more compact, single-volume edition which discusses the scope and development of each provision.

The Constitution of the United States of America; Analysis and Interpretation is prepared by the Congressional Research Service of the Library of Congress and published as a Senate Document.[3] This volume, edited by J.H. Killian and published in 1987, is the eighth annotated edition of the Constitution prepared under congressional direction. The first, in 1913, merely listed citations of Supreme Court cases after each provision. The work grew in scope with each edition, and adopted much of its present form with the 1953 edition, which was edited by the distinguished constitutional law scholar, Edward S. Corwin. The current edition is the third revision since 1953, and discusses Supreme Court cases decided through July 1982. A pocket part supplement, also published in 1987, updates the text with annotations of cases decided through July 1986.[4]

The Library of Congress edition includes the text of the Constitution interspersed with extensive commentary, historical background, legal analysis, and summaries of judicial interpretation of each clause and amendment of the Constitution. The major constitutional decisions of the Supreme Court are discussed in detail, and the footnotes include numerous citations to other relevant cases and scholarly interpretations. Illustration C shows the page on which discussion of the impeachment clause begins.

Unlike the *USCA* and *USCS* indexes to the Constitution, which cover just its text, the Library of Congress edition's index has extensive coverage of topics addressed in its analysis, as well as an alphabetical table listing all cases discussed or noted in the text. The volume also

3. S.Doc. No. 16, 99th Cong., 1st Sess. (1987).

4. S.Doc. No. 9, 100th Cong., 1st Sess. (1987).

Illustration B

Article II, § 4 as printed in *United States Code Service*

Section 4. Removal from office.

The President, Vice President and all civil Officers of the United States, shall be removed from Office on Impeachment for, and Conviction of, Treason, Bribery, or other high Crimes and Misdemeanors.

RESEARCH GUIDE

Federal Procedure L Ed:

Government Officers and Employees, Fed Proc, L Ed, § 40:579.

Am Jur:

63A Am Jur 2d, Public Officers and Employees §§ 211-218.

Annotations:

Executive privilege with respect to Presidential papers and recordings. 19 ALR Fed 472.

Law Review Articles:

Franklin, Romanist Infamy and The American Constitutional Conception of Impeachment. 23 Buff L Rev 313.

Firmage & Mangrum, Removal of the President: Resignation and the Procedural Law of Impeachment. 1974 Duke LJ 1023.

Art II, § 4 CONSTITUTION

Rogers & Young, Public Office as a Public Trust: A Suggestion that Impeachment for High Crimes and Misdemeanors Implies a Fiduciary Standard. 63 Geo LJ 1025.

Hogan, The Impeachment Inquiry of 1974: A Personal View. 63 Geo LJ 1051.

Danielson, Presidential Immunity from Criminal Prosecution. 63 Geo LJ 1065.

Mezvinsky & Freedman, Federal Income Tax Evasion as an Impeachable Offense. 63 Geo LJ 1071.

Williams, The Historical and Constitutional Bases for the Senate's Power to Use Masters or Committees to Receive Evidence in Impeachment Trials. 50 NYU L Rev 512.

Sloan & Garr, Treason, Bribery, Or Other High Crimes and Misdemeanors—A Study of Impeachment. 47 Temp LQ 413.

INTERPRETIVE NOTES AND DECISIONS

No one has ever supposed that the effect of Art II, § 4, was to prevent removal of officers for other causes deemed sufficient by President, and no such inference could be reasonably drawn from its language. Shurtleff v United States (1903) 189 US 311, 47 L Ed 828, 23 S Ct 535.

There is no express provision respecting removals in Constitution, except as Art II, § 4, provides for removal from office by impeachment. Myers v United States (1926) 272 US 52, 71 L Ed 160, 47 S Ct 21 (ovrld on other grounds Humphrey's Exr. v United States, 295 US 602, 79 L Ed 1611, 55 S Ct 869) as stated in Kalaris v Donovan, 225 App DC 134, 697 F2d 376, cert den 462 US 1119, 77 L Ed 2d 1349, 103 S Ct 3088, reh den 463 US 1236, 77 L Ed 2d 1451, 104 S Ct 30 and (ovrld on other grounds Immigration & Naturalization Service v Chadha, 462 US 919, 77 L Ed 2d 317, 103 S Ct 2764 (superseded by statute as stated in EEOC v Westinghouse Electric Corp. (CA3 Pa) 765 F2d 389, 37 CCH EPD ¶ 35361)) as stated in United States v Woodley (CA9 Hawaii) 726 F2d 1328, different results reached on reh, en banc (CA9 Hawaii) 751 F2d 1008.

Because impeachment is available against all civil officers of United States, not merely against President, under Article II, § 4, of Constitution, contention that President is immune from judicial process cannot be based upon any immunities peculiar to President emanating by implication from fact of impeachability. Nixon v Sirica (1973) 159 App DC 58, 487 F2d 700, 19 ALR Fed 343.

Federal judges are "civil officers" within meaning of Article II, § 4. United States v Claiborne (1984, CA9 Nev) 727 F2d 842, cert den (US) 83 L Ed 2d 56, 105 S Ct 113, later proceeding (CA9 Nev) 765 F2d 784, 85-2 USTC ¶ 9821, 18 Fed Rules Evid Serv 1131.

Illustration C

A page from the Library of Congress edition of the Constitution

602 ART. II—EXECUTIVE DEPARTMENT

Sec. 4—Powers and Duties of the President Impeachment

which they can be held responsible must be under the general "federal question" jurisdictional statute, which, as recently amended, requires no jurisdictional amount.[27]

SECTION 4. The President, Vice President and all civil Officers of the United States, shall be removed from Office on Impeachment for, and Conviction of, Treason, Bribery, or other high Crimes and Misdemeanors.

IMPEACHMENT[1]

Few provisions of the Constitution were adopted from English practice to the degree the section on impeachment was. In England, impeachment was a device to remove from office one who abused his office or misbehaved but who was protected by the Crown.[2] It was a device which figured in the plans proposed to the Convention from the first and the arguments went to such questions as what body was to try impeachments and what grounds were to be stated as warranting impeachment.[3] The attention of

---

[27] *See* 28 U.S.C. § 1331. On deleting the jurisdictional amount, *see* P.L. 94-574, 90 Stat. 2721 (1976), and P.L. 96-486, 94 Stat. 2369 (1980). If such suits are brought in state courts, they can be removed to federal district courts. 28 U.S.C. § 1442(a).

[1] Impeachment is the subject of several other provisions of the Constitution. Article I, § 2, cl. 5, gives to the House of Representatives "the sole power of impeachment." Article I, § 3, cl. 6, gives to the Senate "the sole power to try all impeachments," requires that Senators be under oath or affirmation when sitting for that purpose, stipulates that the Chief Justice of the United States is to preside when the President of the United States is tried, and provides for conviction on the vote of two-thirds of the members present. Article I, § 3, cl. 7, limits the judgment after impeachment to removal from office and disqualification from future federal office holding, but allows criminal trial and conviction following impeachment. Article II, § 2, cl. 1, deprives the President of the power to pardon or reprieve in cases of impeachment. Article III, § 2, cl. 3, excepts impeachment cases from the jury trial requirement.

The word "impeachment" may be used to mean several different things. Any member of the House may "impeach" an officer of the United States by presenting a petition or memorial, which is generally referred to a committee for investigation and report. The House votes to "impeach," the meaning used in § 4, when it adopts articles of impeachment. The Senate then conducts a trial on these articles and if the accused is convicted, he has been "impeached." *See* 3 A. Hinds' *Precedents of the House of Representatives of the United States* (Washington: 1907), §§ 2469-2485, for the range of forms.

[2] 1 W. Holdsworth, *History of English Law* (London: 7th ed. 1956), 379-385; Clarke, "The Origin of Impeachment," in *Oxford Essays in Medieval History, Presented to Herbert Salter* (Oxford: 1934), 164.

[3] Simpson, "Federal Impeachments," 64 U. Pa. L. Rev. 651, 653-667 (1916).

includes the texts of proposed amendments which were not ratified; tables of Acts of Congress, state constitutional and statutory provisions, and municipal ordinances which have been held unconstitutional by the Supreme Court; and a list of Supreme Court decisions overruled by subsequent decisions.

The major shortcoming of this otherwise superb work is its infrequent revision and supplementation. Before the current 1987 edition there had been no pocket part for five years. The new volume was already five years out-of-date the day it was published. Unless regular pocket part supplementation is provided, thorough updating will generally require the use of other, more current sources. Although the volume must be used with increasing caution as it ages, it remains an authoritative and useful resource for constitutional research.

d. Annotated State Statutory Codes

State courts frequently apply and interpret the United States Constitution. State laws or governmental actions are often challenged, for example, as being in conflict with the federal constitution. A state court decision is often relevant to research in constitutional issues, particularly as precedent in subsequent litigation in that state. As noted above, the annotations under the provisions of the U.S. Constitution in *USCA* and *USCS* include abstracts of state court decisions, as well as those of the federal courts. In about a dozen states, another valuable source for locating relevant cases is the annotated state code.

Almost every annotated state code contains the text of the U.S. Constitution, in addition to the constitution of that state. While every code annotates the provisions of the state constitution, only a few also annotate the U.S. Constitution. Those that do so provide a valuable service to researchers in their state, by isolating the most relevant case law from the mass of materials found in *USCA* or *USCS.* The annotations include abstracts of both state court decisions and federal cases arising in that state. References to state attorney general opinions, law review articles and other publications may also be provided. Notable among these state codes is the *Official Code of Georgia Annotated,* which devotes an entire volume to a thoroughly annotated U.S. Constitution.

2. SHEPARDIZING THE U.S. CONSTITUTION

References to court decisions applying and construing the provisions of the Constitution can be found in *Shepard's United States Citations* and in each of Shepard's state citators. The first "statute edition" volume of *Shepard's United States Citations* provides references to all federal court decisions citing or discussing each constitutional clause or amendment. Supreme Court cases are listed first, followed by lower federal court decisions arranged by circuit.[5] The

5. Supreme Court decisions since 1956 which apply or interpret particular constitutional provisions are also listed in the *Lawyers' Edition Desk Book*'s "Table of

listings also include citations to the Constitution in federal legislation, treaties, *American Bar Association Journal* articles, and annotations in *ALR, ALR Federal,* and *Lawyers' Edition.* Because the Constitution is the subject of much interpretation and litigation, the bound volume's lists of citations under most provisions are lengthy and bewildering. Citations found in recent paperback supplements may be useful, however, in providing references to current cases that have not yet been covered in annotated editions.

Every Shepard's state citator, including those covering the District of Columbia and Puerto Rico, also includes a section listing references to the U.S. Constitution. The citations in these listings are generally limited to decisions of the particular state's courts and state legislative acts, although some include state attorney general opinions. Federal court decisions, even those from District Courts within the state, are *not* included. These citators can be very useful if one needs to know how a state supreme court or appellate court has applied or interpreted the federal constitution. Since only about a dozen state codes provide state annotations to the U.S. Constitution, *Shepard's* is often the quickest way to find state court decisions. Illustration D shows a typical page from *Shepard's New Mexico Citations,* covering the U.S. Constitution.

3. FINDING COURT INTERPRETATIONS BY SUBJECT

Tools such as annotated texts and citators gather references to cases decided under particular constitutional provisions. If one is unsure of the relevant provision or wants a broader perspective, decisions interpreting and applying the Constitution can also be found by using any of the major case-finding methods discussed in Chapter 4.

Digests, including those in West's American Digest System, arrange headnotes of cases by subject. Although the annotated codes are more effective starting points for constitutional research, the digests can serve as an alternative approach to the same decisions. West's digests include sets covering the Supreme Court, the entire federal court system, and nearly every state court system. One of the topics West uses is "Constitutional Law," although constitutional issues are also addressed under numerous other topics. One can use the "Descriptive–Word Indexes" to find relevant sections, or approach the digest from the key numbers assigned to a known case. Because all of West's federal, regional and state digests follow the same subject outline, it is easy to expand one's research from one jurisdiction to others or to the entire body of published case law. Unlike annotated codes or Shepard's, in which references are limited to cases citing a particular constitution, West's digests provide access to all cases with similar themes whether interpreting provisions of the U.S. Constitution or a state constitution.

Federal Laws, Rules and Regulations Cited and Construed."

Illustration D

Citations to the U.S. Constitution in *Shepard's New Mexico Citations*

UNITED STATES CONSTITUTION

Amend. 1

Preamble
71P2d140

Art. 1
§ 2
48NM261
87NM79
149P2d1003
529P2d745
Cl. 2
79NM578
446P2d445
§ 4
48NM261
87NM79
149P2d1003
529P2d745
§ 6
Cl. 2
88NM244
539P2d1006
§ 7
Cl. 2
93NM718
605P2d223
§ 8
1933p358
1NM583
12NM192
12NM425
13NM558
36NM64
57NM112
70NM90
74NM377
78NM78
84NM629
76P310
78P74
86P551
8P2d103
255P2d317
370P2d811
394P2d141
428P2d617
506P2d786
720P2d1246
Cl. 1
New Mexico Supreme Court decision
57NM112
255P2d317
Cl. 2
75NM450
405P2d932
Cl. 3
New Mexico session law:
1945C107
41NM141
45NM29
49NM337
51NM332
59NM154
59NM201
60NM304
61NM16
64NM330
70NM90
80NM98
81NM724
82NM41
82NM45
82NM436
83NM158
84NM629
85NM381
86NM571
88NM176
89NM133

90NM258
91NM485
93NM23
93NM304
93NM390
93NM747
95NM528
96NM194
99NM553
100NM220
65P2d863
109P2d247
164P2d209
184P2d416
280P2d1045
281P2d654
291P2d607
293P2d977
328P2d589
370P2d811
451P2d1002
472P2d987
475P2d41
475P2d45
483P2d317
489P2d666
506P2d786
512P2d954
525P2d931
538P2d1198
548P2d95
561P2d1351
576P2d291
595P2d1212
599P2d1098
600P2d841
605P2d251
624P2d37
629P2d270
660P2d1035
668P2d1097
716P2d255
720P2d1254
Cl. 4
42NM254
76P2d1139
Cl. 5
52NM74
191P2d996
Cl. 7
85NM753
517P2d75
Cl. 17
1963C262
43NM318
44NM89
52NM303
53NM66
58NM597
63NM185
80NM255
100NM659
92P2d993
98P2d838
197P2d884
201P2d782
274P2d127
315P2d832
454P2d269
674P2d1119
§ 9
90NM25
559P2d402

Cl. 2
77NM420
423P2d611
Cl. 3
97NM662
642P2d1121
Cl. 5
39NM188
43P2d927
Cl. 7
36NM262
13P2d559
§ 10
12NM425
26NM127
32NM404
35NM550
35NM672
44NM556
45NM92
46NM138
50NM30
85NM186
90NM502
97NM661
98NM147
99NM44
100NM225
78P74
189P878
258P209
4P2d643
6P2d205
105P2d1070
111P2d41
123P2d389
168P2d851
510P2d510
565P2d1019
642P2d1120
646P2d574
653P2d875
668P2d1102
Cl. 1
24NM627
29NM311
34NM443
36NM53
37NM385
46NM71
48NM17
49NM234
56NM415
57NM287
58NM250
70NM90
90NM181
100NM345
175P722
222P657
283P900
7P2d940
24P2d253
120P2d619
145P2d219
161P2d714
244P2d1112
258P2d391
270P2d386
370P2d811
561P2d43
670P2d956

Cl. 3
1935p115

Art. 2
29NM455
224P1028
§ 1
14NM205
48NM261
89P267
149P2d1003
§ 2
14NM205
31NM276
48NM261
89P267
242P332
149P2d1003
§ 3
14NM205
89P267

Art. 3
7NM486
11NM378
84NM789
87NM469
91NM434
38P580
68P933
508P2d1276
535P2d1320
575P2d943
§ 1
27NM412
202P524
§ 2
27NM412
42NM115
80NM633
82NM156
84NM789
103NM410
202P524
76P2d6
459P2d159
477P2d332
508P2d1276
708P2d322
Cl. 3
43NM146
46NM134
95NM226
87P2d437
123P2d387
620P2d880

Art. 4
§ 1
1NM573
19NM278
35NM659
37NM415
41NM356
55NM461
57NM93
58NM597
59NM312
60NM432
61NM491
63NM236
65NM200
67NM189
73NM192
73NM261
82NM461

82NM659
83NM591
85NM62
85NM196
85NM260
85NM305
86NM784
89NM235
91NM423
94NM164
94NM800
95NM607
101NM321
101NM338
101NM384
142P918
200P1071
6P2d200
24P2d269
68P2d928
235P2d529
254P2d1059
274P2d127
283P2d1073
292P2d115
303P2d698
316P2d557
334P2d1107
354P2d127
386P2d711
387P2d462
483P2d935
486P2d68
495P2d371
509P2d254
510P2d914
511P2d746
512P2d65
527P2d1222
549P2d1070
575P2d607
608P2d138
617P2d1315
624P2d549
681P2d747
681P2d1116
683P2d66
§ 2
33NM324
73NM267
89NM463
95NM256
101NM73
267P58
387P2d588
553P2d1270
620P2d1281
678P2d701
Cl. 1
56NM407
94NM805
244P2d790
617P2d1320
Cl. 2
56NM407
92NM596
99NM642
101NM72
244P2d790
592P2d512
662P2d643
678P2d700

§ 3
31NM120
44NM547
103NM409
241P1027
105P2d744
708P2d321
Cl. 2
49NM292
59NM77
163P2d257
279P2d624

Art. 5
1933p400

Art. 6
14NM147
65NM200
103NM409
89P239
334P2d1107
514P2d297
708P2d321
720P2d1255
§ 2
57NM112
75NM450
83NM158
83NM463
88NM596
91NM398
91NM485
93NM125
94NM290
95NM198
95NM473
96NM498
97NM330
98NM6
98NM10
98NM277
98NM635
98NM746
99NM11
99NM393
103NM458
255P2d317
405P2d932
489P2d666
493P2d773
544P2d1161
575P2d88
576P2d291
597P2d290
609P2d1244
619P2d1242
623P2d987
632P2d733
639P2d1184
644P2d521
644P2d524
648P2d316
651P2d1279
652P2d1197
653P2d511
658P2d1120
709P2d180
732P2d880

Amendments

Amend. 1 et seq.
86NM784
527P2d1222

Amends. 1 to 10
63NM443
75NM514
75NM757
89NM305
90NM347
92NM170
94NM392
95NM226
96NM190
321P2d628
407P2d356
411P2d234
551P2d1352
563P2d610
584P2d1310
610P2d1214
620P2d880
629P2d266

Amend. 1
1945p316
11NM392
27NM477
41NM318
51NM421
55NM501
56NM56
56NM355
60NM304
63NM267
75NM475
77NM384
82NM347
83NM303
83NM511
85NM234
85NM708
86NM447
86NM543
87NM230
87NM414
88NM162
88NM187
88NM276
88NM284
88NM548
89NM150
89NM305
89NM606
91NM187
91NM250
92NM170
92NM465
92NM622
93NM314
93NM551
94NM99
94NM667
95NM363
95NM704
95NM786
97NM244
97NM627
98NM58
98NM146
98NM235

98NM264
98NM290
98NM398
99NM241
99NM426
99NM717
100NM153
100NM254
101NM43
101NM350
102NM186
102NM501
103NM271
103NM304
72P20
202P988
68P2d168
186P2d512
236P2d949
239P2d1003
244P2d520
291P2d607
317P2d317
406P2d349
423P2d421
481P2d709
491P2d520
494P2d173
511P2d560
516P2d679
525P2d374
525P2d903
531P2d1203
534P2d1126
538P2d804
539P2d207
540P2d206
540P2d214
543P2d1176
548P2d112
551P2d1352
555P2d906
571P2d1190
572P2d1258
584P2d1310
589P2d1056
593P2d63
600P2d258
603P2d285
607P2d636
615P2d984
622P2d268
625P2d1221
626P2d1283
638P2d1089
642P2d613
644P2d1047
646P2d571
647P2d868
648P2d303
648P2d329
649P2d466
656P2d904
659P2d312
663P2d376
667P2d460
669P2d263
677P2d1079
682P2d743
692P2d1332
697P2d501
705P2d677
706P2d515
715P2d459

Continued

In the *United States Supreme Court Digest, Lawyers' Edition* (Lawyers Co-op), it is very easy to determine which digest sections are applicable to particular constitutional provisions. The text of the

Constitution is set out at the beginning of volume 17 of the set, with references after each provision to relevant digest topics and sections.

Other Lawyers Co-op reference tools can also be used to find cases. Many of the annotations in *ALR, ALR Federal* and *Lawyers' Edition* contain extensive discussion of federal constitutional issues, including citations to state court decisions where they are relevant. As indicated above, annotations citing particular constitutional provisions are listed in *Shepard's United States Citations,* and access by subject is available in the five-volume *Index to Annotations.*

The full-text case databases of WESTLAW and LEXIS can also be very useful in finding case law under the Constitution, especially as one often needs to apply the Constitution's broad language to a particular set of circumstances. A computer search can combine the citation of a constitutional section or amendment with relevant factual or legal terms. Tips on using WESTLAW to retrieve cases are included in each of the Constitution volumes in *United States Code Annotated.*

4. SECONDARY SOURCES

Research on federal constitutional problems is often aided by the commentary and analysis of legal scholars. The extensive literature of constitutional law in such secondary sources as encyclopedias, treatises, and periodicals includes works that approach the Constitution from both historical and contemporary viewpoints. While later chapters will deal in depth with secondary sources generally, it is appropriate here to mention a few specific sources that can be of particular help to the constitutional researcher.

An excellent beginning point for analysis of constitutional issues is the *Encyclopedia of the American Constitution* (Macmillan, 1986). This four-volume work, edited by L.W. Levy, K.L. Karst and D.J. Mahoney, includes over two thousand articles, many by leading scholars. More than half of the encyclopedia discusses doctrinal concepts of constitutional law, but there are also articles on specific people, judicial decisions, statutes, and historical periods. Most articles include numerous cross-references to other articles and a short bibliography of further readings. In the final volume there are chronologies of the Constitution's birth and development, a brief glossary, and indexes by case, name and subject.[6]

Two current texts should be noted for their broad coverage of the Constitution with a focus on current issues. L.H. Tribe's *American Constitutional Law,* 2d ed. (Foundation Press, 1988) is probably the most thorough and authoritative one-volume treatment of American constitutional law. R.D. Rotunda, J.E. Nowak, & J.N. Young, *Treatise on Constitutional Law: Substance and Procedure* (West, 3 vols., 1986) is

6. Another recent work attempting comprehensive coverage of major concepts and cases is R.C. Chandler, R.A. Enslen & P.G. Renstrom, *The Constitutional Law Dictionary* (ABC–Clio, 2 vols., 1985–87). The first volume discusses individual rights provisions and the second covers governmental powers. A supplement to volume one was issued in 1987.

also an extensive analysis of constitutional issues, with an abridged hornbook version for students published as *Constitutional Law,* 3d ed. (West, 1986).

Numerous texts have been devoted to specific aspects of the Constitution and to the interpretative decisions of the Supreme Court. Among the many historical treatments of the Court and the Constitution, perhaps the most ambitious is the Oliver Wendell Holmes Devise *History of the Supreme Court of the United States* (Macmillan, 1971–date), under the general editorship of P.A. Freund and S.N. Katz. This multivolume, detailed history, with separate authors for each volume, is still incomplete, only eight of its projected eleven volumes having been issued so far. Each volume covers the major constitutional issues and decisions in its respective period.

Periodical articles are a rich source of scholarly writing on the Constitution and constitutional issues. Subject access to these articles can be gained through the standard legal periodical indexes, to be discussed in Chapter 11, or through one of several bibliographies published in recent years. Two of these bibliographies worth noting are K.L. Hall, *A Comprehensive Bibliography of American Constitutional and Legal History, 1896–1979* (Kraus International, 5 vols., 1984), and B.D. Reams & S.D. Yoak, *The Constitution of the United States: A Guide and Bibliography to Current Scholarly Research* (Oceana, 1987) (also published as volume five of *Sources and Documents of United States Constitutions, Second Series*).

In addition to the numerous relevant articles in law reviews of general coverage, there are several periodicals specializing in constitutional issues, such as *Constitutional Commentary, Harvard Civil Rights–Civil Liberties Law Review,* and *Hastings Constitutional Law Quarterly.* The *Supreme Court Review,* published annually by the University of Chicago, includes scholarly articles on important, recent U.S. Supreme Court decisions, many of which deal with constitutional issues. The first issue of each volume of the *Harvard Law Review* usually contains an extensive analysis by its student editors of the activity of the Supreme Court in the preceding term. This survey, always prefaced by a major introductory article written by a noted scholar, is widely read and often cited. Finally, the *Yearbook of the Supreme Court Historical Society,* published annually by the Society, includes articles, usually in a popular tone, on the history of the Court and the Constitution.

C. HISTORICAL BACKGROUND OF THE FEDERAL CONSTITUTION

The events and discussions leading to the adoption of the Constitution and its amendments are preserved in a variety of reports, journals and other documents. These materials are of continuing importance as courts attempt to apply the terms of an eighteenth century document to changing modern circumstances. The significance of the framers' intent, however, is a subject of considerable dispute.[7]

A particularly useful guide to historical research sources on the Constitution and its amendments is Part VI, "Sources for Constitutional Provisions," of G. Folsom, *Legislative History: Research for the Interpretation of Laws* (University Press of Virginia, 1972; reprinted by Rothman, 1979).

1. DRAFTING AND RATIFICATION

The Constitution of the United States was drafted in Philadelphia in 1787, and ratified by the states between 1787 and 1790. The Constitutional Convention was called to address deficiencies in the Articles of Confederation, which had been in force since 1781. Although the Constitutional Convention did not issue an official record of its proceedings, extensive notes were kept by James Madison and other delegates. The following sources provide useful documentary background on the drafting and adoption of the Constitution:

M. Farrand, *The Records of the Federal Convention of 1787* (Yale University Press, 3 vols., 1911; supplement edited by J.H. Hutson, 1987, supplanting vol. 4, published in 1937). Long the standard source for documents of the constitutional convention, this set includes extensive day-by-day records including notes by major participants and the texts of various alternative plans presented.

P.B. Kurland & R. Lerner, *The Founders' Constitution* (University of Chicago Press, 5 vols., 1987). This set provides references to and excerpts from primary materials illustrative of the political arguments and reasoning of the adopters of the Constitution. Following a first volume devoted to major themes leading up to the Constitution, the next three volumes are arranged by article, section, and clause of the Constitution. Volume 5 deals with the first twelve amendments.[8]

7. The opposing viewpoints may best be represented in speeches given in 1985 by Attorney General Edwin Meese II and Justice William Brennan, Jr. *Compare* Meese, "The Attorney General's View of the Supreme Court: Toward a Jurisprudence of Original Intent," 45 *Pub.Admin.Rev.* 701 (1985) (reprinted with minor changes as "The Supreme Court of the United States: Bulwark of a Limited Jurisdiction," 27 *S.Tex.L.Rev.* 455 (1986)), *with* Brennan, "The Constitution of the United States: Contemporary Ratification," 27 *S.Tex.L. Rev.* 433 (1986). Both speeches are also printed, with others, in *The Great Debate: Interpreting Our Written Constitution* (Federalist Society, 1986).

8. Two earlier, but still useful, compilations of historical documentation are: U.S. Bureau of Rolls and Library, *Documentary History of the Constitution of the United States of America, 1786–1870* (U.S. Department of State, 5 vols., 1894–1905; reprinted by Johnson Reprint Corp., 1965); and Library of Congress. Legislative Reference Service, *Documents Illustrative of the Formation of the Union of the American States,* H.R.Doc. No. 398, 69th Cong., 1st Sess. (1927).

A variety of documents from 1492 to 1977, including major Supreme Court decisions and other primary sources, are reprinted in W.F. Swindler & D.J. Musch, *Sources and Documents of U.S. Constitutions, Second Series* (Oceana, 5 vols., 1982–87).

W.E. Benton, *1787: Drafting the U.S. Constitution* (Texas A & M University Press, 2 vols., 1986). Less comprehensive in scope than *The Founders' Constitution,* this work also reproduces excerpts from participants' notes, arranged by article and section.

The Federalist, containing the essays of James Madison, John Jay and Alexander Hamilton in support of the adoption of the Constitution, has been issued in many editions since its first collected publication in 1788, and remains an indispensable work for the study of the Constitution. The full texts of *The Federalist,* as well as *Documents Illustrative of the Formation of the Union of the American States* (including the Declaration of Independence, the Articles of Confederation, and James Madison's notes on the debates in the Federal Convention of 1787), can be searched online in WESTLAW's "Bicentennial of the Constitution" (BICENT) database.

The debates concerning ratification of the federal Constitution by the state conventions are recorded in a variety of sources, including J. Elliot's *Debates in the Several State Conventions on the Adoption of the Federal Constitution*, 2d ed. (Elliot, 5 vols., 1836–45; reprinted by Ayer, 1987). M. Jensen's ambitious multivolume set, *Documentary History of the Ratification of the Constitution* (State Historical Society of Wisconsin, 7 vols. to date, 1976–date), will be, when completed, the most comprehensive compilation of documents on the ratification of the Constitution by the states.

2. AMENDMENTS

Under the terms of Article V, amendments to the Constitution are proposed by Congress and presented to the states for ratification. The first ten amendments, which are known as the Bill of Rights, were proposed in 1789 and ratified in 1791. Although many other amendments have been suggested over the years, the Constitution has so far been amended only twenty-six times.

Information on the Bill of Rights and other proposed or enacted amendments to the federal Constitution can be found in several sources. Volume five of *The Founders' Constitution,* discussed above, covers the first twelve amendments as well as the original seven articles. The texts of major documents relating to the Bill of Rights appear in B. Schwartz, *The Bill of Rights: A Documentary History* (Chelsea House, 2 vols., 1971). There are also numerous documentary compilations which focus on the history of individual amendments.

A series of books providing information on amendments proposed during successive time periods all have titles beginning with the words *Proposed Amendments to the Constitution*. . . . The first, covering the Constitution's first century, was prepared by H.V. Ames, and published as 2 *Am.Hist.A.Ann.Rep.* (1896) and as H.R.Doc. No. 353, Pt. 2, 54th Cong., 2d Sess. (1897). Later volumes published as Senate documents cover the periods 1890–1926, S.Doc. No. 93, 69th Cong., 1st

Sess. (1926); 1926–63, S.Doc. No. 163, 87th Cong., 2d Sess. (1963); and 1963–68, S.Doc. No. 38, 91st Cong., 1st Sess. (1969). The latest contribution to the series, covering 1969 to 1984, was edited by R.A. Davis and published in 1985 by the Library of Congress.

D. STATE CONSTITUTIONS

Each of the fifty states has its own constitution. These documents vary considerably in length and scope, and most address day-to-day activities of state government in a far more detailed manner than that of the U.S. Constitution. State constitutions can also be a vital tool in ensuring citizens' rights; even where the words in a state document mirror those in the federal Constitution, the judiciary of each state can interpret the terms of its own fundamental law.[9] A state constitution cannot deprive persons of federal constitutional rights, but it can guarantee additional protections not found in federal law.[10]

1. TEXTS

The texts of state constitutions are easily located in any of several sources. Each state's statutory code contains the text of the state's current constitution, along with earlier constitutions and other organic documents. Most useful are the annotated editions of the state codes, which contain *annotated* texts of the state constitution, similar to those for the U.S. Constitution in *USCA* and *USCS.* These annotated editions usually include references to historical background, attorney general opinions, and legislative history. The West state annotated codes can also be used for references, by key numbers, to the West digest system. Illustration E shows the section of the New Mexico Constitution concerning grounds for impeachment, as it appears in *New Mexico Statutes Annotated.* Note the cross-references to other constitutional provisions; annotations of cases and New Mexico Attorney General opinions; citations to law review articles; and references to *Am.Jur.2d, ALR,* and *C.J.S.*[11]

Another source for the texts of state constitutions is *Constitutions of the United States, National and State,* 2d ed. (7 vols., 1974–date),

9. In an influential article Justice William J. Brennan, Jr. urged the independent consideration and application of state constitutional rights. Brennan, "State Constitutions and the Protection of Individual Rights," 90 *Harv.L.Rev.* 489 (1977).

10. For example, the U.S. Supreme Court has held that police are not required to inform a criminal suspect of counsel's efforts to provide legal assistance. *Moran v. Burbine,* 475 U.S. 412 (1986). Several state courts have declined to follow *Burbine* and have held that their state constitutions mandate such a duty. *See, e.g., People v. Houston,* 42 Cal.3d 595, 230 Cal.Rptr. 141, 724 P.2d 1166 (1986); *State v. Stoddard,* 206 Conn. 157, 537 A.2d 446 (1988).

11. Note also in Illustration E that Section 37 prohibits legislators from taking free railroad trips, a provision of less impact today than when the New Mexico Constitution was adopted in 1911. Many state constitutions reflect the prevailing political attitudes and concerns of the times in which they were drafted. For earlier examples, see W.P. Adams, *The First American Constitutions: Republican Ideology and the Making of the State Constitutions of the Revolutionary Era* (University of North Carolina Press, 1980).

Illustration E

A page from the New Mexico Constitution, in *New Mexico Statutes Annotated*

Art. IV, § 36 LEGISLATIVE DEPARTMENT Art. IV, § 37

Sec. 36. [Officers subject to impeachment.]

All state officers and judges of the district court shall be liable to impeachment for crimes, misdemeanors and malfeasance in office, but judgment in such cases shall not extend further than removal from office and disqualification to hold any office of honor, trust or profit, or to vote under the laws of this state; but such officer or judge, whether convicted or acquitted shall, nevertheless, be liable to prosecution, trial, judgment, punishment or civil action, according to law. No officer shall exercise any powers or duties of his office after notice of his impeachment is served upon him until he is acquitted.

Cross-reference. — As to power of impeachment, and exercise thereof, see N.M. Const., art. IV, § 35.

Legislators. — The impeachment route could be used to handle violation by a legislator of N.M. Const., art. IV, § 28 (relating to appointment of legislators to civil office and interests of legislators in contracts with the state or municipalities) or of art. IV, § 39 (relating to bribery or solicitation involving member of the legislature). 1965 Op. Att'y Gen. No. 65-229.

Judicial officers. — Although the supreme court, upon proper recommendation of the board of bar commissioners, could hold an individual subject to discipline, even though he was a judge, insofar as his activities and standing as a member of the bar association were concerned, recommendation by the board to the court regarding a judge's alleged dishonest, illegal or fraudulent act could not as such affect the individual's capacity as a judge during his term of office, inasmuch as the constitution provides the only method for the removal of a judicial officer. In re Board of Comm'rs of State Bar, 65 N.M. 332, 337 P.2d 400 (1959).

Officers appointed by governor are subject to removal by him, whether or not they may be impeached. State ex rel. Ulrick v. Sanchez, 32 N.M. 265, 255 P. 1077 (1926).

Comparable provisions. — Iowa Const., art. VI, § 19.

Montana Const., art. V, § 13.

Utah Const., art. VI, § 19.

Wyoming Const., art. III, § 18.

Law review. — For student symposium, "Constitutional Revision — Judicial Removal and Discipline — The California Commission Plan for New Mexico?" see 9 Nat. Resources J. 446 (1969).

Am. Jur. 2d, A.L.R. and C.J.S. references. — 46 Am. Jur. 2d Judges §§ 18, 19; 63 Am. Jur. 2d Public Officers and Employees §§ 171 to 176.

Physical or mental disability as ground for impeachment, 28 A.L.R. 777.

Power of officer as affected by pendency of impeachment proceeding, 30 A.L.R. 1149.

Offense under federal law or law of another state or country, conviction as vacating accused's holding of state or local office or as ground of removal, 20 A.L.R.2d 732.

Infamous crime, or one involving moral turpitude, constituting disqualification to hold public office, 52 A.L.R.2d 1314.

Conviction, what constitutes, within statutory or constitutional provision making conviction of crime ground of disqualification for, removal from or vacancy in, public office, 71 A.L.R.2d 593.

48 C.J.S. Judges § 27; 67 C.J.S. Officers § 68; 81A C.J.S. States §§ 94 to 101.

Sec. 37. [Railroad passes.]

It shall not be lawful for a member of the legislature to use a pass, or to purchase or receive transportation over any railroad upon terms not open to the general public; and the violation of this section shall work a forfeiture of the office.

Cross-reference. — As to prohibition against use of railroad passes by public officers, see N.M. Const., art. XX, § 14.

Purpose. — This provision was adopted for the primary purpose of eliminating graft upon the part of members of the legislature and to relieve said members of any feeling of obligation toward a railroad company by virtue of possession of a free pass. 1939-40 Op. Att'y Gen. 34.

Use of railroad passes prohibited. — There is no legislation against accepting free passes on railroads, but under this section and N.M. Const., art. XX, § 14, members of the legislature, of the state board of equalization, of the corporation commission, judges of the supreme or district courts, district attorney, county commissioner and county auditor assessor are prohibited from accepting and using passes. 1912-13 Op. Att'y Gen. 22.

Grant or receipt of free passes by motor carrier unlawful. — No carrier is required to transport any state employee or other person free of charge whether traveling on official business or not, and it is unlawful for a motor carrier which is regulated by the state to grant passes to any such person or for such person to accept them. 1937-38 Op. Att'y Gen. 160.

Prohibition inapplicable to railroad employees. — The prohibition does not apply to bona fide employees of the railroad companies or their wives, if they become legislators. 1939-40 Op. Att'y Gen. 34.

The acceptance of a pass from a railroad company by a member of the legislature who is also regularly employed by such company would not be within the contemplation of this provision of the constitution. 1937-38 Op. Att'y Gen. 56.

A railroad employee who becomes a member of the legislature does not come within the purview of this law prohibiting free passes. 1933-34 Op. Att'y Gen. 53.

A.L.R. references. — Evidence of right to free transportation on public conveyance, 3 A.L.R. 387.

Carriers, free passes to public officials or employees, 8 A.L.R. 682.

published by Oceana Publications for the Legislative Drafting Fund of Columbia University. This set collects the constitutions of all the states and territories in looseleaf volumes, kept current by regular supplements and revisions. The publisher has begun but not completed an indexing service for the set. Rather than compiling one comprehensive index for all the constitutions, as it had previously,[12] it plans to issue a series of separate subject indexes in a looseleaf binder. Only two subject indexes have been issued to date: "Fundamental Liberties and Rights: A 50–State Index" (1980), and "Laws, Legislature, Legislative Procedure: A Fifty State Index" (1982), both by B.F. Sachs. A sample page, covering grounds for disqualification of legislators, is shown in Illustration F. If this project is completed, it will provide a comprehensive subject index to the constitutions of the fifty states.

Constitutions for some states are also available online in WESTLAW or LEXIS. When a state's statutes are added to the databases, its constitution is also included. In WESTLAW constitutions are simply included within statutory databases, but in LEXIS one can search in a file containing only the constitution or in one containing both constitutions and statutes. Because state statutory coverage in the systems is increasing, more and more constitutions are becoming available online. When all fifty state constitutions can be searched by computer, comparative research in constitutional provisions will be greatly facilitated.

The *Book of the States,* published biennially by the Council of State Governments, also gives information about proposed state constitutional developments and revisions.

2. CASES AND SECONDARY SOURCES

Each of Shepard's state citators, in its statutory volumes or sections, covers that state's constitution. Shepard's provides references to judicial citations of constitutional provisions in that state's courts and in federal courts. It also includes citations in state session laws, law reviews, and *ALR* annotations. In addition, because proposed amendments to state constitutions are printed in the state session laws, they can also be Shepardized in the session law sections of the state citators. Many proposed amendments are not ratified, so it is useful to be able to check their status in Shepard's.

The traditional subject approaches to case-finding can also be used in research on state constitutional law. The topic "Constitutional Law" is used in West's digests for issues arising under both federal and state constitutions, and many issues of state governmental powers are digested under the topic "States." Numerous *ALR* annotations discuss matters involving state constitutional issues, and the state case law databases in WESTLAW and LEXIS can be used to find documents

12. *Index Digest of State Constitutions,* 2d ed. (Oceana, 1959, with pocket part supplementation through 1967), discontinued, but still useful for earlier coverage.

Illustration F

"Laws, Legislature, Legislative Procedure: A 50-State Survey," in *Constitutions of the United States, National and State*

LEGISLATURE (Cont.)
QUALIFICATIONS/DISQUALIFICATIONS OF MEMBERS (Cont.)

Dual Office Holding (Cont.)

Ineligible to State Office Created During Term

Ala IV 59	Me IV Pt III 10	Ohio II 4
Alas II 5	Md III 17	Okla V 23
Alas XV 15	Mass Am LXV	Ore IV 30
Del II 14	Miss IV 45	SD III 12
Ga III Pt V 7	Mo III 12	Tex III 18
H III 8	Nev IV 8	Utah VI 7
Ill IV 2	NJ IV Sec V 1	Wash II 13
Ind IV 30	NJ XI Sec II 4	W Va VI 15
Iowa III 21	NY III 7	Wis IV 12
Ky 44	ND IV 17	

United States Offices

Alas II 5	Mich IV 8	RI IX 6
Ariz IV Pt II 4	Minn IV 5	SC III 24
Ark V 7	Mo III 12	SD III 3
Colo V 8	Mont V 9	Tenn II 26
Conn III 11	Nebr III 9	Tex III 19
Del II 14	NH II 95	Tex XVI 12
Ga III Pt V 7	NJ IV Sec V 3	Utah VI 6
Ill IV 2	NJ IV Sec V 4	Vt II 54
Iowa III 22	NM IV 3	Wash II 14
Kan II 5	NY III 7	W Va VI 13
Me IV Pt III 11	Ohio II 4	Wis IV 13
Md I 9	Okla V 18	Wyo III 8
Md III 10	Ore II 10	
Mass Am VIII	Pa II 6	

Offices Outside State

Ill IV 2	SD III 3
Iowa III 22	Tex III 19
Md I 9	Tex XVI 12
ND II 37	W Va VI 13
RI IX 6	Wash II 14
SC II 24	

combining citations of constitutional provisions with other particular search terms.

Writings on state constitutional law can be found by using the standard periodical indexes or guides for particular states. Two recent bibliographies of articles and other works are the brief survey "State Constitutional Law Resources," in B.D. McGraw, ed., *Developments in State Constitutional Law* (West, 1985), and the extensive monograph *The Constitutions of the States: A State-by-State Guide and Bibliography to Current Scholarly Research,* by B.D. Reams & S.D. Yoak (Oceana, 1988).

3. HISTORICAL RESEARCH

Unlike the venerable and rarely amended United States Constitution, state constitutions are subject to frequent amendment and revision. The amendment process in many states has been used for quite mundane matters. The Alabama Constitution of 1901, for example, includes well over 400 amendments. Many states have had several constitutional conventions and a number of corporate revisions. Louisiana has had eleven constitutions in its history. On the other hand, nineteen states still operate under an amended version of their original constitution, and the constitutions for Massachusetts, New Hampshire and Vermont date from the eighteenth century.

The most comprehensive source for documents pertaining to state constitutions is the microfiche collection issued by Congressional Information Service, *State Constitutional Conventions, Commissions, and Amendments,* which includes documents issued from 1776 through 1978 for all fifty states. Access to the microfiche is provided by two bibliographies: C.E. Browne, *State Constitutional Conventions from Independence to the Completion of the Present Union, 1776–1959: A Bibliography* (Greenwood Press, 1973), and the two-volume *State Constitutional Conventions, 1959–1978: An Annotated Bibliography* (CIS, 1981).

The major constitutional documents of every state, including enabling acts, acts of admission, and all enacted constitutions, are reprinted in W.F. Swindler, *Sources and Documents of United States Constitutions* (Oceana, 10 vols. in 11, 1973–79). Here the past constitutions and other documents are assembled in chronological order for each state, with background notes, editorial comments on provisions of succeeding constitutions, selected bibliographies on the constitutional history of each state, and indexes.[13]

13. Two older compilations, still valuable for research in early constitutions, are: B.P. Poore, *The Federal and State Constitutions, Colonial Charters, and Other Organic Laws of the United States* (Government Printing Office, 2 vols., 1877); and F.N. Thorpe, *The Federal and State Constitutions, Colonial Charters, and Other Organic Laws of the States, Territories and Colonies Now or Heretofore Forming the United States of America,* 7 vols., H.R.Doc. No. 357, 59th Cong., 2d Sess. (1909).

A.L. Sturm, *A Bibliography on State Constitutions and Constitutional Revision, 1945–1975* (Citizens Conference on State Legislatures, 1975), while out of date, contains useful lists of articles and other secondary sources on constitutional revision generally and in each state.

E. SUMMARY

The impact of judicial interpretation and application of constitutional provisions has had and continues to have significant effect on the development of law in the United States. It is therefore important that research problems be closely examined for possible constitutional issues. The extensive literature and research apparatus described in this chapter provides easy access to the texts of the federal and state constitutions, to relevant judicial decisions under each constitutional provision, and to secondary sources. These resources can be used to cut through the bewildering array of constitutional literature and locate further analysis and interpretation.

F. ADDITIONAL READING

J.A. Barron & C.T. Dienes, *Constitutional Law in a Nutshell* (West, 1986).

C. Black, *People and the Court: Judicial Review in a Democracy* (Macmillan, 1960; reprinted Greenwood Press, 1977).

D.P. Currie, *The Constitution of the United States: A Primer for the People* (University of Chicago Press, 1988).

M. Kammen, *A Machine that Would Go of Itself: The Constitution in American Culture* (Knopf, 1986).

J.K. Lieberman, *The Enduring Constitution: An Exploration of the First Two Hundred Years* (Harper & Row, 1987).

J.S. Williams, *Constitutional Analysis in a Nutshell* (West, 1979).

Chapter 7

LEGISLATIVE HISTORY

A. INTRODUCTION

Legislative history is not history in the usual sense of a narrative record or interpretation of past events. It is rather the process or results of research in the documentary records of a legislature's formulation, consideration and passage or rejection of a proposed law. The phrase as used here describes a research technique or the cumulative product of that research.

Statutory research often includes the determination of a legislature's intent in passing a specific law, or the meaning of particular provisions of a law. Such a search may seek the current status of a proposed law during its pre-enactment consideration by the legislature. Or it may investigate evidence of intent as found in a variety of legislative documents, after the law's passage or rejection. As statutory enactments proliferate and regulate virtually every aspect of human conduct and endeavor, this type of research is an important part of a lawyer's work. Many appellate decisions turn on questions of legislative history, since the ambiguities frequently contained in statutory language are resolved through litigation. Lawyers and informed citizens are also increasingly engaged in activities which seek to influence legislative consideration of pending proposals, and this inevitably requires research in the legislature's actions.

Justice Felix Frankfurter described this trend over forty years ago, as follows:

> As the area of regulation steadily widened, the impact of the legislative process upon the judicial brought into being, and compelled consideration of, all that convincingly illumines an enactment, instead of merely that which is called, with delusive simplicity, "the end result." . . . Legislative reports were increasingly drawn upon, statements by those in charge of legislation, reports of investigating committees, recommendations of agencies entrusted with the enforcement of laws, etc. etc. When Mr. Justice Holmes came to the Court, the U.S. Reports were practically barren of references to legislative materials. These swarm in current volumes. And let me say in passing that the importance that such materials play in Supreme Court litigation carr[ies] far-reaching implications for bench and bar.[1]

The use of legislative history materials has continued to increase dramatically since Frankfurter's time.[2] The ability of lawyers to do effective research in legislative history, unfortunately, has not kept pace.[3]

This chapter describes the methods and sources of research in legislative history. Its primary focus is on the procedures and docu-

1. Frankfurter, "Some Reflections on the Reading of Statutes," 2 *Rec. A.B. City N.Y.* 213, 233 (1947), reprinted in 47 *Colum.L.Rev.* 527, 542–43 (1947).

2. In Supreme Court opinions, for example, the number of citations to legislative history documents per year rose from nineteen during 1938 to over 400 during 1979. Carro & Brann, "The U.S. Supreme Court and the Use of Legislative Histories: A Statistical Analysis," 23 *Jurimetrics J.* 294, 303 (1982).

3. Judge Richard Posner of the Seventh Circuit has recently written:

> Almost three years of reading briefs in cases involving statutory interpretation have convinced me that many lawyers do not research legislative history as carefully as they research case law. It may be that they do not know how. It is more difficult to research legislative history than case law, . . . and I would guess that not one lawyer in a thousand has a real proficiency in it.

R.A. Posner, *The Federal Courts: Crisis and Reform* 339 (Harvard University Press, 1985).

ments of the United States Congress and the finding tools for following Congressional actions. While interpretation of state statutes is no less important, the tools available to determine the intent of state legislatures is far less developed than that of the federal level. What resources do exist on the state level, however, usually follow the general paradigm of the federal legislative system.

B. THE FEDERAL LEGISLATIVE PROCESS

Consideration of legislative history must begin with the legislative process itself—that is, what happens to a bill as it wends its way through Congress or a state legislature. The documents of legislative history must be viewed in the context of the parliamentary practices which produce them. Congressional procedures are quite complex, and the legislative processes of the various states present a wide range of patterns and forms. It is impossible to describe adequately here the variety of possible steps a law may take from its introduction to its passage or defeat, on either the federal or state level. The following brief survey of the stages of Congressional consideration in its simplest form is designed to place the major documents of federal legislative history in their procedural setting. More detailed information about that legislative process can be found in two brief Congressional pamphlets, *How Our Laws Are Made* and *Enactment of a Law: Procedural Steps in the Legislative Process.*[4] Illustrations A–1 and A–2 show the beginning and end of the text of a federal statute, the Foreign Intelligence Surveillance Act of 1978, as it appears in the *Statutes at Large.* The illustrations that follow in this chapter show various documents and finding tools relating to the legislative history of that law.

1. PRELIMINARY CONSIDERATION

Documents relating to particular enactments may exist even before the proposal is introduced as a bill.

Hearings on a problem of legislative concern may be held prior to the introduction of specific bills to remedy that condition. Such hearings may be held either in a session prior to that which finally considers the remedial legislation, or in the session that actually passes on it. Sometimes such hearings continue through several sessions. If one's research into the legislative history of a particular law is limited only to the session of its enactment, relevant and important debates, hearings or reports may be overlooked.

Many bills introduced in Congress stem from Presidential recommendations and may be accompanied by a Presidential message or a memorandum from an executive agency. These documents describe the purpose of proposed legislation and reveal the original intent of its

4. C.J. Zinn, *How Our Laws Are Made,* H.R. Doc. No. 99–158, 99th Cong., 2d Sess. (1986) (rev. and updated by E.F. Willett, Jr.); *Enactment of a Law: Procedural Steps in the Legislative Process,* S.Doc. No. 97–20, 97th Cong., 1st Sess. (1982) (rev. by R.B. Dove).

Illustration A–1

Beginning of the text of the Foreign Surveillance Act of 1978, as printed in the *U.S. Statutes at Large*

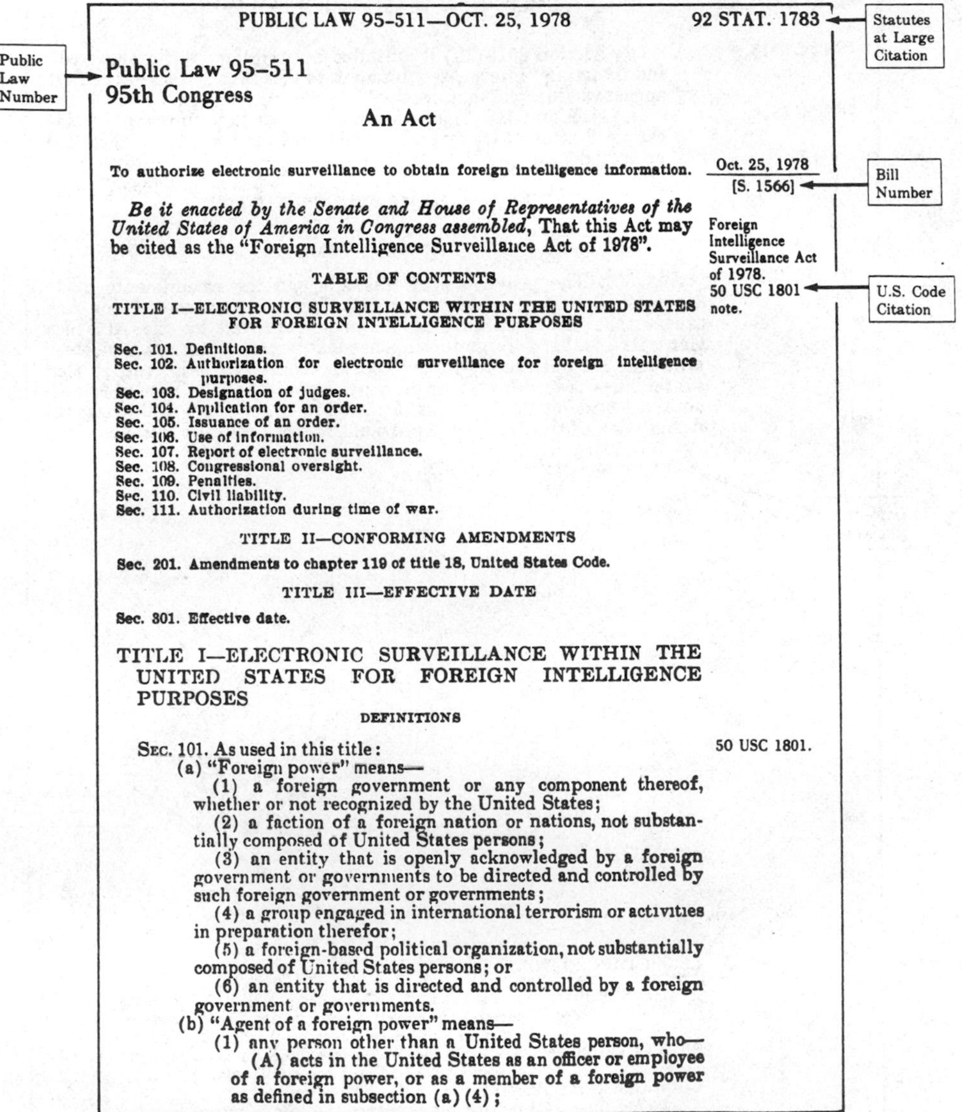

PUBLIC LAW 95-511—OCT. 25, 1978 92 STAT. 1783

Public Law 95-511
95th Congress

An Act

To authorize electronic surveillance to obtain foreign intelligence information. Oct. 25, 1978 [S. 1566]

Be it enacted by the Senate and House of Representatives of the United States of America in Congress assembled, That this Act may be cited as the "Foreign Intelligence Surveillance Act of 1978". Foreign Intelligence Surveillance Act of 1978. 50 USC 1801 note.

TABLE OF CONTENTS

TITLE I—ELECTRONIC SURVEILLANCE WITHIN THE UNITED STATES FOR FOREIGN INTELLIGENCE PURPOSES

Sec. 101. Definitions.
Sec. 102. Authorization for electronic surveillance for foreign intelligence purposes.
Sec. 103. Designation of judges.
Sec. 104. Application for an order.
Sec. 105. Issuance of an order.
Sec. 106. Use of information.
Sec. 107. Report of electronic surveillance.
Sec. 108. Congressional oversight.
Sec. 109. Penalties.
Sec. 110. Civil liability.
Sec. 111. Authorization during time of war.

TITLE II—CONFORMING AMENDMENTS

Sec. 201. Amendments to chapter 119 of title 18, United States Code.

TITLE III—EFFECTIVE DATE

Sec. 301. Effective date.

TITLE I—ELECTRONIC SURVEILLANCE WITHIN THE UNITED STATES FOR FOREIGN INTELLIGENCE PURPOSES

DEFINITIONS

SEC. 101. As used in this title: 50 USC 1801.
(a) "Foreign power" means—
(1) a foreign government or any component thereof, whether or not recognized by the United States;
(2) a faction of a foreign nation or nations, not substantially composed of United States persons;
(3) an entity that is openly acknowledged by a foreign government or governments to be directed and controlled by such foreign government or governments;
(4) a group engaged in international terrorism or activities in preparation therefor;
(5) a foreign-based political organization, not substantially composed of United States persons; or
(6) an entity that is directed and controlled by a foreign government or governments.
(b) "Agent of a foreign power" means—
(1) any person other than a United States person, who—
(A) acts in the United States as an officer or employee of a foreign power, or as a member of a foreign power as defined in subsection (a) (4);

drafters. As such, they are relevant to the search for legislative history, although they are not direct evidence of *legislative* intent. The President's annual State of the Union message is an example of an executive document which proposes various laws in general terms, but there are other Presidential messages which in greater detail describe and urge the passage of individual measures. Such messages are

Illustration A–2

End of text and legislative history summary for Foreign Surveillance Act of 1978, in *Statutes at Large*

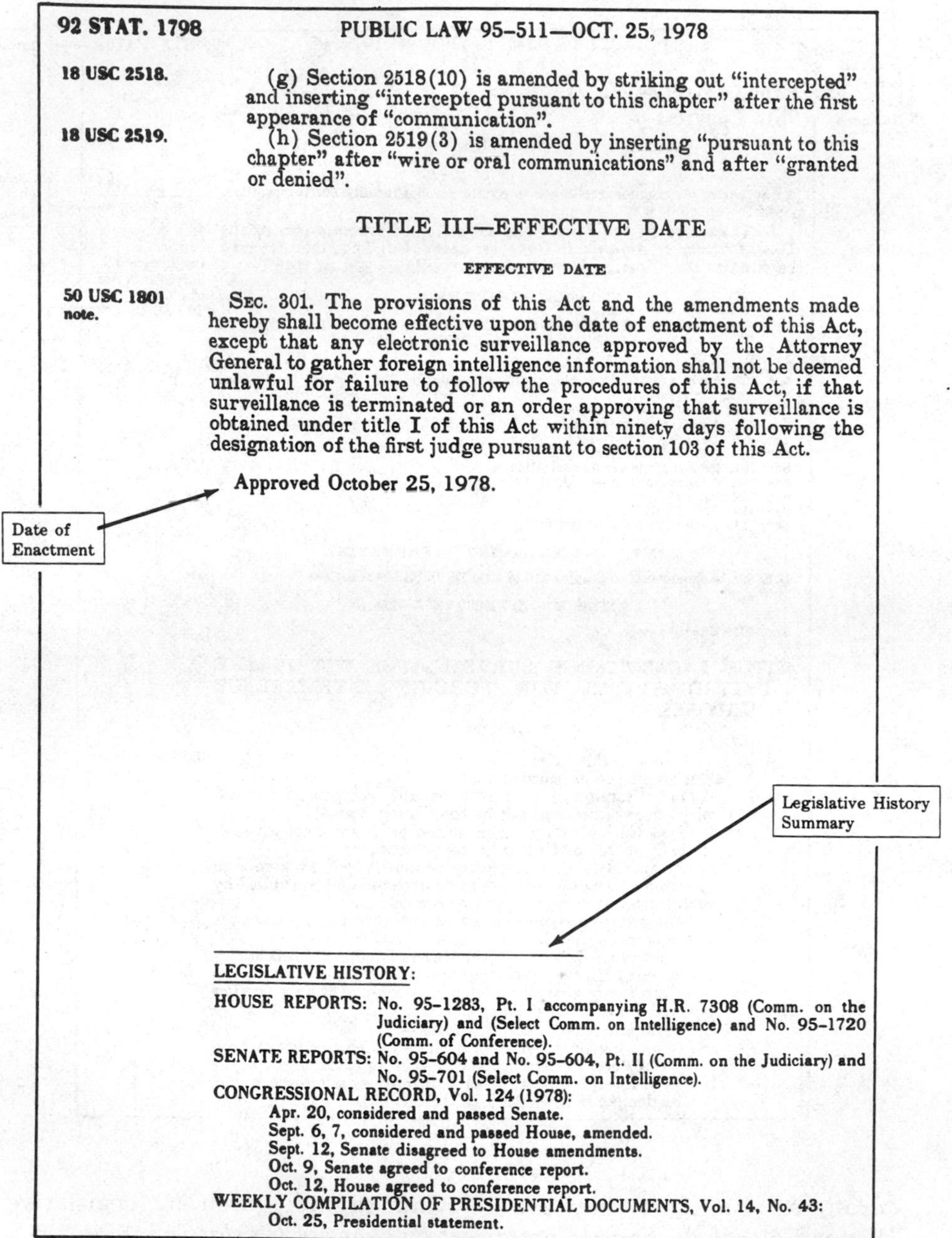

92 STAT. 1798 PUBLIC LAW 95–511—OCT. 25, 1978

18 USC 2518. (g) Section 2518(10) is amended by striking out "intercepted" and inserting "intercepted pursuant to this chapter" after the first appearance of "communication".

18 USC 2519. (h) Section 2519(3) is amended by inserting "pursuant to this chapter" after "wire or oral communications" and after "granted or denied".

TITLE III—EFFECTIVE DATE

EFFECTIVE DATE

50 USC 1801 note. SEC. 301. The provisions of this Act and the amendments made hereby shall become effective upon the date of enactment of this Act, except that any electronic surveillance approved by the Attorney General to gather foreign intelligence information shall not be deemed unlawful for failure to follow the procedures of this Act, if that surveillance is terminated or an order approving that surveillance is obtained under title I of this Act within ninety days following the designation of the first judge pursuant to section 103 of this Act.

Approved October 25, 1978.

LEGISLATIVE HISTORY:

HOUSE REPORTS: No. 95–1283, Pt. I accompanying H.R. 7308 (Comm. on the Judiciary) and (Select Comm. on Intelligence) and No. 95–1720 (Comm. of Conference).

SENATE REPORTS: No. 95–604 and No. 95–604, Pt. II (Comm. on the Judiciary) and No. 95–701 (Select Comm. on Intelligence).

CONGRESSIONAL RECORD, Vol. 124 (1978):
- Apr. 20, considered and passed Senate.
- Sept. 6, 7, considered and passed House, amended.
- Sept. 12, Senate disagreed to House amendments.
- Oct. 9, Senate agreed to conference report.
- Oct. 12, House agreed to conference report.

WEEKLY COMPILATION OF PRESIDENTIAL DOCUMENTS, Vol. 14, No. 43:
- Oct. 25, Presidential statement.

printed and indexed in the *Congressional Record,* and appear in the *Weekly Compilation of Presidential Documents,* the *House* and *Senate*

Journals, and separately as House and Senate Documents. They are further described in Chapter 8, Administrative and Executive Publications. Illustration B shows President Ford's communication transmitting an early draft of the proposed Foreign Intelligence Surveillance Act.

2. CONGRESSIONAL BILLS

Each bill, when introduced, is printed, assigned a bill number, and then referred to a committee of the house in which it is presented. The bill may be amended at any stage of its legislative progress and some bills are amended many times. The bill number is the key to tracing legislative actions prior to enactment and to locating many of the documents reflecting such actions. The finding tools for such research are called *status tables.* They usually list bills by number, identify documents relevant to their consideration, and frequently describe significant legislative actions taken. After enactment, similar tables arranged by public law number recapitulate the steps and documents of the legislative history of each enactment. These tables are discussed in Section C below.

Variations in the text of the bill as it is introduced, as it appears in a committee print, as amended, and as passed, may be helpful in determining its meaning. The deletion or insertion of particular language in the text implies a legislative choice and thus may reveal the intent of the legislature. Almost every printing of a bill represents a distinct step in its progress toward enactment and may ultimately be a significant document in its legislative history.

Congressional bills are individually numbered in a separate series for each house and retain that number through both of the annual sessions of each Congress. A citation to a bill includes the number of the Congress and session in which it was introduced or printed, as follows: S. 1566, 95th Cong., 1st Sess. (1977). At the end of the two-year term of Congress, pending bills lose their active status and must be reintroduced if they are to be considered.

Bills are received in microfiche by government documents depositories, including many law libraries. They can also be obtained individually from the clerk of the House or Senate, from the legislators who sponsor them, or from the clerk of the committee considering them. The texts of a few bills also appear in the *Congressional Record,* but that is not the regular form of publication for bills. A commercial publisher, Congressional Information Service (CIS), issues Congressional bills and resolutions on microfiche beginning with the 74th Congress (1935–36). (CIS also publishes a comprehensive indexing service to Congressional materials since 1970, to be discussed in Section C.2 below, and numerous indexes to and microfiche collections of various other older Congressional documents.) Bill texts are also available online from LEGI–SLATE, a service providing a variety of information

Illustration B

Presidential communication transmitting proposed legislation, printed as a House Document

94th Congress, 2d Session - - - - - - - House Document No. 94–422

FOREIGN INTELLIGENCE SURVEILLANCE
ACT OF 1976

COMMUNICATION

FROM

THE PRESIDENT OF THE UNITED STATES

TRANSMITTING

A DRAFT OF PROPOSED LEGISLATION TO AMEND TITLE 18, UNITED STATES CODE, TO AUTHORIZE APPLICATIONS FOR A COURT ORDER APPROVING THE USE OF ELECTRONIC SURVEILLANCE TO OBTAIN FOREIGN INTELLIGENCE INFORMATION

MARCH 24, 1976.—Referred to the Committee on the Judiciary and ordered to be printed

---

U.S. GOVERNMENT PRINTING OFFICE

57–011 WASHINGTON : 1976

about Congressional activities. LEGI–SLATE and other online services are described in Section C.3 below.[5]

Illustrations C–1 and C–2 represent the first page of different stages of bill number S. 1566, which became the Foreign Intelligence Surveillance Act of 1978. The bill was introduced by Senator Kennedy and referred to the Senate Committee on Judiciary. Illustration C–1 shows the bill after it was reported out by the Judiciary Committee with amendments, and referred to the Select Committee on Intelligence. After its passage by the Senate, the bill was introduced in the House of Representatives, as shown in Illustration C–2.

3. HEARINGS

Hearings are held by standing and special committees of the House and Senate to investigate particular problems or situations of general concern, and also to elicit the views of persons or groups interested in proposed legislation. Hearings may be designed to air a controversial situation, determine the need for new legislation, or bring before the Congress information helpful to its consideration of a pending bill. Hearings do not *have* to be held on every bill, and occasionally legislation is enacted for which hearings have not been held in one or both houses. But that is unusual and, even then, relevant hearings may be found on similar or related bills which may aid in interpreting the provisions of such an enactment.

The hearings, as published, consist of transcripts of testimony before a particular committee or subcommittee, questions by the legislators and answers by witnesses, exhibits submitted by interested individuals or organizations, and sometimes a print of the bill in question. Not every hearing which is held is published. Those that are published are listed in the *Monthly Catalog of U.S. Government Publications,* in *CIS/Index,* and in some of the status tables and legislative services described in Section C below.

As noted above, hearings relevant to the interpretation of a particular enactment may have been held and published by a session of Congress prior to the one which enacted the law in question. Sometimes relevant hearings may extend over several sessions and be published in several parts or volumes. Longer hearings sometimes contain indexes which are helpful in locating specific references.

As evidence of legislative intent, hearings rank below committee reports and the variant texts of bills. The testimony they contain may range from the helpful and objective views of disinterested experts to the partisan comments of interest groups. Although careful research can frequently turn up useful material in published hearings, this source must be used with a critical and discriminating view.

Hearings are generally identified by the number of the Congress and session in which they were held, the name of the committee which

5. Another source for bills is Commerce Clearing House, which supplies subscribers with bills on particular subjects through its expensive *Legislative Reporting Service.*

Illustration C–1

A Senate bill after being reported out by the Judiciary Committee, with amendments, and referred to the Select Committee on Intelligence

95th CONGRESS
1st Session

S. 1566

[Report No. 95–604]

IN THE SENATE OF THE UNITED STATES

May 18 (legislative day, May 16), 1977

Mr. Kennedy (for himself, Mr. Bayh, Mr. Eastland, Mr. Inouye, Mr. McClellan, Mr. Mathias, Mr. Nelson, Mr. Thurmond, Mr. Huddleston, and Mr. Garn) introduced the following bill; which was read twice and referred by unanimous consent to the Committee on the Judiciary, and, if and when reported, then to the Select Committee on Intelligence

November 15 (legislative day, November 1), 1977
Reported by Mr. Kennedy, with amendments

[Omit the part struck through and insert the part printed in italic]

November 15 (legislative day, November 1), 1977
Referred, by unanimous consent, to the Select Committee on Intelligence

A BILL

To amend title 18, United States Code, to authorize applications for a court order approving the use of electronic surveillance to obtain foreign intelligence information.

Be it enacted by the Senate and House of Representatives of the United States of America in Congress assembled, That this Act may be cited as the "Foreign Intelligence Surveillance Act of 1977".

Sec. 2. Title 18, United States Code, is amended by adding a new chapter after chapter 119 as follows:

II

Illustration C–2

Bill as introduced in House of Representatives after passage by the Senate

95TH CONGRESS
2D SESSION

S. 1566

IN THE HOUSE OF REPRESENTATIVES

APRIL 24, 1978

Referred to the Committee on the Judiciary

AN ACT

To amend title 18, United States Code, to authorize applications for a court order approving the use of electronic surveillance to obtain foreign intelligence information.

Be it enacted by the Senate and House of Representatives of the United States of America in Congress assembled, That this Act may be cited as the "Foreign Intelligence Surveillance Act of 1978".

SEC. 2. Title 18, United States Code, is amended by adding a new chapter after chapter 119 as follows:

I

held them, the short title which appears on the cover of the published hearing, the number of the bill being discussed, and the dates covered by the hearing. Hearings are not generally published or numbered in consecutive series, but in recent years more committees have begun to employ convenient numbering arrangements for their published hearings. Illustration D shows the title page for the following Senate hearings: *Foreign Intelligence Surveillance Act of 1978: Hearings before the Subcomm. on Intelligence and the Rights of Americans of the Select Comm. on Intelligence of the United States Senate . . . on S. 1566,* 95th Cong., 2d Sess. (1978).

While hearings are indexed in the official *Monthly Catalog of U.S. Government Publications,* the most useful listings and indexes appear in the commercial publication, *CIS/Index.* Published by Congressional Information Service since 1970, *CIS/Index* has provided a comprehensive finding tool for federal legislative history (described more fully in Section C.2 below). Its annual coverage of hearings includes abstracts of testimony and indexing under the name of each witness. CIS also publishes a detailed retrospective index of hearings held from 1833 to 1969, under the title *CIS US Congressional Committee Hearings Index* (42 vols., 1981–85). This index provides access to hearings by subject, witness name, bill number, and hearing title. For unpublished committee hearings, CIS also publishes two indexes, *CIS Index to Unpublished US Senate Committee Hearings* (5 vols., 1986), covering the period 1823 to 1964, and *CIS Index to Unpublished US House of Representatives Committee Hearings* (2 vols., 1988), covering the period 1833 to 1936. The hearings covered in each of these indexes are also available from CIS in microfiche.

The Library of the United States Senate publishes another series of indexes to the hearings of both houses.[6] These cover the period back to the 41st Congress (1869–71), but provide less detail and fewer points of access than the CIS indexes described above.

4. COMMITTEE REPORTS

The most important documents of legislative history are the reports of the Congressional committees of each house, and the reports of conference committees held jointly by the two houses. The House and Senate committees generally issue a report on each bill when it is sent to the whole house for consideration, or "reported out of committee." These reports reflect the committee's proposal after the bill has been studied, hearings held, and amendments made. They frequently contain the revised text of the bill, an analysis of its content and intent, and the committee's rationale for its recommendations. Sometimes the report also includes a minority statement, if there was disagreement among the committee members. Since most bills die in committee and are never reported out for action, one cannot expect to find a committee report on every bill introduced.

6. *Cumulative Index of Congressional Committee Hearings* (U.S. Government Printing Office, 10 vols., 1935–date). These indexes now seem to be issued biennially, the seventh and latest supplement covering the 96th Congress, 1979–80. See Schmeckebier & Eastin, *Government Publications and Their Use,* 2d rev. ed., at 181–182 (Brookings Institution, 1969), for a description of these indexes.

Illustration D

Senate hearings on S. 1566, the Foreign Intelligence Surveillance Act of 1978

FOREIGN INTELLIGENCE SURVEILLANCE ACT OF 1978

HEARINGS

BEFORE THE

SUBCOMMITTEE ON INTELLIGENCE AND THE RIGHTS OF AMERICANS

OF THE

SELECT COMMITTEE ON INTELLIGENCE

OF THE

UNITED STATES SENATE

NINETY-FIFTH CONGRESS

SECOND SESSION

ON

S. 1566

FOREIGN INTELLIGENCE SURVEILLANCE ACT OF 1978

JULY 19, 21, 1977 AND FEBRUARY 8, 24, 27, 1978

Printed for the use of the Select Committee on Intelligence

U.S. GOVERNMENT PRINTING OFFICE

94-628 WASHINGTON : 1978

For sale by the Superintendent of Documents, U.S. Government Printing Office
Washington, D.C. 20402
Stock Number 052-070-04477-2

If different versions of a proposed enactment have been passed by each house, a conference committee is convened, including members from each house. The conference committee reconciles the differences and produces an agreed compromise for return to both houses and final passage. The reports of these conference committees usually contain the text of the compromise bill. Conference committee reports are another very persuasive source for interpretation.

Committee reports and conference committee reports are generally given more weight than any other documents of legislative history, because they are produced by those members of Congress who have worked most closely with the proposed legislation. There are other materials that could be even more helpful in interpreting statutory language, such as the transcripts of committee markup sessions, in which legislation is first examined in detail, or of conference committee proceedings. Only rarely, however, are such transcripts published or generally available.[7]

Committee reports may also be issued on special investigations, studies and hearings not related to the consideration or reporting of a specific bill. Reports are issued, for example, on nominations to the executive and judicial branches.

The committee reports of each house are published as single pamphlets in separate numerical series for each session of Congress. They are most easily identified and traced by these report numbers, and their citations include the numbers of the Congress and session which issued them, e.g., "S.Rep. No. 701, 95th Cong., 2d Sess. (1978)"; and "H.R.Rep. No. 1283, 95th Cong., 2d Sess. (1978)." Committee reports are listed and indexed in the *Monthly Catalog of U.S. Government Publications* and the *CIS/Index.* The reports are available as a series by subscription from the Government Printing Office, or sometimes individually from the clerk of the committee issuing them or from the clerk of the house. Some can be purchased from the Government Printing Office, but supplies are usually exhausted shortly after publication. One or more committee reports on major enactments are reprinted selectively in *U.S. Code Congressional and Administrative News,* and a few appear also in the *Congressional Record.*

The reports are also published, together with House and Senate documents (another form of Congressional publication described below), in a bound series of volumes popularly called the *Serial Set.* In that form, they can also be located by the volume numbers in which they appear. A retrospective index to the Serial Set, covering the period from 1789 to 1969, is published by the Congressional Information Service under the title *CIS US Serial Set Index* (36 vols., 1975–79). Divided into twelve chronological parts, it provides access by subjects, keywords, and proper names.

7. *See* Wald, "Some Observations on the Use of Legislative History in the 1981 Supreme Court Term," 68 *Iowa L.Rev.* 195, 200–203 (1983).

The following Illustrations show various committee reports on the proposed Foreign Intelligence Surveillance Act of 1978: E, Senate Report; F, House Report; G, House publication of the Conference Report; H, *USCCAN* publication of Committee Reports selectively.

Congressional publications also include "committee prints," which like the committee reports are issued generally in consecutive series for each House, with the numbering sequence beginning over in each session of Congress. Some committee prints are not numbered at all, however, and some are reissued subsequently as House or Senate reports or documents. Committee prints usually contain material prepared specifically for the use of a committee, such as studies done by the committee staff or outside experts, or compilations of statutes in particular areas. Others are statements by members of the committee or its subcommittees on a pending bill. An example of the latter type in 1978 set forth the views of members of a subcommittee of the House Committee on the Judiciary, on the House version of the proposed Foreign Intelligence Surveillance Act.

Like other Congressional documents, committee prints since 1970 are covered in the privately published *CIS/Index.* CIS has also published a comprehensive index to earlier committee prints, from 1830 to 1969, *CIS US Congressional Committee Prints Index* (5 vols., 1980).

5. CONGRESSIONAL DEBATES

Floor debate in Congress on a pending bill can occur at almost any stage of its progress, but typically it takes place after the bill has been reported out by committee. During consideration of the bill, amendments will be proposed and accepted or defeated. Arguments for and against amendments and passage are made, explanations of unclear or controversial provisions are offered, and much of the business of the legislative process is revealed in floor discussion.

Both houses of Congress publish official journals which describe their proceedings in brief form, but these *House* and *Senate Journals* do not report the details of debates. The essential source for this form of legislative history is the *Congressional Record,* which is published daily while either house is in session. The *Congressional Record* provides a more or less verbatim transcript of the legislative debates and proceedings, subject, however, to revision of their remarks by the individual legislators.

The *Congressional Record* has been published since 1873, and is the successor to three earlier series reporting debates of Congress. The chronological record of Congressional debates is contained in the following publications: [8]

Annals of Congress, 1789–1824 (1st Congress to 18th Congress, 1st Session)

8. See Schmeckebier & Eastin, *supra* note 6, at 134–146, for a fuller description of each.

Illustration E

Report of the Senate Select Committee on Intelligence on the Foreign Intelligence Surveillance Act of 1978

Calendar No. 643

95TH CONGRESS } SENATE { REPORT
2D SESSION } { No. 95–701

FOREIGN INTELLIGENCE SURVEILLANCE ACT OF 1978

MARCH 14, (legislative day, FEBRUARY 6), 1978.—Ordered to be printed

Mr. BAYH, from the Select Committee on Intelligence, submitted the following

REPORT

together with

ADDITIONAL VIEWS

[To accompany S. 1566]

The Select Committee on Intelligence, to which was referred the bill (S. 1566) to amend title 18, United States Code, to authorize applications for a court order approving the use of electronic surveillance to obtain foreign intelligence information, having considered the same, reports favorably thereon with amendments and recommends that the bill, as amended, do pass.

AMENDMENTS

On page 1, line 4, strike "1977", and insert in lieu thereof "1978".

On page 3, strike out all after line 5 through the end of line 19, and insert in lieu thereof the following:

(A) any person, other than a United States person, who—

(i) acts in the United States as an officer or employee of a foreign power; or

(ii) acts for or on behalf of a foreign power which engages in clandestine intelligence activities contrary to the interests of the United States, when the circumstances of such person's presence in the United States indicate that such person may engage in such activities in the United States, or when such person knowingly aids or abets any person in the conduct of such activities or conspires with any person knowing that such person is engaged in such activities;

Illustration F

Report of the House Permanent Select Committee on Intelligence on the Foreign Intelligence Surveillance Act of 1978

95TH CONGRESS 2d *Session* } HOUSE OF REPRESENTATIVES { REPORT 95–1283, Pt. I

FOREIGN INTELLIGENCE SURVEILLANCE ACT OF 1978

JUNE 8, 1978.—Ordered to be printed

Mr. BOLAND, from the Permanent Select Committee on Intelligence, submitted the following

REPORT

together with

SUPPLEMENTAL, ADDITIONAL, AND DISSENTING VIEWS

[To accompany H.R. 7308 which on November 4, 1977, was referred jointly to the Committee on the Judiciary and the Permanent Select Committee on Intelligence]

The Permanent Select Committee on Intelligence, to whom was referred the bill (H.R. 7308) to amend title 18, United States Code, to authorize applications for a court order approving the use of electronic surveillance to obtain foreign intelligence information, having considered the same, report favorably thereon with amendments and recommend that the bill as amended do pass.

AMENDMENTS

Strike all after the enacting clause and insert in lieu thereof:

That this act may be cited as the "Foreign Intelligence Surveillance Act of 1978".

TABLE OF CONTENTS

29–228

Illustration G

House of Representatives Conference Report No. 95–1720, on the Foreign Intelligence Surveillance Act of 1978

95TH CONGRESS } HOUSE OF REPRESENTATIVES { REPORT
2d Session } { No. 95–1720

FOREIGN INTELLIGENCE SURVEILLANCE ACT OF 1978

OCTOBER 5, 1978.—Ordered to be printed

Mr. BOLAND, from the committee of conference, submitted the following

CONFERENCE REPORT

[To accompany S. 1566]

The committee of conference on the disagreeing votes of the two Houses on the amendments of the House to the bill (S. 1566) to authorize electronic surveillance to obtain foreign intelligence information, having met, after full and free conference, have agreed to recommend and do recommend to their respective Houses as follows:

That the Senate recede from its disagreement to the amendment of the House to the text of the Senate bill, and agree to the same with an amendment as follows:

In lieu of the matter proposed to be inserted by the House amendments insert the following:

That this Act may be cited as the "Foreign Intelligence Surveillance Act of 1978".

TABLE OF CONTENTS

Illustration H

USCCAN publication of selections of committee reports on the Foreign Intelligence Surveillance Act of 1978

LEGISLATIVE HISTORY
P.L. 95-511

FOREIGN INTELLIGENCE SURVEILLANCE ACT OF 1978

P.L. 95-511, see page 92 Stat. 1783

Senate Report (Judiciary Committee) No. 95-604 (I and II), Nov. 15, 22, 1977 [To accompany S. 1566]

Senate Report (Intelligence Committee) No. 95-701, Mar. 14, 1978 [To accompany S. 1566]

House Report [Intelligence Committee) No. 95-1283, June 8, 1978 [To accompany H.R. 7308]

House Conference Report No. 95-1720, Oct. 5, 1978 [To accompany S. 1566]

Cong. Record Vol. 124 (1978)

DATES OF CONSIDERATION AND PASSAGE

Senate April 20, October 9, 1978

House September 7, October 12, 1978

The Senate bill was passed in lieu of the House bill. The Senate Reports (this page, p. 3970, p. 3973) and the House Conference Report (p. 4048) are set out.

SENATE REPORT NO. 95-604—PART 1
[page 1]

The Committee on the Judiciary, to which was referred the bill (S. 1566) to amend title 18, United States Code, to authorize applications for a court order approving the use of electronic surveillance to obtain foreign intelligence information, having considered the same, reports favorably thereon with amendments and recommends that the bill, as amended, do pass.

* * * * * * * * *

[page 3]

PURPOSE OF AMENDMENTS

The amendments to S. 1566 are designed to clarify and make more explicit the statutory intent, as well as to provide further safeguards for individuals subjected to electronic surveillance pursuant to this new chapter. Certain amendments are also designed to provide a detailed procedure for challenging such surveillance, and any evidence derived therefrom, during the course of a formal proceeding.

Finally, the reported bill adds an amendment to Chapter 119 of title 18, United States Code (Title III of the Omnibus Crime Control and Safe Streets Act of 1968, Public Law 90-351, section 802). This latter amendment is technical and conforming in nature and is designed to integrate certain provisions of Chapters 119 and 120. A more detailed explanation of the individual amendments is contained in the section-by-section analysis of this report.

3904

Register of Debates,	1824–1837 (18th Congress, 2d Session to 25th Congress, 1st Session)
Congressional Globe,	1833–1873 (25th Congress, 2d Session to 42d Congress, 2d Session)
Congressional Record,	1873–date (43d Congress, 1st Session to date)

A bound edition of the *Congressional Record,* in recent years comprising over twenty-five volumes, is published after the end of each session. At the government's notoriously slow publication rate, however, there is currently a six year lag between a session and its coverage in bound volumes. Nonetheless there are differences between the daily issues and the bound volumes, and the latter is the standard and generally accepted source for most research. For one thing, the two editions do not use the same system of pagination: in the daily issues, separate series of page numbers are prefixed with S (Senate), H (House), or E (Extension of Remarks). In the bound edition, all this material is integrated into one sequence. There are other differences in content; for example, from 1955 to 1968, the Extension of Remarks sections, which include extraneous materials, supplements to floor remarks, exhibits and almost anything a legislator wishes to insert in the *Record,* were not even included in the bound volumes. Many libraries provide access to older daily issues on microfilm or microfiche, but references to the *Congressional Record* should be to the final bound edition unless the cited material is available only in the daily edition.

Illustrations I–1 and I–2 show debates in the *Congressional Record* on the Foreign Intelligence Surveillance Act of 1978, I–2 showing the passage of the Act by the Senate.

Since the 80th Congress, each issue of the *Congressional Record* contains a "Daily Digest," which summarizes the day's proceedings, lists actions taken and enactments signed by the President that day, and provides useful committee information. The "Daily Digests" are cumulated and indexed in one volume of the bound edition.

An index to the proceedings, by subjects, names of legislators, and titles of legislation, is included in the *Record* every two weeks. These indexes do not cumulate, however, until the bound edition is published at the end of the session. Illustration J shows two sample columns from that index, both relating to the Foreign Intelligence Surveillance Act of 1978—the left hand column under Senator Kennedy's name, and the right hand column under the name of the Act.

Beginning with the 99th Congress in 1985, the *Congressional Record* can be searched through full-text computer-assisted research. Both LEXIS and WESTLAW have databases with the text of the *Record* since 1985, and it is also available on optical disk. Another online service, LEGI–SLATE, to be discussed in Section C.3 below, provides access to the *Record* of the current Congress in addition to other documents such as bills and committee reports. Summaries (but not

Illustration I-1

Debate in the *Congressional Record* on S. 1566

surveillance to obtain foreign intelligence information.

The Senate proceeded to consider the bill, which was reported from the Committee on the Judiciary with amendments; and from the Select Committee on Intelligence with amendments.

The ACTING PRESIDENT pro tempore. Time for debate on this bill is limited to 2 hours, to be equally divided and controlled by the Senator from Massachusetts (Mr. KENNEDY) and the Senator from South Carolina (Mr. THURMOND), with 1 hour on any amendment, with 30 minutes on any debatable motion or appeal, and with 20 minutes on any point of order.

Mr. BAYH. Mr. President, I ask unanimous consent that the following members of my staff and the staff of the Select Committee on Intelligence be granted privilege of the floor during proceedings on S. 1566 and during the vote on the bill and any amendments: Abe Shulsky, Keith Raffel, Stan Taylor, William G. Miller, Earl Eisenhower, Tom Connaughton, Angelo Codevilla, Walter Ricks, Mark Gitenstein, Mike Epstein, Dave Bushong, Tom Crowley, Sam Bouchard, Patrick Norton, Edward Levine, Tom Moore, David Shaw and John Elliff.

The ACTING PRESIDENT pro tempore. Without objection, it is so ordered.

Mr. KENNEDY. Mr. President, I ask unanimous consent that Ken Feinberg, of my staff, be granted privilege of the floor.

The ACTING PRESIDENT pro tempore. Without objection, it is so ordered.

Mr. GARN. Mr. President, I ask unanimous consent that Eric Haltman, of the Judiciary Committee, be granted privilege of the floor during the debate and votes.

The ACTING PRESIDENT pro tempore. Without objection, it is so ordered.

Mr. GARN. I also ask unanimous consent that Bob Heppler, of Senator HEINZ' staff, and Kay Davies, of Senator DOMENICI's staff, be granted privilege of the floor.

The ACTING PRESIDENT pro tempore. Without objection, it is so ordered. Who yields time?

Mr. KENNEDY. Mr. President, I suggest the absence of a quorum and ask unanimous consent that the time not be charged to either side.

The ACTING PRESIDENT pro tempore. Without objection, it is so ordered. The clerk will call the roll.

The assistant legislative clerk proceeded to call the roll.

Mr. KENNEDY. Mr. President, I ask unanimous consent that the order for the quorum call be rescinded.

The ACTING PRESIDENT pro tempore. Without objection, it is so ordered.

Mr. KENNEDY. I yield myself such time as I might use.

Mr. President, today the U.S. Senate writes a new chapter in the ongoing 10-year debate to regulate foreign intelligence electronic surveillance. In considering S. 1566, the Foreign Intelligence Surveillance Act of 1978, the full Senate at long last has the opportunity to place foreign intelligence electronic surveillance under the rule of law. The abuses of recent history sanctioned in the name of national security and documented in detail by the Church committee highlight the need for more effective statutory controls and congressional oversight.

Recent prosecutions in the Humphrey and Trong cases point out the need for this legislation. Without S. 1566 in place serious constitutional issues are raised in those cases: Is the warrantless surveillance constitutional? and, even if it is, may the Government use the evidence obtained in a subsequent criminal prosecution for espionage? or does the Government, in so doing, violate the provisions of title III? S. 1566 resolves these issues and must be dealt with expeditiously.

We have the major responsibility for seeing to it that history does not repeat itself, that civil liberties and the rights of our citizens are not bargained away in the name of national security.

S. 1566 benefits from broad bipartisan support. It has the overwhelming support of both the Senate Judiciary Committee and the Senate Select Committee on Intelligence. My distinguished colleagues, Senator BAYH, Senator THURMOND, and Senator GARN have been particularly instrumental in the development of this legislation. Working together we have fashioned a product which brings to an end the fruitless and unsatisfactory debate of the past.

S. 1566 has been endorsed and supported not only by this administration, but by the Ford administration as well. Both Attorney General Bell and Attorney General Levi have been most cooperative and helpful in the drafting of the bill. The legislation constitutes a major step forward in bringing needed safeguards to the unregulated area of foreign intelligence surveillance. It is designed to strike a balance between the protection of national security and the protection of our human liberties and rights. It is a recognition, long overdue, that the Congress does have a role to play in the area of foreign intelligence surveillance.

S. 1566—building upon S. 3197, legislation drafted in 1976 with the dedicated help of Attorney General Levi—achieves a major breakthrough in the long debate over foreign intelligence electronic surveillance. It is the culmination of past efforts and present hopes. This legislation would, for the first time, substitute carefully prescribed accountability and oversight for the arbitrariness of the past. The bill would require that all foreign intelligence electronic surveillance in the United States—as well as some overseas interceptions—be subject to a judicial warrant requirement based on probable cause. For an American citizen to be surveilled, there must be probable cause that he is an agent of a foreign power—a citizen acting for or on behalf of a foreign power—and engaging in sabotage, terrorism, or clandestine intelligence activities. It is the courts, not the executive, that would ultimately rule on whether the surveillance should occur. The bill would require that, before such surveillance could occur, a named executive branch official—such as the Secretary of Defense—certify in writing and under oath that such surveillance is necessary to obtain foreign intelligence information.

Mr. President, these statutory provisions are the very heart of the legislation. They relegate to the past the wiretapping abuses visited on Joseph Kraft, Martin Luther King, Jr., and Morton Halperin. They prevent the National Security Agency from randomly wiretrapping American citizens whose names just happen to be on a list of civil rights or antiwar activists.

The legislation provides the type of accountability which has heretofore not existed. It would for the first time expressly limit whatever inherent power the executive may have to engage in electronic surveillance in the United States. In so doing, the bill ends a decade of debate over the meaning and scope of the "inherent power" disclaimer clause currently found in title III.

S. 1566 would also provide civil and criminal sanctions to those who violate its provisions. It requires that all extraneous information—unrelated to the purposes of the surveillance—be minimized. And it mandates that before any information obtained can be used at a subsequent criminal trial, the trial court must again find that all statutory wiretap procedures have been met.

Most of the concerns expressed by some about various provisions of the bill have been satisfactorily resolved in the Senate committees. I and others in the Congress shared these very concerns over the years; thus, for example, either the Attorney General or the Deputy Attorney General must personally sign off on each application; the application must state whether "physical entry is required to effect the surveillance," thereby notifying the court whether or not a break-in is necessary in order to install the surveillance device; use of the information obtained by the surveillance is further restricted—even in the case of non-American citizens—to "lawful purposes"; any testing of new electronic surveillance equipment, tests which are not covered by this legislation, cannot be directed against specific American citizens without their consent.

Most importantly, Mr. President, the issue of the so-called noncriminal standard has been resolved to the satisfaction of all the parties concerned. Both S. 3197 last year, and the bill introduced this year, retained a narrowly restricted provision allowing for electronic surveillance in the absence of a statutory recognition that the activity is criminal.

This provision, as originally drafted, remained a major stumbling block to prompt passage of the legislation. Many were convinced that S. 1566 would establish an unfortunate precedent if statutory recognition were conferred on electronic surveillance in the absence of a showing of criminal conduct. After long and difficult negotiations this crucial issue has been resolved. A special tribute is owed Senator BAYH, Senator GARN, and the other members of the Senate Intelligence Committee for developing alternate language and providing for a criminal standard. The bill now provides for

Illustration I–2

Debate and passage of S. 1566 in the *Congressional Record*

10906 CONGRESSIONAL RECORD — SENATE *April 20, 1978*

deserve our thanks and congratulations.●

The PRESIDING OFFICER. Who yields time?

Mr. KENNEDY. Mr. President, I shall ask for the yeas and nays on passage, so I suggest the absence of a quorum, the time to be evenly divided.

The PRESIDING OFFICER. The time will have to come out of the time of the Senator from South Carolina.

Mr. THURMOND. That is fine. I have no objection.

The PRESIDING OFFICER. Without objection, it is so ordered.

The clerk will call the roll.

The assistant legislative clerk proceeded to call the roll.

Mr. KENNEDY. Mr. President, I ask unanimous consent that the order for the quorum call be rescinded.

The PRESIDING OFFICER. Without objection, it is so ordered.

Mr. KENNEDY. Mr. President, I ask for the yeas and nays on passage of the bill.

The PRESIDING OFFICER. Is there a sufficient second? There is a sufficient second.

The yeas and nays were ordered.

Mr. KENNEDY. I ask for third reading, Mr. President.

The PRESIDING OFFICER. If there be no further amendments to be proposed, the question is on the engrossment and third reading of the bill.

The bill was ordered to be engrossed for a third reading and was read the third time.

Mr. KENNEDY. Mr. President, I suggest the absence of a quorum on the time of the Senator from South Carolina.

Mr. THURMOND. I have no objection.

The PRESIDING OFFICER. The clerk will call the roll.

The assistant legislative clerk proceeded to call the roll.

Mr. KENNEDY. Mr. President, I ask unanimous consent that the order for the quorum call be rescinded.

The PRESIDING OFFICER. Without objection, it is so ordered.

Does the Senator from South Carolina yield back his remaining time?

Mr. THURMOND. Mr. President, I yield back my time and suggest we have a vote on the bill.

The PRESIDING OFFICER. The question is, Shall the bill pass? The yeas and nays have been ordered and the clerk will call the roll.

The assistant legislative clerk called the roll.

Mr. CRANSTON. I announce that the Senator from Colorado (Mr. HASKELL), the Senator from New Hampshire (Mr. McINTYRE), and the Senator from Ohio (Mr. METZENBAUM) are necessarily absent.

I further announce that, if present and voting, the Senator from Ohio (Mr. METZENBAUM) and the Senator from New Hampshire (Mr. McINTYRE) would each vote "yea."

Mr. STEVENS. I announce that the Senator from Idaho (Mr. McCLURE) is necessarily absent.

The result was announced—yeas 95, nays 1, as follows:

[Rollcall Vote No. 128 Leg.]

YEAS—95

Abourezk	Glenn	Morgan
Allen	Goldwater	Moynihan
Anderson	Gravel	Muskie
Baker	Griffin	Nelson
Bartlett	Hansen	Nunn
Bayh	Hart	Packwood
Bellmon	Hatch	Pearson
Bentsen	Hatfield,	Pell
Biden	Mark O.	Percy
Brooke	Hatfield,	Proxmire
Bumpers	Paul G.	Randolph
Burdick	Hathaway	Ribicoff
Byrd,	Hayakawa	Riegle
Harry F., Jr.	Heinz	Roth
Byrd, Robert C.	Helms	Sarbanes
Cannon	Hodges	Sasser
Case	Hollings	Schmitt
Chafee	Huddleston	Schweiker
Chiles	Humphrey	Sparkman
Church	Inouye	Stafford
Clark	Jackson	Stennis
Cranston	Javits	Stevens
Culver	Johnston	Stevenson
Curtis	Kennedy	Stone
Danforth	Laxalt	Talmadge
DeConcini	Leahy	Thurmond
Dole	Long	Tower
Domenici	Lugar	Wallop
Durkin	Magnuson	Weicker
Eagleton	Mathias	Williams
Eastland	Matsunaga	Young
Ford	McGovern	Zorinsky
Garn	Melcher	

NAYS—1

Scott

NOT VOTING—4

Haskell	Metzenbaum
McClure	McIntyre

So the bill (S. 1566), as amended, was passed, as follows:

S. 1566

Be it enacted by the Senate and House of Representatives of the United States of America in Congress assembled, That this Act may be cited as the "Foreign Intelligence Surveillance Act of 1978".

SEC. 2. Title 18, United States Code, is amended by adding a new chapter after chapter 119 as follows:

"Chapter 120.—ELECTRONIC SURVEILLANCE WITHIN THE UNITED STATES FOR FOREIGN INTELLIGENCE PURPOSES

"Sec.

"2521. Definitions.

"2522. Authorization for electronic surveillance for foreign intelligence purposes.

"2523. Designation of judges authorized to grant orders for electronic surveillance.

"2524. Application for an order.

"2525. Issuance of an order.

"2526. Use of information.

"2527. Report of electronic surveillance.

"2528. Congressional oversight.

"§ 2521. Definitions

"(a) Except as otherwise provided in this section the definitions of section 2510 of this title shall apply to this chapter.

"(b) As used in this chapter—

"(1) 'Foreign power' means—

"(A) a foreign government or any component thereof, whether or not recognized by the United States;

"(B) a faction of a foreign nation or nations, not substantially composed of United States persons;

"(C) an entity, which is openly acknowledged by a foreign government or governments to be directed and controlled by such foreign government or governments;

"(D) a foreign-based terrorist group;

"(E) a foreign-based political organization, not substantially composed of United States persons; or

"(F) an entity which is directed and controlled by a foreign government or governments.

"(2) 'Agent of a foreign power' means—

"(A) any person, other than a United States person, who—

"(i) acts in the United States as an officer or employee of a foreign power; or

"(ii) acts for or on behalf of a foreign power which engages in clandestine intelligence activities contrary to the interests of the United States, when the circumstances of such person's presence in the United States indicate that such person may engage in such activities in the United States, or when such person knowingly aids or abets any person in the conduct of such activities or conspires with any person knowing that such person is engaged in such activities;

"(B) any person who—

"(i) knowingly engages in clandestine intelligence gathering activities for or on behalf of a foreign power, which activities involve or may involve a violation of the criminal statutes of the United States;

"(ii) pursuant to the direction of an intelligence service or network of a foreign power, knowingly engages in any other clandestine intelligence activities for or on behalf of such foreign power, which activities involve or are about to involve a violation of the criminal statutes of the United States;

"(iii) knowingly engages in sabotage or terrorism, or activities in furtherance thereof, for or on behalf of a foreign power;

"(iv) knowingly aids or abets any person in the conduct of activities described in subparagraph (B) (i) through (iii) above, or conspires with any person knowing that such person is engaged in activities described in subparagraph (B) (i) through (iii) above: *Provided*, That no United States person may be considered an agent of a foreign power solely upon the basis of activities protected by the first amendment to the Constitution of the United States.

"(3) 'Terrorism' means activities which—

"(A) are violent acts or acts dangerous to human life which would be criminal under the laws of the United States or of any State if committed within its jurisdiction; and

"(B) appear to be intended—

"(i) to intimidate or coerce the civilian population,

"(ii) to influence the policy of a government by intimidation or coercion, or

"(iii) to affect the conduct of a government by assassination or kidnaping.

"(4) 'Sabotage' means activities which would be prohibited by title 18, United States Code, chapter 105, if committed against the United States.

"(5) 'Foreign intelligence information' means—

"(A) information which relates to, and if concerning a United States person is necessary to, the ability of the United States to protect itself against actual or potential attack or other grave hostile acts of a foreign power or an agent of a foreign power;

"(B) information with respect to a foreign power or foreign territory which relates to, and if concerning a United States person is necessary to—

"(i) the national defense or the security of the Nation; or

"(ii) the successful conduct of the foreign affairs of the United States; or

"(C) information which relates to, and if concerning a United States person is necessary to, the ability of the United States to protect against—

"(i) sabotage or terrorism by a foreign power or an agent of a foreign power, or

"(ii) the clandestine intelligence activities of an intelligence service or network of a foreign power or an agent of a foreign power.

"(6) 'Electronic surveillance' means—

"(A) the acquisition by an electronic, mechanical, or other surveillance device of

Illustration J

Congressional Record index, showing references under Senator's name and title of Act.

864
Kennedy, Edward M.

———humanitarian need for food in Laos, 6825
———provide for health and disease prevention (S. 2420), 8069
———provide humanitarian assistance to Lebanon, 9478, 10327
———role of humanitarian assistance, 20454
Foreign Assistance Act: amend (S. 3075), 22536–22538, 22572, 22573, 22763, 22766–22768, 22770, 22808
———authorize development assistance programs (S. 3074), 18944–19849, 18963
———separate authorization for health care and disease prevention, 18945
Foreign assistance and related programs: appropriations (H.R. 12931), 30631, 30876, 30877, 30879, 30880, 30882–30884
Foreign-born children: expeditious naturalization of adopted (H.R. 12508), 30355
Foreign intelligence information: court order approving use of electronic surveillance (S. 1566), 10887, 10888, 10900–10902, 10906, 10910
Foreign Intelligence Surveillance Act: conference on S. 1566 requested, 31531
Foreign Intelligence Surveillance Act of 1978: enact (S. 1566), conference report, 34844–34846
Foreign policy: administration's emphasis on human rights, 2310
———comprehensive nuclear test ban treaty negotiations, 26706
———diplomatic initiatives toward Cyprus, 10337, 10954
———insure Lebanon cease-fire, 20784, 20785
———normalization of relations with People's Republic of China, 27892
Foreign trade: effect of Domestic International Sales Corporation on U.S. imports, 2291
———hearing on Romania's most-favored-nation status, 19905
Fukuda, Takeo: visit of Prime Minister of Japan, 15602
Full Employment and Balanced Growth Act: enact (S. 50; H.R. 50), 34579, 36736, 36738
GAO: stressing conservation in energy planning, 20253
Gasoline stations: display of octane rating (H.R. 130), 12987–12990
Genetic diseases: investigation and study respecting ethical, moral, and legal implications of voluntary testing, 18905
Gilliam, Reginald: tribute, 7251
Government spending: automatic surtax to recoup previous year's deficit, 26391, 26392
Greece: earthquake, 18484
Gutierrez Ruiz, Hector: assassination, 15279
Hagan, Joseph H.: tribute, 22190
Hansen, Senator: tribute, 38059
Hatfield, Senator Paul: tribute, 38057
Health: budget requests for research and development, 5687
———extension of research programs (S. 2450), 1243–1246
Health insurance: national program, 33007–33011
Health Maintenance Organization Amendments: enact (S. 2676), 5670
Health maintenance organizations: revitalize and further encourage development (S. 2534), 3254, 22129–22136, 22140, 22141, 22145, 22147
Health Planning Amendments and Hospital Services Discontinuation Act: enact (S. 2551), 3930
Health services: formula and project grants for preventive (S. 3116), 14595–14599
Health Services Extension Act: enact (S. 2474), 1754–1756
Health Services Extension and Primary Health Care Act: enact (S. 2474), 32494, 32499, 32500, 32506, 32514, 32518–32521, 32524, 32526, 32527, 32529, 32530, 32532–32535, 32537, 32540, 32543, 32544–32548, 32553
Highway and Public Transportation Improvement Act: enact (S. 2953), 10738, 10739
Highway trust fund: abolish, 27120
Highways: air brake standards on drive axles of truck trailers, 5233

585
Foreign Investments

Bill relative to tax treatment of foreign-earned income, 6518
World Development Report, 1978, World Bank, 27490
Tables
East European debt to West (selected data), 26976
Exports and imports (selected data), 27635
Foreign holdings of U.S. debt, by countries (selected data), 12453
Investment in U.S.: selected data, 10314, 10316
U.S. international agreements: selected data, 19240
U.S. Treasury bills, notes, and bonds: estimated total foreign holdings of certain (selected data), 36500, 36501
World economic performance, 1972–1977 (selected data), 32636
World population data sheet—1978, Bureau of the Census, 11194–11197
Worldwide airport restrictions (selected data), 12568
Texts of
Amendment to the Export-Import Bank authorization bill (H.R. 12157), 22953
H.R. 10698, facilitate Coast Guard enforcement of narcotic drug-related crime on high seas, 1894
S. 3384, Agricultural Foreign Investment Information Act, 25653

FOREIGN CURRENCIES
Articles and editorials
End of the Dollar Era, 37908
Floating—Not Sinking—Dollar, 2624
Gold Contracts Useful for Doctors?, 6909
U.S. Moves to Bolster Dollar Falter, 5247
Remarks in House
Dollar: value on foreign markets, 6353
Military personnel: effects of local currency fluctuations on, 5932
Remarks in Senate
International monetary system: changes affecting, 37908

FOREIGN EARNED INCOME ACT
Remarks in House
Enact (H.R. 13488), 31274, 31314, 31320

FOREIGN EMBASSIES
Remarks in Senate
Foreign Mission Solar Energy Demonstration Act: introduction (S. 2472), 1752, 1771

FOREIGN GIFT AND DECORATIONS ACT
Remarks in Senate
Amend, 10100

FOREIGN INTELLIGENCE ELECTRONIC SURVEILLANCE ACT
Analysis
H.R. 13442, bill to enact, 20710
Remarks in House
Enact (H.R. 13442), 20709

FOREIGN INTELLIGENCE SURVEILLANCE ACT
Remarks in House
Enact (H.R. 7308), 21221, 21798, 23995
Enact (S. 1566; H.R. 7308), 28121, 28131, 28158, 28396, 28427, 31623
Enact (S. 1566), conference report, 36409
Report
Conference on bill (S. 1566) enact, 33778

FOREIGN INVESTMENTS
Articles and editorials
Copperweld Corp. Takeover by French Firm, 12735
How U.S. Can Boost Export Trade, Strengthen Dollar, Senator Brooke, 13750
Little Leg Work Will Help the Dollar, 12944
Now, the U.K. Tax Treaty, 13197
Sinking Dollar and the Gathering Storm, 12747
Study Finds Foreign Executives Prefer New York, 19606
Remarks in House
Agricultural Foreign Investment Disclosure Act: enact (H.R. 13356), 25973, 32114
———enact (S. 3384; H.R. 13356), 31671
Foreign banks: Federal regulation of domestic market participation, 26726

full text) of *Record* material since 1981 are also searchable in the database *Congressional Record Abstracts,* available through DIALOG Information Services.

Both the fortnightly index and the cumulative bound index contain very useful "History of Bills and Resolutions" sections, which list all bills introduced in that session and summarize their legislative history. The bound edition also contains a tabular "History of Bills Enacted into Public Law," which is arranged by public law number and provides bill numbers, committee report numbers, and dates and pages of consideration in the *Congressional Record.* Both of these legislative history finding tools are discussed further and illustrated in Section C.5 below.

The value of legislative debates as evidence of legislative intent has been greatly diminished by the contradictory nature of the statements they contain and the calculated use of prepared colloquies designed to manufacture evidence of legislative intent. This practice and the integrity of the *Record* itself have been widely criticized,[9] and courts rely more on committee reports than on legislative debates for aid in statutory interpretation.

6. PRESIDENTIAL APPROVAL OR VETO

After a bill is passed by both houses of Congress, it goes to the President for approval. If the President approves a bill, it becomes law. If the President vetoes a bill, to become law it must be repassed by both houses by a two-thirds majority. The messages or statements issued when the President signs or vetoes particular enactments can shed light on legislative history. Like other Presidential messages to Congress, these documents appear in several places, including the *Congressional Record,* the *Weekly Compilation of Presidential Documents,* the *House* and *Senate Journals,* and as House and Senate Documents. Illustration K shows President Carter's statement on signing the Foreign Intelligence Surveillance Act of 1978, as it appeared in the *Weekly Compilation of Presidential Documents.*

In recent years, President Reagan sometimes used signing statements to convey his interpretation of disputed provisions. These statements have been included in *USCCAN*'s legislative history section beginning in 1986, although their importance in determining legislative intent is subject to dispute.[10]

7. OTHER CONGRESSIONAL DOCUMENTS

Congress publishes many documents as required by law or by special request. These *House* and *Senate Documents* are issued in numerical series which run consecutively through both sessions of each

9. *See* Springer, "The *Congressional Record:* 'Substantially a Verbatim Report?' ", 13 *Gov't Publications Rev.* 371 (1986).

10. *See, e.g.,* Garber & Wimmer, "Presidential Signing Statements as Interpretations of Legislative Intent: An Executive Aggrandizement of Power," 24 *Harv.J. on Legis.* 363 (1987); Greenhouse, "In Signing Bills, Reagan Tries to Write History," *N.Y. Times,* Dec. 9, 1986, at B14.

Illustration K

President Carter's statement on signing S. 1566 into law, as published in the *Weekly Compilation of Presidential Documents*

other agency of the Executive Branch. Current statutes provide the Chief Counsel with sufficient authorities to evaluate small business issues and serve as an ombudsman to small business interests.

I am also concerned by the loan pooling provision in this bill that would authorize private dealers to issue a new class of 100 percent federally guaranteed securities which would compete directly with the Treasury and other federally-backed securities in the bond markets.

I look forward to working with the Congress and the small business community who worked on this bill to develop a program to meet the needs of small business. It is my great hope that early in the next Congress an approach will be fashioned to meet the needs of the small business community, with the full involvement of my Administration.

JIMMY CARTER

Foreign Intelligence Surveillance Act of 1978

Statement on Signing S. 1566 Into Law. October 25, 1978

I am pleased to sign into law today the Foreign Intelligence Surveillance Act of 1978. As I said a year and a half ago at the beginning of the process that produced this bill, "one of the most difficult tasks in a free society like our own is the correlation between adequate intelligence to guarantee our Nation's security on the one hand, and the preservation of basic human rights on the other."

This is a difficult balance to strike, but the act I am signing today strikes it. It sacrifices neither our security nor our civil liberties. And it assures that those who serve this country in intelligence positions will have the affirmation of Congress that their activities are lawful.

In working on this bill, the Congress dealt skillfully with sensitive issues. The result shows our country benefits when the legislative and executive branches of Government work together toward a common goal.

The bill requires, for the first time, a prior judicial warrant for *all* electronic surveillance for foreign intelligence or counterintelligence purposes in the United States in which communications of U.S. persons might be intercepted. It clarifies the Executive's authority to gather foreign intelligence by electronic surveillance in the United States. It will remove any doubt about the legality of those surveillances which are conducted to protect our country against espionage and international terrorism. It will assure FBI field agents and others involved in intelligence collection that their acts are authorized by statute and, if a U.S. person's communications are concerned, by a court order. And it will protect the privacy of the American people.

In short, the act helps to solidify the relationship of trust between the American people and their Government. It provides a basis for the trust of the American people in the fact that the activities of their intelligence agencies are both effective and lawful. It provides enough secrecy to ensure that intelligence relating to national security can be securely acquired, while permitting review by the courts and Congress to safeguard the rights of Americans and others.

This legislation is the first long step toward the goal of establishing statutory charters for our intelligence agencies. I am committed to that goal, and my administration will work with the Congress to achieve it.

Congress. They contain special studies and reports, reprints of Presidential messages, executive agency reports and memoranda, reports of nongovernmental organizations, and a great variety of papers ordered to be printed by either house of Congress. They are listed and indexed in the *Monthly Catalog of U.S. Government Publications,* and since 1970 in the *CIS/Index.* A document is cited by the name of the house issuing it, the number of the Congress and session, and the document number. House and Senate Documents also appear in the *Serial Set* and can be cited to that form by volume number. The *CIS US Serial Set Index,* referred to above, provides access to House and Senate Documents, as well as House and Senate Reports, issued from 1789 to 1969 (with access to later reports and documents through the *CIS/Index*). The value of House and Senate Documents for legislative history is usually negligible, but occasionally a document will have some relevance to a pending bill. An example of such a document, a Presidential communication transmitting a draft version of proposed legislation, was shown in Illustration B earlier in this chapter.

The Senate also issues two confidential series of publications in connection with its special responsibility for treaty ratification. *Senate Treaty Documents* contain the text of treaties sent to the Senate for its advice and consent, together with related messages or correspondence from the President and Secretary of State. *Senate Executive Reports* are issued by the Senate Foreign Relations Committee after its consideration of the treaty. These materials are discussed more fully in Chapter 15.

C. TOOLS FOR COMPILING A FEDERAL LEGISLATIVE HISTORY

To compile the legislative history of a pending bill or of an enacted statute, one must trace each of the actions taken by the legislature with regard to the bills which became law or which shaped the final enactment. The documents reflecting those actions must be located and studied either to ascertain the legislature's understanding of the final language of the enactment or to follow the procedures taken in considering the various proposals leading to the enactment.

The mass of documents comprising the source material for legislative history would be virtually inaccessible were it not for a number of finding tools which are indispensable for such research. No two of them are exactly alike and recourse to several is often necessary to secure adequate information. They are sometimes used to identify and locate a single document or to establish the current status of a pending bill. Most frequently they are used to reconstruct the history of a bill or enactment and to identify all of the documents relevant to its interpretation. As in other fields of legal bibliography, some of these tools are official government documents and others are unofficial commercial publications. The latter are often more useful by reason of their prompt supplementation, better indexing, or greater variety of research aids.

As noted above, the bill number of a proposed law (and even of an already enacted law) is usually the key to searching its legislative history and identifying the documents of that history. Since 1903, the bill number of each federal statute appears above its text or in the opening margin in *Statutes at Large,* and in many of the other sources listed below.[11]

Most of the finding tools to be described are essentially lists by bill number of laws or proposed laws, summarizing the provisions, indicating legislative actions taken from the time of introduction, and providing references to at least some of the documents issued in connection with Congressional consideration of the bill. These lists are frequently called *status tables,* since they indicate the current status of those bills which are still pending. Some of the following aids also include tables arranged by public law number for those bills which were enacted into law.

Which tool should be used in any particular circumstance depends on the resources available and the research needs. The most up-to-date information on current legislation may be found in *Congressional Index* or one of the online bill-tracking services. The most comprehensive coverage of documents relating to laws enacted within the past two decades is usually found in *CIS/Index.* For legislative history information on older laws, the only resource available may be the "History of Bills and Resolutions" in the *Congressional Record* index, which dates back to the nineteenth century.

1. CCH *CONGRESSIONAL INDEX*

Congressional Index, a commercial looseleaf service published since 1937 by Commerce Clearing House, is one of the most popular finding tools for legislative history. It is issued in two volumes for each Congress, and offers these many different approaches: indexes of all public general bills by subject and by sponsor; digests of each bill; a status table of actions taken on bills and resolutions; an index of enactments and vetoes; a table of companion bills; a list of reorganization plans, treaties, and nominations pending; tables of voting records of members of Congress by bill and resolution number; and a weekly report letter on major news and developments in Congress. Its status table section includes references to hearings, an important feature lacking in some other publications.

It should be noted that this service does not, however, contain the actual text of bills, debates, reports or laws. *Congressional Index* is

11. For laws before 1903, bill numbers can be found in E. Nabors, *Legislative Reference Checklist: The Key to Legislative Histories from 1789–1903* (Rothman, 1982). Tables for each Congress provide references from public law numbers and *Statutes at Large* citations to bill numbers.

only a finding tool, but a most useful one, with weekly supplementation and generally good indexing.

Illustration L shows a typical page of the *Congressional Index*'s current status table of Senate bills, with a particularly informative entry for S. 1566, the bill which is the subject of the previous illustrations in this chapter.

2. *CIS/INDEX*

Congressional Information Service has published its unofficial legislative service *CIS/Index* since 1970. *CIS/Index* offers the most complete and detailed indexing and abstracting of the documents of legislative history for each Congressional session. It is supplemented monthly, with quarterly cumulations and annually cumulated bound volumes. The indexes, providing access both by subject and by bill number, provide references to numbers assigned to each document by CIS and used to organize the accompanying abstracts.

From 1970 to 1983, two permanent volumes were issued for each year—an *Index* volume and *Abstracts,* which included a section providing cumulative legislative histories of enacted laws. This legislative history information has since 1984 appeared in a third annual volume, called *Legislative Histories.* There are also four cumulative indexes covering the periods 1970–74, 1975–78, 1979–82, and 1983–86. Further cumulative indexes may be expected in the future.

The service's main contribution to research in legislative history lies in its excellent coverage of published hearings, reports, committee prints and documents. It offers detailed indexing of these sources, as well as abstracts of each hearing, report and document. Illustration M shows the CIS cumulative index for 1975–78, which provides access to listings of various actions and documents relating to the Foreign Intelligence Surveillance Act.

The legislative histories of enactments, in the *Abstracts* volumes until 1983 and the *Legislative Histories* volumes beginning in 1984, include references to bills, hearings, committee reports, debates, committee prints, House and Senate documents, Presidential documents, and all legislative actions. Rather than limiting coverage to a single term of Congress, these histories include references to earlier hearings and other documents on related bills from *prior* Congressional sessions. These are probably the most complete summaries of the legislative history of federal enactments. Illustration N shows the cumulative legislative history of the Foreign Intelligence Surveillance Act of 1978 from the *Abstracts* volume for 1978. Illustration O shows a more comprehensive summary on a related bill in the 1984 *Legislative Histories* volume.

To accompany its index and abstracts, CIS provides microfiche reproductions of all published bills, hearings, reports, committee prints and congressional documents included in *CIS/Index* since 1970. This service is issued regularly and offers the full text of the documents

Illustration L

"Current Status of Senate Bills" table in CCH *Congressional Index*

See also Status of Senate Bills
For digest, see "Senate Bills" Division.

1487
Reptd., amended, S. Rept. No. 95-962 .... 6/28/78
Amended on S. floor (Voice) 9/29/78
Passed S. as amended (Voice) 9/29/78
Amended to contain text of H. 8853 as passed (Voice) 10/3/78
Passed H. as amended (Voice) 10/3/78
Conferees appointed by H. 10/3/78
H. amends. rejected by S. 10/9/78
Conferees appointed by S. 10/9/78
Conf. Rept. filed, H. Rept. No. 95-1778 .... 10/12/78
Agreed to by H. (Roll-call) 10/14/78
Agreed to by S. (Voice) 10/14/78

1493
Hearing in S. 5/10/78
Reptd., amended, S. Rept. No. 95-1412 .... 10/14/78

1503
Passed S. as reptd. (Voice) 1/20/78
To H. Committee on Judiciary 1/23/78
Reptd., amended, H. Rept. No. 95-1747 .... 10/10/78
H. suspension vote postponed 10/10/78
Passed H. as reptd. (Roll-call) 10/12/78
H. amends. agreed to by S. (Voice) 10/13/78

* 1509
Reptd., no amend., H. Rept. No. 95-846 .... 1/23/78
Passed H. as reptd. (Voice) 2/6/78
To President 2/8/78
Approved (P.L. 95-232) 2/17/78

1531
Hearing in H. 3/7/78

1537
Indefinitely postponed by S. 4/24/78

1546
Hearing in S. 4/5/78

1547
Amended on S. floor (Voice) 1/31/78
Text of bill incorporated into H. 7442 .... 1/31/78
Indefinitely postponed by S. 1/31/78

1556
Hearing in S. 6/15/78

1566
Reptd., amended, S. Rept. No. 95-701 .... 3/14/78
Amended on S. floor (Voice) 4/20/78
Passed S. as amended (Roll-call) ... 4/20/78
To H. Committee on Judiciary 4/24/78
Amended to contain text of H. 7308 as passed (Voice) 9/7/78
Passed H. as amended (Voice) 9/7/78
H. amends. rejected by S. 9/12/78
Conferees appointed by S. 9/26/78
S. amends. rejected by H. (Voice) 9/26/78
Conferees appointed by H. 9/26/78
Conf. Rept. filed, H. Rept. No. 95-1720 .... 10/5/78
Agreed to by S. (Voice) 10/9/78
Agreed to by H. (Roll-call) 10/12/78

* 1568
Reptd., amended, S. Rept. No. 95-721 .... 3/23/78
Passed S. as reptd. (Voice) 4/5/78
To H. Committee on Public Works and Transportation 4/6/78
Passed H. in lieu of H. 10838 ...... 5/15/78
Approved (P.L. 95-285) 5/25/78

1570
Hearing in S. (Printed) 1/19/78

* 1582
Amended to contain text of H. 8009 as amended (Voice) 6/29/78
Passed H. as amended (Voice) 6/29/78
H. amends. agreed to by S. (Voice) 7/13/78
To President 7/17/78
Approved (P.L. 95-328) 7/28/78

* 1585
Agreed to by H. (Roll-call) 1/24/78
To President 1/25/78
Approved (P.L. 95-225) 2/7/78

1587
Hearing in S. 3/15/78

1592
Hearing in S. 7/26/78

1613
Reptd., amended, H. Rept. No. 95-1364 .... 7/17/78
Amended to contain text of H. 9622 as passed 2/28/78 (Voice) 10/4/78
Passed H. as amended (Voice) 10/4/78
Conferees appointed by H. 10/4/78
Conferees appointed by S. 10/7/78
H. amends. rejected by S. 10/7/78

* 1617
Bill title amended (voice) 2/28/78
Passed H. as amended (Voice) 2/28/78

Illustration M

Index to *CIS/Index* for 1975 to 1978

Foreign economic relations | **Index of Subjects and Names**

US foreign policy effect on long-term access to Rhodesian mineral resources, 76 H461-87
US intl energy policy, 75 H381-45, 75 J841-27.3
US Intl Trade Commission programs, FY77 authorization, 76 S361-14
US Intl Trade Commission programs, FY78 authorization, 77 S361-12
"U.S.-Mexico Economic Relations: The Role of California", 78 H181-62
US oil firms' foreign ops, 76 S521-46.12
US-Saudi-Israel relations; relationship of Somalia aid to Diego Garcia naval base estab, 77 S381-1.3
US stockpiling policies and intl trade, 76 J952-23
US 200 mile fishing zone, estab, 76 S201-6.1
USDA participation in intl agric commodity negotiations, 75 S163-30
World energy supply and demand projections, 77 H962-23.1, 77 H962-27.1
World market economy system, status assessment, 77 S382-14
see also Balance of payments
see also Blockade
see also Dumping
see also East-West trade
see also Embargoes and boycotts
see also Export controls
see also Foreign assistance
see also Foreign corporations
see also Foreign trade
see also Foreign trade promotion
see also Import restrictions
see also International debts
see also International finance
see also Multinational corporations
see also Tariffs
see also Trade agreements

Foreign exchange
AF ops and maintenance programs to defray costs of dollar devaluation, FY79 approp, 78 S181-35.5
Army ops and maintenance programs to defray costs of dollar devaluation, FY78 approp reprogramming action, 78 S181-48.11
Bd for Intl Broadcasting programs, FY76 authorization, 75 H381-48
Bd for Intl Broadcasting programs to defray costs of dollar decline, supplemental approp FY78, 78 H181-92.24
Currency convertibility problems for US publications sales in Eastern Europe, 77 J891-4.6
Developing countries acceptance of economic reforms as precondition for foreign loans, 78 H241-4.1
DOD military construction and family housing programs to defray costs of dollar decline, supplemental approp FY78, 78 H181-93.5
DOD programs, supplemental approp FY78, 78 H181-26.4
Dollar decline abroad, effect on inflation, 78 S241-57.3
"Dollar Devaluation, Floating Exchange Rates and U.S. Exports", 78 H241-30.4
Dollar stabilization policies, 78 J841-25.1
Dollar's exchange rate decline, analysis, 78 S241-23.2
Domestic intl sales corporations cost-benefit analysis, seminar, 75 S252-25.1
Economic review, Oct 1978, 78 J842-22
Eurodollar market ops and impact on intl finance, 77 J842-5
European Recovery Program extension, 1949, 76 H461-83.3
Exchange rate policy and intl monetary reform, 75 H241-39, 75 H242-11, 75 J842-27
Exchange Stabilization Fund, oversight and Fed budget inclusion, 76 H261-15
Export policy oversight, 78 S241-37
Fed budget and economic overview, FY79, 78 H181-52.2
Fed Reserve Bd intervention to strengthen dollar, 77 H241-41.1
Financial instns restructuring for economic recovery, congressional study plans, 75 H242-17
First concurrent budget resolution, FY79, economic review, 78 S251-6.4
Foreign economic policy objectives, 76 H461-46.3
Foreign economic policy overview, 78 S381-1.3
Illegal African currency transfers allegedly encouraged by Overseas Private Investment Corp, 76 H461-58
IMF Articles of Agreement amendments, congressional authorization, 76 H241-35, 76 S241-69, 76 S243-24, 76 S381-33
IMF gold agreement proposal, rpt, 75 J842-38
IMF guidelines for govtl exchange rates intervention, 77 J841-18
IMF guidelines for govtl exchange rates intervention; Exchange Stabilization Fund, Fed budget inclusion, 78 S241-8
IMF intl currency devs review, 76 H241-22
Intl Communication Agency programs to defray costs of dollar decline, supplemental approp FY78, 78 H181-92.27
Intl exchange rate fluctuations, impact on inflation, 76 S361-22
Intl monetary and energy policy, 76 J841-2
Japan-US relations, background articles, 78 H782-67
Japan-US trade relations, review, 78 S381-30.1
Mexican peso devaluation impact on US Southwest, 77 J841-31
Monetary policy oversight, 78 H241-42.1, 78 H241-42.2
Multinatl corp intl financial transactions, 76 S381-26.1
Multinatl corps transactions during dollar devaluation crisis, 75 S382-24
OPEC oil price increases impact on intl economic stability, 75 H241-5.2, 75 H241-5.3
OPEC oil price peg to spec drawing rights, US economy impact, 77 H242-11
Pres Ford's economic proposals, 75 J841-20.1
Radio Free Europe/Radio Liberty facility leases renegotiation problems relating to currency fluctuations, 76 H461-32.1
State Dept programs to defray costs of dollar decline, FY78 reprogramming actions, 78 H181-92.2
State Dept programs to defray costs of dollar decline, supplemental approp FY78, 78 H181-17.7, 78 H181-92.7, 78 H181-92.8
Tax reductions and revisions, 78 S361-42.1
Trade deficits impact on dollar stability, 78 H781-12
US-held foreign currency accounts, 76 H401-38.2
"U.S.S.R.: Hard Currency Trade and Payments, 1977-78", 77 S402-16
see also Balance of payments
see also Special foreign currency programs

Foreign Gifts and Decorations Act
House of Reps members, officers, and employees acceptance of gifts from foreign govts, rules, 78 H742-1
Senate rules on Sens and employees travel at foreign govt expense, 77 S383-22

Foreign Government Investment Control Act
Foreign investment disclosure and anti-boycott proposals, 75 S241-43
Foreign investment regulation, 75 S261-68

Foreign Income Act
Taxation of Amers working abroad, 78 H783-50

Foreign Intelligence Surveillance Act
Draft text, Pres communic, 76 H520-1
Foreign intelligence electronic surveillance, judicial warrant requirements, 76 S521-40, 76 S523-32, 76 S963-8, 77 H521-26, 77 S421-1, 77 S521-52, 77 S523-43, 77 S523-44, 78 H431-3, 78 H433-3, 78 H433-5, 78 H522-12, 78 S421-3, 78 S423-1, 78 PL95-511

Foreign Investment Act
Foreign investment disclosure and anti-boycott proposals, 75 S241-43
Foreign investment in US, disclosure and regulation requirements, 75 S241-19
Foreign investment regulation, 76 H241-1.2

Foreign Investment Disclosure Act
Foreign investment disclosure and anti-boycott proposals, 75 S241-43
Foreign investment regulation, 75 S261-68, 76 H241-1.3

Foreign Investment Reporting Act
Foreign investment regulation, 75 S261-68

Foreign Investment Review Act
Foreign investment in US, info gathering and review procedures estab, 75 S261-27

Foreign Investment Study Act
Commerce Dept programs, supplemental approp FY75, 75 S181-32
Domestic and Intl Business Admin program, supplemental approp FY75, 75 H181-12.16
Foreign direct investment regulation, 75 S261-68.2
Foreign investment in US, disclosure and regulation requirements, 75 S241-19.1
Foreign investment in US, study authorization, 75 PL93-479
Foreign investment regulation, 76 H241-1.2
Foreign investments in US, Treas and Commerce Depts rpts, 76 S261-56

Foreign Investment Survey Act
US and foreign investments data collection system estab, 76 S263-20

Foreign investments
African dev problems and US aid programs, 78 H461-76.1
AID housing investment guarantee program, FY78 approp, 77 H181-77.7
Arab bank deposit implications for US banks, 76 H461-27.4
Arab-influenced US corp discriminatory practices, 76 H461-27.3

1066 CIS/Four-Year Cumulative Index | Volumes 6 - 9, 1975 - 1978

Illustration N

Cumulative legislative history summary in *CIS/Index* 1978 "Abstracts" volume

318 and related

H721-10; H721-14.
:722-2.

H721-5; H721-38;

S721-18;
:6; S721-27.
H722-2; H722-3.
:-14.
:402-5.
No. 95-949); H723-
ice Report).
No. 95-1140);

124 (1978):
ssed House.
ssed Senate,

nference report.
onference report.

TICLES, duty

'8. 95-2. 1 p.
'3 •Item 575.
774.

f June 30, 1981, the
es on certain metal
metal, and other ar-
r purposes."
tures of mashed or
and salt.
2165 and related

No. 95-1361).
No. 95-1243).
124 (1978):
ssed House.
ssed Senate,

n Senate amend-

ENT OF ENERGY SECURITY AND APPLICATIONS AR ENERGY ATION ACT OF

'8. 95-2. 5 p.
/3 •Item 575.
775.

s for the Department
rity programs for fis-
r purposes."
· R&D on strategic
ations of nuclear en-

1686 and related

; H201-25.
.4; S201-19.5;

Jo. 95-1108).
nd S313-23 (No.
2693).

Congressional Record Vol. 124 (1978):
May 16, 17, considered and passed House.
Sept. 30, considered and passed Senate, amended, in lieu of S. 2693.
Oct. 11, House concurred in Senate amendment.

PL95–510 SMALL BUSINESS ACT, amendment, volunteer programs, establishment and operation.
Oct. 24, 1978. 95-2. 3 p.
• CIS/MF/3 •Item 575.
92 STAT. 1780.

"To amend the Small Business Act by transferring thereto those provisions of the Domestic Volunteer Service Act of 1973 affecting the operation of volunteer programs to assist small business, to increase the maximum allowable compensation and travel expenses for experts and consultants, and for other purposes."

Transfers statutory authority for SBA-administered Service Corps of Retired Executives and Active Corps of Executives.

Legislative history: (H.R. 13418 and related bills):

1978 CIS/Annual:
House Hearings: H721-27.
House Report: H723-7 (No. 95-1375).

Congressional Record Vol. 124 (1978):
Sept. 25, considered and passed House.
Oct. 11, considered and passed Senate.

PL95–511 FOREIGN INTELLIGENCE SURVEILLANCE ACT OF 1978.
Oct. 25, 1978. 95-2. 16 p.
• CIS/MF/3 •Item 575.
92 STAT. 1783.

"To authorize electronic surveillance to obtain foreign intelligence information."

Establishes judicial warrant requirements for executive branch use of electronic surveillance to obtain foreign intelligence information, and restricts the use of such information.

Legislative history: (S. 1566 and related bills):

1973 CIS/Annual:
Senate Hearings: S521-45.

1974 CIS/Annual:
House Hearings: H521-64.

1975 CIS/Annual:
Senate Hearings: S521-35; S521-60.
Senate Committee Print: S522-6.

1976 CIS/Annual:
House Document: H520-1.
House Hearings: H521-15; H521-16.
Senate Hearings: S521-40.
Senate Reports: S523-32 (No. 94-1035, accompanying S. 3197); S963-8 (No. 94-1161, accompanying S. 3197).

1977 CIS/Annual:
House Hearings: H401-4.4; H521-26.
Senate Hearings: S421-1; S521-52.
Senate Committee Print: S522-2.
Senate Reports: S523-43 (No. 95-604); S523-44 (No. 95-604, pt. 2).

1978 CIS/Annual:
House Hearings: H431-3.
Senate Hearings: S421-3.

House Committee Print: H522-12.
House Reports: H433-3 (No. 95-1283, pt. 1, accompanying H.R. 7308); H433-5 (No. 95-1720, Conference Report).
Senate Report: S423-1 (No. 95-701).

Congressional Record Vol. 124 (1978):
Apr. 20, considered and passed Senate.
Sept. 6, 7, considered and passed House, amended.
Sept. 12, Senate disagreed to House amendments.
Oct. 9, Senate agreed to conference report.
Oct. 12, House agreed to conference report.

Weekly Compilation of Presidential Documents Vol. 14, No. 43 (1978):
Oct. 25, Presidential statement.

PL95–512 COMPTROLLER GENERAL ANNUITY ADJUSTMENT ACT OF 1978.
Oct. 25, 1978. 95-2. 3 p.
• CIS/MF/3 •Item 575.
92 STAT. 1799.

"To provide for cost-of-living adjustments in the annuity of a retired Comptroller General, and for other purposes."

Amends Budget and Accounting Act of 1921.

Legislative history: (S. 3412 and related bill):

1978 CIS/Annual:
House Hearings: H401-31.
Senate Hearings: S401-53.
House Report: H403-10 (No. 95-1241, accompanying H.R. 12196).
Senate Report: S403-54 (No. 95-1267).

Congressional Record Vol. 124 (1978):
July 25, H.R. 12196 considered and passed House.
Oct. 9, considered and passed Senate.
Oct. 11, considered and passed House, in lieu of H.R. 12196.

PL95–513 VIETNAM VETERANS WEEK, designation authorization.
Oct. 25, 1978. 95-2. 1 p.
• CIS/MF/3 •Item 575.
92 STAT. 1802.

"Authorizing and requesting the President to designate the seven-day period beginning on May 28, 1979, as 'Vietnam Veterans Week'."

Legislative history: (H.J. Res. 1147):

Congressional Record Vol. 124 (1978):
Oct. 10, considered and passed House.
Oct. 12, considered and passed Senate.

PL95–514 PUBLIC RANGELANDS IMPROVEMENT ACT OF 1978.
Oct. 25, 1978. 95-2. 8 p.
• CIS/MF/3 •Item 575.
92 STAT. 1803.

"To improve the range conditions of the public rangelands."

Amends Federal Land Policy and Management Act of 1976 to provide for management of public grazing lands under Bureau of Land Management. Includes provisions for grazing fees and control of wild horses and burros.

Legisl
bills):
1976
Senat
Senat
pan
1978
House
House
H4
Senat
Cong
June
Sept.
am
Oct.
Oct.
Week
ment
Oct.

PL9

"To
parin
the s
other
In lie
anism
in Fe
Legis
1976
Hous
Hous
co
1977
Sena
1978
Sena
Hous
co
Sena
Cong
Sept.
Oct.
H
in

PL9

"For
Man
ters.
Also
grap
Legi
bill):
1978
Hou
M
13

JANUARY-DECEMBER 1978 **Volume 9, Number 1-12**

Illustration O

Legislative history entry for related Act in *CIS/Index* 1984 "Legislative Histories" volume

Public Law 98-477 **98 Stat. 2209**

Central Intelligence Agency Information Act

October 15, 1984

Public Law

1.1 Public Law 98-477, approved Oct. 15, 1984. (H.R. 5164)

"To amend the National Security Act of 1947 to regulate public disclosure of information held by the Central Intelligence Agency, and for other purposes."

Prohibits search, review, or release, under the Freedom of Information Act (FOIA) of CIA-designated sensitive operational information detailing intelligence sources or methods.

Authorizes search and review of designated sensitive files containing information relating to improper or illegal intelligence activities.

Authorizes search and review of designated sensitive files containing information on special activities when existence of such activities must be disclosed under the FOIA.

Authorizes judicial review of CIA designations of sensitive files.

Requires review for declassification and release of CIA information of historical value.

Requires additional CIA reports to congressional committees for oversight of FOIA processing activities.

Clarifies the relationship between the FOIA and the Privacy Act to prohibit Federal agency use of a Privacy Act exemption as grounds for denial of information otherwise accessible under FOIA provisions.

(CIS84:PL98-477 4 p.)

P.L. 98-477 Reports

98th Congress

2.1 S. Rpt. 98-305 on S. 1324, "Intelligence Information Act of 1983," Nov. 9, 1983.

(CIS83:S423-3 45 p.)
(Y1.1/5:98-305.)

2.2 H. Rpt. 98-726, pt. 1 on H.R. 5164, "Central Intelligence Agency Information Act," May 1, 1984.

(CIS84:H433-2 42 p.)
(Y1.1/8:98-726/pt.1.)

2.3 H. Rpt. 98-726, pt. 2 on H.R. 5164, "Central Intelligence Agency Information Act," Sept. 10, 1984.

(CIS84:H403-20 26 p.)
(Y1.1/8:98-726/pt.2.)

P.L. 98-477 Debate

130 Congressional Record
98th Congress, 2nd Session - 1984

4.1 Sept. 17, 19, H.R. 5164 considered and passed House.

4.2 Sept. 28, H.R. 5164 considered and passed Senate.

P.L. 98-477 Hearings

96th Congress

5.1 "Freedom of Information Act: Central Intelligence Agency Exemptions," hearings before the Subcommittee on Government Information and Individual Rights, House Government Operations Committee, Feb. 20, May 29, 1980.

(CIS81:H401-40 iii+205 p.)
(Y4.G74/7:F87/2.)

5.2 "H.R. 6588, The National Intelligence Act of 1980," hearings before the Subcommittee on Legislation, House Select Intelligence Committee, Mar. 18, 19, 27, Apr. 15, 22, 1980.

(CIS81:H431-2 iv+608 p.)
(Y4.In8/18:In8/2.)

97th Congress

5.3 "Freedom of Information Act, Vol. 1," hearings before the Subcommittee on Constitution, Senate Judiciary Committee, July 15, 22, 31, Sept. 24, Oct. 15, Nov. 12, Dec. 9, 1981.

(CIS82:S521-71 vi+1147 p. il.)
(Y4.J89/2:J-97-50/v.1.)

5.4 "Freedom of Information Act: Appendix, Vol. 2," hearings before the Subcommittee on Constitution, Senate Judiciary Committee, July 15, 22, 31, Sept. 24, Oct. 15, Nov. 12, Dec. 9, 1981.

(CIS82:S521-72 vi+880 p. il.)
(Y4.J89/2:J-97-50/v.2.)

5.5 "Intelligence Reform Act of 1981," hearings before the Senate Select Intelligence Committee, July 21, 1981.

(CIS81:S421-5 iv+90 p.)
(Y4.In8/19:In8/2.)

454 CIS/INDEX Legislative Histories JANUARY-DECEMBER 1984

themselves in a convenient form. A retrospective microfiche collection of Congressional documents before 1969 is also available from CIS, accessible through its indexes to the Serial Set, hearings, and committee prints, described above in Section B.

The CIS coverage of federal legislative history since 1970 can be searched online through DIALOG. The online database is updated each month, like the printed indexes. Computerized access to the pre-1970 documents is available through the *CIS Congressional Masterfile, 1789–1969,* a composite CD–ROM service that incorporates the various retrospective CIS indexes and permits free-text searching.

3. ONLINE LEGISLATIVE RESEARCH SERVICES

The development of a variety of online database services has vastly improved research in legislative history. Several of these have already been described above, such as the various computer-based approaches to the *Congressional Record* and the online version of *CIS/Index.* Several of the specialized federal databases in WESTLAW and LEXIS include selective documents of legislative history of new legislation in those subject fields, with the most comprehensive coverage in federal taxation databases.

Online bill-tracking services are among the most important and timely sources for information on the status of current legislation. LEGI–SLATE is a service of the Washington Post Company covering Congressional developments and updated daily. As mentioned in earlier parts of this chapter, it includes the text of bills, committee reports, and the *Congressional Record* from the current Congress. Relevant legislation can be found by several methods, including subject, sponsor, and keyword. LEGI–SLATE tracks action on each bill day-by-day, providing information such as committee referrals, committee schedules pending, and recorded floor votes. It also lists any article discussing a bill in the *Washington Post, Congressional Quarterly Weekly Report,* and *National Journal.* Coverage of most Congressional action begins with the 96th Congress in 1979.

ELSS (Electronic Legislative Search System) is a bill-tracking service developed by Commerce Clearing House and covering both Congress and the state legislatures. ELSS does not include the full text of documents such as bills and reports, but provides summaries of legislation and information, updated daily, on developments such as committee assignments and floor actions.

Other bill-tracking services are available from Congressional Quarterly (discussed below in Section C.8) and Washington Online. A service available through both WESTLAW and LEXIS is BILLCAST, which summarizes legislation in the current Congress and provides forecasts of each bill's chances of passage. A companion database, BILLCAST ARCHIVES, contains information on earlier terms, beginning with the 99th Congress in 1985.

With the frequent offering of new databases and the demise of others, any description of those available is soon outdated. The use of *current* database directories is essential for determining available resources. Two directories which are updated at least twice each year are: *Data Base Directory* (Knowledge Industry Publications), and *Directory of Online Databases* (Cuadra/Elsevier). The *Directory of Online Databases* is also available through WESTLAW.

4. *DIGEST OF PUBLIC GENERAL BILLS AND RESOLUTIONS*

The *Digest of Public General Bills and Resolutions* has been published since 1936 by the Congressional Research Service of the Library of Congress, and is normally issued twice during each session with occasional supplements. The final issue of the *Digest* for each session, published in two parts after its adjournment, cumulates information from the earlier issues and is invaluable for retrospective research. The *Digest* provides summaries of all bills and resolutions introduced in each session of Congress, with more detailed analyses of those bills which have been reported out of committee. There are indexes by sponsor and by subject. Separate sections of the digest provide coverage of those bills which have been enacted into law (arranged by public law number) and for all other measures receiving action (arranged by bill and resolution number). Following the summary of a bill's provisions is a list of major steps in its consideration. These lists include citations to committee reports issued on the bill, but not to hearings. Illustration P shows the beginning of the entry for S. 1566, when it was enacted as Public Law 95–511.

5. *CONGRESSIONAL RECORD* HISTORY TABLES

The *Congressional Record* provides more than a transcript of debates in the Senate and House. Its fortnightly and final indexes also include useful tables providing information on the status and history of bills. The fortnightly index contains a "History of Bills and Resolutions," which is arranged separately for each house by bill and resolution number. It includes a brief digest of each measure, the name of the sponsor, the committee to which it has been referred, as well as references to debates, legislative actions, committee reports, amendments and passage information. Each entry also provides reference to the page number in the *Congressional Record* at which action is reported. Unfortunately, this status table only lists bills and resolutions which were acted upon during the two-week period preceding the index and does not cumulate all measures introduced in that session. Nor does the table contain references to hearings. However, the coverage of committee reports and debates on each bill listed is complete back to the date of its introduction.

At the end of each session, a completely cumulative "History of Bills and Resolutions" table is published in the *Index* volume of the permanent bound set of the *Congressional Record.* Since publication of the bound edition has been running six years late, the utility of this table, except for historical purposes, has diminished. While tables in recent bound *Congressional Record* volumes may not be as timely or complete as listings in commercial sources such as *CIS/Index,* listings

Illustration P

Entry for Public Law 95–511 in the *Digest of Public General Bills and Resolutions*

10-14-78 Measure presented to President
10-24-78 Public Law 95-508

Public Law 95-509 Approved 10/24/78; H.R. 11686.

Department of Energy National Security and Military Applications of Nuclear Energy Authorization Act - *Title I: National Security Programs* - Authorizes the appropriation of funds to the Department of Energy for specified operating expenses, designated plant and capital equipment costs, and for supplemental authorizations for specified previously authorized projects.

Authorizes the appropriation of funds for research and development concerning: inertial confinement fusion; naval reactor development; nuclear materials security and safeguards; weapons activities; special materials production; defense intelligence and arms control; and program direction and management support related to national security programs.

Title II: General Provisions - Prohibits use of any amount appropriated pursuant to this Act for any program: (1) in excess of the amount actually authorized for that particular program by this Act; or (2) which has not been presented to, or requested of, the Congress, unless a specified period has passed after the Secretary of Energy has given Congress notice of the proposed action or unless the appropriate committee has no objection to the proposed action and so notifies the Secretary before such period elapses.

Prohibits the start of specified plant and capital equipment projects if their current estimated cost exceeds by more than 25 percent the amount authorized for such project. Requires the Secretary: (1) to notify Congress whenever such project cost estimates occur; and (2) not proceed with such projects unless and until additional funds are authorized.

Sets certain limits on the costs of general plant projects which the Secretary is authorized to start.

Makes available for use, when necessary, in all national security programs of the Department of Energy amounts appropriated in this Act for policy and management activities, general plant projects, and plant engineering and design.

Authorizes the Secretary to perform construction design services for any construction project of the Department in support of national security programs which have been presented to, or requested of, Congress in specified amounts. Requires the Secretary to notify Congress at least 30 days before any funds are obligated for design services for projects in which the estimated design costs exceed $300,000.

Allows increases in appropriations authorized in this Act for salary, pay, retirement, or other benefits for Federal employees by such amounts as may be necessary for increases in such benefits authorized by law.

Prohibits the use of funds authorized by this Act for the testing, modernization, rebuilding, or replacement of any component of the B43 bomb. Allows use of such funds for quality and reliability testing and for the replacement of limited life components of such bomb.

Provides directions on future authorization requests.

Requires the Secretary to conduct a study and to report to Congress on the status of all Government-owned, contractor-operated, plant, capital equipment, facilities, and utilities which support the nuclear weapons program, including an analysis of measures required to restore the nuclear weapons complex to a satisfactory condition and a plan containing proposed schedules for carrying out and funding any restoration found to be necessary.

Amends the Department of Energy Organization Act by repealing the provision allowing members of the Armed Forces to be detailed for service in the Department by the Secretary concerned pursuant to cooperative agreements.

Stipulates that none of the funds authorized by this or any Act may be expended for the development of a nuclear warhead for the SM-2 standard missile until an arms control impact statement for such warhead has been filed with the Congress.

5-03-78 Reported to House from the Committee on Armed Services, H. Rept. 95-1108
5-16-78 Measure called up by special rule in House
5-16-78 5-17-78, Measure considered in House
5-17-78 Measure passed House, roll call #326 (348-46)
5-22-78 Referred to Senate Committee on Armed Services
9-30-78 Measure called up by committee discharge in Senate
9-30-78 Measure considered in Senate
9-30-78 Measure passed Senate, amended, in lieu of S. 2693, roll call #433 (68-1)
10-11-78 House agreed to Senate amendment
10-13-78 Measure enrolled in House
10-13-78 Measure enrolled in Senate
10-14-78 Measure presented to President
10-24-78 Public Law 95-509

Public Law 95-510 Approved 10/24/78; H.R. 13418.

Amends the Small Business Act and the Domestic Volunteer Service Act of 1973 to transfer to the Small Business Administration the authority to conduct a program of volunteer assistance for small businesses. Includes the transfer of the SCORE (Service Corps of Retired Executives) and ACE (Active Corps of Executives) programs to the Administration from the ACTION Agency.

Increases the maximum allowable compensation and travel expenses for experts and consultants employed by the Administrator of the Small Business Administration to the maximum amounts payable under the executive schedule for Federal employees.

7-19-78 Reported to House from the Select Committee on Small Business, H. Rept. 95-1375
9-25-78 Measure called up under motion to suspend rules and pass in House
9-25-78 Measure considered in House
9-25-78 Measure passed House
10-11-78 Measure called up by unanimous consent in Senate
10-11-78 Measure considered in Senate
10-11-78 Measure passed Senate
10-13-78 Measure enrolled in House
10-13-78 Measure enrolled in Senate
10-14-78 Measure presented to President
10-24-78 Public Law 95-510

Public Law 95-511 Approved 10/25/78; S. 1566.

Foreign Intelligence Surveillance Act - *Title I: Electronic Surveillance within the United States for Foreign Intelligence Purposes* - Permits the President, acting through the Attorney General, to authorize electronic surveillances for foreign intelligence purposes without a court order in certain circumstances. Requires the Attorney General: (1) to certify that the minimization procedures governing these surveillances meet certain standards; and (2) to forward such procedures to the House and Senate intelligence committees at least 30 days prior to their going into effect. Provides for the Attorney General to direct a specified common carrier to render assistance. Directs the Attorney General to transmit a copy of the certification for electronic surveillance to the appropriate court where it is to be maintained under security measures and remain seal, except in certain circumstances.

Requires the Chief Justice of the United States to designate seven district court judges, who shall constitute a special court, each of whom shall have jurisdiction to hear applications for and grant orders approving electronic surveillance anywhere within the United States. Requires the Chief Justice to designate three Federal judges to comprise a special court of appeals which shall have jurisdiction to hear an appeal by the United States from the denial of any application. Grants the United States a further right to appeal an affirmance of denial to the Supreme Court. Provides that such judges shall serve for a maximum of seven years and shall not be eligible for redesignation.

Requires each application for any order approving electronic surveillance for foreign intelligence purposes to be approved by the Attorney General and to include among other information: (1) the identity of the officer making the application; (2) the authority conferred on the Attorney General by the President and the approval of the Attorney General to make the application; (3) the identity, if known,n of the subject of the surveillance; (4) the fact and circumstances justifying belief that the target of surveillance is a foreign power or an agent of a foreign power; (5) a description of the type of information sought and a certification by one of specified Federal officers that such official deems the information sought to be foreign intelligence information, and information which cannot feasibly be obtained by normal investigative techniques; (6) a statement of the period of time for which the surveillance is required; and (7) a statement of procedures to be taken

for earlier bills can be invaluable. History tables have appeared in *Congressional Record* index volumes since 1873, sixty years before the *Congressional Index* began and almost a century before *CIS/Index.* Illustration Q shows the final "History of Bills and Resolutions" entry for S. 1566, the Foreign Intelligence Surveillance Act of 1978.

Another history table appears in the *Daily Digest* volume of the bound *Congressional Record* set. This table, "History of Bills Enacted into Public Law," lacks the debate entries in the "History of Bills and Resolutions," but is otherwise a useful summary. Illustration R shows this table, with an entry for the Foreign Intelligence Surveillance Act of 1978.

6. LEGISLATIVE CALENDARS

Calendars issued for each house of Congress and for most committees provide current information on the status of pending bills. Although they are primarily internal publications for the use of the legislators, some are distributed to libraries and, because of their frequency of updating, can be useful sources for the current status of bills listed and particularly for information on hearings.

Perhaps the most important feature of any Congressional calendar is the table "History of Bills and Resolutions: Numerical Order of Bills and Resolutions Which Have Been Reported to or Considered by Either or Both Houses," in *Calendars of the United States House of Representatives, and History of Legislation.* This table covers bills in *both* houses, is updated daily, and cumulates legislative information for bills on which some action has been taken. It includes several subsidiary tables and a subject index, but does not fully list debates and hearings. The "Numerical Order" table in the final issue of the House *Calendars* cumulates both sessions at the end of each Congress and is very useful for permanent reference. It is available long before the bound edition of the *Congressional Record* is published, but is less complete than the *Record*'s "History of Bills and Resolutions" since it includes only bills on which action was taken.

7. *STATUTES AT LARGE*

One of the simplest and most readily available places to find legislative history information for enacted laws is in the *Statutes at Large.* As shown above in Illustration A–2, on page 220, at the end of the text for each law there appears a legislative history summary. This summary includes citations of reports from House, Senate, and Conference Committees, lists the dates of consideration and passage in each house, and provides references to presidential statements. It does not, however, provide references to exact *Congressional Record* pages, or to hearings and other relevant documents. This information has appeared at the end of each law only since 1975. From 1963 to 1974, it appeared at the end of each volume in a table, "Guide to Legislative History." The legislative history summaries in *Statutes at Large* are by

Illustration Q

"History of Bills and Resolutions" in annual *Congressional Record* index volume

SENATE BILLS

From the Committee on the Judiciary. Reported with amendment (S. Rept. 95-696), 6234.

S. 1484—For the relief of Michael Bruce Holland.

From the Committee on the Judiciary. Reported (S. Rept. 95-993), 21149.—Referred to Committee on the Judiciary, 22678.—Reported (H. Rept. 95-1701), 33644.—Passed House, 38216.—Examined and signed, 38775, 38082.—Presented to the President, 38084.—Approved [Private Law 95-81], 38086.

S. 1487—To eliminate racketeering in the sale and distribution of cigarettes, and for other purposes.

Cosponsors added, 6992.—From Committee on the Judiciary. Reported with amendment (S. Rept. 95-962), 19275.—Made special order S. Res. 499, 22181.—Amended and passed Senate, 32562.—Amended and passed House (in lieu of H.R. 8853) title amended. House insisted on its amendment and asked for a conference. Conferees appointed, 33281.—Senate disagreed with House amendment and agreed to a conference. Conferees appointed, 34863.—Conference report (H. Rept. 95-1778), submitted in House, 36510.—Conference report considered and agreed to in House, 38284.—Conference report submitted and agreed to in Senate, 37517.—Examined and signed, 38083, 38776.—Presented to the President, 38085.—Approved [Public Law 95-575], 38086.

S. 1493—To amend the Public Works and Economic Development Act to establish a comprehensive program to provide financial and technical assistance to States, local governments, and Indian tribes to manage impacts caused by energy development, and for other purposes.

From the Committee on Environment and Public Works and the Committee on Governmental Affairs. Reported with amendments (S. Rept. 95-1412), 37654.

S. 1500—To designate certain lands in the State of Alaska as units of the National Park, National Wildlife Refuge, National Wild and Scenic Rivers, and National Wilderness Preservation Systems, and for other purposes.

Cosponsors added, 10948, 16537, 19281, 24157.

S. 1503—To provide for the payment of losses incurred as a result of the ban on the use of chemical Tris in apparel, fabric, yarn, or fiber, and for other purposes.

Amended and passed Senate, 207.—Referred to Committee on the Judiciary, 454.—Reported with amendment (H. Rept. 95-1747), 35194.—Debated, 34906.—Rules suspended. Amended and passed House, 36485.—Senate concurred in House amendment, 36726.—Examined and signed, 38776, omitted in Senate.—Presented to the President, 38085.—Presidential veto, 38087.

S. 1509—To provide for the return to the United States of title to certain lands conveyed to certain Indian Pueblos of New Mexico and for such land to be held in trust by the United States for such tribes.

Reported (H. Rept. 95-846), 455.—Passed House, 2373.—Examined and signed, 2507, 2548.—Presented to the President, 2776.—Approved [Public Law 95-232], 4642.

S. 1537—To amend the Federal Aviation Act to authorize appropriations for the Civil Aeronautics Board, to require the Board to recodify its rules, and for other purposes.

Indefinitely postponed, 11106.

S. 1547—To amend the Communications Act of 1934, as amended, with respect to penalties and forfeitures, and to authorize the Federal Communications Commission to regulate pole attachments, and for other purposes.

Amended and passed Senate, 1595.—Passage vitiated. Indefinitely postponed (H.R. 7442 passed in lieu), 1599.

S. 1556—To amend title 38, United States Code, to authorize a program of assistance to States for the establishment, expansion, improvement, and maintenance of veterans' cemeteries.

Cosponsors added, 5374, 13429.

S. 1559—To provide for the reinstatement of civil service retirement survivor annuities for certain widows and widowers whose remarriages occurred before July 18, 1966, and for other purposes.

Cosponsors added, 5817.

S. 1562—For the relief of Datronics Engineers, Inc.

From Committee on the Judiciary. Reported (S. Rept. 95-944), 18433.—Passed Senate, 19184.—Referred to Committee on the Judiciary, 19431.—Reported (S. Rept. 95-1648), 32467.—Passed over, 33236.—Passed House, 38214.—Examined and signed, 38775, 38082.—Presented to the President, 38084.—Approved [Private Law 95-157], 38086.

S. 1563—For the relief of Do Sook Park.

From the Committee on the Judiciary. Reported (H. Rept. 95-1691), 33644.—Passed House, 38215.—Examined and signed, 38775, 38082.—Presented to the President, 38084.—Approved [Private Law 95-118], 38086.

S. 1564—For the relief of Tomiko Fukuda Eure.

From the Committee on the Judiciary. Reported (S. Rept. 95-994), 21149.—Passed Senate, 22050.—Referred to Committee on the Judiciary, 22350.

S. 1566—To amend title 18, United States Code, to authorize applications for a court order approving the use of electronic surveillance to obtain foreign intelligence information.

From the Committee on Intelligence. Reported with amendments (S. Rept. 95-701), 6800.—Debated, 10886.—Amended and passed Senate, 10906.—Referred to Committee on the Judiciary, 11100.—Amended and passed House (in lieu of H.R. 7308), 28427.—Senate disagreed with House amendments, 28895.—House insisted on its amendments and asked for a conference. Conferees appointed, 31623.—Senate agreed to a conference. Conferees appointed, 31531.—Additional conferees appointed, 31614.—Conference report (H. Rept. 95-1720) submitted in House, 33778.—Conference report submitted in Senate and agreed to, 34844.—Conference report agreed to in House, 36409.—Examined and signed, 38771, 37650.—Presented to the President, 38084.—Approved [Public Law 95-511], 38086.

S. 1568—To name the lake located behind Lower Memorial Lock and Dam, Washington, "Lake Herbert G. West, Senior."

From Committee on Environment and Public Works. Reported with amendment (S. Rept. 95-721), 8266.—Amended and passed Senate, title amended, 8767.—Referred to Committee on Public Works and Transportation, 9142.—Passed House (in lieu of H.R. 10838), 13556.—Examined and signed, 13852, 13946.—Presented to the President, 14054.—Approved [Public Law 95-285], 15564.

S. 1571—To incorporate the National Ski Patrol System, Inc.

Cosponsors added, 628, 4177, 8427, 19892, 36866.

S. 1575—To establish a voluntary program to provide farmers protection against loss of farm production when natural or uncontrollable conditions adversely affect such production.

Cosponsors added, 11457.

S. 1582—Relating to the settlement between the United States and the Ak-Chin Indian community of certain water right claims of such community against the United States.

Committee discharged. Amended and passed House (in lieu of H.R. 8099), 19495.—Senate concurred in House amendment, 20754.—Examined and signed, 21148, 21224.—Presented to the President, 21148.—Approved [Public Law 95-328], 23637.

S. 1585—To amend title 18, United States Code, to make unlawful the use of minors engaged in sexually explicit conduct for the purpose of promoting any film, photograph, negative, slide, book, or magazine.

Conference report agreed to in the House, 525—Examined and signed, 718, 901.—Presented to the President, 718.—Approved [Public Law 95-225], 2548.

S. 1587—To amend the nternal Revenue Code of 1954 to exempt certain State and local government retirement systems from taxation, and for other purposes.

Cosponsors added, 728, 25122.

S. 1611—To amend the Internal Revenue Code of 1954 to provide for a deduction for additions to a reserve for product liability losses.

Cosponsors added, 12998.

S. 1613—To improve access to the Federal courts by enlarging the civil and criminal jurisdiction of U.S. magistrates, and for other purposes.

From the Committee on the Judiciary. Reported with amendment (S. Rept. 95-1364), 21224.—Made special order, H. Res. 1322, 26522.—Debated, 32899.—Amended and passed House. House insisted on its amendment and asked for a conference. Conferees appointed, 33549.—Senate disagreed with House amendments and asked for a conference. Conferees appointed, 34659.

S. 1617—To establish a program of ocean pollution research and monitoring, and for other purposes.

Rules suspended. Amended and passed House. Title amended, 5000.—Senate concurs in House amendments, 11230.—Examined and signed, 11361, 11434.—Presented to the President, 11572.—Approved [Public Law 95-273], 12870.

S. 1618—For the relief of Sang Yun Yoon.

From the Committee on the Judiciary. Reported (H. Rept. 95-1690), 33644.—Passed House, 38214.—Examined and signed, 38083, 38776.—Presented to the President, 38085—Approved [Private Law 95-119], 38086.

S. 1624—To authorize an additional Assistant Secretary of Commerce.

From the Committee on Governmental Affairs. Reported with amendments (S. Rept. 95-1048), 23273—Amended and passed Senate, 23817.—Referred to Com-

1663

no means complete, but they are readily available to a researcher studying the text of an act.

Illustration R

"History of Bills Enacted into Public Law" in annual *Congressional Record* "Daily Digest" volume

To declare that the United States holds in trust for the Pueblo of Santa Ana certain public domain lands in New Mexico.	S. 2588 (H.R. 3924)	Feb. 24	IIA	IA	May 25	Aug. 22	95-1219	95-1132	33523	28060	Oct. 4	Sept. 6	Oct. 21	95-498
To declare that the United States holds in trust for the Pueblo of Zia certain public domain lands in New Mexico.	S. 2358 (H.R. 10240)	Dec. 15 1977	IIA	IA	May 25	Aug. 22	95-1220	95-1131	33303	28056	Oct 3	Sept. 6	Oct. 21	95-499
To make specific tariff provisions for ball or roller bearing pillow block, flange, take-up, cartridge, and hangar units.	H.R. 8755	Aug. 4 1977	WM	Fin	July 14	Sept. 26	95-1356	95-1241	29825	32861	Sept. 18	Sept. 30	Oct. 21	95-500
To strengthen the economy of the United States through increased sales abroad of American agricultural products.	S. 3447 (H.R. 10584)	Aug. 23	Agr IR	Agr.	July 10 Sept. 14	Aug. 23	95-1338	95-1142	31301	28558	Sept. 25	Sept. 8	Oct. 21	95-501
To clarify exemption from political organization taxable income for proceeds from bingo and related games.	H.R. 8533	July 26 1977	WM		Sept. 22		95-1608	....	31274	35346	Sept. 25	Oct. 10	Oct. 21	95-502
To authorize payment of transportation expenses by U.S. marshals for persons released in one court for appearance in another court.	S. 2411	Jan. 23	Jud	Jud	Sept. 28	Apr. 25 1977	95-1653	95-760	34866	11832	Oct. 10	Apr. 27	Oct. 24	95-503
Air Transportation Regulatory Reform Act of 1978	S. 2493 (H.R. 12611)	Feb. 6	PWT	CST	May 19	Feb. 6 1977	95-1211	95-631	30718	10698	Sept. 21	Apr. 19	Oct. 24	95-504
To amend Title XI of the Merchant Marine Act, 1936, to permit the guarantee of obligations for financing Great Lakes vessels in an amount not exceeding 87½% of the actual or depreciated cost of each vessel.	H.R. 11658	Mar. 20	MMF		Aug. 25		95-1528	....	33253	34461	Oct. 3	Oct. 6	Oct. 24	95-505
To permit the recovery of replacement costs of motor vehicles and other related equipment and supplies.	H.R. 13767	Aug. 7	GO		Aug. 25		95-1529	....	31190	35373	Sept. 25	Oct. 10	Oct. 24	95-506
To amend and extend programs administered by the Small Business Administration.	H.R. 11318	Mar. 7	SB	SB GA	Mar. 13	Aug. 8 Aug. 23	95-949	95-1070 95-1140	7529	29646	Mar. 20	Sept. 15	Oct. 24	95-507
To extend until the close of June 30, 1981, the existing suspension of duties on certain metal waste and scrap, unwrought metal, and other articles of metal.	H.R. 12165	Apr. 17	WM	Fin	July 14	Sept. 26	95-1361	95-1243	28950	32862	Sept. 12	Sept. 30	Oct. 24	95-508
Authorizing funds for national security programs for the Department of Energy for fiscal year 1979.	H.R. 11686	Mar. 21	AS		May 3		95-1108	....	14115	32802	May 17	Sept. 30	Oct. 24	95-509
To insert in the Small Business Act those provisions of the Domestic Volunteer Service Act which govern the operation of SBA volunteer counseling programs.	H.R. 13418	July 11	SB		July 19		95-1375	....	31268	34446	Sept. 25	Oct. 11	Oct. 24	95-510
To establish procedures for electronic surveillance to obtain intelligence information.	S. 1566 (H.R. 7308)	May 18 1977	Jud Intel	Jud Intel	July 8	Nov. 15 1977 Mar. 14	 95-1283	95-604 95-701	28432	10906	Sept. 7	Apr. 20	Oct. 25	95-511
To provide cost-of-living adjustments in the annuity of a retired Comptroller General.	S. 3412 (H.R. 12196)	Aug. 15	GO	GA	June 1	Oct. 3	95-1241	95-1267	35708	34846	Oct. 11	Oct. 9	Oct. 25	95-512
Authorizing and requesting the President to designate the seven-day period beginning on May 28, 1979, as "Vietnam Veterans' Week".	H.J. Res. 1147	Oct. 4					....	....	34866	36182	Oct. 10	Oct. 12	Oct. 25	95-513
Authorizing funds to improve conditions of the public grazing lands.	H.R. 10587	Jan. 26	IIA	ENR	May 10	July 10	95-1122	95-1237	19507	32820	June 29	Sept. 30	Oct. 25	95-514
To regulate interstate commerce with respect to parimutuel wagering on horseracing.	S. 1185 (H.R. 14089)	Mar. 30 1977	IFC	CST Jud	Oct. 6	Oct. 27 1977 Aug. 14	95-1733	95-554 95-1117	34901	31560	Oct. 10	Sept. 26	Oct. 25	95-515
To extend through June 30, 1981, duty-free entry of crude and refined natural graphite, and through June 30, 1980, duty-free entry of assembled freight cars.	H.R. 10161	Nov. 29 1977	WM	Fin	July 14	Aug. 11	95-1363	95-1114	23674	27407	Aug. 1	Aug. 23	Oct. 25	95-516
Authorizing the Secretary of the Army to return ten paintings to the Navy of the Federal Republic of Germany.	H.R. 11945	Apr. 6	AS	AS	Sept. 18	Oct. 13	95-1575	....	32879	36841	Oct. 2	Oct. 14	Oct. 25	95-517
Designating Gathright Lake on the Jackson River, Virginia, as Lake Moomaw.	H.R. 12112	Apr. 13	PWT	EPW	May 1	Aug. 25	95-1094	95-1165	13556	28061	May 15	Sept. 6	Oct. 25	95-518
To exclude the Librarian of Congress from accruing annual and sick leave.	S. 1626	June 6 1977	POCS	GA	Aug. 16	Aug. 5 1977	95-1496	95-403	29820	28421	Sept. 18	Sept. 9 1977	Oct. 25	95-519
To extend for one year authority to provide benefits to the Philippines for medical care and treatment of eligible veterans.	H.R. 5029	Mar. 14 1977	VA	VA	Mar. 23 1977	May 15	95-111	95-825	10210	15705	Apr. 4 1977	May 26	Oct. 26	95-520

8. *U.S. CODE CONGRESSIONAL AND ADMINISTRATIVE NEWS*

Like the *Statutes at Large,* the West Publishing Company's *United States Code Congressional and Administrative News* publishes the texts of federal acts. It has also been reprinting committee reports on a selective basis since it began in 1941. The major benefit of *USCCAN* in legislative history research is the ready availability it provides, since it is found in many smaller libraries that do not generally collect Congressional materials. For someone wishing a quick overview or needing to check a particular report reference, the material printed in *USCCAN* may prove sufficient. Anyone preparing a complete legislative history, however, will need to use other resources.

Committee reports appear in both the monthly pamphlets and the final bound volumes of *USCCAN.* Before the text of each act, there is a cross-reference to the page on which legislative history documents appear. At the beginning of its legislative history section for each act, *USCCAN* provides references to all reports, including ones it doesn't reproduce, and to dates of consideration and passage in each house. See Illustration H, earlier in this chapter at page 233. In addition, both monthly pamphlets and final bound volumes include a table summarizing the legislative history of enacted laws. Since it does not list pending bills or measures which were not passed, and since it is not as thorough as most of the tables already described, it is at best a secondary tool for tracing legislative history. Illustration S shows the table's entry for Public Law 95–511. The monthly pamphlets also include a table on "Major Bills Pending," an alphabetical subject list of legislation showing dates each bill was reported to or passed by either house. This list, however, does not include references to reports or other documents.

9. CONGRESSIONAL QUARTERLY MATERIALS

Several works on Congressional activities are published by Congressional Quarterly, Inc., including an analytical weekly magazine, a daily newsletter, and an online bill-tracking database. CQ also publishes a variety of separate reference books relating to Congress, the most comprehensive being *Congressional Quarterly's Guide to Congress,* 3d ed. (1982).

The *Congressional Quarterly Weekly Report* offers weekly reporting of Congressional news, with summaries of major legislation and issues and cumulative indexing. *CQ Weekly Report* does not offer the completeness of coverage of the status tables and services previously described, but does include valuable analysis and background discussion of laws and legislative issues which make it popular with political scientists and many general researchers. At the end of each session a *Congressional Quarterly Almanac* volume is published, providing considerable information of permanent research value on Congressional activity during that year.

Illustration S

Legislative History table in 1978 *USCCAN* volume

TABLE 4—LEGISLATIVE HISTORY

Public Law		92 Stat. Page	Bill No.	Report No. 95-		Comm. Reporting		Cong.Rec.Vol.124 (1978) Dates of Consideration and Passage	
No.95-	Date App.			House	Senate	House	Senate	House	Senate
493	Oct. 20	1643	H.R. 11035	1638	none	J	none	Oct. 2	Oct. 5
494	Oct. 21	1648	H.R. 12264	1323	none	IIA	none	Sept. 25	Oct. 9
495	Oct. 21	1649	H.R. 12250	1117	1274	IIA	ENR	June 5,	Oct. 9, 15
				1790	1327	Conf	Conf	Oct. 15	
496	Oct. 21	1660	S. 1081	1459	1157	IIA	IA	Oct. 3	Sept. 8,
						(H.R. 11894)			Oct. 7
497	Oct. 21	1665	H.R. 12051	1605	none	WM	none	Oct. 3	Oct. 7
498	Oct. 21	1672	S. 2588	1219	1132	IIA	IA	Oct. 4	Sept. 6,
						(H.R. 3924)			Oct. 7
499	Oct. 21	1679	S. 2358	1220	1131	IIA	IA	Oct. 3	Sept. 6,
						(H.R. 10240)			Oct. 7
500	Oct. 21	1683	H.R. 8755	1356	1241	WM	F	Sept. 18,	Sept. 30
								Oct. 10	
501	Oct. 21	1685	S. 3447	1338(I)	1142	Agr	ANF	Sept. 25,	Sept. 8,
				1338(II)		IR		Oct. 15	Oct. 11
				1755	1315	Conf	Conf		
						(H.R. 10584)			
502	Oct. 21	1693	H.R. 8533	1608	none	WM	none	Sept. 25,	Oct. 10
								Oct. 13	
503	Oct. 24	1704	S. 2411	1653	760	J	J	Oct. 10	Apr. 27
504	Oct. 24	1705	S. 2493	1211	631	PWT	CST	Sept. 21,	Apr. 19,
				1779		Conf		Oct. 15	Oct. 14
						(H.R. 12611)			
505	Oct. 24	1755	H.R. 11658	1528	none	MMF	none	Oct. 3	Oct. 6
506	Oct. 24	1756	H.R. 13767	1529	none	GO	none	Sept. 25	Oct. 10
507	Oct. 24	1757	H.R. 11318	949	1070	SB	SB	Mar. 20,	Sept. 15,
					1140		GA	Oct. 6	Oct. 10
				1714		Conf			
508	Oct. 24	1774	H.R. 12165	1361	1243	WM	F	Sept. 12,	Sept. 30
								Oct. 10	
509	Oct. 24	1775	H.R. 11686	1108	961	AS	AS / ENR	May 17,	Sept. 30
							(S. 2693)	Oct. 11	
510	Oct. 24	1780	H.R. 13148	1375	none	SB	none	Sept. 25	Oct. 11
511	Oct. 25	1783	S. 1566	1283	604	Int	J	Sept. 7,	Apr. 20,
					701		Int	Oct. 12	Oct. 9
				1720		Conf			
						(H.R. 7308)			
512	Oct. 25	1799	S. 3412	1241	1267	GO	GA	July 25,	Oct. 9
						(H.R. 12196)		Oct. 11	
513	Oct. 25	1802	H.J.Res.	none	none	none	none	Oct. 10	Oct. 12
			1147						
514	Oct. 25	1803	H.R. 10587	1122	1237	IIA	ENR	June 29,	Sept. 30,
				1737		Conf		Oct. 10	Oct. 11
515	Oct. 25	1811	S. 1185	1733	554	IFC	CST	Oct. 10	Sept. 26
					1117	(H.R. 14089)	J		
516	Oct. 25	1816	H.R. 10161	1363	1114	WM	F	Aug. 1,	Aug. 23,
								Oct. 10	Oct. 12
517	Oct. 25	1817	H.R. 11945	1575	none	AS	none	Oct. 2	Oct. 13
518	Oct. 25	1818	H.R. 12112	1094	1165	PWT	EPW	May 15,	Sept. 6
								Oct. 15	
519	Oct. 25	1819	S. 1626	1496	403	POCS	GA	Sept. 18	Sept. 9 *
									Oct. 10
520	Oct. 26	1820	H.R. 5029	111	825	VA	VA	Apr. 4 *	May 26,
								Oct. 13	Oct. 15

*1977.

10001

The *Congressional Monitor* is a reporting service providing daily coverage of *active* legislative proposals. It combines some of the features of the *Daily Digest,* with a selective weekly status table of bills acted upon and a weekly list of published hearings, reports and documents. The *Monitor* summarizes daily proceedings in each house and in the major committees, and offers unofficial projections of forthcoming activity. It does not, however, provide detailed coverage or analysis in depth, and is primarily useful for lobbyists and others needing quick information day by day on legislative activity.

CQ also produces an online service, *Washington Alert,* which covers sessions back to 1983 and includes bill-tracking information, daily Congressional schedules, notices of new Congressional publications, and the text of *CQ Weekly Report.* The *Weekly Report* is also accessible online through LEGI–SLATE.

10. *FEDERAL INDEX*

Federal Index, issued by the National Standards Association, has since 1977 provided an index to numerous government-related publications, including the *Congressional Record;* House and Senate bills, reports and hearings; the *Weekly Compilation of Presidential Documents;* the *Federal Register;* and the *Code of Federal Regulations.* It is published monthly, with annual cumulative volumes, and is also available online through DIALOG. Access is provided in three ways: by government agency involved; by specific governmental functions; and by affected industries, individuals, institutions, and countries.

D. COMPILED LEGISLATIVE HISTORIES

Since the sources of legislative history are scattered among many publications and are published in forms which frequently become unavailable shortly after they are issued, retrospective research is often very difficult. Legislative histories for major legislation, compiled in book form or in microfacsimile, offer a convenient approach to the important documents relating to some laws. At their best, these compilations include bills, hearings, committee reports, committee prints, debates and documents, with detailed indexing. A comprehensive compiled history can save the researcher many hours of library time in retrieving those documents from their disparate sources. Frequently, however, only *some* of the essential documents are included and often indexing is omitted or inadequate.

Compiled legislative histories have been issued by government agencies concerned with the enforcement of particular acts, by commercial publishers, and by trade associations and other private interest groups. Selected legislative histories are also published by the Congressional Research Service of the Library of Congress and the U.S. General Accounting Office. In addition to its general microfiche collections of Congressional documents, CIS can provide full documentation (except debates) of any act since 1970 on either microfiche or paper, through its

"Documents on Demand" service. Commerce Clearing House, through its *Public Laws Legislative Histories on Microfiche* (PLLM) series, also provides pertinent documents beginning with enactments of the 96th Congress (1981).

The most useful finding tool for published compilations is N.P. Johnson's *Sources of Compiled Legislative Histories.*[12] Arranged chronologically by Congress and Public Law number, it provides a single checklist of all available compiled legislative histories from the 1st through the 99th Congress, and is indexed by author, title, and name of act.

Many law firms compile legislative histories of enactments or proposals which are of interest to their clients. To improve access to some of these private files, the Law Librarians' Society of the District of Columbia has prepared the *Union List of Legislative Histories,* 5th ed. (Rothman, 1986), which lists legislative histories held by its member libraries.

E. STATE LEGISLATIVE HISTORIES

The use of legislative history in the interpretation of state legislation, and in statutory research at the state level generally, is no less important than in the federal area. However, the sources for state legislative history and the available research tools are much less adequate and the process is often very frustrating. In most states, it is virtually impossible to collect the necessary documents for a simple legislative history *outside* of the state capitol or its legislative library. Debates are almost never published, bills are usually available only at the legislature and during the session itself, committee reports are published in only a few states, and hearings even less often. Legislative journals are published for most states, but these rarely contain documentation explaining the decision-making process.

Many state legislatures are now covered by commercial legislative services, some of which provide status tables of pending bills. The commercial services often include document ordering options, but they can be quite expensive. In a number of states there are computer-based official or commercial information services for legislative proceedings. These usually include online access to bill tracking and bill digests, and sometimes offer information on legislative documents. For some states, however, there is no convenient method of identifying pending legislation, ascertaining its status, securing copies of documents or abstracts thereof, or tracing legislative proceedings. Recourse must be had to the legislature itself, to the legislative reference library, or to the state library.

12. American Association of Law Libraries Publication Series No. 14 (Rothman, 1988).

Guide to State Legislative and Administrative Materials, 4th ed.,[13] by M.L. Fisher, has vastly improved the process of identifying what documents are available for each state, and from whom they are available. The guide provides detailed information for every state, with addresses and phone numbers of all relevant offices. It also indicates whether each state is covered by a legislative information service, in either printed or online format.

Another useful service, focusing on legislative organization and process generally rather than on specific legislative documents, is L. Hellebust, *State Legislative Sourcebook: A Resource Guide to Legislative Information in the Fifty States* (Government Research Service, annual). This looseleaf tool, first published in 1985, contains eight to ten pages of detailed information on the legislature and legislative process of each state. It also includes references to available information services.

Legal research manuals, describing legislative material, are available for a number of states (see Appendix A at the end of this book), and there are occasional periodical articles describing legislative history research in particular states.[14] The reference staff of a research law library in your state should also be consulted for details as to the local situation.

Some of the annotated state statutory compilations offer legislative session services which, like some looseleaf services with state coverage, include the text of laws enacted during the pending legislative session. These services may also provide some legislative history references, but not on a comprehensive or systematic basis. The *Legislative Reporting Service* of Commerce Clearing House, and its computer-based counterpart ELSS, referred to in Section C.3 above, offer, at considerable cost, custom-tailored information services on proposed legislation in particular subject areas.

Most states now have official or quasi-official agencies devoted to the research and recommendation of new legislation. These include independent law revision commissions, legislatively controlled councils, judicial groups, or academic bodies devoted to legislative study and drafting. The studies and proposals prepared by such agencies frequently result in enactments, although rarely in the exact form proposed. Their publications are an invaluable source of legislative history and may shed considerable light on the interpretation of the resulting enactment. Many of these studies are listed in the monthly *State Government Research Checklist,* published by the Council of State Governments.

13. American Association of Law Libraries Publication Series No. 15 (Rothman, 1988).

14. *See, e.g.,* O'Connor, "The Use of Connecticut Legislative History in Statutory Construction," 58 *Conn.B.J.* 422 (1984); Rhodes & Seereiter, "The Search for Intent: Aids to Statutory Interpretation in Florida—An Update," 13 *Fla.St.U.L.Rev.* 485 (1985); Allison & Hambleton, "Research in Texas Legislative History," 47 *Tex.B.J.* 314 (1984); Comment, "Legislative History in Washington," 7 *U. Puget Sound L.Rev.* 571 (1984).

Although the inaccessibility of legislative documents on state legislation is still an impediment to legal research, the astute researcher can often find useful material by persistent digging and the resourceful use of local libraries.

F. SUMMARY

The many ambiguities in the language of our statutes derive less from the grammatical inadequacies of English prose than from the political compromises necessary to achieve a consensus for enactment. These ambiguities frequently become the focal issues of litigation in both the federal and state courts. Careful research in the documents of legislative history is necessary to ascertain the intent of the legislature in enacting the disputed provisions. Such research also provides sources for the development of arguments for or against particular interpretations.

Research into legislative history is facilitated by the use of a variety of finding tools, indexes and tables, in both official and commercial publications, as well as in an increasing number of online databases. The availability of the legislative documents themselves has been expanded by their inclusion in microfiche collections and computer-based services. Although many of these services are quite expensive, the work of the skilled researcher in federal legislative history can now be done in smaller libraries and away from large urban centers. For legislative research on the state level, the documentary sources are less adequate, but the finding tools for many states are increasing in numbers and expanding in scope.

G. ADDITIONAL READING

R. Dickerson, *The Interpretation and Application of Statutes* (Little, Brown, 1975). The standard text on statutory interpretation.

G.B. Folsom, *Legislative History: Research for the Interpretation of Laws* (University Press of Virginia, 1972; reprinted, Rothman, 1979). Although somewhat dated, this remains the best overall text on research in legislative history.

How Federal Laws Are Made, 2d rev. ed. (WANT Publishing Co., 1985). A brief exposition of Congressional procedures and practices in law-making.

R.S. Lockwood & C.M. Hillier, *Legislative Analysis: With Emphasis on National Security Affairs* (Carolina Academic Press, 1981). A clear overview of the sources and tools of legislative history, focusing for illustrative purposes on one statutory field.

P.C. Schank, "An Essay on the Role of Legislative Histories in Statutory Interpretation," 80 *Law Libr. J.* 391 (1988). an argument that the concept of legislative intent is illusory, and that the use of legislative history in statutory interpretation should be limited to the elucidation of truly ambiguous provisions.

W. Twining & D. Miers, *How to Do Things With Rules: A Primer of Interpretation,* 2d ed. (Weidenfeld & Nicolson, 1982). Part II of this English text is a thoughtful analysis of the interpretation and application of statutory rules. Despite the more restrictive English view of legislative history, the work provides a useful background to this chapter.

Chapter 8

ADMINISTRATIVE AND EXECUTIVE PUBLICATIONS

A. INTRODUCTION

A great number and variety of documents of legal effect and significance are regularly issued by the President, the various offices of the executive branch, and the many independent administrative agencies which have grown up since the establishment of the Interstate

Commerce Commission in 1887. The President has always had a lawmaking function, usually exercised through proclamations and executive orders, and the executive departments have issued regulations within their administrative jurisdictions. The independent agencies developed in response to a need for regulation which could not be met by the established units of government. The existing executive offices were not equipped to handle the administration of new social and economic legislation; Congress could not foresee, much less legislate, the detailed requirements of complex industrial activities; and the courts could not cope with the mass of adjudication required to effectuate and enforce the legislative and regulatory standards. The creation of new agencies and the expansion of existing agencies provided the expertise and specialization necessary for these tasks, and there grew a large body of administrative and executive publications.

The predominant forms of administrative lawmaking resemble the primary sources of statutory and judicial law, such as legislative rules and regulations and adjudicative decisions. Since the regulations of agencies are often considered *subordinate* or *delegated* legislation, and their decisions and rulings are often called *quasi*-judicial, traditionally the publications of administrative agencies have been accorded less weight and authority than statutes and judicial decisions. In many aspects of modern society, however, administrative law plays a powerful role and can be more immediately relevant to day-to-day legal practice than either statutory or judge-made law.

Because the primary forms of administrative law publication are distinct from other materials we have studied, they are explained here in a separate chapter. Administrative law, however, cannot be considered an isolated discipline separate from other forms of lawmaking. Regulations often implement specific statutory provisions, and court decisions are often necessary to clarify the meaning of regulations or to determine the validity of agency decisions. The impact of an agency regulation or decision can be affected, for example, by the legislative history of the governing statute or by judicially imposed due process limitations.

The literature of administrative law also encompasses aids to research, such as indexes, looseleaf services, citators, and a vast literature of treatises, periodicals, monographs, and reports. Looseleafs and secondary materials, to be discussed in subsequent chapters, often treat administrative publications on an equal footing with judicial or statutory publications. Research in administrative law is part of any overall legal research strategy. An understanding of the many forms, official and unofficial, in which administrative materials are published and indexed is essential to the legal researcher.

Most of this chapter focuses on the publications of the federal government. Publication and research methods for agency regulations and decisions are explained, followed by discussion of presidential documents, other publications, and guides and secondary sources useful in administrative law research. State governments have administrative agencies which operate much like federal agencies, but only a brief section at the end of the chapter discusses state administrative research. The variations between states are such that one cannot easily generalize about their publications, and a particular state's administrative materials are best studied individually. The state legal research guides listed in Appendix A provide basic information for the states they cover.

B. REGULATIONS OF FEDERAL ADMINISTRATIVE AGENCIES

As discussed in Chapter 5 the United States Congress enacts detailed legislation on a bewildering variety of subjects. Congress, however, cannot possibly provide for the multitude of possible situations which might arise under its enactments. Members of Congress are not experts in all areas of regulation, and the complexities of the legislative process are not well suited to rational consideration of detailed technical distinctions. Much of the work of creating specific rules to govern conduct is left to agencies specializing in particular activities. These agencies interpret and apply their governing statutes to create highly detailed rules, or regulations, which give specific content to the statutory intent and provide procedures for implementation and enforcement.[1]

These regulations are published by the federal government in the same two basic formats as statutes, chronologically and in a subject arrangement. The *Statutes at Large* presents laws as enacted, and the *United States Code* arranges those laws by subject. Similarly, regulations are published chronologically in the *Federal Register,* which is issued every business day. The same regulations are then published in a more accessible format, arranged by issuing agency and subject, in the *Code of Federal Regulations.*

While the basic method of regulatory publication is analogous to that for statutes, there is little similarity between the research systems. Statutory codes are generally published in bound volumes, with amendments and annotations issued in pocket parts or supplements. Because the great volume of administrative regulation would make such a system impracticable, different methods are employed to update regulations and make sure that current information is available. Research in federal regulations has its own unique procedure, one that is not complex but is different from research approaches discussed previously. The status of a *CFR* section is determined by consulting numerous finding lists for references to *Federal Register* pages. The process may sound laborious, but most of it is mechanical and quite straightforward.

1. The terms "rule" and "regulation" have the same meaning in this context. 1 C.F.R. § 1 (1988). We use "regulation" more often, since there are numerous other "rules" to be reckoned with in legal research, such as court rules or citation rules.

1. THE *FEDERAL REGISTER*

Although executive and administrative agencies are as old as our government, industrialization in the late 19th century led to the creation of many new agencies and expanded the power of existing agencies. The extension of government control during World War I caused an increase in agency regulation, and demonstrated the need for a centralized system of publication.[2] Nothing was done, however, even when the depression and the New Deal brought about a tremendous increase in the amount of agency business. The failure to provide systematic publication of this huge bureaucracy's rules and decisions created a confusing and unjust "government in ignorance of law." [3] Hundreds of executive orders, thousands of regulations, and tens of thousands of pages of other documents of legal effect were issued with no regular method of publication. In many instances no attempt at public notice was even made. A lawyer who wanted to ascertain the applicable rules and their current status had no access to such information.

Public pressure for reform finally came to a head when two cases concerning New Deal regulation of the oil industry reached the Supreme Court, even though they were based on a provision which had been revoked before the lawsuits were begun.[4] The cases proceeded through the courts with no one aware of the regulatory change, until finally the Solicitor General discovered the revocation and informed the parties and the Court. In a criminal case, four Texas oil producers had been indicted and jailed for conspiracy to violate the nonexistent regulation, which the lower court then found unconstitutional. The government's appeal was dismissed on its own motion.[5] A civil suit, known as the "hot oil" case, proceeded to oral argument. There the Justices had several questions about the accessibility of regulations, and asked the government for a supplemental memorandum on the issue within two days.[6] In his opinion for the Court the next month, Chief Justice Hughes noted his dissatisfaction with the government's handling of the matter:

2. An early critic wrote: "In the matter of publication there is a maximum of variety and confusion. Not only is there no general system, but no department has developed a system for itself. Each bureau, and often each local office, has its own methods, or more often lack of method." Fairlie, "Administrative Legislation," 18 *Mich.L.Rev.* 181, 199 (1920).

3. See Griswold, "Government in Ignorance of the Law—A Plea for Better Publication of Executive Legislation," 48 *Harv. L.Rev.* 198 (1934), in which the documentary chaos of the early New Deal is described. This article called for and contributed significantly to the prompt creation of the *Federal Register* and the *Code of Federal Regulations.*

4. *United States v. Smith,* 293 U.S. 633 (1934) (appeal dismissed); *Panama Refining Co. v. Ryan,* 293 U.S. 388 (1935).

5. "Oil Suit Dismissed in Supreme Court," *N.Y. Times,* Oct. 2, 1934, at 6.

6. Wallen, "Complete File of New Deal Laws Lacking," *N.Y. Herald Tribune,* Dec. 12, 1934, at 1. The justices also asked the government to explain why criminal indictments had been obtained under a provision no longer in effect. "Smiles appeared on the usually solemn faces of the justices and the crowd of lawyers that filled the room" when it was admitted that the error was not discovered until a few days before the case was to be argued. Id. at 6.

Whatever the cause of the failure to give appropriate public notice of the change in the section, with the result that the persons affected, the prosecuting authorities, and the courts, were alike ignorant of the alteration, the fact is that the attack in this respect was upon a provision which did not exist.[7]

The furor resulting from the hot oil case provided the final impetus for the enactment of remedial legislation in 1935.

The Federal Register Act[8] was designed to end this chaotic uncertainty by establishing a central repository for the publication of federal proclamations, orders, regulations, notices and other documents of general legal applicability. It initiated a new daily publication, the *Federal Register,* in which such documents must be published. The first *Federal Register* issue was published on Saturday, March 14, 1936. The *Register* 's statutory mandate is to publish the following classes of documents:

(1) Presidential proclamations and Executive orders, except those not having general applicability and legal effect or effective only against Federal agencies or persons in their capacity as officers, agents, or employees thereof;

(2) documents or classes of documents that the President may determine from time to time have general applicability and legal effect; and

(3) documents or classes of documents that may be required so to be published by Act of Congress.

. . . [E]very document or order which prescribes a penalty has general applicability and legal effect.[9]

Publication in the *Federal Register* is deemed to provide any parties affected by a regulation with constructive notice of its contents.[10]

Despite the substantial improvements in access brought about by the Federal Register Act, the decision-making procedures used by the

7. *Panama Refining Co.,* 293 U.S. at 412–13.

8. Ch. 417, 49 Stat. 500 (1935).

9. 44 U.S.C. § 1505(a) (1982). The Administrative Committee of the Federal Register has further defined "document having general applicability and legal effect" as "any document issued under proper authority prescribing a penalty or course of conduct, conferring a right, privilege, authority, or immunity, or imposing an obligation, and relevant or applicable to the general public, members of a class, or persons in a locality, as distinguished from named individuals or organizations." 1 C.F.R. § 1.1 (1988).

10. 44 U.S.C. § 1507 (1982). Justice Jackson sharply criticized the effects of this notice provision:

To my mind, it is an absurdity to hold that every farmer who insures his crops knows what the Federal Register contains or even knows that there is such a publication. If he were to peruse this voluminous and dull publication as it is issued from time to time in order to make sure whether anything has been promulgated that affects his rights, he would never need crop insurance, for he would never get time to plant any crops. Nor am I convinced that a reading of technically-worded regulations would enlighten him much in any event.

Federal Crop Insurance Corp. v. Merrill, 332 U.S. 380, 387 (1947) (Jackson, J., dissenting).

agencies remained unclear and arbitrary. In 1946 Congress passed the Administrative Procedure Act,[11] which gave the public the right to participate in agency rulemaking and significantly expanded the scope of the *Federal Register.* The act provided that notice of proposed rulemaking be published in the *Register,* affording the public the opportunity to comment on the proposed rules.[12] In its January 1, 1947 issue, the *Federal Register* inaugurated a new "Proposed Rule Making" section with proposed standards for grades of canned tangerine juice.[13] Further improvements in publication of notices were added by the Freedom of Information Act,[14] which requires agencies to publish organizational descriptions and policy statements,[15] and the Government in the Sunshine Act,[16] which requires agencies to publish notices of most meetings.[17]

In each issue of the *Federal Register,* material is published in the following order:

(1) Presidential documents (proclamations, executive orders, and other executive documents);

(2) Rules and regulations (documents having general applicability and legal effect);

(3) Proposed rules (texts of proposed regulations, as well as regulatory agendas and notices of hearings);

(4) Notices (documents not concerned with rulemaking proceedings, such as announcements of application deadlines or license revocations); and

(5) Notices of Sunshine Act meetings.

The arrangement of documents in each section of the *Register* is determined by the title of the *Code of Federal Regulations* in which the rules will appear or which they affect. Some documents are published as separate sections at the end of an issue, rather than in their appropriate place, so that issuing agencies can make additional copies available for distribution. Illustration A shows the first of several *Federal Register* pages in which the Food and Drug Administration announces the implementation of a final rule governing children's foaming detergent bath products. The rule amends 21 C.F.R. Part 740, Cosmetic Product Warning Statements. The page shown provides background information, including the citations of previous *Federal Register* documents; subsequent pages print FDA responses to comments received and the text of the rule.

To provide access to its array of documents and notices, each issue of the *Federal Register* also contains a number of finding aids. At the beginning of each issue there is a table of contents arranged by agency

11. Ch. 324, 80 Stat. 237 (1946).

12. 5 U.S.C. § 553 (1982).

13. 12 Fed.Reg. 32 (1947).

14. Act of July 4, 1966, Pub.L. No. 84–487, 80 Stat. 237.

15. 5 U.S.C. § 552(a)(1) (1982).

16. Pub.L. No. 94–409, 90 Stat. 1241 (1976).

17. 5 U.S.C. § 552(e)(3) (1982).

Illustration A

A *Federal Register* page

Federal Register / Vol. 51, No. 108 / Thursday, June 5, 1986 / Rules and Regulations 20471

began to run since they used the phrase, "communicated" to the claimant as the start of the appeal time period. The use of that phrase makes it unclear whether the appeal period starts on the date the notice of the decision is sent to the claimant or when it is received by the claimant. The amendment to the regulation clarifies that the appeal period begins to run from the date the notice is mailed.

The Board has determined that this is not a major rule under Executive Order 12291. Therefore, no regulatory analysis is required. There are no information collections associated with this rule.

A notice of proposed rulemaking was published in the **Federal Register** on February 24, 1986 (51 FR 6422). No comments were received from the public.

List of Subjects in 20 CFR Part 395

Employee benefit plans, Employee protection benefits, Railroad employees, Railroad Retirement.

PART 395—[AMENDED]

Title 20 CFR Part 395 is amended as follows:

1. The authority citation for Part 395 is revised to read:

Authority: 45 U.S.C. 362(1); 45 U.S.C. 797.

§ 395.9 [Amended]

2. Section 395.9 is amended by adding at the end of paragraphs (c)(1) and (d)(1) the following new sentence which reads as follows: Notice shall be deemed to have been communicated to the claimant when it is mailed to the claimant at the latest address furnished by him or her.

Dated: May 28, 1986.
By Authority of the Board.
Beatrice Ezerski,
Secretary to the Board.
[FR Doc. 86-12631 Filed 6-4-86; 8:45 am]
BILLING CODE 7905-01-M

DEPARTMENT OF HEALTH AND HUMAN SERVICES

Food and Drug Administration

21 CFR Part 740

[Docket No. 76N-0486]

Cosmetic Product Warning Statements: Establishment of Effective Date for Label Caution Requirement on Children's Foaming Detergent Bath Products; Response to Comments

AGENCY: Food and Drug Administration.

ACTION: Final rule.

SUMMARY: The Food and Drug Administration (FDA) is announcing that it has completed its reconsideration of 21 CFR 740.17, a regulation that would require that directions for safe use and a caution statement appear on the label of foaming detergent bath products. The agency announced its intention to reconsider this regulation in the **Federal Register** of February 13, 1983 (48 FR 7203). Upon reconsideration, FDA has decided to take the following actions: (1) FDA is denying the petitions of the Cosmetic, Toiletry and Fragrance Association, Inc. (CTFA), and of the Independent Cosmetic Manufacturers and Distributors (ICMD) to revoke the regulation for children's foaming detergent bath products or any such product whose label does not make clear that it is intended for use exclusively by adults. (2) FDA is granting these petitions to revoke the regulation for those products whose labels make clear that they are intended for use exclusively by adults. (3) FDA is establishing a new effective date for the regulation except with respect to those products whose label makes clear that they are intended for use exclusively by adults.

DATES: Effective June 5, 1987. All foaming detergent bath products except those intended for use exclusively by adults that are initially introduced or initially delivered for introduction into interstate commerce on or after June 5, 1987, shall comply with this regulation. FDA is continuing the interim stay of the effective date of 21 CFR 740.17 until June 5, 1987.

FOR FURTHER INFORMATION CONTACT: Heinz J. Eiermann, Center for Food Safety and Applied Nutrition (HFF-440), Food and Drug Administration, 200 C St. SW., Washington, DC 20204, 202-245-1530.

SUPPLEMENTARY INFORMATION: In the **Federal Register** of August 19, 1980 (45 FR 55172), FDA published a final regulation (21 CFR 740.17) that requires that labels of foaming detergent bath products bear a prescribed caution statement and provide adequate directions for safe use. The statement cautions that excessive use of, or prolonged exposure to, foaming detergent bath products may cause irritation to the skin and the urinary tract. It urges consumers to discontinue use of such products if rash, redness, or itching occurs and to consult a physician if irritation persists.

Foaming detergent bath products are commonly identified and recognized by consumers as "bubble baths" or "foaming bath oils." These products are also known by other names such as "foaming bath," "milk foam bath," and "foaming bath powder." To avoid any confusion as to which products are subject to this regulation, FDA has adopted the general term "foaming detergent bath product" for these types of products. FDA has modified § 740.17 to reflect this new terminology.

Section 740.17 was to have gone into effect on August 19, 1981. However, on June 1, 1981, the agency issued a press release announcing its intention to stay this regulation. On February 18, 1983, FDA announced an interim stay of the effective date of the regulation (48 FR 7169).

In addition to issuing the interim stay, FDA proposed to stay the effective date of the regulation while it reconsidered the labeling requirement (48 FR 7203). The agency stated that it was still concerned about the adverse effects of foaming detergent bath products on children when not properly used, but that the petitions of CTFA and ICMD to revoke the labeling requirement had raised issues that merited a full review of the regulation.

In the February 18, 1983 notice of proposed stay, FDA invited interested persons to submit comments, data, or other information on how consumers could be informed of the risks associated with the use of foaming detergent bath products and effectively protected from irritation to the skin and urinary tract that might result from the misuse of these products. The agency asked that comments specifically address the following questions:

1. How may consumers be informed of the risks associated with the use of foaming detergent bath products other than by means of a required label caution statement and directions for safe use?

2. Did the reported adverse reactions associated with foaming detergent bath products marketed for adult use occur predominantly in adults or children?

3. Would a revised regulation applicable only to products intended for use by children provide adequate consumer protection taking into account the possibility of use (or misuse) of adult products as children's products?

4. What costs would be associated with the caution labeling requirements of § 740.17 or the alternatives suggested in comments?

FDA received 17 comments during the comment period on the proposal. Four comments were from consumers, three were from physicians, one was from a consumer organization, two were from cosmetic trade associations, and seven were from cosmetic manufacturers. Six comments were in favor of a caution labeling requirement, one comment recommended that cosmetic foaming

name and listing rules, proposed rules, and notices. Illustration B shows the table of contents for the June 5, 1986 *Federal Register* issue, containing the foaming detergent bath product regulation. Note that cross-references are provided to agency subdivisions if their regulations and notices are listed separately from the agency's.

The table of contents is followed by a list of *CFR* parts affected in that day's issue. In the June 5, 1986 issue, for example, there is one entry under 21 C.F.R., indicating that Part 740 is affected at page 20471. Regular readers of the *Federal Register* can scan this list to see if there are any developments affecting parts of the *Code of Federal Regulations* with which they are concerned.[18]

At the end of each issue, there are finding aids covering more than the specific issue. First there is a list of telephone numbers in the Office of the Federal Register where one may obtain information and assistance on specific topics. Following this is a table of pages and dates for each *Federal Register* issue published during the current month. This can be helpful since the *Register* is usually cited by page number, but page numbers are not listed on the spine or front cover of an issue. The date does appear in those places, so after using the table one can easily find the needed issue. Next comes a cumulative list of *CFR* parts affected during the current month. This list is updated each day to include the developments in that issue, and hence incorporates the items listed in the front of the issue. This table is an important tool for updating regulations, as will be explained in Section B.4 below. Illustration C shows the above three features for a *Federal Register* issue a few days after the issue seen in Illustrations A and B, and including reference to the new FDA regulation. Following the table of *CFR* parts there are a list of public laws received by the Office from Congress and a weekly checklist of current *CFR* volumes.

Each year's output comprises a new volume of the *Federal Register,* with continuous pagination throughout the year. The first volume in 1936 contained 2,400 pages. The size expanded to a peak of 86,405 pages in 1980, and has since subsided to under 50,000 pages by 1986. Although the texts of most final rules are arranged by subject in *CFR,* much of the other material in the *Federal Register* never appears elsewhere.[19] Proposed rules, agency policy statements, discussion of comments received, and descriptive statements on agency organization give the *Register* a permanent reference value, and most large law

18. To a person first confronting the *Federal Register,* it may seem absurd that anyone would regularly read "this voluminous and dull publication," to quote Justice Jackson in *Federal Crop Insurance Corp. v. Merrill, supra* note 10. Lawyers dealing closely with particular agencies or specializing in specific areas of administrative law, however, would be poorly serving their clients if they were unaware of proposed changes that could affect those clients' interests. Examining each issue of the *Federal Register* is the best and most thorough way to stay informed.

19. In *Wiggins Bros., Inc. v. Department of Energy,* 667 F.2d 77 (Temp.Emer.App. 1981), *cert. denied,* 456 U.S. 905 (1982), the court reversed a district court ruling that excluded consideration of *Federal Register* material not published in *CFR* in construing an agency regulation. The court held that the agency's failure to include a preamble in the codified regulation did not mean that the preamble should be disregarded.

Illustration B

A *Federal Register* table of contents page

IV Federal Register / Vol. 51, No. 108 / Thursday, June 5, 1986 / Contents

libraries have a complete backfile, either bound or in microfilm or microfiche editions.

Illustration C

Reader aids in the *Federal Register*

Reader Aids

Federal Register
Vol. 51, No. 110
Monday, June 9, 1986

INFORMATION AND ASSISTANCE

SUBSCRIPTIONS AND ORDERS

Subscriptions (public)	202-783-3238
Problems with subscriptions	275-3054
Subscriptions (Federal agencies)	523-5240
Single copies, back copies of FR	783-3238
Magnetic tapes of FR, CFR volumes	275-1184
Public laws (Slip laws)	275-3030

PUBLICATIONS AND SERVICES

Daily Federal Register

General information, index, and finding aids	523-5227
Public inspection desk	523-5215
Corrections	523-5237
Document drafting information	523-5237
Legal staff	523-4534
Machine readable documents, specifications	523-3408

Code of Federal Regulations

General information, index, and finding aids	523-5227
Printing schedules and pricing information	523-3419

Laws	523-5230

Presidential Documents

Executive orders and proclamations	523-5230
Public Papers of the President	523-5230
Weekly Compilation of Presidential Documents	523-5230

United States Government Manual	523-5230

Other Services

Library	523-4986
Privacy Act Compilation	523-4534
TDD for the deaf	523-5229

FEDERAL REGISTER PAGES AND DATES, JUNE

19747-19816............................2
19817-20244............................3
20245-20436............................4
20437-20606............................5
20607-20792............................6
20793-20952............................9

CFR PARTS AFFECTED DURING JUNE

At the end of each month, the Office of the Federal Register publishes separately a List of CFR Sections Affected (LSA), which lists parts and sections affected by documents published since the revision date of each title.

3 CFR

Proclamations:
5496.................................19817
5497.................................19819

5 CFR

Proposed Rules:
294.................................20833

7 CFR

26.................................20643
52.................................20437
272.................................20793
273.................................20793
400.................................20245
417.................................20246
908.................................20645
1006.................................20446
1007.................................20446
1011.................................20446
1012.................................20446
1013.................................20446
1046.................................20446
1093.................................20446
1094.................................20446
1096.................................20446
1098.................................20446
1099.................................20446
1136.................................19821
1772.................................19822
1951.................................20465

Proposed Rules:
907.................................20664
908.................................20664
1065.................................19846

8 CFR

100.................................19824
103.................................19824
204.................................20794

9 CFR

Proposed Rules:
92.................................20834
145.................................20790
147.................................20790
151.................................19846

12 CFR

265.................................19825

Proposed Rules:
709.................................19848

13 CFR

108.......................20764, 20781
111.................................20247
115.................................20922
121.................................20795
122.................................20248

14 CFR

21.................................20797
25.................................20249
39.........................20249-20251
71............19825, 20801, 20802

Proposed Rules:
21.................................20301
39..........19848, 19849, 20304-20308, 20495
71.................................20834

15 CFR

377.................................20252
385.......................20467, 20468
399.......................20467, 20468

16 CFR

13.......................20469, 20803
303.......................20803, 20807
455.................................20936

Proposed Rules:
13............20498, 20500, 20803

17 CFR

230.................................20254

Proposed Rules:
240.................................20504

19 CFR

10.................................20810
178.................................20810

20 CFR

395.................................20470

Proposed Rules:
10.................................20736
655.................................20516

21 CFR

81.................................20786
82.................................20786
430.................................20262
442.................................20262
510.......................19826, 19828
522.................................20646
558.................................19828
740.................................20471

Proposed Rules:
20.................................19851
182.................................19851
186.................................19851
201.................................19853
314.................................20310

22 CFR

51.................................20475

Proposed Rules:
508.................................20524

23 CFR

658.................................20817

Proposed Rules:
655.................................20840

Access to the *Federal Register* is provided through several different indexes, tables, and computer databases. These research techniques will be discussed in Sections B.3, Finding Regulations, and B.4, Updating and Verifying Regulations. Because most research in administrative regulations requires use of both the *Register* and the *Code of Federal Regulations,* however, we must first introduce the latter publication.

2. *CODE OF FEDERAL REGULATIONS*

When Congress finally sought through the Federal Register Act to control the tremendous mass of chronologically published rules and regulations, it understood the need for a convenient subject arrangement of regulations in force. Section 11 of the act required each agency to compile and publish in the *Register* its then current body of regulations.[20] It was not until an amendment in 1937,[21] however, that a regular form of codification was established. The first edition of the new *Code of Federal Regulations* was published in 1939, and contained regulations in force as of June 1, 1938.

The *Code* is to contain "documents of each agency of the Government having general applicability and legal effect, . . . relied upon by the agency as authority for, or . . . invoked or used by it in the discharge of, its activities or functions." [22] The regulations are codified in a subject arrangement of fifty titles somewhat similar to those employed for federal statutes in the *United States Code.* For example, 26 U.S.C. is the Internal Revenue Code and 26 C.F.R. contains tax regulations, and Title 7 of each code is concerned with agriculture. The titles do not always match, however. Education statutes are in 20 U.S.C. but corresponding regulations are in 34 C.F.R.; Title 40 of *CFR,* dealing with protection of the environment, has no direct statutory counterpart.

Within each title, regulations are arranged by agency, rather than by subject. The titles are divided into *chapters,* each of which is devoted to the regulations of a particular agency. Chapters are numbered with Roman numerals,[23] and sometimes are divided into subchapters designated by capital letters. In the back of every *CFR* volume there is an alphabetical list of federal agencies indicating the *CFR* title and chapter of each agency's regulations.

The regulations of a particular agency are divided into *parts,* each of which consists of a body of regulations on a particular topic or agency function. (Each *Federal Register* issue, you may recall, includes lists of *CFR* parts affected in that issue and during that month.) Parts are further divided into *sections,* the basic unit of the code. A section "ideally consists of a short, simple presentation of one proposition." [24]

20. Ch. 417, § 11, 49 Stat. 500, 503 (1935).

21. Act of June 19, 1937, ch. 369, 50 Stat. 304.

22. 44 U.S.C. § 1510(a) (1982).

23. Chapters in Title 41, Public Contracts and Property Management, and Title 48, Federal Acquisition Regulations System, are designated by Arabic, not Roman, numeral.

24. Office of the Federal Register, *Document Drafting Handbook* 2 (rev. ed. 1986).

The citation identifying a *CFR* section shows the title, the part and the section (but not the chapter), so that 1 C.F.R. § 1.1 is title 1, part 1, section 1.

The first edition of *CFR* consisted of seventeen volumes kept up-to-date through cumbersome bound supplements. For the second edition, delayed by World War II until 1949, a different method of supplementation was instituted: pocket parts, with republication of volumes as necessary.[25] Gradually this approach too became unworkable, as an increasing number of volumes required annual republication. In 1967, the code changed to paperbound volumes published annually. The colors of the volume covers change each year, so annual editions can be readily distinguished from each other.

The current code consists of about two hundred volumes. Rather than reissue the entire set at one time, the Office of the Federal Register revises the set on a quarterly basis. Titles 1–16 contain regulations in force as of January 1 of the cover year; titles 17–27 as of April 1; titles 28–41 as of July 1; and titles 42–50 as of October 1. Because one year's edition gradually supplants the previous year's, a current *CFR* set almost always consists of volumes of two or more colors.

The table of contents for each title lists its chapters; that for each chapter, its parts; and for each part, its sections. In addition, at the beginning of each part the agency provides notes showing the statutory or executive authority under which the regulations in that part are issued. This *authority note* is followed by a *source note,* providing the citation and date of the *Federal Register* in which the part was last published in full. Illustration D shows the beginning of 21 C.F.R. Part 740, Cosmetic Product Warning Statements, with authority and source notes following the table of sections. If an individual section is based on a different authority or, as is the case with 21 C.F.R. § 740.17, was added or amended later than the other sections, a separate authority or source note follows that section. Illustration E shows the page on which the new section appears, followed by a citation to the exact *Federal Register* page on which the regulatory text is printed.

In addition to the regulations which form the main contents of the code, Title 3 consists of the texts of proclamations, executive orders and other presidential documents. These materials will be separately described below in Section D.

Among the *CFR* volumes revised and reissued each year is an "Index and Finding Aids" volume. This volume is just one of several indexes and means of access to the *Code of Federal Regulations,* and will be discussed in the next section.

25. Exec.Order No. 9930, 3 C.F.R. 689 (1943–48); Act of Aug. 5, 1953, ch. 333, 67 Stat. 388.

This chapter focuses on finding current regulations, the ones most often sought in legal practice. For help in doing historical research using older *CFR* editions, consult E.C. Surrency & R.E. Surrency, *The Code of Federal Regulations: Bibliography and Guide to Its Use, 1939–1982* (Oceana, 1986).

Illustration D

The beginning of 21 C.F.R. Part 740

20 of this chapter and the limitations on exemptions in Subpart E of Part 20 of this chapter.

[39 FR 44657, Dec. 24, 1974, as amended at 42 FR 15676, Mar. 22, 1977; 46 FR 38074, July 24, 1981]

§ 730.8 Misbranding by reference to filing: filing does not constitute an admission.

(a) The filing of an experience report does not in any way denote approval of the firm or the cosmetic product by the Food and Drug Administration. Any representation in labeling or advertising that creates an impression of official approval because of such filing will be considered misleading.

(b) The filing of an experience report does not in any way constitute an admission by the person filing the report that the alleged experience was the result of an ingredient or ingredients in the cosmetic product, or of any other fact.

PART 740—COSMETIC PRODUCT WARNING STATEMENTS

Subpart A—General

→ AUTHORITY: Secs. 201(n), 601, 602, 701(a), 52 Stat. 1041, 1054-1055 (21 U.S.C. 321(n), 361, 362, 371(a)); 21 CFR 5.10, 5.11.

→ SOURCE: 40 FR 8917, Mar. 3, 1975, unless otherwise noted.

Subpart A—General

§ 740.1 Establishment of warning statements.

(a) The label of a cosmetic product shall bear a warning statement whenever necessary or appropriate to prevent a health hazard that may be associated with the product.

(b) The Commissioner of Food and Drugs, either on his own initiative or on behalf of any interested person who has submitted a petition, may publish a proposal to establish or amend, under Subpart B of this part, a regulation prescribing a warning for a cosmetic. Any such petition shall include an adequate factual basis to support the petition, shall be in the form set forth in Part 10 of this chapter, and will be published for comment if it contains reasonable grounds for the proposed regulation.

[40 FR 8917, Mar. 3, 1975, as amended at 42 FR 15676, Mar. 22, 1977]

§ 740.2 Conspicuousness of warning statements.

(a) A warning statement shall appear on the label prominently and conspicuously as compared to other words, statements, designs, or devices and in bold type on contrasting background to render it likely to be read and understood by the ordinary individual under customary conditions of purchase and use, but in no case may the letters and/or numbers be less than 1/16 inch in height, unless an exemption pursuant to paragraph (b) of this section is established.

(b) If the label of any cosmetic package is too small to accommodate the information as required by this section, the Commissioner may establish by regulation an acceptable alternative method, e.g., type size smaller than 1/16 inch in height. A petition requesting such a regulation, as an amendment to this section, shall be submitted to the Dockets Management Branch in the form established in Part 10 of this chapter.

[40 FR 8917, Mar. 3, 1975, as amended at 42 FR 15676, Mar. 22, 1977]

Illustration E

21 C.F.R. § 740.17, as revised in 1986

as to render it likely to be read and understood by ordinary individuals under normal conditions of purchase. The warning may appear on a firmly affixed tag, tape, card, or sticker or similar overlabeling attached to the package. The warning shall comply in all other respects with § 740.2, e.g., type-size requirements.

(3) The warning required by paragraph (c)(1) of this section is applicable only to self-pressurized containers that use a chlorofluorocarbon in whole or in part as a propellant to expel from the container liquid or solid material different from the propellant.

(Secs. 301, 402, 403, 501, 502, 505, 507, 512, 52 Stat. 1042-1043 as amended, 1046-1048 as amended, 57 Stat. 463 as amended, 82 Stat. 343-351 (21 U.S.C. 331, 342, 343, 351, 352, 355, 357, 360b); sec. 101(a), 83 Stat. 853 (42 U.S.C. 4332))

[40 FR 8917, Mar. 3, 1975, as amended at 42 FR 22033, Apr. 29, 1977]

§ 740.12 Feminine deodorant sprays.

(a) For the purpose of this section, the term "feminine deodorant spray" means any spray deodorant product whose labeling represents or suggests that the product is for use in the female genital area or for use all over the body.

(b) The label of a feminine deodorant spray shall bear the following statement:

Caution—For external use only. Spray at least 8 inches from skin. Do not apply to broken, irritated, or itching skin. Persistent, unusual odor or discharge may indicate conditions for which a physician should be consulted. Discontinue use immediately if rash, irritation, or discomfort develops.

The sentence "Spray at least 8 inches from skin" need not be included in the cautionary statement for products whose expelled contents do not contain a liquified gas propellant such as a halocarbon or hydrocarbon propellant.

(c) Use of the word "hygiene" or "hygienic" or a similar word or words renders any such product misbranded under section 602(a) of the Federal Food, Drug, and Cosmetic Act. The use of any word or words which represent or suggest that such products have a medical usefulness renders such products misbranded under section 502(a) of the Act and illegal new drugs marketed in violation of section 505 of the Act.

[40 FR 8929, Mar. 3, 1975]

§ 740.17 Foaming detergent bath products.

(a) For the purpose of this section, a foaming detergent bath product is any product intended to be added to a bath for the purpose of producing foam that contains a surface-active agent serving as a detergent or foaming ingredient.

(b) The label of foaming detergent bath products within the meaning of paragraph (a) of this section, except for those products that are labeled as intended for use exclusively by adults, shall bear adequate directions for safe use and the following caution:

Caution—Use only as directed. Excessive use or prolonged exposure may cause irritation to skin and urinary tract. Discontinue use if rash, redness, or itching occurs. Consult your physician if irritation persists. Keep out of reach of children.

(c) In the case of products intended for use by children, the phrase "except under adult supervision" may be added at the end of the last sentence in the caution required by paragraph (b) of this section.

[51 FR 20475, June 5, 1986]

§ 740.18 Coal tar hair dyes posing a risk of cancer.

(a) The principal display panel of the label and any labeling accompanying a coal tar hair dye containing any ingredient listed in paragraph (b) of this section shall bear, in accordance with the requirements of § 740.2, the following:

Warning—Contains an ingredient that can penetrate your skin and has been determined to cause cancer in laboratory animals.

(b) Hair dyes containing any of the following ingredients shall comply with the requirements of this section: (1) 4-methoxy-*m*-phenylenediamine (2,4-diaminoanisole) and (2) 4-methoxy-*m*-phenylenediamine sulfate (2,4-diaminoanisole sulfate).

[44 FR 59522, Oct. 16, 1979]

3. FINDING REGULATIONS

There are several methods of finding federal agency regulations. Both the *Federal Register* and the *Code of Federal Regulations* have indexes prepared by the Office of the Federal Register and by commercial publishing companies, and both are available on WESTLAW and LEXIS. In addition, various tables and cross-references provide access to regulations from relevant statutory provisions, and numerous topical looseleaf services collect and index regulations in their fields.

Ordinarily research into the regulations of a federal agency begins with the *Code of Federal Regulations,* rather than the daily *Federal Register.* A person searching simply for a particular agency's body of regulations can consult the "Alphabetical List of Agencies Appearing in the CFR," printed in the back of every *CFR* volume. Appendix D, at the back of this volume, also lists the *CFR* location of major agencies' regulations.

For more specific searches, the *Code* is accompanied by an annually revised volume entitled *Index and Finding Aids,* most of which consists of an index of subjects and agencies.[26] The index provides references to *parts,* rather than sections, so it is not always as specific as would be desired. It also covers a very broad area in relatively terse fashion, so it is not completely comprehensive and is sometimes difficult to use.[27] There are no entries in the index for "foaming detergent bath products," the specific regulation illustrated earlier. Illustration F, however, shows the index page for "cosmetics," including a subheading for product warning statements and a reference to 21 C.F.R. 740.

Two commercial publishers issue more extensive, annual indexes of the *CFR.* Congressional Information Service has published an *Index to the Code of Federal Regulations* since 1981.[28] In four annual volumes, it provides very detailed indexing of the *CFR* by subject and by geographic location. As in the official index, however, its entries refer to parts rather than to specific sections. Unlike many commercial

26. This index is commercially reprinted by Lawyers Co-op as a supplement to its *USCS* index. A few individual *CFR* volumes also include separate indexes to particular chapters or parts prepared by the regulating agencies. These topical indexes, ranging in length from one page to well over a hundred pages, only cover a small fraction of the regulations in *CFR,* but may prove occasionally useful. They are listed in the *Index and Finding Aids* volume immediately after the subject/agency index.

27. The *Index and Finding Aids* volume was first published in 1979, after an attorney had brought suit to compel the government to publish an analytical subject index to the set. *Cervase v. Office of the Federal Register,* 580 F.2d 1166 (3d Cir. 1978). It was a marked improvement over earlier indexes, and the plaintiff agreed to dismissal of his suit upon its publication. Hood, "Indexing and the Law," 8 *Int'l J.L. Libr.* 61 (1980).

A former director of the Office of the Federal Register admitted after leaving office that "the in-house joke, repeated anytime someone complained about not being able to find something in the *CFR,* was 'tell them they can find anything they need using our index, provided they know which volume it's in and what page it's on.'" Emery, "Foreword," *Index to the Code of Federal Regulations, 1977–1979* vii, vii (Information Handling Services, 1980).

28. Earlier editions of the same index were published for 1977–79 by Information Handling Services and 1980 by Capitol Services International.

Illustration F

A page from the *CFR* "Index and Finding Aids" volume

publications which appear much more quickly than official works, this index is published rather slowly. The index for one year's *CFR* edition generally does not appear until the following autumn.

In 1988, R.R. Bowker began publication of *Code of Federal Regulations Index,* claiming that its guide is the first "designed *specifically* for legal research." It too is quite slow, in that its 1988 edition covers 1986 regulations. The three-volume set includes several indexes for specific subject areas and a title-by-title index, and is supplemented twice during the year. Illustration G shows a sample page from this index.

The *Federal Register* also has both official and commercial indexes. The government's *Federal Register Index* is published monthly, and consists of a consolidation of the entries in each issue's table of contents. Entries are arranged by agency, not by subject. Within each agency's listing, rules, proposed rules and notices are listed alphabetically by subject. Each month's index cumulates those earlier in the year, so the January–February index replaces the January index, and the January–December index serves as the final annual index. A table of *Federal Register* pages and dates, similar to that in each daily issue, appears in the back of each index for the months covered. The index usually does not appear until several weeks after its period of coverage ends.

A much more thorough and current index to the *Register* has been published since 1984 by Congressional Information Service. Its *CIS Federal Register Index* is published weekly, within two or three weeks of the period covered. The weekly issues are cumulated periodically, until the publication of permanent bound semiannual volumes. The index provides thorough coverage of all *Federal Register* documents except Sunshine Act notices, and is divided into four sections: a calendar of effective dates and comment deadlines, and indexes by subjects and names, by *CFR* section numbers affected, and by agency docket numbers. The subject and name index provides access by numerous methods, including general policy area, specific subject matter, agency name, authorizing legislation, and affected industries, organizations, corporations, individuals, or geographic areas. Illustration H shows a reference in the January–June 1986 index to the FDA bubble bath regulation, under the heading "Soap and detergent industry."

An increasingly important means of access to both the *Code of Federal Regulations* and the *Federal Register* is provided by full-text coverage in both WESTLAW and LEXIS. *Federal Register* issues since the summer of 1980 are searchable on both systems, and each new issue is available online within a week of its publication. On LEXIS the *Register* is in the FEDREG file of the GENFED library, and on WESTLAW it is in the FR database. The current edition of the *Code of Federal Regulations* is also available online, in the CFR file on LEXIS and the CFR database on WESTLAW. Both systems also have databases, such as CFR86, containing previous years' editions of *CFR.*

Illustration G

A page from R.R. Bowker's *Code of Federal Regulations Index*

CFR INDEX **FOOD AND DRUGS**

(References are to sections of the 1986 Edition of the CFR.)

LEXIS also has a combined file of both *Register* and *Code,* called ALLREG.

Illustration H

A page from the *CIS Federal Register Index* for the first half of 1986

Index by Subjects and Names **Social Security Act**

SNC Hydro
Electric power small producer appl: FERC *(5/22/N) 18835*

SNG Trading
Natural gas pipeline take-or-pay contract, expedited certificate, and purchased gas billing procedures, revision: FERC–
Petition response
(1/28/N) 3503-3504 (2 items)

Snohomish River
Hydroelectric license appls and actions, descriptive listing: FERC *(2/3/N) 4219*

Snoqualmie River
Hydroelectric license appls and actions, descriptive listing: FERC *(2/26/N) 6787; (4/10/N) 12373*

Snyder Act
Indian educ cost and facilities construction aid, suppl funds distribution methods revision: BIA–
Run-off election *(3/19/PR) 9624*

Soap and detergent industry
Detergent bath products (foaming) label warning statement rqmts, revision: FDA–
Reconsideration re user age *(6/5/R) 20471*

Sobotka and Co.
EPA confidential info transfer to contractors: EPA–
Hazardous waste mgmt regulatory impact and flexibility, rptg, operational, and resources impact analyses, and EIS preparation *(6/24/N) 22976*

Social Science Research Council
Soviet and Eastern European studies programs, grant awards descriptive listing: DOS *(2/11/N) 5137*

Social sciences
Archaeometry Adv Panel, estab: NSF *(3/20/N) 9727*
see also Anthropology
see also History

Social security
Beneficiaries living or working outside US, residency rqmts and foreign work deductions revision: SSA *(3/4/PR) 7452*
Black lung benefit claims, court decisions acquiescence rulings issuance, descriptive listing: SSA *(6/4/N) 20354*
Food stamp program info and appl availability in SSA offices, estab: FNS *(6/9/IR) 20793*
HHS financial aid programs subject to intergovtl review, coverage revision, listings: HHS *(2/11/N) 5103*
SSA funded research projects in New Beneficiary Survey analysis, divorce determinates, and retirement behavior, grants availability: SSA *(4/14/N) 12652*
State and local govt employee social security coverage regs, revision: SSA *(5/29/PR) 19468*
see also Aid to Families with Dependent Children
see also Health insurance
see also Health maintenance organizations
see also Medical assistance
see also Medicare
see also Old-Age, Survivors, and Disability Insurance
see also Social security tax
see also Supplemental Security Income
see also Unemployment insurance
see also Workers compensation

Social Security Act
AFDC and adult aid programs, regs revision: SSA *(3/18/R) 9191*
AFDC programs automated appl processing and info retrieval system costs, Fed cost sharing rqmts revision: SSA *(4/17/R) 13001*
AFDC qtrly awards, State child support collection activities rptg rqmts, revision: SSA *(4/21/R) 13511*
AFDC work incentive program, exemption criteria and sanction policy revision: ETA and OHDS *(3/19/R) 9440*
Black lung benefit claims, court decisions acquiescence rulings issuance, descriptive listing: SSA *(6/4/N) 20354*
Cardiac pacemaker natl registry, estab: FDA and HCFA *(5/6/PR) 16792*
Disability benefits eligibility under social security and SSI, impairment severity determination diagnostic techniques descriptive listing: SSA *(5/29/N) 19413*
Disability ins beneficiary work return prognosis criteria research project, grant availability: SSA *(4/14/N) 12655*
Electronic data processing use by State public aid programs, Fed matching fund rqmts revision: HHS *(1/27/IR) 3337*
FDA authority for cardiac pacemaker registration and testing, delegation: FDA *(5/29/R) 19328*
Food stamp program info and appl availability in SSA offices, estab: FNS *(6/9/IR) 20793*
HCFA authority for cardiac pacemaker registration and testing, delegation: HHS *(1/9/N) 1042*
Home health agencies cost reimbursement under Medicare, costs per visit schedule of limits and wage index for rural and urban areas, revision: HCFA *(5/30/N) 19734*
Maternal and child health projects, grants availability: HRSA *(3/5/N) 7730*
Maternal and child health svcs Fed set-aside, special project grants regs estab: PHS *(3/5/R) 7726*
Medicaid "developmental and related disabilities" definition, revision: HCFA *(5/28/R) 19177*
Medicaid hosp and long-term care facility svcs payment rptg rqmts and determination procedures, revision: HCFA *(2/18/PR) 5728*
Medicaid mandatory second surgical opinion program, estab: HCFA *(6/17/PR) 21933*
Medicaid mentally retarded intermediate care facility stds, revision: HCFA *(3/4/PR) 7520*
Medicaid plan of AK, eligibility determination State longevity bonus disregard disapproval: HCFA–
Reconsideration hearing *(4/28/N) 15847*
Medicaid plan of AL, State resource transfer policy revision disapproval: HCFA–
Reconsideration hearing *(1/2/N) 74*
Medicaid plan of AR, residential care facility svcs coverage capitation fee info rqmt, amdt disapproval: HCFA–
Reconsideration hearing *(6/20/N) 22567*
Medicaid plan of AR, State Prescribed Drug Program pharmacy dispensing fee revision disapproval: HCFA–
Reconsideration hearing *(1/27/N) 3433*
Medicaid plan of CA, income eligibility rqmts revision re alimony and child support exclusion and community property law use, disapproval: HCFA–
Reconsideration hearing *(1/28/N) 3512*
Medicaid plan of CA, State community property laws use and court ordered support payments disregard in eligibility determinations, revision disapproval: HCFA–
Reconsideration hearing *(3/12/N) 8562*
Medicaid plan of CA, State community property laws use in income eligibility determinations, amdt disapproval: HCFA–
Reconsideration hearing *(6/19/N) 22354*
Medicaid plan of MI, eligibility determination revision disapproval: HCFA–
Reconsideration hearing *(4/14/N) 12646*
Medicaid plan of NC, eligibility determination re countable resource limit, revision disapproval: HCFA–
Reconsideration hearing *(1/10/N) 1301*
Medicaid plan of NY, hospice svcs coverage revision disapproval: HCFA–
Reconsideration hearing *(1/2/N) 75*
Medicaid plan of OH, AFDC ineligibility due to sibling income, impact on Medicaid eligibility: HCFA–
Reconsideration hearing *(2/6/N) 4653*
Medicaid plan of SC, AFDC ineligibility due to sibling income, impact on Medicaid eligibility: HCFA–
Reconsideration hearing *(2/6/N) 4653*
Medicaid plan of SD, prospective payment revision effective date disapproval: HCFA–
Reconsideration hearing *(1/6/N) 450*
Medicaid program mentally retarded intermediate care facilities, fire safety stds revision: HCFA *(4/18/R) 13224; (5/12/R-cx) 17340*
Medicaid svcs third party payment liability, State determination rqmts revision: HCFA *(5/28/PR) 19227*
Medicare and Medicaid hosp participation rqmts, revision: HCFA *(6/17/R) 22010*
Medicare and medicaid nursing home recipients health care quality assessment survey procedures, revision: HCFA *(6/13/R) 21550*
Medicare and Medicaid regs re physician conflicts of interest, podiatric svcs, home health care certification, nursing home safety, and speech pathology svcs, revision: HCFA *(6/30/R) 23541*
Medicare claims for periodic interim payments, electronic format submission rqmt estab: HCFA *(1/21/PR) 2736*
Medicare cost reimbursement, competitive medical plans eligibility estab and capitation reimbursement method authorization for HMOs and competitive medical plan patients: HCFA–
Info collection rqmts correction *(4/4/R-cx) 11581*
Medicare costs reimbursement rates for HMO and competitive medical plans, revision: HCFA *(1/6/N) 506*
Medicare diagnosis related group reimbursement classification system, review: HCFA *(3/13/N) 8762*
Medicare diagnosis related group reimbursement classification system, revision: HCFA *(6/3/N) 20192*
Medicare eligibility for rural hospices, direct nursing care rqmt waiver, revision: HCFA *(3/3/PR) 7292*
Medicare end-stage renal disease outpatient dialysis svcs prospective payment system, composite rates and determination method revision: HCFA *(5/13/N) 17537*
Medicare home health care agency per visit costs calculation, estab: HCFA *(3/25/N) 10267*
Medicare hosp-based skilled nursing svcs cost limits schedule, revision: HCFA *(4/1/N) 11234; (5/14/N-cx) 17674; (6/16/N-cx) 21807*
Medicare hosp costs reimbursement, State hosp reimbursement control systems approval rqmts, estab: HCFA *(4/24/R) 15481*
Medicare hosp-specific cost adjustments, revision: HCFA *(3/10/PR) 8208*
Medicare ineligibility re SSI cost of living increases, eligibility stds revision: HCFA *(4/10/R) 12325*
Medicare noncovered svcs, provider liability determination procedures revision: HCFA *(2/21/R) 6222*
Medicare nonphysician medical svcs "inflation-indexed charge", estab: HCFA *(4/4/R-cx) 11582*
Medicare nursing svcs (skilled, freestanding and hosp-based) cost limits schedule revision: HCFA *(4/1/N) 11253; (5/14/N-cx) 17673; (6/16/N-cx) 21807*
Medicare payment determination and disbursement svcs for home health agency providers, tentative assignments to regional intermediaries listing: HCFA *(2/13/N) 5403*
Medicare payments for inpatient hosp svcs, diagnosis related group regs and FY87 rates revision: HCFA *(6/3/PR) 19970; (6/4/PR-cx) 20435; (6/24/PR-cx) 22948*
Medicare physician fee freeze violation penalties, estab: HHS *(5/22/R) 18790*
Medicare physicians outpatient dialysis svcs capitation payment, home/facility treatment capability ratio revision: HCFA *(3/19/N) 9530*
Medicare proprietary health care providers equity capital return allowance rqmts revision, and new home health agency cost limits exception elimination: HCFA *(2/20/PR) 6139*
Medicare prospective reimbursement system for inpatient hosp svcs, FY86 rates revision: HCFA *(5/6/IR) 16772*

Jan. 2-June 30, 1986 CIS Federal Register Index 611

Often one has access to a statute or presidential document and would like to find regulations promulgated under its authority or related to it. A "Parallel Table of Authorities and Rules" in the *Index and Finding Aids* volume provides access. It lists every statute and presidential document cited by an agency as authority for its rules, taken from the rulemaking authority citation in *CFR*. The table consists of separate sections for *United States Code* sections, *Statutes at Large* pages, public law numbers, and presidential documents. Authority citations are provided by the agencies, and may follow different formats; the same statute may be cited by code section by one agency and by public law number by another agency. The table does not reconcile inconsistencies, so it may be necessary to check more than one section to find all references to a statute. The table in the *Index and Finding Aids* volume is current as of January 1st of each year. During the course of the year, both additions to and removals from the list are printed in the monthly pamphlet *LSA: List of CFR Sections Affected.* These monthly lists cumulate until the next annual edition.

One of the simplest ways to find relevant regulations may be to use a looseleaf service or other resource which collects and reprints agency regulations in a particular subject area. If relevant regulations are already collected, there may be no need to search through indexes or computer databases. Topical looseleaf services focusing on the work of particular agencies (such as the Internal Revenue Service or the National Labor Relations Board) provide currently supplemented and well annotated texts of both substantive and procedural regulations of their subject agencies. Appendix D in this volume indicates where the regulations of major agencies can be found in commercial publications.

In addition, procedural regulations of over two dozen agencies are printed in the "Administrative Rules of Procedure" volume of *United States Code Service.* Like the rest of *USCS,* the administrative rules volumes include annotations of interpretive agency and court decisions and references to relevant forms, *ALR* annotations, and other research tools, and are updated by annual pocket parts and interim supplements. Pike and Fischer's *Administrative Law, Second Series, Deskbook* also contains the texts of eight major agencies' procedural regulations under the Administrative Procedure Act.

4. UPDATING AND VERIFYING REGULATIONS

Even though the *Code of Federal Regulations* is reissued every year, at some point during the year each volume will be up to a year or more out of date. Administrative regulations change frequently, and researchers must be able to determine their current status. To make sure that a *CFR* section is still current, and to find any new or proposed rules affecting it, there is a straightforward routine to be followed. It consists of several steps, different and often simpler than the ways cases and statutes are updated.

The first step in updating a *CFR* section is to check for references in a monthly pamphlet entitled *LSA: List of CFR Sections Affected.* Like the daily and monthly lists in each issue of the *Federal Register,*

LSA indicates *Register* pages of any new or proposed rules affecting the *Code.* (As noted in the previous section, *LSA* also includes an update of the Parallel Table of Authorities and Rules.) Under each *CFR* title, there are separate listings for final actions and for proposed rules. Except for proposed rules, references are to exact sections and include a descriptive word or phrase indicating the nature of the change, such as "amended," "removed," or "revised." Illustration I shows a page from the September 1986 *LSA* indicating the revision of 21 C.F.R. § 740.17. The listing of proposed rules is to part, not section, and has no descriptive annotation. The coverage of *LSA* reflects changes back to the last revision of each title. Because *CFR* volumes are updated as of four different dates during the year, this means that the dates covered for each title will vary. In a September pamphlet, for example, coverage of titles 42 through 50 will include an entire year's changes since the previous October 1 *CFR* revision, while coverage of titles 28 through 41 will only have changes from July through September. Because *LSA* cumulates every month, it is not necessary to examine more than the most recent pamphlet to find out about changes since the latest *CFR* revision.

The second step in updating sends us back to the *Federal Register.* Because the latest *LSA* pamphlet does not bring a search completely up to date, a similar list must be consulted in the last *Federal Register* issue of each month not covered in the pamphlet. This list, as shown above in Illustration B, is by part rather than section. A researcher in late October who has examined a September *LSA* pamphlet need only check the "List of CFR Parts Affected in October" in the latest available *Federal Register* issue to be assured that no changes in the regulation have been promulgated.

Finally, updating takes us beyond administrative materials to judicial decisions. There is a chance that the regulation has been challenged in court or interpreted in litigation. *CFR,* however, does not include annotations to decisions construing or applying regulations, and no publisher issues a comprehensive annotated set of federal regulations. In specialized areas, looseleaf services include annotations to regulations. *Shepard's Code of Federal Regulations Citations,* however, is the best source for checking for judicial treatment of regulations. It includes citations of regulations in federal courts since about 1949, in state courts and selected law reviews since 1977, and in *ALR* annotations. Abbreviations similar to those used in Shepard's statutory citators are used to indicate, for example, when a regulation has been found constitutional (C), valid (Va), void or invalid (V), or void or invalid in part (Vp). A page from this citator is shown in Illustration J, indicating the effect of *Sierra Club v. E.P.A.,* 719 F.2d 436 (D.C.Cir.1983) on various subsections of 40 C.F.R. § 51.1. *Shepard's Code of Federal Regulations Citations* also covers presidential proclamations, executive orders, and reorganization plans, as will be discussed below in section D. Several of the topical Shepard's units include coverage of regulations in their subject areas. Some, such as *Shepard's Federal Tax*

Illustration I

An *LSA* page, showing *CFR* sections affected and proposed rules

78 **LSA—LIST OF CFR SECTIONS AFFECTED**

CHANGES APRIL 1 THROUGH SEPTEMBER 30, 1986

TITLE 21 Chapter I—Con. Page

660.105 (a) introductory text amended....15611
680 Authority citation revised....15611
680.4 (c)(1) introductory text amended....15611
680.21 Amended....15611
680.26 Amended....15611
720 Authority citation revised....11444
720.8 Revised....11444
730 Authority citation revised; section authority citations removed....25687
730.2 Revised....25687
730.3 Revised....25687
730.4 (a)(1) revised....25687
740 Authority citation revised....20475
740.17 Revised; eff. 6-5-87....20475
807 Authority citation revised....33032
807.31 (c) revised....33033
814 Added....26364
Technical correction....34589
882 Authority citation revised....12101
882.5830 (c) added....12101
Technical correction....15883
884 Authority citation revised....16649
884.5360 (d) added....16649

Chapter II—Drug Enforcement Administration, Department of Justice

1304.03 (b) corrected....26154
1308.02 (c) revised; (e) and (f) redesignated as (f) and (g); new (e) added....15317
1308.03 (a) revised....15318
1308.11 (g)(1) effective date extended....15474
(g)(2) effective date extended....21912
(g)(3) and (4) effective date extended....28695
(g)(1) removed; (b)(31) through (46) and (g)(2) through (13) redesignated as (b)(32) through (47) and (g)(1) through (12); new (b)(31) added....33593
1308.12 (b)(4) revised....15318
(f) redesignated as (g); new (f) added....17478

Page

1308.52 Added....15318

Title 21—*Proposed Rules:*

1—1250 (Ch. I)....13023, 15653
2....25708
20....19851
60....25338, 34094
74....11054
123....22482
128e....22483
128f....22482
145....33904
150....11054
155....18566, 26268
163....12631, 12632
172....12163, 12632
175....12163, 12632
176....12163, 12632
177....12163, 12632
179....12163, 12632
181....12163, 12632
182....19851
186....19851
201....13023, 19853
314....20310
331....27342, 27344
335....16138, 26170
344....27366
348....27360
357....25899
358....27346
369....16138, 26170
501....11456
630....16620, 25710, 26557
805....16792
812....11266, 12713, 26830, 30675
868....11516, 15916
882....26718, 30675
1301....17494, 30675
1306....17494, 21773
1308....13025, 15501, 22085, 22946, 28725, 28727
1311....30675
1312....30675

TITLE 22—FOREIGN RELATIONS

Chapter I—Department of State

7 Authority citation revised....15319
7.3 (d) redesignated as (e); new (d) added....15319
7.5 (b)(3) redesignated as (b)(4); new (b)(3) added....15319
7.8 Redesignated as 7.9; new 7.8 added....15319
7.9 Redesignated as 7.10; new 7.9 redesignated from 7.8....15319

Illustration J

A page from *Shepard's Code of Federal Regulations Citations*

§§50.4 to 50.10
539F2d986 △1976
564F2d1274 △1977
590F2d1058 *1977

§§50.4 to 50.7
696F2d152 *1982
696F2d172 *1980

§50.4
427US251 *1975
49LE480 *1975
96SC2523 *1975
480F2d974 *1972
572F2d1153 *1976
572F2d1290 *1976
621F2d800 *1976
659F2d1242 *1980
684F2d1010 △1982
696F2d157 *1981
715F2d326 *1982
739F2d1075 *1982
352FS706 △1972
364FS241 △1973
445FS1072 △1975
483FS1008 *1979
49ChL363 *1981
69VaL617 *1971
89YLJ1493 *1979

§50.4(a)
752F2d1447 *1983

§50.4(b)
659F2d1240 *1980
696F2d152 *1982
752F2d1447 *1983

§50.5
427US251 *1975
49LE480 *1975
96SC2523 *1975
480F2d974 *1972
572F2d1153 *1976
572F2d1290 *1976
621F2d800 *1976
659F2d1242 *1980
696F2d157 *1981
739F2d1075 *1982
752F2d1447 *1983
352FS706 △1972
364FS241 △1973
445FS1072 △1975
89YLJ1493 *1979

§50.6
Va655F2d322 *1979

696F2d163 *1982
364FS241 △1973
445FS1072 △1975
466FS1335 △1979
NM
681P2d732 *1982
690P2d452 *1982
46LCP(3)84 *1982

§50.7
696F2d163 *1982
364FS241 △1973
445FS1072 △1975
466FS1335 △1979
34PaC565 △1978
Pa
384A2d283 △1978
49ChL363 *1981
46LCP(3)84 *1982

§§50.8 to 50.11
C540F2d1130 *1975
383FS142 △1974

§50.8
504F2d654 △1974
598F2d1167 △1979
361FS1398 △1972
400FS559 *1972
427FS1351 △1977
445FS1072 △1975
552FS678 *1981

§50.9
499F2d294 *1973
504F2d654 △1974
759F2d551 *1984
364FS241 △1973
400FS559 *1972
445FS1072 △1975
387Mas388 *1981
Mass
439NE804 *1981
129PaL1063 *1980

§50.9(a)
Va665F2d1181 *1980

§50.10
659F2d1248 *1980
400FS559 *1972
445FS1072 △1975

§50.11
480F2d974 *1972
Va655F2d323 *1979

400FS559 *1972
445FS1072 △1975
30CLA777 *1982

§50.12
705F2d512 *1982
84CR595 *1983

Part 51
421US67 *1974
426US169 *1975
43LE739 *1974
48LE560 *1975
95SC1476 *1974
96SC2008 *1975
477F2d502 △1973
489F2d396 *1972
499F2d293 △1974
500F2d252 △1974
508F2d744 △1975
547F2d130 △1976
621F2d263 △1980
Vp636F2d351 *1978
659F2d1240 *1980

682F2d629 △1982
490FS1146 △1980
46LCP(3)181 *1980
73NwL440 *1977
AEn§10.10
SI§7.27

§51.1
Vp719F2d442 *1982

§51.1(n)
481F2d169 *1972
489F2d394 *1972
507F2d918 △1974
73NwL398 *1977

§51.1(p)
426US181 *1975
48LE566 *1975
96SC2013 *1975
535F2d1322 *1975

§51.1(q)
FRCI§13.14

§51.1(ff)
Va719F2d460 △1983

§51.1(gg)
Va719F2d464 △1983

§51.1(hh)
V719F2d451 △1983

§51.1(ii)(2)
Vp719F2d467 △1983

§51.1(ii)(2)(ii)
C719F2d443 △1983

§51.1(ii)(3)
V719F2d443 △1983

§51.1(jj)
Va719F2d443 △1983

§51.1(kk)
719F2d443 △1983

§51.2
30CLA761 *1981

§51.2(b)
427US266 *1975
49LE488 *1975
96SC2530 *1975
481F2d169 *1972
500F2d252 △1974
504F2d676 △1974
352FS706 △1972
424FS1219 *1975
450FS808 *1975
460FS1316 *1975

§51.2(d)
427US266 *1975
49LE488 *1975
96SC2530 *1975
481F2d169 *1972
500F2d252 △1974
504F2d676 △1974
515F2d216 *1972
424FS1219 *1975
450FS808 *1975
460FS1316 *1975

§51.3
478F2d880 △1973
682F2d642 △1982
FRCI§6.04

§51.3(a)
659F2d1243 *1980

§51.3(b)(1)(iii)
499F2d293 △1974

§51.3(b)(2)
478F2d880 △1973

* followed by a year refers to the CFR edition, if cited. If not cited,
△ followed by a year indicates the date of the citing reference

Citations, include citations to regulations in topical reporters, such as *American Federal Tax Reports,* but coverage unfortunately does not extend to administrative agency decisions applying or interpreting regulations.

Occasionally a researcher will have a citation to a *CFR* section no longer appearing in the current code. The section or its part might have been repealed or simply transferred to another location in the code. In order that one can determine just what has happened to missing sections, each *CFR* volume contains a list of all changes occurring in its contents since January 1, 1973. These changes are listed by year, at the back of the volume. The entries are the same as those appearing in *LSA* pamphlets, but are limited to the sections in each particular volume. Changes in the entire code before 1973 are listed in separate, hardbound volumes, entitled *List of CFR Sections Affected, 1949–1963* and *1964–1972.*

5. SUMMARY: USING THE FEDERAL REGISTER SYSTEM

According to a recent federal court decision, attorneys "may be presumed to understand how to use the Federal Register system." [29] This presumption can be satisfied by a familiarity with the standard means of finding and verifying the status of agency regulations. A basic search for current regulations ordinarily covers the following steps:

(a) Using the general index to the *Code of Federal Regulations* or one of the commercial indexes to the code, or searching the CFR database on either LEXIS or WESTLAW, to determine the titles and sections of relevant regulations.

(b) Examining the text of the regulations in the latest revised edition of its *Code* volume.

(c) Inspecting the latest monthly pamphlet of *LSA: List of CFR Sections Affected* to determine whether the relevant sections have been affected by later changes. The latest *LSA* pamphlet includes all changes from the current *CFR* edition through the end of the month indicated on its cover.

(d) Examining the cumulative "List of CFR Parts Affected" in the most recent issue of the *Federal Register.* This list updates *LSA* and indicates all changes published during the current month. (Depending on how current the latest *LSA* pamphlet is, it may also be necessary to check the final issue of the previous month.)

29. *National Federation of Federal Employees v. Devine,* 591 F.Supp. 166, 169–70 (D.D.C.1984). At issue was whether a supplemental *CFR* volume had to be published when the 1984 edition of Title Five included Office of Personnel Management regulations which had been barred by Congress and declared void before ever taking effect. While noting that a *Federal Register* notice was sufficient to apprise attorneys of what regulations were in force, the court held that a supplemental volume was necessary "to assure that less sophisticated users of the Code are able to have ready access to the regulations currently in effect. Nonattorney users of the Code cannot be expected to be able to engage in legal research such as that done by an attorney." *Id.* at 170.

(e) Checking the citations found in steps (c) and (d) in the *Register* itself to evaluate the substance of the changes.

(f) Using *Shepard's Code of Federal Regulations Citations* to determine whether the current status of the regulation has been affected by any court decisions.

There are ways to save some of these steps. A looseleaf service reprinting regulations in a particular subject area should frequently update and cumulate *CFR* changes appearing in the *Federal Register,* so that its subject arrangement of regulations would be more current than the latest *CFR* edition. A LEXIS or WESTLAW search in the *Federal Register* database for citations of particular *CFR* parts would retrieve changes and proposed changes and eliminate the need to examine *LSA* or the *Register*'s lists of *CFR* parts affected.

C. DECISIONS OF FEDERAL ADMINISTRATIVE AGENCIES

Among the functions of most administrative agencies is the exercise of quasi-judicial power in determining cases and questions arising under their statutes and regulations. These adjudications usually involve a fact-finding process and the application of agency regulations to particular situations or problems. Agency decisions may follow lengthy formal hearings or consist of rulings on specific submitted inquiries.

As administrative agencies grew during the 1930's and assumed more decision-making authority, they came under increasing attack as to their fairness, efficiency, and procedural methods. In 1939 President Roosevelt asked the Attorney General to appoint a committee to study agency procedures, and in 1941 the extensive final report of the Attorney General's Committee on Administrative Procedure was submitted to Congress.[30] The pressure for reform culminated in enactment of the Administrative Procedure Act in 1946.[31] The Act strengthened procedural safeguards, established minimum standards to ensure fairer hearings, and provided a framework for judicial review of agency action.[32]

Under the Administrative Procedure Act, most agency hearings are conducted by an administrative law judge, who has a role very similar to that of a trial judge and issues the initial decision of the agency. That decision can be appealed to a higher authority within the agency, such as the secretary of the department or the commission, and review of a final agency decision can generally be sought in federal court. The

30. *Administrative Procedure in Government Agencies: Report of the Committee on Administrative Procedure, Appointed by the Attorney General, at the Request of the President, to Investigate the Need for Procedural Reform in Various Administrative Tribunals and to Suggest Improvements Therein,* S.Doc. No. 8, 77th Cong., 1st Sess. (1941).

31. Ch. 324, 80 Stat. 237 (1946).

32. 5 U.S.C. §§ 551–559, 701–706 (1982).

statutes creating and empowering most major agencies provide that actions for review be brought in the United States Court of Appeals.[33]

Most federal agencies write formal opinions to justify or explain their decisions, and these are often published in both official and unofficial sources. Such opinions are very much like those issued by courts, both in form and method of publication. An agency decision can be an important document in interpreting a regulation or statute, or in applying regulations to particular facts. Although most agencies do not consider themselves strictly bound by their prior decisions under the doctrine of stare decisis, the decisions do have considerable precedential value for attorneys practicing before an agency or appealing an agency decision. Whenever one is working in an area within the cognizance of a federal agency, that agency's decisions are an important primary legal source.

1. OFFICIAL REPORTS

Over two dozen federal agencies, including all the major regulatory commissions, publish official reports of their decisions, in a form very similar to official court reports. Most decisions are first published in various preliminary forms such as releases, printed slip decisions, and advance pamphlets. Usually these are cumulated after a considerable time lag into permanent bound volumes in numbered series. Appendix D, at the end of this volume, includes a listing by agency of official reports.

It is not easy to generalize about publication of agency reports. Some series, such as *Agriculture Decisions,* are published only in pamphlets. The Federal Communications Commission ceased its *Reports* series in 1986, and now publishes a paperback *FCC Record* which combines decisions with notices and other documents. On the other hand, the Interstate Commerce Commission ceased publication of advance sheets in 1984 when its printing facility closed, but at the same time began a second series of its *Interstate Commerce Commission Reports* bound volumes (I.C.C.2d).

Some agency reports are not published in either pamphlets *or* bound volumes, but are instead made available in less expensive formats such as microfiche. The Civil Aeronautics Board issued bound reports for forty years, before issuing one softcover volume in 1978 and then converting to microfiche. Similarly, the Occupational Safety and Health Review Commission stopped publishing bound reports after 1975. Its decisions are available on microfiche or in commercial series published by the Bureau of National Affairs and Commerce Clearing House. Other agencies do not publish official reports at all. Like states that have discontinued official court reports, they rely on commercial publishers to keep the public informed more quickly and economically than they could.

33. The model for these provisions is the Federal Trade Commission Act of 1914, ch. 311, § 5, 38 Stat. 717, 720 (current version at 15 U.S.C. § 45(c) (1982)).

When official reports are published, they almost always contain tables of cases and other aids to provide access to their contents. Some contain tables of statutes or regulations cited, and most have indexes of some sort, although their quality and depth vary widely. *Federal Trade Commission Reports* has a very brief index in each volume, while *Decisions of the Employees' Compensation Appeals Board* has an extensive digest with lengthy descriptive entries. Just as lawyers in each state must familiarize themselves with the resources of their jurisdiction, those practicing before a particular agency need to learn the resources it offers.

Somewhat different from other agency decisions are the *Opinions of the Attorneys General of the United States.* Written in response to inquiries from federal government officials, attorney general opinions are advisory in nature and not binding. Nonetheless they are usually accepted as persuasive, and thus fall between the categories of primary and secondary authority. The publication of attorney general opinions has dropped precipitously, however, since the presidency of Franklin D. Roosevelt. Hardly any formal opinions of the attorney general are now issued, and instead the Justice Department's Office of Legal Counsel issues informal opinions. The opinions of this office were not generally available until publication of the first volume of *Opinions of the Office of Legal Counsel,* covering 1977.

2. UNOFFICIAL SOURCES

In addition to the various official reports, the decisions of many agencies are also published commercially, either in looseleaf services or in numbered series of bound volumes. Looseleaf editions have several advantages over the official reports. They are issued much more quickly, are better indexed, and are often supplemented by editorial discussion or integrated into other relevant source materials. Appendix D in this volume, in addition to listing official reports, indicates which looseleaf services print the decisions of each major regulatory agency. A more extensive discussion of looseleafs is contained in Chapter 10.

An increasing number of agency decisions are available online in WESTLAW and LEXIS. Recent decisions of most major regulatory commissions are included in topical databases. Both WESTLAW and LEXIS, for example, have energy law libraries containing Federal Power Commission decisions from 1931 to 1977 and Federal Energy Regulatory Commission decisions since 1977, and Nuclear Regulatory Commission decisions from 1975 to date. Attorney General opinions since 1791 are available on either system. Appendix D indicates dates of WESTLAW and LEXIS coverage of major agencies as of this volume's preparation, but coverage continues to expand. New agencies are added to the systems, and older materials are added to existing databases. When beginning research in a specialized area, it is often worthwhile to determine whether there is a suitable topical database or library and, if so, to learn about its contents.

Some agency decisions are also available in topical reporters. Pike & Fischer's *Administrative Law, Second Series* consists primarily of judicial decisions reviewing agency action, but each volume contains a number of agency decisions on issues relating to administrative procedure. Other reporters, such as *Public Utilities Reports,* also contain a mixture of court and agency decisions.

3. FINDING AGENCY DECISIONS

A person conducting general legal research will rarely find references to administrative agency decisions, for they are usually not covered by such standard tools as *ALR,* legal encyclopedias, or West digests. If one is doing research in an area subject to agency action, however, it is important to find out whether the topic has been affected by any agency adjudications. To do so, it is necessary to use one of the specialized research tools of the regulated area. Often the best place to start is one of the unofficial sources described above. A looseleaf service will have a thorough index offering integrated treatment of administrative, legislative, and judicial action, and most major looseleafs reprint agency decisions, particularly if official reports are slow or lacking altogether. Topical databases in WESTLAW and LEXIS often include both court and agency decisions.

For particular agencies, the indexes contained in official reports may prove useful, but the fact that they rarely cumulate for more than one volume makes the task cumbersome. Each volume of *Nuclear Regulatory Commission Issuances,* for instance, contains indexes to cases, regulations, and statutes cited, as well as a general subject index and a facility index.

Some administrative decisions can be found by using standard legal research tools. In its topical citators, Shepard's includes agency citations of federal court cases. A researcher who has found a relevant Court of Appeals case, for example, can use *Shepard's Federal Energy Law Citations* to find citations to it in *F.E.R.C. Reports* and *N.R.C. Issuances.* Shepard's does *not* include agency citations of statutory provisions, but *United States Code Service* includes administrative decisions among its case annotations. Illustration K shows a page of *USCS* with numerous annotations from *Agriculture Decisions.* Finally, scholarly secondary sources such as law review articles will frequently combine discussion of agency and court decisions, providing both citations and commentary.

4. UPDATING AND VERIFYING AGENCY DECISIONS

Precedent may not have a determinative role in administrative adjudication, but it is always important to know if a decision has been overturned in judicial review or disapproved by a later agency decision. Although methods of finding agency decisions are not as standard and

Illustration K

A *USCS* page, including annotations of administrative decisions

AGRICULTURAL ADJUSTMENT 7 USCS § 608c

CODE OF FEDERAL REGULATIONS

This section is no longer cited as authority for:
7 CFR Part 909, 951, 952, 954–957, 1071, 1073, 1104, 1135, 140–1199, 1202–1206, 1208–1260.

RESEARCH GUIDE

Annotations:

Propriety of Federal District Court's enforcement, or injunction against violation, of agriculture order, regulation, or agreement under 7 USCS § 608a(6). 74 ALR Fed 276.

INTERPRETIVE NOTES AND DECISIONS

10.5. Confidentiality of information

1. Constitutionality

Practice of compensating prune producers for sale of reserve prunes at end of year when reserve is liquidated and fact that price is set by administrative committee under authority of Secretary of Agriculture is authorized by authority of executive branch in exercise of its powers under Commerce Clause, to regulate prices when Congress so mandates; price fixing is not taking without just compensation since producers do receive just, although perhaps not ideal, compensation and price is set by committee which is elected to represent interests of producers as well as of industry in general. Prune Bargaining Asso. v Butz (1975, ND Cal) 444 F Supp 785, affd (CA9 Cal) 571 F2d 1132, cert den 439 US 833, 58 L Ed 2d 128, 99 S Ct 113.

2. Handler defined, generally [7 USCS § 608c(1)]

Interim relief cannot be granted where under terms of Marketing Order, term "handler" is synonymous with "shipper", meaning any person who ships fresh tomatoes produced in production area in current of commerce within regulated area or between any point in regulated area and any point outside thereof, and petitioner has failed to allege facts showing that under these terms it is "handler" subject to order. Re M & R Tomato Distributors, Inc. (1982) 41 Ag Dec 33.

3. —Milk handler

Dairy co-operative is handler within meaning of 7 USCS § 608c and must therefore take administrative route to contest order of Secretary where, by its own admission, co-operative is association of milk producers that transports, processes, and distributes milk for sale to public. United States v United Dairy Farmers Cooperative Asso. (1979, CA3 Pa) 611 F2d 488.

5. Notice and hearing on proposed order [7 USCS § 608c(3)]

Produce handlers can challenge unlawful agency action under Agricultural Adjustment Act (7 USCS §§ 601 et seq.) to ensure that Act's objectives will not be frustrated; however, power granted to producers by Act to protect their interests demonstrates lessened need to rely on handlers, and when Secretary is acting within his designated powers, producers' sole opportunities for protest are hearing on proposed order and opportunity to vote on its approval; and thus judicial review is precluded to orange growers seeking to compel Secretary to terminate federal marketing order under which handling of oranges in that area is regulated by administrative committee which determines percentage of total crop that may be made available for commercial shipment by handlers, where it is not alleged that Secretary acted outside his statutory authority. Pescosolido v Block (1985, CA9 Cal) 765 F2d 827.

6. Findings and issuance of order [7 USCS § 608c(4)]

Nothing in Agricultural Marketing Agreement Act prohibits employee of Department of Agriculture from acting as both investigator and decision maker; milk marketing order promulgated pursuant to 7 USCS § 608c was not invalid because same Department of Agriculture employee who met with representatives of dairy co-operative before hearing and helped draft proposed order also helped Secretary of Agriculture write his final decision. Marketing Assistance Program, Inc. v Bergland (1977) 183 App DC 357, 562 F2d 1305.

7. Termination and suspension of orders [7 USCS § 608c(16)]

District Court did not have mandamus jurisdiction over action by orange farmers seeking to compel Secretary to terminate federal marketing order, under which handling of oranges in geographic area is regulated by administrative committee which determines, among other things, percentage of total crop that may be made available for commercial shipment by handlers, thereby precluding farmers from marketing all oranges that they grow, since (1) mandamus would essentially permit farmers to seek reopening of proceedings they brought pursuant to 7 USCS §§ 601 et seq. that have been finally concluded, (2) permitting attack would allow future plaintiffs continually to protest validity of order even after statutory procedures have been followed merely by claiming change of circumstance and (3) § 608c(16)(B) provides adequate alternative remedy in form of vote of simple majority of affected producers, which will effectively terminate order. Pescosolido v Block (1985, CA9 Cal) 765 F2d 827.

8. Amendments of orders [7 USCS § 608c(17)]

Findings and evidence are required under 7 USCS § 608c(17) only when Secretary promulgates order or makes change in order, not when Secretary merely continues in effect provision that has previously been validly promulgated; provisions of Agriculture Adjustment Act (7 USCS §§ 601 et seq.) applicable to issuance of orders are equally applicable to issuance of amendments to orders, thus before order can be amended, Secretary must make discretionary finding that amendment will tend to effectuate declared policy of Act. Re Oaktree Farm Dairy, Inc. (1979) 38 Ag Dec 113.

10.5. Confidentiality of information

Orange handlers are not entitled to injunction enjoining United States from releasing list of names and addresses of orange growers in several states, which list was generated by government in connection with grower referendum under 7 USCS § 608c(19), since (1) § 608c does not provide for any confidentiality of information gained under section, (2) disclosure would not violate § 608d, in that list was not prepared to determine if handlers were in compliance with marketing orders, but was compiled for referendum purposes only and (3) even if list was compiled pursuant to § 608d, release is still permissible under § 608d(2), in that list qualifies as "general statement" which does not identify information furnished by any particular person; further, list is not exempt from disclosure under any statutory exemptions of Freedom of Information Act (5 USCS § 552(b)). Ivanhoe Citrus Asso. v Handley (1985, DC Dist Col) 612 F Supp 1560.

11. Generally

Congressional mandate that Secretary shall prescribe different terms in certain circumstances cannot be transposed into antithesis, that is, that Secretary shall prescribe uniform provisions in absence of such circumstances. Re Oaktree Farm Dairy, Inc. (1979) 38 Ag Dec 113.

12. Classification, generally

14. —Miscellaneous

Order provisions which require handlers to account for butterfat and skim milk separately and to pay for overages and shrinkages of butterfat and skim milk at applicable class prices are in accordance with law. Re Moser Farms Dairy, Inc. (1982) 41 Ag Dec 7.

15. Minimum prices

Secretary complied with 7 USCS § 608c(18) which provides that before he may modify minimum price which handlers must pay to producers under 7 USCS § 608c(5)(A) he must fix reasonable prices based upon hearing record which considers prices of feed, available

[See "Caution" on p. 3 for §§ affected by P.L.'s 100-202 & 203]

readily accessible as case-finding methods, updating techniques are becoming increasingly uniform.

Most major agencies receive coverage in one of Shepard's specialized citators or in *Shepard's United States Administrative Citations,* which consists of a compilation of citations to decisions and orders of a dozen federal administrative departments, courts, boards and commissions. *Administrative Citations* indicates when decisions of agencies such as the Federal Communications Commission or the Interstate Commerce Commission have been cited in later agency reports, in federal court opinions, and in selected law reviews. Signal references like those used in Shepard's court citators indicate the precedential effect of later agency and court decisions. In addition, the set provides cross-references between several series of official agency reports and commercial looseleaf services. Parallel citations for FCC decisions, for example, are provided in *Public Utilities Reports* and *Radio Regulation. Shepard's U.S. Administrative Citations* can be searched in print or online through LEXIS.

Some agencies, such as the Federal Energy Regulatory Commission, are covered both in *Shepard's U.S. Administrative Citations* and in a topical citator, such as *Shepard's Federal Energy Law Citations.* Several agencies, however, are covered only in specialized citators. *Decisions and Orders of the National Labor Relations Board* appears in *Shepard's Federal Labor Law Citations,* for example, and *Administrative Decisions under Immigration and Nationality Laws* is covered in *Shepard's Immigration and Naturalization Citations.* In the specialized citators, administrative decisions appear both as cited and citing material; one can find later court and agency citations of an agency decision, as well as agency citations of judicial decisions. The major topical citators, in the labor, patents, and tax fields, are included in the online versions of Shepard's available through WESTLAW and LEXIS.

For some agencies there are other tools besides Shepard's for updating and verifying decisions. *Decisions and Orders of the National Labor Relations Board* and several Internal Revenue Service publications are covered by Auto–Cite, the citation verification system available through LEXIS. Selected other administrative decisions are also included, if they are published in one of the several looseleaf reporters within Auto–Cite's coverage. One can use Auto–Cite to verify a Federal Trade Commission decision, for example, only if it is published in the CCH *Trade Cases.*

Tax researchers have several choices. Both administrative and judicial materials are covered not only in *Shepard's Federal Tax Citations,* but also in citator services in both CCH's *Standard Federal Tax Reports* and Prentice Hall's *Federal Taxes.* Unlike Shepard's, these citators provide both names and citations of citing cases instead of simply the pages of citing references. Cited revenue rulings and treasury decisions are listed by number, and cited cases are arranged alphabetically.

Finally, other, more obscure means of updating may exist for the decisions of a particular agency. In the front of each volume of

Decisions of the United States Department of the Interior, for example, there is a cumulative table of all Interior cases which have been overruled or modified since the beginning of the reports series. If specialized resources such as this exist, a researcher working extensively with an agency's decisions should eventually stumble upon them.

It is important to keep in mind when working with administrative materials, whether decisions or regulations, that agency actions are reviewable by the courts. Judicial decisions may set standards and determine limitations on administrative action. Many of the most important procedural safeguards of agency rulemaking and adjudication have resulted from decisions of the Supreme Court and the U.S. Courts of Appeals. Methods of access and updating discussed in this chapter focus specifically on the regulations and decisions of the agencies themselves, but should not be used to the exclusion of case-finding techniques discussed in earlier chapters. Substantive and procedural areas can be researched through digests or *ALR* annotations, and case databases on LEXIS or WESTLAW can be searched for references to a specific administrative regulation or decision.

D. PRESIDENTIAL DOCUMENTS

Thus far we have discussed the regulations and decisions of administrative agencies, which are part of the executive branch of the federal government and operate under the supervision of the President. In addition, the President has the power to veto legislation passed by Congress and the duty to enforce enacted laws. The President also has a wide-ranging lawmaking authority in his or her own right, as the nation's agent of foreign relations and its military commander. In fulfilling these roles and functions, the President issues executive orders, proclamations, and other documents of legal effect.

1. EXECUTIVE ORDERS AND PROCLAMATIONS

Two basic forms of executive fiat are used to perform presidential functions pursuant to statutory authority or inherent powers. These are *executive orders* and *proclamations.* Proclamations are general announcements of policy issued to the nation as a whole, and are commonly associated with ceremonial occasions such as observance of National Bowling Week, 1987,[34] or National Skiing Day, 1988.[35] A few substantive proclamations deal with trade policy or tariff issues. Executive orders cover a wide range of issues and are generally issued to government officials. The two types of document have substantially the same legal effect.[36]

34. Proclamation No. 5596, 3 C.F.R. § 1 (1987).

35. Proclamation No. 5756, 3 C.F.R. § 185 (1987).

36. For an historical overview of the development of the use of these presidential documents, see House Committee on Government Operations, 85th Cong., 1st Sess., *Executive Orders and Proclamations: A Study of a Use of Presidential Powers* (Comm. Print 1957).

Executive orders and proclamations are effective upon publication in the *Federal Register.* The Office of the Federal Register assigns a number to each, in separate series for orders and proclamations. This number is the official and permanent means of identifying the document. Presidential documents are the first items appearing in each *Register* issue, in a larger typeface and more legible format than any of the other material. Their titles are listed under the alphabetical heading "Presidential Documents" in the table of contents and in the monthly indexes, and their numbers are listed in the tables of *CFR* parts affected in the particular issue and for the month. They are also listed by number in the monthly pamphlet *LSA: List of CFR Sections Affected.* Illustration C, earlier in this chapter, includes two proclamations in its list of *CFR* parts affected.

At the end of each year executive orders and proclamations are compiled and published in Title 3 of the *Code of Federal Regulations,* which becomes the standard source for these documents. Because each annual edition of Title 3 is a unique set of documents rather than an updated codification, older volumes remain part of the current *CFR* set.[37] Documents from the years 1936 to 1975 have been recompiled into multiyear hardcover editions.[38]

Each annual compilation of Title 3 includes several useful finding aids. Tables 1 to 3 list the year's proclamations, executive orders, and other presidential documents appearing in the *Federal Register* and *CFR.* Table 4 lists presidential documents affected during the year by later executive or congressional action. Table 5 lists statutes cited as authority for presidential documents, and consists of four separate sections, for title of act, *Statutes at Large* citation, *United States Code* citation, and Public Law number.[39] This accommodates the various ways in which laws are cited in documents, but means the researcher must check under any applicable headings for pertinent references. Following the tables there is a subject index. For years before 1976 these finding aids have been cumulated so that each table and index covers several years of documents, including separate volumes providing consolidated coverage for the thirty years from 1936 to 1965.

All executive orders and proclamations published in the *Federal Register* are also published in the *U.S. Code Congressional and Administrative News* and *USCS Advance. USCCAN* bound volumes have reprinted all orders and proclamations since 1943. In both monthly

37. Beginning with the 1985 compilation, the Title 3 pamphlet has had a white cover to distinguish it from other *CFR* volumes and to inhibit the tendency to discard it upon receipt of the new year's edition.

38. There is also a two-volume set, *Proclamations and Executive Orders: Herbert Hoover, March 4, 1929 to March 4, 1933,* compiling pre-*Federal Register* documents for one president.

39. The reverse process, references from presidential documents to the statutes they implement, is provided by tables in all three editions of the United States Code. In the official *U.S. Code,* Table VI lists executive orders that implement general and permanent law as contained in the Code; and Tables VII and VIII list proclamations and reorganization plans set out in the *Code.* These tables appear as Table IV through VI in *USCA* and *USCS.*

pamphlets and bound volumes of *USCCAN,* Table 7 lists proclamations and Table 8 executive orders, and the index lists documents both by subject and under the headings "executive orders" and "proclamations."

Proclamations back to 1846, but *not* executive orders, are printed in *Statutes at Large.* Some proclamations and orders issued under the specific authority of a statute are also published in the *United States Code* (and its annotated editions, *USCA* and *USCS*), following the text of the authorizing section.

Proclamations and executive orders are also available on LEXIS and WESTLAW. Although coverage is subject to expansion, as of 1988 LEXIS had all presidential documents since January 20, 1981, and WESTLAW had executive orders dating back to 1936 and other presidential documents since 1984.

The standard tool for retrospective research in presidential documents, published by Congressional Information Service in 1987, is the *CIS Index to Presidential Executive Orders and Proclamations.* Part one of this set covers 1787 to 1921 in ten volumes. Part two, also ten volumes, provides coverage from 1921 through 1983, up to the beginning of the publisher's *CIS Federal Register Index.* The set covers both numbered and unnumbered documents, and includes indexes by subject, personal name, and date. Lists of interrelated executive orders provide cross-references between orders affecting or affected by other orders. A reference bibliography describing each document is arranged numerically to correspond with the accompanying set of microfiche reproducing all items indexed.

The Office of the Federal Register publishes a useful volume, *Codification of Presidential Proclamations and Executive Orders,* which arranges proclamations and orders by subject in fifty titles similar to those in *CFR.* It contains executive orders and proclamations of general applicability and continuing effect issued from January 20, 1961 to January 20, 1985, with amendments incorporated into the texts of documents. Orders and proclamations are printed in numerical order within each of the fifty titles. The volume also includes valuable disposition tables, listing all proclamations and orders issued from 1961 to 1985 and indicating their current status. Amendments and revocations are listed, as well as the title and page locations of documents included in the codification.

Judicial and law review citations to proclamations and executive orders are included in the coverage of *Shepard's Code of Federal Regulations Citations.* Presidential documents receive treatment similar to regulations, with symbols indicating the effect of court decisions on the documents' validity.

2. OTHER PRESIDENTIAL DOCUMENTS

While executive orders and proclamations are the most usual forms of presidential documents, the President does issue a variety of other documents of legal effect. The President issues administrative orders, transmits messages to Congress, and makes executive agreements with other countries. While these documents may be less common than executive orders and proclamations, some familiarity with them is often necessary.

Administrative orders: A variety of other documents are printed in the *Federal Register* along with executive orders and proclamations, but not included in either numbered series. These documents, such as memoranda, notices, letters, and presidential determinations, are treated similarly to orders and proclamations. They are included in the table of contents and indexes under "Presidential documents," and are cited by date under Title 3 in the lists of *CFR* parts affected and in *LSA.* They are also reprinted in the annual cumulation of 3 C.F.R. in a separate section following executive orders. Table 3 in each annual volume lists these documents by date. Unlike proclamations and executive orders, however, they are generally not reprinted in *USCCAN,* and because there is no standardized numbering system they are not covered in Shepard's citators.

Reorganization plans: A reorganization plan consists of a presidential proposal for changes in the form of agencies, and can abolish or transfer agency functions. Until recently a plan became law automatically unless either chamber of Congress passed a resolution disapproving it, and so was a powerful means of executive action. In 1983, however, the Supreme Court found such one-house legislative vetoes to be unconstitutional,[40] and a reorganization plan must now be approved by both houses of Congress to take effect.[41] Perhaps because it is no longer as efficient a device, the reorganization plan has fallen into disuse.

Reorganization plans are designated by year and plan number within that year, and published in several places. Upon taking effect they appear in the *Federal Register,* in Title 3 of *CFR,* in the *Statutes at Large,* and unofficially in *USCCAN.*[42] They are also published in Title 5 of the *United States Code,* following the particular Reorganization Act under which they were authorized. *USCA* and *USCS* include notes, presidential messages, and executive orders relating to the plans, and are therefore often the most useful research sources. Reorganization plans, like proclamations and executive orders, can be traced in *Shepard's Code of Federal Regulations Citations.* They can also be traced in *Shepard's United States Citations* under their *Statutes at Large* or *U.S. Code* citations.

40. *Immigration and Naturalization Service v. Chadha,* 462 U.S. 919 (1983).

41. Reorganization Act Amendments of 1984, 5 U.S.C. § 906 (Supp. IV 1986).

42. When submitted to Congress, reorganization plans are printed in the *Congressional Record* and in the House and Senate documents series. These are the best sources for plans that have not passed Congress.

Messages to Congress: Communications to Congress by the President are typically made in the form of presidential messages. They may propose new legislation, explain vetoes, transmit reports or other documents, or convey information about the state of national affairs or some matter of concern. Most messages are printed as Congressional documents. They are also printed and indexed in the *Congressional Record* and in the House and Senate journals. A few important ones appear in *USCCAN.* These documents have some value in developing legislative histories of particular statutes.

Presidential statements upon signing legislation into law may also have some relevance in legislative history research. These signing statements, which since 1986 are printed in *USCCAN,* are discussed in Chapter 7, Legislative History, at page 238.

Executive agreements: The President makes executive agreements with other countries, under the authority to conduct foreign affairs. Unlike treaties, they do not require the advice and consent of the Senate. In recent years, more and more diplomatic arrangements have been made through these convenient methods. Because their purposes and publication methods are basically the same as treaties, the two forms of international agreement will be discussed in Chapter 15.

3. COMPILATIONS OF PRESIDENTIAL PAPERS

The most comprehensive source for current presidential documents is the *Weekly Compilation of Presidential Documents,* which has been published by the Office of the Federal Register since 1965. The *Weekly Compilation* includes nominations, announcements, and transcripts of speeches and press conferences, as well as orders, proclamations, and other legally significant documents. Each weekly issue contains an index to all material in the current quarter, and there are cumulated annual indexes.

An annual volume, *Public Papers of the President,* has since the beginning of the Carter presidency cumulated all material in the *Weekly Compilation* in a final, bound format. Earlier, somewhat more selective *Public Papers* volumes have been published for Presidents Hoover, Truman, Eisenhower, Kennedy, Johnson, Nixon, and Ford.[43] The official set contains only annual indexes, but the commercially published *Cumulated Indexes to the Public Papers of the Presidents of the United States* (K.T.O. Press, 1977–79; Kraus International, since 1979) provides single-volume coverage of each administration.

The papers of earlier presidents are available in various forms. Congress created a Joint Committee on Printing in 1895,[44] and one of its first projects was a comprehensive collection of presidential papers. The resulting ten-volume set, *A Compilation of the Messages and Papers*

43. While Franklin D. Roosevelt's papers have not been included in the official series, they have been edited by S.I. Rosenman and commercially published as *The Public Papers and Addresses of Franklin D. Roosevelt,* (Random House, 13 vols., 1938–50).

44. Act of January 12, 1895, ch. 23, 28 Stat. 601.

of the Presidents, 1789–1897, was edited by James D. Richardson and published in 1896–97. The Bureau of National Literature and Art reissued the set in numerous later editions, supplementing it into the 1920's.

E. OTHER FEDERAL GOVERNMENT INFORMATION

Regulations, agency decisions, and presidential documents are among the most legally significant of federal government publications, but they constitute only a small fraction of the information available. This section briefly summarizes some other resources, and discusses ways of finding out about the government and its agencies.

1. DIRECTORIES AND INFORMATION GUIDES

The best single source for general information about the structure, authority, personnel and functions of a federal agency is the *United States Government Manual.* The *Government Manual* was first published in 1935 by the National Emergency Council and is now published annually by the Office of the Federal Register. It is an official compendium of descriptive data about all three branches of the government. Along with relatively brief coverage of Congress and the courts, there is current and encyclopedic information about every bureau, office, agency, commission, and board of the executive branch. The entries include citations of authorizing legislation, descriptions of agency powers and functions, and lists of key personnel. Detailed name and subject/agency indexes provide easy reference access. An appendix lists executive agencies and functions which have been abolished, transferred or terminated since March 4, 1933. Illustration L shows a sample page from the *Manual.*

Another useful directory is the *Federal Regulatory Directory,* 5th ed. (Congressional Quarterly, 1986). Most of this directory focuses on thirteen major agencies, with more summary treatment of other regulatory agencies. The entries explain the organization and functions of agencies, discuss current topics related to their activities, and provide telephone contacts and information sources.[45] *Federal Yellow Book,* published quarterly by Washington Monitor, has no descriptive text but contains an extensive and very current listing of personnel and telephone numbers. The official *Congressional Directory* is less frequently updated, but also contains addresses and telephone numbers for personnel in departments and independent agencies.

45. Congressional Quarterly also publishes *Washington Information Directory* annually. This compendium is divided into broad subject-area chapters. Its listings provides sources of information in three categories: (1) executive branch agencies, (2) Congress, and (3) non-governmental organizations.

Illustration L

The beginning of a *U.S. Government Manual* entry

POSTAL RATE COMMISSION

1333 H Street NW., Washington, DC 20268–0001
Phone, 202–789–6800

Janet D. Steiger	*Chairman*
Maureen Drummy	*Special Assistant*
Gerald E. Cerasale	*Legal Adviser to the Chairman*
Bonnie Guiton	*Vice Chairman*
Ferrell D. Carmine	*Special Assistant*
Henry R. Folsom	*Commissioner*
(Vacancy)	*Special Assistant*
John W. Crutcher	*Commissioner*
Leonard Merewitz	*Special Assistant*
Patti Birge Tyson	*Commissioner*
W. Lawrence Graves	*Special Assistant*
Charles L. Clapp	*Chief Administrative Officer and Secretary*
David F. Stover	*General Counsel*
Stephen L. Sharfman	*Assistant General Counsel*
Robert Cohen	*Director, Office of Technical Analysis and Planning*
Charles C. McBride	*Assistant Director, Office of Technical Analysis and Planning*
Stephen A. Gold	*Director, Office of the Consumer Advocate*
Cyril J. Pittack	*Personnel Officer*

[For the Postal Rate Commission statement of organization, see the *Code of Federal Regulations,* Title 39, Part 3002]

The major responsibility of the Postal Rate Commission is to submit recommended decisions to the United States Postal Service on postage rates and fees and mail classifications. In addition, the Commission may issue advisory opinions to the Postal Service on proposed nationwide changes in postal services; initiate studies and submit recommendations for changes in the mail classification schedule; and receive, study, and issue recommended decisions or public reports to the Postal Service on complaints received from the mailing public as to postage rates, postal classifications, postal services on a substantially nationwide basis, and the closing or consolidation of small post offices.

The Postal Rate Commission is an independent agency created by chapter 36, subchapter I of the Postal Reorganization Act (84 Stat. 759; 39 U.S.C. 3601–3604), approved August 12, 1970, as amended by the Postal Reorganization Act Amendments of 1976 (90 Stat. 1303).

The Postal Rate Commission promulgates rules and regulations and establishes procedures and takes other actions necessary to carry out its functions and obligations. Acting upon requests from the United States Postal Service, or on its own initiative, the Commission recommends to the Board of Governors of the United States Postal Service changes in rates or fees in each class of mail or type of service. It submits recommended decisions on establishing or changing the mail classification schedule, and holds such hearings on the record as are required by law and are necessary to arrive at sound and fair recommendations. The Commission has appellate jurisdiction to review Postal Service determinations to close or consolidate small post offices.

Sources of Information

Rules of Practice and Procedure The Postal Rate Commission's Rules of Practice and Procedure governing the

2. OTHER GOVERNMENT PUBLICATIONS

In addition to their regulations and decisions, all agencies issue other materials containing a great deal of information relating to their legal business. Agency publications can be found by using the Government Printing Office's *Monthly Catalog of United States Government Publications,* the most comprehensive guide and index to federal government documents. It has been published since 1895, and in recent years is very thoroughly indexed by subject, title, title keyword, and agency. The importance of the *Monthly Catalog* is twofold. It is the main source for determining what the government publishes, and it provides the Superintendent of Documents classification numbers used to shelve documents in most large libraries. There are annual indexes, and several cumulative multiyear indexes have been published.[46] The *Monthly Catalog* can also be searched online through DIALOG.

Annual reports can be important information sources about the work of an agency. They may describe important litigation and include statistics concerning cases handled, prosecutions, settlements and dispositions. Often they discuss new enforcement policies, and interpret agency statutes or proposed amendments. Occasionally an agency may use its annual report as the vehicle for a special review or history of its work.

Almost every agency also produces pamphlets and monographs explaining its structure and operation, and varying from short, popular descriptions to detailed administrative handbooks. An example of such a survey is *The Department of State Today* (1988). Many agencies also publish periodicals of general interest in their field of activity, such as the *Federal Reserve Bulletin* and *Social Security Bulletin,* as well as technical journals and newsletters. J.L. Andriot, *Guide to U.S. Government Publications* (Documents Index, annual) lists the published series and periodicals for all agencies, both current and defunct. Almost two hundred major periodicals are indexed in the *Index to U.S. Government Periodicals* (Infordata, 1970–date, quarterly with annual cumulations).

Many of the agencies and commissions issue special studies, reports, and monographs on major problems.[47] Sometimes these include compiled legislative histories of statutes enforced by the agency.[48] Statistical studies and series can be particularly useful for lawyers

46. A 15–volume cumulative subject index for 1900 to 1971 was published by Carrollton Press in 1973–75, and the Government Printing Office published a two-volume cumulative index for 1971–76 in 1981. Subsequent official cumulative indexes have been issued on microfiche, but bound cumulative indexes are published by Oryx Press for 1976–80 (6 vols., 1987) and 1981–85 (7 vols., 1988).

47. Access to government reports is sometimes eased by use of *Popular Names of U.S. Government Reports,* 4th ed. (Library of Congress, 1984). This table identifies reports known by short or unofficial titles, such as the subject or the name of a commission chairperson.

48. The National Labor Relations Board has issued compilations of the legislative histories of the National Labor Relations Act of 1935 (1948), the Labor Management Relations Act of 1947 (1948), and the Labor Management Reporting and Disclosure Act of 1959 (1959), each in two volumes, which are classics of this type.

needing social science data. *American Statistics Index* (Congressional Information Service, monthly with annual cumulations, 1974–date) provides comprehensive coverage of statistical publications of the federal government. *Government Reports Announcements and Index* (National Technical Information Service, 1975–date, and predecessors with different titles since 1946) provides author and subject access to technical and scientific reports and studies. Field 5 (of 22 subject fields), Behavioral and Social Sciences, is of particular value in legal research. Paper or microfiche copies of the documents indexed can be ordered from NTIS.

3. UNPUBLISHED INFORMATION

While the focus of this book is material that is generally published or available, the government has a vast store of additional documentation that it does not publish, such as internal records, data collected on individuals, and staff studies. The Freedom of Information Act [49] and the Privacy Act [50] have dramatically expanded access to government files. Although government resistance to applications and suits under the acts has increased since their passage, these laws have been quite effective in opening new areas of fact-finding for those involved in legal research.

Several books explain the procedures for gaining access to government records under these laws. They discuss the history and interpretation of the acts, explain procedures for filing requests and suing to compel disclosure, and provide the citations of relevant regulations and sample forms. Among these are:

B.A. Braverman & F.J. Chetwynd, *Information Law: Freedom of Information, Privacy, Open Meetings, Other Access Laws* (Practising Law Institute, 2 vols., 1985).

J.D. Franklin & R.F. Bouchard, *Guidebook to the Freedom of Information and Privacy Acts,* 2d ed. (Clark Boardman, 1987).

J.T. O'Reilly, *Federal Information Disclosure: Procedures, Forms and the Law* (Shepard's/McGraw–Hill, 2 vols., 1977–date).

A recently published concise handbook on the acts is *A Citizen's Guide on Using the Freedom of Information Act and the Privacy Act of 1974 to Request Government Records,* H.R.Rep. No. 199, 100th Cong., 1st Sess. (1987). The guide includes sample request forms, but does not cover procedures for filing suit after denial of a request.

F. STATE ADMINISTRATIVE MATERIALS

State administrative publications receive only brief treatment in this chapter for two reasons. First, because the availability of these materials varies widely from state to state, any discussion must necessarily be quite general. Second, state administrative documents tend to emulate the patterns of federal administrative publication, so a person

49. 5 U.S.C. § 552 (1982).

50. 5 U.S.C. § 552a (1982).

familiar with federal research can usually adapt readily to a particular state's materials.

The regulatory bodies of the various states affect their citizens no less profoundly than does the federal bureaucracy. State agencies set and enforce public health and housing standards, fix and regulate utility rates and practices, govern labor and business activities, and perform many other functions. Unfortunately problems of access and control are not always met with sufficient resources or interest to make administrative materials regularly available. In some states the requirements of public notice are almost at the same primitive level as in the federal government before 1935.

Many states have administrative codes and registers similar to the *CFR* and *Federal Register,* but some states publish neither. Some states publish decisions of selected agencies, or issue other documents of legal significance. A large part of the process of doing state administrative research is determining just what publications exist for a particular state. The best place to find this out may be a state-specific legal research guide, if one exists for the particular state. Appendix A, at the end of this volume, lists the available guides. M.L. Fisher, *Guide to State Legislative and Administrative Materials,* 4th ed. (Rothman, 1988) includes information on the availability in each state of administrative regulations, executive orders, and attorney general opinions.

Virtually all of the states publish state manuals, or "bluebooks," providing basic information about the government, its agencies, and its functions and officials. Although their quality and scope vary widely, these books have somewhat the same utility in state administrative law research as does the *United States Government Manual* for federal matters. The titles of these manuals can be found in a bibliography, *State Bluebooks and Reference Publications* (Council of State Governments, 1983), which also lists directories, statistical abstracts, manuals, and other reference works.

For a survey of the officers, agencies, functions, practices and statistics in all the states, *The Book of the States* (Council of State Governments, biennial) is very helpful. A thorough reference tool on state governmental operations, it includes legal, political and statistical information from every state. The *Municipal Year Book* (International City Management Association, annual) performs a similar function for governments on a local level.

Names and addresses of state administrative personnel are available in the *National Directory of State Agencies* (National Standards Association, annual) or *State Administrative Officials Classed by Function* (Council of State Governments, annual).

1. REGULATIONS

The availability of state rules and regulations has improved considerably in recent years. In 1965 only fourteen states published administrative codes.[51] Forty states and the District of Columbia now publish subject compilations of administrative regulations, more or less resembling *CFR.* Many of these are issued in a looseleaf format with periodic updating. Some of these codes are very easily accessible, but the arrangement and indexing of others can be cumbersome and confusing even to experienced users.

All but five of the states that publish codes supplement them with weekly or monthly registers. Three states still have not published codes, but issue registers containing new regulations. Seven states have neither code nor register. For states without regularly published regulations, the issuing agency must be contacted to obtain copies of specific documents. Appendix B, at the end of this volume, indicates the existence of administrative codes and registers for each state.

A few commercial looseleaf services also contain state administrative regulations in particular subject areas. *Environment Reporter* (Bureau of National Affairs), for example, includes state regulations governing air and water quality, mining, solid waste, and land use in its "State Laws" volumes. A person doing research in the regulations of more than one state or seeking to compile a survey of state regulations would do well to start by consulting "State Administrative Regulations Research," in C. Nyberg & C. Boast, *Subject Compilations of State Laws, 1979–1983* 11 (Greenwood Press, 1984).

2. DECISIONS

Some state agencies publish official reports of their decisions, similar to those of federal bodies. The most common are the reports of state tax commissioners, public utility commissions, banking commissions, insurance commissions, and labor agencies. Advance sheets are quite rare, although some agencies issue their decisions *only* in separate slip form. Occasionally state administrative decisions may be found in specialized subject reporters and looseleaf services, and a growing number of state agency decisions are included on WESTLAW and LEXIS.

State attorney general opinions are often an important resource in interpreting and applying statutory provisions. These opinions are similar in form and purpose to those of the United States Attorney General, but in most states they are used much more frequently.[52] They are typically published in annual or biennial volumes by the state (with a considerable time lag), and are also available currently on microfiche from Hein. For several states, Shepard's citators include attorney general opinions as citing material, so one can find opinions discussing particular cases or statutes. Many of the annotated state codes also include references to relevant opinions. Both LEXIS and

51. Cohen, "Publication of State Administrative Regulations—Reform in Slow Motion," 14 *Buffalo L.Rev.* 410, 421 (1965).

52. State attorney general practices are surveyed in Heiser, "The Opinion Writing Function of Attorneys General," 18 *Idaho L.Rev.* 9 (1982).

WESTLAW have databases containing state attorney general opinions, with coverage in most states beginning in 1977.

3. OTHER DOCUMENTS

Like the federal government, state governments publish a variety of documents such as reports, studies, and periodicals. A few states issue periodic lists of recent publications, and some issue annual catalogs. The most complete source for all states is the *Monthly Checklist of State Publications,* which since 1910 has recorded state documents received at the Library of Congress. Publications are listed by state and indexed by subject.

Index to Current Urban Documents (Greenwood Press, quarterly, 1972–date), provides access to documents issued by cities, counties, and other regional agencies. The index is arranged geographically with a subject index, and the documents themselves are available from the publisher on microfiche.

G. SUMMARY

The development of administrative agencies on both federal and state levels has added a massive literature of administrative regulations and decisions to the essential resources of legal research. With the growth of the executive branch generally, the legal documentation flowing from the exercise of Presidential powers has further enlarged the range of these materials. The increased sophistication of indexing and access aids in the *Federal Register* and the *Code of Federal Regulations,* commercial publications of administrative documents such as looseleaf services, and online access through WESTLAW and LEXIS have made these materials easily available to the researcher. Even state regulations and decisions are now more accessible through the proliferation of state administrative codes and registers, and their partial coverage in looseleafs and databases. What had been a wilderness of confusion and frustration has blossomed into a fertile field for the astute researcher.

H. ADDITIONAL READING

H. Ball, *Controlling Regulatory Sprawl: Presidential Strategies from Nixon to Reagan* (Greenwood Press, 1984).

E. Gellhorn & B.B. Boyer, *Administrative Law and Process in a Nutshell,* 2d ed. (West, 1981).

A Guide to Federal Agency Rulemaking (Administrative Conference of the United States, 1983).

K.F. Warren, *Administrative Law in the Political System,* 2d ed. (West, 1988).

Chapter 9

COURT RULES AND PRACTICE

A. INTRODUCTION

While much of legal literature focuses on substantive rights, an equally important aspect of the law deals with the processes under which parties come before courts to settle disputes. These processes are the focus of law school classes on civil procedure and of the burgeoning body of material on court rules and practice. Neither substance nor procedure would serve much purpose without the other. As Roscoe Pound succinctly explained: "Procedure is the means; full, equal and exact enforcement of substantive law is the end." [1]

For centuries the rules governing court proceedings were developed piecemeal through case law, eventually creating the arcane and formalistic pleading rituals of the Court of Chancery in Dickens' *Bleak House.* Reforms within the past century have considerably changed court

1. Pound, "The Etiquette of Justice," 3 *Proc.Neb.St.B.A.* 231, 231 (1909).

procedures, making them simpler and more flexible.[2] In any area of thought shaped by lawyers and judges, however, there are bound to be unforeseen complexities and differences of interpretation. Rules that may appear straightforward must be applied in light of the large body of case law that has developed. There is also an extensive secondary literature to guide litigants through the intricate maze of court proceedings, and formbooks designed to provide the proper format for pleadings and other court documents. This chapter provides a survey of the sources available for finding the texts of court rules and discovering the judicial and secondary sources that can aid one's passage through the courts.

B. COURT RULES

Court rules are designed to guide and regulate the conduct of business before the courts. They range from purely formal details, such as the format to be followed in preparing a brief, to matters of substantial importance, such as grounds for appeal, time limitations, and the types of motions and appeals which will be heard. Court rules may specify or limit available remedies, and may thus affect rights in significant ways.

Each jurisdiction has its own requirements and procedures for the promulgation of court rules. Some involve action by special conferences of judges; others require action or approval by the highest court of the jurisdiction. Some court rules are statutory and are created by legislatures, while some require a combination of judicial action and legislative approval. While courts are traditionally considered to have inherent power to control the conduct of their affairs, court rules are generally promulgated under authority granted by the legislature and are considered a form of delegated legislation.

1. FEDERAL RULES

Federal procedure is not necessarily more important than any other, but it is discussed first for two reasons. Not only does it affect more people than the procedure of any individual state, but its forms and methods of publication have been very influential on the states. An increasing number of states have chosen to model their procedural rules on those established for the federal courts in the past half-century.

Since its first session Congress has expressly given the federal courts power to make rules governing their procedures.[3] In 1822 the

2. "The practically universal trend of reform has been in favor of less binding and strict rules of form enforced upon the litigants and their counsel and with a large measure of discretion accorded to the trial judge in directing the course of a particular lawsuit." C.E. Clark, "The Handmaid of Justice," 23 *Wash.U.L.Q.* 297, 308 (1938).

3. Section 17 of the Judiciary Act of 1789 gave the new federal courts the power "to make and establish all necessary rules for the orderly conducting [of] business in the said courts, provided such rules are not repugnant to the laws of the United States." Ch. 20, § 17, 1 Stat. 73, 83.

Supreme Court promulgated its first set of rules for procedures in equity,[4] but it did not issue general rules for actions at law until well into the twentieth century. A 1934 Act of Congress gave the Court authority to combine equity and law into one federal civil procedure and to make and publish rules governing federal actions.[5] The resulting Federal Rules of Civil Procedure were adopted by the Supreme Court in December 1937 and became effective September 16, 1938.

The new rules were a widely acclaimed success in modernizing federal civil practice. Attorney General Robert H. Jackson wrote in his 1940 report to Congress that the rules had created "probably the simplest form of civil procedure yet devised in any jurisdiction in which Anglo–Saxon jurisprudence prevails."[6] But he went on: "Criminal procedure, however, still remains largely in a chaotic and archaic state. Many technicalities dating back a century or two are still in full vigor in the Federal courts."[7] Congress had given the Supreme Court authority to promulgate rules governing criminal appeals in 1933,[8] and in 1940 it passed a law providing for rules with respect to criminal trial court proceedings.[9] The Federal Rules of Criminal Procedure went through several drafts before finally becoming effective on March 21, 1946.

The criminal rules governed proceedings both before and after verdict, but appeals in civil cases continued to be handled differently in each circuit. Finally in 1966 Congress amended 28 U.S.C. § 2072 to empower the Supreme Court to prescribe rules for the Courts of Appeals in civil actions.[10] The Federal Rules of Appellate Procedure, governing both civil and criminal proceedings, took effect on July 1, 1968.

The last of the four major sets of rules governing federal court proceedings had a rather different origin. In 1972 the Supreme Court submitted proposed Federal Rules of Evidence to Congress, which passed a law preventing them from taking effect until expressly approved.[11] One problem was that the proposed rules covering evidentia-

The Supreme Court's first rules, at its first meeting in February 1790, dealt mostly with qualification of attorneys who wished to practice before it. 2 U.S. (2 Dall.) 399 (1790). A rule five years later ordered that "the Gentlemen of the Bar be notified, that the Court will hereafter expect to be furnished with a statement of the material points of the Case, from the Counsel on each side of a Cause." 3 U.S. (3 Dall.) 120 (1795).

4. 20 U.S. (7 Wheat.) v (1822).

5. Act of June 19, 1934, ch. 651, 48 Stat. 1064 (current version at 28 U.S.C. § 2072 (1982)).

6. *Annual Report of the Attorney General of the United States,* H.R.Doc. No. 9, 77th Cong., 1st Sess. 5 (1940).

7. *Id.*

8. Act of Feb. 24, 1933, ch. 119, 47 Stat. 904, as amended by Act of Mar. 8, 1934, ch. 49, 48 Stat. 399 (current version at 18 U.S.C. § 3772 (1982)).

9. Act of June 29, 1940, ch. 445, 54 Stat. 688 (current version at 18 U.S.C. § 3771 (1982)).

10. Act of Nov. 6, 1966, Pub.L. No. 89–773, 80 Stat. 1323.

11. Act of Mar. 30, 1973, Pub.L. No. 93–12, 87 Stat. 9.

ry privileges were seen as substantive rather than procedural in nature, and thus outside the scope of the Court's rulemaking authority.[12] Congress enacted its own amended version of the rules, which became law on July 1, 1975, and gave the Supreme Court authority to make amendments other than those creating, abolishing or modifying privileges.[13]

The Supreme Court has also issued rules for more limited circumstances. Rules governing bankruptcy proceedings were promulgated under the authority of the Bankruptcy Act of 1898,[14] and have undergone several revisions and changes. The current rules, under the new Bankruptcy Code,[15] became effective August 1, 1983.

An important resource in applying federal court rules is the accompanying commentary by the Advisory Committee that drafted the original rules or a later committee that drafted and proposed an amendment.[16] These notes usually consist of a few paragraphs discussing the history of procedure under prior law and the purpose of the new rule or amendment, and provide a sort of "legislative history" analogous to congressional committee reports. Advisory Committee notes are often an invaluable first step in interpreting rule provisions. In most versions of the major sets of rules, these important notes are printed immediately following the text of each rule.

Finally, in addition to the sets of rules applying to the federal courts in general, there are rules governing proceedings in particular courts. The Supreme Court and specialized courts such as the Claims Court have their own sets of rules, and individual Courts of Appeals and District Courts promulgate supplementary rules for local practice. Any federal court can establish rules for the conduct of its business, as long as they are not inconsistent with Acts of Congress or rules prescribed by the Supreme Court.[17]

These various rules governing federal court proceedings are rarely far from hand in any law library. They can be found in online

12. 28 U.S.C. § 2072 specifies that rules promulgated by the Supreme Court "shall not abridge, enlarge or modify any substantive right." *See* Goldberg, "The Supreme Court, Congress, and Rules of Evidence," 5 *Seton Hall L.Rev.* 667 (1974).

13. Act of Jan. 2, 1975, § 2(a)(1), Pub.L. No. 93–595, 88 Stat. 1926, 1948 (codified at 28 U.S.C. § 2076 (1982)).

14. Ch. 541, § 30, 30 Stat. 544. This section was repealed in 1964, when Supreme Court rulemaking power in bankruptcy was brought into conformity with its power to make other court rules. Act of Oct. 3, 1964, Pub.L. No. 88–623, 78 Stat. 1001 (codified as amended at 28 U.S.C. § 2075 (1982)).

15. Title 11, U.S.C. (1982), enacted and codified by the Bankruptcy Reform Act of 1978, Pub.L. No. 95–598, 92 Stat. 2549.

16. Under a 1958 Act, a permanent Committee on Rules of Practice and Procedure of the Judicial Conference of the United States studies the federal rules on a continuous basis and recommends changes as necessary. Act of July 11, 1958, Pub.L. No. 85–513, 72 Stat. 356 (codified at 28 U.S.C. § 331 (1982)).

17. 28 U.S.C. § 2071 (1982). The Supreme Court may also exercise its inherent supervisory power to ensure that local rules are consistent with principles of right and justice. *See, e.g., Frazier v. Heebe,* 482 U.S. 641 (1987), *on remand,* 825 F.2d 89 (5th Cir.1987) (prohibiting Eastern District of Louisiana from requiring that a member of its bar live or maintain an office in Louisiana).

databases and in numerous publications, both unannotated and annotated. The sheer number of resources about to be described may be bewildering at first, but different versions serve different purposes. The proper source to use depends on the research needs in a particular situation. Sometimes one just needs to consult the text of a set of rules, but often it is necessary to have references to judicial decisions or expert commentary. Table 1, on the following pages, lists the locations of rules in the tools discussed below.

a. *Unannotated Texts*

A variety of resources contain the texts of federal court rules. The *United States Code* publishes both the rules and Advisory Committee notes for the major sets of rules. An appendix to Title 28, Judiciary and Judicial Procedure, contains the Federal Rules of Civil Procedure, Appellate Procedure, and Evidence, as well as rules governing proceedings in the Supreme Court and several specialized courts. The Federal Rules of Criminal Procedure appear in an appendix to Title 18, Crimes and Criminal Procedure, and Bankruptcy Rules and Official Forms are in an appendix to Title 11, Bankruptcy. The official *U.S. Code,* however, is always at least two or three years out of date when it is published, so it cannot be relied upon for coverage of current developments or changes.

Several commercially published sources also contain the texts of the major rules, updated on a more timely basis. The "National Volume" of *Federal Procedure Rules Service* (Lawyers Co-operative, annual) contains the text and Advisory Committee notes for all major rules, along with references to textual references in the publisher's encyclopedia *Federal Procedure, Lawyers Edition* (to be discussed below in Section D).

The major rules are also published annually in pamphlets by West, *Federal Civil Judicial Procedure and Rules* and *Federal Criminal Code and Rules.* As the titles indicate, these books contain the texts of relevant statutes as well as numerous sets of court rules. Bankruptcy rules are available in pamphlets issued annually both by West (*Bankruptcy Code, Rules and Forms*) and by Lawyers Co-op (*Bankruptcy Code, Rules & Official Forms*). Both editions also include relevant statutes, the Federal Rules of Civil Procedure, and the Federal Rules of Evidence.[18]

Volume 16A, "Rules," of the *Cyclopedia of Federal Procedure,* 3d ed. (Callaghan) contains the text of the rules but no Advisory Committee notes. The Rules of Civil Procedure and Appellate Procedure can also be found in the "Finding Aids" volume of Callaghan's *Federal Rules Service,* a very useful resource for research on judicial decisions relating to the rules (to be discussed in Section C).

18. A third paperback for bankruptcy practice is published by Matthew Bender and called the "Collier Pamphlet Edition." It consists of two volumes, one for the bankruptcy code and one for the rules and forms.

Federal rules are also available online in both LEXIS and WESTLAW. LEXIS has files in its GENFED library containing the four major sets of rules (Civil Procedure, Criminal Procedure, Appellate Procedure, and Evidence). Historical notes and Advisory Committee comments are included as well as texts. A group file, RULES, combines these individual files with rules for the U.S. Tax Court and U.S. Claims Court. WESTLAW's USC database includes the texts of all rules printed in *USCA* in addition to sections of the code itself, and its FRULES database consists only of the rules. WESTLAW includes numerous specialized sets of rules not in LEXIS, but its databases do not yet include all Advisory Committee notes.

While not as widely applicable as the major sets of federal rules, rules for specific courts can be just as important in the day-to-day practice of law. In addition to the *United States Code* and other sources, Supreme Court rules also are printed in Commerce Clearing House's looseleaf *Supreme Court Bulletin.* The rules of individual lower federal courts are not quite as widely published as rules promulgated by the Supreme Court. The most comprehensive source for all circuit and district court rules is "Federal Local Court Rules," three looseleaf volumes published by Callaghan as an adjunct to its *Federal Rules Service* and supplemented six times a year. Most of the set consists of rules for individual U.S. District Courts, arranged by state, but the third volume includes rules and internal operating procedures for the Courts of Appeals.

The rules of individual courts are also available in several other places. *Federal Procedure Rules Service* publishes eleven separate "Circuit Volumes," corresponding to the eleven numbered U.S. Courts of Appeals. Each volume contains the rules of its circuit and of each district within the circuit. Rules for the District of Columbia Circuit appear in the Third and Fourth Circuit volumes, and Federal Circuit rules are in the Second, Third and Fourth Circuit volumes. The rules volume of the *Cyclopedia of Federal Procedure* also includes rules of circuits, but not districts.

The handiest source for rules of the district courts in a particular state, and of the circuit within which that state lies, will frequently be a state court rules pamphlet published by West or Michie. These pamphlets, published for over thirty states to accompany annotated state codes, contain rules of both state and federal courts, and will be discussed further in the "state rules" section, below.

Finally, it is important that practitioners be aware of and be able to find proposed and recent amendments to rules. For the major rules sets, the Supreme Court submits newly adopted amendments to Congress. The texts of the amendments, accompanied by Judicial Conference Advisory Committee notes, are printed by Congress as House Documents. The same material is reproduced in full in advance sheets for West's *Supreme Court Reporter, Federal Reporter, Federal Supplement,* and *Federal Rules Decisions,* with its inclusion

Table 1

Published and online locations of various sets of federal court rules

		Annotated Editions		
	United States Code Annotated	*United States Code Service*	*Supreme Court Digest, L.Ed.*	*Moore's Rules Pamphlets*
Federal Rules of Civil Procedure	Title 28 Appendix	Rules volumes	Vol. 18	Vol. 1
Federal Rules of Criminal Procedure	Title 18 Appendix	Rules volumes	Vol. 19	Vol. 3
Federal Rules of Appellate Procedure	Title 28 Appendix	Rules volumes	Vol. 17	Vol. 1 (unannotated)
Federal Rules of Evidence	Title 28 Appendix	Title 28 Appendix	Vol. 20	Vol. 2
Bankruptcy Rules and Official Forms	Title 11 Appendix	Rules volumes	Vol. 17	
Rules of the Supreme Court of the U.S.	Title 28 Appendix	Rules volumes	Vol. 17	Vol. 1 (unannotated)
Rules of individual U.S. Courts of Appeals	Title 28 Appendix	Rules volumes	Vol. 21	
Rules for the Trial of Misdemeanors before U.S. Magistrates	Title 18 Appendix	Rules volumes	Vol. 19	Vol. 3
Rules Governing Sections 2254 and 2255 (habeas corpus) Proceedings	Title 28 following §§ 2254, 2255	Rules volumes	Vol. 19	Vol. 3
Rules of the Judicial Panel on Multidistrict Litigation	Title 28 following § 1407	Rules volumes	Vol. 22	
Rules of the U.S. Claims Court	Title 28 Appendix	Rules volumes	Vol. 22	
Rules of the U.S. Court of International Trade	Title 28 Appendix	Rules volumes	Vol. 22	
Rules of the U.S. Tax Court	Title 26 following § 7453	Rules volumes	Vol. 22	
Rules of the U.S. Court of Military Appeals	Title 10 following § 867	Rules volumes	Vol. 22	

Table 1 (Continued)

Unannotated Editions

United States Code	*Federal Procedure Rules Service*	*Cyclopedia of Federal Procedure*	West rules pamphlets	LEXIS Library/File	WESTLAW Database and search term
Title 28 Appendix	National volume	Vol. 16A	Civil, Bankruptcy	GENFED/ FRCP or RULES	USC or FRULES ci(frcp)
Title 18 Appendix	National volume	Vol. 16A	Criminal	GENFED/ FRCRP or RULES	USC or FRULES ci(frcrp)
Title 28 Appendix	National volume	Vol. 16A	Civil, Criminal	GENFED/ FRAP or RULES	USC or FRULES ci(frap)
Title 28 Appendix	National volume	Vol. 16A	Civil, Criminal, Bankruptcy	GENFED/ FRE or RULES	USC or FRULES ci(frev)
Title 11 Appendix			Bankruptcy		USC or FRULES ci(br)
Title 28 Appendix	National volume	Vol. 16A	Civil, Criminal		USC or FRULES ci(scr)
	Individual circuit volumes	Vol. 16A			USC or FRULES ci(cta#r)
Title 18 Appendix	National volume	Vol. 16A	Criminal		USC or FRULES ci(usmr)
Following Title 28 §§ 2254, 2255	National volume	Vol. 16A	Civil, Criminal		USC or FRULES ci(225#c)
Following Title 28 § 1407	National volume		Civil		USC or FRULES ci(rpjpml)
Title 28 Appendix	3d & 4th Circuit volumes	Vol. 16A		GENFED/ CLRUL or RULES	USC or FRULES ci(ctclt)
Title 28 Appendix	Second Circuit volume				USC or FRULES ci(citr)
Title 26 Appendix				GENFED/ TAXRUL or RULES	USC or FRULES ci(tcr)
Title 10 Appendix					USC or FRULES ci(cma)

prominently noted on the pamphlet covers. Any attorney monitoring the advance sheets for current case developments should thus be on notice of any prospective change in the rules. The advance sheets for the *Federal Reporter* also include amendments to the rules of individual Courts of Appeals. The monthly pamphlets for *U.S. Code Congressional and Administrative News* and *United States Code Service Advance* contain not only all these amendments, but those for other federal courts and administrative tribunals as well.

b. Annotated Texts

Annotated editions of the rules contain not only Advisory Committee comments but headnotes of relevant cases. Both annotated federal codes provide comprehensive coverage of rules, and two less extensive annotated editions of court rules are also published.

Both *United States Code Annotated* and *United States Code Service* treat the rules in similar fashion to statutes and provide extensive annotations of relevant decisions. In *USCA,* the eighty-six Federal Rules of Civil Procedure fill eleven volumes, and in *USCS* they occupy almost seven volumes. The rules are located in the sets in different places: *USCA* includes the rules at the same place they appear in the *U.S. Code,* following the code titles to which they are most closely related. *USCS* publishes several unnumbered "Court Rules" volumes, which are generally shelved at the end of the set. The one exception is the Federal Rules of Evidence; because they were enacted by Congress, *USCS* prints them as an appendix volume to Title 28. Both *USCA* and *USCS* also include annotated editions of the rules of the Supreme Court, of the thirteen individual circuits, and of specialized federal courts. Like the rest of the sets, the volumes of court rules are updated by annual pocket parts and by interim pamphlets.

As it does with statutes, *USCA* includes extensive cross-references to related material such as other federal rules, the publisher's treatise *Federal Practice and Procedure,* and *West's Federal Forms.* The notes to each section also provide relevant digest key numbers and *C.J.S.* section numbers. The bulk of each volume consists of case headnotes, arranged by subject after each rule. Illustration A shows a page from *USCA* containing the text of Federal Rules of Appellate Procedure rule 38, concerning frivolous appeals.

USCS provides the same rules text and Advisory Committee notes, along with cross-references to other rules and statutes and to its publisher's other works. These references include Lawyers Co-op's federal practice encyclopedia, *Federal Procedure, Lawyers' Edition,* as well as *Am.Jur.2d* and annotations in *ALR* and *U.S. Supreme Court Reports, Lawyers' Edition.* The notes following some rules also include references to other Lawyers Co-op texts and law review articles. Illustration B shows rule 38 of the Federal Rules of Appellate Procedure as it appears in *USCS.*

Illustration A

Federal Rules of Appellate Procedure rule 38, in *USCA*

Rule 38. Damages for Delay

If a court of appeals shall determine that an appeal is frivolous, it may award just damages and single or double costs to the appellee.

Notes of Advisory Committee on Appellate Rules

Compare 28 U.S.C. § 1912 [section 1912 of this title]. While both the statute and the usual rule on the subject by courts of appeals (Fourth Circuit Rule 20 [rule 20, U.S.Ct. of App. 4th Cir., this title] is a typical rule) speak of "damages for delay," the courts of appeals quite properly allow damages, attorney's fees and other expenses incurred by an appellee if the appeal is frivolous without requiring a showing that the appeal resulted in delay. See Dunscombe v. Sayle, 340 F.2d 311 (5th Cir., 1965), cert. den., 382 U.S. 814, 86 S.Ct. 32, 15 L.Ed.2d 62 (1965); Lowe v. Willacy, 239 F.2d 179 (9th Cir., 1956); Griffin Wellpoint Corp. v. Munro-Langstroth, Inc., 269 F.2d 64 (1st Cir., 1959); Ginsburg v. Stern, 295 F.2d 698 (3d Cir., 1961). The subjects of interest and damages are separately regulated, contrary to the present practice of combining the two (see Fourth Circuit Rule 20) to make it clear that the awards are distinct and independent. Interest is provided for by law; damages are awarded by the court in its discretion in the case of a frivolous appeal as a matter of justice to the appellee and as a penalty against the appellant.

Cross References

Damages and costs on affirmance, see section 1912 of this title.

Library References

Federal Civil Procedure ⚷2747.

C.J.S. Federal Civil Procedure §§ 1292, 1294.

West's Federal Forms

Motion, see § 747.10.

Notes of Decisions

---

1. Purpose

This rule operates both to compensate winners of judgments in district court for expense and delay of defending against meritless arguments in court of appeals and also to deter such appeals and thus to preserve appellate court calendar for cases worthy of consideration. Ruderer v. Fines, C.A.Ill.1980, 614 F.2d 1128.

This rule is designed to penalize litigants whose appeal is frivolous and to compensate those who have been put to

Illustration B

Rule 38 in *USCS*

RULES OF APPELLATE PROCEDURE **Rule 38, n 1**

Rule 38. Damages for Delay

If a court of appeals shall determine that an appeal is frivolous, it may award just damages and single or double costs to the appellee.

HISTORY; ANCILLARY LAWS AND DIRECTIVES

Other provisions:

Notes of Advisory Committee on Appellate Rules. Compare 28 USC § 1912. While both the statute and the usual rule on the subject by courts of appeals (Fourth Circuit Rule 20 is a typical rule) speak of "damages for delay," the courts of appeals quite properly allow damages, attorney's fees and other expenses incurred by an appellee if the appeal is frivolous without requiring a showing that the appeal resulted in delay. See Dunscombe v Sayle, 340 F2d 311 (5th Cir 1965), cert den, 382 US 814, 15 L Ed 2d 62 (1965); Lowe v Willacy, 239 F2d 179 (9th Cir 1956); Griffin Wellpoint Corp. v Munro-Langstroth, Inc., 269 F2d 64 (1st Cir 1959); Ginsburg v Stern, 295 F2d 698 (3rd Cir 1961). The subjects of interest and damages are separately regulated, contrary to the present practice of combining the two (see Fourth Circuit Rule 20) to make it clear that the awards are distinct and independent. Interest is provided for by law; damages are awarded by the court in its discretion in the case of a frivolous appeal as a matter of justice to the appellee and as a penalty against the appellant.

CROSS REFERENCES

Damages and costs on affirmance, 28 USCS § 1912.

RESEARCH GUIDE

Federal Procedure L Ed:

Appeal, Certiorari, and Review, Fed Proc, L Ed, §§ 3:773, 3:774, 3:776.

Am Jur:

5 Am Jur 2d, Appeal and Error § 1024.
9A Am Jur 2d, Bankruptcy § 897.
48A Am Jur 2d, Labor and Labor Relations §§ 1636, 1685.

Annotations:

What circumstances justify award of damages and/or double costs against appellant's attorney under 28 USCS § 1912, or Rule 38 of the Federal Rules of Appellate Procedure. 50 ALR Fed 652.

INTERPRETIVE NOTES AND DECISIONS

1. Generally
2. Purpose
3. Availability to non-prevailing party
4. "Frivolous"
5. Circumstances justifying award
6. —Appeal taken to delay payment of judgment
7. —Knowledge of non-maritorious claim
8. —Abuse of appellate process
9. —Repetition of previously determined claim
10. Circumstances not justifying award
11. Awards against counsel

1. Generally

Court of Appeals cannot characterize as "friv-

229

Two other annotated editions of federal rules are less comprehensive, but may sometimes provide a more manageable introduction to heavily litigated provisions. *Moore's Rules Pamphlets* (Matthew Bender) consist of three annually published paperbound volumes containing annotated texts of the four major sets of federal rules, as well as Supreme Court rules and rules governing misdemeanor and habeas corpus proceedings. After each rule and excerpts from Advisory Committee notes, only selected leading cases are annotated. The pamphlets also include references to relevant sections in *Moore's Federal Practice* (to be discussed in Section D, below).

The six "Rules" volumes of the *U.S. Supreme Court Digest, Lawyers' Edition,* republished in 1987, contain the annotated texts of all major rules sets and rules for several individual courts, but the only decisions annotated are those of the Supreme Court of the United States. This version is thus of limited value in extensive case research, but provides summaries of the Supreme Court's authoritative decisions more quickly than any other source. The volumes also provide references from each rule to relevant sections of the *Supreme Court Digest, Federal Procedure, Lawyers' Edition,* and *Federal Procedural Forms, Lawyers' Edition.*

Finally, multivolume treatises on the federal rules, such as *Federal Practice and Procedure* and *Moore's Federal Practice* (to be discussed below in Section D), can also be considered annotated editions of the rules. They are frequently arranged by rule number, and include the rule texts and Advisory Committee notes as well as extensive analyses of interpretive cases.[19]

2. STATE RULES

The forms of promulgation and publication of state court rules vary from state to state. In states where legislative acts determine court procedures, these "rules" appear as part of the state's statutory code. In states where rules are promulgated by the judiciary alone, until recently they often appeared only in elusive pamphlets or in the state reports.[20] Increasingly, however, publishers of annotated codes recognize the importance of court rules and include them within their scope of coverage. Even when court rules are not legislative in nature, they receive the same treatment as statutes and are published in a fully annotated, regularly supplemented format. For many state codes, the rules volumes are published in a softcover format and reissued

19. Shorter, one-volume editions of four sets of rules are published by Clark Boardman in an annually updated looseleaf format. For each rule, the text and Advisory Committee notes are accompanied by "practice comments" discussing the rule and its application. The four volumes are: J. Patchan, *Federal Rules of Bankruptcy,* 3d ed. (1988); T.A. Coyne, *Federal Rules of Civil Procedure* (1982); M.G. Hermann, *Federal Rules of Criminal Procedure,* 2d ed. (1980); and P.F. Rothstein, *Federal Rules of Evidence,* 2d ed. (1978).

20. A few states provide for official publication of their court rules on a regularly updated basis, either as part of codes of administrative regulations or separately. Volumes 22(A)–22(C) of the *Official Compilation of Codes, Rules and Regulations of the State of New York* consist of court rules, and the Administrative Code Editor for Iowa publishes the looseleaf *Iowa Court Rules.*

annually. Illustration C shows a page of the court rules volume of Michie's *Utah Code Annotated* covering damages for frivolous appeals.

Illustration C

A page from the court rules volume of the *Utah Code Annotated*

Rule 33 RULES OF THE UTAH SUPREME COURT

Rule 33. Damages for delay or frivolous appeal; recovery of attorney's fees.

(a) **Damages for delay or frivolous appeal.** If the court shall determine that a motion made or appeal taken under these rules is either frivolous or for delay, it shall award just damages and single or double costs, including reasonable attorney's fees, to the prevailing party.

(b) **Disciplinary action for inadequate representation.** The court may take appropriate disciplinary action against counsel who inadequately represents his client on appeal.

Advisory Committee Note. — This rule is designed to ensure that parties and their counsel understand that frivolous or clearly unmeritorious appeals may result in the imposition of single or double costs, including attorney's fees, and damages, as well as disciplinary action against counsel.

Paragraph (a). In the event that a motion made during an appeal or the appeal, itself, is determined to be frivolous or undertaken for delay, this paragraph makes mandatory the imposition of just damages and single or double costs, including a reasonable attorney's fee. The paragraph adopts Rule 38, FRAP, regarding frivolous appeals, but enlarges the federal rule to include the mandatory imposition of costs for delay.

Paragraph (b). This paragraph acknowledges the inherent power of the supreme court to discipline counsel in appellate proceedings who the court determines has inadequately represented his or her client. The paragraph is drawn, in part, from Rule 15(c), U.S. Tenth Circuit Court of Appeals. See also Rule 40 involving discipline of counsel and of a party who appears pro se.

NOTES TO DECISIONS

ANALYSIS

Frivolous appeal.
Cited.

Frivolous appeal.

A husband's appeal from a judgment relating to alimony and distribution of marital property was frivolous, where there was no basis for the argument presented and the evidence and law was mischaracterized and misstated. Eames v. Eames, 735 P.2d 395 (Utah 1987).

For purposes of Subdivision (a), a "frivolous" appeal is one having no reasonable legal or factual basis as defined in R. Utah S. Ct. 40(a). Lack of good faith is not required. O'Brien v. Rush, 744 P.2d 306 (Utah Ct. App. 1987).

Cited in Calfo v. D.C. Stewart Co., 717 P.2d 697 (Utah 1986); Amica Mut. Ins. v. Schettler, 738 P.2d 641 (Utah 1987); Harker v. Condominiums Forest Glen, Inc., 740 P.2d 1361 (Utah Ct. App. 1987); Brown v. Harry Heathman, Inc., 69 Utah Adv. Rep. 36 (Ct. App. 1987).

COLLATERAL REFERENCES

Am. Jur. 2d. — 5 Am. Jur. 2d Appeal and Error § 912.

C.J.S. — 5 C.J.S. Appeal and Error § 1358.

A.L.R. — Inherent power of federal district court to impose monetary sanctions on counsel in absence of contempt of court, 77 A.L.R. Fed. 789.

Key Numbers. — Costs ⇐ 259 to 263.

Note the Advisory Committee comments, case annotations, and references to both major legal encyclopedias (*Am.Jur.2d* and *C.J.S.*), *ALR* annotations, and West digest key numbers.

For many states, court rules are even more readily accessible than statutes. Besides being published in annotated volumes as part of state codes, court rules are also issued in annual, *unannotated* pamphlets designed for ready desktop reference. The West Publishing Company publishes such pamphlets for virtually every state in which it publishes an annotated code, and for several other states as well. As noted earlier, these rules pamphlets are valuable sources not only for state court rules but for the rules of federal courts sitting in that state. Some state court rules are available online through WESTLAW or LEXIS, with additional databases being regularly added.

In some states, annotated editions of court rules are also published separately as part of practice treatises. For example, two volumes of West's *Colorado Practice* consist of an annotated edition of the Colorado Civil Rules, complete with case annotations, cross-references, and extensive commentary. For Colorado, there are thus four places in which rules of civil procedure are published: in the two *Colorado Practice* volumes; another annotated edition in the official *Colorado Revised Statutes;* and unannotated in both a pamphlet published by West and a looseleaf volume published by Michie.

Appendix B in this volume lists sources for state court rules other than statutory compilations. To learn about available resources, it may also help to consult one of the state legal research guides listed in Appendix A. Once the rules are found, locating applicable provisions is not always easy, as it depends on quality of organization and indexing. A steadily increasing number of states, however, have rules modeled on the various federal rules, particularly the Federal Rules of Civil Procedure and the Federal Rules of Evidence. A researcher who knows the relevant rules provision in federal court can easily check the comparable provision in another state.[21]

For civil matters, one can use Federal Rules of Civil Procedure numbers to find relevant state provisions even if the state rules bear no relation to the Federal Rules. Each Circuit Volume of Lawyers Co-op's *Federal Procedure Rules Service* includes a "Comparator," which correlates the provisions of the Federal Rules of Civil Procedure to the court rules or statutory provisions for each state within the circuit.

21. The civil procedural systems of all fifty states and the District of Columbia were recently surveyed in Oakley & Coon, "The Federal Rules in the State Courts: A Survey of State Court Systems of Civil Procedure," 61 *Wash.L.Rev.* 1367 (1986).

Several works provide rule-by-rule comparisons of federal and state evidence provisions: *Evidence in America: The Federal Rules in the States* (Michie, 4 vols., 1987); "State Correlation Tables," in *Federal Rules of Evidence Service* (Callaghan) "Finding Aids" volume; and "State Adaptation of the Federal Rules of Evidence," 5 *Weinstein's Evidence* (Matthew Bender).

C. JUDICIAL INTERPRETATIONS OF RULES

While annotated editions of rules provide references to judicial decisions, there are other tools for finding cases construing and applying court rules. Some of these tools have already been introduced in earlier chapters, but their specific focus on court rules is discussed at greater length here.

1. CITATORS

The "statutes" unit of all jurisdictional Shepard's citators can be used to determine the current status and judicial treatment of federal and state court rules. *Shepard's United States Citations,* statute edition, provides coverage of every set of federal rules listed in Table 1 above (except U.S. Court of Military Appeals rules, which are in *Shepard's Military Justice Citations*). It also includes citations to the rules of several other specialized courts and of individual United States District Courts. Since annotated editions of very few district court rules are published, this may be the only way to find interpretive cases.

Shepard's U.S. Citations indicates amendments to each rule, as well as citations in federal court decisions, annotations, or *American Bar Association Journal* articles.[22] Just as with federal statutes, coverage of federal rules in *U.S. Citations* does not extend to references in either law review articles or state court decisions. Articles in some law reviews are listed in *Shepard's Federal Law Citations in Selected Law Reviews,* and citing state cases appear in each Shepard's *state* unit.

For the four major sets of federal rules, one can use *Shepard's Federal Rules Citations* to find changes in rules and both federal and state citing cases. Less comprehensive in coverage than the rules section of *Shepard's U.S. Citations,* this citator covers only the Federal Rules of Civil Procedure, Criminal Procedure, Evidence, and Appellate Procedure. For these rules, however, it provides citations in *both* federal and state courts. In addition, *Federal Rules Citations* reprints the portions of individual state citators covering state rule provisions similar to each federal rule. Researchers can thus learn how courts in different jurisdictions have interpreted identical or similar provisions, and perhaps find cases useful as persuasive authority. Law review citations to federal rules are *not* included, but coverage of citing material for state rules is identical to that in the state Shepard's volume and does include selected periodicals. Illustration D shows a page from this publication containing citations to rule 38 of the Federal Rules of Appellate Procedure and to several state provisions based on rules 37 and 38.

Coverage of state court rules, whether or not similar to federal rules, is contained in full in each of Shepard's state citators. Changes

22. One can also find Supreme Court cases citing a federal court rule by using the "Table of Federal Laws, Rules and Regulations Cited and Construed" in the *Lawyers' Edition Desk Book.*

Illustration D

Coverage of federal and state rules in *Shepard's Federal Rules Citations*

FEDERAL RULES OF APPELLATE PROCEDURE

Art. 7 Rule 38

567F2d915
616F2d406
702F2d753
743F2d644
69FRD311
Ala
445So2d300
Alk
640P2d818
Colo
37CoA258
547P2d943
DC
507A2d551
Ill
69IlA54
104IlA424
25IlD519
60IlD155
386NE2d
[1183
432NE2d
[1054
Me
342A2d270
360A2d519
Mass
20MaA765
482NE2d880
CRCL§1.15
MFP§8.14

Alabama Rules of Appellate Procedure 1975 as Amended 1977

Rule 37
333So2d797
397So2d89
445So2d300
456So2d67

Alaska Rules of Appellate Procedure 1980 as Amended 1981

Rule 509
A1982July1

Colorado Appellate Rules 1984

Rule 37
37CoA258
37CoA495
547P2d943
552P2d36
1973CoL(6)
[29

District of Columbia Court of Appeals 1971 General Rules

Rule 37
507A2d557

Montana Rules of Appellate Civil Procedure 1966 as Amended 1983

Rule 31
164Mt479
525P2d19
622P2d1027
700P2d609

Nevada Rules of Appellate Procedure 1973 as Amended 1983

Rule 37
91Nev563
92Nev317
92Nev601
540P2d100
549P2d752
555P2d842

North Dakota Rules of Appellate Procedure 1973

Rule 37
356NW2d104
50NDR6

Tennessee Rules of Appellate Procedure 1979 as Amended 1981

Rule 41
597SW2d909
45TnL163
46TnL100

FEDERAL

Rule 38
Cir. D.C.
464F2d835
473F2d94
593F2d1223
662F2d874
Cir. 1
416F2d415
424F2d1072
484F2d923
503F2d313
525F2d2
582F2d135
588F2d846
589F2d21
609F2d33
619F2d153
642F2d5
664F2d6
707F2d28
722F2d873
728F2d4
730F2d834
731F2d74
733F2d10
737F2d145
744F2d892
746F2d92
746F2d927
748F2d49
749F2d102
753F2d169
754F2d49
757F2d1359
763F2d471
774F2d30
33BRW450
Cir. 2
422F2d1279
440F2d1080
457F2d237
469F2d1119
489F2d321

503F2d887
513F2d832
535F2d677
538F2d918
546F2d495
554F2d540
562F2d870
575F2d1011
578F2d467
579F2d692
588F2d1
605F2d36
608F2d928
613F2d21
613F2d385
617F2d19
620F2d348
625F2d448
636F2d31
636F2d908
641F2d1363
659F2d303
671F2d724
678F2d392
680F2d2
682F2d337
687F2d571
688F2d884
689F2d380
697F2d494
707F2d692
708F2d77
713F2d892
734F2d954
740F2d202
748F2d124
751F2d83
751F2d117
751F2d552
754F2d99
758F2d62
759F2d1032
763F2d69
763F2d517
766F2d61
766F2d94
770F2d18
774F2d574
93FRD352
52BRW989
Cir. 3
432F2d386
518F2d641
520F2d270
652F2d347
754F2d490
771F2d70
Cir. 4
409F2d1071
459F2d684
613F2d52
678F2d482
716F2d1417
737F2d409
748F2d915
750F2d1238
400FS65
53FRD39
Cir. 5
421F2d686
466F2d173
511F2d612
520F2d1042
536F2d1032
543F2d1106
567F2d1317

593F2d614
614F2d1028
614F2d1084
615F2d693
617F2d440
629F2d1116
632F2d648
639F2d306
642F2d1000
648F2d293
652F2d415
661F2d72
678F2d24
678F2d31
679F2d87
702F2d61
704F2d812
706F2d739
707F2d115
709F2d911
712F2d199
714F2d25
714F2d430
722F2d194
722F2d210
723F2d1164
724F2d472
725F2d1016
737F2d1418
744F2d408
746F2d306
746F2d1086
749F2d201
749F2d221
752F2d126
752F2d1063
754F2d1272
761F2d1115
764F2d263
765F2d497
770F2d556
771F2d893
598FS753
78FRD192
Cir. 6
435F2d1193
463F2d752
489F2d19
705F2d800
709F2d1088
712F2d244
713F2d197
728F2d359
735F2d974
746F2d1188
752F2d200
753F2d1360
756F2d40
756F2d473
764F2d1190
765F2d589
558FS475
23BRW911
Cir. 7
494F2d860
517F2d552
568F2d553
614F2d1132
627F2d766
652F2d716
667F2d585
678F2d720
684F2d504
688F2d37
689F2d645
697F2d202

704F2d1003
715F2d1154
732F2d563
736F2d1143
737F2d582
739F2d270
741F2d906
744F2d1278
746F2d1322
747F2d1176
747F2d1179
752F2d279
755F2d519
757F2d810
765F2d89
765F2d102
769F2d450
773F2d862
774F2d751
775F2d183
45FRD303
Cir. 8
480F2d1297
546F2d233
550F2d1113
639F2d458
669F2d564
703F2d317
705F2d1018
712F2d1224
734F2d1321
744F2d660
748F2d500
750F2d55
751F2d242
752F2d1306
755F2d697
762F2d707
771F2d421
772F2d400
Cir. 9
471F2d1342
475F2d766
555F2d223
560F2d414
567F2d860
578F2d251
592F2d505
602F2d865
614F2d684
616F2d446
644F2d802
651F2d675
653F2d403
653F2d1332
659F2d1389
661F2d118
679F2d182
680F2d61
680F2d1271
681F2d623
681F2d1243
687F2d290
694F2d185
694F2d192
695F2d381
696F2d1235
699F2d485
704F2d1115
706F2d1027
707F2d430
712F2d1326
716F2d574
717F2d466
719F2d1451
726F2d1417

729F2d656
733F2d710
735F2d350
735F2d1137
736F2d525
736F2d1288
736F2d1383
736F2d1396
739F2d444
739F2d1467
740F2d764
751F2d1103
752F2d435
752F2d1406
753F2d744
755F2d1373
756F2d748
756F2d1379
758F2d373
758F2d416
758F2d1348
760F2d1005
760F2d1052
764F2d670
764F2d1300
764F2d1324
764F2d1328
765F2d942
765F2d1449
766F2d1348
772F2d547
Cir. 10
424F2d149
460F2d508
570F2d1375
612F2d499
616F2d464
624F2d969
683F2d339
733F2d88
733F2d720
733F2d735
733F2d737
744F2d73
744F2d1448
753F2d835
767F2d721
769F2d647
769F2d667
771F2d474
539FS756
Cir. 11
694F2d251
703F2d499
706F2d1115
751F2d1155
764F2d1389
765F2d1084
769F2d708
773F2d1215
774F2d446
775F2d1556
Cir. Fed.
692F2d1382
722F2d1555
728F2d1460
733F2d1573
739F2d622
741F2d1378
745F2d629
748F2d662
754F2d343
758F2d1584
765F2d1102
767F2d894
769F2d754

769F2d1558
CCPA
529F2d1348
ECA
727F2d1580
731F2d907
100FRD543
101FRD556
5ClC294
DC
150ADC326
153ADC383
193ADC69
213ADC318
249ADC342
250ADC327
411A2d351
Ill
143IlA351
NY
108NYA439
489NYS2d
[571
Ore
295Or806
671P2d101
Wis
100Wis2d349
302NW2d513
50ARF652s
50ARF653n
CRCL§1.15
MFP§8.14

Alabama Rules of Appellate Procedure 1975 as Amended 1977

Rule 38
335So2d176
336So2d1357
337So2d6
347So2d1359
351So2d591
360So2d284
368So2d291
374So2d355
378So2d738
378So2d1139
379So2d1265
381So2d90
387So2d201
391So2d122
395So2d1000
397So2d156
399So2d307
402So2d1007
404So2d692
410So2d87
417So2d158
426So2d848
428So2d71
429So2d599
442So2d88

Continued

581

in rules are noted, as well as citations in federal and state court decisions, selected law reviews, annotations, and (in some states) attorney general opinions.

2. REPORTERS AND DIGESTS

While standard case reporters such as official reports and the components of the National Reporter System include many decisions dealing with the application of court rules, there are also specialized reporters for cases decided under the federal rules. West's *Federal Rules Decisions* (cited as F.R.D.) began publication in 1940 as an offshoot of the *Federal Supplement,* and includes the texts of U.S. District Court decisions that construe the Federal Rules of Civil Procedure and the Federal Rules of Criminal Procedure. Its cases do not also appear in the *Federal Supplement. F.R.D.* is by no means an exclusive source of procedural opinions, since many *F.Supp.* opinions also involve procedural issues and since neither Supreme Court nor Courts of Appeals decisions are included. *Federal Rules Decisions* is just an additional component of West's National Reporter System, sharing coverage of the U.S. District Courts with the voluminous *Federal Supplement.* It differs from most reporters in that it includes not just cases but also relevant articles, speeches, and the proceedings of judicial conferences.

Like other West reporters, *Federal Rules Decisions* appears first in advance sheets which then cumulate into bound volumes. Each volume and advance sheet includes West's standard editorial features, such as tables of cases and key number digests. A notable feature is the list of federal court rules cited in *any* National Reporter System unit during the volume or advance sheet's period of coverage. This list covers specialized rules, the Federal Rules of Evidence, and the Federal Rules of Appellate Procedure as well as civil and criminal rules. It is a particularly valuable feature in recent advance sheets, where the comprehensive list of current cases may provide more up-to-date coverage than the latest Shepard's pamphlet. Illustration E shows a page from this list in a recent *Federal Rules Decisions* volume.

A competing commercial reporter for decisions construing federal rules has been published since 1939 by Callaghan & Co., and recently began its third series. *Federal Rules Service* provides the texts of court decisions interpreting the Federal Rules of Civil Procedure and the Federal Rules of Appellate Procedure. Cases are published first in looseleaf format and then in bound volumes. The looseleaf cases are accompanied by current case and digest tables and a "Current Material Highlights" pamphlet, summarizing the holdings of important recent cases.

Federal Rules Service includes cases from all levels of the federal court system, not just district courts. Most of the decisions also appear in one of West's reporters, but some are not published anywhere but *Fed.R.Serv.* Each case is given one or more headnotes assigned to

Illustration E

List of rules cited, in a *Federal Rules Decisions* volume

STATUTES AND RULES

FEDERAL RULES OF EVIDENCE—Continued

Rule	
404(b)	845 F.2d 683
404(b)	845 F.2d 760
404(b)	845 F.2d 880
404(b)	681 F.Supp. 766
406	842 F.2d 1335
407	118 Ill.Dec. 589, 521 N.E.2d 1282
408	683 F.Supp. 783
408	747 S.W.2d 711
411	751 P.2d 964
501	842 F.2d 244
501	119 F.R.D. 421
501	83 B.R. 739
601	680 F.Supp. 1084
602	843 F.2d 18
606(b)	841 F.2d 1074
606(b)	843 F.2d 485
606(b)	843 F.2d 1456
606(b)	680 F.Supp. 1084
606(b)	746 S.W.2d 167
607	841 F.2d 1474
608	420 N.W.2d 145
608(b)	842 F.2d 1245
608(b)	420 N.W.2d 145
609	842 F.2d 201
609	844 F.2d 582
609	366 S.E.2d 274
609(a)(1)	844 F.2d 500
609(a)(2)	844 F.2d 500
611(a)(1)	841 F.2d 818
612	119 F.R.D. 4
612	119 F.R.D. 297
614(b)	841 F.2d 818
615	14 Cl.Ct. 551
615(2)	842 F.2d 476
702	842 F.2d 203
702	842 F.2d 1380
702	844 F.2d 863
702	845 F.2d 356
702	680 F.Supp. 408
702	682 F.Supp. 535
702–704	842 F.2d 1380
703	842 F.2d 1380
703	845 F.2d 356
703	83 B.R. 977
703	118 Ill.Dec. 589, 521 N.E.2d 1282
704	843 F.2d 383
704(b)	842 F.2d 1021
705	118 Ill.Dec. 589, 521 N.E.2d 1282
706	680 F.Supp. 928
706(a)	680 F.Supp. 928
801	681 F.Supp. 813
801(c)	842 F.2d 77
801(c)	842 F.2d 343
801(c)	842 F.2d 1319
801(c)	844 F.2d 660
801(c)	680 F.Supp. 1165
801(c)	682 F.Supp. 920
801(d)(1)(B)	842 F.2d 1319
801(d)(1)(B)	845 F.2d 938
801(d)(2)(A)	842 F.2d 77
801(d)(2)(B)	843 F.2d 1070
801(d)(2)(B)	84 B.R. 653
801(d)(2)(D)	844 F.2d 264
801(d)(2)(D)	844 F.2d 660
801(d)(2)(D)	680 F.Supp. 1165
801(d)(2)(E)	841 F.2d 1320
801(d)(2)(E)	842 F.2d 210
801(d)(2)(E)	842 F.2d 343
801(d)(2)(E)	842 F.2d 515
801(d)(2)(E)	842 F.2d 868
801(d)(2)(E)	842 F.2d 1380
801(d)(2)(E)	843 F.2d 78
801(d)(2)(E)	843 F.2d 432
801(d)(2)(E)	843 F.2d 1070
801(d)(2)(E)	844 F.2d 529
801(d)(2)(E)	844 F.2d 1347
801(d)(2)(E)	844 F.2d 1397
801(d)(2)(E)	845 F.2d 782
802	842 F.2d 210
802	680 F.Supp. 1165
802	683 F.Supp. 337
803	682 F.Supp. 920
803(3)	841 F.2d 1014
803(3)	842 F.2d 82
803(3)	844 F.2d 209
803(6)	843 F.2d 226
803(6)	843 F.2d 618
803(6)	680 F.Supp. 521
803(6)	84 B.R. 874
803(18)	841 F.2d 429
803(18)	681 F.Supp. 1344
803(24)	843 F.2d 618
803(24)	680 F.Supp. 521
803 note	841 F.2d 429
804	682 F.Supp. 920
804	746 S.W.2d 352
804(b)(5)	844 F.2d 537
805	842 F.2d 1335
805	845 F.2d 938
901	84 B.R. 653
901(a)	841 F.2d 1408
901(a)	84 B.R. 653
901(b)(4)	680 F.Supp. 1258
902	842 F.2d 304
1002	842 F.2d 968
1004	842 F.2d 968
1006	83 B.R. 977
1101(a)	83 B.R. 898

FEDERAL RULES OF APPELLATE PROCEDURE

Rule	
4	844 F.2d 411
4	421 N.W.2d 473
4(a)	841 F.2d 513
4(a)	844 F.2d 1485
4(a)(1)	842 F.2d 755
4(a)(1)	843 F.2d 1504
4(a)(1)	845 F.2d 256
4(a)(1)	845 F.2d 492
4(a)(1)	683 F.Supp. 513
4(a)(4)	843 F.2d 1504
4(a)(4)	845 F.2d 256
4(a)(4)	84 B.R. 665
4(a)(4)(iii)	843 F.2d 1504
4(a)(5)	683 F.Supp. 513
4(a)(5)	85 B.R. 32
4(b)	842 F.2d 755
4(b)	843 F.2d 1146
4(b)	845 F.2d 492
10(a)	842 F.2d 1074
22(b)	845 F.2d 501
24	843 F.2d 268
24(a)	843 F.2d 268
26(a)	845 F.2d 492
26(b)	845 F.2d 117
28(a)(4)	841 F.2d 918
28(a)(4)	844 F.2d 628
28(c)	844 F.2d 401
38	841 F.2d 635
38	841 F.2d 732
38	841 F.2d 908
38	842 F.2d 951
38	843 F.2d 172
38	843 F.2d 293
38	843 F.2d 1024
38	843 F.2d 1050
38	844 F.2d 646
38	845 F.2d 364
38	845 F.2d 794
38	84 B.R. 658
39(a)	119 F.R.D. 440
41	844 F.2d 916
46(c)	845 F.2d 202

XLVIII

specific rules and numbered subject subdivisions within each rule, and these headnotes are arranged numerically in the accompanying *Federal*

Rules Digest. A "Finding Aids" volume includes cumulative tables of cases and the outline of the publisher's classification system for each rule, known as the "Federal Index" or "Findex." The second edition of the *Federal Rules Digest* covers the years 1938–54, and the current third edition covers 1954 to date. Because the digest is arranged by rule and within rule by subject, its purpose is similar to that of the case annotations in *USCA* or *USCS:* a comprehensive collection of headnotes for cases decided under each provision. Illustration F shows a page of the digest covering the Federal Rules of Appellate Procedure provision on frivolous appeals.

In 1979 Callaghan began a separate reporting service for the new evidence rules, the *Federal Rules of Evidence Service,* providing similar coverage of evidentiary issues. As with the *Federal Rules Service,* most cases are also published in one of the West federal reporters, although a few appear only in *Fed.Rules Evid.Serv.* The service is accompanied by the *Federal Rules of Evidence Digest,* which arranges the case headnotes by subject within each rule. A "Finding Aids" volume includes the text of the rules, a table of cases, the "Findex" or digest classification system, and state correlation tables providing information on state rules of evidence based on or similar to the Federal Rules. In addition to recent cases, the "Current Material" volume contains finding aids and a monthly "Current Material Highlights."

D. SECONDARY SOURCES

The general secondary sources in legal literature, such as law review articles and encyclopedias, contain a great deal of information on procedural matters. There are also numerous specialized resources dealing specifically with the intricacies of court rules and practice.

1. FEDERAL PRACTICE

The technical nature of the various federal rules and their importance in legal practice has led to the development of a number of excellent commentaries on the rules. These include two comprehensive treatises by distinguished scholars in the fields of federal courts and procedure: *Federal Practice and Procedure* and *Moore's Federal Practice.*

Federal Practice and Procedure (West, 24 vols. to date in 36, 1969–date) is an extensive treatment of federal procedural and jurisdictional issues. The set consists of four components covering the Federal Rules of Criminal Procedure, the Federal Rules of Civil Procedure, jurisdiction and related matters, and the Federal Rules of Evidence (still in progress). The volumes covering the rules sets are organized by rule. The entire set is commonly referred to as "Wright & Miller," after two of its principal authors, Professors Charles Alan Wright of the University of Texas and Arthur R. Miller of Harvard Law School. In actuality, however, each component is the work of a different set of authors. The criminal volumes are written by Wright alone; the civil volumes

Illustration F

A page from Callaghan's *Federal Rules Digest*

RULE 38

DAMAGES FOR DELAY

AP–38.1 Frivolous appeals

AP–38.1 Frivolous appeals

COURTS OF APPEALS

Rule 73(d) providing for a discretionary award of damages for delay upon the affirmance of a money judgment is a matter of procedure rather than of substantive law, and is controlling over a state rule requiring a mandatory award of damages in the amount of 10 %. Nordmeyer v. Sanzone, 7 FR Serv2d 1221, 315 F2d 780 (CA 6th, 1963).

Rule 38 of the Federal Rules of Appellate Procedure permits in highly unusual instances the imposition of sanctions because of a clear showing of bad faith on the part of an appellant, to penalize litigants and to compensate those who have been put to the expense of answering wholly frivolous appeals. Where defendant in simple contract action filed three appeals (in addition to numerous post-trial motions) in an obvious attempt to avoid execution of a lawful judgment, plaintiff's motion for an award of 10% of the original judgment ($4500) and $598.70 in costs of the third appeal would be granted pursuant to Appellate Rule 38. Fluoro Elec. Corp. v. Branford Associates, 18 FR Serv2d 174, 489 F2d 320 (CA 2nd, 1973).

Where, (1) after an order of the NLRB compelling an employer to abide by the results of an election and bargain in good faith with the union had been enforced by the court of appeals and certiorari denied by the Supreme Court, (2) and the employer's motion filed with the NLRB to reopen the record and revoke the certification of the election was denied as lacking in merit, (3) and the employer's action seeking the same relief in the district court was denied for want of jurisdiction, the assessment of double costs and an award of attorney fees on appeal from the district court's order was appropriate under Appellate Rule 38. Both Congressional policy against district court involvement in NLRB controversies and relevant case law were clearly contrary to the employer's position. If the law is to be fulfilled, it must be obeyed. Monroe Auto Equipment Co., Hartwell Division v. National Labor Relations Board, 20 FR Serv2d 956, 511 F2d 611 (CA 5th, 1975).

Where an alien's petition to set aside a deportation order was so utterly frivolous and completely without merit as to permit the conclusion that it was filed solely as a delaying tactic by petitioner's counsel, who was well aware of its meritlessness, double costs would be assessed personally against the petitioner's attorney. While the double costs would normally be assessed against the

by Wright, Miller and M.K. Kane; the jurisdiction volumes by Wright, Miller and E.H. Cooper; and the evidence volumes by Wright and K.W.

Graham, Jr. For each rule, *Federal Practice and Procedure* provides extensive discussion of its history, purpose, and application generally and in specific situations. The text includes copious footnotes to cases and other materials. The set is updated by annual pocket parts, and second edition volumes have since 1982 been supplanting original volumes. There is one index covering the civil and jurisdictional components, but the other parts are separately indexed.

The other major treatise, *Moore's Federal Practice,* 2d ed. (Matthew Bender, 13 vols. in 34, 1948–date), is published in a looseleaf format, revised annually by replacement pages and supplements. The set is named after its primary author, Professor James William Moore of Yale Law School, who has had numerous coauthors at different times and on various volumes. Like *Federal Practice and Procedure, Moore's* devotes several volumes to a rule-by-rule analysis of the Federal Rules of Civil Procedure, with other volumes focusing on other matters such as jurisdiction, the Federal Rules of Criminal Procedure, the Federal Rules of Evidence, and Supreme Court practice. The set includes a detailed three-volume index and one volume listing statutes and rules cited.[23]

Two other multivolume treatments of federal practice are organized not by specific rule but more generally, by subject. Lawyers Co-operative publishes an encyclopedia similar in format to its *Am.Jur.2d* but designed specifically for federal practice: *Federal Procedure, Lawyers' Edition* (40 vols., 1982–date). It consists of eighty alphabetically arranged chapters, some of which focus on procedural issues (Access to District Courts, New Trial) and some on topical areas of federal law (Atomic Energy, Job Discrimination). The chapters deal with civil, criminal and administrative practice, and include checklists, synopses of law review articles, and texts of relevant statutes. The text also includes references to *Federal Procedural Forms, Lawyers' Edition* and other units of the publisher's Total Client–Service Library. The set is updated by annual pocket parts, and includes a three-volume index and a table of statutes, rules and regulations cited.

The other comprehensive work, *Cyclopedia of Federal Procedure,* 3d ed. (Callaghan, 17 vols. in 23, 1951–date), is arranged topically rather than alphabetically. Its ninety-one chapters are divided into five parts (courts and jurisdiction; civil trial practice; criminal procedure; appeal and review; and particular actions and proceedings) and organized topically within each part. Like most of the other works described in this section, its text summarizes the ruling law and its footnotes provide extensive references to cases. Both text and footnotes are updated in annual pocket parts. In addition to an index, the set

23. A similar but less voluminous work is also available from the same publisher. J.W. Moore, A.D. Vestal & P.B. Kurland, *Moore's Manual: Federal Practice and Procedure* (3 vols., 1962–date) is arranged by subject rather than by rule, but contains much of the same text as the larger work. Each section in the *Manual* provides cross-references to more comprehensive treatment in *Moore's Federal Practice.*

includes volumes containing the texts of relevant statutes and court rules and the *Manual for Complex Litigation, 2d.*[24]

Each of the above comprehensive works attempts to span the scope of federal practice issues. More highly focused treatments of specific subject areas may be more helpful for detailed research. For example, L.B. Orfield & M.S. Rhodes, *Orfield's Criminal Procedure under the Federal Rules,* 2d ed. (Lawyers Co-operative, 7 vols., 1985–88), is an extensive treatise limited to federal criminal practice. The text discusses for each rule the history of its drafting, the law prior to its adoption, and judicial developments. The final volume consists of a table of cases and an index, and annual pocket parts keep the set up to date.

A number of works focus on the Federal Rules of Evidence. One of the principal drafters of the rules, Judge Jack B. Weinstein, has written with M.A. Berger a multivolume treatise explaining the intent and application of each provision, *Weinstein's Evidence: Commentary on Rules of Evidence for the United States Courts and Magistrates* (Matthew Bender, 7 vols., 1975–date). It includes both a subject index and an author/title index (of works cited in the text), as well as tables of cases and of statutes and rules. A similar multivolume rule-by-rule analysis is D.W. Louisell & C.B. Mueller, *Federal Evidence* (Lawyers Co-op, 5 vols., 1977–date). Less comprehensive but handier one-volume treatments include M.H. Graham, *Handbook of Federal Evidence,* 2d ed. (West, 1986), and S.A. Saltzburg & K.R. Redden, *Federal Rules of Evidence Manual,* 4th ed. (Michie, 1986). Each of these works is updated annually or more frequently.

Procedural guides for particular courts are also published. One work designed specifically for attorneys practicing before the Supreme Court is R.L. Stern, E. Gressman, & S.M. Shapiro, *Supreme Court Practice,* 6th ed. (Bureau of National Affairs, 1986). The book includes extensive discussions of the Court's policies and procedures, and also contains forms, checklists and Supreme Court Building floor plans.

2. STATE-SPECIFIC AND GENERAL WORKS

State practice manuals and procedural aids, containing such material as the text of court rules, commentaries on the rules, annotations of court decisions, and model forms keyed to the rules, are published for virtually every state. Some of the larger states have two or more competing publications of this kind. The best of these are updated regularly, either with looseleaf filings, pocket part supplements, or complete annual revisions. They provide useful, current information

24. The *Manual,* prepared under the auspices of the Federal Judicial Center, recommends procedures for judges and lawyers coping with complicated civil matters, such as class actions, antitrust cases, or mass disaster tort litigation. It is also published as a supplementary pamphlet to *Federal Practice and Procedure* (West, 1985); as volume 1, part 2 of *Moore's Federal Practice* (Matthew Bender, 1986); and separately as a paperback (Commerce Clearing House, 1985) and a looseleaf volume (Clark Boardman, 1986).

regarding the local rules of practice, and are essential tools for the lawyer's daily work.

West and several other publishers offer multivolume sets on practice in particular states. Some of these are commentaries on procedural rules, while others are series of individual subject treatises in a uniform format, with legal forms and practice checklists. New York, for example, has two major treatises on procedural issues, *Carmody–Wait 2d Cyclopedia of New York Practice* (Lawyers Co-op, 35 vols., 1965–date) and *New York Civil Practice* (Matthew Bender, 37 vols., 1963–date). *Carmody–Wait 2d* focuses first on general civil practice, with several volumes discussing issues arising through the course of litigation, and then has separate volumes dealing with specific matters such as real property and matrimonial actions. *New York Civil Practice* is composed of separate units for practice in different types of actions, such as under the Estates, Powers and Trusts Law or in Family Court Proceedings. Bender also publishes a separate, 11–volume *New York Criminal Practice* (1973–date). Several shorter works summarize practice issues in New York, such as the *Weinstein, Korn and Miller CPLR Manual,* 2d ed. (Matthew Bender, 1980) and D.D. Siegel, *Handbook on New York Practice* (West, 1978). All of these works are regularly updated by either pocket parts or looseleaf supplements.

Another source for practical information on state practice is through continuing legal education materials. Many states publish materials from their C.L.E. programs, often in a looseleaf format. Recent publications of the Illinois Institute for Continuing Legal Education, for example, include *Defending Illinois Criminal Cases, Illinois Civil Discovery Practice, Illinois Product Liability Practice,* and *Real Estate Litigation.* Books such as these provide clear, step-by-step assistance for practitioners in a particular jurisdiction. They are usually updated or replaced periodically, although not always as frequently as works from major commercial publishers.

One of the easiest ways to learn about available treatises, practice manuals, and C.L.E. materials in a particular state is to consult a legal research guide for that state. These guides are listed in Appendix A, at the back of this volume. While not published for every state, there are guides for most major jurisdictions.

Procedural manuals and treatises published for a general national audience can also be of immense practical value, although they are related to no specific procedural rules. Among these are the practice adjuncts to *American Jurisprudence* such as *Am.Jur. Trials* and *Am. Jur. Proof of Facts.* Both of these multivolume sets contain articles on specific issues in litigation, and contain numerous cross-references to other products in Lawyers Co-op's "Total Client–Service Library."

The first six volumes of *Am.Jur. Trials* constitute an extensive treatise on general aspects of trial preparation and procedure. Ensuing volumes, which are issued periodically, consist of "Model Trials." Individual articles in each volume describe unique aspects of specific types of litigation, on issues from compensation for multiple sclerosis to defective automobile door latches. There are over two dozen volumes of "Model Trials," and the set has a two-volume index.

Am.Jur. Proof of Facts, now in its third series, contains articles on specific evidentiary issues, and provides sample interrogatories and examinations. Individual articles describe the elements of proof required for establishing particular facts in judicial proceedings, and outline useful procedures. A three-volume index covers all three series.

A similar collection of articles on trial practice in very specific areas is *Causes of Action* (Shepard's, 1983–date), which includes extensive references to law review articles, legal encyclopedias, digests, and annotations. Works such as these may be little used in academic research, but they are important time-saving resources for practicing lawyers.

E. PRACTICE FORMS

Many writings must follow certain conventions to have legal significance or to have a desired effect. This is true not only of documents such as contracts and wills,[25] but also of forms used in court practice such as briefs or pleadings. Model forms have been prepared to aid lawyers in following proper drafting procedures for hundreds of years. Model writs for use in pleading appeared in manuscripts of the *Registrum Brevium* as early as 1227. The publication of model forms has evolved and is today a major component of legal literature. Forms are included as part of many procedural treatises, and are published separately in comprehensive collections. Some jurisdictions even have prescribed official forms that must be used for certain pleadings or motions.

For federal practice there are several multivolume collections of forms, published in conjunction with the practice treatises described in the preceding sections. The counterparts to Wright & Miller and *Moore's Federal Practice* are *West's Federal Forms* (7 vols. in 12, 1951–date) and *Bender's Federal Practice Forms* (5 vols. in 16, 1952–date).[26] Both sets have forms arranged by rule for practice in the U.S. District Courts as well as in the Courts of Appeals and the Supreme Court. *West's* includes separate volumes for bankruptcy and admiralty practice forms. The forms in both sets are accompanied by explanatory comments and references, and updated by pocket parts or looseleaf supplements. Illustration G shows a sample brief in *Bender's* on the issue of frivolous appeals under rule 38.

Like *Federal Procedure, Lawyers' Edition, Federal Procedural Forms, Lawyers' Edition* (Lawyers Co-op, 21 vols., 1975–date) is arranged alphabetically by subject and includes numerous cross-refer-

25. Forms for transactional documents will be discussed below in Chapter 13.

26. Bender also publishes a less extensive *Federal Practice Forms* (4 vols., 1964–date) to accompany its *Moore's Manual.*

Illustration G

A form from *Bender's Federal Practice Forms*

Form No. 4998.25

FEDERAL RULES OF APPELLATE PROCEDURE, RULE 38[1]

Brief in Support of Motion for Double Costs and Attorney's Fees—Frivolous Appeal[2]

UNITED STATES COURT OF APPEALS
. . . . Circuit

(Title of Action) No. . . . .

Brief in Support of Motion for Double Costs and Attorney's Fees—Frivolous Appeal

[*For format and other contents of Brief, see Form No. 4998, supra.*]

POINT I. APPELLEE IS ENTITLED TO AN AWARD OF DOUBLE COSTS AND REASONABLE ATTORNEY'S FEES

Only recently, this Court announced that its "patience with frivolous appeals is at an end." (*Citations*). Appellee submits that this is a frivolous appeal.

An appeal is frivolous when the result is obvious, or the arguments are wholly without merit. (*Citations*). The Federal Rules of Appellate Procedure provide that "[i]f a court of appeals shall determine that an appeal is frivolous, it may award just damages and single or double costs to the appellee." Fed. R. App. P. 38. To the same effect is 28 U.S.C. § 1912, which allows an award of damages where parties deliberately seek to delay resolution of a dispute. (*Citations*).

To avoid an award of double costs and reasonable attorney's fees, an appellant must do more than submit unsubstantiated claims. (*Citations*). Where even a minimal amount of research would have revealed the weaknesses of appellant's position in a . . . . (*type of action*) action, the appeal has been found frivolous. (*Citations*). Similarly,

[1] *See* Cases and Comments Concerning Rule 38, *supra.*

[2] Form adapted from papers in Yale Univ. v. Lown Enter., Inc. No. 86-7871 (2d Cir. 1987).

(Rel.47-12/87 Pub.090)

ences to *USCS, CFR,* and the publisher's encyclopedias and annotations. Like the *Cyclopedia of Federal Procedure,* the *Nichols Cyclopedia of Federal Procedure Forms* (Callaghan, 4 vols. in 6, 1952–date) tracks civil and criminal proceedings through the course of litigation. Each chapter is divided into two sections, "suggestions and reminders" and sample forms.

Legal forms are an essential part of most state practice manuals, discussed above. In addition, many states have separately published collections of forms. Two volumes of *Virginia Forms* (Michie, 5 vols., 1978–88), for example, focus on civil litigation, while criminal procedure occupies part of another volume. Another publication, R.J. Bacigal, *Virginia Criminal Procedure Forms* (Harrison, 1984), provides more extensive coverage of criminal matters. Some states have officially promulgated forms, such as *California Judicial Council Forms,* published annually as an adjunct to *West's Annotated California Codes.*

Although not keyed to the practice of any particular jurisdiction, general formbooks can still be very useful in preparing for litigation. *American Jurisprudence Pleading and Practice Forms,* rev. ed. (Lawyers Co-operative, 37 vols., 1967–date) is an extensive collection of forms for such matters as complaints, motions, and orders. Its forms are accompanied by explanatory text, case annotations, and cross-references to other Lawyers Co-op publications, as well as tables providing statutory and rules references for each jurisdiction. It is arranged alphabetically by subject, and has a two-volume index. Other series are designed for specific stages of litigation, such as *Bender's Forms of Discovery* (16 vols. in 20, 1963–date), which includes ten volumes of sample interrogatories by subject. Practice forms appear as well in many specialized treatises and manuals.

F. MODEL JURY INSTRUCTIONS

Publications of jury instructions are an important aid to both practicing trial lawyers and judges. Before a jury is sent out to weigh the evidence, the judge instructs its members on the applicable law. Proposed instructions are frequently drafted and submitted to the judge by opposing counsel, and the outcome of a case may turn on which instructions are chosen. Collected examples of jury instructions have been published since the late nineteenth century.[27]

Cases have frequently been overturned on appeal due to inadequate or erroneous instructions. To reduce the chances of error, many states have prepared standardized, approved instructions to be used in common situations. These instructions are known by various designations,

27. F. Sackett, *Instructions from the Court to the Jury in Jury Trials* (Jameson & Morse, 1881). A book published the previous year concluded with an example of an instruction *not* to be followed. It began: "Gentlemen of the Jury: The investigation of guilt and the punishment of crime are a painful, but a highly important duty. God has so ordered it, and we worms of the dust must recognize what He has ordered." S.D. Thompson, *Charging the Jury: A Monograph* 176 (W.H. Stevenson, 1880).

including *model, pattern,* or *approved* jury instructions. The first published set of these instructions was in California, *Book of Approved Jury Instructions,* in 1938. By now there are model instructions for practically every state.[28] In some states model jury instructions are used by judges only as guides, but in others the instructions must be read verbatim if applicable. Some sets of model instructions are promulgated by the state supreme courts, while others are unofficial products of bar or judicial associations.

For the federal courts there is no general set of approved instructions, although some sets of pattern instructions have been published for individual circuits. There are, however, two sets of commercially published, unofficial instructions covering both criminal and civil cases. E.J. Devitt, C.B. Blackmar, & M.A. Wolff, *Federal Jury Practice and Instructions* (West, 3 vols., 1977–date) is an authoritative work with explanatory comments and notes of relevant cases. Its two volumes of criminal instructions are in a 1977 third edition, and its civil instructions in a 1987 fourth edition volume. An interim index pamphlet covers all three volumes. L.B. Sand et al., *Modern Federal Jury Instructions* (Matthew Bender, 4 vols., 1985–date) is a similar work, consisting of sample instructions, comments, and case notes. There are two volumes each for civil and criminal instructions, with separate indexes and tables for the two components.

G. SUMMARY

Access to court rules, both federal and state, is available in a variety of sources. The most useful forms of publication are those which provide commentary and citations to court decisions interpreting and applying the rules. The extensive literature of practice manuals and formbooks is closely related to court rules. These materials describe the procedures to be followed in litigation and usually include the texts of rules as well as forms, commentary, and annotations to court decisions. They are an essential component of the working library of every practitioner.

The literature of court rules and practice is sometimes seen as dry and overly concerned with technical minutiae. This is a valid criticism, particularly when rules prescribe rigid and formalistic processes to be followed in all cases. Even so, a lawyer must be familiar with governing rules and procedures in order to avoid compromising clients' interests. As Justice Hugo Black complained thirty-five years ago: "Judicial statistics would show, I fear, an unfortunately large number of meritorious cases lost due to inadvertent failure of lawyers to conform to procedural prescriptions having little if any relevancy to

28. Recent, comprehensive listings of published jury instructions, arranged by state, are: Nyberg and Boast, "Jury Instructions: A Bibliography Part I: Civil Jury Instructions," *Legal Reference Services Q.,* Spring/Summer 1986, at 5; and Nyberg, Williams and Boast, "Jury Instructions: A Bibliography Part II: Criminal Jury Instructions," *Legal Reference Services Q.,* Fall/Winter 1986, at 3.

substantial justice."[29] Simplification and flexible application of rules, however, can allow them to achieve the salutary purpose Justice Black enunciated: "The principal function of procedural rules should be to serve as useful guides to help, not hinder, persons who have a legal right to bring their problems before the courts."[30]

H. ADDITIONAL READING

C.E. Clark, *Procedure—the Handmaid of Justice* (West, 1965). Collected essays of Judge Charles E. Clark of the Second Circuit, Reporter for the Advisory Committee which drafted the Federal Rules of Civil Procedure and lifelong advocate of procedural reform.

J.B. Weinstein, *Reform of Court Rule–Making Procedures* (Ohio State University Press, 1977). Theories of court rules, by a principal drafter of the Federal Rules of Evidence; based in part on an article with the same title, 76 *Colum.L.Rev.* 905 (1976).

29. Order Adopting Revised Rules of the Supreme Court of the United States, 346 U.S. 945, 946 (1954) (Black, J., dissenting).

30. *Id.*

Chapter 10

LOOSELEAF SERVICES

A. INTRODUCTION

Any resource which is relied upon as presenting the current state of legal developments must be kept up-to-date, or it is of little use to the practicing lawyer. The most prevalent means of updating in legal publications is the pocket part, but many materials are published in binders so that individual pages or sections can simply be replaced or added. Annotated codes for several states are published in this format, as are numerous state administrative codes and some treatises and formbooks. The looseleaf publishing format is an ingenious response to our legal system's constant state of change. Through the periodic insertion of new pages and the removal of superseded material, the looseleaf volume is continuously being reedited to reflect the current state of the law.

A *service,* as used in the context of legal research, monitors current developments in a particular subject area and provides researchers with a diverse collection of source materials. The looseleaf format has proved ideal for this purpose. A looseleaf service publisher reproduces the relevant primary sources in a particular field (statutes, decisions, regulations, rulings, etc.), arranges them topically in binders, and unifies this material with explanatory text, several types of indexes and finding lists, and a method of organization appropriate to the subject being covered. A looseleaf service contains all the primary sources in its subject area, and is in effect a mini-library in one field of law.

The first looseleaf services were introduced early in this century by the Corporation Trust Company, a predecessor of Commerce Clearing House. They reported developments in Congress and the Supreme Court, much as CCH's *Congressional Index* and *Supreme Court Bulletin* do today. The first service to focus on a specific subject area followed immediately upon authorization of federal income taxes in 1913, and within a decade there were at least three competing services on federal tax laws. The increase in regulatory activity in the 1930's led to a great proliferation of services in other areas, such as labor relations, as the laws changed rapidly and were otherwise unavailable. There are now hundreds of services covering subject areas throughout the legal field, with tax services remaining the most highly sophisticated and widely used.[1]

The major attributes of looseleaf services are the promptness with which they notify researchers of developments and provide copies of new authorities, and the access they permit through several forms of indexing. These same attributes are shared and refined by online databases, which can be updated several times a day and permit full-text searching. Online services are undoubtedly the successors to looseleaf publications, although both printed and electronic methods of information retrieval will have their place in most libraries for the foreseeable future.

B. TYPES OF LOOSELEAF SERVICES

Looseleaf services are published in a variety of sizes, shapes and configurations. They use varied schemes of organization, and it is difficult to offer a general description or a single research model valid for all services. There are, however, common features of which a researcher should be aware.

Published looseleaf services are generally issued in one of two formats, which we will call *newsletter-type* and *interfiled* services. The two styles of service serve different purposes and are useful for different matters. The newsletter-type service is most useful in areas where it is important to monitor current information from a variety of sources. An interfiled service is better suited to areas such as tax law, in which new matters apply a specific body of doctrine and must be considered in connection with earlier interpretations. To be a useful tool, either type of service must be updated with great frequency.

1. For a brief history of this form of publication, see Neal, "Loose-Leaf Reporting Services," 62 *Law Libr.J.* 153, 153–56 (1969).

Many of the most highly respected looseleafs are updated weekly, while others are supplemented fortnightly or monthly. A publication which is only supplemented quarterly or less frequently is not generally an effective current awareness tool.

Although there are well over a dozen significant publishers of legal looseleaf services, three firms dominate the field: Bureau of National Affairs, Commerce Clearing House, and Prentice Hall. The three publishers compete in a number of fields, particularly labor law and taxation. A researcher working regularly in a particular subject area can feel free to rely on one service for most needs, but should have some familiarity with each available service in the field. The competing sources on a particular subject do not overlap completely, and material found in one will not necessarily appear in another.[2]

1. NEWSLETTER–TYPE SERVICES

The newsletter-type looseleaf service utilizes packets of new material to be filed as a unit or series of units, supplementing rather than displacing previously filed material. These units or releases can be read through as a single periodical publication, like a newsletter, and thereby serve a "current awareness" function. The newsletter-type service is distinguished from the interfiled service, in which individual pages are filed *in place of* superseded pages, which are then discarded. The releases of a newsletter-type service do not replace older pages, but are merely added to the accumulation of previous releases.

Typical of the newsletter-type form are most of the services of the Bureau of National Affairs (BNA). *United States Law Week* is BNA's most widely known service, although it is different from most in that it does not cover a particular subject. The four major sections of *U.S. Law Week* summarize general legal developments, provide excerpts from recent court decisions, track Supreme Court proceedings, and reprint the full text of all Supreme Court opinions. Separate indexes are issued on a regular basis to cover the general law and Supreme Court sections of the service. Other BNA services cover more specialized areas, such as antitrust, environmental law, or labor relations. Most of these services include a summary of recent developments and provide the text of some of the major primary sources in the field, such as new court decisions, administrative agency decisions, statutory changes, and new regulations.

Some BNA services, such as *Antitrust & Trade Regulation Report* and *Securities Regulation & Law Report,* consist only of newsletter-type releases. Others include both sequentially filed pages reporting recent developments and reference volumes containing primary sources such as statutes and regulations. In these services, new developments are

2. Because of the intense competition in the field, the publishers offer a variety of special services to subscribers. BNA, for example, has a "BNA Plus" service which can provide the full text of any document referred to in any of its publications. A document delivery service can be expensive, but may be necessary when a particularly elusive decision or ruling is needed.

filed newsletter-style, and pages with changes in statutes or regulations are interfiled to replace old pages. These publications blur the distinction between newsletter-type and interfiled services, and can be considered hybrids combining the best of both forms. The *Environment Reporter,* for example, has both a "Current Developments" volume and several sets of binders such as "Federal Regulations," "State Air Laws," and "State Water Laws."

Several BNA services also include separate sections containing the full text of court and administrative decisions. These decisions have a permanent reference value and are often cumulated and reprinted in bound reporter volumes. Court decisions on environmental issues are first published in a looseleaf "Decisions" volume of the *Environment Reporter* and then cumulated into bound *Environment Reporter Cases* volumes. The looseleaf volumes of the *Labor Relations Reporter* contain cases which are later published in five separate bound series: *Fair Employment Practice Cases, Individual Employment Rights Cases, Labor Arbitration Reports, Labor Relations Reference Manual,* and *Wage and Hour Cases.* Cases generally have the same volume and page citation in both looseleaf and bound formats, as is standard with most reporter advance sheets and volumes. This permits cases cited upon first publication to be located easily by readers months or years later.

The current developments material generally receives a final cumulative index at the end of each six months or year, but is not reprinted in a bound format by the publisher. Because the news reports may contain information not published elsewhere, however, many libraries bind and retain their copies.

Illustration A shows a typical first page from the "Current Report" section of a newsletter-type service, BNA's *Product Safety & Liability Reporter.* Note the summaries of topics discussed in the issue, and the industry checklist at the bottom of the page. Both items provide references to fuller discussions on the pages indicated. The first summary and the first entry in the checklist relate to all-terrain vehicles (ATVs), which will be the focus of other illustrations in this chapter.

2. INTERFILED SERVICES

Looseleaf services that are updated by interfiling new pages and removing superseded pages are perhaps the most common and familiar type. New pages usually replace existing pages, providing new documentation, revisions, and corrections, and can also be used to incorporate entirely new sections into the service to represent new areas of concern. Instead of pamphlets, as used in newsletter-type services, new material in an interfiled service is usually made up of individual sheets.

Because it consists of an assortment of new material, corrections, and inserted changes, the loose collection of pages that makes up a new release in an interfiled service generally is not read as a current awareness service. However, many releases include a "report letter"

Illustration A

The first page of a *Product Safety & Liability Reporter* (BNA) weekly issue

PRODUCT SAFETY & LIABILITY REPORTER®

A weekly review of consumer safety developments

Volume 16, Number 18 THE BUREAU OF NATIONAL AFFAIRS, INC. April 29, 1988

HIGHLIGHTS OF CURRENT REPORT

THE CONSENT DECREE on all-terrain vehicles is approved by U.S. District Judge Gerhard Gesell with amendments agreed to by the parties under which the Consumer Product Safety Commission will set up a central repository of ATV information and have a greater ability to seek administrative remedies if the settlement is not carried out (p. 389; text of judge's order, p. 425) ... The CPSC decides to request an additional $1.53 million for its fiscal 1989 budget for ATV activities (p. 390).

NO FEDERAL PRE-EMPTION of vaccine claims was intended by Congress, the U.S. Court of Appeals for the Fourth Circuit holds, remanding a DPT vaccine case for consideration of failure-to-warn and design defect claims (p. 395; text, p. 421).

REASSIGNMENTS OF CPSC EMPLOYEES by Chairman Terrence M. Scanlon has "hurt the Commission's ability to protect consumers from unsafe products," Rep. James J. Florio (D-NJ) charges in releasing a new report on the agency by the General Accounting Office (p. 391).

CLAIMS OF INJURIES from the drug DES that were time-barred at the time of the 1980 *Sindell* decision establishing market share liability were not revived by that landmark ruling, the California Supreme Court decides (p. 396) ... A Minnesota state trial judge dismisses a boy's claim that he was injured because his grandmother used DES while she was pregnant with his mother (p. 397) ... A New York appellate court upholds denial of summary judgment to seven DES manufacturers who contended that they did not manufacture the drugs used by the plaintiffs' mothers (p. 399).

MARKUP OF HR 1115, the product liability bill sponsored by Rep. Bill Richardson (D-NM), is set to begin May 3 in the full House Energy and Commerce Committee (p. 398).

RISKS OF SMOKING ARE QUANTIFIED by a former research director of the Committee for Tobacco Research during the Cipollone trial. A plaintiff's attorney says the statement is the first of its kind (p. 398).

WARNINGS ON CHOKING RISKS presented by small toys and toy parts would be required under a bill introduced by Rep. Sam Gejdenson (D-Conn) (p. 391).

WOODEN BABY SWINGS that may come unglued are being replaced free of charge by Hedstrom Corp., the CPSC announces (p. 391).

AUTOMATIC RESTRAINTS must be installed in convertibles on the same schedule as in other passenger cars, the National Highway Traffic Safety Administration decides, denying petitions for reconsideration for extension of the Sept. 1, 1989, deadline (p. 393).

MAKERS OF MOTOR HOMES from the 1984–86 model years built on General Motors chassis are asked by NHTSA to recall the vehicles because of a possible fire hazard (p. 393).

A CLAIM OF DEFECTIVE DESIGN of a motorcycle due to lack of a crash bar was properly rejected by the trial judge for lack of evidence, a Maryland appellate court holds (p. 399).

PENDING RULEMAKING ACTIONS are listed in the semiannual regulatory agendas published by the CPSC and NHTSA (p. 392; text, pp. 401, 407).

INDUSTRY CHECKLIST

Section 1

or similar bulletin that describes the new developments in a summary manner and provides references to the location of new matter. This report letter is accompanied by filing instructions, so that the new pages can properly be inserted into the binders. Obviously, if filing is not done regularly or is done without due care, researchers cannot find needed material and the service is useless. Illustration B shows the filing instructions from CCH's *Products Liability Reports,* a typical interfiling service. Note the addition of new annotations and current court decisions, and the updating of the case table and index.

Because new material is added to the body of an interfiled service, page numbers cannot simply be sequentially numbered the way they are in a newsletter-type service or other periodical. To provide access to contents, whether pages are added or not, publishers must have a consistent way of numerically designating a particular block of material. Many interfiled services do not use page numbers as their basic points of reference, but refer instead in summaries and indexes to material by *paragraph number.* A "paragraph" in looseleaf terminology is a term of art and does not necessarily refer to the traditional single block of type. It can designate any quantity of material, and often consists of several pages. Each new court decision, for example, is often assigned a paragraph number. This can be confusing, since in many services each page contains both a page number at the top and a paragraph number at the bottom. Even experienced looseleaf users can be misled when the paragraph and page numbers are somewhat similar. Note in Illustration B, for example, that new material in paragraphs 3310 to 3335 is being added, on pages 3199–5 to 3333. Remember when using services that employ paragraph numbering systems that the numbers in index entries and cross-references designate paragraphs, not pages.

Just as with newsletter-type services, there are some sections of many interfiled services which report new court and agency decisions in full. For some services these decisions are reissued in a permanent bound format, but other services simply issue "transfer binders" for the storage of older material. Without the expense of additional bound volumes, this allows continued access to older material and permits the size of the main binders to remain manageable.

The major looseleaf services on federal taxation, CCH's *Standard Federal Tax Reports* and Prentice Hall's *Federal Taxes,* use an interfiled system. Both are arranged by section of the Internal Revenue Code, and gather for each code section the statutory text, legislative history information, regulations, commentary, and annotations of decisions and rulings. Another interfiled looseleaf, discussed above in Chapter 7, is CCH's *Congressional Index.* The addition of new pages allows lists of pending bills, status tables, and indexes by subject and bill sponsor to be updated on a regular basis.

Most interfiled services utilize the same binders year after year, with textual changes made as necessary and new material filling the space left by the removal of older decisions. A few services, like the major tax services, issue a new set of binders each year. The sets from previous years are frequently retained in larger libraries, and can be

Illustration B

Filing instructions for an issue of *Products Liability Reports* (CCH)

CONTENTS

—1—

	Pages Not Required	Pages in This Report
Table of Cases		
Current Case Table.	381—391	381—391
Defense • Practice and Procedure		
Annotations reflecting recent decisions (¶ 3310—3335); *Chart of Negligence Statutes of Limitations.*	3199-5—3215-13 3471—3472	3199-5—3333 3471—3472
Strict Liability		
Subsequent action noted (¶ 4030.4503, 4095.4527, 4280.8504).	4039—4040 4085-57—4085-58 4409-7—4410	4039—4040 4085-57—4085-58 4409-7—4410

—2—

	Pages Not Required	Pages in This Report
Cumulative Index		
Cumulative Index to Current Decisions.	4901—4914	4901—4915
Current Decisions		
New decisions begin at ¶ 11,880.	34,149—34,150	34,149—34,186
Last Report Letter		
This is Report No. 658.	No. 657	No. 658

COMMERCE, CLEARING, HOUSE, INC.

useful for historical research or for determining the state of the law at a particular time.

3. ELECTRONIC SERVICES

The words you are now reading are printed in ink on paper. This form of communication is not yet obsolete, but other technologies are increasingly used for legal information. A "book," no longer necessarily a physical item, can consist of information electronically stored and retrieved. A "looseleaf" service does not necessarily require loose leaves or binders, but can be retrieved electronically and displayed on a screen.

The major looseleaf publishers have been in the process for several years of making their major reporters accessible online. The full texts of several BNA reporters, including *United States Law Week, Antitrust & Trade Regulation Report, Chemical Regulation Reporter, Environment Reporter, Government Employee Relations Reporter, International Trade Reporter, Patent, Trademark & Copyright Journal, Pension Reporter,* and *Securities Regulation & Law Report* are available on both WESTLAW and LEXIS. In addition, there are BNA databases which are updated each working day with new developments, such as *Banking Daily, International Trade Daily, Daily Labor Report, Pension and Benefits Daily, Securities Law Daily,* and *Daily Tax Report. BNA Tax Updates* provides even more current information, supplementing the *Daily Tax Report* with new developments twice each day.

While WESTLAW and LEXIS do not have as many services from Commerce Clearing House as from BNA, they do provide access to its *Blue Sky Law Reporter* and to the daily *CCH Tax Day: Federal* and *CCH Tax Day: State.* WESTLAW and LEXIS also provide access to numerous databases from Tax Analysts, Inc., including the weekly *Tax Notes* and the daily *Tax Notes Today.*[3]

The online counterpart to Prentice Hall's *Federal Taxes* is PHINet. It includes the full text of tax cases and various IRS documents such as private letter rulings, revenue rulings, and revenue procedures, as well as news of current developments.[4] Prentice Hall current income tax materials are available on WESTLAW, which also provides gateway access to the entire PHINet system.

In addition to providing access to other companies' services, WESTLAW performs a similar function with its "Topical Highlights" databases. These databases, in the fields of antitrust, bankruptcy,

3. *Tax Notes* is also published as a weekly newsletter, with summaries of documents which are supplied in full text on microfiche. It thus performs the basic functions of a looseleaf service—current commentary and analysis, with convenient access to primary sources—in an innovative way.

4. Prentice Hall also makes tax primary sources available on optical disk. The disk format is very useful for low-cost full-text searching, but is better designed for retrospective collections of documents than for current information. Unless new disks are issued regularly, the format lacks the frequent supplementation which is an essential component of a looseleaf service.

corporations and securities, environmental law, financial services, products liability, and utilities, provide brief synopses of recent decisions of interest, as well as new legislative and administrative developments. For most cases, the full text can be retrieved simply by typing the command "FIND" while viewing the summary. Like a looseleaf, this electronic service provides both editorial current awareness and access to original documents.

In a broader sense, the legal database systems function somewhat like looseleaf services, in that they gather a wide variety of primary and secondary sources in one location.[5] Topical libraries in WESTLAW and LEXIS generally include statutes, regulations, court and administrative decisions, and secondary materials. Browsing between databases online is not that different from paging through a looseleaf volume, but there is one major difference. The editors of a printed looseleaf service gather material on a particular subject in one place. Online retrieval is determined by the specific combination of terms used by the researcher. While this permits a greater precision, it also requires a greater level of expertise, both in online searching techniques and in the subject area. For an overview of sources in a particular area, the printed service may be much more efficient. Just as thorough case research involves using both databases and printed resources such as digests and annotations, topical research should take advantage of the attributes of both online and printed services.

C. COMMON LOOSELEAF FEATURES

Looseleaf services vary greatly in approach, format, and method of organization, but they have some common advantages over most other legal publications. Some features, such as diversity of primary sources and prompt supplementation, are shared by printed services and electronic databases. Editorial features, such as explanatory text and subject indexing, are particular advantages of published services.

1. DIVERSITY OF PRIMARY SOURCES

Most of the publications described in earlier chapters contain one primary legal source, often with references to one or more other sources. The annotated statutory codes, for example, are quite versatile, but contain the full text of only legislative provisions, with brief abstracts of decisions and citation references to legislative history and secondary sources. Looseleaf services are unique in providing a variety

5. The most recent technology in electronic legal database systems is CD-ROM (compact disc read-only memory). 200,000 pages or more of primary and secondary source materials are electronically printed on a small laser-read disc which can be translated by a properly outfitted personal computer. For example, West CD-ROM Libraries (TM), introduced in 1988, provide comprehensive sets of materials for a given field of research. A single library might contain statutes, regulations, treatises, practice materials, forms, and cases. West CD-ROM Libraries and WESTLAW are integrated to allow the user access to both online updates and the full array of WESTLAW databases. Current offerings include libraries for Bankruptcy, Federal Tax, Federal Government Contracts and Civil Procedure.

of primary sources in full text. These include statutes, regulations, court rules, and both judicial and administrative decisions. A frequently supplemented looseleaf service is often the *first* available published source for such documents. Online services make documents available even faster, since instead of printing and mailing them they simply have to add them to a database.

In the products liability field, for example, both BNA and CCH services provide primary sources. BNA's *Product Safety & Liability Reporter* includes two "Reference File" binders containing federal acts and regulations on matters such as consumer products and motor vehicles, and its weekly report includes the texts of selected court decisions. Illustration C shows the first page of a United States District Court decision on all-terrain vehicles, published in the BNA reporter the same week it was announced.

CCH's *Products Liability Reports* has a much more extensive collection of court decisions, providing a regular reporting service. Illustration D shows the beginning of an opinion on ATVs published in the CCH reporter and now found in the 1986–87 transfer binder. Note that this case has been designated ¶ 11,118, and that its citation in the *Federal Supplement* is provided after the name. The headnotes are prepared by CCH and include "back references" to paragraphs within *Products Liability Reports* where further information on specific issues can be found.

Products Liability Reports also provides the texts of relevant federal and state laws. The first headnote in Illustration D includes a reference to ¶ 91,316, which is a section of the Idaho Product Liability Reform Act. Illustration E shows the beginning of this act, as printed in the CCH reporter.

2. EXPLANATORY TEXT

In addition to the primary sources of law, services also provide descriptive and explanatory sections to aid the researcher in understanding the primary sources and their legal effect, in integrating and synthesizing them, and in using them in practice. These sections are often straightforward and concise, since they are designed more for rapid assimilation by working attorneys than for lengthy consideration by academics. The textual material, prepared by the publishers' editorial staffs, is usually competently and accurately done, but it is not considered authoritative and is generally not quoted or cited in briefs.

Some of the editorial text appears in report letters accompanying the pages in interfiled services, and is designed merely to summarize current news and be discarded within weeks. Other text provides more extensive discussion, and is retained and indexed. In interfiled services, the editorial text is updated and revised by new pages as necessary. In newsletter-type services, "current reports" provide information on developments in the field. Illustration F shows a page of the "Current Report" section of BNA's *Product Safety & Liability Reporter*,

Illustration C

A court decision, as printed in *Product Safety & Liability Reporter* (BNA)

DECISION OF U.S. DISTRICT COURT IN *U.S. v. AMERICAN HONDA MOTOR CO.* [DC DC, April 27, 1988]

IN THE UNITED STATES DISTRICT COURT
FOR THE DISTRICT OF COLUMBIA

UNITED STATES OF AMERICA
Plaintiff,

v.

AMERICAN HONDA MOTOR CO., INC.; HONDA MOTOR CO., LTD.; HONDA RESEARCH & DEVELOPMENT CO., LTD.; YAMAHA MOTOR CO., LTD.; YAMAHA MOTOR CORP., U.S.A.; SUZUKI MOTORS CO., LTD.; U.S. SUZUKI MOTOR CORP.; KAWASAKI HEAVY INDUSTRIES LTD.; KAWASAKI MOTORS CORP., U.S.A.; POLARIS INDUSTRIES, L.P.
Defendants.

Civil Action No. 87-3525

MEMORANDUM AND ORDER

GESELL, District Judge:

The Court has before it for approval or disapproval a proposed Final Consent Decree[1] which may terminate this litigation.

The complaint was filed December 30, 1987, against five distributors of all-terrain vehicles ("ATVs"). A preliminary injunction was simultaneously filed by consent, approved by the Court and became immediately effective. The proposed Final Consent Decree was filed on March 14, 1988 and was served on various interested consumer groups and others who had notified the Court of possible objections and had been designated *amici*[2] with full rights to brief and argue. After briefing by all concerned, extensive oral argument was heard on April 18, 1988.

The complaint is the culmination of a protracted investigation by the Consumer Product Safety Commission ("CPSC") and others into deaths and serious injuries associated with ATVs. These vehicles are widely sold throughout the United States by one or more of the defendants to children and adults for recreational or utility purposes. ATVs are distributed in a variety of models, both three-wheeled and four-wheeled. They are characterized by large, low-pressure tires, a relatively high center of gravity, straddle seating and handlebar steering, and are intended for operation over rough and varied off-highway terrain by a single individual.

Prior to the filing of the complaint, the danger of death or serious injury associated with the operation of ATVs received public attention and considerable comment. In May, 1985, CPSC published in the *Federal Register* an Advance Notice of Proposed Rulemaking which included a preliminary determination that ATVs may present an unreasonable risk of injury. Advance Notice of Proposed Rulemaking, 50 Fed. Reg. 23,139 (May 31, 1985). The same month hearings also commenced on the alleged hazards before subcommittees of both the Senate and the House of Representatives. The Commission received some 3,000 comments in response to its Advance Notice, held public hearings and then directed a Task Force to investigate, to monitor developments and to report in 18 months. The Task Force Report, a voluminous document, was presented to CPSC on September 30, 1986. In December, 1986, CPSC voted to initiate the present action by invoking Section 12 of the Consumer Protection Safety Act ("CPSA"), 15 U.S.C. §2061, which contemplates direct emergency action by the United States in federal district court. No formal opportunity was provided for the industry to rebut the Task Force Report. Thus, full development of the applicable facts was left to trial of this case without benefit of a contested administrative record under the following circumstances.

In February, 1987, CPSC formally referred the matter to the Department of Justice to seek a judicial declaration that ATVs present an "imminent and unreasonable risk of death, serious illness, or severe personal injury." 15 U.S.C. §2061(a). The Department commenced trial preparation with a staff of ten attorneys, aided by the 12,000-page Task Force Report. Various related hearings and notices were initiated by the CPSC in the interim. The CPSC also participated, as did some consumers and dealer groups, at further hearings scheduled by the Senate Commerce Committee.

Settlement discussions were initiated by the United States and defendants in December, 1987, with the encouragement of the Senate Commerce Committee and they proceeded rapidly. These discussions were directed at promptly addressing the government's evaluation of the situation, which in its view called for immediate relief that would focus consumer attention on what it perceived to be the hazards posed, particularly for children and inexperienced operators, by the deceptively benign appearance and unique handling characteristics of ATVs. When the complaint alleging the necessity of abating this "grave hazard" was filed, agreement had already been reached between the parties on the preliminary injunction designed to provide interim relief — but only until a more definitive final consent decree could be fully negotiated and perfected. The Court then allowed the parties to withhold taking normal litigation steps for a few weeks to determine whether or not they could, as they expected, agree on a final consent decree. The proposed Final Consent Decree and judgment were filed in March, 1988, and these court proceedings looking toward approval or disapproval commenced shortly thereafter.

The Court is required to determine, in its discretion, whether or not the Final Consent Decree settlement, on balance, is by its terms fair, adequate, reasonable and in the general public interest. This task does not require the Court

[1] In fact, two proposed Final Consent Decrees have been submitted, one for the four defendants which are wholly-owned American subsidiaries of Japanese concerns, American Honda Motor Co., Inc., Yamaha Motor Corp., U.S.A., U.S. Suzuki Motor Corp., and Kawasaki Motors Corp., U.S.A., and another for the American-owned concern, a smaller, regional distributor, Polaris Industries, L.P. The proposed consent judgments contemplate dismissal of the parent Japanese companies, without prejudice. No distinction will be drawn between the two Final Consent Decrees in this Memorandum and they are discussed as if one.

[2] The *amici* participating in this case are as follows: American, Academy of Pediatrics, American Public Health Association, Frederic Booth, Public Citizen, Consumer Federation of America, and United States Public Interest Research Group; the states of Alaska, Arkansas, California, Colorado, Connecticut, Delaware, Florida, Hawaii, Illinois, Indiana, Iowa, Kentucky, Maine, Maryland, Massachusetts, Michigan, Minnesota, Missouri, Montana, Nebraska, Nevada, New Jersey, New York, North Carolina, North Dakota, Oklahoma, Oregon, Tennessee, Texas, Vermont, West Virginia, and Wisconsin; and the United States Senator from the State of New York, the Honorable Alfonse M. D'Amato.

providing information on an ATV class action which had recently been filed.

Illustration D

A court decision, as printed in *Products Liability Reports* (CCH)

[¶ 11,118] Galen B. GREEN and Deborah A.Green, Plaintiffs v. A.B. HAGGLUND AND SONER; Nordic Tracked Vehicles, Inc., dba Tracks Unlimited; and Dyna-Haul, Ltd., Defendants.

U.S. District Court, District of Idaho. No. 84-1360. May 2, 1986. 634 F.Supp. 790.

Seller's Liability—All-Terrain Vehicle—Sufficiency of Evidence

Liability of a seller of an all-terrain vehicle for injuries sustained during a test drive could not be determined, as a matter of law, because issues of fact remained as to whether the seller had made express warranties, had had a reasonable opportunity to inspect the vehicle or had altered or modified the vehicle. Absent evidence of these circumstances, the seller would be relieved of liability under § 6-1407 of the Idaho Products Liability law.

Back references.—¶ 4120; 4243.30; 91,316.

Breach of Warranty—Oral Statements—Lack of Sales Agreement

Despite the absence of a consummated sales agreement, representations made by a seller of an all-terrain vehicle constituted express warranties upon which a passenger injured during a test drive of the vehicle could sue to recover for personal injuries. Warranty provisions of the Uniform Commercial Code did not require the existence of a sales agreement, only that any promises form part of the basis of the bargain. A bargain was struck when the passenger agreed to participate in a test drive to further consider purchasing the vehicle, and the seller represented that the vehicle would perform in a particular manner. Under these circumstances, statements made by the seller constituted express warranties.

Back references.—¶ 1080; 1355.

Breach of Warranty—All-Terrain Vehicle—Privity Requirement

The privity requirement was eliminated in a breach of warranty action for personal injuries brought against a seller of an all-terrain vehicle by a passenger who was injured during a test drive.

Back references.—¶ 1210.13; 1355.

Damages—Loss of Consortium—Children's Claim

Idaho does not recognize a cause of action brought on behalf of children seeking to recover damages for loss of a parent's love, care, companionship and guidance.

Back reference.—¶ 3310.

For Plaintiffs: Craig L. Meadows and Wayne B. Slaughter, Jr., of Hawley, Troxell, Ennis & Hawley, Boise, Idaho.

For A.B. Hagglund & Soner: Blaine Evans, Robert J. Koontz and Bruce C. Jones, of Evans, Keane, Koontz, Boyd & Ripley, Boise, Idaho.

For Dyna-Haul, Ltd.: R.B. Rock, Larry C. Hunter, of Moffatt, Thomas, Barrett & Blanton, Boise, Idaho.

For Nordic Tracked Vehicles, Inc.: Brian K. Julian, of Quane, Smith, Howard & Hull, Boise, Idaho.

[All-Terrain Vehicle]

I. Introduction

RYAN, J.: This action arises from an accident which occurred during the demonstration of an all-terrain vehicle, Model BV206, manufactured by Defendant A.B. Hagglund and Soner (Hagglund). The accident occurred in August 1983. At the time of the accident, Plaintiff Galen Green was a Bureau of Land Management (BLM) employee and was participating in the demonstration by riding in the BV206. Green was injured when the BV206 was unable to negotiate a steep hill.

On April 23, 1986, the court heard oral argument on the following pending motions:

1. Defendant Tracks Unlimited's Motion for Summary Judgment.

2. Defendant Hagglund's Motion for Partial Summary Judgment.

3. Defendant Hagglund's Motion for Leave to File Cross-claims Against Dyna-Haul, Ltd., and Nordie Tracked Vehicles, Inc.

4. Defendant Hagglund's Motion to Allow Jury Inspection of the Accident Scene.

II. Discussion

A. *Summary Judgment Standards*

Summary Judgment is appropriate only where there is no genuine issue of material fact and the moving party is entitled to judgment as a matter of law. Fed.R.Civ.P. 56. Necessarily, conflicting factual testimony is not properly resolved on a motion for summary judgment. Further, the record must be examined in the light most favorable to, and all inferences from the evidence must be drawn in favor of, the nonmoving parties. *Lew v. Kona Hospital,* 754 F.2d 1420, 1423 (9th Cir.1985).

B. *Defendant Tracks Unlimited's Motion for Summary Judgment*

Tracks Unlimited (Tracks) seeks summary judgment primarily on the grounds that Idaho Code § 6-1407 insulates it from liability.

The liability limitation of Section 6-1407 is not applicable where Tracks (1) has made express warranties; (2) has had a reasonable opportunity to inspect the product in a manner which would or should, in the exercise of reason-

Illustration E

A state statute, as printed in *Products Liability Reports* (CCH)

IDAHO

References are to Idaho Code, as amended.

IDAHO PRODUCT LIABILITY REFORM ACT

***Added by Laws* 1980, *Ch.* 225, *approved March* 28, 1980, *effective July* 1, 1980.**

[¶ 91,310]

Sec. 6-1401. Scope. The previous existing applicable law of this state on product liability is modified only to the extent set forth in this act.

[¶ 91,311]

Sec. 6-1402. Definitions. (1) "Product seller" means any person or entity that is engaged in the business of selling products, whether the sale is for resale, or for use or consumption. The term includes a manufacturer, wholesaler, distributor, or retailer of the relevant product. The term also includes a party who is in the business of leasing or bailing such products. The term "product seller" does not include:

(a) A provider of professional services who utilizes or sells products within the legally authorized scope of its professional practice. A nonprofessional provider of services is not included unless the sale or use of a product is the principal part of the transaction, and the essence of the relationship between the seller and purchaser is not the furnishing of judgment, skill, or services;

(b) A commercial seller of used products who resells a product after use by a consumer or other product user, provided the used product is in essentially the same condition as when it was acquired for resale; and

(c) A finance lessor who is not otherwise a product seller. A "finance lessor" is one who acts in a financial capacity, who is not a manufacturer, wholesaler, distributor, or retailer, and who leases a product without having a reasonable opportunity to inspect and discover defects in the product, under a lease arrangement in which the selection, possession, maintenance, and operation of the product are controlled by a person other than the lessor.

(2) "Manufacturer" includes a product seller who designs, produces, makes, fabricates, constructs, or remanufactures the relevant product or component part of a product before its sale to a user or consumer. It includes a product seller or entity not otherwise a manufacturer that holds itself out as a manufacturer. A product seller acting primarily as a wholesaler, distributor, or retailer of a product may be a "manufacturer" but only to the extent that it designs, produces, makes, fabricates, constructs, or remanufactures the product before its sale.

(3) "Product" means any object possessing intrinsic value, capable of delivery either as an assembled whole or as a component part or parts, and produced for introduction into trade or commerce. Human tissue and organs, including human blood and its components, are excluded from this term. The "relevant product" under this chapter is that product, or its component part or parts, which gave rise to the product liability claim.

(4) "Claimant" means a person or entity asserting a product liability claim, including a wrongful death action, and, if the claim is asserted through or on behalf of an estate, the term includes claimant's decedent. "Claimant" includes any person or entity that suffers harm.

(5) "Reasonably anticipated conduct" means the conduct which would be expected of an ordinary reasonably prudent person who is likely to use the product in the same or similar circumstances.

[¶ 91,312]

Sec. 6-1403. Length of time product sellers are subject to liability. (1) Useful safe life.

(a) Except as provided in subsection (1)(b) hereof, a product seller shall not be subject to liability to a claimant for harm under this chapter if the product seller proves by a preponderance of the evidence that the harm was caused after the product's "useful safe life" had expired.

"Useful safe life" begins at the time of delivery of the product and extends for the time during which the product would normally be likely to perform or be stored in a safe manner. For the purposes of this chapter, "time of delivery" means the time of delivery of a product to its first purchaser or lessee who was not engaged in the business of either selling such products or using them as component parts of another product to be sold.

(b) A product seller may be subject to liability for harm caused by a product used beyond

Illustration F

Summaries of current developments in *Product Safety & Liability Reporter* (BNA)

75

Current Report

Sports and Recreation

CLASS ACTION REFUND SUIT FILED AGAINST ATV MANUFACTURERS BY TLPJ

A nationwide consumer class action suit seeking a refund for all current owners of three-wheel all-terrain vehicles was filed Jan. 13 in federal district court in Philadelphia by Trial Lawyers for Public Justice, a Washington, D.C., public interest law firm.

The lawsuit alleges violations of the federal racketeering statute, fraud, breach of warranty, and violations of state consumer protection statutes. The defendants are the four Japanese companies that sell the vast majority of ATVs — Honda, Yamaha, Suzuki, Kawasaki — along with their United States subsidiaries and American ATV manufacturer Polaris Industries. Together these firms have sold more than 2.3 million ATVs currently in use throughout the U.S.

The Consumer Product Safety Commission and the Department of Justice announced Dec. 30 they had reached a preliminary consent agreement with the ATV makers under which they will stop the sale of three-wheel models, provide warnings and training to consumers, but stopped short of ordering the companies to recall the vehicles from consumers' hands (16 PSLR 3; text, 60).

"Once again, plaintiffs' trial lawyers have stepped in to protect consumers when the government has failed to do its job," TLPJ Executive Director Arthur Bryant said in announcing the suit. "These machines are ticking time bombs — every three days, two people die from using them. If a refund is available, millions of ATVs will be returned and hundreds of thousands of injuries and deaths will be prevented."

Lead counsel in the suit are TLPJ Sponsor Harold E. Kohn and Dianne M. Nast of Kohn, Savett, Klein & Graf, Philadelphia. Co-counsel are TLPJ founder Sidney W. Gilreath, and TLPJ Executive Director Arthur H. Bryant.

"The manufacturers should have voluntarily recalled all of these vehicles and offered full refunds years ago," Nast said. "It is unfortunate that it will take litigation to achieve that result."

TLPJ is supported by over 550 of plaintiffs' trial lawyers in the United States and specializes in precedent-setting and socially significant litigation. TLPJ developed and successfully prosecuted the landmark lawsuit against W.R. Grace & Co. for contaminating the drinking water in Woburn, Mass., and causing the deaths of eight children. Last November, TLPJ filed the first lawsuits in the country against the lead industry on behalf of children who suffered lead poisoning from eating lead-based paint (15 PSLR 898).

Budget

CONTRACTS HIT HARD AS COMMISSION CUTS FY 1989 BUDGET TO MEET OMB MARK

Contracts for a number of projects were eliminated by the Consumer Product Safety Commission at a Jan. 13 session in order to meet its Fiscal Year 1989 budget mark of $32,917,000 set by the Office of Management and Budget.

A total of $1,132,000 in reductions of contract funding was proposed by the staff and approved by the commission as part of an effort to trim nearly $3 million from the agency's fiscal 1989 budget request of $36.1 million. Some $2 million in reductions in the commission's FY 1988 budget were approved by CPSC last week (16 PSLR 45). The following contract reductions were authorized by the commission for fiscal 1989:

National Electronic Injury Surveillance System: $120,000
Computer utilization costs: $100,000
All-terrain vehicle work: $200,000
Publication distribution: $25,000
Product safety assessments (kept at 1988 level): $50,000
Toxicity support: $15,000
Economics special studies: $20,000
State and local contracts: $25,000
Ongoing and seasonal projects: $22,000
Planning and evaluation: $40,000
Bicycles project: $75,000
Riding mowers project: $220,000
Indoor air quality project: $200,000
Health sciences laboratory equipment: $20,000

Salaries also will be cut by $1,221,000. In addition, six full-time positions will be eliminated in accordance with the CPSC appropriations bill for FY 1988 (16 PSLR 4), including two from media relations, one from the Office of General Counsel, one from the Chairman's office, and one from the Office of the Executive Director. Three full-time employees from the Office of Information and Public Affairs have already been "redistributed."

In addition, operating costs for such items as the CPSC telephone Hotline, printing, and travel, will be slashed by $459,000, and common costs, such as rents, telephone, and postage, will be cut by $371,000.

OUTLOOK '88 ADVANCE ORDERS

Later in January, *Product Safety & Liability Reporter* will publish an analysis of the important issues to be decided in 1988 by Congress, the federal agencies, and the courts. This "Outlook for Product Safety and Liability in 1988" is part of one of a series of five Outlook '88 reports prepared by BNA editors. All of these reports are sent to subscribers to BNA's *Daily Report for Executives*, and selected portions appear in other BNA services.

Now you can order the complete set of Outlook '88 reports and find out what to expect in the coming year. Outlook '88 will give you a head start on planning for changes in fields such as taxes, employee benefits, environmental compliance, banking, securities, trade, antitrust, and intellectual property.

To order the complete Outlook '88 series ($50) or the individual reports ($20 each) on (1) Economics, (2) Tax, (3) Trade and Competitiveness, (4) Energy, Environment, and Chemicals, or (5) Regulatory Policy (including product safety and liability), call BNA PLUS at 800-452-7773 or (202) 452-4323.

1-15-88

Services occasionally extend explanations and analyses into lengthy, separately published items, such as the "Outlook for Product Safety and Liability in 1988" advertised in the lower right corner of Illustration F. Some of these separate booklets are issued to subscribers as part of a looseleaf service. BNA's *Environment Reporter*, for example, has included several special reports such as *The Clean Water Act Amendments of 1987* and *Superfund II: A New Mandate* (1987). The tax looseleafs prepare "bulletins" or "extra editions" on a regular basis to explain new laws, to reprint important Congressional documents, or to provide editorial explanations of specific topics of current concern.

Some secondary aspects of looseleaf services are designed not for analysis or explanation but as means of access to primary sources. Much of CCH's *Products Liability Reports,* for example, consists of a digest-type outline of the law on various procedural aspects of the field and on particular types of products, with reprinted case headnotes. Illustration G shows the page on which ¶ 4243, analysis of recreational and utility vehicles, begins. A very brief overview is followed by headnotes from cases, arranged by product type. ATV case headnotes would appear under ¶ 4243.30 with jeeps and 4–wheel drives. Note in the case shown earlier in Illustration D that the same headnote which referred to the Idaho Product Liability Reform Act also includes a reference to ¶ 4243.30. The paragraph numbers accompanying the other headnotes in the case provide access to sections on other issues such as breach of warranty or damages.

Some looseleaf publications do little more than provide copies of particular primary source documents. Similarly, many online databases simply load the full text of new documents without editorial comment. If they are prompt and reliable, such publications and databases serve an important function. A looseleaf *service,* however, integrates primary sources into a cohesive body of material, and provides its readers with organization and analysis.

3. THOROUGH AND VARIED INDEXING

There are several different approaches for retrieving information from a looseleaf service, in addition to scanning current reports for recent developments. These include a variety of subject indexes, tables of cases, and finding lists for statutes and administrative materials. A major advantage of looseleaf services is the variety and promptness with which they provide access to their contents. A greater number of access points means generally that a service can handle a wider variety of research needs.

Many services provide more than one subject index. A very general index may have only a few broad entries to direct users to the sections of the service in which particular large topics begin. In CCH services, this is called the "Rapid Finder" index. As shown in Illustration H, *Products Liability Reports* contains a "Rapid Finder Index to Products," which provides speedy access to the coverage of ATVs at ¶ 4243.30.

More extensive indexing is found in a general or "topical" index, which includes far more entries and subdivisions. A thorough topical index may occupy a hundred pages or more. New material is added to

Illustration G

Annotations to cases in *Products Liability Reports* (CCH)

¶ 4243 Recreational and Utility Vehicles

Although strict liability has been imposed upon manufacturers, sellers, distributors and lessors of recreational-type vehicles, many courts have recognized the obvious dangers associated with most of these vehicles. For example, motorcycle manufacturers are not required to equip their products with crash bars or other leg protection devices because there is no duty to produce the safest possible product, only one that is not unreasonably dangerous (.5028). A user's knowledge of the hazardous character of the product (.5009) and awareness of optionally available crash bars relieve manufacturers of liability for defective design (.5005).

The second collision or crashworthiness doctrine, originally applicable to automobiles only, has been extended to include recreational vehicles (.4008, .5006).

Annotations to ¶ 4243 Appear Topically Below, as Follows:

.10 Bicycle.—A retailer was strictly liable for the misassembly of a bicycle whose front wheel wobbled, causing its rider to fall and sustain injury. *Means v. Sears, Roebuck & Co.* (Mo. Ct. App. 1976) PRODUCTS LIABILITY REPORTS ¶ 7662, aff'd (Mo. Sup. Ct. 1987) 550 S.W.2d 780.

.15 Golf carts.—A seller of a motor-powered golf cart could be held liable to a renter of the cart for injuries sustained when the cart collapsed. The seller could reasonably anticipate that the cart would be rented to and used by members of the general public. *Simpson v. Powered Products of Michigan, Inc.* (1963) PRODUCTS LIABILITY REPORTS ¶ 5148, 24 Conn.Sup. 409, 192 A.2d 555.

.1501 The issue of strict liability was correctly submitted to a jury in a case involving a golf cart, which overturned, pinning its victim beneath. The vehicle was found to be unreasonably dangerous, but not unavoidably unsafe. The golf cart could have been improved in several ways by the manufacturer. *Blevins v. Cushman Motors* (Mo. Sup. Ct. 1977) PRODUCTS LIABILITY REPORTS ¶ 7919, 551 S.W.2d 602, *aff'g* (Mo. Ct. App. 1976) PRODUCTS LIABILITY REPORTS ¶ 7758.

.1502 A golfer, who was injured when a motorized golf cart overturned and fell on him, was entitled to a jury determination of the liability of the country club that rented the cart to him and the manufacturer of the cart. Strict liability could not be contracted away by an exculpation clause in the rental ticket for the cart. Assumption of risk was not a defense because there was no evidence that the golfer had unreasonably proceeded to use the cart with knowledge of its instability as designed. His operation of the cart at full speed was not patent misuse. Finally, his evidence raised a genuine issue as to the identification of the alleged manufacturer of the cart. *Sipari v. Villa Olivia Country Club* (1978) PRODUCTS LIABILITY REPORTS ¶ 8338, 63 Ill.App. 3d 985, 380 N.E.2d 819.

.1503 A jury should have considered whether the absence of a warning rendered a golf cart that had a propensity to tip over "substantially dangerous" to the user in determining whether a manufacturer was strictly liable. Although the "unreasonably dangerous" standard was inapplicable in manufacturing and design defect cases, this did not preclude weighing such considerations in a failure to warn action. *Cavers v. Cushman Motor Sales, Inc.* (1979) PRODUCTS LIABILITY REPORTS ¶ 8535, 95 Cal.App.3d 338, 157 Cal.Rptr. 142.

.30 Jeeps/4-wheel drives/All terrain vehicles (ATVs).—A manufacturer of a jeep was not liable for injuries to a pedestrian struck when the driver hit the accelerator instead of the brake allegedly because of the positioning of the pedals. The manufacturer was not under a duty to make an accident-proof vehicle and the mere fact that the particular accident would not have occurred if the vehicle had been designed differently did not establish a breach of design duty. *Wells v. Jeep Corp.* (Wyo. Sup. Ct. 1975) PRODUCTS LIABILITY REPORTS ¶ 7408, 532 P.2d 595.

.3001 A manufacturer and a distributor of a jeep were not liable for the fire under the hood near the carburetor while a second-hand purchaser was driving because there was no proof that the defect which caused the fire existed when the jeep left their hands. *St. Paul Mercury Ins. Co. v. Jeep Corp.* (Mont. Sup. Ct. 1977) PRODUCTS LIABILITY REPORTS ¶ 8082, 372 P.2d 588.

.3002 There was no proof that the steering mechanism of a 1976 Custom Jeep was defective, and the manufacturer was not liable for the death and injuries of its passengers. The injured had argued that the steering had locked, causing the Jeep to roll over in a one-car accident. *Jensen v.*

Illustration H

A page from the "Rapid Finder Index" in *Products Liability Reports* (CCH)

RAPID FINDER INDEX

to

PRODUCTS

References are to paragraph (¶) numbers.

See also topical indexes in this division.

Italicized references are to "Strict Liability" division.

a service every week or two, but this main index is hardly revised that often. To avoid this prohibitive expense while still providing prompt subject access to new material, many services use "layered indexing." The main index (sometimes called a "Master Index") is supplemented by a frequently revised *updating* index called "Current Index" or "Latest Additions." This updating index provides access only to material issued since the last revision of the main index. Some looseleaf services employ three or more different indexes (a main index, a supplement revised monthly or quarterly, and a current supplement revised weekly), although the necessity of consulting three indexes is often cumbersome. Needless to say, however, in any subject approach to a service it may be necessary to check in each of the indexes. Each index should notify users to refer to the service's other indexes, ideally at the top of every page.

CCH's *Products Liability Reports* is a service with three, and sometimes four, subject indexes. The "Topical Index" provides references to the main sections of the service (as shown in Illustration G), where analyses and case summaries appear. This index is supplemented by a "Topical Index to Prior Decisions," which provides subject access to cases with headnotes that have not yet been incorporated into the subject arrangement. Illustration I shows a page from this index, providing several very specific subject references to the Idaho case shown earlier. Note that the topical index includes entries not only for products but for specific jurisdictions (Alabama, Alaska), theories of recovery (alternative liability), and procedural matters (amendment of pleadings). A "Current Topical Index" provides access to recent material, and is updated every few months. A sample page is shown in Illustration J. Like the other sample index page, it includes notices that references are to paragraph numbers (not pages) and that the other indexes should also be consulted. Finally, between revisions of the "Current Topical Index," the service may also have a "Latest Additions Topical Index," updated every two to four weeks.

A different form of indexing, used in some services, is designed for the user who already knows the paragraph location of relevant material. This index is frequently called the "cumulative" index. It operates like a citator, providing references directly from the text to new material. Illustration K shows a "Cumulative Index" page from *Products Liability Reports,* providing a reference from ¶ 4243 (recreational and utility vehicles) to ¶ 11,118 (the Idaho case shown earlier). This index is updated, as noted at the top of the page, by a frequently revised "Cumulative Index to Current Decisions." Obviously, these cumulative indexes cannot be used when first searching a service for a subject. For the experienced user who knows the classification of relevant matter, however, they provide a shortcut eliminating the need to consult the subject indexes.

Finally, most looseleaf services also include specific indexes for particular types of legal materials they contain. These "finding lists"

Illustration I

A page from the "Topical Index to Prior Decisions" in *Products Liability Reports* (CCH)

152 **Topical Index** 646 3-88

References are to paragraph (¶) numbers.
See also pages 101 and 251.

AIRCRAFT—continued
. passenger bridge collapse
. . ball/screw assembly . . . (Utah)10,272
. proximate cause
. . helicopter . . . (Va.)11,001
. punitive damages
. . reckless disregard standard . . . (Wis.)10,366
. *res ipsa loquitur*
. . control and multiple defendants . . . (Cal.)9763
. similar occurrence evidence
. . statistical analyses . . . (Cal.)11,140
. statutory violation
. . FAA certification . . . (Cal.)10,386

ALABAMA
. adequacy of warnings
. . insulin . . . 10,787
. automobile fuel tank
. . proximate cause . . . 10,888
. breach of warranty
. . combine . . . 9725
. . IUD user, notice . . . 10,500
. chemical
. . implied warranties . . . 11,052
. dry cleaning solvent
. . duty to warn . . . 11,396
. . implied warranty . . . 11,396
. . unavoidably unsafe product . . . 11,396
. duty to inspect
. . used truck . . . 10,964
. duty to warn
. . brucellosis vaccine . . . 10,727
. . tire explosion . . . 10,714
. embossing/printing machine
. . unguarded nip points . . . 9790
. expert testimony
. . qualifications of auto mechanic . . . 9808
. fabric press
. . assumption of risk . . . 11,152
. fire code
. . sailboat . . . 10,798
. forging press
. . government immunity . . . 10,870
. house
. . privity . . . 10,817
. implied warranties
. . chemical . . . 11,052
. . dry cleaning solvent . . . 11,396
. industry standards
. . hip prosthesis . . . 11,065
. insulin
. . adequacy of warnings . . . 10,787
. IUD
. . notice of breach of warranty . . . 10,499
. motorcycle
. . duty to warn . . . 11,148
. . proximate cause . . . 11,148
. privity
. . house . . . 10,817
. sailboat
. . fire code recommendations . . . 10,798
. . similar occurrences . . . 10,798
. . subsequent remedial measures . . . 10,798
. school bus
. . unreasonably dangerous requirement . . . 11,090
. similar occurrences
. . sailboat . . . 10,798
. statute of limitations
. . embossing/printing machine . . . 9790
. subsequent remedial measures
. . "mast warnings" for boats . . . 10,798
. truck
. . AEMLD . . . 10,964
. . duty to inspect . . . 10,964
. unavoidably unsafe product
. . dry cleaning solvent . . . 11,396

ALABAMA—continued
. wooden pallet
. . identity of tortfeasor . . . 11,484

ALASKA
. attorney's fees
. . assessment against consumer . . . 9788
. foam insulation
. . emission of noxious fumes . . . 9840
. garage door opener
. . design defect . . . 11,061
. indemnification
. . active negligence . . . 9655
. non-contractual indemnification
. . concurrently negligent tortfeasors . . . 9602
. notice of breach
. . consumer's filing of complaint . . . 9840
. prescription drug
. . duty to warn . . . 11,530
. statutory violations
. . acetylene cylinder . . . 9655
. superseding cause
. . air tank explosion . . . 10,842

ALL-TERRAIN VEHICLES
. breach of warranty
. . lack of sales agreement . . . (Ida.)11,118
. . oral statements as expressed warranty . . . (Ida.)11,118
. . privity requirement, personal injury . . . (Ida.)11,118
. damages
. . loss of parental consortium . . . (Ida.)11,118
. seller's liability
. . sufficiency of evidence . . . (Ida.)11,118

ALTERATION OF PRODUCTS
. plastic extruding machine
. . seller's alteration of safety device . . . (Mich.)9955
. seat belts
. . reinstallation . . . (Mich.)10,653

ALTERNATIVE LIABILITY
. wheel rim assemblies
. . unidentified product . . . (Mich.)10,710

AMENDMENT OF PLEADINGS
. foam insulation
. . joinder of defendant . . . (Alas.)9840
. . personal injury count . . . (Alas.)9840
. punitive damages claim
. . prejudicial error . . . (Fla.)9752
. relation-back
. . adding negligence counts . . . (Ill.)9956
. . naming DES manufacturer . . . (R.I.)9757

AMMUNITION
. grenade
. . *res ipsa loquitur* . . . (Tex.)10,984

AMUSEMENT RIDES
. cause of action
. . strict liability of operator . . . (N.H.)10,202
. damages
. . parental loss of child's society . . . (N.H.)10,202
. water slides
. . 11-year-old boy's assumption of risk . . . (Ga.)9988

ANIMAL FEED
. economic loss
. . calf growers . . . (Ill.)10,334
. . feed company business . . . (Ill.)10,334
. hog food
. . warnings and instructions . . . (Mich.)10,178

ANIMALS
. cattle
. . UCC preemption of earlier statute . . . (N.D.)9854

AIR

014—75
[E7386]

Illustration J

The first page of a "Current Topical Index" in *Products Liability Reports* (CCH)

CURRENT TOPICAL INDEX

References are to Paragraph (¶) Numbers.

See also "Topical Index to Prior Decisions" and "Topical Index."

Illustration K

A "Cumulative Index" page from *Products Liability Reports* (CCH)

4966 **Cumulative Index** 645 3-88

See also Cumulative Index to Current Decisions

From Compilation Paragraph No.			To Current Decisions Paragraph No.
4241	.19	Evidence of defective condition of tire as cause of accident (La Ct App)	11,336
	.25	Circumstantial evidence of manufacturing defect (Miss Sup Ct)	11,436
	.26	Excessiveness of punitive damages award against wheel rim assembly manufacturer (CA-8)	11,418
	.26	Sufficiency of evidence of tire defect as cause of accident (DC Mo)	11,523
	.33	Concert of action theory against tire rim component manufacturers (DC NY)	11,335
	.45	Proof of loss of earnings and manufacturing defect in tire blowout action (CA-5)	11,375
	.45	Worker's contributory negligence in multi-piece wheel explosion (CA-5)	11,128
4242		Government contractor defense in airplane crash action (DC NY)	11,022
	.10	Ejection seat as proximate cause of death (DC Mo)	11,196
	.10	Recovery of purely economic losses (DC NY)	11,386
	.10	Replacement of aircraft aft hanger as alteration of product (NY Sup Ct App Div)	11,274
	.10	Viability of implied warranty claim after adoption of strict liability (CA-11)	11,154
	.50	Application of government contractor defense in military air crash (DC Tex)	11,086
	.50	Application of government contractor defense (DC Pa)	11,195
	.50	Government contractor defense against defective helicopter engine (DC Pa)	11,441
	.50	Proof that defect in helicopter caused fatal crash (La Ct App)	11,281
	.70	Economic loss from fishing boat engine defect (DC NJ)	11,269
	.70	Economic loss recovery against manufacturer of boat engine (DC La)	11,517
	.70	Economic loss recovery for damage caused by defective components (CA-5)	11,526
	.70	Evidence of defectively designed throttle/shift control system (Cal Ct App)	11,251
	.70	Foreseeability of misuse in jet boat motor mount action (Iowa Ct App)	11,076
	.70	Use of large horsepower motor as misuse of boat steering mechanism (Miss Sup Ct)	11,380
4243	.30	Application of crashworthiness doctrine when jeep did not cause accident (CA-4)	11,193
	.30	Unreasonably dangerous requirement and proximate cause issues in pick-up truck action (Minn Ct App)	11,337
	.35	Application of consumer expectation test of defectiveness (Wash Sup Ct)	11,233
	.35	Continued viability of implied warranty in tort recovery (Wash Sup Ct)	11,233
	.35	Duty to warn in mini trail bike action (Wash Sup Ct)	11,233
	.35	Proximate cause of mini trail bike injuries (Wash Sup Ct)	11,233
	.50	Duty to warn passengers on one-person motorcycle (Ala Sup Ct)	11,385
	.50	Economic loss for damage to cam chain tensioner bolt (NY Sup Ct App Div)	11,206
	.50	Industry custom as determining manufacturer's duty to warn of windshield's aerodynamic dangers (Ala Sup Ct)	11,148
	.50	Lack of standard equipment crash bars as design defect (Ga Ct App)	11,467
	.50	Motorcycle without crash bars as unreasonably dangerous (Ill App Ct)	11,243
	.50	Necessity of proximate cause showing in injured rider's duty to warn claim (Ariz Ct App) Vac'd and rem'd (Ariz Sup Ct)	10,819; 11,531
	.50	Open and obvious danger of motorcycle without crash bars (Ill App Ct)	11,243
	.50	Operator's assumption of risk for inadequate headlamp beam and lack of crash bars (Ga Ct App)	11,467
	.50	Proof that motorcycle design caused injuries under risk benefit test (Cal Ct App)	11,348
	.50	Seller's liability for defective ATV (DC Ida)	11,118
4244	.15	Sufficiency of evidence of defect as cause of mobile home fire (Idaho Ct App)	11,174
4245	.50	Federal preemption of worker's action against railroad tank car maker (NJ Super Ct App Div)	11,400
4246	.15	Adequacy of dump trailer manufacturer's warning of power line contact dangers (Pa Super Ct)	11,394
	.15	Assumption of risk, design defect and foreseeability issues in driver's method of descent (La Ct App)	11,343
	.15	Comparative fault application to defective tank trailer walkboard (La Ct App)	11,155
	.15	Defective design of tanker-trailer (Ga Ct App)	11,246
	.15	Driver's assumption of open and obvious risk of falling from top of oil-slick trailer (DC Miss)	11,078
	.15	Manufacturing defect in tractor-trailer's rear wheel suspension system (DC Ky)	11,556
4248		Constitutionality of repose statute in posthole digger action (Tenn Sup Ct)	11,136
		Manufacturing defect in skidder-tractor and worker's comparative fault (CA-5)	11,557
		Repose statute as bar in hoist sheave guard injury action (CA-6)	11,127
	.10	Evidence of design defect in action for scissors-lift platform fall (Fla Dist Ct App)	11,132
	.10	Skyhook manufacturer's liability as successor corporation (DC Md)	11,200
	.10	Subsequent remedial measures by nonparty employer (Cal Ct App)	11,115
	.10	Worker's assumption of risk in executing hazardous maneuver (Colo Ct App)	11,222
	.20	Can conveyor system component manufacturer's duty to warn (Ohio Ct App)	11,333
	.20	Component suppliers' liability (NY Sup Ct App Div)	11,165
	.20	Component supplier's liability for completed conveyor (Wash Ct App)	11,305
	.25	Disregard of warnings as proximate cause of worker's injury (CA-6)	11,521
	.25	Ironworker's contribution to injuries from defective crane (CA-5)	11,266
	.25	Successor corporation's liability for crane (DC Colo)	11,063

¶ 4241

009—34

[E7388]

enable one to locate a known document directly without having to refer to the subject indexes. The most prevalent are tables of cases. Like the other indexes, the case tables are published in a layered format. The main case table is infrequently revised, but is updated by a "current" case table and perhaps a "latest additions" case table. Illustration L shows the beginning of the "Case Table" in *Products Liability Reports,* including a cross-reference to the beginning page of the "Current Case Table." Note that the table provides case citations not only in *Products Liability Reports* but in official and National Reporter System volumes, for decisions published in those sources. The table also provides information on subsequent developments in cases, such as denial of *certiorari.* In addition to the paragraph number of the case itself, the table provides references to the subject paragraphs where the headnotes are reprinted. Some services have not only case tables, but finding lists for statutes, regulations, rulings, agency directives, and other documents.

A much simpler indexing system is employed in a newsletter-type service, since there is not such a myriad of information of which to keep track. Illustration M shows a page from a semiannual index for BNA's *Product Safety & Liability Reporter,* providing references to pages on which news reports and primary source documents appear. Entries include the text of the decree shown above in Illustration C and the report of the filing of the class action suit shown in Illustration F.

4. PROMPT SUPPLEMENTATION

As noted earlier, the frequent supplementation of looseleaf services makes them the first available source for many legal documents. They appear long before the standard compilations of statutes, and are usually the first published source of both judicial and administrative decisions. Most court decisions are available sooner electronically on either WESTLAW or LEXIS, however, and administrative regulations are published first in the daily *Federal Register.*

Many of the major services include weekly releases, and may even distribute special issues to cover particularly important developments between releases. Other services are updated biweekly or monthly, and provide reasonably current awareness of new developments. A publication updated quarterly or annually is rarely current enough to be considered a true looseleaf service.

Because of the topical arrangement and layered indexing, the new material is usually easily accessible as soon as it is filed. Even though main indexes do not reflect new matter, each new release often includes a "Latest Additions" index incorporating coverage of that week's reported developments.

5. INSTRUCTIONS FOR USE

Looseleaf services are designed to fit particular subject areas, and are not all arranged the same. Some, like the major tax services, are

Illustration L

The first page of the "Case Table" in *Products Liability Reports* (CCH)

CASE TABLE

References are to paragraph (¶) numbers.

See also "Current Case Table" at page 381.

A

A. & A. MACHINERY CORP.: CITY MACHINE & MFG. CO. v.
(DC NY 1967) Products Liability Reports ¶ 5777 .... ¶ 1070.331

AAA MOBILE HOMES, INC.: FONDER v.
(Wis S Ct 1977) Products Liability Reports ¶ 8049 .... ¶ 3040.5101; 3340.1032

A. B. CHANCE CO.: HOFFMAN v.
(DC Pa 1972) Products Liability Reports ¶ 6742, 339 FSupp 1385
—2nd opin (DC Pa 1972) Products Liability Reports ¶ 6820 .... ¶ 3390.3901; 4030.3901

A. B. CHANCE CO.: HOGUE v.
(Okla S Ct 1978) Products Liability Reports ¶ 8356, 592 P2d 973 .... ¶ 4250.0031; 4360.3701

A. B. CHANCE CO.: SOUTH v.
(1981) Products Liability Reports ¶ 9134, 96 Wash2d 439, 635 P2d 728 .... ¶ 4360.4904

ACF INDUSTRIES, INC.: VANSKIKE v.
(CA-8 1981) Products Liability Reports ¶ 9127, 665 F2d 188 ...... ¶ 3310.4517; 4060.2601; 4170.263; 4242.455
—cert den (1982) 455 US 1000, 102 SCt 1632, 71 LEd2d 867

A. E. FINLEY & ASSOCIATES, INC. v. MEDLEY
(Fla Dist Ct App 1962) 14 Negligence Cases (2d) 732, 141 So2d 613 .... ¶ 1610.82

A. E. STALEY MFG. CO.: FIORENTINO v.
(Mass Ct App 1981) Products Liability Reports ¶ 8989, 416 NE2d 998 .... ¶ 1765.052

A. F. E. INDUSTRIES, INC.: SHANKS v.
(Ind S Ct 1981) Products Liability Reports ¶ 8905, 416 NE2d 833 .... ¶ 4095.1504; 4265.42

A. H. ROBINS CO., INC.: BALLEW v.
(CA-11 1982) Products Liability Reports ¶ 9403, 688 F2d 1325 .... ¶ 4380.11

A.H. ROBINS CO., INC.: CALDWELL v.
(DC Pa 1984) Products Liability Reports ¶ 10,067, 577 FSupp 796 .... ¶ 4380.3911

A.H. ROBINS CO., INC.: CONDON v.
(Neb S Ct 1984) Products Liability Reports ¶ 10,038 ... . ¶ 4380.2802

A.H. ROBINS CO., INC.: DAVIS v.
(NY S Ct App Div 1984) Products Liability Reports ¶ 9999, 473 NYS2d 182 .... ¶ 4380.3319

A. H. ROBINS CO., INC.: DORTCH v.
(1982) Products Liability Reports ¶ 9437, 59 OrApp 310, 650 P2d 1046 .... ¶ 4390.3803

A.H. ROBINS CO., INC.: FITZPATRICK v.
(1984) Products Liability Reports ¶ 9915, 99 AppDiv 2d 478, 470 NYS2d 415 .... ¶ 4380.3318

A.H. ROBINS CO., INC.: HANSEN v.
(1983) 113 Wis 2d 550, 335 NW2d 578 Products Liability Reports ¶ 9689
—after certification (CA-7 1983) Products Liability Reports ¶ 9761, 715 F2d 1265 .... ¶ 4380.5102

A.H. ROBINS CO., INC.: HILLIARD v.
(1983) Products Liability Reports ¶ 9828, 148 CalApp3d 374, 296 CalRptr 117 .... ¶ 3290.0502; 4095.0521; 4232.0503; 4362.0502

A. H. ROBINS CO., INC.: KNAYSI v.
(CA-11 1982) Products Liability Reports ¶ 9332, 679 F2d 1046 .... ¶ 4380.3312

A.H. ROBINS CO., INC.: KRISTELLER v.
(DC NY 1983) Products Liability Reports ¶ 9733, 560 FSupp 831 .... ¶ 380.3314

A.H. ROBINS CO., INC.: LINDSEY v.
(1983) Products Liability Reports ¶ 9506, 91 AppDiv 2d 150
—aff'd (NY Ct App 1983) *sub nom Martin v. Edwards Laboratories,* Products Liability Reports ¶ 9872, 469 NYS2d 973 .... ¶ 4380.33

A.H. ROBINS CO., INC.: MACK v.
(DC Ariz 183) Products Liability Reports ¶ 9941, 573 FSupp 149
—aff'd (CA-9 1985) Products Liability Reports ¶ 10,493 .... ¶ 4380.0301

A.H. ROBINS CO., INC.: NEUHAUSER v.
(DC Ind 1983) Products Liability Reports ¶ 9940, 573 FSupp 8 .... ¶ 4380.1503

A.H. ROBINS CO., INC.: PALMER v.
(Colo S Ct 1984) Products Liability Reports ¶ 10,085 .... ¶ 4232.0602

A.H. ROBINS CO., INC.: PHILPOTT v.
(CA-9 1983) Products Liability Reports ¶ 9713, 710 F2d 1422 .... ¶ 4390.3804

Products Liability Reports
013—47

AHR
[E7389]

Illustration M

A page from a *Product Safety & Liability Reporter* (BNA) semiannual index

2 (PSLR) PRODUCT SAFETY & LIABILITY REPORTER — Jan. 1-June 24, 1988

organized around particular code provisions. Others are arranged topically. Indexes may appear at the beginning of the first volume or the end of the last volume. The two-volume *Products Liability Reports* is a relatively simple service but can be rather confusing, even after several of its features have been described and illustrated. To make maximum use of a service, the user has to gain some familiarity with what it offers and where. A service's organizational scheme cannot always be learned by a superficial scanning of the contents, but every service includes an instructional section. This section, usually called "How to Use This Service," is located either in the first binder or with the main index. This brief guide describes the contents, the various means of access, and any special features. A few minutes with these instructions will inevitably repay itself in time saved and frustration avoided.

D. FINDING LOOSELEAF SERVICES BY SUBJECT

There are several ways to discover what looseleaf services may be available in a particular subject field. At the back of this volume, in Appendix E, there is a selected list of major services by subject. Because new services are frequently introduced, be aware that published lists can soon become out of date.

An annually revised list of looseleaf publications, which includes regularly supplemented services but also lists numerous other publications issued in post binders (including those supplemented infrequently or not at all), is: A.L. Eis, *Legal Looseleafs in Print* (Infosources Publishing). This list provides subscription and cost information as well as the frequency of supplementation. Entries are arranged alphabetically, and indexed by subject.

Pamphlets issued by the major looseleaf publishers list their services, and frequently include general instructions for use. BNA's *Reporter Services and Their Use* (1980) provides an extensive introduction to major BNA services, and describes the history and use of looseleaf services generally. WESTLAW and LEXIS directories of electronic services are both printed in pamphlet form and accessible online.

E. SUMMARY

Looseleaf services have a reputation for providing a current statement of the law, regularly and thoroughly updated. In 1987, a judicial nominee testifying before the Senate Judiciary Committee was asked why it took him ten years to announce that he had repudiated earlier controversial views. He responded: "Senator, I don't usually keep issuing my new opinions every time I change my mind. I just don't. If I revisit the subject, . . . I revisit it, but I don't keep issuing looseleaf services about my latest state of mind." [6]

6. Robert H. Bork, quoted in "Excerpts from Questioning of Judge Bork by Senate Committee Chairman," *N.Y. Times*, Sept. 16, 1987, at A27, A28.

The looseleaf service is still the most versatile form of legal publishing, combining a variety of primary legal sources, secondary editorial analysis and explanation, frequent supplementation, and a number of indexing approaches. A looseleaf service, whether printed or online, can save considerable time and steps in the research process. It is not, however, the only resource to be consulted in most research situations. After checking the latest developments in a service, one can use these leads to continue the research in other sources and tools. The statutes can be checked in an annotated code for notes of other decisions and for references to legislative history and to secondary sources. The decisions can be found in West reporters, and the digest topics and key numbers found there used for digest searching. Cases, statutes, and regulations should all be Shepardized to determine their current authority and to obtain later cases which have cited them. A variety of secondary sources (periodical articles, treatises, encyclopedias) can be explored. The looseleaf service can provide an excellent start, but invariably must be followed by research in the primary sources it cites, in citators for verification, and then in secondary sources for explanation and amplification.

F. ADDITIONAL READING

G.L. Richmond, *Federal Tax Research: Guide to Materials and Techniques,* 3d ed. (Foundation Press, 1987), Section L, "Looseleaf Services, Encyclopedias and Treatises." An in-depth discussion of services in the tax field.

Sherman, "The Company That Loves the U.S. Tax Code," *Fortune,* Nov. 26, 1984, at 58. An inside look at Commerce Clearing House, a leading looseleaf publisher.

Stern, "In Acquiring Looseleaf Services, Caveat Emptor," *Legal Times,* June 27, 1983, at 18. A practical consumer's guide to looseleaf publications generally.

Chapter 11

LEGAL PERIODICALS

A. INTRODUCTION

Most of the materials discussed in preceding chapters have been *primary* legal sources (cases, statutes, and administrative law) and their basic finding tools. We now turn to those descriptive or explanatory materials which are commonly designated *secondary* sources. Although several features of the primary sources in their published forms, such as the headnotes preceding reported decisions and the annotations following statutory code sections, are secondary in nature, they relate to the primary sources and have been treated as part of those sources. Looseleaf services, discussed in Chapter 10, are a combination of primary and secondary material. Now we move further from the primary sources, and deal with materials that are *entirely* secondary in nature, with only citations to, analysis of, or quotations from, the primary sources.

It is important to note that secondary source materials have two functions. They *provide citations to primary source material*. One can use secondary sources as finding tools to obtain references to decisions and statutes that may open fruitful lines of research. The second and most important function, at least from their authors' point of view, is to *describe, explain, or analyze issues of law or legal developments.* Periodical articles, encyclopedias and treatises can help one unfamiliar with a particular area of law by introducing basic concepts and terminology, and by summarizing and synthesizing numerous, sometimes contradictory, primary sources.

The narrative simplicity of some secondary sources may, however, carry disadvantages. Secondary sources which seek to provide clear and concise statements of law often oversimplify complicated concepts and describe as settled and fixed a body of law which is in fact unsettled and changing. Many text writers are more comfortable with order and certainty, while the law is in reality often disordered and uncertain. The researcher is cautioned to use secondary sources for what they can provide, but to beware of these dangers. Secondary materials also lack the authority of primary sources of law. The quality of the work or the author's reputation may give a particular text considerable recognition, but that is quite different from the authority carried by a primary legal source.

This chapter and the next explore several of the most commonly used secondary sources. Legal periodicals are discussed first, due to their importance in advocacy, research, and legal thinking generally.

B. TYPES OF LEGAL PERIODICALS

The best modern legal periodicals provide sophisticated analysis of current legal issues, historical research, results of empirical studies, interdisciplinary treatment of legal problems, and citations to primary and other secondary sources. Legal periodical literature ranges from the theoretical essays and serious scholarship in academic law reviews to the practical "how to do it" articles in bar journals. By their nature, purpose and format, legal periodicals fall into several distinct categories.

1. ACADEMIC LAW REVIEWS

The most serious and highly reputed legal periodicals are those produced at the major American law schools. Since the late 19th century, academic law reviews have been an increasingly important intellectual force. These journals provide the most thorough presentation of new legal developments and issues, and the most serious analysis of important decisions and statutes. They are cited extensively by the courts and by scholars, and provide researchers a wealth of primary citations.

Among scholarly periodicals, law school reviews are unique in serving an important educational function as well as providing the major forum for publication of scholarship and research. The field of law is unusual in that its most prestigious journals are edited by students who have not attained their first professional degree. These journals are so well accepted as pedagogical tools that every accredited law school in the United States publishes at least one review, despite the fact that most require substantial subsidy. The faculty and administration of every law school are concerned about the quality of the school's periodical, since the reputation of the school will be judged in part on the respect accorded its review.

The "law review experience" is considered a superb learning opportunity for student editors and contributors. Nor is the student role in editing the review merely nominal. At most schools, students exercise complete control over the acceptance of articles and rigorously maintain editorial standards, often ruffling professorial feathers by insisting upon changes in submitted manuscripts. The student editor exercises considerable authority in dealing with authors.

The student response to the prestige and educational benefit engendered by participation in law review editing has been to seek more opportunities for that experience. As a result, more and more schools have supported the creation of additional journals, which, unlike the school's first publication, focus on specific subject areas.[1] This development has allowed a greater number of students to participate in journal activities, but has also raised concerns about the proliferation of legal periodicals and the maintenance of their quality.

A distinctive characteristic of law school reviews is their uniformity of format. These journals typically consist of three sections. The first contains "lead articles," normally written by scholars or practitioners, and usually consisting of intensive explorations of somewhat narrow legal topics or issues. They carry extensive footnoting, sometimes with hundreds of citations,[2] the checking of which is part of the drudgery candidates for editorial positions must endure. These footnotes give the law reviews great value as case-finding tools. One might assume that the value of the text of a law review article would naturally outweigh the value of its footnotes, but the opposite is often true. Remember that a major goal of most legal research is finding primary sources on a specific issue. If you find a law review article on a research topic, you can utilize its footnote citations. An author and a team of law student editors may have worked months to gather citations to every relevant source. Even the most banal text may ride atop a mother lode of useful footnotes. Illustration A shows a typically footnote-laden law review page.

1. For example, in addition to the *California Law Review,* the University of California School of Law, Boalt Hall, publishes: *Berkeley Women's Law Journal, Ecology Law Quarterly, High Technology Law Journal, Industrial Relations Law Journal,* and *International Tax and Business Lawyer.*

2. Jacobs, "An Analysis of Section 16 of the Securities Exchange Act of 1934," 32 *N.Y.L.Sch.L.Rev.* 209 (1987), contains 4,824 footnotes.

Footnotes in legal writing are the subject of an extensive literature. *See* Austin, "Footnotes as Product Differentiation," 40 *Vand.L.Rev.* 1131 (1987), and works cited in its footnotes.

Illustration A

A sample law review page

California Law Review

VOL. 56 JANUARY 1968 No. 1

Symposium: Drugs and the Law

INTRODUCTION

Let the Earth bring forth Grass . . . .
Genesis 1:11

The drug drama has many scenes. Some people stage it as a cultural movement,[1] embodying its own language,[2] literature,[3] music,[4] art,[5] morals,[6] and dress.[7] To some it is the great religious phenomenon of our time,[8] to others but a passing passion for hedonism.[9] Still others consider

1 "Whatever their meaning and wherever they may be headed, the hippies have emerged on the U.S. scene . . . as a wholly new subculture . . . ." TIME, July 17, 1967, at 18.

2 As part of their lexicon of drugs, initiates use such terms as "dope" (signifying all drugs), "acid" (LSD), "smack" (heroin), "speed" (amphetamines), "roach" or "reefer" (marijuana cigarette), "goof balls" (barbiturates), and various terms for marijuana—"pot," "grass," "Acapulco Gold," "Panama Black," "Mex," and "Cambodian Red." See San Francisco Chronicle, Oct. 31, 1967, at 1, col. 2; Chapman, Oakland Tribune, Nov. 5, 1967, at 20-21 (Parade Section); San Francisco Chronicle, Nov. 1, 1967, at 1, col. 3.

3 *See, e.g.*, C. BAUDELAIRE, THE ESSENCE OF LAUGHTER AND OTHER ESSAYS, JOURNALS, AND LETTERS (1956); W. S. BURROUGHS, NAKED LUNCH (1959); TIBETAN BOOK OF THE DEAD (Evans-Wentz ed. 1957); A. GINSBERG, KADDISH AND OTHER POEMS, 1958-1960 (1961); A. HUXLEY, BRAVE NEW WORLD (1946); A. HUXLEY, DOORS OF PERCEPTION (1954); BHAGAVAD-GITA (F. Edgerton transl. 1944); J. KEROUAC, ON THE ROAD (1957); K. KESEY, ONE FLEW OVER THE CUCKOO'S NEST (1962); H. M. MCLUHAN, UNDERSTANDING MEDIA (1964); F. RABELAIS, GARGANTUA AND PANTAGRUEL (1928); J. R. R. TOLKIEN, THE HOBBIT (1937); A. WATTS, THE JOYOUS COSMOLOGY (1962).

4 Consider the music of the following groups, all of which have been "busted" at one time or another on charges of possessing hallucinogens: The Rolling Stones, The Grateful Dead, The Lovin' Spoonful, Canned Heat, and the Electric Flag. *See* Berkeley Barb, Oct. 6, 1967, at 2, col. 1; San Francisco Chronicle, Oct. 28, 1967, at 2, col. 4; San Francisco Chronicle. Oct. 23, 1967, at 3, col. 8; San Francisco Chronicle, Oct. 31, 1967, at 5, col. 6. The Beatles have also admitted to having used hallucinogenic drugs. San Francisco Chronicle, July 25, 1967, at 3, col. 7.

5 San Francisco Chronicle, July 16, 1967, § 6 (Magazine), at 26, col. 1.

6 Consider the communal, often promiscuous, sometime nudist life in such settlements as Morning Star in Northern California, Drop City near Trinidad, Colorado, Timothy Leary's colony of Millbrook in New York, and the Haight-Ashbury in San Francisco. See TIME, July 7, 1967, at 18, A-F. See also San Francisco Chronicle, Nov. 7, 1967, at 1, col. 5. To the extent that drug subculture localizes in isolated enclaves, it may be entitled to special legal consideration of the kind granted nudist colonies.

7 See TIME, July 7, 1967, at 18, A.F.

8 *See* note 50 *infra*.

9 San Francisco Chronicle, Nov. 2, 1967, at 1, col. 2.

Of course, the text of the article can be most valuable. It may help explain or clarify an issue or may provide useful analysis that can be cited as persuasive authority. Occasionally, new concepts or theories appear first in the periodical literature, are debated and developed there, and are later adopted by the courts or legislatures.[3]

The second component of most law reviews is the "Note and Comment" section, which contains student writing.[4] *Comments* are generally similar to articles in style and purpose, although usually narrower in focus. They have the same extensive footnoting as articles, and can thus also be used for primary source finding. As the work of students rather than experienced scholars, they have less impact as persuasive authority and often appear without author attribution.[5] *Notes* usually follow comments in most reviews; they tend to be shorter, and are frequently devoted to analysis of a single new case or statute.

The third section of academic law reviews is usually devoted to book reviews, although in most journals this component has declined in length and importance. The long delay in the publication of these book reviews diminishes their impact; occasionally the review is so late that the book has already gone out of print. Instead of traditional concise reviews limited to analysis of a book's merits, the modern trend is for book reviewers to use the forum for lengthy discussions of their own theories on a subject. Timeliness is not as essential for extended reviews of this type. A leading source of current reviews is the *Michigan Law Review,* which has since 1978 devoted one issue a year entirely to book reviews.

The law reviews which are generally open to articles on any legal topic do vary that pattern on occasion. "Symposium" issues, which focus on a particular topic or development, have become increasingly popular. (The page shown in Illustration A is introducing a symposium issue.) Some law reviews also publish annual surveys of legal developments in their states or circuits. Individual subjects are assigned to different authors, either to scholars or practitioners specializing in that field, or to students. The *Annual Survey of American Law* began as part of the *New York University Law Review,* but since 1963 has been issued as a separate publication. Although national in coverage, it has served as a model for similar state surveys.

There are a few subject-specialized academic journals that are not student-edited, or on which students play only a secondary role. These include the *American Journal of Legal History* at the Temple University School of Law, *Tax Law Review* at the N.Y.U. School of Law, and at

3. The classic example is Brandeis & Warren, "The Right to Privacy," 4 *Harv.L. Rev.* 193 (1890).

4. A few law school journals are entirely intramural, publishing *only* student work. These lack the prestige of those containing outside articles and are less likely to be cited as persuasive authority, but they provide a forum and an incentive for student writing.

5. Student comments in most reviews are signed at the end. Some reviews, however, have begun providing standard author attribution for student work. In 1986 the *Stanford Law Review* announced that it would begin citing student-written material by author rather than generically as "Comment" or "Note." President's Page, 39 *Stan.L.Rev.* 1 (1986).

least four journals at the University of Chicago Law School.[6] The professionally edited academic law journals are highly respected but few, and student-edited reviews remain the dominant source for legal scholarship.

Increasingly law school journals have come under attack for their sheer proliferation. Critics contend that the growing number of reviews and the publish-or-perish system of promotion and tenure for law faculty have produced a mass of superfluous and "unnecessary" literature. Many of these critics also assail the dry and ponderous style of law review prose. See, for example, this widely quoted comment from over fifty years ago:

> There are two things wrong with almost any legal writing. One is its style. The other is its content. That, I think, about covers the ground. . . . The average law review writer is peculiarly able to say nothing with an air of great importance. When I used to read law reviews, I used constantly to be reminded of an elephant trying to swat a fly.[7]

Despite such criticism the academic law reviews flourish, and remain among the most important resources for legal thinking.

Finally, a word must be said about the central role played by the major law reviews in establishing norms for the citation of the law. *A Uniform System of Citation*, 14th ed. (1986), the "Bluebook" which haunts the dreams of first-year law students, is produced jointly by the Columbia Law Review, the Harvard Law Review Association, the University of Pennsylvania Law Review, and the Yale Law Journal.[8] It decrees not only the telegraphic forms by which sources are generally cited, but general rules governing the use of introductory signals, the omission or inclusion of parenthetical information, typefaces, and a host of other matters.

Citation rules provide the uniformity that allows writers and readers to focus on substance rather than puzzle over form.[9] The rules are meant to clarify or simplify expression, but slavish devotion can lead instead to elaborate obfuscation. It is important to remember that the Bluebook rules govern writing *in law reviews*. In order that

6. *Crime and Justice: An Annual Review of Research; Journal of Law and Economics; Journal of Legal Studies;* and *Supreme Court Review*.

7. Rodell, "Goodbye to Law Reviews," 23 *Va.L.Rev.* 38 (1936).

8. *But see* Aside, "Don't Cry over Filled Milk: The Neglected Footnote Three to *Carolene Products*," 136 *U.Pa.L.Rev.* 1553, 1565–66 (1988) (suggesting that Bluebook is so mysterious that it could only have been produced by an advanced extraterrestrial race).

9. "Let us consider what purposes are served by having a system of citation forms rather than a free-for-all. There are four. The first is to spare the writer or editor from having to think about citation form; he memorizes the book of forms, or uses its index . . . . The second purpose, which is self-evident, is to economize on space and the reader's time. The third, which is in tension with the second, is to provide information. The fourth is to minimize distraction." Posner, "Goodbye to the Bluebook," 53 *U.Chi.L.Rev.* 1343, 1344 (1986). Appended to this essay at page 1353 is the first edition of *The University of Chicago Manual of Legal Citation*, an alternative, concise set of citation rules which has become known as the "Maroon Book."

students learn proper legal citation form, they also govern most written work in law school. In the real world of legal practice, however, other rules may apply. Some state courts, for example, have their own citation rules which conflict with the Bluebook. Generally, it is reasonable to deviate from Bluebook form for a purpose such as providing additional information to the reader. Using nonstandard form for no apparent reason is like using bad grammar; it just distracts readers and makes them think the writer don't know better.

Periodicals themselves are generally cited in a manner similar to primary sources, with the volume number preceding an abbreviation for the journal's name, followed by the beginning page number of the article and then the date. Thus the page shown in Illustration A is 56 *Calif.L.Rev.* 1 (1968). Some of the abbreviations for journal names are convenient and easy to decipher. Others can be bewildering to the uninitiated. The *Harvard Civil Rights—Civil Liberties Law Review* is cited, for example, as "Harv. C.R.–C.L. L. Rev." Standard abbreviations for full titles and individual words are listed in the Bluebook, and in dictionaries to be discussed in Chapter 13.

2. BAR ASSOCIATION PERIODICALS

Most national and state bar associations and many local and specialized bar groups publish journals. Although they primarily focus on the interests of their membership, some have achieved a broader audience and even a national reputation. While bar journals were once not considered scholarly literature, in recent years those devoted to particular types of practice have attained a respect equal to that of the specialized academic journals. Local bar journals have generally remained of interest only to practitioners in the region represented, or to researchers interested in a specific jurisdiction.

The numerous publications of the American Bar Association are the most important of the bar journals. The *American Bar Association Journal* publishes some articles on substantive legal topics, usually shorter and of a more popular nature than the law reviews, and contains much news about the Association, the legal profession generally, and national legal developments. Most American Bar Association sections also issue their own publications. Some, in the form of academic journals, are perhaps the most important and respected of bar association periodicals.[10] Others are in the form of newsletters or glossy magazines.

10. These include *Administrative Law Review* (Section of Administrative Law); *American Criminal Law Review* (Section of Criminal Justice); *Antitrust Law Journal* (Section of Antitrust Law); *Business Lawyer* (Section of Corporation, Banking and Business Law); *Family Law Quarterly* (Section of Family Law); *International Lawyer* (Section of International and Comparative Law); *Labor Lawyer* (Section of Labor and Employment Law); *Public Contract Law Journal* (Section of Public Contract Law); *Real Property, Probate and Trust Journal* (Section of Real Property, Probate and Trust Law); *Tax Lawyer* (Section of Taxation); *Tort & Insurance Law Journal* (Section of Tort and Insurance Practice); and *Urban Lawyer* (Section of Urban, State and Local Government Law).

State, county and city bar journals occasionally contain useful coverage of legal developments in their area, but, with a few exceptions, are of only local interest. Most notable is the *Record of the Association of the Bar of the City of New York,* which contains not only useful research articles and important bar addresses,[11] but also well-prepared, monthly bibliographies on topics of current interest.

Some of the periodicals of specialized bar associations, such as the *I.C.C. Practitioner's Journal* and the *Journal of the Patent Office Society,* often provide significant sources of information on legal developments in their subject fields. While typically less scholarly in tone than the academic law reviews, they can offer help to a researcher whose problem falls into an area of their expertise.

For many years bar publications were not included in the major indexes because they were not viewed as sufficiently "scholarly." Attitudes toward the proper balance of scholarly and practical information in legal practice and education have shifted, however, and the vast majority of these publications are now indexed and available to the researcher.

3. COMMERCIAL JOURNALS AND NEWSLETTERS

In the 19th century most major legal periodicals were commercially published. By the turn of the century, however, academic law journals had become dominant, and commercial publications became limited to a relatively few topical journals that fell into lower esteem. Several commercial periodicals, particularly those published by Commerce Clearing House, have survived as subject-specialized journals.

A more recent development in commercial periodical publication is the growth of numerous topical newsletters. As lawyer specialization has increased, publishers have found a market for journals in narrow, highly technical practice areas. Some newsletters are published by public interest groups, but most are high-priced commercial ventures. Issued weekly or monthly, newsletters focus on recent developments in specific areas, often providing brief abstracts of judicial, administrative and legislative actions. These publications serve primarily as a source of current information and can be very useful for the busy practitioner. Because of their brevity, transitory interest, and lack of serious analysis, they tend to have little permanent research value. Sometimes, however, they may be the most important source on new, relatively limited topics such as vaccine liability or asbestos poisoning. *Legal Newsletters in Print* (Infosources, annual) provides descriptions of and subscription information for well over 1,000 newsletters. It is arranged alphabetically, but a subject index provides access to newsletters on particular legal topics.

11. Justice Frankfurter's influential "Some Reflections on the Reading of Statutes," later reprinted in the *Columbia Law Review,* appeared first in 2 *Rec.A.B. City N.Y.* 213 (1947).

4. LEGAL NEWSPAPERS

Although legal newspapers have been in existence for a long time,[12] the most interesting recent addition to the field of commercial periodicals has been the development of national legal newspapers. Recognizing the size and affluence of the market represented by the legal profession in this country, publishers now issue three national legal news journals, two of which are weekly newspapers: the *National Law Journal* and *Legal Times.* Both have attracted considerable advertising and a substantial audience. The *National Law Journal* was launched in 1978 by the publisher of the highly successful daily, the *New York Law Journal,* and offers national coverage of the legal profession and legal issues generally. It features articles on prominent attorneys, noteworthy trends in litigation, professional controversies, and developments in both substantive and procedural law. Regular, continuing features keep readers posted on certain subject specialties, current periodical literature, and professional gossip. Special supplements also cover various aspects of the economics and technology of law practice.

Legal Times (formerly *Legal Times of Washington*) also began publication in 1978 and focuses on developments in Washington, D.C. It reports on administrative agencies, regulatory activities, and important rulings and regulations. It also covers legislative and judicial news, and is perhaps the most serious in tone of the three national periodicals.

The third national legal journal is the *American Lawyer,* which began in 1979. This monthly publication tends to concentrate on personalities, and has been called the *People* magazine of legal publishing. By focusing on exposés and lighter issues, it has attracted a wide readership. One of its most popular features is the annual issue in which law student summer clerks rate the law firms at which they've worked.

Local legal newspapers continue to serve the bench and bar of the larger metropolitan areas, primarily publishing dockets, calendars, and local court announcements. Some also include court orders, dispositions of motions, and decisions of lower courts which may not be reported elsewhere. They contain legal advertisements that are required by statute or court order to be published in local newspapers. The legal articles and essays published in a few of these newspapers have long been elusive, because they have not been covered by the *Index to Legal Periodicals.* The *Legal Resource Index,* however, covers several newspapers, including the three national tabloids discussed above and daily legal newspapers from Chicago, Los Angeles, and New York.

12. The *Legal Intelligencer,* published in Philadelphia for the bench and bar of that city since 1843, is the oldest continuously published legal newspaper in the country.

The following bibliography of legal newspapers published throughout the country lists them by city and state: A.R. Ashmore, "Checklist of Legal Newspapers in the United States," 74 *Law Libr.J.* 543 (1981).

C. ACCESS TO LEGAL PERIODICAL ARTICLES

The researcher usually approaches legal periodicals in search of a particular item or information about a particular topic. Since a very current article is often most useful, prompt and effective access is crucial. Although there have been shortcomings in legal periodical indexing in the past, the current situation is quite encouraging. The legal researcher can choose from a number of approaches, as competing publishers provide indexes in a variety of print and electronic formats, and citators and full-text databases offer alternative approaches to finding relevant articles.

Many standard legal research tools which are primarily designed for other purposes also carry references to periodical articles. Among these are many of the annotated codes, *ALR* annotations, encyclopedias, and some looseleaf services. These materials, discussed elsewhere in this book, can be very useful for finding relevant articles.

1. H.W. WILSON COMPANY INDEXES

For many years the only general index for legal periodical literature was the H.W. Wilson Company's *Index to Legal Periodicals.* Begun in 1908, *I.L.P.* indexes several hundred of the most important legal periodicals in the same format used in other familiar Wilson products such as *Readers' Guide to Periodical Literature. I.L.P.* indexes articles by author and subject, before 1961 in separate sections and since then merged into one alphabetical arrangement. Until 1983, however, full bibliographic information appeared *only* under subject entries. The author entries consisted merely of subject heading cross-references, each followed by the first letter of the article's title. This meant that a searcher looking for a specific article by an author had to turn to the appropriate subject heading and then scan its listings to find the title and location of the article. This inconvenience was only ameliorated by the fact that most searches *did* begin with the subject entry. Illustrations B–1 and B–2 show the nature of *I.L.P.* before 1983. Two of the author entries in Illustration B–1 provide references to a subject listing in Illustration B–2.

As legal literature grew more sophisticated, *I.L.P.* became the target of increasing criticism and was eventually challenged by a competitor in 1980. Prodded by market forces, the Wilson Company has extended coverage to a greater number and variety of journals and introduced new subject headings. In 1982 *I.L.P.* began using Bluebook form for all journal titles, and in 1983 author entries began providing full information on each article. One doing retrospective research must be aware that different *I.L.P.* volumes have different features, but

Illustration B–1

A page from the 1982–83 *Index to Legal Periodicals*

SUBJECT AND AUTHOR INDEX 53

BONDS—*Continued*

Demand debentures—must time to repay be allowed after demand for payment? Ronald Elwyn Lister Limited v. Dunlop Canada Limited [Judgment of May 31, 1952, S Ct Can (unrep)] A. M. Kaufman. 20 Alta L Rev 486-93 '82
Foreign financings by U.S. companies. W. B. Taylor. 41 N Y U Inst on Fed Tax 26.1-.26 '83
Impact of the Tax Equity and Fiscal Responsibility Act of 1982 on the treatment of zero coupon bonds. D. R. Nave. 60 Taxes 763-7 O '82
Industrial development bonds after TEFRA. G. J. Winston. 61 Taxes 20-7 Ja '83
Model simplified indenture. 38 Bus Law 741-813 F '83
Municipal antifraud liability under the federal securities laws upon issuance of tax-exempt industrial development bonds. J. R. Tandler. 24 Wash U J Urb & Contemp L 193-212 '83
New look of municipal bonds. M. E. Godwin. 68 ABA J 1580+ D '82
Original issue discount and the foreign investor—more uncertainty about United States Treasury bills. S. M. Shajnfeld. 36 Tax Lawyer 293-345 Wint '83
Recent developments on tax exemptions. B. P. Friel, N. P. Arkuss. 14 Urb Law 899-918 Fall '82
Tax allocation bonds in California after Proposition 13. A. P. Schuster, P. R. Recht. 14 Pac L J 159-79 Ja '83
Tax aspects of recent innovative financings—strategies for existing discount debt and for new securities. Recent innovative financing techniques—an addendum. D. H. Walter. 60-61 Taxes 995-1009 D '82; 154-5 Mr '83
Tax-exempt finance in Georgia—recent developments. H. S. Poe, J. W. Lowe. 18 Ga St B J 20-2+ Ag '81
United States savings bonds: the unique legal aspects of a little-understood investment. A. Levatino-Donoghue. 71 Ill B J 114-21 O '82

BONET RAMON, Francisco
Compar law (S)
Liab without fault (S)

BONFIELD, Arthur Earl
Adm law—State (S)
Adm proc—State (R)
Legal educ: teaching (S)

BONILLA, William
Judges (J)

BONNER, David
Deportation (C)
Terrorism (C)

BONNIE, Edward S.
Animals (E)
Corrupt prac (C)
Narcotics (C)

BONNIE, Richard J.
Crim law (D)
Crim responsibility (M)
Narcotics (D)

BONOVITZ, Sheldon M.
Corporate liquidation (T)
Inc tax: corp distr—US (T)

BONVENTRE, Vincent Martin
Self-incrimination (A)

BOOKER, Daniel I.
Antitrust law: sp industries, etc (A)
Labor law (A)

BOOKER, Keven
Aliens (A)
Colonies (A)
Const law—Australia (S)

BOOKSTAVER, David R.
Inherit taxes (S)

BOOTH, David
Magistrates and magistrates' cts (F)

BOOTH, Richard S.
Mines and minerals (I)
Pollution: air (I)

BOOTH, Robert T.
Oil and gas (R)

BOOTHBY, Lee
Discrimination (R)
Freedom of relig (R)

BORCHARD, William M.
Copyright (C)
Entertainment (P)

BORDEN, Arthur M.
Corp: consol and merger (G)
Securities: state reg (G)

BORDONI, R. Daniel
Labor law (D)

BORJAS, George J.
Adm agencies—US (P)
Discrimination (P)
Politics (P)
Wages (P)

BORK, Robert H.
Antitrust law (I)

BORKOWSKI, Andrew
Damages (A)
Personal injuries (A)
Wills (A)

BORNSTEIN, Tim
Ind arb (O)

BOROWITZ, Albert I.
Antitrust law (S)
Legal hist (P)

BOROWSKY, Philip
Damages (P)
Verdicts (P)

BORRIE, Gordon
Adm law (R)
Antitrust law: for (C)
Consumer protect (L)
Trade reg (L)

BOSANAC, Paul
Collective bargaining (C)

BOSHKOFF, Douglass G.
Bankruptcy: discharge (L)
Compar law (L)

BOSS, Amelia H.
Equipment leasing (L)
Secured trans (L)

BOSS, Hugh M.
Corp: consol and merger (S)
Real property (S)

BOSSONS, John
Pub finance (G)

BOST, Thomas G.
Inc tax: evasion and avoidance—US (I)
Real property (I)

BOTEIN, Michael
Antitrust law: sp industries, etc (N)
Radio and tv (C)

BOTHE, Michael
Legal educ: teaching (T)
War (A)

BOUCHARD, Philip W.
Biog (Thompson)

BOULTBEE, Jack
Tax shelters (T)

BOUNDARIES
Beagle Channel arbitration [(1978) 17 ILM 634] D. W. Greig. 7 Austl Y B Int'l L 332-85 '81
Boundary and resource issues: modes de règlement des différends entre le Canada et les États-Unis en matière de frontières et de ressources maritimes. C. C. Emanuelli. 1 Can-U S L J 36-66 Summ '78
Criminal law: sailing away with the fourth amendment: Morales v. State, 407 So. 2d 321 (Fla) 12 Stetson L Rev 837-47 Wint '83
Critique of boundary provisions in the Law of the Sea Treaty. H. D. Hedberg. Reply. V. E. McKelvey; Rejoinder. H. D. Hedberg. 12 Ocean Dev & Int'l L 337-48 '83

Illustration B–2

Another *I.L.P.* page from 1982–83, showing cross-references from author entries in Illustration B–1

SUBJECT AND AUTHOR INDEX 321

NAMES

Equal protection of the sexes in Kentucky: the effect of the Hummeldorf [Hummeldorf v. Hummeldorf, 616 S W 2d 794 (Ky)] decision on a woman's right to choose her surname. 9 N Ky L Rev 475-98 '82

NAMIBIA

Namibia and Zimbabwe: decolonisation and the rule of international law. R. H. F. Austin. 35 Current Legal Prob 203-32 '82

Question of Namibia. P. D. Maynard. 6 W I L J 245-55 O '82

NAMIBIA (South West Africa)

Settlement of the Namibian dispute: the United States role in lieu of U.N. sanctions. 14 Case W Res J Int'l L 543-71 Summ '82

NAPIER, B. W.

Employer and employee (I)
Injunctions (I)

NAPIER, Brian

Employer and employee (D)

NAPIER, W. G. F.

Ombudsman (N)
Social welfare (O)

NARCOTICS –

Analysis of federal drug-related civil forfeiture. 34 Me L Rev 435-58 '82

Anglo-American cooperation in the suppression of drug smuggling. J. Siddle. 31 Int'l & Comp L Q 726-47 O '82

Assessment of the effects of marijuana decriminalization with minimal resources. R. R. Clayton. 10 Contemp Drug Prob 447-61 Wint '81

Attempting to have in possession. K. E. Dawkins. 5 Otago L Rev 172-81 '81

Brennan [Brennan v. Illinois Racing Bd. 245 N E 2d 881 (Ill)] revisited: trainer's responsibility for race horse drugging. R. H. Garrison, J. N. Klein. 70 Ky L J 1103-30 '81/'82

Conceptual issues in marijuana decriminalization research. H. B. Kaplan. 10 Contemp Drug Prob 365-82 Wint '81

Constitutional law—criminal procedure—searches and seizures—police officers who have probable cause to believe a stopped automobile contains contraband do not need a warrant to search all containers and packages discovered within the automobile that may conceal the contraband.—United States v. Ross, 102 S Ct 2157. 51 U Cin L Rev 897-912 '82

Constitutional law—overbreadth and vagueness—in a pre-enforcement challenge, a drug paraphernalia law which does not reach constitutionally protected conduct and which is reasonably clear in its application will pass constitutional muster. Village of Hoffman Estates v. Flipside, Hoffman Estates, Inc., 102 S Ct 1186. 60 U Det J Urb L 338-48 Wint '83

Constitutionality of anti-drug paraphernalia laws—the smoke clears. 58 Notre Dame L Rev 833-62 Ap '83

Constructive possession of illegal drugs: the inferential leap from joint occupancy to joint control: Brown v. State, 412 So. 2d 420 (Fla) 12 Stetson L Rev 512-25 Wint '83

Corrupt Horse Racing Practices Act of 1980: a threat to state control of horse racing. E. S. Bonnie. 70 Ky L J 1159-79 '81/'82

Criminal forfeiture: attacking the economic dimension of organized narcotics trafficking. 32 Am U L Rev 227-55 Fall '82

Criminal procedure—fourth amendment—warrantless earch of any container found in automobile held permissible. United States v. Ross, 102 S Ct 2157. 66 Marq L Rev 161-77 Fall '82

Crucial variables in marijuana decriminalization research. J. A. Inciardi. 10 Contemp Drug Prob 383-90 Wint '81

D.E.A. drug courier profile: history and analysis. P. S. Greene. B. W. Wice. 22 S Tex L J 261-85 '82

Death of a headshop: Texas' new Drug Paraphernalia Act. 34 Baylor L Rev 247-67 Spr '82

Decriminalization of marijuana—a brief overview of research-relevant policy issues. R. C. Petersen; The meaning of "decriminalization": a review of the law. R. J. Bonnie; Marijuana decriminalization: the processes and prospects of change. E. Josephson; A review of the effects of the decriminalization of marijuana. D. Maloff; Critique of marijuana decriminalization research. W. R. Cuskey; Trends in cannabis use among American states with different and changing legal regimes, 1972-77. W. Saveland, D. F. Bray. 10 Contemp Drug Prob 363-361 Fall '81

Design features for an optimal assessment of the effects of marijuana decriminalization. L. D. Johnston. 10 Contemp Drug Prob 463-80 Wint '81

Drug paraphernalia laws: clearing a legal haze. 13 Cum L Rev 273-306 '82/'83

Drug trafficking at airports—the judicial response. 36 U Miami L Rev 91-114 N '81

First century: the history of nonmedical opiate use and control policies in Canada, 1870-1970. R. Solomon, M. Greene. 20 U W Ont L Rev 307-36 D '82

Head shops—legitimate governmental interest in regulating the sale of drug paraphernalia receivers judicial recognition—Village of Hoffman Estates v. Flipside, Hoffman Estates, Inc. 102 S Ct 1186, 5 Campbell L Rev 231-47 Fall '82

How open are open fields? United States v. Oliver [686 F 2d 356] 14 U Tol L Rev 133-63 Fall '82

Implementation of international narcotics control: the struggle against opium cultivation in Pakistan. 6 B C Int'l & Comp L Rev 199-241 Wint '83

Judicial schizophrenia: an involuntarily confined mental patient's right to refuse antipsychotic drugs. 51 UMKC L Rev 74-106 Fall '82

Multivariate view of marijuana decriminalization research. P. M. Bentler. 10 Contemp Drug Prob 419-33 Wint '81

Possession of minute drug quantity. J. K. Bentil. 126 S J 388-90 Je 11 '82

Potential problems and suggested solutions in marijuana decriminalization research: a longitudinal view. R. T. Campbell. 10 Contemp Drug Prob 435-46 Wint '81

Quasi-experimentation: an introduction to its priority questions and mechanics. T. D. Cook, R. B. Straw. 10 Contemp Drug Prob 391-418 Wint '81

Search and seizure—airport drug seizures: how the federal courts strike the fourth amendment balance. 58 Notre Dame L Rev 663-82 F '83

NASH, Martin J.

Inc tax: partnerships—US (N)

NATBONY, William

Inc tax: trusts—US (C)
Inherit taxes (C)

NATHAN, Charles M.

Corp: consol and merger (L)
Securities: tender offers (L)

NATHAN, Max, Jr

Compar law (F)
Factors (F)
Secured trans (F)

NATHANSON, David C.

Taxation—Can (R)

NATION, Rosemary

Oil and gas (W)

NATIONAL defense

Critique of United States nuclear deterrence theory. K. C. Kennedy. 9 Brooklyn J Int'l L 35-66 Wint '83

"D" notice system. J. Jaconelli. 1982 Pub L 37-42 Spr '82

NATIONAL PARKS. SEE PARKS AND MONUMENTS

NATIONAL SECURITY. SEE SUBVERSIVE ACTIVITIES

NATIONALITY. SEE CITIZENS AND CITIZENSHIP

NATIONALIZATION OF INDUSTRY. SEE EXPROPRIATION AND NATIONALIZATION

NATIVE law

See also
Indians

Indian and Inuit family law and the Canadian legal system. B. W. Morse. 8 Am Indian L Rev 199-257 '80

Jurisdiction: conflicts of law and the Indian reservation: solutions to problems in Indian civil jurisdiction. 8 Am Indian L Rev 861-86 '80

NATURAL DEATH. SEE RIGHT TO DIE

NATURAL GAS. SEE OIL AND GAS

there is little doubt that today's index is a much improved research tool. Illustration C shows the form of entry in today's *Index to Legal Periodicals.*

Besides the main author/subject index, every volume also has an alphabetical Table of Cases, listing decisions which have been the subjects of law review notes. Volumes since 1980 contain a similar Table of Statutes as well. These tables do not list *every* article which discusses a particular decision or statute, and do not include the titles of those listed. They are useful, however, when the focus of research is a specific primary source. *I.L.P.* also contains a list of book reviews, arranged by authors of the books reviewed. Illustration D shows a page from the Table of Cases in a recent *I.L.P.* volume.

I.L.P. cumulated into triennial volumes until 1979, and has been issued in annual volumes since then. These volumes are supplemented by pamphlets, issued every month except September, which cumulate quarterly. In the front of every volume and pamphlet are lists of abbreviations used and journals indexed. A separate volume, *Index to Legal Periodicals: Thesaurus* (1988), is an extensive list of subject headings, with cross-references from headings not used in the index and a variety of broader, narrower and related terms listed under headings the index does use. The *Thesaurus* can be useful for clarifying a search topic or suggesting related avenues of research.

For coverage beginning in 1981, the same information in the published index is also available electronically, both online and in CD–ROM (compact disc read-only memory). Access to *I.L.P.* is available through both WESTLAW and LEXIS, and as part of WILSONLINE, H.W. Wilson's online research system. The online versions of *I.L.P.* offer much greater speed and flexibility than the printed volumes and pamphlets, although searchers usually are billed for each use. A researcher trained in WESTLAW or LEXIS searching techniques can easily find all recent articles combining two research interests, for example, or all articles with a particular word in their titles.

I.L.P. is available in LEXIS's LAWREV and LEXREF libraries, and as the ILP database on WESTLAW. These databases are currently not available to law school libraries on their discounted subscriptions, but they are accessible to law firms and other commercial subscribers. WILSONLINE provides the same information but uses a different system of searching techniques. It also is not widely used in law school libraries, although a number of law firms and general research libraries are subscribers.

The CD–ROM version of *I.L.P.* is part of H.W. Wilson's WILSONDISC program. This version allows much the same speed and ease as computerized research, without the expense of online search charges. Several approaches to searching are available, for novice and experienced users. A new disc updating and cumulating index coverage is issued quarterly (not monthly), but the WILSONDISC system can

Illustration C

A page from the 1987–88 *Index to Legal Periodicals*

SUBJECT AND AUTHOR INDEX 435

Narcotics—*cont.*
Substance abuse and the law: a symposium. Drug testing in sports. S. F. Brock, K. M. McKenna; Drug testing of athletes and the United States constitution: crisis and conflict. J. O. Cochran; Chemical dependency in the legal profession: Oregon's response. N. Robart; The cocaine impaired lawyer. R. P. O'Keefe; Psychiatric and chemical dependency treatment of minors: the myth of voluntary treatment and the capacity to consent. B. Balos, I. Schwartz; The minimum drinking age for young people: an observation. M. P. Rosenthal. 92 *Dick. L. Rev.* 505-663 Spr '88
Synthetic drugs legislation: broadening the classifications by defining "controlled substance analog" as a percentage of common structural elements. 64 *U. Det. L. Rev.* 775-94 Summ '87
Trends and issues in juvenile confinement for psychiatric and chemical dependency treatment. M. Jackson-Beeck, I. M. Schwartz, A. Rutherford. 10 *Int'l J.L. & Psychiatry* 153-65 '87
The war on drugs: in search of a breakthrough: a symposium. Introduction: in search of a breakthrough in the war on drugs. S. Wisotsky; Breaking the impasse in the war on drugs: a search for new directions. N. E. Zinberg; Towards new perspectives on drug control: a negotiated settlement to the war on drugs. D. A. J. Richards; Why the drug war is unstoppable. T. Szasz; Vice policy in a liberal society: an analysis of the impasse in the war on drugs. M. A. R. Kleiman; A proposal for regulation and taxation of drugs. L. Grinspoon; The war on drugs: predicting the status quo. J. Kaplan; The national strategy—an overview. L. Kellner; Roundtable discussion and questions from the audience. Coda: what impasse? A skeptical view. P. Reuter; Milestones in the war on drugs. Writings by contributors: a selective listing. Other suggested reading: an essential bibliography on drug law and policy. 11 *Nova L. Rev.* 891-1052 Spr '87

Nardolilli, Michael A.
Fire now, prove it later: the Merit Systems Protection Board's new hearing regulations as a toothless shark. 34 *Fed. B. News & J.* 206-12 Je '87

Nardulli, Peter F.
The societal costs of the exclusionary rule revisited. 1987 *U. Ill. L. Rev.* 223-39 '87

Nash, Brian T.
Software industry disputes: an analysis of resolution methodologies. 2 *Software L.J.* 29-76 Wint '87

Nasseri, Kurosh
The multimodal convention. 19 *J. Mar. L. & Com.* 231-60 Ap '88

Natale, Richard
Going Hollywood: writing screenplays, producing TV shows, dominating the boardrooms—lawyers are suddenly center stage. 7 *Cal. Law.* 39-43 S '87

Natelson, Robert G.
Comments on the historiography of condominium: the myth of Roman origin. 12 *Okla. City U.L. Rev.* 17-58 Spr '87
Mending the social compact: expectancy damages for common property defects in condominiums and other planned communities. 66 *Or. L. Rev.* 109-52 '87

Nathan, Irvin B.
Strengthening the independent counsel law requires judicial review of the Attorney General's decisions; by I. B. Nathan, D. P. Gersch. 25 *Am. Crim. L. Rev.* 199-227 Fall '87

Nathan, John A.
Alabama's interstate banking legislation. 49 *Ala. Law.* 80-5 Mr '88

Nathan, Rabindra S.
Controlling the puppeteers: reform of parent-subsidiary law in New Zealand. 3 *Canterbury L. Rev.* 1-34 '86

Nathan, Richard
The enforceability of post-employment noncompetition agreements formed after at-will employment has commenced: the "afterthought" agreement; by J. H. Leibman, R. Nathan. 60 *S. Cal. L. Rev.* 1465-577 S '87

National defense
Some observations on the attitude of west-European governments to the development of defensive weapons in outer space. D. Goedhuis. 15 *J. Space L.* 101-17 '87

National Highway Traffic Safety Administration (U.S.) *See* United States. National Highway Traffic Safety Administration

National Labor Relations Board (U.S.) *See* United States. National Labor Relations Board

National parks *See* Parks and monuments

National security
Alien departure control—a safeguard for both the exercise of fundamental human rights and national security. 28 *Va. J. Int'l L.* 159-93 Fall '87
'Allo, 'allo, 'allo, who's in charge here then?. P. Gill. 9 *Liverpool L. Rev.* 189-201 '87
Current United States economic policy and national security considerations in the export of technology to the People's Republic of China. 23 *Willamette L. Rev.* 813-42 Fall '87
Entick v. Carrington [(1765) 19 St. Tr. 1030] in the 1980s. C. Gearty. 137 *New L.J.* 470-2 My 22 '87
Failures in the interagency administration of national security export controls. 19 *Law & Pol'y Int'l Bus.* 537-77 '87
Judicial review, the royal prerogative and national security. C. F. Forsyth. 36 *N. Ir. Legal Q.* 25-32 Spr '85
Keeping secrets: the Church Committee, covert action, and Nicaragua. 25 *Colum. J. Transnat'l L.* 601-45 '87
National security: muting the "vital criticism". A. Lewis. 34 *UCLA L. Rev.* 1687-702 Je/Ag '87
National security vs. access to computer databases: a new threat to freedom of information. J. J. Berman. 2 *Software L.J.* 1-15 Wint '87
Le nouveau mandat d'enquête créé par la Loi sur le Service canadien du renseignement de sécurité. D. A. Bellemare. 16 *Rev. Gén.* 335-61 '85
Parliamentary privilege, Zircon and national security. A. W. Bradley. 1987 *Pub. L.* 488-95 Wint '87
Prior restraints: the Pentagon Papers Case [New York Times Co. v. United States, 91 S. Ct. 2140] revisited. S. Godofsky, H. M. Rogatnick. 18 *Cum. L. Rev.* 527-55 '88
Rethinking the state secrets privilege. C. Brancart. 9 *Whittier L. Rev.* 1-26 '87
Statutory improvements to the foreign availability process for high technology national security export controls. 27 *Va. J. Int'l L.* 575-602 Spr '87
United States dependence on imports of four strategic and critical minerals: implications and policy alternatives. G. K. Jones. 15 *B.C. Envt'l Aff. L. Rev.* 217-94 Wint '88
The value of a secret: compensation for imposition of secrecy orders under the Invention Secrecy Act. G. L. Hausken. 119 *Mil. L. Rev.* 201-55 Wint '88

National self-determination
The independence of Western Samoa—some conceptual issues. A. Quentin-Baxter. 17 *Vict. U. Well. L. Rev.* 345-72 S '87
La politica del derecho internacional de descolonizacion en el caso de Puerto Rico. C. Rivera Lugo. 25 *Rev. D.P.* 55-78 Jl/O '85
The process of self-determination and Micronesia's future political status under international law. N. Hirayasu. 9 *U. Hawaii L. Rev.* 487-532 Fall '87
The right to rebel. T. Honoré. 8 *Oxford J. Legal Stud.* 34-54 Spr '88
Settlement in the Middle East: what would it look like and can we get there from here? a roundtable discussion. 77 *Am. Soc'y Int'l L. Proc.* 271-87 '83

National territory
See also
Boundaries
Military occupation
Territorial waters

Nationality *See* Citizenship

Nationalization of industry *See* Expropriation and nationalization

Native Americans *See* Indians

Native peoples *See* Indigenous peoples

NATO *See* North Atlantic Treaty Organization

Natter, Raymond
Glass-Steagall Act reform: the next banking issue on the Congressional agenda. 35 *Fed. B. News & J.* 185-91 My '88

Natural death *See* Right to die

Natural gas *See* Oil and gas

Natural law
See also
Liberty
Algernon Sidney on public right. E. Dumbauld. 10 *U. Ark. Little Rock L.J.* 317-38 '87/'88
The conflict between reason and will in the legislation of surrogate motherhood. D. De Marco. 32 *Am. J. Juris.* 23-46 '87
The constitution and the Declaration of Independence: natural law in American history. E. J. Melvin. 31 *Cath. Law.* 35-49 Wint '87

Illustration D

A table of cases in the *Index to Legal Periodicals*

TABLE OF CASES

324 Liquor Corp. v. Duffy, 107 S. Ct. 720
27 *Washburn L.J.* 184-93 Fall '87

A

A.A. Sales, Inc.; Crumb v., 188 U.S.P.Q. 447 (N.D. Cal. 1975), rev'd per memorandum, No. 75-3265 (9th Cir. Mar. 15, 1977)
11 *Colum.-VLA J.L. & Arts* 635-68 Summ '87
A. Bottacchi S.A. De Navegacion; Schiffahrtsgesellschaft Leonhardt & Co. v., 732 F.2d 1543
36 *Ala. L. Rev.* 663-99 Wint '85
A.E. Dayton Servs. Ltd.; Polkey v., [1987] 3 W.L.R. 1153; 1987 Indus. R.L.R. 503
47 *Cambridge L.J.* 21-4 Mr '88
17 *Indus. L.J.* 41-4 Mr '88
A.G. Sec. v. Vaughan, The Times, Dec. 28, 1987
104 *Law Q. Rev.* 173-5 Ap '88
A. J. Dunning & Sons (Shopfitters) Ltd. v. Sykes & Son (Poole) Ltd., [1987] 2 W.L.R. 167
1987 *Conv. & Prop. Law. (n.s.)* 214-17 My/Je '87
A.T. Massey Coal Co. v. International Union, United Mine Workers, 799 F.2d 142
89 *W. Va. L. Rev.* 825-35 Spr '87
Abbott v. Burke, 477 A.2d 1278 (N.J.)
40 *Rutgers L. Rev.* 193-239 Fall '87
Abbott Laboratories; Martin v., 689 P.2d 368 (Wash.)
55 *Miss. L.J.* 195-211 Mr '85
Abbott Laboratories; McCormack v., 617 F. Supp. 1521
29 *Ariz. L. Rev.* 155-64 '87
Abdulmajid; Wilhelmina Models v., 413 N.Y.S.2d 21
17 *Golden Gate U.L. Rev.* 169-96 Summ '87
ABKCO Music, Inc. v. Harrisongs Music, Ltd., 722 F.2d 988
5 *Loy. Entertainment L.J.* 245-9 '85
Abourezk v. Reagan, 785 F.2d 1043
21 *Cornell Int'l L.J.* 147-79 Wint '88
62 *N.Y.U. L. Rev.* 149-200 Ap '87
Abrams; McCray v., 750 F.2d 1113
8 *Crim. Just. J.* 147-57 '85
55 *Miss. L.J.* 389-411 Je '85
Abramson; FBI v., 102 S. Ct. 2054
86 *Mich. L. Rev.* 620-45 D '87
Abston v. Woodard, 437 So. 2d 1261 (Ala.)
36 *Ala. L. Rev.* 355-72 Fall '84
Ackermann v. Levine, 788 F.2d 830
11 *Suffolk Transnat'l L.J.* 159-71 Fall '87
Adams; Mennonite Bd. of Missions v. 103 S. Ct. 2706
36 *Ala. L. Rev.* 969-1002 Summ '85
48 *La. L. Rev.* 535-93 Ja '88
89 *W. Va. L. Rev.* 961-96 Summ '87
Adamson v. Ricketts, 789 F.2d 722
17 *Golden Gate U.L. Rev.* 77-88 Spr '87
Adeeb, In re, 787 F.2d 1339
7 *Rev. Litigation* 97-112 Fall '87
Adickes v. Kress, 90 S. Ct. 1598
6 *Rev. Litigation* 227-62 Summ '87
Administrative Hearing Comm'n; Brown Group v., 649 S.W.2d 874 (Mo.)
44 *J. Mo. B.* 111-17 Mr '88
Adolf; State ex rel. Honda Research and Dev. Co., Ltd. v., 718 S.W.2d 550 (Mo.)
52 *Mo. L. Rev.* 715-32 Summ '87
Adolph; State of Missouri ex rel. Wichita Falls Gen. Hosp. v., 728 S.W.2d 604 (Mo.)
92 *Dick. L. Rev.* 393-9 Wint '88
Aetna v. Lavoie, 106 S. Ct. 1580
9 *Am. J. Trial Advocacy* 439-58 Spr '86
AFGE, Local 916; Pham v. 799 F.2d 634
40 *Okla. L. Rev.* 361-406 Fall '87
AFSCME v. Washington, 770 F.2d 1401
29 *How. L.J.* 669-82 '86
Aguilar v. Felton, 105 S. Ct. 3232
50 *Alb. L. Rev.* 811-42 Summ '86
31 *Cath. Law.* 77-98 '87
4 *Hum. Rts. Ann.* 239-68 Fall '86
17 *J.L. & Educ.* 1-33 Wint '88
Aguillard; Edwards v., 107 S. Ct. 2573
21 *Akron L. Rev.* 255-66 Fall '87
101 *Harv. L. Rev.* 189-99 N '87
21 *J. Mar. L. Rev.* 449-53 Wint '88
62 *Tul. L. Rev.* 261-7 N '87
22 *U. Rich. L. Rev.* 149-82 Wint '88
34 *Wayne L. Rev.* 265-302 Fall '87
Ahlers, In re, 794 F.2d 388
63 *N.D.L. Rev.* 405-28 '87
23 *Tulsa L.J.* 37-76 Fall '87
Ahmanson; Heckman v., 214 Cal. Rptr. 177
18 *Tex. Tech. L. Rev.* 1083-119 '87
Aillon v. State, 363 A.2d 49 (Conn.)
61 *Conn. B.J.* 215-30 Ag '87
Air Crash Disaster near New Orleans, Louisiana on July 9, 1982, In re, 821 F.2d 1147
62 *Tul. L. Rev.* 813-20 Mr '88
Air France v. Saks, 105 S. Ct. 1338
10 *Suffolk Transnat'l L.J.* 361-75 Spr '86
Air Line Pilots Ass'n, Int'l v. United Air Lines, Inc., 614 F. Supp. 1020
15 *Transp. L.J.* 435-51 Summ '87
Ake v. Oklahoma, 105 S. Ct. 1087
1987 *Army Law.* 15-23 O '87
29 *How. L.J.* 609-24 '86
55 *Miss. L.J.* 287-328 Je '85
12 *Okla. City U.L. Rev.* 385-413 Summ '87
20 *U. Mich. J.L. Ref.* 907-42 Spr '87
Akron Center for Re-productive Health v. Rosen, 633 F. Supp. 1123
25 *J. Fam. L.* 816-26 '86/'87
Aktion Maritime Corp. of Liberia v. Kasmas & Bros. Ltd. (The Aktion), [1987] 1 Lloyd's L.R. 283
1987 *Lloyd's Mar. & Com. L.Q.* 410-14 N '87
AKZO Chemie BV; Engineering and Chem. Supplies (Epsom and Gloucester) Ltd. v., 28 O.J. E. Comm. (No. L 374) 1
17 *Ga. J. Int'l & Comp. L.* 271-302 Summ '87
Al-Kandari v. J. R. Brown & Co., [1987] 2 W.L.R. 469
103 *Law Q. Rev.* 346-53 Jl '87
Al Tech Specialty Steel Corp. v. United States, 651 F. Supp. 1421
11 *Fordham Int'l L.J.* 208-31 Fall '87
Alabama; Heath v., 106 S. Ct. 433
38 *Ala. L. Rev.* 153-70 Fall '86
63 *Chi.-Kent L. Rev.* 175-88 '87
9 *Crim. Just. J.* 147-63 Fall '86
Alabama; Swain v. 85 S. Ct. 824
15 *Am. J. Crim. L.* 263-302 Spr '88
Alad Corp.; Ray v., 560 P.2d 3 (Cal.)
10 *Am. J. Trial Advocacy* 393-407 Fall '86
Alameda-Contra Costa Transit Dist.; Wirta v., 434 P.2d 982 (Cal.)
10 *Comm/Ent L.J.* 829-58 Spr '88
Alan R. Pulver & Co.; County Personnel (Employment Agency) Ltd. v., [1987] 1 All E.R. 289
1988 *Conv. & Prop. Law. (n.s.)* 67-70 Ja/F '88
Albers; Whitley v., 106 S. Ct. 1078
14 *New Eng. J. on Crim. & Civ. Confinement* 155-68 Wint '88
32 *Wash. U.J. Urb. & Contemp. L.* 231-45 Summ '87
Albert v. Yale Univ., No. 232497 (Conn. Super. Ct. filed Oct. 25, 1984)
31 *St. Louis U.L.J.* 875-901 O '87
Alcon (Puerto Rico) Inc., 32 FERC ¶ 61, 247 (1985)
7 *Energy L.J.* 101-9 '86
Aldon Accessories Ltd. v. Spiegel, Inc., 738 F.2d 548
10 *Comm/Ent L.J.* 591-621 Wint '88
62 *N.Y.U. L. Rev.* 373-403 My '87
135 *U. Pa. L. Rev.* 1281-320 Je '87
Aldoupolis v. Globe Newspaper Co., 500 N.E.2d 794 (Mass.)
21 *Suffolk U.L. Rev.* 929-34 Fall '87
Alexander v. Choate, 105 S. Ct. 712
20 *Loy. L.A.L. Rev.* 1471-525 Je '87
Alexander v. Gardner-Denver Co., 94 S. Ct. 1011
82 *Nw. U.L. Rev.* 109-43 Fall '87
9 *U. Hawaii L. Rev.* 605-41 Fall '87

automatically connect to the online database and run the same search to find more current citations.

For *I.L.P.* coverage until 1981, the *only* available access is through printed volumes. Indexing since 1981 is available in three different formats (print, online, and CD–ROM), each of which presents advantages and disadvantages. The crucial point to remember is that all three contain the same information. For some searches, the printed volumes or pamphlets may be as quick and effective as electronic means. For others, the flexibility of online searching can save enormous amounts of time. It is ideal to be familiar with all three methods, in order to make informed decisions about searching choices. The printed form of *I.L.P.* is still the most widely used, however, and in many settings is the only option available.

2. INFORMATION ACCESS COMPANY INDEXES

By 1980 dissatisfaction with the problems of the old version of *I.L.P.* had crested. With the encouragement of the American Association of Law Libraries a new index for legal materials was launched by the Information Access Company (IAC). The *Current Law Index* (*C.L.I.*), which began in January 1980, provides access to over seven hundred legal and law-related periodicals. It greatly expanded coverage and introduced many practice-oriented periodicals into the world of indexed items. *C.L.I.* uses detailed Library of Congress subject headings, with extensive subheadings and cross-references.

Current Law Index is similar in structure to the *Index to Legal Periodicals*, but includes separate subject and author/title indexes. Full bibliographic entries for articles appear under both subject and author. (The author/title section lists titles of books reviewed, but *not* article titles.) *C.L.I.* also contains case and statute tables that function like their counterparts in *I.L.P.*. Entries in these tables include authors and titles as well as citations, so they are a bit more descriptive than the *I.L.P.* tables. There is no separate book review section, but reviews are indexed under both the author and title of the book reviewed in the regular author/title section. One added feature of its book review coverage is the assignment of "grades" based on the degree of favor expressed in the review. Illustrations E–1 and E–2 show pages from the subject and author/title sections of a *Current Law Index* volume.

The *Legal Resource Index* (*L.R.I.*), a companion publication to *C.L.I.*, provides the same information in addition to coverage of several legal newspapers not included in *C.L.I.*[13] It is issued in microfilm, which is loaded into a motorized reader. Each month a new cumulative microfilm reel is distributed, so the researcher need only check one place to find all index references since January 1980. *L.R.I.*, like *C.L.I.*, cannot be used for pre–1980 searches. It is more expensive than the standard printed indexes, and therefore not as widely available.

13. The following newspapers are indexed in *L.R.I.* but not *C.L.I.*: *Chicago Daily Law Bulletin, Legal Times, Los Angeles Daily Journal, National Law Journal, New Jersey Law Journal, New York Law Journal,* and *Pennsylvania Law Journal–Reporter.*

Illustration E-1

A page from the subject index in the 1987 *Current Law Index*

HUMAN RIGHTS WORKERS SUBJECT INDEX

HUMAN rights workers
The generals' bonfires: the death of Rodrigo Rojas in Chile. by Marjorie Agosin
9 Human Rights Quarterly 423-425 Aug '87
HUMAN risk assessment *see*
Health risk assessment
HUMAN skeleton
Estimating age at death from immature human skeletons: an overview. by Douglas H. Ubelaker
32 Journal of Forensic Sciences 1254-1263 Sept '87
Racial variation in the sternal extremity of the rib and its effect on age determination. by Mehmet Yasar Iscan, Susan R. Loth and Ronald K. Wright
32 Journal of Forensic Sciences 452-466 March '87
see also
Forensic anthropology
Skeletal maturity
HUMAN T-cell leukemia lymphoma virus
see also
Human immunodeficiency viruses
HUMAN T-cell leukemia virus type III antibodies *see*
Human immunodeficiency virus antibodies
HUMAN T-cell lymphotropic virus type III antibodies *see*
Human immunodeficiency virus antibodies
HUMAN T-cell lymphytropic virus *see*
Human immunodeficiency viruses
HUMAN welfare *see*
Humanitarianism
HUMANE societies *see*
Charitable societies
Child welfare
HUMANE treatment of animals *see*
Animals, Treatment of
HUMANISM
The religion of secular humanism. by Leo Pfeffer
29 Journal of Church and State 495-507 Aut '87
War between the faiths: secular humanist books banned. by Paul Reidinger
73 American Bar Association Journal 128(1) June 1 '87
Judge Hand's holy war. (Judge W. Brevard Hand) by Francis Wilkinson
9 American Lawyer 111(4) May '87
Religious fundamentalism and the public schools. (editorial) by James E. Wood Jr.
29 Journal of Church and State 7-17 Wntr '87
Secular humanism, the establishment clause, and publie education by Eric C. Freed
61 New York University Law Review 1149-1185 Dec '86
Secular humanism and scientific creationism: proposed standards for reviewing curricular decisions affecting students' religious freedom. (Symposium: the Tension between the Free Exercise Clause and the Establishment Clause of the First Amendment) by Nadine Strossen
47 Ohio State Law Journal 333-407 Spr '86
see also
Classical philology
Learning and scholarship

-cases
Secular humanism as a religion within the meaning of the First Amendment. (case note) Grove v. Mead School District 753 F.2d 1528 (9th Cir. 1985) by Julie A. Scheib
61 Tulane Law Review 453-467 Dec '86
HUMANITARIANISM
Reexamining the doctrine of humanitarian intervention in light of the atrocities in Kampuchea and Ethiopia. (Pacific Basin issue) by Michael J. Bazyler
23 Stanford Journal of International Law 547-619 Summ '87
Humanitarian law. (speech given Feb. 27, 1987 in Wellington at seminar on Current issues in Humanitarian Law) (transcript) by F.D. O'Flynn
New Zealand Law Journal 73(2) March '87
Intervention in Grenada. by Samuel R. Maizel
35 Naval Law Review 47-86 Spr '86
HUMANITARIANS *see*
Philanthropists
HUMANITIES
see also
Philosophy
HUMANITY
Human nature as a ground for absolute prohibitions by Gary M. Atkinson
31 American Journal of Jurisprudence 137-172 Ann '86
see also
Charity
HUMANITY, Religion of *see*
Positivism
HUMANIZATION of work life *see*
Quality of work life
HUMANS *see*
Man
HUME, Basil Cardinal
Integrity and the law. (delivered at Westminster Cathedral on 14 July 1985 to Catholic lawyers attending ABA London meeting) (transcript) by Basil Cardinal Hume
Law and Justice 5-8 Wntr-Spr '86
HUMORS, Body *see*
Body fluids
HUMPHREYS, Richard H.
Memorial to Professor Richard H. Humphreys: colleague, friend, teacher. (Delaware) by Robert J. Bruce
12 Delaware Journal of Corporate Law 1-3 Wntr '87

HUNGARY
Enterprise organization of East European socialist countries - a creative approach. (Eason-Weinmann Center for Comparative Law Eighth Annual Symposium: An Examination of the Unity and Diversity within the Socialist Legal Family) by Kresimir Sajko
61 Tulane Law Review 1365-1382 June '87
Law-making as administrative behaviour: the case of investment regulation in Hungary. by Andras Sajo and Gyorgy Csillag
15 International Journal of the Sociology of the Law 209-223 May '87
Legislative arrangements relevant to alcohol treatment in Hungary. by Zsuzsanna Elekes
14 Contemporary Drug Problems 113-123 Spr '87
HUNGER

-addresses, essays, lectures
Robert F. Drinan. (keynote speaker on the world hunger problem) (World Food Day Food and Law Conference: the Legal Faces of the Hunger Problem) by Robert F. Drinan
30 Howard Law Journal 211-221 Spr '87

-conferences and congresses
The relationship of law to the hunger problem: foreword. (World Food Day Food and Law Conference: the Legal Faces of the Hunger Problem) by Goler Teal Butcher
30 Howard Law Journal 193-203 Spr '87

-demographic aspects
The role of law: equity between urban and rural groups. (World Food Day Food and Law Conference: the Legal Faces of the Hunger Problem) by Ann Seidman and Robert B. Seidman
30 Howard Law Journal 425-439 Spr '87

-evaluation
Do liberals bloat the hunger problem? by Glenn C. Loury, J.A. Parker, Charles B. Rangel and Mickey Leland
Business and Society Review 60-64 Spr '84

-government policy
Food aid: how it works in this country and its effect on recipient countries. (World Food Day Food and Law Conference: the Legal Faces of the Hunger Problem) by Carol Lancaster
30 Howard Law Journal 311-319 Spr '87
Hungry people and the allocation process: the adequacy of the legislative standard. (World Food Day Food and Law Conference: the Legal Faces of the Hunger Problem) by Lewis Gulick and Roy A. Stacy *30 Howard Law Journal 323-336 Spr '87*
The policy variables needed to address the hunger problem. (World Food Day Food and Law Conference: the Legal Faces of the Hunger Problem) by John W. Mellor
30 Howard Law Journal 269-284 Spr '87
The proposed African Famine Recovery and Development Fund Act. (World Food Day Food and Law Conference: the Legal Faces of the Hunger Problem) (panel discussion) by David Shear, Mark L. Edelman and Alexander Shakow
30 Howard Law Journal 355-374 Spr '87
The African countries: implications of the debt crisis. (World Food Day Food and Law Conference: the Legal Faces of the Hunger Problem) by Chandra Hardy *30 Howard Law Journal 469-472 Spr '87*
The Sudan-Horn region. (the right to food - the legal and policy framework: three case studies) (World Food Day Food and Law Conference: the Legal Faces of the Hunger Problem) by Fantu Cheru
30 Howard Law Journal 455-460 Spr '87
U.S. food aid legislation: its perspective, the American farmer or hungry people; and its structure, purposes and conclusions. (World Food Day Food and Law Conference: the Legal Faces of the Hunger Problem) by J. Dirck Stryker
30 Howard Law Journal 301-309 Spr '87

-international cooperation
Closing. (the right to food: what must be done) (World Food Day Food and Law Conference: the Legal Faces of the Hunger Problem) by Djibril Diallo *30 Howard Law Journal 485-488 Spr '87*
The International Monetary Fund and the right to food. (World Food Day Food and Law Conference: the Legal Faces of the Hunger Problem) by Philip Alston
30 Howard Law Journal 473-482 Spr '87
The role of the church and private voluntary organizations. (World Food Day Food and Law Conference: the Legal Faces of the) by Martin M. McLaughlin
30 Howard Law Journal 381-386 Spr '87

-political aspects
The current reality of food surplus and the geography of hunger. (World Food Day Food and Law Conference: the Legal Faces of the Hunger Problem) by Maurice Williams
30 Howard Law Journal 251-257 Spr '87
The definition and structure of the hunger problem. (World Food Day Food and Law Conference: the Legal Faces of the Hunger Problem) by Robert J. Berg *30 Howard Law Journal 259-266 Spr '87*
The relationship of political human rights to the hunger problem. (World Food Day Food and Law Conference: the Legal Faces of the Hunger Problem) by James C.N. Paul
30 Howard Law Journal 413-420 Spr '87

-sociological aspects
The human faces of the hunger problem. (Africa) (World Food Day Food and Law Conference: the Legal Faces of the Hunger Problem) by C. Payne Lucas *30 Howard Law Journal 285-295 Spr '87*

-statistics
Role of FAO in ending world hunger. (United Nations Food and Agriculture Organization) (World Food Day Food and Law Conference: the Legal Faces of the Hunger Problem) by Roger Sorenson
30 Howard Law Journal 387-391 Spr '87
HUNGER strikes
The end of a hunger strike. (New South Wales)
8 Legal Service Bulletin 136-137 June '83
The Frolova case: a practitioner's view. (Symposium. the Enforcement of Human Rights Norms: Domestic and Transnational Perspectives) by Anthony A. D'Amato
1 New York Law School Journal of Human Rights 33-50 Ann '83
HUNT, Alan
Critical legal studies and social theory - a response to Alan Hunt. by Martin Krygier
7 Oxford Journal of Legal Studies 26-39 Spr '87
HUNT, H.L., family
Borrowers fight back with lender liability. by Debra Cassens Moss
73 American Bar Association Journal 64(7) March 1 '87
HUNT, Robert S.
Dedication to Professor Robert S. Hunt. (U. of Washington School of Law) by William R. Andersen, Stephen J. Dwyer, William T. Hart, Desmond Heap, James Willard Hurst and John R. Price
62 Washington Law Review 612-630 Oct '87
HUNTER, E. Marshall
Reflections. (by Texas lawyers and judges on 50 years in law practice)
49 Texas Bar Journal 1235(3) Dec '86
HUNTING
Walden v. Hensler: a recent analysis of claim of right. (Queensland) by Philip Jamieson
17 Queensland Law Society Journal 47(3) Feb '87
see also
Subsistence hunting

-cases
Limitation on Indians' hunting rights in Idaho. (case note) State v. Cutler 708 P.2d 853 (Idaho 1985) by Stan J. Tharp
23 Idaho Law Review 553(2) Spr '87
Tribal hunting and fishing rights fail to survive eession of treaty land. (case note) Oregon Department of Fish & Wildlife v. Klamath Indian Tribe 105 S. Ct. 3420 (1985) by Elizabeth Ann O'Brien
13 Ecology Law Quarterly 593-608 Wint '86
HUNTING guns
see also
Shotguns
HUNTING, Job *see*
Job hunting
HUNTING law *see*
Game-laws
HUNTING, Primitive
see also
Subsistence hunting
HUNTINGTON'S chorea
see also
Dementia
HURD, Douglas
Back into the cupboard. (thoughts on abolishing the right to remain silent) (Great Britain) (editorial)
131 Solicitors' Journal 1195 Sept 11 '87
HURLBURT, W. H.
Harmonization of provincial legislation in Canada. (Symposium: Harmonization of Provincial Legislation in Canada; the Elusive Goal) by Arthur L. Close
12 Canadian Business Law Journal 425-432 May '87
HURRICANE protection
see also
Agricultural credit
Disaster relief
Flood control
Insurance, Disaster
Public works
Zoning
HUSBAND and wife
see also
Antenuptial contracts
Community property
Conjugal violence
Desertion and non-support
Dowry
Marital property
Marriage law
Married women
Putative spouse
Separation (Law)
Support (Domestic relations)

-cases
Interspousal wiretapping: should state law or federal statute govern? (case note) Lizza v. Lizza 631 F. Supp. 529 (E.D.N.Y. 1986) by Sharon K. Smith
10 Hamline Law Review 255-277 Feb '87
The new application of an old remedy: the abrogation of interspousal immunity. (case note) Townsend v. Townsend 708 S.W.2d 646 (Mo. 1986) by Patricia R. Jensen
55 UMKC Law Review 323-334 Wntr '87
Surviving spouses' rights uncertain. (case note) Sullivan v. Burkin 460 N.E.2d 572 (Mass. 1984) by Walter J. Jenkins
27 Boston College Law Review 855-881 July '86

400

The information in *L.R.I.* is also available in both online and CD–ROM versions. Online access is available on both LEXIS and

Illustration E-2

A page from the author/title index in the 1987 *Current Law Index*

FRECKELTON, IAN — AUTHOR/TITLE INDEX

Derryn Hinch: martyr or menace. (journalist charged with contempt of court over his broadcasts of child-molesting priest case) (Victoria)
11 Legal Service Bulletin 190-192 Aug '86
Reforming the jury system. (Australia)
11 Legal Service Bulletin 138-140 June '86
Possession and importation of narcotics offences: a major change to the law. (Australia)
11 Legal Service Bulletin 36-37 Feb '86

FRECKELTON, Ian R.
Focusing on the police. (includes related article on seminar series) (Australia)
61 Law Institute Journal 708(2) July '87
The trial of the expert. by Ian R. Freckelton rev by John Olle grade A
61 Law Institute Journal 740(1) July '87

FRED, Alford C.
Science and the revenge of nature: Marcuse and Habermas. by Alford C. Fred rev by Donald Rothbert grade B *97 Ethics 500 Jan '87*

FREDERICK, Howard H.
Cuban-American radio wars: ideology in international telecommunications. by Howard H. Frederick rev by Douglas A. Boyd grade A
31 Journal of Broadcasting & Electronic Media 220-222 Spr '87

FREDERICK, Jeffrey T.
Using juror surveys to solve problems at trial.
29 For the Defense 8-12 Aug '87

FREDERICK, Phillip D.
Videotaped depositions - a primer for defense trial counsel *29 For the Defense 8-14 Nov '87*

FREDERICK, Robert E.
Is greed America's new creed? (are ethics given enough emphasis in the business schools)
Business and Society Review 4-13 Spr '87

FREDERICKS, James M.
Excess insurer's duty to defend after primary insurer settles within policy limits. (case note)
70 Marquette Law Review 285-319 Wntr '87

FREDMAN, Sandra
Teachers' Pay and Conditions Act 1987. (Great Britain)
16 Industrial Law Journal 107-110 June '87
The right to strike: policy and principle. (Great Britain) *Law Quarterly Review 176-182 April '87*
Deregulating pay: the Wages Act 1986. (Great Britain) *Public Law 551-561 Wint '86*
Labour law and industrial relations in Great Britain. by B.A. Hepple and Sandra Fredman rev by David Lewis grade B *20 Law Teacher 229-230 Summ '86*

FREDRICK, Thomas W.
Indemnification and liability of corporate directors and officers.
43 Journal of the Missouri Bar 287(6) July-Aug '87

FREDRICKSON, Robin Smith
Tort liability for AIDs?
24 Houston Law Review 957-990 Oct '87

Free Alister, Dunn and Anderson: the Ananda Marga conspiracy case.
by Tim Anderson rev by Marcus Einfeld grade A
10 Legal Service Bulletin 237-239 Oct '85
by Tim Anderson rev by Lynn Buchanan grade A
10 Legal Service Bulletin 239-240 Oct '85

Free flow of information: a new paradigm.
by Achal Mehra grade B
19 New York University Journal of International Law and Politics 504-505 Wntr '87
by Achal Mehra grade B
19 Vanderbilt Journal of Transnational Law 935 Fall '86

FREE, Frank
Fly from evil. by Frank Free rev by Charles Alan Wright grade B *33 Practical Lawyer 91(5) Oct '87*

Free government in the making.
by Alpheus Thomas Mason and Gorden E. Baker grade A
59 New York State Bar Journal 60(2) May '87

FREED, Doris Jonas
Family law in the fifty states: an overview.
20 Family Law Quarterly 439-587 Wntr '87

FREED, Eric C.
Secular humanism, the establishment clause, and public education
61 New York University Law Review 1149-1185 Dec '86

FREED, Michael J.
Antitrust in the Seventh Circuit from the plaintiff's perspective. *1 Antitrust 28-32 Wntr '87*

FREED, Roy N.
Legal interests relation to software programs. (reprinted from Jurimetrics Journal, Summer 1985)
2 Computer Law & Practice 141-154 May-June '86

FREEDLAND, Mark R.
The contract of employment: the role of public law. (Ireland)
12 Industrial Law Journal 43-45 March '83

FREEDMAN, Benjamin
Purpose and function in government-funded health coverage.
12 Journal of Health Politics, Policy and Law 97-112 Spr '87

FREEDMAN, Bradley J.
Obtaining evidence from Canada: the enforcement of letters rogatory by Canadian courts.
21 University of British Columbia Law Review 351-387 Spr '87

FREEDMAN, Frances Schanfield
Passing off in Quebec.
45 La Revue du Barreau 641-652 Sept-Oct '85

FREEDMAN, Henry A.
The good cause exception to the AFDC child support cooperation requirement.
21 Clearinghouse Review 339-346 Aug-Sept '87

FREEDMAN, Judith
Profit and prophets: law and accountancy practice on the timing of receipts; recognition under the earnings basis (schedule D, cases 1 & 2), continued. (Great Britain)
British Tax Review 104-133 May-June '87
Profit and prophets - law and accountancy practice on the timing of receipts - recognition under the earnings basis (Schedule D, Cases I & II) (Great Britain)
British Tax Review 61-79 March-April '87

FREEDMAN, Lawrence R.
Confidentiality in mediation: the need for protection. (Symposium on Critical Issues in Mediation Legislation)
2 Ohio State Journal on Dispute Resolution 37-45 Fall '86

FREEDMAN, Lawrence Zelic
Perspectives on terrorism. by Jonah Alexander and Lawrence Zelic Freedman rev by Karen F. Botterud grade A
8 ASILS International Law Journal 151-152 Wint '84

FREEDMAN, Maryann Saccomando
The president's message. (anti-discrimination disciplinary rule approved by N.Y. bar House of Delegates) (president's page)
59 New York State Bar Journal 3(2) Oct '87

FREEDMAN, Monroe H.
The aftermath of Nix v. Whiteside: slamming the lid on Pandora's box. (response to article by Brent Appel)
23 Criminal Law Bulletin 25-29 Jan-Feb '87
Legal ethics and the suffering client. (Brendan F. Brown Lecture and Response)
36 Catholic University Law Review 331-336 Wntr '87
Advances in prosecutors' ethics.
1 Criminal Justice 15-18 Wntr '87
Nix v. Whiteside: is incrimination by counsel constitutional? (transcript)
12 Social Responsibility 34-46 Ann '86

FREEDMAN, Philip
Service charges: law & practice. by Philip Freedman, Eric Shapiro and Robert W. Maas grade B
131 Solicitors' Journal 407 March 27 '87

FREEDMAN, Samuel
The law as literature. (Shumiatcher lecture - 9-21-84)
49 Saskatchewan Law Review 319-327 Summ '84

FREEDMAN, Warren
Frivolous lawsuits and frivolous defenses. by Warren Freedman grade B *23 Trial 120(1) Nov '87*
International products liability. by Warren Freedman rev by Gary D. Fox grade C
23 Trial 113(2) Sept '87

Freedom.
by William Safire rev by Paul Reidinger grade B
73 American Bar Association Journal 140(2) Nov 1 '87

Freedom and equality: the moral basis of democratic socialism.
by Keith Dixon rev by Mark D. Stohs grade C
97 Ethics 679-680 April '87

Freedom, feminism, and the state: an overview of individualist feminism.
by Wendy McElroy rev by Siegrun F. Fox grade B
47 Public Administration Review 436(3) Sept-Oct '87

Freedom for the college student press: court cases and related decisions defining fourth estate boundaries.
by Louis E. Ingelhart rev by Walter E. Volkomer grade B
8 Communications and the Law 57-60 June '86
by Louis E. Ingelhart rev by Edward R. Hines grade C
15 Journal of Law and Education 509-511 Fall '86

Freedom of expression: a critical analysis.
by Martin H. Redish rev by Deborah Jones Merritt grade A
3 Constitutional Commentary 234-243 Wntr '86

Freedom of expression in Japan: a study in comparative law, politics, and society.
by Lawrence Ward Beer rev by Samuel Krislov grade A
3 Constitutional Commentary 622-624 Summ '86

Freedom of information.
by Peter W. Bayne rev by Jack Waterford grade B
10 Legal Service Bulletin 83-84 April '85

Freedom of speech.
by Eric Barendt rev by Colin Warbrick grade B
36 International and Comparative Law Quarterly 419-421 April '87
by Eric Barendt rev by Melissa H. Maxman grade D
85 Michigan Law Review 947-952 April-May '87
by Eric Barendt rev by George Rutherglen grade A
7 Oxford Journal of Legal Studies 115-124 Spr '87
by Eric Barendt rev by Laurence Lustgarten grade A *Public Law 122-124 Spr '87*

Freedom of speech basis and limits.
by Gerry Maher rev by George Patterson grade B
31 Journal of the Law Society of Scotland 434(1) Nov '86

Freedom of speech in the United States.
by Thomas L. Tedford rev by John Moeller grade A *3 Constitutional Commentary 600(5) Summ '86*

Freedom, state security and the rule of law: dilemmas of the apartheid society.
by A.S. Mathews rev by Christopher Forsyth grade A *46 Cambridge Law Journal 368 July '87*

FREEGARD, Michael
The Berne Convention, compulsory licensing and collecting societies. (a conference to celebrate the centenary of the Berne Convention, 1886-1986)
11 Columbia - VLA Journal of Law & the Arts 137-155 Fall '86

FREELAND, Mark S.
Selective contracting for hospital care based on volume, quality, and price: prospects, problems, and unanswered questions.
12 Journal of Health Politics, Policy and Law 409-426 Fall '87

FREEMAN, Alan
A critical legal look at corporate practice. (edited and revised version of talk given at A.B.A. convention in Chicago, Aug. 1984)
37 Journal of Legal Education 315-326 Sept '87

FREEMAN, Andrew D.
A critique of economic consistency
39 Stanford Law Review 1259-1270 May '87

FREEMAN-BURNEY, Melodie
Jurisdiction under the Bankruptcy Amendments of 1984: summing up the factors. (case note)
22 Tulsa Law Journal 167-200 Wint '86

FREEMAN, Eric T.
The Twenty-first Amendment and the Commerce Clause: what rationale supports Bacchus Imports.
13 Hastings Constitutional Law Quarterly 361-387 Wntr '86

FREEMAN, Janet L.
Defining serious bodily injury in aggravated assault and kidnapping cases. (case note)
48 Montana Law Review 179-191 Wntr '87

FREEMAN, Kelly A.
Conflicts of interest in class action representation vis-a-vis class representative and class counsel.
33 Wayne Law Review 141-158 Fall '86

FREEMAN, Louis S.
Some early strategies for the methodical disincorporation of America after the Tax Reform Act of 1986: grafting partnerships onto C corporations, running amok with the master limited partnership concept, and generally endeavoring to defeat the intention of the draftsmen of the repeal of General Utilities. (39th Annual Federal Tax Conference of the University of Chicago Law School, October 29-31, 1986) *64 Taxes 962-990 Dec '86*
Pension investments in real estate
1 Journal of Taxation of Investments 155-169 Wntr '84

FREEMAN, M.D.A.
Dealing with domestic violence. by M.D.A. Freeman grade A *131 Solicitors' Journal 1184 Sept 4 '87*
Lloyd's introduction to jurisprudence: 5th ed. by Lord Lloyd of Hampstead and M.D.A. Freeman rev by Peter Ingram grade B
38 Northern Ireland Legal Quarterly 105-107 Spr '87
Lloyd's introduction to jurisprudence: 5th ed. by Lord Lloyd of Hampstead and M.D.A. Freeman rev by Bernard George grade B
15 Anglo-American Law Review 246-248 Jul-Sep '86
After Warnock - whither the law? (ethics of using human embryos in research) (Great Britain)
39 Current Legal Problems 33-55 Ann '86

FREEMAN, Mark
Admiralty. (Fifth Circuit Survey: July 1985 - May 1986)
18 Texas Tech Law Review 263-320 March '87

FREEMAN, Martha
Alternatives to the old up and out: associates who fail to become partners are getting new job descriptions. *8 California Lawyer 44(4) Dec '87*
Teaching computers to think like lawyers. (artificial intelligence) *7 California Lawyer 36(8) Oct '87*
Desktop publishing: boon or bauble?
7 California Lawyer 65(3) Sept '87
Designer law offices. (Cal.)
6 California Lawyer 31(3) Dec '86

FREEMAN, Michael D.A.
The law and practice of custodianship. by Michael D.A. Freeman rev by Margaret Rutherford grade A
17 Family Law 72-73 Feb '87
England: the trumping of parental rights. (Annual Survey of Family Law 1985)
25 Journal of Family Law 91-102 Oct '86
State, law and the family: critical perspectives. by Michael D.A. Freeman rev by Belinda Meteyard grade B
12 Journal of Law and Society 239-241 Summ '85

1076

WESTLAW, as well as through other commercial database vendors. In each system, the database offers the same advantages of speed and flexibility as the online *I.L.P.* The index is found in the "LGLIND" file on LEXIS and the "LRI" database on WESTLAW. The online *Legal Resource Index* is updated daily.

IAC's CD-ROM product, LegalTrac, presents the entries on the microfilm *L.R.I.* in a much more convenient format. Rather than scanning through a microfilm reel, a researcher uses a keyboard to go immediately to a particular index location. Relevant entries are then printed out by machine rather than jotted down by hand. As yet, however, LegalTrac does *not* provide the sophisticated searching techniques of online databases, such as refining searches or combining terms in specified proximities. It is an easy and enjoyable tool for new users, but a fairly primitive application of CD–ROM technology. LegalTrac is updated monthly by a new cumulative disc.

3. ONLINE FULL–TEXT RETRIEVAL

For several years, both LEXIS and WESTLAW have been adding the text of legal periodicals to their databases. This means that every word in the text and footnotes of an article is available for searching. Thus it is possible to construct searches similar to those used for case-finding to retrieve secondary discussions of legal topics. A fifty-page article which focuses for a few pages on a particular issue may not be indexed under that subject, but the discussion can be found using a full-text search. Although many newly developing legal topics do not fit the subject headings established by the indexes, a full-text search can retrieve any article using a term such as "medical waste" or "poison pill." The researcher can then immediately browse the specific portions of the articles containing the relevant terms.

The two systems have somewhat different policies for inclusion of law review articles. LEXIS chooses a group of periodicals it considers important and puts the complete text of every issue online in its LAWREV library. It currently covers about four dozen journals, consisting mostly of major academic reviews but including a few A.B.A. publications. Coverage of most journals begins in about 1982. WESTLAW, in addition to providing full coverage for most of these journals, monitors a much larger range of periodicals and includes specific articles that it feels are of importance to practicing lawyers. It has a database designated "TP" for all articles, as well as smaller databases for articles in specific subject areas and from individual journals. Because West chooses among articles, however, the fact that a journal title is listed as a WESTLAW database is no guarantee that a particular article is available online.

Coverage in the two systems overlaps, and neither is comprehensive, so a thorough online search involves checking in both systems. Even if no article online is quite on point, footnote references matching a search query can often lead to numerous relevant articles in other journals or in volumes predating online coverage, as well as works published as monographs or in journals outside the legal field.

4. CITATORS

Shepard's Citations serves two important purposes with respect to periodical research. One can Shepardize a primary source such as a case or statute to find journal articles in which it is cited. One can also Shepardize a law review article to find both primary sources and other articles in which *it* is cited.

In addition to their value for verifying the status of primary sources, Shepard's citators for each jurisdiction also track a selected group of legal periodicals and include citing references from these periodicals in their coverage of cases, constitutions, statutes, and court rules. Thus a researcher Shepardizing an authority can easily find articles which may provide helpful analysis or explanation.

To find periodical citations to state primary sources, one must use the individual state unit of Shepard's. While the scope of coverage in Shepard's *regional* citators includes cases from other states, it excludes law reviews. The *state* unit, however, generally covers any law reviews and bar journals published within the state, as well as nineteen major national law reviews and the *American Bar Association Journal.*

The only periodical generally covered in *Shepard's United States Citations* or *Shepard's Federal Citations* is the *A.B.A. Journal.*[14] A separate publication, *Shepard's Federal Law Citations in Selected Law Reviews,* provides access to law review articles since 1973 discussing federal primary sources, including the *U.S. Reports* and lower federal court reporters, the Constitution, the U.S. Code, and federal court rules. There is, unfortunately, *no* section for citations to Supreme Court decisions before they appear in the official *U.S. Reports,* so the citator is of little use for research on recent Court decisions. Coverage consists of the same nineteen law reviews which are treated in every state citator. A listing of the reviews in the citator's preface indicates the specific volumes of each within its scope.

Finally, whereas law review articles are within the scope of *citing* sources in the above Shepard's publications, they are the *cited* sources in *Shepard's Law Review Citations.* This citator lists by volume and page periodical articles, comments and notes since 1947 in over 180 law reviews, and indicates citations in other articles or in federal and state court decisions beginning in 1957. This enables the researcher who is interested in a particular article, a position taken therein, or its author, to locate related judicial decisions and periodical articles. Illustration F shows a sample page from this citator, including three citations to the symposium introduction shown in Illustration A.

Reference to particular articles or authors can also be found in the case and law review databases on WESTLAW and LEXIS, simply by using an author's name or an article title as a search term. A full-text

14. As noted above in Chapter 3, supplementary volumes 8 through 12 of *Shepard's U.S. Citations,* published in 1988, include retrospective coverage of law review articles since 1973 citing Supreme Court decisions, listed under all three citations. As of this writing, however, this coverage is not continued in current pamphlets.

Illustration F

A page from *Shepard's Law Review Citations*

CALIFORNIA LAW REVIEW — Vol. 56

- 695 -
56CaL1526
45DJ146

- 702 -
18CLA476
32LJ16
9SDL533
19WnL1091

- 728 -
5C3d500
Calif
96CaR566
487P2d1206
56CaL1557
49DJ26
25FLR24
68McL524

- 780 -
1CnL128

- 856 -
56CaL1532
49DJ34
19HLJ426
23HLJ1433
1972LF236

- 899 -
45JUL595

- 911 -
23MiL150
117PaL379

- 926 -
390US642
20LE205
88SC1282

- 977 -
1970DuL471

- 1020 -
482F2d939
588F2d8
669F2d1117
741F2d936
261CA2d397
17CA3d1134
Alk
670P2d1163
Calif
67CaR800
95CaR570
117CaR846
Mo
530SW479
29AkL131
29LLR78
71McL130
58OLR458
131PaL120
46StJ412
58TuL411
56WsL270

- 1059 -
2CA3d765
2C3d9
Calif
84CaR177
465P2d65

- 1065 -
Calif
66CaR139

- 1067 -
55CaL1275

- 1078 -
Vt
258A2d836

- 1100 -
Calif
82CaR868

- 1123 -
Calif
71CaR523

- 1163 -
Calif
84CaR177
465P2d65

- 1204 -
56CaL1207
17DR53
16WnL34
19WnL23

- 1229 -
23VLR547

- 1247 -
8CA3d162
131CA3d47
70C2d228
1C3d166
3C3d212
11C3d365
12C3d552
20C3d272
24C3d59
24C3d476
28C3d820
38C3d443
64NCA38
Calif
74CaR228
75CaR719
81CaR627
82CaR598
86CaR818
90CaR28
113CaR457
116CaR253
142CaR421
154CaR425
156CaR25
171CaR612
182CaR230
212CaR477
449P2d164
460P2d499
474P2d996
521P2d449
526P2d261
572P2d35
592P2d1177
595P2d603
623P2d173
696P2d1319
Fla
355So2d1250
NC
306SE815
58CaL82
62CaL1031
64CaL263
71CaL1142
17CLA287
22CLA814
70CR1325
10Day747
31DeP795
44GW716
49GW245
21HLJ291
25HLJ33
29HLJ11
29HLJ99
29HLJ129
29HLJ155
96HLR1189
47JBC618
15JMR647
16KLR306
11LoyL302
29MB465
32MeL21
55NDL713
16SFR201
14W&M69

- 1284 -
61ABA479
23Buf604
27Buf257
72CaL1184
11CoL2322
60Cor1000
69CR535
69CR1348
70CR1149
27DeP11
9Hof1435
89HLR646
38LCP224
43LJ29
26StnL43
27StnL839

- 1361 -
Wyo
474P2d303
53Cor1055
20HLJ496

- 1396 -
423F2d944
464F2d779
17CA3d977
8C3d240
30CoA364
260Or178
3WAp308
4WAp904
58Wis2d598
81W2d28
Calif
95CaR392
100CaR102
104CaR512
502P2d8
Colo
492P2d865
Iowa
210NW618
Ore
489P2d955
RI
295A2d685
Wash
474P2d917
484P2d1165
499P2d11
Wis
207NW312
17CLA764
18DeP458
32LCP586
51NbL530
64NwL608
64NwL628
5SFR227
20StnL1138
1969UtLR8

- 1419 -
11AzL44

- 1452 -
57KLJ367

Vol. 56

- 1 -
396F2d29
54ILR710
20SR566

- 17 -
273CA2d487
Calif
78CaR152
56VaL1101

- 37 -
71C2d42
Calif
77CaR9
453P2d449

- 54 -
1984AzS675
21Buf612
52BUR336
25EmJ869
45FR1337
11GGU535
30HLJ991
48JUL131
31KLR556
8ONU328
127PaL1232
5RCL78
28RLR871
8SFR13
5SMJ51
56VaL1037
20VR933
32W&L67
79YLJ212

- 74 -
273CA2d487
53H342
Calif
78CaR152
Haw
493P2d315
18Cth13

- 86 -
396F2d599
273CA2d487
Calif
78CaR152
18Cth13
75DLR38

- 100 -
75DLR38
83HLR343

- 116 -
50FRD32
63Ap2d33
49CA3d26
105CA3d320
290Or66
Calif
122CaR221
164CaR592
NY
407NYS2d [209
Ore
618P2d1271
9AlkR43
25AzL24
1980BYU76
56CaL12
56CaL149
69CaL943
69Cor42
70Cor811
79CR290
87DLR288
27DR241
52FR51
9Goz709
31HLJ640
97HLR854
44ILJ506
67ILR955
70ILR181
10InLR773
14JMJ645
15LoyC397
34MB399
74McL1282
56SCL1232
16SFR21
32SLJ1233
20SR566
42TLQ293
54TxL1214
59VaL23
25VLR133
33VLR1297
6WSR21

- 149 -
50FRD347
Ky
458SW157
Tex
502SW858
12BCR258
51ILJ586
70ILR214
67MnL346
45MoL580
58NYL875
42OBJ2040
27OR358
27SCR843
23SLJ296
34SLJ13
21StLJ53
42TLQ333
48TxL407
54TxL1214
60VaL1358
25VLR133
6WSR21

- 251 -
293FS331
5C3d594
18C3d740
Calif
96CaR607
135CaR350
487P2d1247
557P2d934
35ChL592
1969Tol396
1978UtLR [648

- 260 -
392US125
20LE976
88SC1965
29C3d807
94Ida395
376Mas45
109NH31
Calif
176CaR307
632P2d960
Idaho
488P2d865
Mass
379NE583
NH
241A2d800
13AzL569
26AzL650
19Buf177
59CaL330
27CLA605
22CWL234
48FR409
5GaL445
37GW232
84HLR1084
21HUL191
1982IlLR607
38LCP525
1970LF351
1979LF8
67McL286
69McL204
83McL181
56MnL161
58MqL256
51NDL545
70NwL892
16Pcf381
41PitL675
3PLR292
10PLR405
11PLR465
30RLR351
55VaL579
4Val35
11Val200
15WFL214
25W&M8
1979WLQ [438
1979WLQ [769
79YLJ1314

- 343 -
393US494
405US327
21LE726
31LE271
89SC753
92SC1084
319FS111
324FS1190
17C3d922
60Wis2d502
Calif
132CaR415
553P2d575
Wis
211NW10
11AzL385
11AzL629
11AzL631
35BR17
41BR771
8GaL381
39GW186
23HLJ1018
23HLJ1089
53ILJ209
18KLR509
19LoyR30
57MnL307
65NwL618
47NYL163
23SLJ509
48StJ107
23StnL480
25StnL41
4Tol439
24VLR1105
51WsL660

- 365 -
393US488
21LE723
89SC750
11AzL630
39GW238
23HLJ1093
53ILJ208
18KLR589
65NwL618
47NYL175
23StnL482
24VLR1105

- 371 -
393US500
21LE729
89SC756
22CA3d596
60Wis2d502
Calif
97CaR872
99CaR162
Wis
211NW11
11AzL631
39GW237
23HLJ1089
87HLR325
53ILJ225
18KLR592

- 379 -
405US45
405US55
31LE29
31LE35
92SC822
398F2d708
408F2d591
440F2d595
447F2d254
292FS918
311FS938
318FS241
325FS814
352FS442
17CLA977
57Cor405
22HLJ362
82HLR384
22MeL7
10SDL113
46TxL1051
54VaL1386
55VaL483
55VaL507

179

search is only as limited in scope as the databases of citing documents, and one can find references to *any* published work of interest—articles in early or obscure law reviews, journal literature in other disciplines, treatises, monographs, or literature. Three separate searches would have to be performed to find federal decisions, state decisions, and law review articles, though, so *Shepard's Law Review Citations* is usually a more cost-effective tool for articles within its coverage.

5. OTHER PERIODICAL INDEXES

Although the major indexes described earlier achieve reasonably comprehensive coverage of American law reviews, there are numerous relevant articles which may not be found there. Among these are articles from other countries, in specialized disciplines, or in general-interest periodicals, as well as new articles which have yet to receive full indexing coverage. There are additional indexes to fill these needs.

As noted above, coverage in the *Current Law Index* and the *Legal Resource Index* begins in 1980. For articles before that date, the *Index to Legal Periodicals* is the only general means of access. *I.L.P.* began in 1908, and adopted its present format and volume numbering in 1926. The major index for access to earlier articles is *An Index to Legal Periodical Literature* (6 vols., 1888–1933). The index is known as "Jones–Chipman," after the compiler of the first two volumes (Leonard A. Jones) and the remaining four (Frank E. Chipman). The first volume provides retrospective coverage from 1770 to 1886.[15]

The *Index to Foreign Legal Periodicals,* published under the auspices of the American Association of Law Libraries, offers comprehensive access to over three hundred periodicals, primarily from countries outside the common law system. It indexes journals published outside the United States, the United Kingdom, and the Commonwealth, as well as articles in selected American and Commonwealth journals on international law, comparative law, or the domestic law of other countries. Its coverage, therefore, overlaps to some extent with the standard periodical indexes. Many of its articles are in languages other than English, but it is a very useful place for *any* researcher to begin work on an international law problem.

The *Index to Foreign Legal Periodicals* is published quarterly, formerly with triennial cumulative bound volumes, now cumulating annually. It is divided into four sections: (1) subject index, (2) geographical index, (3) book review index, and (4) author index. The geographical and author sections contain cross-references to entries in the subject index. To save space journal titles are indicated by alphanumeric codes, but a table in the front of each volume and pamphlet indicates full titles. Illustration G shows entries in the subject index.

The *Index to Foreign Legal Periodicals* has been criticized for the limited number of journals indexed. Because of the wide range of international and foreign journals and the variety of languages involved, however, only a small percentage can be included. In recent

15. The development of legal periodical indexes is discussed in Leiter, "A History of Legal Periodical Indexing," *Legal Reference Services Q.*, Spring 1987, at 35.

Illustration G

A page from the subject index in the 1986 *Index to Foreign Legal Periodicals*

326 ■ *SUBJECT INDEX: DOMICILE & RESIDENCE*

Spain
Los delitos de infidelidad en la custodia de documentos.
J.-S. Salom Escrivá. *R160 42:2477-2508 '86*

■ DOMICILE & RESIDENCE

Domicile and habitual residence.
A. Iyer. *S30 6:115-129 '85*

Austria
Darf der Landesgesetzgeber den Begriff »ordentlicher Wohnsitz« selbständig regeln?
R. Thienel. *O5 41:357-362 '86*

Ist der Landesgesetzgeber zuständig, den Begriff "ordentlicher Wohnsitz" selbständig zu regeln?
R. Häussl. *O5 40:750-753 '85*

Bulgaria
Semeĭnoto zhilishte sled razvod.
N. Gachev. *S45 35:13-19 Ja '86*

Liechtenstein
Das Bürgerrecht im Wandel der Zeit.
A. Ospelt. *L25 Sondernummer 7:147-155 '86*

Netherlands
Het begrip "hoofdverblijf" in de Vreemdelingenwet.
A. Andriesen & T. Wolff. *N5 61:640-644 '86*

South Africa (Republic)
Divorced abroad: still married here.
E. Kahn. *T35 1986:1-17*

USSR
"Foreigners in the USSR: the ins and outs of Soviet law" or recent developments in Soviet legislation on the legal status of foreigners.
W.B. Simons. *R44 12:273-307 '86*

USA
Taxation of the dual-resident alien: the interaction of section 7701(b) and the United States income tax treaties. [In English & French]
L.J. Schreyer & C.W. Cope. *R235 1986:45-58*

■ DRUG ADDICTION

Criminalidade sem fronteiras: O tráfico de estupefacientes e de substâncias psicotrópicas.
A.G. Lourenço Martins. *B15 no.351:35-58 '85*

Le juge face à la toxicomanie: répression et/ou traitement?
R. Screvens. *R245 66:933-946 '86*

Piercing offshore bank secrecy laws used to launder illegal narcotics profits: the Cayman Islands example.
J.I. Horowitz. *T2 20:133-165 '85*

America
Using the organization of American states to control international narcotics trafficking and money laundering.
B. Zagaris & C. Papavizas. *R315 57:119-132 '86*

Argentina
Algunas consideraciones acerca de la incriminación de la tenencia de estupefacientes.
T. García Torres. *L20 1985(B):1055-1059*

Austria
Die Drogenproblematik in Österreich aus der Sicht der Suchtgiftgesetznovelle 1985.
G. Peternell. *L25 7:61-66 '86*

Belgium
Le juge face à la toxicomanie: répression et/ou traitement?
R. Screvens. *R245 66:933-946 '86*

Germany, Western
Beteiligung an vorsätzlicher Selbstgefährdung – BGHSt 32, 262 und BGH, NStZ 1984, 452.
W. Stree. *J107 25:179-184 '85*

Fragen des Betäubungsmittelstrafrechts.
H.W. Schmidt. *M20 39:969-974 '85*

Sind Dealer Mörder? Kriminalstrategische und dogmatische Anmerkungen.
H. Schäfer. *Middendorf collection. 221-256*

Netherlands
Drugbeleid: paradoxaal en een dubbele moraal.
L.J.S. Wever. *D6 1986:436-440*

Hedendaagse drugbestrijding; kosten en risico's.
H.J. van Vliet. *D6 1986:476-486*

Poland
Zjawisko narkomanii w Polsce a projekt ustawy o zapobieganiu i zwalczaniu narkomanii.
P. Zakrzewski. *N70 40:69-81 Je '84*

Spain
Prevención y control de drogas en las Fuerzas Armadas: aspectos legales.
E. Calderón Susín. *R160 42:3985-3994 '86*

Turkey
Uyuşturucu maddeler ve suç siyaseti.
K. Bayraktar. *I75 51:45-64 '85*

years the *Index* has made an effort to add new journals, particularly those from Asia and Africa. A major format change in 1986 and an improvement in timeliness have made the *Index to Foreign Legal Periodicals* an excellent research aid. A supplement published in 1987 provides a systematic arrangement of subject headings, an alphabetical list of subjects with extensive cross-references, and sections translating the English subject terms into French, German and Spanish.

Commonwealth legal periodicals are covered in the standard indexes described earlier, but there are several other indexes for specific countries which include many more periodicals:

(a) *Legal Journals Index* (Legal Information Resources, 1986–date, monthly with quarterly and annual cumulations). Covers over 150 British law journals.

(b) *Index to Canadian Legal Literature* (Carswell, two retrospective volumes published in 1981, with bound and looseleaf supplements). Includes monographs and periodical articles.

(c) *Index to Canadian Legal Periodical Literature* (1961–date, three quarterly issues, cumulating with the fourth quarter in an annual volume).

(d) *Current Australian and New Zealand Legal Literature* (Law Book Co., 1973–date, quarterly, noncumulating).

(e) *Index to Indian Legal Literature* (Indian Law Institute, 1963–date, semiannual, with annual cumulations).

Works such as these are discussed more fully in treatments of English and Canadian legal research.

Another important index of secondary legal materials was the *Annual Legal Bibliography,* published by the Harvard Law Library from 1961 to 1981. This index (which cumulated monthly *Current Legal Bibliography* issues) provided only subject access by broad topical headings, but covered a very wide range of publications. All periodicals and monographs the library acquired, domestic, foreign and international, were indexed. Thus, almost two thousand periodicals in law and related fields were indexed, more than twice the number covered by the *Index to Legal Periodicals* and the *Index to Foreign Legal Periodicals* combined. The only regular tool which indexed both texts and monographs during its period, the *Annual Legal Bibliography* was perhaps the most ambitious universal index to legal sources ever attempted. Its termination in 1981 left a major gap in the apparatus of legal research. The *National Legal Bibliography* (Hein, 1984–date) has filled the gap for monographic literature, but it is unlikely that a tool like the *Annual Legal Bibliography* will be seen again. The entire 21-year run has been cumulated and reissued on microfiche by the Law Library Microform Consortium as the *Harvard Legal Bibliography, 1961–1981.* New "Quick Survey Tables" permit researchers to find all entries for particular jurisdictions.

There are also indexes and abstracting services for particular subject areas. The field of taxation is particularly well covered by a variety of specialized tools. Two major access tools are:

(a) *CCH Federal Tax Articles*—a looseleaf reporter, issued in monthly installments, containing abstracts of tax articles and conference papers, arranged by section of the Internal Revenue Code. Four bound volumes cover articles from 1954 to 1984.

(b) *Index to Federal Tax Articles* (Warren, Gorham & Lamont)—a comprehensive index, by author and subject, of periodical articles and other publications in all fields of taxation. Developments from 1913 to 1974 are covered in three volumes, and more recent articles are listed in three additional cumulative volumes and quarterly supplements.

In addition, the *Monthly Digest of Tax Articles* (Newkirk Products) contains condensed versions of recent journal articles on taxation.

Articles too new to be indexed in the *Current Law Index* and the *Index to Legal Periodicals* are covered in the weekly *Current Index to Legal Periodicals,* published by the Marian G. Gallagher Law Library of the University of Washington. By using a much smaller list of about ninety broad subject headings, this index is able to notify users of recent publications on a very current basis. In addition to its subject index, the *Current Index* lists the contents of the journal issues covered each week. The *Current Index to Legal Periodicals* covers nearly three hundred law reviews. Recent issues are available for searching on WESTLAW, allowing full access by title keywords or author names. Illustration H shows a sample page from the *Current Index.*

For readers who prefer scanning the recent issues of periodicals for current awareness, there are services which photocopy the actual contents pages of recent legal periodicals. These current contents services enable the reader to know what is being published in the law reviews (at least by author and title). Many law school libraries photocopy contents pages for the perusal of their own faculty and staff, and several pamphlet services are published commercially. One of the most prominent is *Legal Contents* (formerly called *Contents of Current Legal Periodicals*), published monthly by Management Contents. Competitors offering similar weekly services are *Law Review Access* and *Law Review Ink.*

To fill the gap created by the limited coverage of the *Index to Legal Periodicals,* another index was begun in 1958 to cover both legal periodicals excluded from *I.L.P.* and a wide range of nonlegal periodicals carrying articles of interest to lawyers and others engaged in legal research. The *Index to Periodical Articles Related to Law,* published by Glanville, currently consists of three bound cumulative volumes covering the years 1958–68, 1969–73, and 1974–78. Each volume contains a list of subjects under which articles are indexed and a list of the authors of articles. The bound volumes are supplemented by quarterly issues, which cumulate into an annual compilation in each Fall issue. These volumes and issues covering 1958 through 1988 are scheduled for replacement in 1989 by a cumulative thirty-year *Index* volume.

Illustration H

The first page of a *Current Index to Legal Periodicals* issue

CURRENT INDEX TO LEGAL PERIODICALS
Marian Gould Gallagher Law Library
University of Washington

Joseph David Rudman, Editor
Muriel A. Quick, Program Assistant

Copyright 1988, Marian Gould Gallagher Law Library

Key to Citations----November 25, 1988

Colum. J. Envtl. L.	13	Columbia Journal of Environmental Law, No. 2, Pp. 153-403, 1988.
Dick. L. Rev.	93	Dickinson Law Review, No. 1, Fall, 1988.
Geo. L.J.	76	Georgetown Law Journal, No. 5, June, 1988.
Law & Pol'y	10	Law & Policy, Nos. 2 & 3, April/July, 1988.
Loy. L.A.L. Rev.	22	Loyola of Los Angeles Law Review, No. 1, November, 1988.
Nw. U.L. Rev.	82	Northwestern University Law Review, No. 3, Spring, 1988.
Okla. L. Rev.	41	Oklahoma Law Review, No. 2, Summer, 1988.
Pac. L.J.	20	Pacific Law Journal, No. 1, October, 1988.
Rev. Litigation	7	The Review of Litigation, No. 3, Summer, 1988.
Suffolk U.L. Rev.	22	Suffolk University Law Review, No. 1, Spring, 1988.
Vand. L. Rev.	41	Vanderbilt Law Review, No. 5, October, 1988.
Wash. L. Rev.	63	Washington Law Review, No. 4, October, 1988.

- -

ADMINISTRATIVE LAW

Hirshman, Linda R. Postmodern jurisprudence and the problem of administrative discretion. 82 Nw. U.L. Rev. 646-704 (1988).

Trager, Susan M. Emerging forums for groundwater dispute resolution in California: a glimpse at the second generation of groundwater issues and how agencies work towards problem resolution. 20 Pac. L.J. 31-74 (1988).

White, Martin B. Due process in federal debt collection by offset: two concepts and a case study. 41 Okla. L. Rev. 195-233 (1988).

Article III and due process limitations on the FSLIC's adjudicatory role during its receiverships. 76 Geo. L.J. 1845-1866 (1988).

AGENCY

Clarifying the peculiar risk doctrine: the rule restated. 20 Pac. L.J. 197-219 (1988).

Property law--sellers incur liability for real estate broker's commission where conveyance fails due to defective title. (Bennett v. McCabe, 808 F.2d 178, 1st Cir. 1987.) 22 Suffolk U.L. Rev. 250-256 (1988).

AIR AND SPACE LAW

Aviation: the rule for admissibility: building a balance between the interests of air safety and the interests of aviation litigation. 41 Okla. L. Rev. 265-289 (1988).

ARTS

Siegel, Neil F. The resale royalty provisions of the Visual Artists Rights Act: their history and theory. 93 Dick. L. Rev. 1-22 (1988).

BANKING LAW

Article III and due process limitations on the FSLIC's adjudicatory role during its receiverships. 76 Geo. L.J. 1845-1866 (1988).

Bank financed precious metals trading--is it just another precious metals scam? 93 Dick. L. Rev. 107-141 (1988).

BANKRUPTCY LAW

Deferred cash payments to secured creditors in cram down of Chapter 11 plans: a matter of interest. 63 Wash. L. Rev. 1041-1061 (1988).

CIVIL RIGHTS

Sander, Richard H. Individual rights and demographic realities: the problem of fair housing. 82 Nw. U.L. Rev. 874-939 (1988).

Civil rights--the First Circuit refines evidentiary burdens under Title VII where plaintiff presents direct evidence of discrimination. (Fields v. Clark University, 817 F.2d 931, 1st Cir. 1987.) 22 Suffolk U.L. Rev. 131-137 (1988).

Constitutional law--affirmative action plan considering gender as a factor in promotion decisions constitutional. (Johnson v. Transportation Agency, Santa Clara County, 107 S. Ct. 1442, 1987.) 22 Suffolk U.L. Rev. 159-167 (1988).

Constitutional law: employment discrimination--emerging judicial standards for careful construction of affirmative action remedies. 41 Okla. L. Rev. 289-313 (1988).

Constitutional law--race conscious promotion order survives Fourteenth Amendment challenge. (United States v. Paradise, 107 S. Ct. 1053, 1987.) 22 Suffolk U.L. Rev. 176-183 (1988).

The scope of the *Index to Periodical Articles Related to Law* was limited in 1979 to exclude law journals, which began receiving broader coverage in the new *Current Law Index.* Coverage now includes substantial English-language articles not included in *C.L.I., I.L.P.,* the *Index to Foreign Legal Periodicals,* the *Legal Resource Index,* or LegalTrac.

With the expansion of legal research into many interdisciplinary areas, indexes from related fields, such as the *Public Affairs Informa-*

tion Service, Social Sciences Index, and *Social Sciences Citation Index,* have become increasingly important to lawyers and other users of legal materials. These indexes are described in Chapter 14, Nonlegal Research Sources.

D. SUMMARY

Periodicals are among the most important secondary sources in legal research. They can serve as sources of persuasive authority or as repositories of citations to other materials. Long accessible through traditional indexing, the recent competition stimulated by new databases and citators has improved access considerably. A search of the legal periodical literature should be a regular part of the sophisticated lawyer's research strategy.

E. ADDITIONAL READING

B.H. Cane, "The Role of Law Review in Legal Education," 31 *J.Legal Educ.* 215 (1981).

D.B. Maggs, "Concerning the Extent to Which the Law Review Contributes to the Development of the Law," 3 *S.Cal.L.Rev.* 181 (1930).

Chapter 12

ENCYCLOPEDIAS, RESTATEMENTS, AND TEXTS

A. INTRODUCTION

The secondary source materials discussed in this chapter are designed primarily to *explain* legal concepts, and are less concerned than the periodical literature with analysis and abstract theory. This material offers the researcher assistance in understanding the meaning of a particular primary source, in deciphering the complex interactions of different primary sources, or in learning the basic terminology and doctrines of an area of law.

Encyclopedias, Restatements and texts can support research in three ways. First, they may provide persuasive authority which an advocate can cite to reinforce an interpretation of the law. Not all secondary sources are considered authoritative, however, so one must take care to evaluate a source before relying on it. Second, they may clarify and summarize the state of the law in a manner that makes sense out of the seeming chaos at the heart of many legal problems. A source that is not persuasive to a court may still be quite helpful in elucidating important issues, acquainting the user with pertinent vocabulary, and providing the needed background to the primary sources. The third function is that of citation gathering. Some publications provide citations to numerous authorities to support their textual arguments. Regardless of the strength of the commentators' analysis, this gathering of authorities leads to relevant primary sources and thereby provides a useful starting point in research.

The researcher's use of these materials may combine all three functions. One might turn to secondary sources seeking only background information, but through these sources discover and use relevant authorities. With experience in a substantive legal area, one comes to know its research landscape well. One learns which sources to trust, which authors to cite with authority, and which sets to turn to for background.

B. ENCYCLOPEDIAS

Legal encyclopedias are among the most frequently used reference sets in some law school libraries. They are organized much like general encyclopedias, with an alphabetic arrangement of broad topics and access provided by detailed subject indexes. Legal encyclopedias attempt to describe systematically the entire field of American legal doctrine. They do not generally emphasize the historical or social aspects of the legal system.

At one time the encyclopedias were viewed as serious and reliable statements of law, and were frequently cited by the courts, but their use as authority by law students, lawyers, and most judges has declined. The reasons for this are their emphasis on case law and their neglect of statutes and regulations, their tendency to oversimplify and generalize, and their failure to reflect change and subtlety in legal development. In recent decades, they have come to be viewed primarily as research tools, useful for case-finding and as introductions to research, but not as independent authority.

Originally the legal encyclopedia was designed to describe the developments in all areas of the common law, by summarizing case holdings. As the nature of law became more complex and the interplay of statutes, cases, and administrative rules and regulations increased, meaningful discussion based on cases alone grew more and more difficult. As the law in the fifty states and at the federal level became more particularized, it was impossible to provide a grand "national" summary. Finally, with the publication of over a hundred thousand cases a year, it became a futile exercise to incorporate all "new" cases into the set. The text of the encyclopedia was made very bland and general to avoid gross error, and the long lists of accompanying case citations became an impediment rather than an aid to clarity.

The legal encyclopedia today can help as a background tool or a lead to citations, but very few courts consider it as persuasive authority. With these limitations understood, the two national legal encyclopedias can still be used, where appropriate, in one's research plan.

1. *CORPUS JURIS SECUNDUM*

Corpus Juris Secundum, part of the West Publishing Company's interrelated research system, began publication in 1936 and over the course of twenty years superseded its predecessor, *Corpus Juris* (72 vols., 1911–37). *Corpus Juris* is now rarely consulted for its text, but is still referred to occasionally in checking citations or quotations from earlier sources. Its footnote citations are by and large not repeated in *C.J.S.,* so the older set is still useful for historical research.

C.J.S. currently consists of 101 numbered volumes contained in 157 physical volumes. Both the text volumes and the General Index volumes are updated annually by pocket parts. When the amount of material in its pocket part requires it, a volume is revised and sometimes expanded into two volumes, incorporating the accumulated supplementary material.

The grand concept of *Corpus Juris Secundum* is described in the "Explanation" at the front of each of the original volumes, sixty-one of which are still in the current set:

> *Corpus Juris Secundum* is . . . a complete restatement of the entire body of American Law. The clear-cut and exhaustive propositions comprising the text are supported by all the authorities from the earliest times to date.

Corpus Juris Secundum thus claims to reflect all published case law in its discussions of legal topics. In this, it continues the West Publishing Company's philosophy of "comprehensiveness." Many pages of *C.J.S.* contain more material in footnotes than text. Illustration A shows a typical page from the "Prisons and Rights of Prisoners" topic in a recently revised volume of *Corpus Juris Secundum.* The page shown is part of section 115, "Law Libraries and Access to Legal Material—Adequacy."

C.J.S. contains 433 topical articles in an alphabetical arrangement, ranging from "Abandonment" to "Zoning." Within each article, the subject is presented in a logical sequence, with a topical analysis at the beginning outlining the contents. Numerous case citations in the footnotes provide references to court decisions supporting the statements in the text. Because *C.J.S.* attempts to cover all American jurisdictions, and because it is designed for a wide range of readers, the text tends to be general and simplistic in its analysis. To reflect the real complexity of each topic would require that the encyclopedia be of an unmanageable size and be supplemented more frequently than the

Illustration A

A sample page from *Corpus Juris Secundum*

§ 115 PRISONS 72 C. J. S.

Materials from outsiders.

Officials may prohibit prisoners from receiving legal materials from outsiders other than publishers or publication suppliers, where suitable alternatives are available.[49]

c. Access to Library

A denial of physical access to the library by the prisoners, as well as a time limitation may be justified by security considerations, and particular needs of the prisoners.

A denial of physical access to the library [50] or the placement of physical restraints upon an inmate attending the library [51] may be justified by security considerations. Where a prisoner is denied physical access to a library but is allowed to request specific legal material by name, courts have held both that such procedure is [52] and is not [53] adequate, depending upon the circumstances. Restricted confinement inmates need not be afforded the same legal resources as other inmates, so long as they are afforded meaningful access to the courts.[54] However, it has been said that such inmates must be given opportunities for legal research equivalent to those provided other inmates, even if provided by different means.[55] Courts sometimes require that officials establish a satellite library for inmates in restricted confinement.[56]

There is no right of unlimited access to a prison law library.[57] The paramount consideration in evaluating a time limitation upon library use is whether prisoners can perform meaningful legal research.[58] Time limitations must be reasonable.[59] The amount of library access to which a particular prisoner is entitled may depend upon his particular needs.[60] An isolated incident of denial of library access does not make out a constitutional violation.[61] The validity of a time limitation may depend upon the availability and quality of assistance provided for library utilization.[62] Under some circumstances, inmates serving as jailhouse lawyers for others must be given access to the library beyond that given inmates generally.[63] The validity of various time limitations upon the use of a library has been adjuciated.[64]

Short-term facility contents

U.S.—Fluhr v. Roberts, D.C.Ky., 460 F.Supp. 536.

49. U.S.—Guajardo v. Estelle, C.A.Tex., 580 F.2d 748.

50. U.S.—Williams v. Wyrick, C.A.Mo., 747 F.2d 1231.

51. Assistance

Prisoner was not denied meaningful access to the courts as result of the physical restraints since prisoner was accompanied by a "clerk" who would obtain books for him and perform other requests and was permitted the use of both hands when he desired to type.

U.S.—Tubwell v. Griffith, C.A.Miss., 742 F.2d 250.

52. U.S.—Stewart v. Gates, D.C.Cal., 450 F.Supp. 583, remanded 618 F.2d 117.

Or.—State v. Smith, 675 P.2d 1060, 66 Or.App. 374, review denied 683 P.2d 1370, 297 Or. 339.

Outcamp housing

La.—Martin v. Phelps, App., 380 So.2d 164.

Restricted confinement inmate

U.S.—Lovell v. Brennan, D.C.Me., 566 F.Supp. 672, affirmed 728 F.2d 560—Wojtczak v. Cuyler, D.C.Pa., 480 F.Supp. 1288—Frazier v. Ward, D.C.N.Y., 426 F.Supp. 1354.

53. U.S.—Jones v. Diamond, C.A.Miss., 594 F.2d 997, on rehearing 636 F.2d 1364, amended on other grounds 101 S.Ct. 3141, 453 U.S. 911, 69 L.Ed.2d 993, certiorari dismissed 102 S.Ct. 27, 453 U.S. 950, 69 L.Ed.2d 1033—Brown v. Winston, C.A.Va., 584 F.2d 1336.

Toussaint v. McCarthy, D.C.Cal., 597 F.Supp. 1388—Canterino v. Wilson, D.C.Ky., 562 F.Supp. 106.

54. U.S.—Kendrick v. Bland, D.C.Ky., 586 F.Supp. 1536.

55. U.S.—Wojtczak v. Cuyler, D.C.Pa., 480 F.Supp. 1288.

56. U.S.—Cepulonis v. Fair, C.A.Mass., 732 F.2d 1.

57. U.S.—Boston v. Stanton, D.C.Mo., 450 F.Supp. 1049.

58. U.S.—Cruz v. Hauck, C.A.Tex., 627 F.2d 710.

59. Ariz.—Berry v. Department of Corrections, App., 697 P.2d 711, 144 Ariz. 318.

60. U.S.—O'Bryan v. Saginaw County, Michigan, D.C.Mich., 437 F.Supp. 582, entered final judgment 446 F.Supp. 436, remanded 620 F.2d 303, on remand 529 F.Supp. 206, affirmed 741 F.2d 283.

61. U.S.—Burrascano v. Levi, D.C.Md., 452 F.Supp. 1066, affirmed 612 F.2d 1306.

62. U.S.—Cruz v. Hauck, C.A.Tex., 627 F.2d 710—Williams v. Leeke, C.A.S.C., 584 F.2d 1336, certiorari denied 99 S.Ct. 2825, 442 U.S. 911, 61 L.Ed.2d 276.

Canterino v. Wilson, D.C.Ky., 562 F.Supp. 106.

N.Y.—Ford v. LaVallee, 390 N.Y.S.2d 269, 55 A.D.2d 799, appeal denied 362 N.E.2d 627, 41 N.Y.2d 802, 393 N.Y.S.2d 1027.

63. U.S.—Wetmore v. Fields, D.C.Wis., 458 F.Supp. 1131.

Jailhouse lawyers are discussed generally supra § 108.

64. U.S.—Nadeau v. Helgemoe, C.A.N.H., 561 F.2d 411, appeal after remand 581 F.2d 275.

Robbins v. South, D.C.Mont., 595 F.Supp. 785—Oliver v. Marks, D.C.Pa., 587 F.Supp. 884.

N.D.—Jensen v. Satran, 303 N.W.2d 568.

annual pocket parts allow. The simplified text, however, can provide an introduction to an area that is unfamiliar to the researcher, and can explain the basic concepts and terminology that underlie a field of law.

Access to *Corpus Juris Secundum* can be achieved in three ways. The simplest way is to have a reference to a *C.J.S.* section from one of West's other publications, such as an annotated code, or online from Insta–Cite, West's citation verification system. Without such a reference, one can go directly to one of the topics (a list of all topics is printed at the beginning of the set) and scan its table of contents for the appropriate section. At the beginning of each topic, a general "Analysis" lists its major subdivisions and is followed by a detailed "Sub–Analysis" listing every section.

Preferably, one can use the five-volume General Index at the end of the set to locate the relevant topic, and then use the individual index for that topic, at the back of its volume, to find relevant sections. The General Index usually provides references to exact sections, but it is often worthwhile to use an individual topic index to refine an inquiry. The General Index was last revised in 1981, and is supplemented by annual pocket parts. The topic indexes in volumes recompiled since the latest General Index revision *must* be used, since the General Index's references to sections in earlier, replaced volumes are obsolete. Illustration B shows a typical page from the title index for "Prisons and Rights of Prisoners," which was revised in 1987.

Because *C.J.S.* is a West publication, it not only shares West's comprehensive approach, but also provides lateral citations to other West publications. If a West digest "key number" covers a topic under discussion, that number is cited. *C.J.S.* thus provides not only footnote citations directly to relevant cases, but also a research key that can be used in any of the West digests to locate more cases on the same issue. For the earliest volumes, these key numbers are found only in pocket parts.

Most *C.J.S.* volumes also provide definitions of important terms and legal maxims, which are listed in the regular alphabetical sequence of articles and defined with citations to multiple case authorities. Definitions in older volumes are updated in their pocket parts, but the feature has been eliminated from new replacement volumes issued since 1986.

Although *C.J.S.* volumes are replaced from time to time, and occasional supplementary volumes are issued for newer topics such as products liability or securities regulation, many volumes have not been recompiled for over thirty years. Pocket parts supplement the text and add citations to new cases, but one must constantly refer from the text to the pocket part to bring narrative and references up to date. West has worked in the past decade to modernize the set, and recent replacement volumes have a cleaner, less stifling layout of text and footnotes. It is hoped that this effort will extend rapidly to the remaining volumes, since *C.J.S.* is not likely to be replaced by another total revision. To include references to *all* cases in a new edition would be virtually impossible. If *Corpus Juris Tertium* (*C.J.T.*?) were ever to appear, it would require a more selective conceptual base.

Illustration B

A *Corpus Juris Secundum* index page

PRISONS AND RIGHTS OF PRISONERS 72 C.J.S.

754

2. *AMERICAN JURISPRUDENCE 2D*

American Jurisprudence 2d, popularly known as *Am.Jur.2d,* is the general legal encyclopedia published by the Lawyers Co-operative Publishing Company. It supersedes *American Jurisprudence* (66 vols., 1936–60), which had in turn superseded *its* predecessor, *Ruling Case Law* (38 vols., 1914–31).

Am.Jur.2d differs from *Corpus Juris Secundum* in several respects. It includes some 82 numbered volumes contained in 118 books, as opposed to the over 150 volumes of *C.J.S.* Part of this difference in size relates to *Am.Jur.2d's* more "selective" approach to the use of footnote references. Whereas *C.J.S.* claims to provide citations to *every* relevant case, *Am.Jur.2d* provides fewer case citations but includes references to *ALR* annotations and other Lawyers Co-op research aids. Citations to those sources eliminate the need to cite every case summarized therein, and keep the footnotes from overpowering the text. Illustration C shows a page from the *Am.Jur.2d* topic "Penal and Correctional Institutions," discussing the issue of prisoner access to law libraries.

The number of topics covered by *Am.Jur.2d* (430) is almost the same as in *C.J.S.* In providing access to these topics, *C.J.S.* and *Am. Jur.2d* are quite similar. *Am.Jur.2d* begins each topic with a detailed scope note, general cross-references, and an outline of sections. There is a four-volume General Index covering the entire set, and each individual volume has indexes for the articles in that volume. As with *C.J.S.,* it is necessary at times to use both the General Index and a topic index to find relevant sections. Illustration D shows a page from the *Am.Jur.2d* General Index.

There are several other notable differences between *C.J.S.* and *Am. Jur.2d.* One is the New Topic Service binder in *Am.Jur.2d,* which allows the publisher to introduce new topics into the encyclopedia without having to reissue an entire volume. Through the New Topic Service, *Am.Jur.2d* reacts more quickly to changes in the law and to newly developing legal fields. The New Topic Service supplements the whole set, containing articles on matters such as "Alternative Dispute Resolution" and "Real Estate Time-Sharing" until they can be incorporated into a revised volume.

Am.Jur.2d focuses slightly more on statutes than *C.J.S.* Examples of this include the statutory coverage reflected in the New Topic Service, the use of three volumes (33, 34, and 34A) for federal taxation, and the "Tables of Statutes and Rules Cited" in every *Am.Jur.2d* volume. These tables, however, are limited to *federal* statutes, *federal* rules, and Uniform and Model Laws. Coverage of state statutes, unfortunately, remains minimal.

Am.Jur.2d is part of the Lawyers Co-op research system, the Total Client–Service Library. As such, it provides citations to *ALR* and a variety of other Lawyers Co-op research tools, some of which are described briefly below. Both legal encyclopedias illustrate the general tendency of their publishers to provide extensive references to their

Illustration C

A sample page from *American Jurisprudence 2d*

§ 75 PENAL AND CORRECTIONAL ETC. 60 Am Jur 2d

nished with a court-appointed attorney.[32] However, due process does not require that an accused awaiting trial and represented by counsel also have access to a law library,[33] and even though a prisoner who represents himself is confined in a maximum security cell without access to a law library, his right of access is not infringed, where he has two appointed standby attorneys with whom he refuses to discuss his defense and from whom he could receive legal materials.[34]

§ 76. —Limitations on time for use of library

In view of the fact that establishing a library for inmates is but one method of providing inmates constitutionally adequate access to the courts,[35] prison rules that the library is open for use for only 30 hours per week and that a maximum of four inmates could be in the library at any one time are reasonable regulations which do not necessarily impede access to the courts, where the prisoners failed to show specifically how those policies hampered their legal activities.[36]

§ 77. Access to legal research materials

A state department of corrections regulation providing for an exclusive list of legal reference books for use by prisoners violates indigent prisoners' rights to equal protection and to access of the courts, where the library established by the list is inadequate for the needs of indigent prisoners who are unable to take advantage of state laws permitting them to communicate with private counsel and to buy personal law books, and the denial of prisoners' rights which the inadequate library caused was not justified by the state's countervail-

32. Spates v Manson (CA2 Conn) 644 F2d 80; Crawford v Smith (Utah) 578 P2d 1282.

A system provided by the state was constitutionally adequate, since the state combined its law library program with state funded programs designed to provide trained legal assistance to prisoners contesting the legality or conditions of their confinement. Under state law, prisoners in a state prison could seek the appointment of competent counsel to assist them concerning any legal matter relating to their incarceration if they did not already have a court-appointed lawyer. Williams v Leeke (CA4 SC) 584 F2d 1336, cert den 442 US 911, 61 L Ed 2d 276, 99 S Ct 2825.

As to inmates' right of access to court, generally, see § 65.

Practice Aids.—Access to legal assistance. 22 Am Jur Trials 1, Prisoners' Rights Litigation § 64.

—Class action complaint by prisoners to enjoin enforcement of discriminatory prison regulations regarding prison law library. 5 Federal Procedural Forms, L Ed, Civil Rights § 10:161.

33. State v Downing, 251 Or 515, 446 P2d 519.

34. Wilkie v State, 98 Nev 192, 644 P2d 508.

35. § 65.

36. Jensen v Satran (ND) 303 NW2d 568.

Where prisoners in the general prison population were experiencing no more than one day's delay in obtaining access to the prison law library, where every time they went to the library they had about 3 hours in which to work on legal matters, and where those inmates confined in the segregated ward were allowed 49 hours per week in which to study law and prepare legal documents in their cells, adequate time had been afforded for the purpose of preparing complaints, petitions, or applications in which the inmates desired to test the legality of their confinement, since such pleadings are factual in content and the inclusion therein of legal argument is inappropriate. Hatfield v Bailleaux (CA9 Or) 290 F2d 632, cert den 368 US 862, 7 L Ed 2d 59, 82 S Ct 105.

As to inmates' right of access to court, generally, see § 65.

Practice Aids.—Access to legal materials. 22 Am Jur Trials 1, Prisoners' Rights Litigation § 64.

—Class action complaint by prisoners to enjoin enforcement of discriminatory prison regulations regarding prison law library. 5 Federal Procedural Forms, L Ed, Civil Rights § 10:161.

other publications. These cross-references often make it worthwhile for the researcher to work within a single publisher's system, at least in the initial stages of research.

Illustration D

An *American Jurisprudence 2d* index page

AMERICAN JURISPRUDENCE 2d

1074

Some of Lawyers Co-op's research tools are closely identified with *Am.Jur.2d,* and are often shelved next to it, because their titles begin with the words *American Jurisprudence.* One of these, the *Am.Jur.2d Deskbook,* is a handy compendium of legal statistics and other information. It is published as an adjunct to the encyclopedia, but is discussed separately in Chapter 13 with other legal factbooks and reference tools. Other Lawyers Co-op publications with "Am.Jur." in their titles are separate multivolume sets. *Am. Jur. Proof of Facts* and *Am.Jur.Trials,* both of which analyze specific trial practice issues, are discussed in Chapter 9, Court Rules and Practice, as is *Am.Jur.Pleading and Practice Forms. Am.Jur.Legal Forms 2d,* which contains examples of business and transactional forms, will be discussed with other formbooks in Chapter 13.

3. STATE ENCYCLOPEDIAS

Jurisdictional legal encyclopedias are also published for some individual states. These state encyclopedias are arranged much like the national legal encyclopedias, emphasizing the case law, and to a lesser extent the statutory law, of particular states. Several are published by either West or Lawyers Co-op, and tend to follow the pattern set by their publisher's national encyclopedia. Often disparaged by legal researchers, the state encyclopedias can actually be quite useful in their treatment of jurisdictionally specific concepts, such as community property or oil and gas law. A researcher unfamiliar with the domestic law of another jurisdiction can use that state's encyclopedia for a quick overview of the locally accepted interpretations, with extensive footnotes to primary sources. The state encyclopedias published by West or Lawyers Co-op, as might be expected, also provide cross-references to other tools of their respective publisher. The following state encyclopedias are currently published:

California Jurisprudence 3d (Lawyers Co-op)
Florida Jurisprudence 2d (Lawyers Co-op)
Encyclopedia of Georgia Law (Harrison)
Illinois Law and Practice (West)
Indiana Law Encyclopedia (West)
Maryland Law and Practice (West)
Michigan Civil Jurisprudence (Callaghan)
Michigan Law and Practice (West)
New York Jurisprudence 2d (Lawyers Co-op)
Strong's North Carolina Index 3d (Lawyers Co-op)
Ohio Jurisprudence 3d (Lawyers Co-op)
Pennsylvania Law Encyclopedia (West)
Tennessee Jurisprudence (Michie)
Texas Jurisprudence 2d (Lawyers Co-op)
Michie's Jurisprudence of Virginia and West Virginia (Michie)

This list of encyclopedias is limited to multivolume works, in which alphabetically arranged topics provide comprehensive coverage of a state's legal doctrines. Many states have other tools, sometimes called "Practice Series," which cover broad areas of state law in a thorough fashion. These works are discussed above in Chapter 9, Court Rules and Practice. To some extent, the outlines prepared for bar review courses are the modern form of topical summary once provided by legal encyclopedias. Anyone setting out to practice law in a jurisdiction should become familiar with the available resources describing and summarizing its legal doctrines.

C. RESTATEMENTS OF THE LAW

Over the last fifty years, the Restatements of the Law, prepared under the auspices of the American Law Institute, have become one of the most frequently cited, widely respected, and yet controversial secondary legal authorities. They are a unique form of legal literature, covering only ten specific fields of law: agency, conflict of laws, contracts, foreign relations law, judgments, property, restitution, security, torts, and trusts. All of the Restatements, except those on restitution and security, have been issued in second editions.

1. HISTORY AND PURPOSE

The American Law Institute was organized in 1923 for the purpose of summarizing and defining, or *restating,* major legal doctrines. Its members are among the most distinguished lawyers, judges and legal scholars in the country. The Institute's object in preparing the Restatements was:

> to present an orderly restatement of the general common law of the United States, including in that term not only the law developed solely by judicial decision, but also the law that has grown from the application by the courts of statutes that were generally enacted and were in force for many years.[1]

Some members of the Institute hoped that the Restatements would achieve such authority that they would relieve the burden of research in the numerous volumes of court reports. For many reasons that hope was never realized, and the considerable authority achieved by the first series of Restatements has actually been decreasing.

The first series of Restatements required over twenty years to complete, and after thirty years of effort the second series is still unfinished. The first component of a *third* series, *Restatement (Third) of the Foreign Relations Law of the United States,* was published in 1987. The process of preparing a Restatement involves an initial draft by the Reporter, an outstanding scholar in the subject field. The draft is reviewed by a committee of Advisors, who are also noted specialists, and the resulting text is then reviewed by the Council of the American Law Institute and further revised. The next version, the *tentative draft,* is distributed to all members of the Institute, considered, debated and often further amended at their annual meetings. The text may be returned to the Reporter for revision or redrafting before the final version is ultimately adopted. The tentative drafts are often treated as

1. Wolkin, "Restatements of the Law: Origin, Preparation and Availability," 21 *Ohio B.A.Rep.* 663, 663 (1949).

a form of legislative history of the Restatements, and are frequently cited to explain, support, or attack particular Restatement rules.[2]

Although the Restatements have no official legal status, and their reception and acceptance have varied from field to field, they have been successful on the whole and have had considerable influence on the courts. While often criticized for stating what the law *ought to be,* rather than what it *is,* some Restatements have led to needed changes in the law.[3]

2. COVERAGE AND FORMAT

The field of law covered by each Restatement is divided into a logical arrangement of numbered chapters, each chapter examining a major aspect of the field. Most chapters are then divided into topics and titles, and finally into numbered sections, each of which deals with a general principle of law. In the *Restatement (Second) of Contracts,* for example, chapter three concerns mutual assent in the formation of contracts, topic two focuses on manifestation of intent, and section 21 deals with intention to be legally bound. The section numbering is continuous throughout each Restatement, so only the section number is included in a citation: *Restatement (Second) of Contracts* § 21 (1981).

Each section begins with a statement of the principle of law, printed in boldface type (thus often called the "black letter" rule or principle). If a caveat to the rule is necessary, it follows the statement of the rule. Then, an explanatory comment is set forth, with one or more illustrations of the rule in the form of hypothetical applications.[4] These comments are followed in most Restatements (Second) and in the *Restatement (Third) of Foreign Relations Law* by Reporter's Notes, which provide background information on the development of the section, and cite court decisions, statutes, treatises and periodical articles, both in support of and contrary to the stated rule. Illustrations E-1 through E-3 show these components in Section 21 of the *Restatement (Second) of Contracts.*

2. Transcripts of A.L.I. discussions of drafts are printed in the *Proceedings* of the Institute. Like the drafts themselves, these provide insights into the rationale for the formulation of a Restatement as adopted.

A full bibliography of the drafts and other documentation for the several Restatements is published as section five of M.S. Zubrow, *Pimsleur's Checklist of Basic American Legal Publications,* Am.A.L.Libr. Pubs.Series No. 4 (Rothman, 1984).

3. A Director of the American Law Institute has defended the Restatements' frequent adoption of the "best" rule rather than a majority rule, by asserting that the Institute was "not obliged to govern its appraisals by a count of jurisdictions." Wechsler, "The Course of the Restatements," 55 *A.B.A.J.* 147, 150 (1969).

4. The assertions, counter-assertions, and cautions embodied in the Restatements have been parodied in the following hypothetical Restatement of the law on the power to regulate interstate commerce: "*Black letter text:* Congress has power to regulate interstate commerce. *Comment:* The states may also regulate interstate commerce, but not too much. *Caveat:* How much is too much is beyond the scope of this Restatement." Attributed to Professor Thomas Reed Powell, by Freund, "Review of Federalism," in E.N. Cahn, ed., *Supreme Court and Supreme Law* 86, 96-97 (Indiana University Press, 1954).

Illustration E-1

Restatement (Second) of Contracts **black-letter text, comment and illustrations**

§ 21. Intention to Be Legally Bound

Neither real nor apparent intention that a promise be legally binding is essential to the formation of a contract, but a manifestation of intention that a promise shall not affect legal relations may prevent the formation of a contract.

Comment:

a. Intent to be legally bound. Most persons are now aware of the existence of courts and rules of law and of the fact that some promises are binding. The parties to a transaction often have a reasonably accurate understanding of the applicable law, and an intention to affect legal relations. Such facts may be important in interpreting their manifestations of intention and in determining legal consequences, but they are not essential to the formation of a contract. The parties are often quite mistaken about particular rules of law, but such mistakes do not necessarily deprive their acts of legal effect.

Illustrations:

1. A draws a check for $300 payable to B and delivers it to B in return for an old silver watch worth about $15. Both A and B understand the transaction as a frolic and a banter, but each believes that he would be legally bound if the other dishonestly so asserted. There is no contract.

2. A orally promises to sell B a book in return for B's promise to pay $5. A and B both think such promises are not binding unless in writing. Nevertheless there is a contract, unless one of them intends not to be legally bound and the other knows or has reason to know of that intention.

b. Agreement not to be legally bound. Parties to what would otherwise be a bargain and a contract sometimes agree that their legal relations are not to be affected. In the absence of any invalidating cause, such a term is respected by the law like any other term, but such an agreement may present difficult questions of interpretation: it may mean that no bargain has been reached, or that a particular manifestation of intention is not a promise; it may reserve a power to revoke or terminate a promise under certain circumstances but not others. In a written document prepared by one party it may raise a question of misrepresentation or mistake or overreaching; to avoid such questions it may be read against the party who prepared it.

The parties to such an agreement may intend to deny legal effect

See Appendix for Court Citations and Cross References

Illustration E-2

Continuation of Restatement comment and illustrations

to their subsequent acts. But where a bargain has been fully or partly performed on one side, a failure to perform on the other side may result in unjust enrichment, and the term may then be unenforceable as a provision for a penalty or forfeiture. See §§ 185, 229, 356. In other cases the term may be unenforceable as against public policy because it unreasonably limits recourse to the courts or as unconscionably limiting the remedies for breach of contract. See §§ 178–79, 208; Uniform Commercial Code §§ 2–302, 2–719 and Comment 1.

Illustrations:

3. A, an employer, issues to B, an employee, a "certificate of benefit", promising stated sums increasing yearly, payable to a named beneficiary if B dies while still in A's employ. The certificate provides that it "constitutes no contract" and "confers no legal right." The quoted language may be read as reserving a power of revocation only until B dies.

4. A and B, two business corporations, have a contract by which B is the exclusive distributor in a certain territory of goods made by A. By a detailed written agreement they agree to continue the distributorship for three years. The writing provides that it is not to be a legal agreement or subject to legal jurisdiction in the law courts. The written agreement may be read and given effect to terminate the prior contract and to prevent any legal duty arising from the making of the agreement or from the acceptance of orders under it; but it does not excuse B from paying for goods delivered under it.

c. Social engagements and domestic arrangements. In some situations the normal understanding is that no legal obligation arises, and some unusual manifestation of intention is necessary to create a contract. Traditional examples are social engagements and agreements within a family group. See §§ 189–91. Where the family relation is not close, valuable services rendered in the home may make binding an express or implied promise to pay for the services; but even in such cases it would often be understood that there is no legal obligation while the agreement is entirely executory on both sides. See Comment *a* to § 19, Comment *b* to § 32.

Illustrations:

5. A invites his friend B to dinner in his home, and B accepts. There is no contract. If A promised B a fee for attending and entertaining other guests, and B did so, there would be a contract to pay the fee.

Illustration E-3

Reporter's Note for *Restatement (Second) of Contracts* § 21

6. A, a husband, is living in harmony with his wife, B. Before A leaves on a trip, A and B assess B's financial needs and agree that A will remit a fixed sum per month to support her. There is no contract.

REPORTER'S NOTE

This Section is new; compare former § 20. See 1 Williston, Contracts § 21 (3d ed. 1957); 1 Corbin, Contracts § 34 (1963).

Comment a. See Sulzbach v. Town of Jefferson, 83 S.D. 156, 155 N.W.2d 921 (1968); Wyoming Farm Bureau v. Smith, 259 F. Supp. 870, 873 (D. Mont. 1966), aff'd, 377 F.2d 918 (9th Cir. 1967); Bailey v. West, 105 R.I. 61, 249 A.2d 414 (1969). The relationship of this Section to §§ 18–20 is illustrated by Sulzbach v. Town of Jefferson, supra, in which a third party testified that the defendant said to him: "would I contact [the plaintiffs] and ask if they would take care of the work for him." This was held to be a sufficient manifestation of assent to constitute an offer that could be (and was) accepted by plaintiffs' performance without notice of acceptance, and regardless of whether defendant was "conscious of the legal relationship which [his] words or acts [gave] rise to." Illustration 1 is based on Keller v. Holderman, 11 Mich. 248, 83 Am. Dec. 737 (1863); see also Kilpatrick Bros. v. International Business Mach. Corp., 464 F.2d 1080 (10th Cir. 1972), and cases there cited. Illustration 2 is based on Illustration 2 to former § 20.

Comment b. Illustration 3 is based on Tilbert v. Eagle Lock Co., 116 Conn. 357, 165 A. 205 (1933); see also Mabley & Carew Co. v. Borden, 129 Ohio St. 375, 195 N.E. 697 (1935), 49 Harv. L. Rev. 148 (1935). A well-known case holding that there is no contract is Meyerson v. New Idea Hosiery Co., 217 Ala. 153, 115 So. 94 (1927); compare Spooner v. Reserve Life Ins. Co., 47 Wash.2d 454, 287 P.2d 735 (1955), involving a claim for an annual bonus by a living employee, where the court distinguished cases of death benefits. Illustration 4 is based on Rose & Frank Co. v. J. R. Crompton & Bros., [1923] 2 K.B. 261 (C.A.). As Comment *b* indicates, most of the arguments against enforcing a "not binding" clause are based on unfairness to one party. This argument is especially strong in pension plan disputes, see discussion of Illustration 3; cf. 42 A.L.R.2d 461 (1955). It is less strong in business transactions involving parties of roughly equal bargaining power, but in one such case a court found a duty to bargain in good faith despite language in a letter of intent that "[i]f the parties fail to agree . . . they shall be under no obligation to one another." Itek Corp. v. Chicago Aerial Indus., 248 A.2d 625 (Del. 1968), on remand, 257 A.2d 232 (1969); see Knapp, Enforcing the Contract to Bargain, 44 N.Y.U.L. Rev. 673 (1969).

Comment c. Illustration 6 is based on Balfour v. Balfour, [1919] 2 K.B. 571 (C.A.); contracts within the family present problems more of family law than of the law of contracts, and legal attitudes toward matrimonial contracts are currently in flux. See authorities cited in Reporter's Note to § 19, Comment *a*, and Edmiston, How to Write Your Own Marriage

See Appendix for Court Citations and Cross References

The three earliest Restatements (Second), for agency, torts and trusts, did not include the Reporter's Notes after each section. Instead these notes were printed in separate Appendix volumes, which also contained notes of court citations to the first series of Restatements and to tentative drafts, and cross-references to relevant West key numbers and to *ALR* annotations. Some later Appendices also provide these cross-references, but most concentrate on notes of court citations to either Restatement series.

A general index volume covers the contents of every Restatement in the *first* series. A general index for the second series has not been prepared, but each of the individual Restatements in the second or third series has its own index. (In recent Restatements, these indexes are preceded by various tables, including cases cited in Reporter's Notes and cross-references from earlier Restatement provisions.) Because each Restatement covers a discrete topic, it is rarely difficult to determine which index to consult. The table of contents of a Restatement can also be used to find material on specific topics. As with digests and statutory codes, however, this analytical approach tends to be less than satisfactory for researchers who are not familiar with a Restatement's format and contents.

3. TREATMENT IN CASES AND PERIODICAL ARTICLES

The Restatements have been the subject of much comment and analysis in both court decisions and periodical articles. Such comments, discussing a Restatement's development, applying its principles to particular situations, or criticizing its position, may be useful in determining the scope and value of Restatement doctrine.

Court citations of Restatements can be found in the Appendices to individual Restatements, as noted above.[5] Citing cases are listed for each Restatement section, with a brief explanation of the nature of the citation. "Cit. in sup.," for example, means that the section was cited to support a proposition. A paragraph-length summary of each case is also provided. In older volumes these summaries were simply reprinted headnotes of particular points of law, but in recent years they are more extensive and summarize entire decisions. Illustration F shows notes of citing cases to § 21 of the *Restatement (Second) of Contracts.*

These Appendices are kept up to date by annual pocket parts or supplementary pamphlets, and by revised or added volumes as necessary. An additional semiannual pamphlet, *Interim Case Citations to*

5. Case citations were formerly printed in a separate *Restatement in the Courts* series covering all the Restatements. This series consists of several volumes covering citations through 1975, but it has now been superseded by the individual Appendices. The "Permanent Edition" of the *Restatement in the Courts,* covering 1932 to 1944, has some historical value, in that it includes a glossary of terms defined in the Restatements and a history of the American Law Institute and the Restatements.

Volumes of state court annotations for some of the Restatements were also issued for some states, in the same format as the *Restatement in the Courts.* These were not issued for all states, nor for all of the Restatements, and have not been kept up to date.

Illustration F

Court citations to *Restatement (Second) of Contracts* § 21, as noted in Appendix volume

the case when the bank failed to correct it at trial. Pine River State Bank v. Mettille, 333 N.W.2d 622, 630.

Miss.1982. Cit. in disc. An action was brought against an insured and an additional insured to recover delinquent insurance premiums. The trial court rendered judgment for the insurer. The additional insured appealed and the state supreme court reversed. The court held that even though the insured was required to have the appellant named as an additional insured in its insurance policies as a term of its franchise agreement with the additional insured, and there was some correspondence between the insurer and the additional insured concerning the status of various policies, in the absence of a contractual relationship between the parties, the additional insured was not liable for the default in the payment of insurance premiums by the person who obtained the insurance. A. Copeland Enterprises v. Pickett & Meador, Inc., 422 So.2d 752, 754.

The following cases have cited or referred to § 21B of the Tentative Drafts. This is now § 21 of the Official Draft.

C.A.4, 1979. Cit. in sup., com. (b) cit. in sup. A foreign corporation sued two domestic corporations and others for breach of contract and tortious interference with a contractual relationship. On appeal from the lower court's grant of summary judgment in favor of the defendants, the appellate court reversed and remanded. This court stated that summary judgment was inappropriate when material issues of fact existed as to whether the parties had manifested mutual assent to the bargained exchange necessary for the formation of the contract, whether the approval of the foreign government was intended to be a precondition to acceptance of the domestic corporation's offer, and when the existence of agency powers was questionable. The court continued to state that it could not be said, as a matter of law, that the terms of the domestic corporation's offer were so uncertain as to preclude binding acceptance nor that the parties had manifested an intention to form a contract only after their oral agreements had been reduced to an integrated writing. Charbonnages de France v. Smith, 597 F.2d 406, 414.

Mass.1979. Cit. in diss. op. A patient brought a medical malpractice action against her doctor for the negligent performance of a tubal ligation and for breach of contract. Evidence at the trial included the plaintiff's testimony that she had told the doctor that she did not want any more children and that the doctor had responded by stating that the effects of the operation were permanent. The defendant offered testimony that after the surgery he had again told the plaintiff that the results of the surgery were permanent. Subsequently, the plaintiff had another child. Testimony concerning postoperative conversations between the plaintiff and her doctor were not allowed into evidence. The court directed a verdict in favor of the defendant on the negligence count and a jury found in favor of the defendant on the contract claim. The plaintiff appealed the jury verdict. This court held that the evidence did not warrant submission of the case to the jury concerning the breach of contract issue because even if all of the excluded testimony had been admitted at the trial, the evidence would not have supported a conclusion that the doctor had promised a specific result from the operation. The court stated that the doctor's statements were designed to make sure that the plaintiff knew the operation was irreversible in character but that the words used by the doctor were not promissory in nature. The dissenting opinion argued that there were sufficient facts in dispute for the case to be submitted to the jury and that the evidence concerning the defendant's admissions should not have been excluded. The dissent argued that the doctor had reason to know what the plaintiff's intentions were and so he should have to bear the risk if his statements were misunderstood. The dissent stated that a contract may have been created even though the parties did not speak in terms of warranties or guarantees. Clevenger v. Haling, 397 Mass. 154, 394 N.E.2d 1119, 1125.

Okl.App.1980. Com. (c) cit. in disc. The plaintiffs, husband and wife, sought to recover for services rendered to the husband's deceased mother. The plaintiffs asserted that the defendant, the husband's brother, had orally agreed that if the plain-

the Restatements of the Law, provides more current coverage of recent cases which have not yet been treated in full.

The *Annual Reports* of the American Law Institute, which are published separately and also reprinted in the annual *Proceedings,* include bibliographies of articles published during the preceding year on the various Restatements. The legal periodical indexes also provide access to such articles. The *Index to Legal Periodicals* lists articles about the Institute generally under "American Law Institute," but articles about an individual Restatement are found only under the general heading for the subject area. The *Current Law Index* and *Legal Resource Index* also list general articles under "American Law Institute," and refer to analyses of particular Restatements both by subject and under the name of the Restatement.

Both cases *and* articles mentioning specific Restatement sections can also be found by using *Shepard's Restatement of the Law Citations.* This work covers references to any of the Restatement series in published federal and state court decisions, in the *American Bar Association Journal,* and in nineteen major law reviews (the same reviews covered in *Shepard's Federal Law Citations in Selected Law Reviews* and every Shepard's state unit). The citator subdivides each Restatement section, indicating when a particular comment, caveat or illustration has been cited. Unlike most of Shepard's citators, it does not use any introductory signals to indicate the citing sources' approval or disapproval of the cited provisions. Illustration G shows a page in this citator listing section 21 of the *Restatement (Second) of Contracts.*

In researching Restatement positions, it is important to remember that many rules can be found in more than one Restatement series, usually assigned different section numbers. Some Restatement (Second) provisions are new, but others repeat or modify sections of the first series. It may be necessary, therefore, to look for decisions and articles under *both* citations in the Restatement Appendices or in *Shepard's Restatement of the Law Citations.* Cross-references between appropriate sections are easy to find; Reporter's Notes in the second and third series refer to earlier section numbers, and tables in recent volumes convert older citations to their modern counterparts.

The American Law Institute has an almost obsessive concern with the extent to which the Restatements have been cited by the courts. Tables in its *Annual Reports* provide statistics of court citations every year, and A.L.I. publicity for the Restatements focuses on the quantity of such citations. The Restatements are accorded unusual respect and attention by the courts and the bar, but remain a *secondary* authority.

D. TEXTS

From the earliest periods of English law, text writers have produced commentaries, guides, and summaries of the developing case law and legislation. Treatises in common law legal systems have never

Illustration G

Court and law review citations to *Restatement (Second) of Contracts*, as noted in *Shepard's Restatement of the Law Citations*

§ 1

CONTRACTS, SECOND

Contracts
2nd Series
598FS1580
611FS950
16MaA81
Idaho
706P2d1367
Mass
448NE1316
5AL513n

§ 1
15BRW194
48BRW677
142Az576
147CA3d110
148CA3d321
48CC676
88IlA970
114IlA186
217Neb814
144Vt207
101W2d549
Ariz
691P2d667
Calif
195CaR12
195CaR865
Ill
411NE94
448NE1023
Vt
475A2d1077
Wash
682P2d876
70CaL214
67Cor742
67Cor793
81CR111
Comment b
67Cor742
Comment f
17MaA121
Mass
456NE772

§ 2
602F2d53
155CA3d506
19MaA357
61NY112
20OA118
101W2d549
102W2d230
Calif
202CaR618
Mass
474NE1134
NY
460NE1081
472NYS2d
[596
Ohio
484NE1373
Wash
682P2d876
685P2d1088
70CaL306
52ChL932
67Cor794
97HLR690
94YLJ1040
Comment b
613FS523
102Wis2d186
Ariz
709P2d592
Wis
306NW658
94YLJ1040
Comment c
97HLR692
Comment d
602F2d53
97HLR692

§ 3
735F2d1427
745F2d1493
579FS1430
5BRW33
39BRW60
134Az563
147CA3d110
48CC676
96Il2d526
232Kan699
144Vt209
Ariz
658P2d216
Calif
195CaR12
Ill
451NE861
Kan
659P2d831
Vt
475A2d1077
70CaL297
67Cor743
67Cor793
Comment c
735F2d1427
67Cor742

§ 4
743F2d1025
530FS1133
581FS972
142Az576
145Az114
90NYAD966
15OA8
20OA118
Ariz
691P2d667
700P2d501
NY
456NYS2d
[557
Ohio
484NE1373
W Va
317SE512
70CaL306
67Cor793
Comment a
741F2d1515
19MaA141
Mass
472NE1351
94YLJ1015
Comment b
667F2d672
110IlA642
Ill
443NE605
Ind
452NE1004
Iowa
314NW397
346NW491
67Cor794
94YLJ1015

§ 5
180Ct94
Conn
429A2d809
Me
432A2d752
67Cor743
67Cor794
96HLR1181
98HLR1171
Comment a
760F2d13
Comment b
304PaS431
336PaS600
Me
450A2d988
Pa
486A2d427

§ 6
763F2d663
35BRW944
198Col447
Colo
601P2d1372
25CLA190
67Cor642

§ 7
687F2d933
759F2d471
556FS1338
568FS1120
102FRD773
27BRW246
35BRW578
59NY443
Ind
452NE1000
NY
452NE1219
465NYS2d
[891

§§ 12
to 16
70CaL217

§ 12
Comment f
68MnL173

§ 13
Tex
699SW602

§§ 14 to 16
98HLR1405

§ 14
92YLJ789

§ 15
85PaC56
Pa
481A2d984
67Cor667
67Cor706
67Cor795
81CR151
95HLR748
Comment a
85PaC57
Pa
481A2d985
Comment b
Illustra-
tion 1
85PaC58
Pa
481A2d985
Comment c
60NYAD368
85PaC59
NY
401NYS2d
[588
Pa
481A2d985

§ 16
95HLR769

§§ 17 to 19
Va
326SE676

§ 17
460US862
75LE607
103SC1608
51USLW
[4397
687F2d1256
735F2d1427
758F2d681
580FS1191
26BRW76
28BRW593
147CA3d110
48CC676
393Mas652
99Nev598
Calif
195CaR12
Del
468A2d1303
Mass
473NE180
Nev
668P2d263
70CaL217
67Cor642
67Cor786
Comment b
70CaL217
Comment c
Va
326SE676

§ 18
554FS324
94YLJ1041

§ 19
703F2d539
711F2d1206
735F2d1433
755F2d1267
765F2d735
530FS1133
554FS324
581FS972
613FS522
88IlA970
88Wis2d642
Ill
411NE94
Iowa
277NW771
Minn
330NW695
67MnL1133
Comment a
142Az576
Ariz
691P2d667
67Cor795
94YLJ1021
Illustra-
tion 1
94YLJ1022
Comment b
102Wis2d187
Wis
306NW658
67Cor794
Comment c
Minn
330NW695
Comment d
613FS523

§ 20
735F2d1433
760F2d13
761F2d1122
533FS345
571FS339
583FS961
607FS140
26BRW76
28BRW593
Alk
645P2d151
Ariz
707P2d321
Idaho
708P2d934
NM
679P2d266
67Cor757
67Cor795
66MnL294
36StnL1126
94YLJ1057
Comment c
Idaho
708P2d934
Comment d
67Cor768
67Cor800
94YLJ1058
Illustra-
tions
1 to 4
67Cor800
Illustra-
tion 4
Tex
695SW790

§ 21
768F2d1228
187Ct414
102Wis2d187
Conn
446A2d804
Minn
333NW630
Miss
422So2d754
Wis
306NW659
67Cor676
67Cor798

§ 22
735F2d1428
579FS1426
613FS521
134Az563
147CA3d110
48CC676
188Ct587
337PaS67
Ariz
658P2d216
Calif
195CaR12
Conn
452A2d640
Pa
486A2d483
Comment a
Fla
418So2d375

§ 23
700F2d500
Comment b
700F2d500
737F2d1504
Comment c
155CA3d507
Calif
202CaR619
Comment e
737F2d1504

§ 24
701F2d1263
761F2d1121
778F2d465
415FS453
544FS1347
15BRW194
35BRW944
139Az212
57MdA536
58MdA57
284Or369
57PaC641
333PaS207
Ariz
677P2d1320
Del
498A2d156
Ind
478NE1245
Md
470A2d1325
472A2d112
Ore
587P2d998
Pa
426A2d1290
482A2d246
Utah
622P2d787
65Cor344
Comment a
15OA9
20OA118
Ohio
484NE1373

§ 25
580FS144
104IlA510
17MaA121
300Md253
63NCA692
103NYAD708
10OA215
507Pa122
Ala
363So2d994
Ill
432NE1127
Mass
456NE772
Md
477A2d786
NC
306SE149
NY
478NYS2d10
Ohio
461NE327
Pa
488A2d599
81CR62

§ 26
703F2d1368
126IlA235
57MdA536
58MdA57
66OrA840
20OS106
333PaS207
Ala
363So2d994
Ill
466NE1249
Iowa
249NW637
Md
470A2d1325
472A2d112
Ohio
443NE164
Ore
676P2d904
Pa
482A2d246
67Cor795
Comment a
67Cor795
Comment b
99Ida400
333PaS207
Idaho
582P2d1078
Pa
482A2d246
Illustra-
tion 1
333PaS207
Pa
482A2d246
Comment d
703F2d539
703F2d1368

§ 27
756F2d935
596FS383
300PaS55
332PaS7
35WAp171
Pa
445A2d1296
480A2d1157
499A2d1076
Wash
665P2d1385
Comment a
108Ida190
112IlA254
332PaS8
Idaho
697P2d1204
Ill
445NE463
Pa
480A2d1157
Comment b
596FS1092
112IlA254
Ill
445NE463
Comment c
677F2d154
777F2d80
108Ida189
Idaho
697P2d1203
Comment d
677F2d154

§ 28
31BRW343
101IlA258
126IlA235
331PaS339
Ill
427NE1346
466NE1249
Pa
480A2d1063
Comment b
126IlA235
Ill
466NE1249
Comment c
558FS188

162

achieved the authoritative status of commentaries in civil law systems, but they continue to be an important part of our legal literature. By restating and synthesizing decisions and statutes, legal texts seek to impose order on the chaos of individual precedents. They also summarize historical developments, analyze and explain apparent discrepancies and inconsistencies, predict future changes, and provide practical guidance for the conduct of legal business by the legal profession and the lay public. From the first printed lawbooks in the 15th century to the multitude of volumes pouring from the presses today, legal texts have been characterized by a wide range of quality, style, and purpose.

1. TYPES OF TEXTS

Texts are used extensively by practitioners, scholars, and students for various purposes. Some trace the history of the field covered, synthesize complex legal developments, and provide a relatively clear statement of the law in a difficult or changing field. Others serve primarily as pragmatic reference guides for practicing lawyers in specialized areas. Another increasingly popular type of text provides a general introduction to a legal subject for the student, in a form typified by the West Publishing Company's hornbook and Nutshell series.

a. The Encyclopedic Treatise

As distinguished from the increasingly sophisticated forms used for primary sources and finding tools, the basic structure of the treatise has remained surprisingly constant—a narrative text, following the main areas of the subject in a more or less logical sequence; documentation to support the stated principles, by footnote citations to relevant cases or other primary sources; occasionally, an appendix of illustrative primary sources; and finally an index. When designed for the practical guidance of either the bar or the general public, the treatise may also include model forms for particular legal transactions or procedures.

Although the components of the treatise have changed relatively little, the breadth of coverage of individual works has narrowed considerably in recent years. The comprehensive, almost encyclopedic scope of works like Sir William Blackstone's *Commentaries on the Laws of England* (Clarendon Press, 4 vols., 1765–69) [6] and its American counterpart, James Kent's *Commentaries on American Law* (Halsted, 4 vols., 1826–30), has not been duplicated in modern times, and such broad treatments are unlikely to be attempted again. The texts of this century have been devoted to single subjects, and, even there, extensive multivolume treatments of an entire field like *Wigmore on Evidence*,[7]

6. For a comprehensive bibliography of the many editions of the *Commentaries*, Blackstone's writings, and works based on Blackstone's *Commentaries*, see C.S. Eller, *The William Blackstone Collection in the Yale Law Library, A Bibliographical Catalogue* (Yale University Press, 1938).

7. J.H. Wigmore, *A Treatise on the System of Evidence in Trials at Common Law* (Little, Brown, 4 vols., 1904–05). Current edition is *Evidence in Trials at Common Law*, 4th ed. (Little, Brown, 11 vols. in 13, 1961–88, with annual pocket supplements), revised by J.T. McNaughton (vol. VIII),

Williston on Contracts,[8] *Corbin on Contracts,*[9] and *Scott on Trusts*[10] seem to be a disappearing form. With a few exceptions, scholarly treatises are now focusing on increasingly narrow areas of law.[11]

Multivolume texts covering a single field exhaustively are still occasionally being written, either as a long-term project by one or two distinguished scholars, or as collaborative efforts by groups of writers. A fourth edition of *Scott on Trusts* has recently been published, as was a fifth edition of A.J. Casner, *Estate Planning* (Little, Brown, 9 vols., 1984–88). P. Areeda & D.F. Turner, *Antitrust Law* (Little, Brown, 7 vols. to date, 1978–date with annual bound supplement) is a major work in progress. Other current examples are the procedural treatises discussed in Chapter 9: *Moore's Federal Practice,* 2d ed. (Matthew Bender, 1948–date); Wright & Miller, *Federal Practice and Procedure* (West, 1969–date); and *Federal Procedure, Lawyers Edition* (Lawyers Co-op, 1982–date). These massive works are usually kept current by annual pocket parts, and are designed for scholars, students, and practicing lawyers. They have some of the characteristics of legal encyclopedias, and are often supplemented by forms, court rules, and other aids to practice.

On a slightly less ambitious scale, West has begun publishing some two- to four-volume treatises, expanding coverage of topics addressed in student hornbooks. Recent examples include W.R. LaFave, *Search and Seizure,* 2d ed. (4 vols., 1987), W.H. Rodgers, Jr., *Environmental Law: Air and Water* (2 vols., 1986), and R.D. Rotunda, J.E. Nowak, & J.N. Young, *Treatise on Constitutional Law* (3 vols., 1986).

Many treatises are issued in a looseleaf format to facilitate supplementation. Some of these are standards in their fields, such as *Moore's Federal Practice* or L.P. King et al., *Collier on Bankruptcy,* 15th ed. (Matthew Bender, 13 vols., 1979–date). It is important to remember, though, that these are not the same as looseleaf *services,* which are updated weekly or monthly. Most looseleaf treatises are supplemented annually, at the same frequency as bound volumes with pocket parts, and undue reliance should not be placed on their currency.[12] It is not publishing format but timeliness, thoroughness, clarity, and insight that make a treatise a valuable resource.

J.H. Chadbourn (vols. II–VII and IX), and P. Tillers (vols. I and IA).

8. S. Williston, *The Law of Contracts* (Baker, Voorhis, 5 vols., 1920–22). Current edition is *A Treatise on the Law of Contracts,* 3d ed. (Baker, Voorhis, 22 vols., 1957–79, with annual pocket supplements), by W.H.E. Jaeger.

9. A.L. Corbin, *Corbin on Contracts: A Comprehensive Treatise on the Rules of Contract Law* (West, 8 vols., 1950–51). Currently 12 vols., with infrequent supplementation by C.K. Kaufman.

10. A.W. Scott, *The Law of Trusts* (Little, Brown, 4 vols., 1939). Current edition is by W.F. Fratcher, (Little, Brown, 6 vols., 1987–88, with annual bound supplement).

11. This trend is described in Simpson, "The Rise and Fall of the Legal Treatise: Legal Principles and the Forms of Legal Literature," 48 *U.Chi.L.Rev.* 632 (1981).

12. Advantages and disadvantages of the looseleaf format are summarized in Moore, "Quality of Looseleaf Treatises: Analysis of the Publisher's Contributions," 8 *Legal Reference Services Q.* 209 (1988).

b. *Scholarly Monographs*

Most scholarly monographs tend to be narrow in scope and usually one volume in length, as distinguished from the encyclopedic multivolume treatises (many of which are also scholarly in approach). Typically, scholarly monographs are critical texts and examine the law analytically rather than just descriptively. They are rarely supplemented, but are occasionally revised and published in successive editions. Although issued by many publishers, they come most often from university presses or academic institutes. These texts tend to focus heavily on the historical background, underlying causes and policies, and future directions of particular legal subjects. Monographs often tend to be more interdisciplinary in nature than other legal writings.

c. *Hornbooks and Student Texts*

Since the end of the 19th century, American legal education has used the Socratic method of instruction, with the student participating actively in the learning process. When this teaching method is combined with casebooks which generally avoid explanation so that students must reach conclusions on their own, it is easy to see the market for books which present clear, concise summaries of the law. Several types of books meet the need.

"Hornbook" is the name given to a straightforward one-volume statement of the law on a specific subject. Such a volume can be used by the law student to clarify and organize the course material. Typically, a hornbook is written by an authority in the field. The main purpose of a hornbook is to be clear, not necessarily definitive, but several have become accepted by the courts as persuasive authority and are widely used by the bar. A leading example is William Prosser's classic *Handbook of the Law of Torts.*[13]

Hornbooks are organized in sections with detailed tables of contents, alphabetic lists of cases discussed, and topical indexes. Occasionally they are updated by pocket parts or supplementary pamphlets. Two widely used series of hornbooks are published by the Foundation Press and West Publishing Company. Each series offers at least one title on every major law school subject.

The West Publishing Company also produces a series called "Nutshells." These are paperback volumes, each devoted to a clear exposition of a single legal subject. They are much shorter and less exhaustive than hornbooks. Nutshells can be excellent introductions to new areas, but are not generally cited as authority. A list of current Nutshells appears in the front of each volume in the series.

d. *Practice Guides*

Many texts are designed primarily for practitioners in particular fields of law. The most widely used of this type are the procedural

13. First edition published by West in 1941. Current edition is W.P. Keeton et al., *Prosser and Keeton on the Law of Torts,* 5th ed. (West, 1984).

manuals issued commercially for particular jurisdictions. Supplementation is important in these publications, and is furnished by looseleaf inserts, pocket parts, or new editions every year. Model forms are provided, either in the text itself or in supplementary volumes. Court rules and civil practice acts are also frequently included.

Several publishers issue multivolume sets of practice books for various states, often including volumes on both procedural and substantive law. Some of the substantive law volumes in these series are major subject treatises, but with a single-jurisdiction emphasis. West is the largest publisher in this format and offers such sets for about two dozen states.

e. Law for the General Public

Among the oldest forms of legal texts are handbooks of law for the layperson. These were published in England in the first century of printing and have continued in popularity. New versions still appear almost every year.

Justice of the Peace manuals and similar guides for peace officers and town officials, most of whom did not have formal legal training, were common in England and America. In the nineteenth century many such works for the general public were published under the title *Every Man His Own Lawyer,* and there was at least one *Every Woman Her Own Lawyer,* by G. Bishop (Dick & Fitzgerald, 1858). These texts tended to be general introductions to the law and often included simplified instructions for conducting legal business, with model forms for specific transactions.

In recent years, there has been an increasing emphasis on self-lawyering, particularly in matters such as organizing a business, writing a will, avoiding probate, collecting a debt, and getting a divorce. Many of these guides suffer from oversimplification, lack of supplementation, and failure to reflect variation in the requirements of different jurisdictions. Some, however, are relatively reliable when used with caution for their intended purpose. Nolo Press is one publisher of well-prepared, regularly updated guides, although many of its works are written specifically for California. The organized bar, as might be expected, has opposed publications which in its view involve the unauthorized practice of law, and in a few instances has brought legal actions against them.[14] By and large, however, such efforts to demystify areas of the law and make them comprehensible to the general public are slowly succeeding.

2. FINDING TEXTS

The simplest method for locating a legal text on a particular research topic is to learn of one through the case law or periodical

14. *See, e.g., State v. Winder,* 42 A.D.2d 1039, 348 N.Y.S.2d 270 (1973); *New York County Lawyers' Ass'n v. Dacey,* 28 A.D.2d 161, 283 N.Y.S.2d 984 (1967), *rev'd,* 21 N.Y.2d 694, 287 N.Y.S.2d 422, 234 N.E.2d 459 (1967).

literature in a particular area of law. A treatise which is regularly cited as authority is likely to offer cogent analysis, well supported with references to further resources.

Several printed guides list or describe the basic works in specific areas of law. J.A. McDermott, ed., *Recommended Law Books,* 2d ed. (American Bar Association, 1986), is an annotated, highly selective bibliography of basic materials in almost five dozen subject areas. Designed specifically for practicing lawyers, its entries include excerpts from book reviews and critical comments from specialists in each field. The *Encyclopedia of Legal Information Sources* (Gale Research, 1988) lists treatises, textbooks, and numerous other resources under 460 law-related subjects, but includes no annotations.

Bibliographies on specific subjects can be found by using the *Legal Bibliography Index,* edited and published by W.S. Chiang and L.E. Dickson. In cumulative volumes covering 1978–82 and 1983–87, extensive subject indexes list bibliographies appearing in treatises, monographs or periodicals, or as separate publications. Most of the bibliographies indexed provide references not only to texts, but also to articles and other resources.

A thorough state legal research guide does more than provide information on a jurisdiction's legal system and primary sources. It also describes or lists the treatises and practice materials available for the jurisdiction. Appendix A, at the end of this volume, lists state legal research guides and bibliographies.

There are also more general works listing all available law books by subject. While these rarely differentiate well between basic treatises and more specialized studies or monographs, they can be useful for thorough searches. R.R. Bowker publishes *Law Books and Serials in Print* (3 vols., annual), in the same format as its general *Books in Print.* N. Triffin, ed., *Law Books in Print,* 5th ed. (Glanville, 6 vols., 1987) also lists books by author, title and subject, and is updated three times a year by *Law Books Published.*

An even more comprehensive approach is taken by P.D. Ward & M.A. Goldblatt, *National Legal Bibliography* (Hein, 1984–date), which lists all books newly acquired by major research law libraries throughout the United States. Monthly subject indexes give the researcher immediate notice of a wide range of current legal materials, and annual volumes also contain title and name indexes. A separate Part II for government documents, in a similar format, was added in 1986. *National Legal Bibliography* also publishes subject listings of books in particular fields. For example, a law firm might subscribe to a quarterly list of newly acquired books on securities regulation.

To find books on a particular subject, of course, one can also turn to a library's card catalog or online catalog. Given the variety of classifications and subject systems employed in libraries across the country, it is difficult to offer detailed instruction on how to use libraries to locate texts. Researchers should enlist the assistance of reference librarians and refer to relevant guides in their own libraries.

Two online bibliographic databases contain enormous amounts of information on legal material. RLIN (Research Libraries Information Network), a system based at Stanford University, reflects the holdings of many major research libraries (e.g., Harvard, Yale, Columbia, Michigan, Berkeley, and the Los Angeles County Law Library). Each time a member library adds a book to its collection, and catalogs it, the relevant information is put into the RLIN database. Many retrospective projects have been carried out to put older materials into the database as well. A competing system, OCLC (Online Computer Library Center), includes many law firm libraries and smaller law school libraries as members. Both systems also include records of the holdings of the Library of Congress. These systems create enormous online union catalogs listing all the books held by members, with information concerning which libraries hold which titles. One can determine whether any member library holds a particular volume by author or title. By using these two systems, researchers can gain access to the holdings of libraries throughout the United States, greatly increasing their ability to locate relevant texts. Often these systems are not available to the public and must be used by asking a librarian.

E. SUMMARY

In this chapter we have described three important genres of secondary source material. Encyclopedias, Restatements and texts can be helpful in providing background, are occasionally valuable as sources of authority, and are always useful for finding citations and perhaps other research leads. The researcher is cautioned to consider the nature of the work being used and the value of the material. One must be always mindful of the dangers inherent in relying on others' work. An essential component of legal research is synthesizing information in applying it to one's own concern or interest.

F. ADDITIONAL READING

J.H. Merryman, "The Authority of Authority," 6 *Stan.L.Rev.* 613 (1954).

J.H. Merryman, "Toward a Theory of Citations: An Empirical Study of the Citation Practice of the California Supreme Court in 1950, 1960 and 1970," 50 *S.Cal.L.Rev.* 381 (1977).

Chapter 13

OTHER LEGAL RESEARCH SOURCES

A. INTRODUCTION

This chapter presents a potpourri of very useful tools. All fall into the general category of legal research materials, but they have eluded categorization in preceding chapters. They do not contain primary source materials, and they generally do not analyze legal developments. Dictionaries are used to find a needed definition; directories help locate the address of a lawyer or judge. The use of language and communication with other lawyers and judges are essential to a lawyer's work; hence these are important aids.

Other materials described in this chapter such as formbooks and appellate records and briefs can be useful models for the preparation of legal documents. They have different origins: formbooks are published for this very purpose, while briefs are research by-products of specific litigation. They can save time and effort in legal practice, and often suggest new approaches to particular problems.

B. LEGAL DICTIONARIES

The complexity of legal terminology and the necessity for accuracy and precision in the use of words and phrases of legal significance have made law dictionaries an important tool of the lawyer's craft. The nuances and ambiguities of legal language have been a source of humor, anger, and misunderstanding on the part of the general public, and have often created great animosity toward the legal profession. There has been a movement for many years to change the wording of statutes and documents such as form contracts from legalese to plain English. Even everyday words, however, may have a different meaning in legal use.

The law dictionary is an essential aid to legal research. Karl Llewellyn once described its importance for the law student as follows:

> You are outlanders in this country of the law. You do not know the speech. It must be learned. Like any other foreign tongue, it must be learned: by seeing words, by using them until they are familiar; meantime, by constant reference to the dictionary. . . . Does *nisi prius* mean *unless before?* Or *traverse* mean an upper gallery in a church? I fear a dictionary is your only hope—a law dictionary—the one volume kind you can keep ready on your desk. . . . The life of words is in the using of them, in the wide network of their long associations, in the intangible something we denominate their feel. But the bare bones to work with the dictionary offers; and without those bare bones you may be sure the feel will never come.[1]

The first legal dictionary published in this country was an 1812 edition of John and William Rastell's *Les Termes de la Ley,* a successor to the oldest English law dictionary, published in 1527 by the older John Rastell. For almost a hundred years, the numerous editions of John Bouvier's *A Law Dictionary*[2] were most popular among American lawyers. Today, there are a number of American legal dictionaries of varying purpose and scope.

1. K.N. Llewellyn, *The Bramble Bush: On Our Law and Its Study* 41 (Oceana, 1951).

2. First published in 1839 (T. & J.W. Johnson, 2 vols.). The final edition was *Bouvier's Law Dictionary and Concise Encyclopedia,* 3d rev. (8th ed.) by F. Rawle (West, 3 vols., 1914).

1. *BLACK'S LAW DICTIONARY*

The two major legal dictionaries most used in the United States are *Black's Law Dictionary,* 5th ed. (West, 1979) and *Ballentine's Law Dictionary,* 3d ed. (Lawyers Co-op, 1969). Each presents in a single volume an alphabetical arrangement of terms that are of special relevance to the law. Both provide definitions that include, where possible, citations to relevant precedents. Each has attained a measure of recognition for reliability, although neither is viewed as particularly scholarly. Illustration A shows the definitions of the Latin term *res ipsa loquitur* in *Black's* and *Ballentine's.*

The fifth and latest edition of *Black's Law Dictionary* incorporates many improvements over the preceding editions. It includes ten thousand revised or new entries, such as brain death, ombudsman, palimony, and environmental impact statement. In addition to its availability in published form, the dictionary can be searched by computer on WESTLAW. The online version, unfortunately, is not

Illustration A

Res ipsa loquitur defined in *Black's* and *Ballentine's* law dictionaries

Res ipsa loquitur /ríyz ípsə lówkwədər/. The thing speaks for itself. Rebuttable presumption or inference that defendant was negligent, which arises upon proof that instrumentality causing injury was in defendant's exclusive control, and that the accident was one which ordinarily does not happen in absence of negligence. Res ipsa loquitur is rule of evidence whereby negligence of alleged wrongdoer may be inferred from mere fact that accident happened provided character of accident and circumstances attending it lead reasonably to belief that in absence of negligence it would not have occurred and that thing which caused injury is shown to have been under management and control of alleged wrongdoer. Hillen v. Hooker Const. Co., Tex.Civ.App., 484 S.W.2d 113, 115. Under doctrine of "res ipsa loquitur" the happening of an injury permits an inference of negligence where plaintiff produces substantial evidence that injury was caused by an agency or instrumentality under exclusive control and management of defendant, and that the occurrence was such that in the ordinary course of things would not happen if reasonable care had been used.

Black's Law Dictionary, 5th ed. (1979) p. 1173.

res ipsa loquitur (rēz ip'sa lo'qui-ter). The thing speaks for itself. The rule that proof that the thing which caused the injury to the plaintiff was under the control and management of the defendant, and that the occurrence was such as in the ordinary course of things would not have happened if those who had its control or management had used proper care, affords sufficient evidence, or, as sometimes stated by the courts, reasonable evidence, in the absence of explanation by the defendant, that the injury arose from, or was caused by, the defendant's want of care. 38 Am J1st Negl § 295.

The three essential elements of the doctrine of res ipsa loquitur are: (1) the instrumentality must be under the control or management of the defendant; (2) the circumstances, according to common knowledge and experience, must create a clear inference that the accident would not have happened if the defendant had not been negligent; and (3) the plaintiff's injury must have resulted from the accident. Lewis v Wolk, 312 Ky 536, 228 SW2d 432, 16 ALR2d 974.

The term means "the thing speaks for itself," and that means the thing or instrumentality involved speaks for itself. It clearly does not mean the accident speaks for itself. It means that when the initial fact, namely what thing or instrumentality caused the accident has been shown then, and not before, an inference arises that the injury or damage occurred by reason of the negligence of the party who had it under his exclusive control. The inference of negligence arising from the initially established fact compels the defendant, in order to relieve himself of liability, to move forward with his proof to rebut the inference of negligence. Travelers Ins. Co. v Hulme, 168 Kan 483, 213 P2d 645, 16 ALR2d 793.

Ballentine's Law Dictionary, 3d ed. (1969) pp. 1104–5.

regularly updated but simply contains the text of the printed 1979 volume.

Black's provides translations, definitions, and pronunciation aids for foreign and difficult words and phrases, including many Latin, Norman French, Saxon, and other ancient legal maxims. With the decline in the general knowledge of Latin, many maxims are now impenetrable to most researchers, without assistance. The maxims are listed alphabetically, by their *first* word, in the main listing of words in each dictionary, usually with no reference from any other word in the maxim. This is often confusing when the first word is insignificant and not within the researcher's recollection.[3]

Black's includes an extensive table of abbreviations, covering law reports, legal periodicals and other legal publications, and has several other appendices providing the text of the Constitution and information on Supreme Court justices and British regnal years.

2. *BALLENTINE'S LAW DICTIONARY*

Although older and slightly smaller than *Black's, Ballentine's Law Dictionary* is an excellent comprehensive dictionary. It contains many of the same features as *Black's,* such as coverage of legal maxims; pronunciation aids; citations of decisions and other sources; and a somewhat shorter table of abbreviations. *Ballentine's* cites frequently to *ALR* annotations and to the Lawyers Co-op encyclopedia *American Jurisprudence 2d.* Until the new, fifth edition of *Black's,* many felt that *Ballentine's* definitions and citations were more current than *Black's,* but now the comparison is much more difficult. Both still contain some outdated references, and each has modern words and phrases lacking in the other. *Ballentine's* current edition is now twenty years old, however, and its use appears to be decreasing. Publication of a new edition may reverse this trend.

3. *WORDS AND PHRASES*

A *judicial* dictionary draws its definitions of words and phrases from judicial decisions. A definition from a court is authoritative legally even if suspect lexicographically. *Black's* and *Ballentine's* both base much of their work on decisions, but attempt to integrate various judicial pronouncements into one definition.

The most comprehensive American judicial dictionary is *Words and Phrases,* the West Publishing Company's encyclopedic collection of abstracts of cases which have interpreted or defined words and phrases. These abstracts are taken from the headnotes printed in West's National Reporter System, and summarize the judicial definitions of specific terms. Some decisions define words in issue in contractual disputes,

3. There are a few other sources of maxims. Perhaps the most comprehensive and detailed is H. Broom, *A Selection of Legal Maxims, Classified and Illustrated,* 10th ed. by R.H. Kersley (Sweet & Maxwell, 1939), based on English law. *Latin for Lawyers,* 3d ed. (Sweet & Maxwell, 1960) and *Latin Words & Phrases for Lawyers* (Law and Business Canada, 1980) also define or translate Latin maxims.

while others construe statutory language. *Words and Phrases* is a ninety-volume set covering federal and state courts, kept up to date with annual pocket parts. The set consists simply of the case abstracts, with no text, commentary, synthesis or evaluation. Since courts keep redefining certain terms, multiple entries for many words are found. There are well over a hundred pages devoted to the term *res ipsa loquitur.* Often the best first place to look is in the pocket part, where recent definitions are located. Even more current definitions can be found through tables appearing in the advance sheets and bound volumes of all West reporters. Illustration B shows a page from a *Words and Phrases* pocket part, including several definitions of *res ipsa loquitur* as a rule of evidence.

In addition to the *Words and Phrases* set, West publishes "Words and Phrases" tables as part of each of its federal and state digests. These tables provide citations to cases but do not reprint headnotes. For definitions in a specific jurisdiction, the state digest's "Words and Phrases" may be the best place to look first.

It should also be noted that both LEXIS and WESTLAW, with full text retrieval capability, can be used as crude judicial dictionaries, since one can retrieve every use of a particular word in an opinion. While the definition of a common word would be buried in a veritable avalanche of other, irrelevant uses, in some circumstances, particularly where unusual words or phrases are involved, such a search may be helpful. The "digest" field on WESTLAW is often useful in increasing the precision of searches of this type.

4. OTHER DICTIONARIES

Other law dictionaries, considerably shorter than the major dictionaries described above, are also published. Illustration C shows the definitions of *res ipsa loquitur* in several of these works.

The best small dictionary in the opinion of many is S.H. Gifis, *Law Dictionary,* 2d ed. (Barron's, 1984). Although quite limited in coverage compared to *Black's* or *Ballentine's,* its selection is careful and astute, and it contains a high percentage of the most important older legal words and phrases and the most frequently used modern terminology. The definitions are clear and concise, and the case citations are often more recent than those in the two major dictionaries. It also includes references to treatises and periodical articles. Gifis is also author of *Dictionary of Legal Terms: A Simplified Guide to the Language of Law* (Barron's, 1983).

D. Oran, *Law Dictionary for Non–Lawyers,* 2d ed. (West, 1985) is a good small dictionary for the general public. Others of similar size and approach can be found in any law library.

K.R. Redden & E.L. Veron, *Modern Legal Glossary* (Michie, 1980) is a substantial modern dictionary, devoted exclusively to the definition of legal *terms, phrases and concepts* rather than *words.* It also includes the names of professional associations, government agencies and inter-

Illustration B

A page from a *Words and Phrases* pocket part supplement

exercised, rule of evidence is that accident speaks for itself, "res ipsa loquitur," that is to say, a presumption of negligence arises from fact of accident itself. Brechtel v. Gulf States Elevator Corp., La.App., 195 So.2d 403, 406.

The doctrine of "res ipsa loquitur" is a rule of evidence designed to secure a just consideration of cases involving injury or damage to those who suffer them through unusual or extraordinary circumstances and applies where court finds that, due to the fact that knowledge concerning cause of accident is peculiarly within possession of defendant, plaintiff is unable to produce proof of the specific act of negligence involved. Kramer v. R. M. Hollingshead Corp., 71 A.2d 139, 140, 141, 6 N.J.Super. 255.

"Res ipsa loquitur" is rule of evidence allowing inference of negligence from proven facts; it is based on theory of probability where there is no direct evidence of defendant's conduct, permitting common sense inference of negligence from happening of the accident. Gicking v. Kimberlin, 2 Dist., 215 Cal. Rptr. 834, 835, 170 C.A.3d 73.

Doctrine of "res ipsa loquitur" is a rule of circumstantial evidence which applies when the facts shown suggest the negligence of the defendant as the most plausible explanation of an accident. Lemon v. Fein, La.App. 4 Cir., 467 So.2d 548, 552.

Doctrine of "res ipsa loquitur" is simply rule of evidence whereby negligence may be inferred upon proof that character of the accident is such that it would not ordinarily occur in the absence of negligence and that the instrumentality causing the injury had been under the management and control of the defendant. Martin v. Petta, Tex.App. 2 Dist., 694 S.W.2d 233, 239.

"Res ipsa loquitur" is rule of circumstantial evidence under which jury may infer negligence in absence of direct evidence to that effect. Newkirk v. National R.R. Passenger Corp., D.C.Ill., 618 F.Supp. 1422, 1424.

RES IPSA LOQUITUR CASE

"Res ipsa loquitur case" is ordinarily merely one kind of case of circumstantial evidence, in which jury may reasonably infer both negligence and causation from mere occurrence of event and defendant's relation to it. Weeden v. Armor Elevator Co., Inc., 468 N.Y.S.2d 898, 901, 97 A.D.2d 197.

RES IPSA LOQUITUR DOCTRINE

When instrumentality which causes injury, without any fault of injured person, is, at time of injury, under such control by defendant that it would be unlikely that other negligence could have occurred which would have operated as an intervening proximate cause of the injury, and injury is such as in the ordinary course of things does not occur if one having such control uses proper care, then, under "res ipsa loquitur doctrine," law infers negligence on part of the one in control as cause of injury. Knowlton v. Sandaker, 436 P.2d 98, 103, 150 Mont. 438.

The "res ipsa loquitur doctrine" is that when an instrumentality which causes injury, without any fault of injured person, is under exclusive control of defendant at time of injury, and injury is such as in ordinary course of things does not occur if the one having such control uses proper care, then the law infers negligence on part of the one in control as the cause of the injury. Jackson v. William Dingwall Co., 399 P.2d 236, 241, 145 Mont. 127.

"Res ipsa loquitur doctrine" is that where a thing which causes injury without fault of the injured person is shown to be under the exclusive control, actual or constructive, of a defendant, and the injury is such as, in the ordinary course of things, does not occur if the one having control uses proper care, then the injury is presumed to have arisen from defendant's negligence or want of care. Great Am. Indem. Co. v. Ford, La.App., 122 So.2d 111, 113.

RESIST

In statute proscribing the resistance or obstruction of peace officer in performance of duty, "obstruct" is more broad than "resist," and includes putting obstacles in path of officers completing their duties; however, initial question is whether alleged violation of statute, although possibly within statute, constitutes a hindrance of official duties. State v. Hauan, Iowa App., 361 N.W.2d 336, 339.

The word "resist" is derived from the Latin, and its etymological meaning is "to stand against" or "to withstand"; and to constitute offense of resisting arrest, there must be actual opposition or resistance, making necessary, under circumstances, use of force and threats unaccompanied by force, and mere words do not constitute resistance. State v. Avnayim, 185 A.2d 295, 298, 24 Conn.Sup. 7, 1 Conn.Cir. 348.

As respects statute making it unlawful for any person to knowingly and willfully resist or oppose any officer of State or any person authorized by law in serving or attempting to execute any legal writ, rule, order, or process whatsoever, or to knowingly and willfully resist any such officer in discharge of his duties without, such writ, rule, order, or process, word "resist" means to oppose and describes opposition by direct action and quasi-forcible means; it is limited to obstructive conduct but does not require employment of actual violence or direct force; it is sufficient that person charged engaged in actual opposition to officer through use of actual or constructive force making it reasonably necessary for officer to use force to carry out his duty, and, although words or even threats alone do not constitute resistance, threats accompanied by present ability and apparent intention to execute them will be sufficient. State v. Donner, Iowa, 243 N.W.2d 850, 854.

It is not required that complainant use physical resistance in refusing to submit to an act of sexual penetration by force; in the context of sex offenses, "resist" means physical struggle by the complainant with the actor. State v. Heinzer, Minn.App., 347 N.W.2d 535, 537.

RESISTANCE

See, also,

Earnest Resistance.
Unreasonable Resistance.

"Resistance" means withstanding the force or effect of or the exertion of oneself to counteract or defeat. Landry v. Daley, D.C.Ill., 280 F.Supp. 938, 959.

national organizations; foreign phrases; famous trials; popular names of cases and statutes; biographical notes on important legal figures;

Illustration C

Res ipsa loquitur defined in four legal dictionaries

RES IPSA LOQUITUR *(rēz ip'sa lo'qui-ter)*—Lat: the thing speaks for itself. A rule of **evidence** whereby **negligence** of the alleged wrongdoer may be inferred from the mere fact that the accident happened, provided: (1) the occurrence is the kind of thing that does not ordinarily happen without negligence; (2) the occurrence must have been caused by an agency or instrumentality within the exclusive control of the defendant; (3) the occurrence was not due to contribution or voluntary action by the plaintiff. Prosser, Torts 214 (4th ed. 1971). The rule may not apply when direct evidence of negligence exists. See 270 So. 2d 900, 904. "The gist of it, and the key to it, is the inference, or process of reasoning by which the conclusion is reached. This must be based upon the evidence given, together with a sufficient background of human experience to justify the conclusion. It is not enough that plaintiff's counsel can suggest a possibility of negligence. The evidence must sustain the **burden of proof** by making it appear more likely than not." Prosser, Torts 212 (4th ed. 1971). The procedural effect of successfully invoking the doctrine is to shift the **burden** of going forward with the evidence, which normally attaches to the plaintiff, to the defendant, who is thereby charged with introducing evidence to refute the presumption of negligence which has been created.

S.H. Gifis, *Law Dictionary*, 2d ed. (Barron's, 1984) p. 407.

RES IPSA LOQUITUR (Latin—the thing speaks for itself). A doctrine of tort law which allows the plaintiff to rely on circumstantial evidence to raise an inference of negligence. If he cannot come forward with proof of negligence, the plaintiff may avoid a directed verdict for the defendant by showing that (1) the injury in question generally results from negligence, and (2) the defendant was in sole control of the instrumentality which caused the injury. Although Res Ipsa establishes a Prima Facie case for negligence, the jury may still find for the defendant. '

K.R. Redden & E.L. Veron, *Modern Legal Glossary* (Michie, 1980) p. 445.

res ipsa loquitur (= the thing speaks for itself) is known in G.B. but is far more common in the U.S., where it has become familiar enough that *res ipsa case* and even *resipsy* have become lawyers' elliptical colloquialisms. *Res ipsa loquitur* is one of those LATINISMS that have become so common in lawyers' ARGOT, or more specifically as a TERM OF ART, that their usefulness is unquestioned. The last syllable is sometimes misspelled *-or* or *-er*.

The tendency toward the elliptical dropping of the final word in the phrase is illustrated in this specimen: "The doctrine of *res ipsa* does not relieve the plaintiff of the burden of proving negligence." Kramer, *The Rules of Evidence in Negligence Cases* 35 (3d ed. 1963).

B.A. Garner, *A Dictionary of Modern Legal Usage* (Oxford University Press. 1987) p. 479.

6. *Res ipsa loquitur* ("the thing speaks for itself") is a **rebuttable presumption** (a conclusion that can be changed if contrary evidence is introduced) that a person is **negligent** if the thing causing an accident was in his or her control only, and if that type of accident does not usually occur without negligence. It is often abbreviated "res ipsa" or RIL. [pronounce: rez ip-sa lock-we-tur]

D. Oran, *Law Dictionary for Non-Lawyers*, 2d ed. (West, 1985) p. 267.

and bibliographic entries. It is not a substitute for a word dictionary, but is a useful supplementary reference book to *Black's* or *Ballentine's*.

One of the most useful and entertaining of legal dictionaries is Bryan A. Garner's *A Dictionary of Modern Legal Usage* (Oxford University Press, 1987). While this work does not attempt to define all legal terms, it is an excellent guide to terms commonly used and misused in legal writing. Many of its entries crusade wittily against legal jargon and gobbledygook.

In late 1988, the Oxford University Press and the University of Texas School of Law launched a project to produce an unabridged *Oxford Law Dictionary,* applying the historic and scholarly approach of the *Oxford English Dictionary* to legal terminology. The project, to span a decade, may produce the first authoritative, historical law dictionary. Bryan Garner, author of *A Dictionary of Modern Legal Usage,* will serve as editor-in-chief.

A project is also underway at Macmillan to produce a truly "modern" legal dictionary without the obsolete arcana that fill so many pages of *Black's* and *Ballentine's.*

Dictionaries in several fields related to law (e.g., criminology, economics, finance, and political science) often contain words and phrases not likely to be found in law dictionaries, and can be quite useful. Some of these are described in Chapter 14, Nonlegal Research Sources.

C. OTHER LANGUAGE TOOLS

A variety of reference works other than dictionaries provide very useful assistance in the writing and reading of legal prose.

1. LEGAL WRITING AIDS

Much of a lawyer's work is written communication, from client letters to memoranda to court briefs. Some lawyers write well, of course, but the general state of legal writing has been deplored in a steady flow of books and articles.

There are several handbooks available for those interested in creating comprehensible documents. Two recent, well-reviewed treatments are V.R. Charrow & M.K. Erhardt, *Clear and Effective Legal Writing* (Little, Brown, 1986) and M.B. Ray & J.J. Ramsfield, *Legal Writing: Getting It Right and Getting It Written* (West, 1987). Other works which may be helpful include D. Mellinkoff, *Legal Writing: Sense and Nonsense* (Scribner/West, 1982), and R.C. Wydick, *Plain English for Lawyers,* 2d ed. (Carolina Academic Press, 1985).[4] One of

4. Wydick's book is based on an article of the same name at 66 *Calif.L.Rev.* 727 (1978). A recent survey of legal writing, including a selective bibliography of books and articles, is Gopen, "The State of Legal Writing: *Res Ipsa Loquitur,*" 86 *Mich.L. Rev.* 333 (1987).

the most valuable tools for legal writing is Garner's *Dictionary of Modern Legal Usage,* described above.

There are two modern *legal* equivalents of Roget's popular thesaurus, providing alternatives for words commonly used in legal writing and argument. W.C. Burton, *Legal Thesaurus* (Macmillan, 1980) is in two parts, like Roget's. The first part lists the main words alphabetically, with the form indicated (noun, verb, adjective, or adverb), followed by their synonyms and alternatives, and a helpful listing of associated concepts and foreign phrases. The second part is an index which provides references from the secondary words to the main words in the first part. W. Statsky, *Legal Thesaurus/Dictionary* (West, 1985) provides substantially the same coverage in one alphabet, with cross-references, and hence is somewhat easier to use.

A quotation containing a well-turned phrase or illustration often makes a point more clearly and succinctly than numerous citations to more weighty authority. There are several modern books of *legal* quotations, including P.C. Cook, *Treasury of Legal Quotations* (Vantage Press, 1961); E.C. Gerhart, *Quote It! Memorable Legal Quotations* (Clark Boardman, 1969); S. James & C. Stebbings, *A Dictionary of Legal Quotations* (Croom Helm/Macmillan, 1987); M.F. McNamara, *2,000 Famous Legal Quotations* (Aqueduct Books, 1967); and D. Shrager & E. Frost, *The Quotable Lawyer* (Facts on File, 1986). General quotation books such as *Bartlett's Familiar Quotations,* 15th ed. (Little, Brown, 1980), may also be of use.

2. GUIDES TO ABBREVIATIONS

Because of the extensive abbreviation of legal publications in citations, there is often need for tables of abbreviations to identify the source cited. As noted above, both of the two major law dictionaries, *Ballentine's* and *Black's,* contain tables of abbreviations. *A Uniform System of Citation* (the "Bluebook") also contains several lists of abbreviations, but none as comprehensive as those in the dictionaries or in separately published abbreviations dictionaries.

The most current and comprehensive American source for interpreting abbreviations is D.M. Bieber, *Dictionary of Legal Abbreviations Used in American Law Books,* 2d ed. (Hein, 1985). M.D. Powers, *The Legal Citation Directory* (Franas Press, 1971) is limited to U.S. federal and state reports and attorney general opinions, but it has entries for both abbreviations and reporters, and provides forms used by both law reviews and courts. D. Raistrick, *Index to Legal Citations and Abbreviations* (Professional Books, 1981) is a British publication, and provides the best coverage of early English reports. It also includes many abbreviations from the United States and other countries.

For researchers trying to *write* citations rather understand them, abbreviated forms for courts and legal publications are provided in M.M. Prince, ed., *Bieber's Dictionary of Legal Citations,* 3d ed. (Hein, 1988).

Many law books include their own tables of abbreviations for works cited therein. Before using extrinsic aids such as those described above, it may save time and needless confusion to check the front of the volume in which a citation is found, for the full designation of the abbreviated reference. This is particularly important in Shepard's citators. Shepard's often uses abbreviations found nowhere else, sometimes even using the same abbreviation in different citator units to designate different publications.

D. LEGAL REFERENCE BOOKS

Legal encyclopedias such as *Am.Jur.2d* and *C.J.S.* have already been discussed in Chapter 12. These massive sets describe specific legal doctrines, but do not analyze institutional aspects of the legal system or its history. There are a few specialized encyclopedias of this latter sort, including S.H. Kadish, ed., *Encyclopedia of Crime and Justice* (Free Press, 4 vols., 1983); L.W. Levy, K.L. Karst & D.J. Mahoney, eds., *Encyclopedia of the American Constitution* (Macmillan, 4 vols., 1986); and R.J. Janosik, ed., *Encyclopedia of the American Judicial System* (Scribner, 3 vols., 1987).

One of the broadest and yet most concise of encyclopedic works is D.M. Walker, *Oxford Companion to Law* (Oxford University Press, 1980). It contains thousands of relatively short articles on legal institutions, events, individuals, cases and statutes. It focuses primarily on English law, but offers a wide range of information on American subjects and the law of various countries. Many of the articles provide citations to other sources for further research. Its breadth of coverage, lively style, and conciseness make it very useful for quick reference, particularly on historical topics.

West's Guide to American Law: Everyone's Legal Encyclopedia (West, 12 vols., 1983–85, and 1987 supplement) offers extensive coverage of many American legal issues and institutions. Designed for a lay audience, it contains straightforward definitions of many legal terms and brief articles on famous people and events. Unlike most legal reference materials, it is heavily illustrated. Some of its articles are written by renowned authorities, while others are simply reprinted from government sources. For lawyers and law students, the set's primary value is as quick background reference on unfamiliar topics.

A variety of ready-reference compendia are published, the legal equivalents of the *World Almanac.* These volumes generally play little role in scholarly research, but can be very handy for someone seeking a specific fact or statistic about the legal system.

The *American Jurisprudence 2d Deskbook* (Lawyers Co-op, 1979) is published as an adjunct to the legal encyclopedia, and supplemented by an annual pocket part. It is divided into seven parts, and contains historical legal documents, information on court systems and the legal profession, statistical data, tables of law reports, and much other useful reference material.

Similar works are *The Lawyer's Almanac* (Law & Business, 1985), and S. Wasserman & J.W. O'Brien, eds., *Law and Legal Information Directory,* 5th ed. (Gale Research, 1988). Both include sections on the legal profession, legal education, the judiciary, government agencies, statutes, and commonly used abbreviations. *Shepard's Lawyer's Reference Manual* (1983, with annual pocket part), summarizes the laws of each state on a variety of topics, outlines state court systems, and provides information on federal and state agencies.

E. LEGAL DIRECTORIES

Directories of lawyers, judges, law firms, and law libraries are extremely useful tools for a variety of purposes, including job hunting, referral of legal matters, and background information about a particular lawyer or judge. There are many different kinds of law directories, ranging from simple lists of lawyers in a particular jurisdiction to publications offering detailed biographical coverage of the bench and bar.

1. *MARTINDALE–HUBBELL LAW DIRECTORY*

This annual multivolume directory, published by Martindale–Hubbell, Inc., is by far the most extensive and widely used source of information on American attorneys, with more selective coverage of Canadian and other foreign lawyers. In addition to providing information on individual attorneys and law firms, the *Martindale–Hubbell Law Directory* contains a wide range of information on a variety of legal topics. The 1989 edition is in eight volumes.

The first seven volumes are an alphabetic arrangement of the fifty states. Each volume has two sources of information. First there is a "Geographical Bar Roster," which is an alphabetical list of attorneys by city. These entries include the date of birth, date of admission to the bar, and the college and law school attended by each attorney. These latter items are provided by a code number; one must consult a table at the front of the volume to convert the number into useful information. Both individual attorneys and law firms are listed. Listings for attorneys affiliated with firms have cross-references to the firm listings.

The second source of information, comprising most of each volume, is called the "Biographical Section." It consists of display advertisements purchased by law firms. Its coverage is far more limited than the Geographical Bar Roster in the front of the volume, although virtually all large law firms purchase space here, as do a great many medium and small firms. Firm listings are arranged by city and then alphabetically by firm name. They list areas of specialty, provide references and include biographical information on each lawyer in the firm. It is important to remember that this information is an advertisement drawn from questionnaires prepared by members of the law firm, and may not be objective. Firm listings in the Geographical Bar Roster indicate the page location of fuller treatments in the Biographical Section.

Geographical and biographical sections for Canadian and international lawyers are in volume seven of the eight-volume set, as is a Biographical Section for corporate legal departments. Following the regular Geographical Bar Rosters in each volume are separate Patent Lawyers' Rosters, for each state and foreign country.

The last volume of *Martindale–Hubbell* is called "Law Digest." This volume contains brief summaries of the laws of all fifty states and U.S. territories, Canada and its provinces, and over fifty other countries, including the law of the European Economic Communities. These digests are not official or definitive statements of the law, but they are prepared by reputable attorneys in the individual states and countries and are usually quite well done. They are too limited for serious research, but most provide citations for further research and are handy guides for superficial inquiries. Each discusses the same specified topics, so the digests can be a handy starting place for comparative research on a subject within their scope. The last volume of *Martindale–Hubbell* also contains the texts of Uniform and Model Acts, American Bar Association codes (including the Model Rules of Professional Conduct), and selected international conventions. Illustration D shows a sample page from a *Martindale–Hubbell* state law digest.

2. OTHER NATIONAL AND INTERNATIONAL DIRECTORIES

A national legal directory of much more limited scope than *Martindale–Hubbell* is *Who's Who in American Law* (Marquis, biennial). Prepared by the publisher of *Who's Who in America,* this volume includes biographies of prominent attorneys, judges, and legal scholars.

A new *online* national directory of attorneys being introduced in 1989 is the WESTLAW Lawyer's Referral Directory. Updated on a continuous basis, the directory's entries on lawyers and law firms include addresses, telephone numbers, specialties, education, and various other information. Among the advantages of an online directory are the ability to retrieve a list of firms practicing in a particular specialty or to find attorneys by name without having to know in what state and city they practice.

There are several other national directories of lawyers and law firms. Two that provide fuller treatment of large firms are *Law & Business Directory of Major U.S. Law Firms* (Law & Business, 2 vols., 1984) and *American Lawyer Guide to Leading Law Firms* (Am–Law, 2 vols., 1983). The *National Law Journal Directory of the Legal Profession* (New York Law, 1984) provides coverage of major firms geographically and of smaller specialized firms by specialty. All three of these

Illustration D

The first page of a *Martindale-Hubbell* state law digest

ALASKA LAW DIGEST

Revised for 1989 edition by

ROBERTSON, MONAGLE & EASTAUGH, A Professional Corporation, of the Alaska Bar.

(Citations unless otherwise noted are to Alaska Statutes [AS], with 1986 revisions. Rules of Civil Procedure are cited: Civ. R.P., Rule of Criminal Procedure: Crim. R.P.)

Note: Not all legislation approved by Governor at time of going to press. This revision covers Session Laws adopted and approved by Governor up to June 6, 1988. Any later legislation affecting topics in Digest will be reflected in Supplement.

Uniform Probate Code and 1975 Official Amendments adopted. See topic Wills.

ABSENTEES:

Care of Property.—If owner of property disappears and cannot be found after reasonable inquiry, on application of any person who would be an heir if such absentee were dead, a guardian for the estate may be appointed. (13.26.165). See topics Death; Descent and Distribution.

Process Agent.—No statutory provision.

Escheat.—When a person dies intestate, without heirs, leaving real or personal property in the state, or when no claim of ownership has been made to bank deposits, cash, or personal property for more than seven years, the property escheats to state. The property may be sold by the state. Escheated property may be recovered within seven years by an action in superior court by a person not a party to the prior escheat proceedings and who had no knowledge thereof, and who can establish a claim. (09.50.070-110).

ACCORD AND SATISFACTION:

In absence of statute, common law applies. See topic Commercial Code.

Pleading.—Assert affirmative defense. (Rule 8[c], Civ. R.P.).

ACKNOWLEDGMENTS:

Uniform Acknowledgment Act not adopted.

Within State.—Acknowledgments may be made within State of Alaska before any justice, judge, magistrate, clerk or deputy clerk of court, notary public, postmaster or other authorized officer. (09.63.010). Fee is not regulated by statute.

Outside State.—Notarial acts, including acknowledgments, performed outside state will be recognized if performed by authorized notary public, justice, judge, magistrate, clerk or deputy clerk of court of record in place in which notarial act is performed, officer of foreign service of U.S., consular agency, or person authorized by regulation of Department of State, or other persons authorized to perform notarial acts in place in which act is performed. (09.63.050).

Persons in or with U.S. Armed Forces.—Commissioned officer in active service with armed forces or person authorized by regulation of armed forces to perform notarial acts may take acknowledgments for merchant seamen of U.S., member of armed forces of U.S., person serving with or accompanying armed forces of U.S. or his dependants. (09.63.010).

Real Estate Conveyances, Within State.—Acknowledgments may be made within state of Alaska before any clerk of court, notary public, postmaster, or commissioner by subscribing witness or handwriting. Officer must endorse on instrument certificate of acknowledgment and date it was taken under his hand. (34.15.150).

Real Estate Conveyances, Outside State, But Within U.S.—Acknowledgments may be made within any state, territory, or district of U.S. outside of Alaska, before any judge of court of record, justice of peace, notary public, or other officer authorized to take acknowledgments by law of jurisdiction in which taken. (34.15.160).

Real Estate Conveyances, Outside U.S.—Conveyance executed in foreign country may be acknowledged under laws of Alaska. (34.15.180).

General Requirements as to Taking.—Officer taking acknowledgment must certify that person acknowledging appeared before him and acknowledged execution of instrument and that person acknowledging was known to person taking acknowledgment or person taking acknowledgment must have satisfactory evidence that person acknowledging was person described in and who executed instrument.

General Requirements of Certificates.—Certificate must conform to laws and regulations of state or other place in which acknowledgment is taken or certificate must contain words "acknowledged before me" or their substantial equivalent. (09.63.080). For real estate, endorsement by officer taking acknowledgment of certificate of acknowledgment and date of making acknowledgment. (34.15.150).

Attorneys in Fact.—Uniform Durable Power of Attorney Act not adopted. Uniform Probate Code applies. (13.26.325-13.26.330).

Corporations.—No special provisions.

Foreign Acknowledgments.—Conveyance may be executed according to laws of foreign country and execution of it acknowledged under 09.63.050-09.63.130.

Effect of Acknowledgment.—Entitles conveyance to be read in evidence without further proof or recorded and filing is constructive notice of conveyance's contents to subsequent purchasers or mortgagees. (34.15.260).

Proof by Subscribing Witness or Handwriting.—Proof of execution of an instrument may be made before any officer authorized to take an acknowledgment thereof by a subscribing witness thereto, who must state his own residence, and that he knew the person described in, and who executed the instrument. Officer must either personally know witness or have satisfactory proof of his identity. (34.15.210). Conveyance may be proved before superior court by proving handwriting of grantor and a subscribing witness. (34.15.220).

Authentication.—Certificates of acknowledgment shall be recognized if certificate is in form prescribed by laws and regulations of state or other place in which acknowledgment is taken or certificate contains words "acknowledged before me" or their substantial equivalent. (09.63.080).

Form.—No form is specifically required by statute. Statute includes five forms from Uniform Recognition of Acknowledgments Act for various types of acknowledgments. (09.63.100).

Alternative to Acknowledgment or Proof.—Matter required or authorized to be supported, evidenced, established or proven by sworn statement, declaration, verification, certificate, oath or affidavit, in writing of person making it (other than deposition, acknowledgment, oath of office, or oath required to be taken before specified official other than notary public) may be supported, evidenced, established or proven by person certifying in writing under penalty of perjury that matter is true. Certification shall state date and place of execution, fact that notary public or other official empowered to administer oath is unavailable and following: "I certify under penalty of perjury that the foregoing is true." (09.63.020).

Validation.—Defective acknowledgments of deeds, contracts, leases, powers of attorney, mortgages and other instruments pertaining to real property validated, provided no suit to change, set aside or reform instrument filed in court of record in judicial district wherein property located within ten years from date of instrument or of acknowledgment; judicial sales deeds, executors' and administrators' sales and deeds, and defective tax deeds also validated. (34.25.010).

ACTIONS:

Rules of Civil Procedure (Civ. R.P.) based upon Federal Rules, control in Superior and district courts. See topic Practice.

Equity.—Distinction between actions at law and suits in equity is abolished. There is but one form of action, which is denominated a civil action.

Civil actions against State authorized. (09.10.010).

Commencement.—By filing a complaint with court. (Rule 3 Civ. R.P.).

Parties.—Every action must be prosecuted in the name of the real party in interest, except that an administrator or executor, a trustee of an express trust, or a person expressly authorized by statute, may sue without joining with him the person for whose benefit the action is prosecuted; but these provisions do not authorize the assignment of a thing in action not arising out of contract. (Civ. R.P. 17[a]).

Heirs of decedent, whose names and addresses are unknown, may be proceeded against as "the unknown heirs of" such decedent in any action or suit relating to real property in Alaska. (09.45.750).

Class Actions.—One or more as fairly represents a class may sue or be sued when right to be enforced is: joint, common or secondary when owner of primary right refuses to enforce; several, when object of action is adjudication of claims which affect property; or several when common question of law or fact affects common rights and relief sought. Uniform Class Actions Act not adopted. (Rule 23 Civ. R.P.).

Intervention.—As a matter of right or by permission depending whether applicant would be bound by a judgment or main action has common questions of law or fact. (Rule 24 Civ. R.P.).

Interpleader.—Persons having claims against plaintiff may be joined as defendants and required to interplead when their claims expose plaintiff to double liability. (Rule 22 Civ. R.P.).

Third Party Practice.—Defendant as third party plaintiff may serve complaint on person not a party who may be liable to defendant on plaintiff's claim. (Rule 14 Civ. R.P.).

See note at head of Digest as to 1988 legislation covered.

works, unfortunately, have not been issued in new editions for several years. In the rapidly changing world of legal practice, they are now quite dated.

Several other national directories are less descriptive but are updated annually. These include the *Bar Register* (Bar Register Co.); the *Lawyers' List* (Law List Publishing); and *The American Bar, the Canadian Bar, the International Bar* (Reginald Bishop Forster & Associates). Additional directories with an international scope are *Allen's International Directory of English Speaking Attorneys* (National Legal Directory Publishing, 1986); *International Lawyers* (International Lawyers Co., annual); *International Law List* (Corper–Mordaunt Co., annual); and *Kime's International Law Directory* (annual). The last two of these are British publications.

The *American Bar Association Directory* (annual) lists addresses and officers for A.B.A. sections and divisions, as well as numerous affiliated organizations. The *Directory of Law Teachers* (Association of American Law Schools, annual) includes biographies of faculty members of all accredited law schools in the United States, preceded by a list of those schools, with addresses, phone numbers, and faculty rosters. The *Directory of Law Libraries* (American Association of Law Libraries, annual) lists law libraries by state and city with addresses and phone numbers.

3. SPECIALIZED AND LOCAL DIRECTORIES

With the specialization of law practice, directories of lawyers practicing in particular fields of law have become important for the referral of legal matters. Such directories are published both by specialized bar associations and commercial organizations. They vary in scope and detail, but are almost always based on information supplied by the listed individuals and firms. Some sections of the American Bar Association also publish rosters which are often used as specialized directories.

A specialized directory, like a general directory, must be current to be of value. The following are a few examples of regularly updated specialized directories:

Directory of Lawyer Referral Services (American Bar Association, annual);

Directory of Legal Aid and Defender Offices in the United States (National Legal Aid and Defender Association, annual);

Law & Business Directory of Bankruptcy Attorneys (Prentice Hall Law & Business, annual; available online in WESTLAW);

Law & Business Directory of Corporate Counsel (Prentice Hall Law & Business, 2 vols., biennial; available online in WESTLAW);

Markham's Negligence Counsel (Markham Publishing, annual);

National Directory of Prosecuting Attorneys (National District Attorneys Association, biennial);

Probate Counsel (Royal Publishing, annual).

A variety of state and regional directories of lawyers provide information on practitioners in specific geographical areas. Over two dozen are published by the Legal Directories Publishing Co. These include directories for individual states (e.g., *Illinois Legal Directory*) and for regions (e.g., the *Mountain States Legal Directory*). Because of their pale blue covers, they are often called "Bluebook" directories. They contain listings of federal and state officials in the jurisdiction; names and addresses of federal, state and local courts, judges and court officers; a listing of lawyers and law firms, by county and city; and advertisements for specialized legal support services. These "Bluebooks" include some practitioners not listed in *Martindale–Hubbell.*

There are also bar directories issued by other commercial publishers, such as the *Parker Directory of California Attorneys* (Parker & Son, annual), and by state and local bar associations.

4. JUDICIAL DIRECTORIES

Although judges are listed in most of the national and jurisdictional directories described above there are a number of excellent directories and biographical works focusing specifically on the judiciary. Perhaps the most important of these is *Almanac of the Federal Judiciary* (LawLetters, 2 vols., 1984–date), a regularly updated looseleaf publication. Volume one covers all district court judges, and volume two covers circuit court judges and Supreme Court justices. Detailed biographies include each judge's major publications and noteworthy rulings, along with media coverage and lawyers' evaluations of the judge's ability and temperament.

The *Federal Judiciary Almanac* (Wiley, annual) is a thorough and more traditional biographical directory of the federal bench, with statistical information for each district. It can be searched online through LEXIS. *Judicial Staff Directory* (Congressional Staff Directory, annual) provides listings of federal court personnel, including U.S. Attorney and U.S. Marshal staffs, and brief biographies of judges and staff members. I.J. Waldman, ed., *Federal Judges & Justices* (Rothman, 1987–date, updated monthly) is a current listing of nominations, confirmations, elevations, resignations, and retirements of the federal judiciary. The *United States Court Directory* (Administrative Office of the U.S. Courts, semiannual) provides names, addresses and telephone numbers.

The American Bench (Reginald Bishop Forster & Associates, biennial) is a substantial biographical directory of both federal and state courts, covering almost every judge in the United States. It also includes information on the structure and jurisdiction of various courts. *BNA's Directory of State Courts, Judges, and Clerks*, 2d ed. (BNA, 1988), does not include biographical information, but has a very extensive listing of state court personnel with addresses and telephone numbers. Both *The American Bench* and the BNA directory have personal name indexes, handy for tracking down the titles and courts of particular judges. The BNA directory also has convenient one-page charts of each state's court system, showing routes of appeal. Similar charts are included in *Want's Federal–State Court Directory* (WANT Publishing, annual), a slim paperback providing addresses and telephone numbers of federal judges and of major state courts and officials.

F. FORMBOOKS

Because of the repetitive nature of many legal transactions, the use of model forms has always been common among lawyers in all times and places. Single printed forms for a variety of transactions have been prepared and sold by legal stationers in this country since the 18th century. Individual practitioners and law firms revise and re-use forms prepared in the course of their practice. It would be an enormous waste of time and effort (and probably a dangerous practice) to draft every form anew, without regard to standard forms which incorporate the experience of others, legal precedents and statutory requirements. On the other hand, simply copying standard forms, without the modifications necessary for the specific facts and circumstances of each transaction, would be a gross violation of professional responsibility.

Modern law publishing has developed standard forms into a major segment of legal literature. Legal forms are still published and sold singly and in pads, but the publication of formbooks in separate volumes, in sets, and in massive encyclopedias now offers a sophisticated and often bewildering array of selections to the drafter. Formbooks are annotated with notes of decisions and with explanations of the tax consequences of particular forms. Sets are issued for particular subjects and specific jurisdictions, and keyed to applicable statutes. As with other legal publications, formbooks must be supplemented frequently to reflect changes in the legal requirements on which they are based.

Several large multivolume sets of legal forms are published for the two principal purposes which forms generally serve. *Practice forms,* designed for litigation procedures or other business before courts and administrative agencies, have already been discussed in Chapter 9. *Transactional forms* are also published extensively. These are instruments designed for specific legal transactions, such as contracts, leases, wills, and deeds.

One of the largest sets of transactional forms is *American Jurisprudence Legal Forms 2d* (Lawyers Co-op, 33 vols., 1971–date). It has an extensive two-volume general index, annotations to cases, statutes and other primary sources, notes on tax consequences, and references to other Lawyers Co-op publications. Forms are assigned to broad subject headings, which are arranged alphabetically from "Abandoned Property" to "Zoning." The set includes a "Federal Guide to Legal Forms" in two looseleaf volumes; other volumes are supplemented by annual pocket parts.

West's Legal Forms, 2d ed. (West, 30 vols., 1981–86, with pocket part supplementation) is similar to *Am. Jur. Legal Forms,* but includes both practice forms and instruments. It is also organized differently, with separate sections devoted to forms for specific types of practice instead of a single alphabetical arrangement. "Business Organizations," for example, occupies the first six volumes.

Other sets of comparable scope and coverage are J. Rabkin & M.H. Johnson's *Current Legal Forms with Tax Analysis* (Matthew Bender, 10 vols. in 22, 1968–date, with looseleaf supplementation) and *Nichols Cyclopedia of Legal Forms Annotated,* (Callaghan, 10 vols. in 29, 1936–date, with pocket part supplementation).

Many formbooks are issued for specialized practice or for the drafting of instruments in specific subject fields. Among the most common of this type are those for real estate transactions, corporate practice, wills and estates, matrimonial practice, and, more recently, for practice under the Uniform Commercial Code. At least three multivolume formbooks are geared specifically to U.C.C. articles and sections. Typical specialized formbooks include *Fletcher Corporation Forms Annotated* (Callaghan, 7 vols. in 19, 1972–date) and *Municipal Legal Forms* (Callaghan, 4 vols. in 8, 1976–date).

Computer-produced forms, which can be custom-designed for each transaction, are a recent development in legal drafting. Many lawyers use word-processing equipment to store and retrieve both complete forms and individual provisions for particular instruments, greatly expediting drafting tasks. A variety of software packages that provide forms for lawyers' use is now available. Such products are regularly reviewed in the legal newspapers and practice journals.

G. RECORDS AND BRIEFS

At the appellate level of litigation, attorneys present their arguments in written briefs. Oral arguments are held in most cases, but they are usually less extensive than briefs, which afford the best opportunity to persuade the court. The briefs contain arguments on the points of law at issue, with citations to supporting primary sources and secondary authorities. In some cases, *amicus curiae* ("friend of the court") briefs are also filed with the permission of the court, by persons or groups interested in the outcome of the case. Counsel for the appellant also prepares and files a full record of the proceedings below, including the trial transcript and pre-trial documents.

Appellate records and briefs are documents of substantial research value.[5] Court decisions are based on the arguments presented, and opinions are written in response to specific points made in the briefs.

5. Not all briefs are documents of substantial value. One particularly disreputable effort caused the Indiana Supreme Court to establish a minimum standard: "A brief is not to be a document thrown together without either organized thought or intelligent editing on the part of the briefwriter." *Frith v. State,* 263 Ind. 100, 104, 325 N.E.2d 186, 189 (1975).

Appellate decisions can therefore be best understood in light of the briefs and the record of the case below. These documents can also be used to develop arguments in similar cases, to study the appellate process generally, or to learn about earlier stages of particular litigation.

1. U.S. SUPREME COURT

Copies of the records and briefs of the Supreme Court of the United States are distributed to about twenty law libraries throughout the country on a regular basis. They arrive long after the end of the Court's term, however, and are often incomplete. Most researchers, therefore, rely on commercial microform publication of Supreme Court briefs. Several publishers have issued microfilm or microfiche editions of records and briefs going back to the Court's beginnings; Congressional Information Service is the major supplier of current records and briefs on microfiche. Its set includes petitions for writs of *certiorari* and other papers on cases the Court has declined to hear, as well as full records of cases argued and decided. Most large law libraries now receive microfiche copies of Supreme Court records and briefs, within a few weeks after oral argument or summary disposition.[6]

Filings in all cases orally argued since the 1979 term are also available online through LEXIS, in the BRIEFS file of its GENFED library. Briefs are often available on LEXIS before they arrive in libraries on microfiche, but they are still only released *after* oral argument.

Complete oral arguments before the U.S. Supreme Court since the 1953 term are available on microfiche from University Publications of America. That publisher also issues briefs and oral arguments on a very selective basis in the field of constitutional law in book form under the title, *Landmark Briefs and Arguments of the Supreme Court of the United States.* Tape recordings of oral arguments have been available from the National Archives since 1955, with several limitations. They are available three years after decision of the case, only for scholarly or instructional purposes, and only with permission upon application to the Marshal of the Supreme Court.

2. OTHER COURTS

The records and briefs of lower federal courts and of state courts are not as widely available as those for the Supreme Court. Most circuits of the U.S. Courts of Appeals distribute their records and briefs to a few law libraries in their region, although some have no distribution. Microfiche editions for the Second Circuit and the District of Columbia Circuit have expanded the distribution of their records and

6. The holdings of libraries around the country as of 1982 are listed in Teitelbaum, "United States Supreme Court Briefs and Records: An Updated Union List," *Legal Reference Services Q.*, Fall 1982, at 9.

briefs considerably, but attempts to provide complete coverage of the Courts of Appeals briefs on microfiche have not succeeded.[7]

The records and briefs of the high court in most states, and of the intermediate appellate courts in a few states, are available at several libraries in each of the states. Inquiry can be made to each court to determine where its briefs are deposited. Microfilm or microfiche editions are also available for the records and briefs of the high courts of a very few states.[8]

Many students mistakenly assume that there are "briefs" for every case. Most cases are simply not appealed, and much litigation at the trial court level does not produce any written submissions on points of law. There may be papers submitted to support or oppose specific motions, such as motions to dismiss or for summary judgment, but there is no single set of "briefs" as exists in most appellate actions. For some cases there may be an extensive written record, but this material is generally only available from the clerk of the court or through the attorneys involved.

H. SUMMARY

This chapter reviews a variety of tools for legal reference and finding tools. Some, like the dictionaries, provide access to authorities. Others, like the directories, provide reference information. Formbooks and records and briefs can be useful tools for working attorneys. All are part of the arsenal of research materials with which every lawyer should be familiar.

I. ADDITIONAL READING

Comment, "Jurisprudence by Webster's: The Role of the Dictionary in Legal Thought," 39 *Mercer L.Rev.* 961 (1988).

D. Mellinkoff, "The Myth of Precision and the Law Dictionary," 31 *UCLA L.Rev.* 423 (1983).

F.R. Shapiro, "Legal Data Bases and Historical Lexicography," *Legal Reference Services Q.*, Winter 1983, at 85.

7. For holding libraries as of 1983, see Teitelbaum, "United States Courts of Appeals Briefs and Records," *Legal Reference Services Q.*, Fall 1983, at 67.

8. The two remaining installments in Professor Teitelbaum's union list are "State Courts of Last Resort's Briefs and Records: An Updated Union List," *Legal Reference Services Q.*, Summer/Fall 1985, at 187; and "Intermediate Appellate State Courts' Briefs and Records: An Updated Union List," 8 *Legal Reference Services Q.* 159 (1988).

Chapter 14

NONLEGAL RESEARCH SOURCES

A. INTRODUCTION

Most practicing lawyers spend very little of their time on what we might call doctrinal research. Only a few concentrate on appellate practice and deal regularly with constitutions, statutes, and case law. Others, engaged in less lofty research pursuits, are more likely to be doing research on such topics as the viability of a particular truck brake lining system or land movement problems at an office building site. Thus guidance in the basics of general research may be valuable for many prospective lawyers.

This chapter does not aspire to being a comprehensive guide to general research, but tries to provide a basic introduction to major nonlegal research and reference works. Each of the many works cited can lead to other useful sources of information.

Just as the legal researcher constantly questions the basis of the authority being used (Is it a primary source? Is it a useful persuasive authority? Is it a source that must be updated and verified?), so the researcher in a factual area must always be aware of the origin or reliability of the information found. The vigilant researcher always evaluates the veracity and timeliness of the source in hand.

This chapter focuses on printed and online resources, but a person with subject expertise in an area may often be a better source of information than a book or database. Good lawyers become experts at getting to the most useful source, which often is a knowledgeable human being who can provide precisely the information needed. Such a person will also be able to direct one to the most authoritative research tools in the field. The directories to be discussed in Section C can provide valuable names and phone numbers.

Naturally the information in this chapter will become dated as soon as it is printed. New reference sources and databases are issued constantly, and existing ones are updated. When you begin a research project, it is well worth checking with a reference librarian to ensure that you are getting the most current data and using the best available resources.

B. GENERAL INFORMATION

This section discusses some of the major sources of general information in nonlegal areas. Its suggestions are selective and illustrative, rather than comprehensive. Most of these sources are in the reference collection of any major public or academic library, and many are included in larger law library collections.

1. ENCYCLOPEDIAS AND FACTBOOKS

Encyclopedias are primarily useful to a researcher with little or no knowledge of a subject area. Although seldom authoritative, an encyclopedia can provide a researcher with sufficient background on a subject to make reasonable decisions about additional research.

General encyclopedias such as the *Encyclopedia Americana* (Grolier, 30 vols., revised annually) and *Encyclopaedia Britannica,* 15th ed. (32 vols., revised annually),[1] are primarily designed for a mass audience, including high school students. They can be useful, however, as introductions to unfamiliar fields or for specific information on well-settled topics. Some of the longer essays are quite technical and the bibliogra-

1. The current edition of the *Encyclopaedia Britannica* consists of the single *Propaedia* volume (outlining all human knowledge); the ten-volume *Micropaedia* (containing over one hundred thousand short "ready-reference" articles); the nineteen-volume *Macropaedia* of over four thousand longer articles, many of which include selective bibliographies; and a two-volume index. This unusual format disturbs some users who prefer the traditional approach of the still highly regarded, but considerably outdated, 9th (25 vols., 1875–89) and 11th (29 vols., 1911) editions.

phies can provide leads to authoritative works in the field. Access by the traditional alphabetical arrangement of articles is supplemented by detailed general indexes. Older revisions of most encyclopedias are updated by annual yearbooks, but these become cumbersome to use as their number increases.

A one-volume general encyclopedia can be very helpful for quick reference, particularly if it is based on scholarly sources. One of the best of these is the *New Columbia Encyclopedia,* 4th ed. (Columbia University Press, 1975).

Specialized subject encyclopedias are generally more scholarly than the general encyclopedias, and frequently feature articles by leading authorities in the particular field. They are designed for serious researchers who may not be familiar with the field. They frequently also provide leads for further research. Dozens of subject encyclopedias are published. Two of the most important are the *Encyclopaedia of the Social Sciences* (Macmillan, 15 vols., 1930–35) and the *International Encyclopedia of the Social Sciences* (Macmillan, 18 vols., 1968–80). The newer edition of this encyclopedia is often the first place to look, but it does not completely supersede its predecessor. Both cover anthropology, economics, geography, history, law, political science, psychiatry, psychology, sociology, and statistics, with signed articles written by experts in each field.[2] The articles provide clear expositions of basic concepts and include selected bibliographies of sources.

The New Palsgrave: A Dictionary of Economics (Macmillan, 4 vols., 1987) is a major new encyclopedic treatment of its subject, with authoritative articles and extensive bibliographies. Other specialized encyclopedias which may be of use include the *Dictionary of American History* (Scribner's, 8 vols., 1976), *Dictionary of the History of Ideas* (Scribner's, 5 vols., 1973–74), *Encyclopedia of Philosophy* (Macmillan, 8 vols., 1967), *International Encyclopedia of Education* (Pergamon, 10 vols., 1985), *International Encyclopedia of Psychiatry, Psychology, Psychoanalysis & Neurology* (Van Nostrand Reinhold, 12 vols., 1977), and *McGraw–Hill Encyclopedia of Science and Technology,* 6th ed. (McGraw–Hill, 20 vols., 1987; available online in WESTLAW). This is but a sampling of important specialized encyclopedias; others are available for every major discipline. The section below on "Research Guides and Bibliographies" provides information on ways to identify subject encyclopedias.

For some research problems, an encyclopedic treatment is neither needed nor helpful. Often one simply needs basic facts or figures. Several factbooks designed specifically for lawyers have already been described in Chapter 13, at pages 417–418. A more general work, such as the annual *World Almanac and Book of Facts,* may quickly provide just the information needed. The *World Almanac* and its competitors

2. In the *Encyclopaedia of the Social Sciences,* for example, the article on "Common Law" is written by Roscoe Pound; "Lawlessness" is by Jerome Frank; and "Supreme Court, United States" is by Felix Frankfurter.

provide a wide range of data on politics, sports, awards, current events, weather, and virtually every field of general interest.

Factual compendia are published for many specialized fields, by government agencies, trade associations, and commercial publishers. Examples include *Aerospace Facts and Figures* (Aerospace Industries Association of America, annual), *Insurance Facts* (Insurance Information Institute, annual), *Yearbook of Agriculture* (U.S. Department of Agriculture, annual), and deskbooks for a variety of professions. Like subject encyclopedias, these factbooks can be found through resources described in "Research Guides and Bibliographies," below.

2. DICTIONARIES

In addition to the *legal* dictionaries previously described in Chapter 13, the following general dictionaries of the English language are valuable reference tools for lawyers and are readily available in most libraries.[3]

The *Random House Dictionary of the English Language,* 2d unabridged ed. (1987) is the newest unabridged dictionary. Its 315,000 entries provide extensive treatment of the origin and meaning of words, and its recent publication date suggests its inclusion of most terms which have entered the language in the past few years.

Webster's Third New International Dictionary of the English Language, Unabridged (Merriam–Webster, 1961) is an older but somewhat more thorough work. It has over 450,000 entries, and to many scholars is the authoritative dictionary of American English. The dictionary has not been revised in almost thirty years, but reprintings include new words in an "Addenda Section" at the beginning of the volume.

The researcher interested in the development of the English language should consult the *Oxford English Dictionary,* 2d ed. (Oxford University Press, 20 vols., 1989). This massive dictionary offers encyclopedic treatment of more than 600,000 words and phrases. Most entries include representative quotations illustrating usage in relevant historical periods and reflecting changes in meaning.

There are many specialized subject dictionaries that may be of use to the legal researcher confronted with a problem in an unfamiliar or technical area. A few examples are: J.E. Schmidt, *Attorneys' Dictionary of Medicine and Word Finder* (Matthew Bender, 4 vols., 1962–date); *Banking Terminology,* 2d ed. (American Bankers Association, 1985); *Dictionary of Criminal Justice Data Terminology,* 2d ed. (U.S. Bureau of Justice Statistics, 1981); A. Gilpin, *Dictionary of Economics and Financial Markets,* 5th ed. (Butterworths, 1986); L.E. Davids, *Dictionary of Insurance,* 6th ed. (Rowman & Allanheld, 1984); D.D. Runes, ed., *Dictionary of Philosophy,* rev. ed. (Philosophical Library, 1983); W. Laqueur, *A Dictionary of Politics,* rev. ed. (Free Press, 1974); *McGraw–*

3. Many more specialized dictionaries can be identified by use of a comprehensive bibliography of such sources, A.M. Brewer, ed., *Dictionaries, Encyclopedias and Other Word–Related Books,* 4th ed. (Gale Research, 3 vols., 1987).

Hill Dictionary of Scientific and Technical Terms, 3d ed. (1984); and G.A. Theodorson & A.G. Theodorson, *A Modern Dictionary of Sociology* (Crowell, 1969).

The three leading dictionaries for the social sciences generally are J. Gould & W.L. Kolb, *A Dictionary of the Social Sciences* (Free Press, 1964); G.D. Mitchell, *A New Dictionary of the Social Sciences* (Aldine, 1979), and B.B. Wolman, *Dictionary of Behavioral Science,* 2d ed. (Academic Press, 1988).

To locate other dictionaries in specific fields, consult Brewer's bibliography (footnote 3 above), a guide to the literature of a particular discipline, or a general guide to reference books.

3. RESEARCH GUIDES AND BIBLIOGRAPHIES

Just as this book might be of use to an economist looking for information on statutory publication, other fields have similar research aids that provide an understanding of *their* research sources. In addition, there are general guides to research methodology and to reference literature in all disciplines.

One of the best short treatments available is A.L. Todd, *Finding Facts Fast,* 2d ed. (Ten Speed Press, 1979), which provides a brief introduction to the principles of good research and discusses a wide range of reference sources. Other recent guides include J.K. Gates, *Guide to the Use of Libraries and Information Sources,* 6th ed. (McGraw–Hill, 1988); T. Mann, *Guide to Library Research Methods* (Oxford University Press, 1987); and M. McCormick, *New York Times Guide to Reference Materials,* rev. ed. (Times Books, 1985).

The basic source for determining what published reference materials exist in all disciplines is E.P. Sheehy, ed., *Guide to Reference Books,* 10th ed. (American Library Association, 1986). Sheehy lists and describes basic tools such as dictionaries, encyclopedias, bibliographies, research guides, directories, and periodical indexes in hundreds of areas of study. Section A covers general reference works, and Sections B through E cover the various branches of the humanities; social and behavioral sciences; history and area studies; and science, technology, and medicine. The fastest way to get some sense of the literature of an unfamiliar discipline is often through the *Guide to Reference Books'* overview. Because it covers all subject areas, discussion is quite cursory and not of consistent reliability. Any reference source attempting such comprehensive coverage would suffer from some unevenness, however, and Sheehy's *Guide* is a reliable starting point. Illustration A shows a page of the *Guide to Reference Books.*

For specific fields, there are other useful and more descriptive guides to research sources. The most comprehensive guide to the social sciences is W.H. Webb et al., *Sources of Information in the Social Sciences,* 3d ed. (American Library Association, 1986). This guide provides references to treatises, sources of statistics and empirical data, specialized dictionaries, handbooks, the principal journals in each field,

Illustration A

A page from Sheehy's *Guide to Reference Books*, 10th ed.

CG379 Social Sciences | Economics | General Works

Includes general information, statistics, and trade directories.
F2131.W47

Yugoslavia

Statisticki godisnjak Jugoslavije. 1954– . Beograd, Savezni Zavod za Statistiku, 1954– . Annual. **CG379**

Title varies.

Name of issuing agency varies.

Detailed statistics on a wide range of topics, with comparative figures for recent years.

The Federal Statistical Office of Yugoslavia also issues a *Statistical yearbook of the Socialist Federal Republic of Yugoslavia* . . . English text (Beograd, 1955–). This is a translation key to be used with original tables in *Statisticki godisnjak;* no figures from the tables are reproduced therein. HA1631.A34

Yugoslavia. Direktsīja Drzhavne Statīstīke. Statisticki godisnjak. Annuaire statistique. Knjiga 1–9, 1929–38/39. Beograd, 1932–39. **CG380**

In Serbian and French. HA1631.A3

Statistical pocket-book of Yugoslavia. 1955– . Beograd, 1955– . Annual. **CG381**

At head of title: Federal Institute for Statistics.

Also published in Serbo-Croatian, Russian, German, and French.

Aims to present in concise form "the essential and general statistical information on Yugoslavia, socialist republics and socialist autonomous provinces."—*[p.3]*. HA1631.S8

Zambia

Zambia. Central Statistical Office. Statistical year-book, 1967– . Lusaka, [1968?]– . Annual. **CG382**

Includes tables on population and housing, health, education, labor, agriculture, transport, commerce and industry, trade, finance, etc. HA1977.R48A33

CH

Economics

◆This area is a large one under which many related subjects are grouped: business and business management, commerce, finance and banking, insurance, labor and industrial relations, and various others. Many large libraries, both public and academic, will have special departments devoted to one or several of these subject fields, and in most large cities there will be pertinent special libraries, usually connected with large business or banking concerns. These libraries will have many more specialized sources than can be listed here.

In this section are included some of the bibliographies, indexes, dictionaries, and handbooks from which, or about which, information may be sought in a large general library.

Documents issued by the federal government are particularly useful in the field of economics. Only a few of the many valuable publications of the various departments and bureaus can be listed here. The U.S. Bureau of Labor Statistics, the Bureau of the Census, the Department of Commerce and its various bureaus, including the now defunct Bureau of Foreign and Domestic Commerce, and many others are prolific publishers. For further information consult the *Monthly catalog of United States government publications* (AG51).

GENERAL WORKS

Guides

Information sources in economics. Ed., John Fletcher. 2d ed. London, Butterworths, [1984]. 339p. **CH1**

1st ed. (1971) had title: *The use of economics literature.*

An attempt by British librarians and economists "jointly to view the literature of economics and provide a guide to it."—*Introd.* Introductory chapters on libraries and literature searches are followed by chapters on types of resources—bibliographies, periodicals, documents of national governments and international organizations, statistics, bibliographic and numeric databases. Thirteen chapters on various subject areas of economics were written by economists to suggest the most useful sources. Strong British emphasis. HB71.I53

Maltby, Arthur. Economics and commerce: the sources of information and their organisation. London, Bingley; [Hamden, Conn.], Archon Books, 1968. 239p. **CH2**

A bibliographical survey intended primarily as a text for the British Library Association examination. Z7164.E2M38

Bibliography

Amstutz, Mark R. Economics and foreign policy: a guide to information sources. Detroit, Gale, [1977]. 179p. (International relations information guide ser., v.7) **CH3**

An annotated bibliography of over 750 English-language books and articles on the political economy of international relations, grouped into chapters on international political economy and economic relations, politics and trade, regional integration, politics and the international monetary system, politics and foreign aid, foreign private investment, imperialism, and the economics of war and defense. Final chapter covers bibliographies and journals. Author, title, and subject indexes. Z7164.E17A48

Batson, Harold Edward. A select bibliography of modern economic theory, 1870–1929. London, Routledge, 1930. 224p. (Repr.: N.Y., Kelley, 1968) **CH4**

An annotated bibliography of books and periodical articles; listing is by subject and by author. Z7164.E2B3

Black, Robert Dionysius Collison. A catalogue of pamphlets on economic subjects published between 1750 and 1900 and now housed in Irish libraries. N.Y., Kelley, 1969. 632p. **CH5**

Comprises a union catalog of "pamphlets of economic interest published anywhere between the 1st January, 1750 and the 31st December, 1900" (*Introd.*) and now housed in one or more of the 17 cooperating libraries. Chronological arrangement with author and title indexes. Z7164.E2B6

Braeuer, Walter. Handbuch zur Geschichte der Volkswirtschaftslehre; ein bibliographisches Nachschlagewerk. Frankfurt am Main, Klostermann, [1952]. 224p. **CH6**

An international bio-bibliography of the history of political economy from ancient and medieval times to the modern day, with biographical sketches of important economists. Includes books, dissertations, and periodical articles.

and indexing and abstracting services. It first treats the literature relating to the social sciences generally and then gives detailed coverage to the literature of economics and business administration, sociology, psychology, political science, history, anthropology, education, and geography. These broad social science disciplines are further divided into appropriate subtopics. The volume has a very detailed index to help find related materials in more than one discipline, an important aid because of the increasingly interdisciplinary nature of so many access tools and information sources.

Although less comprehensive than Webb, other guides also provide useful introductions to social science resources. F.L. Holler, *Information Sources of Political Science,* 4th ed. (ABC–Clio, 1986), provides an organized approach to the literature of the social sciences, covering political science, history, anthropology, sociology, psychology, economics, and geography, with annotated references. T. Li, *Social Science Reference Sources: A Practical Guide* (Greenwood Press, 1980) is a useful compendium describing over 800 social science reference sources, including archives, databases and unpublished materials as well as the standard sources.

Comprehensive coverage of information on corporations and other aspects of business is found in L.M. Daniells, *Business Information Sources,* rev. ed. (University of California Press, 1985). The book includes chapters on statistics, management, finance, marketing, and specific fields such as insurance and banking. Extensively annotated entries cover not just basic handbooks, indexes and directories, but also major monographs and studies. J. Woy, *Encyclopedia of Business Information Sources,* 7th ed. (Gale Research, 1988), is alphabetically organized by industry or topic. Its entries are less detailed than those in Daniells, but it is a useful listing of yearbooks, directories, periodicals, databases, and statistical sources for specific industries.

Similar research guides for most other disciplines can be found in Sheehy's *Guide to Reference Books.*

If a distinction between research guides and bibliographies can be made, it is that guides are generally more descriptive and more selective in coverage. Bibliographies can be important resources when one is looking not for an overview of an area but for references to specific information sources. Many bibliographies of varying scope, coverage and detail, with or without annotations and evaluations, are published in every discipline. Most are not updated and therefore decrease in value as time passes after their publication. Those which are issued periodically or supplemented regularly are particularly useful for following the literature in particular fields or on specific problems. Major bibliographies are listed in the *Guide to Reference Books,* and others can be found through tools such as specialized research guides or library catalogs.

The *International Bibliography of the Social Sciences,* prepared by UNESCO's International Committee for Social Science Documentation, is perhaps the most comprehensive social science bibliography of books, periodical articles, government publications, and pamphlets in many languages. Each of its four subject series is issued in annual volumes, with indexes by author and subject in English and French:

International Bibliography of Economics (Aldine, 1955–date).

International Bibliography of Political Science (Aldine, 1953–date).

International Bibliography of Social and Cultural Anthropology (Aldine, 1955–date).

International Bibliography of Sociology (Aldine, 1952–date).

There is unfortunately a one- or two-year delay in the publication of these annual bibliographies.

C. INFORMATION ON INSTITUTIONS AND PEOPLE

Often it is necessary to find out about particular libraries, associations or individuals, such as opposing parties in litigation, potential business partners, or expert witnesses. Names, addresses, telephone numbers, and background information can be found in a variety of directories. Legal directories have already been described in Chapter 13, and this section briefly discusses general directory resources. Directories in specific fields can be found by referring to the *Guide to American Directories,* 11th ed. (B. Klein Publications, 1982), or J.E. Towell, ed., *Directories in Print,* 6th ed. (Gale Research, 2 vols., 1989). The latter includes over 10,000 publications and databases, and contains references to directories from nearly eighty foreign countries. An English counterpart to these tools is *Current British Directories,* 11th ed. (CBD Research, 1988).

1. LIBRARIES

While most of the basic reference tools discussed in this chapter can be found in law libraries or general research libraries, more specialized resources are often located only in libraries with strong collections in specific subject fields. Two standard library directories provide information about collections, indicating where fruitful research can be undertaken. These directories can also be useful if one is not familiar with the library resources of an area.

The *American Library Directory* (Bowker, 2 vols., annual) lists more than 30,000 libraries in the United States. Entries, arranged geographically by state and city, provide addresses, telephone numbers, hours of opening, size, special services, and subject areas of concentration. One can use this directory to find information about virtually any library in the country.

L. Ash & W.G. Miller, *Subject Collections,* 6th ed. (Bowker, 2 vols., 1985), is a similar guide, arranged by subject rather than location. Its listings include both libraries concentrating on a particular subject and special subject collections contained in larger libraries. Entries under each subject are arranged geographically.

Most private libraries provide access to serious researchers, although a letter of introduction from an institution such as a law school or bar association may be necessary. Preliminary telephone inquiry as to such requirements and as to hours of access is usually desirable.

2. ORGANIZATIONS

Trade or professional associations are often useful sources of information on their subject field. The American Bar Association, for example, publishes several journals, creates standards for the legal profession, and compiles and issues legal statistics and directories. Associations in other fields are no less active. Many associations have staff members, including librarians, who respond to written and telephone inquiries from the press, the public, and researchers.

The standard, multivolume directory for finding associations of all kinds is the *Encyclopedia of Associations* (Gale Research, 4 vols., annual). It lists over 20,000 organizations in eighteen broad categories, from trade associations to fan clubs. Legal and public affairs organizations are included. Entries provide addresses and telephone numbers, as well as information about membership, organization activities, and publications. The index lists associations under full names and keywords, and there are separate geographic and executive indexes. Illustration B shows a typical page from this encyclopedia.

A separate *Encyclopedia of Associations* volume, *International Organizations,* provides similar coverage of 3,000 groups which are international in scope and headquartered outside the United States. There are also seven regional editions of *Encyclopedia of Associations: Regional, State and Local Organizations,* covering 50,000 additional nonprofit groups. The entries in each regional edition are arranged by state and city. The various components of the *Encyclopedia of Associations* are also available through online databases and on compact disc.

National Trade and Professional Associations of the United States (Columbia Books, annual) is a paperback volume of less extensive scope than the *Encyclopedia of Associations.* It does, however, contain basic information on major national industrial and business organizations. Its entries are arranged alphabetically and indexed by subject, location, budget, and acronym.

There are many other directories for particular types of organizations. Two that may be helpful to researchers are the *Foundation Directory,* 11th ed. (Foundation Center, 1987), which provides information on foundation purposes, assets, and grants; and *Research Centers Directory,* 11th ed. (Gale Research, 1987), a subject guide to over 9,000 university-related and other nonprofit research organizations. The *Directory of British Associations,* 9th ed. (CBD Research, 1988), provides basic and concise information on organizations in the United Kingdom.

Illustration B

A sample page from the *Encyclopedia of Associations*

4891 ENCYCLOPEDIA OF ASSOCIATIONS, 23rd Edition - 1989 Page 428

4891 NATIONAL ADVOCATES SOCIETY (Attorneys) (NAS)
c/o Robert Martwick
203 N. LaSalle, Suite 1600 Phone: (312) 368-8900
Chicago, IL 60601 Robert Martwick, Contact
Founded: 1933. **Members:** 1000. **Budget:** Less than $25,000. American lawyers of Polish heritage. Bestows awards; maintains speakers' bureau. **Committees:** Charitable; Educational; Scholarship. **Publications:** (1) Bulletin, annual; (2) Directory, triennial. **Formerly:** Polish American Legal Society. **Convention/Meeting:** annual conference - 1988 Aug. 3-7, Colorado Springs, CO; 1989 July 26-30, Hyannis, MA.

4892 NATIONAL ASSOCIATION OF BENCH AND BAR SPOUSES (Attorneys) (NABBS)
5617 Congress Blvd. Phone: (504) 928-1663
Baton Rouge, LA 70808 Harriet A. Pitcher, Pres.
Founded: 1951. **Members:** 400. **Regional Groups:** 4. Chapters: 28. Spouses of attorneys united to conduct civic, cultural, and social activities in order "to enhance the prestige of the legal profession" and to encourage fellowship among attorneys' spouses. Sponsors conferences and child advocacy programs; maintains Dorothy Atkinson Legal Scholarship Fund for college students interested in careers in law. **Publications:** (1) Newsletter, semiannual; (2) Membership Directory, annual; also publishes historical brochure and program aids. **Affiliated With:** National Bar Association. **Formerly:** National Association of Barristers' Wives; (1987) National Barristers' Wives. **Convention/Meeting:** annual - in conjunction with NBA. 1988 Aug. 8-13, Washington, DC; 1989 Oakland, CA.

4893 NATIONAL ASSOCIATION OF BLACK WOMEN ATTORNEYS (NABWA)
3711 Macomb St., N.W., 2nd Fl. Phone: (202) 638-5715
Washington, DC 20016 Mabel D. Haden, Pres.
Founded: 1972. **Members:** 250. **Staff:** 1. **Regional Groups:** 7. Black women who are members of the bar of any U.S. state or territory; associate members include law school graduates, paralegals, and law students. Seeks to: advance jurisprudence and the administration of justice by increasing the opportunities of black and non-black women at all levels; aid in protecting the civil and human rights of all citizens and residents of the U.S.; expand opportunities to women lawyers through education; promote fellowship among women lawyers. Provides pre-law and student counseling; serves as job placement resource for firms, companies, and others interested in the field. Holds regional seminars; sponsors competitions; bestows awards and scholarships. Maintains hall of fame; offers charitable program. **Computerized Services:** Data base; directory. **Publications:** (1) NABWA News, bimonthly; (2) Souvenir Booklet, annual. **Convention/Meeting:** semiannual conference.

4894 NATIONAL ASSOCIATION OF REPUBLICAN ATTORNEYS (NARA)
53-50 194th St. Phone: (718) 357-8848
Fresh Meadows, NY 11365 Thomas Robert Stevens, Pres.
Acts as a forum for networking; charters new Republican law student associations.

4895 NATIONAL ASSOCIATION OF WOMEN LAWYERS (Attorneys) (NAWL)
750 N. Lake Shore Dr. Phone: (312) 988-6186
Chicago, IL 60611 Patricia O'Mahoney, Exec.Dir.
Founded: 1911. **Members:** 1200. Lawyers who have been admitted to practice in any state or territory of the U.S. Presents Toch Membership Trophy annually to member who endorses most new members during the year. Maintains 17 committees. **Publications:** (1) Presidents Newsletter, quarterly; (2) Women Lawyers Journal, quarterly; (3) Membership Directory, biennial. **Affiliated With:** American Bar Association; International Bar Association; International Federation of Women Lawyers. **Absorbed:** Women Lawyers Club. **Convention/Meeting:** annual conference - always February. 1989 Denver, CO; 1990 Los Angeles, CA. Also holds midyear regional meeting.

4896 NATIONAL BAR ASSOCIATION (Attorneys) (NBA)
1225 11th St., N.W. Phone: (202) 842-3900
Washington, DC 20001 John Crump, Exec.Dir.
Founded: 1925. **Members:** 10,000. **Budget:** $500,000. **Regional Groups:** 12. **Local Groups:** 60. Minority (predominantly black) attorneys, members of the judiciary, law students, and law faculty. Programs and involvements represent the interests of members and the communities they serve. Offers specialized education and research programs. Presents annual C. Francis Stradford Award; maintains reference library. **Divisions:** Commercial Law; Lawyer Referral Program. **Publications:** (1) Bulletin, monthly; (2) Newsletter, monthly; (3) Magazine, quarterly; (4) Annual Journal; (5) Annual Report. **Convention/Meeting:** annual (with exhibits) - 1988 Washington, DC; 1989 Oakland, CA; 1990 Houston, TX; 1991 Indianapolis, IN.

4897 NATIONAL CONFERENCE OF BAR PRESIDENTS (Attorneys) (NCBP)
750 N. Lake Shore Dr. Phone: (312) 988-5346
Chicago, IL 60611 W. Stell Huie, Exec. Officer
Founded: 1950. **Members:** 830. **Staff:** 2. **Budget:** $50,000. Presidents, presidents-elect, and past presidents of state, local, and specialty bar associations. Provides a forum for exchange of ideas; seeks to stimulate work in bar associations, and encourages closer coordination of bar activities with the American Bar Association (see separate entry). Sponsors speakers and panel discussions. Publishes NCBP Best Projects of 1981. **Convention/Meeting:** semiannual - always February and August, in conjunction with the ABA. 1988 (next) Toronto, ON, Canada; 1989 Denver, CO and Honolulu, HI; 1990 Los Angeles, CA and Chicago, IL; 1991 Seattle, WA and Atlanta, GA; 1992 Dallas, TX and San Francisco, CA.

4898 NATIONAL CONFERENCE OF BLACK LAWYERS (Attorneys) (NCBL)
126 W. 119th St. Phone: (212) 864-4000
New York, NY 10026 Wilhelm Joseph, Dir.
Founded: 1968. **Members:** 1000. **Staff:** 6. **Local Groups:** 15. Attorneys throughout the U.S. and Canada united to use legal skills in the service of black and poor communities. Maintains projects in legal services to community organizations, voting rights, and international affairs; provides public education on legal issues affecting blacks and poor people. Researches racism in law school and bar admissions. Conducts programs of continuing legal education for member attorneys. Maintains general law library. Compiles statistics; maintains lawyer referral and placement services. Provides speakers' bureau on criminal justice issues, international human rights law, and civil rights practice. Presents awards. **Sections:** Bar Development; Criminal Justice; Delivery of Legal Services; Economic and Social Rights; International Affairs and World Peace; Political Rights; Racially Targetted Violence; Rights of Women. **Publications:** Notes, quarterly. **Affiliated With:** International Association of Democratic Lawyers. **Convention/Meeting:** annual - always late summer or early fall.

4899 NATIONAL CONFERENCE OF WOMEN'S BAR ASSOCIATIONS (Attorneys) (NCWBA)
113 W. Franklin St. Phone: (301) 752-3318
Baltimore, MD 21201 Carol T. Shaner, Exec.Dir.
Founded: 1983. **Members:** 110. **Staff:** 1. State and local women's bar associations. Promotes the interests of women lawyers. Serves as a forum for information exchange among women's bar associations. Maintains National Conference of Women's Bar Associations Foundation. Bestows community service awards. **Computerized Services:** National Clearinghouse of Women's Bar Associations. **Publications:** NCWBA Newsletter, quarterly. **Convention/Meeting:** semiannual - in conjunction with the American Bar Association.

4900 NATIONAL LAWYERS CLUB (Attorneys) (NLC)
1815 H St., N.W. Phone: (202) 638-3200
Washington, DC 20006 Earl W. Kintner, Pres.
Founded: 1959. **Members:** 2469. Private legal club.

4901 NATIONAL LAWYERS GUILD (Attorneys) (NLG)
853 Broadway, Suite 1705 Phone: (212) 260-1360
New York, NY 10003 Barbara Dudley, Exec.Dir.
Founded: 1937. **Members:** 9000. **Budget:** $270,000. **Regional Groups:** 120. Lawyers, law students, legal workers, and jailhouse lawyers dedicated to seeking economic justice, social equality, and the right to political dissent. Serves as national center for progressive legal work providing training programs to both members and nonmembers. Sponsors skills seminars in different areas of law. Maintains speakers' bureau; offers legal referrals. Caucus: Third World. **Committees:** Affirmative Action/Anti-Discrimination; Civil Liberties; Committee on Native American Struggles; Criminal Law; International; Labor; Law Students in Action; Rural Justice; Summer Projects; Theoretical Studies. **Projects:** Central American Refugee Defense Fund; Grand Jury; National Immigration; Visa Denial. **Subcommittees:** AIDS Network; Cuba; Disinformation and Information Restriction; Faculty Network; Gay Rights; IADL Representative; International Debt Crisis; International Law; Middle East; Peace and Disarmament; Philippines; Puerto Rico; Relations-International Organization; Southern Africa; Work and Welfare. **Task Forces:** Anti-Repression; Anti-Sexism; Central America; Chile; Economic Rights; Ireland; Military Law; Movement Support Network; National Prison Network. **Publications:** (1) Bulletin, monthly; (2) Guild Notes, quarterly; (3) Guild Practitioner, quarterly; (4) Referral Directory, biennial. **Convention/Meeting:** annual.

4902 PROTESTANT LAWYERS ASSOCIATION OF NEW YORK (Attorneys) (PLANY)
187 Hicks St., Apt. 4C Phone: (718) 624-4082
Brooklyn, NY 11201 Ilse G. Coe, Pres.
Founded: 1950. **Members:** 75. **Budget:** Less than $25,000. Attorneys and judges of Protestant religious background; membership centered in New York City area. Sponsors dinner meetings with speakers of legal, political, and/or religious background and occasional joint meetings with the Guild of Catholic

3. CORPORATIONS

A wide variety of directories provide information on corporations and companies. The major American directories are *Standard and*

Poor's Register of Corporations, Directors, and Executives (3 vols., annual), which covers about 40,000 companies, and the *Million Dollar Directory* (Dun's Marketing Services, 5 vols., annual), which covers well over 100,000 companies. *Standard and Poor's* provides brief data about directors and officers, and both works include indexes by geographic location and Standard Industrial Classification (SIC) code. For information on manufacturers, the *Thomas Register of American Manufacturers and Thomas Register Catalog File* (21 vols., annual) is a useful resource. It lists, by product and alphabetically, over 100,000 U.S. manufacturers.

For financial information on corporations, *Moody's Manuals* are perhaps the best known source. Moody's Investors Service publishes eight separate annual manuals covering different industries or exchanges, providing information on the assets and operations of publicly traded companies and on other securities.[4] Each manual is supplemented by a weekly or biweekly update. Comprehensive access is provided by *Moody's Complete Corporate Index.*

Large amounts of business information are available electronically. One of the most widely used databases is *Disclosure,* which provides continually updated financial and textual information on 11,000 companies, with information drawn from S.E.C. filings. *Disclosure* is accessible in a variety of formats, including online database and compact disc. Dun and Bradstreet Credit Service, with financial information on several million U.S. businesses, is available on WESTLAW through a gateway.

4. INDIVIDUALS

Directories and biographical sources for lawyers and judges have already been described in Chapter 13. Most other professions have similar reference tools, and the following additional sources provide general coverage of prominent individuals in all fields of activity.

Two general indexes provide information on *where* to find biographical data. The *Biography and Genealogy Master Index,* 2d ed. (Gale Research, 8 vols., 1980, with annual supplements), provides access to over four million entries in several hundred biographical directories. *Biography Index* (H.W. Wilson, 1946-date) provides references to biographical material appearing in over 2,000 periodicals. It is published monthly and cumulates in annual and three-year volumes.

Who's Who in America (Marquis, 2 vols., biennial) is the most widely used and respected compendium of contemporary American biographies. It consists of reasonably accurate information on prominent Americans, based on data submitted by the subjects. Since some individuals are more prolix (or accomplished), the length and detail of entries vary. A one-volume supplement is published between editions.

4. The *Moody's Manuals* are: *Bank and Finance Manual; Industrial Manual; International Manual; Municipal and Government Manual; OTC Industrial Manual; OTC Unlisted Manual; Public Utilities Manual;* and *Transportation Manual.*

The same publisher provides four biennial regional collections in the same format, each containing many entries not in the national version: *Who's Who in the East, Who's Who in the Midwest, Who's Who in the South and Southwest,* and *Who's Who in the West.* In addition to these geographical *Who's Who* editions and *Who's Who in American Law* (discussed above in Chapter 13), Marquis also produces *Who's Who of American Women* and *Who's Who in Finance and Industry* (both irregular). A competing publisher, R.R. Bowker, issues *American Men and Women of Science* and *Directory of American Scholars* (both revised irregularly). Similar collections for religious, ethnic, and professional groups are issued by other publishers, usually without a regular pattern of revision.

Biographical dictionaries are published on a more or less regular basis for many foreign countries, including the British *Who's Who* (Black/St. Martin's, annual); *Wer ist Wer, Das Deutsche Who's Who* (Arani) and *Who's Who in Germany* (Oldenbourg) (both issued irregularly); *Who's Who in France* (Lafitte, biennial); and *Who's Who in Japan* (International Culture Institute, annual). *International Who's Who* (Europa, annual) and *Who's Who in the World* (Marquis, biennial) offer global coverage.

There are several sources for biographical information on deceased individuals. For figures of historical importance, two classic biographical encyclopedias are considered most authoritative. For Americans, there is the *Dictionary of American Biography* (Scribner's, 20 vols., 1928–37), with seven supplements to date covering to 1965, and its abridgment, *Concise Dictionary of American Biography,* 3d ed. (1980). For English subjects the leading source is the *Dictionary of National Biography* (Oxford University Press, 22 vols., 1912–59), with decennial supplements covering through 1980, and the *Concise Dictionary* (2 vols., 1953–82). *Notable American Women 1607–1950* (Belknap Press, 3 vols., 1971), modelled after *D.A.B.,* is an excellent retrospective biographical encyclopedia of distinguished American women. A one-volume supplement, *The Modern Period* (1980), has also been published.

Marquis, publisher of *Who's Who in America,* also produces *Who Was Who in America.* Consisting of an *Historical Volume 1607–1896* (1963) and eight supplementary volumes to date, covering the period from 1897 to 1985, this set is a useful source of basic data on over 100,000 deceased Americans. The entries in the later volumes are largely based on the original entries for each individual in *Who's Who in America.* A separate cumulative index covers all volumes.

D. STATISTICS

The use of statistical data is extensive in modern litigation and legal research, on issues from asbestos claims to zoning impact. There are many sources of statistics, but the most important are federal government agencies such as the Bureau of the Census and the Bureau of Labor Statistics. Before relying on statistical data, a researcher should check its source for bias, currency and reliability.

The *Statistical Abstract,* an annual publication of the Bureau of the Census since 1879, is the most versatile and reliable compendium of statistics on political, economic, social and demographic subjects.[5] Its statistics are drawn from various sources, most produced by government agencies. It is well indexed and gives sources for all of its tables and summaries, making it easy to go from the *Abstract* to more in-depth coverage in a specific agency's or organization's publications. Illustration C shows a typical page from the *Abstract,* providing statistics from the Administrative Office of the U.S. Courts, the U.S. Department of Justice, and the National Center for Juvenile Justice.

The United Nations publishes several major statistical sources of international scope. The *Statistical Yearbook* provides a variety of information on industrial and social matters, while the *Demographic Yearbook, Industrial Statistics Yearbook, International Trade Statistics Yearbook,* and *National Accounts Statistics* focus on more specific areas. Each of these annual publications provides excellent comparative data for individual nations around the globe. They contain exhaustive and authoritative information, although some appear after a substantial delay.

The most comprehensive index of statistical sources is provided by three Congressional Information Service publications:

American Statistics Index (1973–date, with retrospective coverage to early 1960s), covering publications of the United States government;

Statistical Reference Index (1980–date), covering publications from sources other than the U.S. Government, such as state governments and trade associations; and

Index to International Statistics (1983–date), covering publications of international organizations.

All three are issued monthly in *Index* and *Abstracts* pamphlets, with annual bound volumes, in formats similar to that used for Congressional publications by the *CIS/Index.* Their extensive indexes provide access to thorough, descriptive abstracts. Each index is supplemented by a microfiche library of the actual publications abstracted. Illustration D shows a page from an *American Statistics Index* issue, including abstracts of Administrative Office of the U.S. Courts publications.

Another useful index to statistical publications is *Statistics Sources,* 12th ed. (Gale Research, 2 vols., 1988), a subject guide which includes coverage of statistical data available through online databases or in machine-readable form.

5. Retrospective coverage is found in *Historical Statistics of the United States, Colonial Times to 1970* (U.S. Govt. Printing Office, 2 vols., 1975). Its twenty-six chapters cover broad subject areas, accessible by detailed subject and time period indexes.

Illustration C

A typical page in the *Statistical Abstract*, 1988 ed.

No. 298. U.S. District Courts—Defendants Charged With Violations of Drug Abuse Prevention and Control Act: 1980 to 1986

[For years ending **June 30**]

ITEM	MARIHUANA					DRUGS					CONTROLLED SUBSTANCES (prescribed drugs)				
	1980	1983	1984	1985	1986	1980	1983	1984	1985	1986	1980	1983	1984	1985	1986
Defendants disposed of	**1,690**	**3,806**	**3,179**	**3,984**	**3,989**	**3,290**	**3,692**	**4,548**	**5,595**	**7,321**	**1,363**	**1,666**	**1,464**	**1,598**	**1,624**
Not convicted	569	792	667	854	904	749	601	786	868	1,009	276	281	279	246	257
Dismissed [1]	483	676	516	709	777	620	481	668	692	813	234	236	237	200	221
Convicted	1,121	3,014	2,512	3,130	3,085	2,541	3,091	3,762	4,727	6,312	1,087	1,385	1,185	1,352	1,367
By guilty plea and nolo contendere	772	2,379	1,895	2,523	2,637	1,830	2,334	2,935	3,839	5,125	848	1,061	963	1,138	1,126
Imprisonment, total [2]	**754**	**1,921**	**1,841**	**2,036**	**2,048**	**1,945**	**2,493**	**3,049**	**3,701**	**5,058**	**780**	**1,035**	**866**	**1,049**	**1,046**
Regular sentence	555	1,416	1,344	1,512	1,594	1,410	1,942	2,326	2,885	4,169	582	792	636	810	838
Avg. sentence (mo.)	47.2	55.1	54.4	53.2	55.7	60.8	70.8	71.8	69.6	73.1	46.5	62.2	67.6	69.3	81.2
Other sentences to prison [2]	199	505	497	524	454	535	551	723	816	889	198	243	230	239	208
Probation, total	**341**	**973**	**616**	**938**	**902**	**588**	**583**	**661**	**960**	**1,148**	**303**	**337**	**307**	**287**	**303**
Avg. sentence (mo.)	37.9	27.9	42.0	31.2	33.4	39.9	40.8	44.3	39.7	41.6	37.2	38.0	43.4	40.5	43.7
Fine only	20	94	11	83	91	4	8	4	3	15	3	6	3	6	2
Other [3]	6	26	44	73	44	4	7	48	63	91	1	7	9	10	16

[1] Includes defendants committed under 28 USC 2902, Narcotic Addict Rehabilitation Act of 1966. [2] Split or mixed sentences of prison and probation in the same case as well as indeterminate and Youth Corrections Act sentences are included under total imprisonment and other sentences to prison. [3] Includes deportation, suspended sentences, imprisonment for four days or less or for time already served, remitted and suspended fines and life sentences.

Source: Administrative Office of the U.S. Courts, *Annual Report of the Director.*

No. 299. Federal Prosecutions of Public Corruption: 1974 to 1986

[As of **Dec. 31.** Prosecution of persons who have corrupted public office in violation of Federal Criminal Statutes]

PROSECUTION STATUS	1974	1975	1976	1977	1978	1979	1980	1981	1982	1983	1984	1985	1986
Total: [1] Indicted	291	255	563	507	557	687	721	878	729	1,073	936	1,182	1,192
Convicted	217	179	380	440	409	555	552	730	671	972	934	997	1,027
Awaiting trial	5	27	199	210	205	187	213	231	186	222	269	256	246
Federal officials: Indicted	59	53	111	129	133	128	123	198	158	[2] 460	408	563	596
Convicted	51	43	101	94	91	115	131	159	147	[2] 424	429	470	523
Awaiting trial	1	5	1	32	42	21	16	23	38	58	77	90	83
State officials: Indicted	36	36	59	50	55	58	72	87	49	81	58	79	88
Convicted	23	18	35	38	56	32	51	66	43	65	52	66	71
Awaiting trial	-	5	30	33	20	30	28	36	18	26	21	20	24
Local officials: Indicted	130	139	194	157	171	212	247	244	257	270	203	248	232
Convicted	87	94	100	164	127	156	168	211	232	226	196	221	207
Awaiting trial	4	15	98	62	72	67	82	102	58	61	74	49	55

- Represents zero. [1] Includes individuals who are neither public officials nor employees but who were involved with public officials or employees in violating the law, not shown separately. [2] Increases in the number indicted and convicted between 1982 and 1983 resulted from a greater focus on federal corruption nationwide and more consistent reporting of cases involving lower-level employees.

Source: U.S. Department of Justice, *Federal Prosecutions of Corrupt Public Officials, 1970–1980* and *Report to Congress on the Activities and Operations of the Public Integrity Section*, annual.

No. 300. Children's Cases Disposed of by Juvenile Courts: 1970 to 1983

[For definition of delinquency cases, see text, section 5. Dependency and neglect cases are all cases referred to the court for some form of neglect or inadequate care on the part of parents or guardians. See also *Historical Statistics, Colonial Times to 1970*, series H 1119–1124]

ITEM	Unit	1970	1975	1978	1979	1980	1981	1982	1983
Population 10–17 years old [1]	1,000	32,614	33,960	32,276	31,643	31,171	30,725	29,914	29,345
Delinquency cases, excluding traffic	1,000	1,052	1,317	1,359	1,374	1,445	1,350	1,292	1,276
Per 1,000 population 10–17 years old	Rate	32.3	38.8	42.1	43.4	46.4	44.0	43.2	43.5
Male	1,000	800	1,002	1,055	1,058	1,121	1,024	990	980
Female	1,000	252	315	304	316	324	326	303	295
Percent of total cases	Percent	24.0	23.9	22.4	23.0	22.4	24.1	23.4	23.1
Population under 18 years old [1]	1,000	70,810	68,314	65,982	65,335	64,908	64,405	63,763	63,812
Dependency and neglect cases	1,000	133	143	158	157	153	185	172	196
Per 1,000 population under 18 years old	Rate	1.9	2.1	2.4	2.5	2.3	2.9	2.7	3.1

[1] U.S. Bureau of the Census estimates of civilian population as of July 1.

Source: National Center for Juvenile Justice, Pittsburgh, PA, *Juvenile Court Statistics*, annual. (Copyright.)

Illustration D

A page of abstracts in the *American Statistics Index*

United States Courts

18202
ADMINISTRATIVE OFFICE OF THE U.S. COURTS
Current Periodicals

18202-2 REPORT OF THE PROCEEDINGS OF THE JUDICIAL CONFERENCE OF THE U.S., SEPT. 14, 1988
Semiannual. 1988.
vii+p. 49-120. † ASI/MF/3
•Ju10.10:988-2.

Semiannual report on proceedings of the Judicial Conference of the U.S. held Sept. 14, 1988. Conference is held in spring and fall to review criminal law and courts administration; recommend and approve staff levels, regulations, and procedures; and make recommendations to Congress.

Administrative areas include judicial ethics and codes of conduct; jury, probation, and magistrates systems; bankruptcy and other special courts; and public defenders and community public defender organizations. Report usually includes some supporting data on staff and budgets.

Proceedings of both Judicial Conference meetings, together with the *Annual Report of the Director of the Administrative Office of the U.S. Courts*, are later reprinted in one volume. For description of 1987 combined report, see ASI 1988 Annual (or 1988 Monthly Supplement 3) under 18204-8.

18204
ADMINISTRATIVE OFFICE OF THE U.S. COURTS
Annuals and Biennials

18204-3 FEDERAL COURT MANAGEMENT STATISTICS, 1988
Annual. Sept. 1988.
6+167 p. Foldouts. †
ASI/MF/4 •Ju10.14:988.
LC 83-647695.

Annual report presenting statistical profiles showing court workloads and management data, for each of the 12 Federal courts of appeals and the 94 district courts, years ending June 30, 1983-88.

Contents: introduction and explanation of format (p. c-f); profile for each circuit court of appeals, with summary and national profile (p. 2-29); and profile for each district court, by circuit, with summary for each circuit and national profile (p. 33-167).

Circuit Courts. Profiles show the following data for each U.S. court of appeals, with national rankings:

a. Overall workload and actions per judicial panel: appeals filed and terminated by category (prisoner, other civil, criminal, administrative); and appeals pending.

b. Actions per active judge: terminations on merit and procedure; and written decisions signed, unsigned, and without comment.

c. Number of judgeships and panels, sitting senior judges, and vacant judgeship months; and median time from filing to disposition.

d. Other judgeship workload: applications for interlocutory appeals; pro se mandamus petitions; and petitions for rehearing.

District Courts. Profiles show the following data for each court, with circuit and national rankings:

a. Workload: cases filed, terminated, pending, and percent change; number of judgeships; and number of vacant judgeship months.

b. Actions per judgeship: civil and criminal filings, pending cases, weighted filings, terminations, and trials completed.

c. Median time from filing to disposition, for civil and criminal cases, and from issue to trial (civil only); number and percent of civil cases pending 3 years or more; and number and percent of triable defendants in pending criminal cases.

d. Jurors present for jury selection; and percent not selected, serving, or challenged.

e. Civil and criminal filings, by type of offense.

Data are for years ending June 30, 1983-88.

Previous report, for 1987, is described in ASI 1987 Annual under this number.

18224
SPECIAL COURTS
Annuals and Biennials

18224-1 U.S. CLAIMS COURT STATISTICAL REPORT for the Court Year Oct. 1, 1987-Sept. 30, 1988
Annual. [1988.] 4 p.
U.S. Claims Court †
ASI/MF/3

Annual report for FY88 on U.S. Claims Court caseloads. Contains narrative summary and 3 tables showing petitions filed, disposed of, and pending at beginning and end of year, and number of plaintiffs involved, by type of case; value of claims and judgments; and appeals filed, pending at beginning of year, and dispositions by type.

Report has been issued since 1962.

Previous report, for FY87, is described in ASI 1987 Annual under this number.

18224-3 U.S. TAX COURT ANALYSIS OF CASES CLOSED (BY DOCKETS), Oct. 1, 1987-Sept. 30, 1988
Annual. [1988.] 2 p.
U.S. Tax Court † ASI/MF/3

Annual report for FY88 on U.S. Tax Court caseloads. Presents data on small tax, declaratory judgment, and all cases.

Contains 2 tables showing number of dockets and amount of deficiencies (tax due), by disposition and type of decision (stipulation, dismissal, opinion, mandate), FY88.

18224-5 U.S. TAX COURT, FY88 ANNUAL REPORT
Annual. Nov. 1988. 19 p.
U.S. Tax Court † ASI/MF/3

Annual report for FY88 on U.S. Tax Court activity. Contains narrative summary (p. 1); and 18 tables, described below (p. 2-21).

Two pages containing confidential information have been deleted from this report.

Report has been issued since FY73.

A summary report is also issued (see 18224-3).

TABLES:

[Data are for FY79-88, unless otherwise noted. Declaratory judgment cases are usually shown by type, including employee retirement plans, tax-exempt organizations and private foundations, and Government bonds.]

18224-5.1: Tax Court Activity

1-2. Total and small tax cases filed, closed, transferred (small tax only), and pending. (p. 2-3)

3. Petitions filed by attorneys and taxpayers, by case type. (p. 4.)

ASI 1989 **Supplement 1 77**

E. PERIODICALS AND NEWSPAPERS

Legal periodicals and newspapers, and their indexes, have been described above in Chapter 11. Nonlegal periodicals however, have become increasingly important in law-related research. This section describes a few directories for identifying such publications, and some of the major periodical indexes and databases that provide access to their contents.[6]

1. DIRECTORIES

Periodical directories are used to find journals that concentrate on a specific subject or industry, or to get more information on a specific publication. Several standard works with overlapping coverage compile information on large numbers of journals and newspapers.

Ulrich's International Periodicals Directory (Bowker, 3 vols., annual) is arranged by subject, with an index by title. It covers over 100,000 titles, including irregular serials and annuals. In addition to publication data, its entries indicate the indexing and abstracting sources which cover each periodical. *Ulrich's* is available online as well as in print.

The Serials Directory (EBSCO, 3 vols., annual), available in print and on compact disc, is comparable in scope to *Ulrich's,* and provides international coverage with excellent indexing.

Another extensive guide to U.S. and Canadian periodicals is the *Standard Periodical Directory* (Oxbridge Communications, biennial). It lists over 60,000 titles in an alphabetical subject arrangement, with a title index.

Newsletters, which may provide the most current news in specialized areas, are covered in *Newsletters in Print* (Gale Research, annual). Over 10,000 newsletters are indexed, with detailed content and subscription information.

The most useful source for coverage of newspapers is the *Gale Directory of Publications* (annual, formerly known as *Ayer's Directory*). It lists newspapers by state and city, and provides useful demographic and economic information on the markets they serve. The *Gale Directory* also lists trade publications and those designed for particular religious and ethnic groups.

2. PUBLISHED INDEXES

There are numerous indexes to periodical literature, varying enormously in scope and style of indexing. In this section only a few general indexes are discussed.

Readers' Guide to Periodical Literature, the H.W. Wilson Company's index to about 175 popular periodicals of general interest, is probably the most widely used periodical index in the world. It is issued biweekly, with quarterly and annual cumulations, and provides indexing by author and subject.

6. Further information on specific fields can be obtained from *Indexes, Abstracts and Digests* (Gale Research, 1982), a guide to some 6,000 aids for searching the contents of books, periodicals, and documents, and its update service, *Abstracting and Indexing Services Directory.*

H.W. Wilson is the publisher of many indexes, including the *Index to Legal Periodicals,* and someone familiar with one Wilson product may find comfortable similarities in its other indexes. Other Wilson indexes of possible interest are: *Social Sciences Index* and *Humanities Index* (both 1974–date, continuing the earlier combined *Social Sciences and Humanities Index*); *Business Periodicals Index* (1958–date); and *Applied Science & Technology Index* (1958–date).

Since 1976, the *Magazine Index* has been published on microfilm by Information Access Company (IAC), on the same basis as that publisher's *Legal Resource Index.* It indexes about four hundred magazines, twice the number covered by *Readers' Guide,* and provides more points of access to their contents than its traditional competitor. The microfilm is revised and updated monthly, and permanent microfiche cumulations are issued to permit reduction of the main microfilm index. IAC also publishes *National Newspaper Index* (1979–date) in a similar format. It covers the *Christian Science Monitor, Los Angeles Times, New York Times, Wall Street Journal,* and *Washington Post.*

The *New York Times* has a unique research value as the most comprehensive newspaper of record in this country, and its index is frequently used by lawyers to locate information on individuals, institutions, or events. The *New York Times Index* has coverage back to 1851, and is now issued semimonthly, with annual cumulations. Several other major newspapers, such as the *Los Angeles Times* and the *Washington Post,* also have their own indexes. These indexes are less significant than they once were, however, with the full text of these newspapers now available online.

Public Affairs Information Service (PAIS, 1915–date) indexes over one thousand periodicals published in English throughout the world, and selective books, documents and pamphlets. Its focus is primarily on political science, economics, government, legislation, and other social sciences. The *PAIS Bulletin* is published monthly, with quarterly cumulations and annual bound volumes. Since 1972, PAIS has also issued a *Foreign Language Index,* on a quarterly basis, for French, German, Italian, Portuguese, and Spanish periodicals in the fields of economics and public affairs.

There are many specialized indexing and abstracting services covering current writing and developments in particular disciplines. One of the best known is *Psychological Abstracts* (American Psychological Association, 1927–date); there are similar services in virtually every other discipline. The following few examples illustrate the variety of other services:

Anthropological Literature: An Index to Periodical Articles and Essays (Redgrave Publishing Co., 1979–date)

Historical Abstracts . . . Bibliography of the World's Periodical Literature (ABC–Clio, 1955–date)

Index Medicus (National Library of Medicine, 1960–date)

Index of Economic Articles in Journals and Collective Volumes (R.D. Irwin, 1961–date)

International Political Science Abstracts (Blackwell, 1951–date)

Sociological Abstracts (1952–date)

Indexes for other disciplines can be identified through use of the research guides described earlier in the chapter, including Sheehy's *Guide to Reference Books.*

Among the most important research tools developed in recent years are the citation indexes prepared by the Institute for Scientific Information, *Science Citation Index* (1961–date, with retrospective coverage to 1954), *Social Sciences Citation Index* (1973–date, with coverage to 1956), and *Arts and Humanities Citation Index* (1978–date, covering since 1975). Like *Shepard's Citations,* these indexes allow a researcher to identify publications which refer to previously published books and articles. They also provide "Permuterm" title keyword indexes which can be used to find articles on particular topics. The *Social Sciences Citation Index* provides comprehensive coverage of over a thousand journals from every field of social science, including many legal periodicals, and selective coverage of monographs and over two thousand additional journals.

Citation indexes are complex, computer-produced services which require some patience to learn. It is often necessary to refer from one part of an index to another to find desired information. This can be time-consuming, and frustrating if it leads to numerous marginal or irrelevant references. The *Social Sciences Citation Index,* however, provides access to many sources on law-related issues which are not available through the legal periodical indexes described in Chapter 11.

3. ELECTRONIC INDEXES

WESTLAW and LEXIS, providing full-text access to cases and other documents and electronic services such as citation verification, have dramatically changed the nature of legal research. The impact of computers in other areas of research has perhaps been less dramatic but is no less important. Electronic retrieval of information is now available for many other fields, and can play a significant role in nonlegal research.

Most indexing and abstracting tools discussed in the preceding section are available for searching by computer. Online literature searches tend to yield more recent citations than printed volumes, dispensing with the need for a new edition or supplement to be compiled, printed, and distributed. Computer searches can usually be performed more quickly and often provide more varied and sophisticated approaches. In an index database, the searcher can go beyond single subject headings and find specific combinations of words appearing in titles, abstracts, or subject descriptors.

CD–ROM (compact disc read-only memory) technology also offers searching convenience and cumulated information, although in many cases it is neither as flexible nor as current as online databases. On the other hand, online research usually involves a per-search fee, whereas discs require no telecommunications or mainframe computer time. For a researcher who incurs a fee for online searching but has free access to a disc system, the latter may be considerably more cost-effective.

Most of the periodical indexes from H.W. Wilson (including *Readers' Guide*) are available both online (WILSONLINE) and in CD–ROM (WILSONDISC). IAC's general-interest counterpart to its LegalTrac disc system is InfoTrac, and its *Magazine Index* and *National Newspaper Index* are also searchable online. *PAIS* is available in a variety of electronic formats as well.

There are perhaps more specialized abstracting and indexing services available online than are published, since some databases have no print counterpart. DIALOG Information Services, a leading vendor of online information, provides access to several hundred databases. Besides the IAC databases and *PAIS,* two of the most important for legal researchers are PSYCINFO (the online version of *Psychological Abstracts*) and MEDLINE (the online version of *Index Medicus*). *Social Scisearch,* the online counterpart to the *Social Sciences Citation Index,* can be used without flipping from volume to volume, making it considerably easier to use than the cumbersome print version. DIALOG also provides access to numerous other useful databases, including the online versions of the *Encyclopedia of Associations* and *Ulrich's International Periodicals Directory.*

Competing vendors offer additional databases and many of the same ones that are available through DIALOG. In general, online searching procedures in bibliographic and index databases are not as simple and straightforward as those for WESTLAW or LEXIS. It is advisable, and often necessary, to seek assistance from a reference librarian, as to both available databases and appropriate search techniques.

4. FULL–TEXT DATABASES

Although index databases provide greater speed and flexibility than printed materials, they are less versatile than full-text databases. Researchers no longer need to rely on indexers' assignment of subject classifications to documents, and instead can create their own individualized search terminology. The danger remains that relevant documents will be missed, but not because an indexer did not see their relevance to a particular issue.

Law students and attorneys should be familiar with the full-text searching capabilities of LEXIS and WESTLAW. NEXIS, Mead Data Central's general-interest counterpart to its LEXIS service, provides similar access to a variety of nonlegal materials, including over a hundred newspapers, magazines, newsletters, and wire services. NEXIS contains the full text of the *New York Times,* the *Washington Post,* and the *Los Angeles Times,* as well as numerous trade and business journals and newsletters. An attorney needing current news or background material can search NEXIS for references to a particular person, company, or product. The searching procedures used in NEXIS are the same as those for LEXIS, so it is a much easier system for lawyers and law students to use than most online databases.

A similar full-text system, VU/TEXT, is available to WESTLAW subscribers. VU/TEXT coverage includes over two dozen newspapers from throughout the country, and operates in a similar fashion to NEXIS. It lacks the *New York Times* and its authoritative coverage of national and international issues, but provides broader coverage of local issues in the home states of its newspapers. Its searching techniques are *not* identical to WESTLAW's, so inexperienced users often need some assistance.

WESTLAW also can provide access to DIALOG and to Dow Jones News/Retrieval, which contains *Wall Street Journal* articles and a variety of other business and financial information. As with VU/TEXT, searching these systems requires use of *their* commands and logic, not WESTLAW's.

F. SUMMARY

This chapter has been a brisk tour through the vast literature of general reference materials, stopping only at a few standard resources. Our intention has been to provide some highlights and a background for further investigation.

While most students enter law school with some experience in nonlegal research at the undergraduate level, many let their skills atrophy through years of working only with legal materials. This is unfortunate, since a lawyer who can work with all kinds of information is better able to serve clients' needs than one whose vision is limited to the law.

Chapter 15

U.S. PRACTICE IN INTERNATIONAL LAW [1]

A. INTRODUCTION

Up to now, this book has focused on research in the law of the United States. In this chapter, we broaden our view and look at legal materials affecting our relations with other countries. The field of international law encompasses two different branches, *public* and *private* international law. Public international law regulates the relations between national states. Private international law (in this and some other countries often called "conflicts of law") consists of those rules and practices which determine *where,* and *by whose law,* controversies involving the law of more than one state are resolved, and how foreign judgments are enforced.

1. Excerpted from Chapter 15, International Law, of *How to Find the Law,* 9th ed.

In approaching a research problem in international law, one can begin with a reference work, a law review article, or a treatise, for general information and for help in analyzing the issues involved. Next one should determine whether there are treaties in force which deal with the subject matter. If so, the legislative history of a treaty and its interpretation by the courts may be important. If there is no treaty, the researcher should explore resources such as case law, statutes, or other documents determining or reflecting national practice.

For American lawyers and law students, those materials which reflect United States practice in international law are the most important and most frequently consulted research sources in this field. Aside from the specialized treaty literature, most of the other materials have been discussed in earlier chapters. Their further treatment here will focus on special features and finding aids for international law research.

B. TREATIES

Treaties and *conventions* [2] are formal agreements between countries and constitute one of the major sources of international law. Treaties are called *bilateral* when they are made between two countries, and *multilateral* when more than two parties are involved. Article VI of the United States Constitution states that treaties, like federal statutes, are the "supreme law of the land" and are binding on all judges. Since treaties and statutes have the same legal effect, a treaty can supersede earlier statutes, and a statute can abrogate a prior treaty as controlling law within the United States.

Treaties are initiated, drafted, and negotiated to agreement by the executive branch, but require approval by a two-thirds vote of the Senate. After Senate approval, they are ratified and proclaimed by the President. The determination of the effective date of a treaty is sometimes confusing because of the several significant dates involved in treaty-making [3] and because the effective date for international implementation may differ from that for domestic authority (i.e., when it becomes the "law of the land"). Generally, the effective date of a treaty for international purposes is that specified in the treaty itself, and such specification is increasingly common in modern treaties, usually in the final clause. In the absence of a specified date in the treaty, the date on which ratifications are exchanged is considered the effective date.[4] For domestic purposes, a self-executing treaty becomes law when it is proclaimed by the President.

2. Little distinction seems to exist today between the two terms, but *convention* tends to be used primarily for multilateral agreements.

3. For example, the date of signing; the date on which ratifications are exchanged with the other signatory; the effective date specified in the treaty; the date of approval by the Senate; the date of ratification by the President; and the date of proclamation.

4. To add to the confusion of dates, lists of treaties are often arranged by date of signing rather than by effective date.

Executive agreements are made with other countries by the President under the authority to conduct foreign affairs, and are similar in form and effect to treaties. However, unlike treaties, such agreements do not require the advice and consent of the Senate, and hence are often used to avoid the delay and controversy entailed in obtaining Senate approval. Most of the following discussion of sources and research procedure applies to both treaties and executive agreements.

The typical steps in research on a United States treaty include the following: (1) finding an authoritative text of the treaty; (2) determining whether it is in force and with what parties and reservations; (3) interpreting the treaty, including its legislative history and judicial interpretation; and (4) verifying and updating its current status.

A treaty is usually referred to by its title, in most instances indicating its subject matter, at least in general terms. A citation to a treaty includes its name; the date of its signing; the parties, if there are three or fewer; and references to the main sources of publication. For example, Illustration Ashows the first page of a treaty which is cited as: Protocol on the Northern Pacific Halibut Fishery, Mar. 29, 1979, United States–Canada, 32 U.S.T. 2483, T.I.A.S. No. 9855.

1. FORMS OF PUBLICATION

Until 1950, United States treaties appeared regularly after proclamation in the volumes of the *Statutes at Large.* Beginning in 1950, treaties and executive agreements have been published in a separate chronological series, called *United States Treaties and Other International Agreements* (cited as U.S.T.). *UST* includes the text of each treaty in the languages of each signatory. Several volumes of *UST* are issued annually, with a noncumulating index by subject and country in each volume. Publication of treaties in *UST* is now about eight years behind schedule.

Prior to their appearance in *UST,* treaties and executive agreements are published in a slip form series consisting of consecutively numbered, individually paginated pamphlets, each containing the text in the language of all parties. This series, begun in 1945, is called *Treaties and Other International Acts Series* (cited as T.I.A.S.) and constitutes the first authoritative publication of these documents.[5] There is considerable delay between the proclamation of a treaty or agreement and its publication in this form, now running about five years late.

Before ratification and publication in *TIAS,* the text of a treaty or agreement is usually issued on the date of signing in a Department of State press release. Another early source of the treaty text, *Senate Treaty Documents,* will be discussed below with other legislative history materials on pages 457–460.

5. *TIAS* is a successor to two earlier separate series, *Treaty Series* (1908–45) and *Executive Agreement Series* (1929–45).

Illustration A

The beginning of a treaty, as published in *United States Treaties and Other International Agreements*

CANADA

Preservation of Halibut Fishery of Northern Pacific Ocean and Bering Sea

Protocol, with annex, amending the convention of March 2, 1953;
Signed at Washington March 29, 1979;
Transmitted by the President of the United States of America to the Senate August 10, 1979 (S. Ex. DD, 96th Cong., 1st Sess.);
Reported favorably by the Senate Committee on Foreign Relations February 19, 1980 (S. Ex. Rep. No. 96–27, 96th Cong., 2d Sess.);
Advice and consent to ratification by the Senate March 20, 1980;
Ratified by the President March 31, 1980;
Ratified by Canada June 23, 1980;
Ratifications exchanged at Ottawa October 15, 1980;
Proclaimed by the President November 11, 1980;
Entered into force October 15, 1980.
With agreed minute.

BY THE PRESIDENT OF THE UNITED STATES OF AMERICA

A PROCLAMATION

CONSIDERING THAT:

The Protocol Amending the Convention between the United States of America and Canada for the Preservation of the Halibut Fishery of the Northern Pacific Ocean and Bering Sea, with Annex, signed at Washington on March 29, 1979, the text of which Protocol, with Annex, in the English and French languages, is hereto annexed;

The Senate of the United States of America by its resolution of March 20, 1980, two-thirds of the Senators present concurring therein, gave its advice and consent to ratification of the Protocol, with Annex;

The Protocol, with Annex, was ratified by the President of the United States of America on March 31, 1980, in pursuance of the advice and consent of the Senate, and was duly ratified on the part of Canada;

73–811 O (2483) TIAS 9855

The monthly *Department of State Bulletin* is another useful source of pre-ratification treaty information. It includes a regular section, "Treaties—Current Actions," with information on negotiations, Congressional status, developments between signing and ratification, and finally ratification and proclamation. Illustration B shows an example of this feature.

Selected treaties also appear in *International Legal Materials,* published bimonthly since 1962 by the American Society of International Law. *International Legal Materials* contains the texts of only major treaties, but includes drafts of some proposed treaties before they become final. It often provides the text of a treaty long before it is published in either of the official sources.

The various editions of the United States Code contain a few important treaties which relate directly to statutory provisions, such as the Universal Copyright Convention and the Warsaw Convention. The *U.S. Code* and *USCA* print these treaties following relevant statutory provisions, while *USCS* includes them in an "Administrative Rules of Procedure" volume. Treaties in *USCA* and *USCS* are followed by annotations of interpretive decisions.

Some treaty collections on particular subjects have been published by commercial publishers. Examples of these include the CCH looseleaf service, *Tax Treaties,* which prints U.S. treaties relating to income and estate taxation as well as background material on treaties in force and pending. I.I. Kavass & A. Sprudzs, *Extradition Laws and Treaties* (Hein, 2 vols., 1979–date) contains all U.S. extradition treaties in force, arranged by the names of the cosignatory countries.

International organizations publish treaty series, which include United States treaties when the U.S. is a member of the organization (e.g., *United Nations Treaty Series* and *O.A.S. Treaty Series*).

The following retrospective treaty collections provide a convenient means for locating specific treaties, as well as sources for historical research in U.S. treaties generally:

(a) C.I. Bevans, comp., *Treaties and Other International Agreements of the United States of America, 1776–1949* (Department of State, 13 vols., 1968–75). This definitive collection makes recourse to the *Statutes at Large* unnecessary, although the *Statutes at Large* text remains authoritative for treaties published therein.[6] The first four volumes of *Bevans* contain multilateral treaties, arranged chronologically by date of signature; the next eight volumes include bilateral treaties, arranged alphabetically by country; and volume 13 contains indexes by country and subject.

(b) *Statutes at Large.* A compilation of treaties entered into by the United States between 1778 and 1845 appears in volume 8 of

6. *Bevans* supersedes two predecessors: W.M. Malloy, *Treaties, Conventions, International Acts, Protocols, and Agreements Between the U.S.A. and Other Powers* (U.S. G.P.O., 4 vols., 1910–38), and H. Miller, *Treaties and Other International Acts of the U.S.A.* (U.S.G.P.O., 8 vols., 1931–48).

Illustration B

A sample "Treaties—Current Actions" page in the monthly *Department of State Bulletin*

TREATIES

Current Actions

MULTILATERAL

Arbitration
Convention on the recognition and enforcement of foreign arbitral awards. Done at New York June 10, 1958. Entered into force June 7, 1959; for the U.S. Dec. 29, 1970. TIAS 6997.
Accession deposited: Bahrain, Apr. 6, 1988.

Aviation
Convention on international civil aviation. Done at Chicago Dec. 7, 1944. Entered into force Apr. 4, 1947. TIAS 1591.

Protocol on the authentic trilingual text of the convention on international civil aviation (TIAS 1591), with annex. Done at Buenos Aires Sept. 24, 1968. Entered into force Oct. 24, 1968. TIAS 6605.
Adherence deposited: Marshall Islands, Mar. 18, 1988.

Convention on offenses and certain other acts committed on board aircraft. Done at Tokyo Sept. 14, 1963. Entered into force Dec. 4, 1969. TIAS 6768.
Accession deposited: Ukrainian S.S.R., Feb. 29, 1988.

Convention for the suppression of unlawful seizure of aircraft. Done at The Hague Dec. 16, 1970. Entered into force Oct. 14, 1971. TIAS 7192.
Accession deposited: Cameroon, Apr. 14, 1988.

Expositions
Protocol revising the convention of Nov. 22, 1928, relating to international expositions, with appendix and annex. Done at Paris Nov. 30, 1972. Entered into force June 9, 1980.
Notification of denunciation: El Salvador, Oct. 5, 1987; effective Oct. 5, 1988.

Finance—Investment Guarantees
Convention establishing the multilateral investment guarantee agency, with annexes and schedules. Done at Seoul Oct. 11, 1985. Entered into force Apr. 12, 1988.
Acceptance deposited: U.S., Apr. 12, 1988.

Finance—International Fund for Agricultural Development
Agreement establishing the international fund for agricultural development. Done at Rome June 13, 1976. Entered into force Nov. 30, 1977. TIAS 8765.
Accession deposited: Trinidad and Tobago, March 24, 1988.

Fisheries
Pacific Island regional fisheries treaty, with annexes and agreed statement. Done at Port Moresby Apr. 2, 1987.[1] [Senate] Treaty Doc. 100–5.
Ratifications deposited: Kiribati, Jan. 19, 1988; Niue, Feb. 15, 1988; Palau, Nov. 6, 1987.

Marine Pollution
Convention for the protection and development of the marine environment of the wider Caribbean region, with annex. Done at Cartagena Mar. 24, 1983. Entered into force Oct. 11, 1986. [Senate] Treaty Doc. 98–13.
Proclaimed by the President: Apr. 19, 1988.

Nuclear Test Ban
Treaty banning nuclear weapon tests in the atmosphere, in outer space, and under water. Done at Moscow Aug. 5, 1963. Entered into force Oct. 10, 1963. TIAS 5433.
Ratification deposited: Pakistan, Mar. 3, 1988.

Pollution
Montreal protocol on substances that deplete the ozone layer, with annex. Done at Montreal Sept. 16, 1987.[1] [Senate] Treaty Doc. 100–10.
Signatures: Byelorussian S.S.R., Jan. 22, 1988; Israel, Jan. 14, 1988; Luxembourg, Jan. 29, 1988; Morocco, Jan. 7, 1988.
U.S. instrument of ratification signed by the President: Apr. 5, 1988.
Ratification deposited: U.S., Apr. 21, 1988.
Acceptance deposited: Mexico, Mar. 31, 1988.

Rubber
International natural rubber agreement, 1987, with annexes. Done at Geneva Mar. 20, 1987.[1] [Senate] Treaty Doc. 100–9.
Signatures: Finland, Norway, Sweden, Dec. 21, 1987.

Sugar
International sugar agreement, 1987, with annexes. Done at London Sept. 11, 1987. Entered into force provisionally Mar. 24, 1988.
Notifications of provisional application: Guatemala, Dec. 17, 1987; Swaziland, Jan. 29, 1988; Thailand, Mar. 28, 1988; Zimbabwe, Mar. 30, 1988.
Acceptances deposited: Japan, Norway, Dec. 21, 1987.
Accession deposited: Barbados, Apr. 4, 1988; Togo, Mar. 30, 1988.
Approval deposited: European Economic Community (EEC), Dec. 18, 1987.

Timber
International tropical timber agreement, 1983, with annexes. Done at Geneva Nov. 18, 1983. Entered into force provisionally Apr. 1, 1985; for the U.S. Apr. 26, 1985.
Ratification deposited: Ecuador, Jan. 19, 1988.

Trade—Textiles
Arrangement regarding international trade in textiles, with annexes. Done at Geneva Dec. 20, 1973. Entered into force Jan. 1, 1974. TIAS 7840.

Protocol extending the arrangement regarding international trade in textiles of Dec. 20, 1973, as extended. Done at Geneva July 31, 1986. Entered into force Aug. 1, 1986; for the U.S. Aug. 5, 1986.
Acceptance deposited: Costa Rica, Mar. 14, 1988.

BILATERAL

Bahamas
Treaty on mutual assistance in criminal matters, with related notes. Signed at Nassau June 12 and Aug. 18, 1987.[1] [Senate] Treaty Doc. 100–17.
Transmitted to the Senate: Apr. 13, 1988.

Belgium
Treaty on mutual legal assistance in criminal matters. Signed at Washington Jan. 28, 1988.[1] [Senate] Treaty Doc. 100–16.
Transmitted to the Senate: Mar. 29, 1988.

Agreement concerning relief from double taxation on income derived from the operation of ships and aircraft. Effected by exchange of notes at Washington Oct. 14, 1987, and Mar. 21, 1988. Entered into force Mar. 21, 1988.
Supersedes agreement of Jan. 28, 1936 (49 Stat. (pt. 2), 3871), and agreement of July 18, 1953 (TIAS 2858).

Colombia
Agreement relating to trade in cotton sateen fabrics, with annexes. Effected by exchange of notes at Bogota Jan. 6 and Mar. 1, 1988. Entered into force Mar. 1, 1988; effective Apr. 1, 1987.

Dominican Republic
Agreement amending special access agreement of Dec. 18, 1986, as amended, relating to trade in cotton, wool, and manmade fiber textiles and textile products. Effected by exchange of notes at Washington Mar. 22 and Apr. 8, 1988. Entered into force Apr. 8, 1988.

Egypt
Agreement amending agreement of Dec. 7 and 28, 1977 (TIAS 8973), as amended, relating to trade in textiles and textile products. Effected by exchange of notes at Cairo Mar. 7 and 14, 1988. Entered into force Mar. 14, 1988.

Memorandum of understanding concerning the exchange of scientists and engineers and mutual cooperation in research and development, procurement, and logistic support of defense equipment, with annex. Signed at Washington Mar. 23, 1988. Entered into force Mar. 23, 1988.

France
Agreement amending and extending the interim agreement of Feb. 24, 1987, relating to the employment of dependents of official government employees. Effected by exchange of notes at Paris Dec. 31, 1987. Entered into force Dec. 31, 1987.

Grenada
Agreement concerning the establishment of a radio relay station of the U.S. Information Agency (Voice of America) on the Island of Grenada. Signed at St. George's Sept. 29, 1987.
Entered into force: Mar. 23, 1988.

the *Statutes at Large.* Another compilation, of treaties in force as of 1873, appears in volume 18, accompanying the *Revised Statutes* of 1873. Volume 64, the last to contain treaties, includes a complete list of all treaties appearing in the *Statutes at Large,* arranged by country.

(c) C.J. Kappler, comp., *Indian Affairs: Laws and Treaties* (U.S.G.P.O., 7 vols., 1904–79), vol. 2, "Treaties." This is probably the best collection of treaties between the United States and the Indian nations. Volume 7 of the *Statutes at Large* contained a collection of Indian treaties from 1778 to 1842, and later Indian treaties appeared in subsequent *Statutes at Large* volumes.

(d) C.L. Wiktor, ed., *Unperfected Treaties of the United States of America, 1776–1976* (Oceana, 6 vols., 1976–84). This work contains treaties which never became effective, with a legislative history summary and analysis of each treaty.

2. INDEXES

Since most collections of United States treaties are published in chronological arrangements, finding aids providing access by subject and country are essential. Because treaties may be modified or terminated, the determination of their current status is a necessary part of treaty research. The following publications serve one or both of those functions for United States treaties.

Treaties in Force (Department of State, annual) is the most important current index to U.S. treaties and agreements in force. It indicates treaties in force for the United States as of January 1 of each year. Its entries include citations to all of the major treaty publications, including *Bevans,* the *Statutes at Large,* and the *League of Nations Treaty Series* for older treaties, and *TIAS, UST,* and the *United Nations Treaty Series* for more recent treaties. Each issue is divided into two parts. The first part lists bilateral treaties alphabetically by country and then, under each country, by subject. The second section lists multilateral treaties alphabetically by subject, and indicates which nations are parties to each treaty. Illustrations C–1 and C–2 show sample pages from each of these parts. *Treaties in Force* is updated between annual editions by the "Treaties—Current Actions" feature of the *Department of State Bulletin.*

A commercially published *Guide to the United States Treaties in Force* (Hein, 2 vols., annual), edited by I.I. Kavass and A. Sprudzs, provides access points beyond those of the official *Treaties in Force.* Part I provides a numerical list of all treaties in force and a subject index covering both bilateral and multilateral treaties. Illustration D shows a page from this index, with references to *TIAS* numbers in the volume's numerical list. Part II lists multilateral treaties chronologically and indexes them by country.

Several retrospective indexes provide subject access to all U.S. treaties, whether or not they are still in force. Each of the following cumulative indexes covers a different class of documents:

Illustration C-1

A list of bilateral treaties between the United States and Canada, in the annual *Treaties in Force*

CANADA (Cont'd)

Agreement concerning the test and evaluation of United States defense weapons systems in Canada. Exchange of notes at Washington February 10, 1983; entered into force February 10, 1983.
TIAS 10659.

Mutual logistical support agreement, with annexes. Signed at Stuttgart February 11, 1983; entered into force February 11, 1983.
TIAS 10658.

Agreement regarding modernization of the North American Air Defense System, with memorandum of understanding. Exchange of notes at Quebec March 18, 1985; entered into force March 18, 1985.
TIAS

NOTES:
[1] Provisions are terminated to the extent that they are inconsistent with the agreement of August 16, 1971 (TIAS 7173). See also agreements of June 13, 1955 (TIAS 3452), June 15, 1955 (TIAS 3453) and September 27, 1961 (TIAS 4859).
[2] See also agreements of April 13, 1959 (TIAS 4208) and July 13, 1959 (TIAS 4264).

ECONOMIC AND TECHNICAL COOPERATION

Agreement relating to post-war economic settlements. Exchange of notes at Washington November 30, 1942; entered into force November 30, 1942.
56 Stat. 1815; EAS 287; 6 Bevans 292; 119 UNTS 305.

EMPLOYMENT (See also LABOR; SOCIAL SECURITY)

Arrangement relating to the employment of dependents of government employees. Exchange of notes at Washington June 4 and 12, 1980; entered into force June 12, 1980.
TIAS 10693.

ENERGY

Memorandum of understanding for cooperation in the research and development of tar sands (oil sands) and heavy oil. Signed at Washington, Edmonton and Ottawa June 4, 1979; entered into force June 4, 1979.
30 UST 7278; TIAS 9585.

EXTRADITION

Treaty on extradition, as amended by exchange of notes of June 28 and July 9, 1974.[1] Signed at Washington December 3, 1971; entered into force March 22, 1976.
27 UST 983; TIAS 8237.

NOTES:
[1] Applicable to all territories.

FINANCE

Agreement relating to exemptions from exchange control measures. Exchange of notes at Ottawa June 18, 1940; entered into force June 18, 1940.
54 Stat. 2317; EAS 174; 6 Bevans 182; 203 LNTS 41.

FIRE PROTECTION

Agreement relating to the participation of the Provinces of New Brunswick and Quebec in the north-eastern interstate forest fire protection compact. Exchange of notes at Washington January 29, 1970; entered into force January 29, 1970.
21 UST 415; TIAS 6825; 753 UNTS 43.

Agreement concerning cooperation in the detection and suppression of forest fires along the boundary between the Yukon Territory and Alaska with memorandum of agreement. Exchange of notes at Washington June 1, 1971; entered into force June 1, 1971.
22 UST 721; TIAS 7132; 793 UNTS 77.

Arrangement on mutual assistance in fighting forest fires. Exchange of notes at Ottawa May 4 and 7, 1982; entered into force May 7, 1982.
TIAS 10436.

FISHERIES

Agreement adopting, with certain modifications, the rules and method of procedure recommended in the award of September 7, 1910, of the North Atlantic Coast Fisheries Arbitration. Signed at Washington July 20, 1912; entered into force November 15, 1912.
37 Stat. 1634; TS 572; 12 Bevans 357.

Convention for the extension to halibut fishing vessels of port privileges on the Pacific Coasts of the United States of America and Canada. Signed at Ottawa March 24, 1950; entered into force July 13, 1950.
1 UST 536; TIAS 2096; 200 UNTS 211.

Convention for the preservation of the halibut fishery of the Northern Pacific Ocean and Bering Sea. Signed at Ottawa March 2, 1953; entered into force October 28, 1953.
5 UST 5; TIAS 2900; 222 UNTS 77.

Amendment:
March 29, 1979 (32 UST 2483; TIAS 9855).

Convention on Great Lakes fisheries. Signed at Washington September 10, 1954; entered into force October 11, 1955.
6 UST 2836; TIAS 3326; 238 UNTS 97.

Amendment:
April 5, 1966 and May 19, 1967 (18 UST 1402; TIAS 6297).

Agreement concerning fishing off the west coast of Canada, with annex. Exchange of notes at Washington March 29, 1979; entered into force March 29, 1979.
30 UST 4067; TIAS 9448.

Treaty on Pacific Coast albacore tuna vessels and port privileges, with annexes. Signed at Washington May 26, 1981; entered into force July 29, 1981.
TIAS 10057.

Treaty concerning Pacific salmon, with annexes and memorandum of understanding. Signed at Ottawa January 28, 1985; entered into force March 18, 1985.
TIAS

HEALTH AND SANITATION

Arrangement concerning quarantine inspection of vessels entering Puget Sound and waters adjacent thereto or the Great Lakes via the St. Lawrence River. Exchange of notes at Ottawa October 10 and 23, 1929; entered into force October 23, 1929.
47 Stat. 2573; EAS 1; 6 Bevans 35; 96 LNTS 167.

Memorandum of understanding on the monitoring of food, beverage and sanitary services provided on common carriers operating between the United States and Canada. Signed at Ottawa and at Washington August 20 and September 8, 1975; entered into force September 8, 1975.
28 UST 884; TIAS 8485.

HIGHWAYS

Agreement providing for the construction of a military highway to Alaska. Exchange of notes at Ottawa March 17 and 18, 1942; entered into force March 18, 1942.
56 Stat. 1458; EAS 246; 6 Bevans 261; 101 UNTS 205.

Agreement relating to the southern terminus of the Alaska Highway. Exchange of notes at Ottawa May 4 and 9, 1942; entered into force May 9, 1942.
57 Stat. 1373; EAS 380; 6 Bevans 274; 101 UNTS 215.

Agreement relating to the construction of flight strips along the Alaska Highway. Exchange of notes at Ottawa August 26 and September 10, 1942; entered into force September 10, 1942.
57 Stat. 1375; EAS 381; 6 Bevans 282; 101 UNTS 221.

Agreement relating to the construction of the Haines-Champagne section of the Alaska Highway. Exchange of notes at Ottawa November 28 and December 7, 1942; entered into force December 7, 1942.
57 Stat. 1377; EAS 382; 6 Bevans 295; 101 UNTS 227.

Agreement relating to access to the Alaska Highway. Exchange of notes at Ottawa April 10, 1943; entered into force April 10, 1943.
57 Stat. 1274; EAS 362; 6 Bevans 319; 21 UNTS 237.

Agreement relating to the designation of the highway from Dawson Creek, British Columbia, to Fairbanks, Alaska, as the "Alaska Highway". Exchange of notes at Washington July 19, 1943; entered into force July 19, 1943.
57 Stat. 1023; EAS 331; 6 Bevans 324; 29 UNTS 289.

Agreement relating to cooperation in reconstruction of Canadian portions of the Alaska Highway. Exchange of notes at Ottawa January 11 and February 11, 1977; entered into force February 11, 1977.
28 UST 5303; TIAS 8631.

Illustration C–2

A list of multilateral treaties and conventions in *Treaties in Force*, indicating parties to each agreement

FINANCIAL INSTITUTIONS (Cont'd)

NOTES:
[1] With reservation.
[2] With declaration.
[3] With a statement.
[4] Applicable to Land Berlin.
[5] Extended only to Kingdom in Europe.

Proces-verbal of rectification of the agreement establishing the Asian Development Bank. Signed at New York November 2, 1967.
18 UST 2935; TIAS 6387; 608 UNTS 380.

Agreement amending the agreement establishing the African Development Bank,[1] with annexes. Adopted by the Board of Governors at Abidjan May 17, 1979;[2] entered into force May 7, 1982; for the United States January 31, 1983.
TIAS
States which are parties:
Angola
Argentina
Austria[3]
Belgium[3]
Benin
Botswana
Brazil[3]
Burkina Faso
Burundi
Cameroon
Canada[3] [4]
Cape Verde
Central African Rep.
Chad
China
Comoros
Congo
Denmark[3] [5]
Djibouti
Egypt
Equatorial Guinea
Ethiopia
Finland[3]
France[3]
Gabon
Gambia, The
Germany, Fed Rep.[3] [4] [6]
Ghana
Guinea
Guinea-Bissau
India[3] [4]
Italy[3] [4]
Ivory Coast
Japan[3] [4]
Kenya
Korea, Rep.[3]
Kuwait[3]
Lesotho
Liberia
Madagascar
Malawi
Mali
Mauritania
Mauritius
Morocco
Mozambique
Netherlands[3] [4]
Niger
Nigeria
Norway[3] [4] [5]
Portugal[3]
Rwanda
Sao Tome & Principe
Saudi Arabia[3]
Senegal
Seychelles
Sierra Leone
Somalia
Spain[3]
Sudan
Swaziland
Sweden[3] [4] [5]
Switzerland[3] [4]
Tanzania
Togo
Tunisia
Uganda
United Kingdom[3] [4] [5]
United States[3] [4]
Yugoslavia[3]
Zaire
Zambia
Zimbabwe

NOTES:
[1] The agreement establishing the African Development Bank, done at Khartoum, August 4, 1963, entered into force September 10, 1964 (510 UNTS 3 and 569 UNTS 353 (corr.)).
[2] The amendments to the agreement, which provide for non-regional membership, were adopted at Abidjan by resolution 05–09 of May 17, 1979 of the Board of Governors and concluded at Lusaka on May 7, 1982. Algeria and Libya are parties to the agreement establishing the Bank but not parties to the 1979 amendments.
[3] Non-regional members.
[4] With reservation(s).
[5] With declaration(s).
[6] Applicable to Berlin (West).

FISHERIES (See also CONSERVATION; SEALS; WHALING)

Convention on fishing and conservation of living resources of the high seas. Done at Geneva April 29, 1958; entered into force March 20, 1966.
17 UST 138; TIAS 5969; 559 UNTS 285.
States which are parties:
Australia
Belgium
Burkina Faso
Cambodia
Colombia
Denmark[1]
Dominican Rep.
Fiji
Finland
France
Haiti
Jamaica
Kenya
Lesotho
Madagascar
Malawi
Malaysia
Mauritius
Mexico
Netherlands
Nigeria
Portugal
Sierra Leone
Solomon Is.
South Africa
Spain[2]
Switzerland
Thailand
Tonga
Trinidad & Tobago
Uganda
United Kingdom[2]
United States[3]
Venezuela
Yugoslavia

NOTES:
[1] With reservation.
[2] With a statement.
[3] With an understanding.

Amended agreement for the establishment of the Indo-Pacific Fisheries Council. Approved at the 11th Session of the Conference of the Food and Agriculture Organization, Rome, November 23, 1961; entered into force November 23, 1961.
13 UST 2511; TIAS 5218; 418 UNTS 348.
Parties:
Australia
Bangladesh
Burma
Cambodia
France
Hong Kong
India
Indonesia
Japan
Korea
Malaysia
Nepal
New Zealand
Pakistan
Philippines
Sri Lanka
Thailand
United Kingdom
United States
Vietnam, Socialist Rep.

Convention for the establishment of an Inter-American Tropical Tuna Commission, with exchange of notes of March 3, 1950. Signed at Washington May 31, 1949; entered into force March 3, 1950.
1 UST 230; TIAS 2044; 80 UNTS 3.
States which are parties:
France
Japan
Nicaragua
Panama
United States

International convention for the high seas fisheries of the North Pacific Ocean, with annex and protocol. Signed at Tokyo May 9, 1952; entered into force June 12, 1953.
4 UST 380; TIAS 2786; 205 UNTS 65.
States which are parties:
Canada
Japan
United States

Amendments:
November 17, 1962 (14 UST 953; TIAS 5385).

Illustration D

A page from the combined subject index to bilateral and multilateral treaties in *A Guide to the United States Treaties in Force*

406
Finance-Food and Agriculture Organization

Guide to Treaties in Force
Subject Reference Index

Finance, Bilateral, continued

Philippines TIAS 1612
TIAS 2151
TIAS 4715
Unnumbered:
July 1985
Poland TIAS 7557
TIAS 8164
TIAS 10255
Unnumbered:
Nov. 1924 (AD 230)
June 1932 (AD 350)
Romania Unnumbered:
Dec. 1925 (AD 258)
June 1932 (AD 353)
Mar. 1983
Feb. 1984
Senegal TIAS 10475
Unnumbered:
Aug. 1983
Aug. 1984
June 1985
Sierra Leone Unnumbered:
Aug. 1985
Somalia Unnumbered:
May 1985
Spain TIAS 2123
Sudan TIAS 9952
TIAS 10437
Jan. 1984
Dec. 1984
Togo TIAS 9740
Unnumbered:
Sept. 1981
Nov. 1983
Turkey TIAS 4111
TIAS 9361
TIAS 9783
TIAS 9786
TIAS 9909
TIAS 10091
TIAS 10131
TIAS 10432
Uganda Unnumbered:
May 1982
Mar. 1983
United Kingdom TIAS 1545
TIAS 2909
TIAS 3962
Unnumbered:
June 1923 (AD 222)
June 1932 (AD 345)
Yugoslavia TIAS 3142
TIAS 3254
TIAS 3255
TIAS 3487
TIAS 4150
TIAS 7298
Unnumbered:
May 1926
Zaire TIAS 8731
TIAS 9405
TIAS 9416
TIAS 9553
TIAS 9907
TIAS 10108
TIAS 10141

Finance, Bilateral, Zaire, continued

Unnumbered:
July 1982
May 1984
Dec. 1985
Zambia Unnumbered:
Dec. 1983
Dec. 1985

FINANCIAL INSTITUTIONS
See also FINANCE

Multilateral

African Development Bank Unnumbered:
May 1979
Asian Development Bank TIAS 6103
TIAS 6387
Inter-American Development Bank TIAS 4397
TIAS 6591
TIAS 6920
TIAS 7437
TIAS 8383
Unnumbered:
Jan. 1977
International Bank for Reconstruction and Development TIAS 1502
TIAS 5929
International Development Association TIAS 4607
International Finance Corporation TIAS 3620
TIAS 4894
TIAS 7683
International Monetary Fund TIAS 1501
TIAS 6748
TIAS 8937

FIRE PROTECTION

Bilateral

Canada TIAS 6825
TIAS 7132
TIAS 10436

FISHERIES
See also CONSERVATION, SEALS, SHELLFISH, and WHALING

Multilateral

Atlantic tunas TIAS 6767
Conservation, high seas TIAS 5969
Indo-Pacific Fisheries Council TIAS 5218
Inter-American Tropical Tuna Commission TIAS 2044
North Pacific Ocean TIAS 2786
TIAS 5385
TIAS 9242
Salmon, conservation TIAS 10789

Bilateral

Bulgaria Unnumbered:
Sept. 1983

Fisheries, Bilateral, continued

Canada TS 572
TIAS 2096
TIAS 2900
TIAS 3326
TIAS 6297
TIAS 9448
TIAS 9855
TIAS 10057
Unnumbered:
Jan. 1985
China, People's Republic of Unnumbered:
July 1985
Colombia Unnumbered:
Oct. 1983
Denmark Unnumbered:
June 1984
European Economic Community Unnumbered:
Oct. 1984
German Democratic Republic TIAS 10687
Iceland Unnumbered:
Sept. 1984
Japan TIAS 10480
Unnumbered:
June 1984
Korea, Republic of TIAS 10571
Poland Unnumbered:
Aug. 1985
Portugal TIAS 9929
Spain TIAS 10581
USSR TS 298
TIAS 7575
TIAS 7663
TIAS 8022
TIAS 8528
TIAS 10531
Unnumbered:
July 1985
United Kingdom TS 572
TIAS 10545

FOOD AID CONVENTION

Multilateral

TIAS 10015
Unnumbered:
Apr. 1983

FOOD AND AGRICULTURE ORGANIZATION
See also AGRICULTURE, ECONOMIC AND TECHNICAL COOPERATION, FISHERIES, PEACE CORPS and POPLAR COMMISSION

Multilateral

TIAS 4803
TIAS 5229
TIAS 5506
TIAS 5987
TIAS 6421
TIAS 6902

(a) I.I. Kavass & M.A. Michael, *United States Treaties and Other International Agreements Cumulative Index 1776–1949* (Hein, 4 vols., 1975), a comprehensive index of the pre-*UST* treaties in the

Bevans compilation. Each of the four volumes is a separate index, providing access to treaties by number, date, country, and topic.

(b) I.I. Kavass & A. Sprudzs, *UST Cumulative Index 1950–1970* (Hein, 4 vols., 1973), a similar set covering the first twenty years of the *UST* series. Supplemented by two bound volumes covering to 1979 and a looseleaf *UST Cumulative Indexing Service.*

(c) I.I. Kavass & A. Sprudzs, *Current Treaty Index* (Hein, annual), an index to treaties which have been published in slip form and assigned *TIAS* numbers but have not yet appeared in *UST.*

(d) I.I. Kavass & A. Sprudzs, *Unpublished and Unnumbered Treaties Index* (Hein, annual), covering recent treaties with neither *TIAS* nor *UST* citations.

3. LEGISLATIVE HISTORY

Treaties, even more than statutes, contain ambiguities which often lead to controversy in interpretation and application. The documents of legislative history produced during Senate consideration of United States treaties are a major source for clarification of the treaty text. Hence research in these documents is often an integral part of treaty research.[7]

Research in legislative history of treaties focuses on proceedings in the Senate, because the House of Representatives plays no role in Congressional consideration of treaties. Most of the documents produced by the Senate have already been discussed in Section B of Chapter 7, Legislative History, and need not be treated here. Two series of confidential Senate documents were not discussed in that chapter, however, because they relate specifically to treaty consideration.

Senate Treaty Documents, called *Senate Executive Documents* before 1981, contain the texts of treaties as transmitted to the Senate for its advice and consent, along with accompanying messages from the President and the Secretary of State.[8] These documents, appearing in a *numerical* series for each Congress,[9] are often confidential when printed and thus are not distributed beyond the Senate and not listed in the *Monthly Catalog of U.S. Government Publications.* When the Senate releases them from secrecy, they are published and distributed. Treaties may be pending before the Senate for several sessions before

7. The value of Senate materials in determining the intent of treaty parties is the subject of dispute. *See United States v. Stuart,* ___ U.S. ___, ___, 109 S.Ct. 1183, 1193–1197 (1989) (Scalia, J., concurring).

Detailed treatment of the legislative history of U.S. treaties can be found in Chapter VII of G.B. Folsom, *Legislative History: Research for the Interpretation of Laws* (University Press of Virginia, 1972; reprinted by Rothman, 1979).

8. Presidential messages upon signing, ratification, or proclamation of treaties may also be helpful in interpreting treaty actions. These messages are generally printed in the *Weekly Compilation of Presidential Documents,* which is discussed in Chapter 8.

9. Senate Executive Documents were identified by alphabetical designations.

approval, but Treaty Documents retain their original numerical designation.

The other treaty-related Senate publications are *Senate Executive Reports,* which are the single most authoritative legislative source for interpretation. Senate Executive Reports, issued by the Senate Foreign Relations Committee after its consideration of individual treaties, contain the committee's analysis of a treaty and its recommendation as to approval by the whole Senate. These, and a few Executive Reports from other committees on matters such as judicial and ambassadorial nominations, are published in a separately numbered series for each Congress.

In addition to their general distribution when the Senate's injunction of confidentiality is lifted, Treaty Documents and Senate Executive Reports also appear in the Congressional Information Service microfiche collection of legislative documents and selectively in *International Legal Materials,* the *Department of State Bulletin,* and *USCCAN.*[10]

For tracing the legislative history of treaties and in identifying the relevant documentary sources of that history, several finding aids are particularly useful.

(a) CCH *Congressional Index.* This looseleaf service, discussed above in Chapter 7, includes a status table of treaties pending before the Senate. This table, updated weekly, is one of the most valuable sources for determining the present status of pending treaties and learning of actions taken. Listings include references to hearings, Executive Reports, and ratifications. Treaties are listed chronologically by the session of transmittal and then by Treaty Document number (or Executive Document letter if transmitted before 1981). An index of subjects and countries precedes the list of treaties. A typical page is shown in Illustration E.

(b) *CIS/Index.* This important index of Congressional publications, also discussed in Chapter 7, includes some coverage of treaties, but does not include legislative history summaries like those provided for statutes. Access points to treaty information, however, include the Index of Subjects and Names, Index of Titles, and Indexes of Report Numbers and Document Numbers.

(c) *Legislative Calendar* of the Senate Foreign Relations Committee. This official status table of matters before the Senate committee contains one of the best lists of pending treaties with actions taken thereon, but it is less widely available than the CCH and CIS services. Its information on hearings is particularly useful. The final edition for each Congress, or "Cumulative Record," includes a list of committee publications for that Congress.

(d) *Congressional Quarterly Weekly Report.* This publication, devoted to congressional activity generally, also includes useful informa-

10. Early Senate Executive Reports can be found in *Reports of the Committee on Foreign Relations, 1789–1901,* S.Doc. No. 231, 56th Cong., 2d Sess. (8 vols., 1901).

Illustration E

A page from the Treaties section of *Congressional Index* (CCH)

The Annex addresses the intentional dumping of plastic garbage from ocean-going vessels. An amendment involves an understanding that the U.S. Government shall make every reasonable effort to have the Gulf of Mexico designated a "special area."

Injunction of secrecy removed: 2/17/87

In Foreign Relations Committee: 2/17/87

Ordered reported: 9/24/87

Reported: S. Ex. Rept. No. 100-8, 10/14/87

Ratified: 11/6/87

100-5, Treaty Document No. (6/18/87)—Fishing and fisheries—Pacific island nations—Tuna fishing

The Treaty on Fisheries Between the Governments of Certain Pacific Island States and the Government of the United States of America, with annexes and agreed statement, resolves a fisheries dispute with several Pacific Island states as a result of conflicting laws regarding jurisdiction over highly migratory tuna.

The treaty ensures the effective conservation and management of tuna and secures access for U.S. fishermen to the tuna stocks wherever they migrate beyond the island states' coastal waters. Among other things, the treaty provides for the issuance of regional licenses for tuna fishing and the collection of data on tuna catches.

Injunction of secrecy removed: 6/18/87

In Foreign Relations Committee: 6/18/87

Ordered reported: 10/21/87

Reported: S. Ex. Rept. No. 100-9, 10/22/87

Ratified: 11/6/87

100-6, Treaty Document No. (6/25/87)—Crime and criminal procedures—Extradition—West Germany

The Supplementary Treaty to the Treaty Between the United States of America and the Federal Republic of Germany Concerning Extradition amends the 1978 treaty by excluding from the scope of the political offense exception serious offenses typically committed by terrorists.

Examples of such offenses are murder, manslaughter, kidnapping, use of a destructive device capable of endangering life or causing grievous bodily harm, and attempt of conspiracy to commit such offenses.

Injunction of secrecy removed: 6/25/87

In Foreign Relations Committee: 6/25/87

100-7, Treaty Document No. (6/26/87)—Communications—Radio regulations

The Regional Agreement for the Medium Frequency Broadcasting Service in Region 2, with annexes and a Final Protocol (containing a statement of reservation made by the U.S.), establishes a Plan of frequency assignments and associated procedures designed to enable the International Telecommunication Union member countries of Region 2 (essentially, the Western Hemisphere) to protect each other's radio broadcasting services in the medium frequency band ("AM radio") from mutually caused objectionable interference.

The statement of reservation made by the U.S. addresses the level of objectionable interference to U.S. stations from various countries in the Region (particularly Cuba).

Injunction of secrecy removed: 6/26/87

In Foreign Relations Committee: 6/26/87

tion on treaties. In addition to occasional special reports on major treaties, the well-indexed *Weekly Report* includes the actual text of important treaty documents, chronologies, summaries of debates and messages, and general information about current treaties.

(e) *Congressional Record* indexes. The fortnightly and bound volume indexes to the *Congressional Record* include a listing of treaty actions and discussions appearing in the *Record.* These references appear under the heading "Treaties" in the alphabetical subject index and also occasionally under the name of a particular treaty or its subject matter. Although inconvenient to use, the *Congressional Record* indexes can be helpful for retrospective research into a particular treaty's legislative history. Their coverage, however, is limited to material appearing in the *Record.*

(f) *CIS Index to US Senate Executive Documents & Reports* (Congressional Information Service, 2 vols., 1987). This finding aid to treaty materials predating coverage in the *CIS/Index* is in two parts. One volume is a chronological bibliography of Senate Executive Documents and Reports from 1818 to 1969, and the other contains a series of indexes—by subject, title, and document and report number. As with its other services, CIS also publishes microfiche copies of all indexed documents and reports.

4. OTHER RESEARCH AIDS

Treaty research is facilitated by a number of other publications and services. These include:

(a) *Popular name tables.* Popular names of treaties and agreements can be translated into their official *UST, TIAS* or *Statutes at Large* citations in *Shepard's Acts and Cases by Popular Names: Federal and State,* in the index volume to *Bevans' Treaties and Other International Agreements,* and in the *UST Cumulative Indexes.*

(b) *Glossary of International Treaties,* by Y. Renoux & J. Yates (Elsevier, 1970). Although not limited to U.S. treaties, this dictionary of treaty terms in Dutch, English, French, German, Italian, Russian and Spanish is a useful aid for the American researcher.

(c) *Computer services.* While neither WESTLAW nor LEXIS provides access to treaties generally, both systems contain databases of U.S. tax treaties. More important, however, is the capacity to use treaty titles or citations as search terms in other databases. This is one of the best ways to locate judicial decisions and secondary sources which have interpreted or discussed a treaty's provisions.

(d) *Digests of International Law.* The Department of State's *Digest of International Law,* by M.M. Whiteman (U.S.G.P.O., 15 vols., 1963–73) and its supplementation since 1973 by the annual volumes of the *Digest of U.S. Practice in International Law* are invaluable for background information and interpretation of major treaties. These publications and earlier digests are discussed more fully below on pages 464–466.

5. VERIFICATION AND UPDATING

Since treaties are subject to judicial interpretation, legislative action, or amendment, their current status must be verified, as with other primary sources. *Shepard's United States Citations,* statute edition, can be used to locate relevant citing *federal* court decisions, statutes affecting the treaty, or amendment by later treaty. For treaties up to 1949, their listing is by *Statutes at Large* citation. After 1950, a separate section of the citator lists treaties by *UST* citation or by *TIAS* number (if not yet published in *UST*). Illustration F shows a page of *Shepard's U.S. Citations* listing references to recent treaties in both *UST* and slip form.

Shepard's U.S. Citations does not include any citing *state* court cases. As with federal statutes, the Shepard's citator for each state includes a listing of U.S. treaties with references to citations in state court decisions. Surprisingly, more citations to treaties occur in state court decisions than in federal decisions.

United States Code Service includes an unnumbered volume with the spine title "Notes to Uncodified Laws and Treaties." This volume lists multilateral treaties by date of signing and bilateral treaties by country, and provides annotations of federal and state court decisions discussing or interpreting them. Its coverage, however, is far more limited than *Shepard's.*

As noted above, WESTLAW and LEXIS can also be used to obtain judicial decisions referring to treaties. This is done by using the treaty's title or citation as a search term. The systems' multistate databases are particularly valuable for this purpose, since a manual search for citing state cases would require consulting fifty separate editions of *Shepard's Citations.* Unfortunately, online searches will not reveal amendments or changes in status of the treaty itself.

C. CASE LAW

In addition to the publication of judicial decisions reflecting U.S. practice in international law in the standard American court reports, there are several specialized reporters containing such cases, and a few specialized case-finding aids for those decisions.

A convenient source for reprints of U.S. federal and state court decisions since 1783 is *American International Law Cases* (Oceana, 1971–date), now in its second series. Cases are arranged by subject, and the set includes a looseleaf index. Selected decisions on international law from U.S. courts also appear in the bimonthly *International Legal Materials,* in the periodicals *American Journal of International Law* and *International Lawyer,* and in *International Law Reports,* a comprehensive reporter of national and international tribunals.

The U.S. Court of International Trade was established in 1980 as successor to the U.S. Customs Court, with enlarged jurisdiction. Its decisions are reported officially in *U.S. Court of International Trade*

Illustration F

A page from *Shepard's U.S. Citations* covering recent treaties

UNITED STATES TREATIES AND OTHER INTERNATIONAL AGREEMENTS

VOL. 30

—3643—
CIT
617FS1083

10324
CIT
617FS1083

—3644—

Art. 18
Subsec. C
CIT
617FS1083

—3872—
ETIAS10274

—3927—
ATIAS10234

—5253—
GICL§ 10.22

—6099—
GICL§ 10.13

—6263—
Cir. 5
668F2d806
Cir. 9
631F2d121

Art. 3
Subsec. 3
Cir. 9
631F2d122
Subsec. 8
Cir. 5
464FS212
Cir. 9
631F2d122

Art. 4
Subsec. 1
Cir. 5
464FS212
Cir. 9
631F2d123

Art. 5
Cir. 5
464FS212
Cir. 6
C630F2d473
Cir. 9
631F2d123
684F2d1345

—6541—
CIT
505FS205

—7223—

Art. 9
Subsec. 5
CtCl
688F2d751

Art. 14
CtCl
688F2d751

—7323—
Cir. DC
665F2d1159

Art. 6
Cir. DC
731F2d932

Art. 8
Subsec. c
Cir. DC
731F2d924

Art. 9
Subsec. a
Cir. DC
731F2d924

—7565—
ATIAS10605

Vol. 31

—513—

Art. 2
Subsec. 4
CIT
618FS499

Art. 5
Subsec. 1
CIT
618FS501
Subsec. 3
CIT
618FS497
Subsec. 9
CIT
618FS499

9620
CIT
592FS1323

—515—

Art. 5
Subsec. 3
CIT
614FS1243

—892—

Art. 4
Subsec. 3
Cir. 2
699F2d77

—944—

Art. 6
Cir. 9
603FS719

Art. 7
Cir. 2
649F2d917

Art. 8
Cir. 2
500FS1385

Art. 17
Cir. 9
603FS719

—2071—
CIT
515FS776

Art. 8
CIT
515FS776
Subsec. a
CIT
515FS777

—2097—
ETIAS10105

—4810—
ATIAS10447

—4919—
CIT
618FS501

Art. 3
Cir. Fed.
750F2d931

Art. 9
Subsec. 1
Cir. Fed.
750F2d931

—5059—
Cir. 2
500FS1384
Cir. 5
623F2d1100

Art. 9
Cir. 5
623F2d1106

—5135—
CIT
544FS890

Art. 57
CIT
544FS895

Art. 58
CIT
544FS895

—5619—
Cir. 2
500FS1385

—5668—
54LE704
98SC814
Cir. 9
560FS135
CtCl
688F2d765
GICL§ 10.16

Art. 9
Subsec. 4
54LE704
98SC814

Art. 10
Subsec. 2
Subd. b
¶1
CtCl
688F2d748

Art. 14
CtCl
688F2d765

Art. 28
CtCl
688F2d752
Subsec. 2
Subd. b
¶2
CtCl
688F2d748

Vol. 32

—322—
53USLW
[4273

—975—
ATIAS10447

—1241—
Cir. Fed.
773F2d1219

—1924—
ETIAS10200

—1935—
Cir. DC
545FS617

Art. 13
Subsec. 2
CtCl
688F2d751

—2071—
Cir. Fed.
751F2d1242
CIT
583FS594

TIAS 9883
ATIAS10363

TIAS 9896
ETIAS10232

TIAS 9903

Art. 11
Subsec. 2
Cir. DC
731F2d936

Art. 12
Cir. DC
731F2d932
Subsec. 1
Cir. DC
731F2d932

TIAS 9935
ATIAS10269

TIAS 9938
Cir. DC
103FRD48

TIAS 9942
ATIAS10196

TIAS 10029
Cir. 6
591FS124
Cir. 8
567FS163
Cir. 11
585FS862
ClCt
1ClC145
6ClC119

TIAS 10030
Cir. 11
768F2d1241

Art. 3
Cir. 11
768F2d1241
Subsec. 8
Cir. 11
768F2d1247
Subsec. 9
Cir. 11
768F2d1241

Art. 10
Subsec. 10
Subd. b
Cir. 11
768F2d1245

TIAS 10031

Art. 11
Subsec. 2
Subd. e
Cir. 11
768F2d1244

Art. 12
Cir. 11
768F2d1245

Art. 13
Cir. 11
768F2d1245

Art. 14
Cir. 11
768F2d1245

Art. 15
Cir. 11
768F2d1241
Subsec. 1
Cir. 11
768F2d1244
Subsec. 2
Cir. 11
768F2d1242
Subsec. 3
Cir. 11
768F2d1242

Art. 16
Cir. 11
768F2d1245

Art. 18
Cir. 11
768F2d1245

Art. 19
Cir. 11
768F2d1245

TIAS 10032

Art. 16
Subsec. 2
Cir. 11
768F2d1244

TIAS 10038

Art. 9
ClCt
6ClC127

Art. 11
Subsec. 2
Subd. e
ClCt
6ClC127

Art. 15
Cir. 6
574FS716
591FS124
Cir. 8
567FS164
Cir. 9
592FS702
Cir. 10
565FS1020
Cir. 11
585FS862
Cir. Fed.
761F2d690
ClCt
6ClC119
Subsec. 1
Cir. 6
574FS716
591FS124
Cir. 8
567FS164
Cir. 9
592FS702
Cir. 10
565FS1020
ClCt
6ClC127
Subsec. 2
Cir. 6
574FS716
591FS124
Cir. 8
567FS164
Cir. 9
592FS702
Cir. 10
565FS1020
Cir. 11
585FS863
ClCt
1ClC145
6ClC120

Subsec. 3
Cir. 6
574FS716
591FS124
Cir. 8
567FS164
Cir. 10
565FS1020
ClCt
6ClC127
Subsec. 4
Cir. 6
574FS716
ClCt
6ClC146

Art. 19
Cir. 2
621F2d1200

TIAS 10042

Art. 10
Subsec. 9
Cir. DC
C580F2d1072

Art. 11
Cir. 5
679F2d380
715F2d1001
Subsec. 1
Cir. 5
715F2d1010
557FS342
Subsec. 2
Cir. 5
715F2d1012
Subsec. 3
Cir. 5
715F2d1012
Subsec. 5
Cir. 5
715F2d1011
Subsec. 6
Cir. 5
715F2d1010
495FS181
557FS342
Subsec. 7
Cir. 5
715F2d1011
Subsec. 8
Cir. 5
715F2d1012

Art. 13
Cir. DC
C580F2d1055
Cir. 3
80FRD120

TIAS 10044
ClCt
6ClC146

Art. 3
Cir. 6
591FS124
Cir. 11
585FS862
Subsec. 9
Cir. 6
591FS124

TIAS 10045

Art. 9
Subsec. 5
Cir. 2
609FS233
Subsec. 9
ClCt
6ClC127

Art. 10
ClCt
6ClC138

Art. 16
ClCt
6ClC137
Subsec. 2
ClCt
6ClC137

TIAS 10046
ClCt
6ClC130

Art. 8
ClCt
6ClC130

Art. 9
Cir. 6
574FS715
Cir. 8
567FS163
Cir. 10
565FS1020

Art. 10
Cir. 5
495FS180
557FS341

TIAS 10047
ClCt
6ClC119

TIAS 10048
Cir. DC
C580F2d1056
676F2d721
Cir. 2
572F2d919
621F2d1200
Cir. 3
80FRD119
Cir. 4
526FS765
Cir. 5
607F2d120
643F2d1111
652F2d419
715F2d1010
495FS181
557FS341
Cir. 8
455FS403
567FS163
Cir. 9
592FS702
Cir. Fed.
761F2d689
ClCt
6ClC119

Reports, and commercially in the *Federal Supplement.* The decisions of the previous court can be found in the *U.S. Customs Court Reports* (85 vols., 1938–80), and in the *Federal Supplement* beginning in 1956.

Judgments of the Court of International Trade are reviewable by the U.S. Court of Appeals for the Federal Circuit, which in 1982 replaced the Court of Customs and Patent Appeals. The Federal Circuit's decisions on international trade are published in *U.S. Court of Appeals for the Federal Circuit International Trade Cases* and in the *Federal Reporter.* Its predecessor's decisions appear in *Court of Customs and Patent Appeals Reports* (69 vols., 1910–82), and in the *Federal Reporter* from 1929 to 1982. The decisions of all of these courts are available online in LEXIS and WESTLAW as well.

The decisions of several United States administrative agencies frequently relate to international law issues. These include the Federal Maritime Administration and its predecessor, the U.S. Maritime Commission; the International Trade Commission; the National Transportation Safety Board; and the Treasury Department. Treasury Department decisions on international trade matters are printed in *Customs Bulletin and Decisions* (1967–date), which succeeded *Treasury Decisions under Customs and Other Laws* (101 vols., 1899–1966). Decisions of the International Trade Commission are available through specialized international databases in both WESTLAW and LEXIS. *International Trade Reporter Decisions* (BNA, 1980–date) includes both judicial and administrative decisions.

The several official digests of international law which have been prepared by the Department of State are described below on pages 464–466. These digests provide discussions of leading American decisions in international law and include tables of cases or authorities cited.

Just as judicial decisions relating to international law can also be found in the court reports and case databases described above in Chapter 2, the standard updating and case-finding tools described in Chapters 3 and 4 can likewise be used to identify and verify the authority of decisions relevant to international law problems.

D. STATUTES AND REGULATIONS

Domestic legislation is often relevant in international law, since many federal statutes and administrative regulations relate to international matters. Discussion of the published sources for these materials can be found above in Chapters 5 and 8, respectively. U.S. Code titles 8 (Aliens and Nationality), 15 (Commerce and Trade), 19 (Customs Duties), 22 (Foreign Relations and Intercourse), 33 (Navigation and Navigable Waters), 46 (Shipping) and 50 (War and National Defense) are particularly important in this regard.

The many looseleaf services published on international taxation and international trade (see listings in Appendix E) are additional, useful research sources for legislation and regulations in those fields.

Selected statutes and legislative documents also appear in *International Legal Materials,* in the "Official Documents" section of the

American Journal of International Law, and in the *International Lawyer.*

E. SECONDARY SOURCES

A wide range of secondary materials is available for research in U.S. international law. These materials can offer introductions to unfamiliar fields, scholarly analysis of broad areas or narrow issues, historical background, or current commentary on recent international disputes and problems. Their authority may be weighty or negligible. Some publications are also useful as finding tools, leading the researcher to primary sources or authoritative discussions in the scholarly literature.

1. DIGESTS

Several encyclopedic digests of international law published by the Department of State have been among the most authoritative sources of information of U.S. practice.[11] These digests combine textual analyses of international matters with extensive excerpts and summaries of treaties, judicial decisions, and other documents. The most current edition is M.M. Whiteman, *Digest of International Law* (15 vols., 1963–73). Although its arrangement is somewhat confusing and it lacks an overall table of contents, the general index and finding aids in the last volume make the set reasonably accessible. The text focuses largely on developments from the 1940's to the 1960's, after which Whiteman's *Digest* is supplemented in other sources. The Department of State's *Digest of United States Practice in International Law* (annual, 1973–date) reports on more recent developments. The annual *Digest* volumes are issued several years after the period covered, but they are in turn supplemented quarterly by the *American Journal of International Law* feature, "Contemporary Practice of the United States Relating to International Law." "Contemporary Practice" is arranged in the same scheme as the *Digest of United States Practice* and includes digests of major current documents. Illustration G shows a sample page from Whiteman's *Digest of International Law.*

Since Whiteman's *Digest* does not cumulate or replace its predecessors, the earlier Department of State digests retain their research value, particularly for historical coverage:

J.L. Cadwalader, comp., *Digest of the Published Opinions of the Attorneys–General and of the Leading Decisions of the Federal Courts, with Reference to International Law, Treaties, and Kindred Subjects,* S.Exec.Doc. 46, 44th Cong., 2d Sess. (1877).

F. Wharton, ed., *A Digest of the International Law of the United States, Taken from Documents Issued by Presidents and Secre-*

11. For detailed descriptions of these digests, see "Guide to International Legal Research," 20 *Geo.Wash.J.Int'l L.* 1, 209–219 (1986); and A.W. Rovine, "U.S. International Law Digests: Some History and a New Approach," 67 *Am.J.Int'l L.* 314 (1973).

Illustration G

A sample page from Whiteman's *Digest of International Law*

Chapter XII

FISHERIES[1]

INTRODUCTION

§ 1

A considerable body of law has been and is evolving on the subject of fisheries and other marine resources of the sea. Impetus for the development of law with respect to the exploitation and conservation of these riches of the sea has arisen in part as a result of the development in the techniques both for exploring and exploiting these resources and for their conservation. This is not the place to assemble data on the developing techniques for exploration and exploitation of the living resources of the sea. It is, however, more and more appropriate for a work devoted to the subject of international law to treat of agreements evolved for the conservation of the living resources of the sea and their orderly exploration and exploitation with a view to assisting and encouraging the more intelligent use of the resources of the sea.

Developing law

By article 2 of the Convention on the High Seas, concluded at the First United Nations Conference on the Law of the Sea, held at Geneva in 1958, it was recognized that:

> "The high seas being open to all nations, no State may validly purport to subject any part of them to its sovereignty. Freedom of the high seas is exercised under the conditions laid down by these articles and by the other rules of international law. It comprises, *inter alia*, both for coastal and non-coastal States:
>
> "(1) Freedom of navigation;
> "(2) Freedom of fishing;
> "(3) Freedom to lay submarine cables and pipelines;
> "(4) Freedom to fly over the high seas.
>
> These freedoms, and others which are recognized by the general principles of international law, shall be exercised by all States with reasonable regard to the interests of other States in their exercise of the freedom of the high seas."

Freedom of fishing

[1] In this connection, see prior U.S. digests of international law, particularly: III Wharton, *International Law Digest* (2d ed., 1887), ch. XIII, pp. 38 ff.; I Moore, *International Law Digest* (1906), ch. V, pp. 767 ff.; I Hackworth, *Digest of International Law* (1940), ch. V, pp. 783 ff.

(932)

taries of State, and from Decisions of Federal Courts and Opinions of Attorneys–General, S.Misc.Doc. 162, 49th Cong., 1st Sess. (3 vols., 1886; 2d ed., 1887).

J.B. Moore, comp., *A Digest of International Law, as Embodied in Diplomatic Discussions, Treaties, and Other International Agreements, International Awards, the Decisions of Municipal*

Courts, and the Writings of Jurists . . ., H.R.Doc. 551, 16th Cong., 2d Sess. (8 vols., 1906; reprinted by AMS Press, 1970). Covers developments from 1776 to 1906, superseding Cadwalader and Wharton.

G.H. Hackworth, comp., *Digest of International Law,* (U.S.G.P.O., 8 vols., 1940–44; reprinted by Garland, 1973). Covers developments from 1906 to 1939.

2. RESTATEMENTS

The American Law Institute, as part of its project to restate American law in a number of fields, has issued two successive editions of its *Restatement of the Foreign Relations Law of the United States.* The *Restatement (Second)* was published in 1965, and the current *Restatement (Third),* 2 vols., in 1987. Only tentative drafts of a *first* Restatement were published.

Although the Restatements have no official status, they have been given considerable authority as reflecting U.S. practice, by American courts, scholars and international lawyers. The illustrations, comments, cross-references and tentative drafts leading up to the final versions all add to the research value of these publications.

For the American position on issues of private international law, the *Restatement (Second) of Conflict of Laws* (American Law Institute, 4 vols., 1971–80) provides similar coverage.

Procedures for locating judicial decisions and periodical articles citing particular provisions of these Restatements are described in Chapter 12.

3. PERIODICALS AND TREATISES

Almost all major law reviews publish articles from time to time on international law topics. In addition, the number of American periodicals devoted specifically to this field has vastly increased with the proliferation of topical law school journals. While the *American Journal of International Law* and *International Lawyer* remain the leading publications, over forty academic journals are now issued on one or another aspect of international law or trade. Almost all of these are indexed in the standard legal periodical indexes discussed in Chapter 11, including the *Current Law Index/Legal Resource Index,* the *Index to Legal Periodicals,* and the *Index to Foreign Legal Periodicals.*

Several dozen journals are also published in the related fields of foreign affairs and international politics. These journals, such as *Foreign Affairs* (1922–date, five times a year), *Foreign Policy* (1970–date, quarterly), *International Organization* (1947–date, quarterly), *World Affairs* (1837–date, quarterly), and *World Politics* (1948–date, quarterly), are accessible through the general and social science periodical indexes discussed in Chapter 14.

Numerous treatises and monographs on various aspects of international law provide convenient discussions and reflections of American practices and positions in this field. These include scholarly analyses, practitioner-oriented handbooks, and student texts. The procedures for finding treatises described in Chapter 12 provide guidance in identifying relevant treatises in specific areas.

4. FOREIGN RELATIONS DOCUMENTATION

In addition to the current documentary publications described above, several historical series (some on a continuing basis) are useful sources for research in U.S. international practice and foreign relations.

International Legal Materials (American Society of International Law, bimonthly, 1962–date) includes a variety of executive and legislative documents, judicial decisions, and drafts and final texts of many treaties. It continues a similar compilation which appeared as the *Supplement to the American Journal of International Law* (1907–55). Beginning in 1956, when the *Supplement* was discontinued, a few important documents appear in the "Official Documents" section of the *American Journal of International Law.*

Foreign Relations of the United States is a mammoth series of official documents, prepared since 1861 by the Historical Office of the Department of State, providing a comprehensive record of material relating to American foreign relations. There is a time lag of about twenty-five years between the dates of documents and their publication in this series.

The Department of State also publishes documentary compilations on a more current basis. These include: *A Decade of American Foreign Policy: Basic Documents, 1941–1949* (1950); *American Foreign Policy: Basic Documents, 1950–1955* (2 vols., 1957); *American Foreign Policy: Current Documents* (annual volumes covering 1956–67); and *American Foreign Policy: Basic Documents, 1968–1980* (3 vols., 1983).[12] The *Current Documents* series was resumed in 1981 with annual volumes and microfiche supplements. There is a delay of from two to five years from the document dates to the publication of these volumes. The monthly *Department of State Bulletin,* as noted above, is a useful current source for selected documents.

F. SUMMARY

As part of the governing body of federal law of the United States, international agreements can be a focus of research for any lawyer. One need not have an "international practice" to require a sound

12. Similar compilations, with both documentation and commentary, were commercially published under the title *American Foreign Relations: A Documentary Record,* (New York University Press, annual, 1971–78), which combined two series issued by the Council on Foreign Relations: *Documents on American Foreign Relations* (annual, 1938–70), and the narrative *The United States in World Affairs* (annual, 1931–70). *American Foreign Relations* is no longer being published.

understanding of the purposes and means of research into treaties, conventions, and related sources of international law.

On the other hand, this brief chapter on U.S. practice presents but a small portion of the documentation of the law of nations and of transnational activities. Anyone representing clients with interests in other countries will also require familiarity with other sources of international agreements and adjudications, as well as with resources for researching the domestic law of other nations. It may be possible to master American legal research in a few short years, but a lifetime of learning awaits the international legal scholar.

G. ADDITIONAL READING

T. Buergenthal & H.G. Maier, *Public International Law in a Nutshell* (West, 1985).

"Guide to International Legal Research," 20 *Geo.Wash.L.Rev.* 1 (1986).

M.W. Janis, *An Introduction to International Law* (Little, Brown, 1988).

Chapter 16

RESEARCH STRATEGIES[1]

A. INTRODUCTION

[R]esearch requires the poetic quality of the imagination that sees significance and relation where others are indifferent or find unrelatedness; the synthetic quality of fusing items theretofore in

1. This chapter was written by Daniel P. Dabney, Reference Department, School of Law (Boalt Hall), University of California, Berkeley.

isolation; above all the prophetic quality of piercing the future, by knowing what questions to put and what direction to give to inquiry.[2]

The preceding chapters in this book discuss in detail particular types of legal research sources—court reports, statutory codes, treatises, and so forth. They need to be discussed individually because each has its own virtues and peculiarities. But mastering any one research tool, or even all of them, is not enough to make one a competent researcher. It is equally important to learn *when* to use each, and how to put together a research strategy.

B. A FIVE-STEP APPROACH TO LEGAL RESEARCH

Legal research calls for judgment and creativity. It is very dangerous to adopt a formulaic approach, since no one search strategy works best for all questions. Perhaps the best advice this book can give on legal research is "be flexible."

But a beginning researcher needs some help getting started. Until you know the basic rules, it is not easy to determine when those rules should be broken. Here, then, are some general guidelines for use until you begin to develop your own research style and preferences.

1. ANALYZE THE FACTS AND FRAME THE QUESTION

Real research questions begin with clients, not with books. From the client, the lawyer learns some of the facts of the case and the ends to be achieved. Part of the lawyer's job is to find out what the law is and how it will affect the client's case. This is legal research.

In most cases, however, the sources of law are not organized by fact, nor even by the object to be achieved. They are collections of legal doctrines and theories, and the literature of the law reflects this. Before you can begin to do research, you need to extract from the facts of the case one or more propositions of legal doctrine.

Here is an illustration: Smith asks his lawyer, "Can Jones legally build a fence across the road leading to my farm?" Smith's lawyer cannot simply go to the law books, look under "fences", and find the applicable law. Smith's question must first be translated into a legal theory that either permits Smith to use the road or prohibits Jones from obstructing it. Smith's lawyer needs to know what legal theories are available, and what facts are necessary to support each one. After considering all of the facts in light of the available legal theories, Smith's lawyer might determine that Smith's question is best considered as a matter of "prescriptive easement." The research will probably focus on some element of the theory, such as: "Is open use of an

2. Frankfurter, "The Conditions for, and the Aims and Methods of, Legal Research," 15 *Iowa L.Rev.* 129, 134 (1930).

estate presumed to be adverse for the purpose of establishing a prescriptive easement?" This is not a question that Smith would have thought to ask, which is one of the reasons Smith needed a lawyer.

Turning statements of fact into propositions of legal theory is one of the most difficult things that lawyers do. Much of the curriculum in many law schools (especially in the first year) is directed toward developing this ability.

Framing the question is not just the first step in the research process—it is a continuous part of that process. You cannot really be sure that you have asked the right question until you have found the answer. In order to frame the question, you need to know something about the law. As you learn more about the law, it is only natural that your view of the question will change. Whenever something you find sheds new light on the work you have already done, you should be willing to return to an earlier step and refine your work. This is particularly true of this first step, framing the question. If something you read gives you a new perspective, stop for a moment and reframe the issue. Otherwise you may waste your time by researching the wrong question.

2. GET AN OVERVIEW OF THE SUBJECT AREA

For beginners, and for experienced researchers starting to work in a new area, the next step is to get an overview of the general area of law that includes the question. This can be viewed as an extension of framing the question—there are no hard and fast lines to be drawn between the steps. In this part of your search, you are not so much concerned with finding the answer to your specific question as with finding where the answer is likely to lie, and with learning enough to recognize the answer when you see it.

The knowledge needed in the overview step corresponds roughly to the content of a basic law school course in the subject area. A good way to get an overview is to read the books with which law students prepare for exams. Among the most popular of these are single-volume treatises called "hornbooks" and "Nutshells." These and similar texts are available from the West Publishing Company and other publishers. Not all publications aimed at law students are good sources for research overviews; study guides known as "outlines" are distinctly less helpful, and law school casebooks are usually of no help at all.

Many larger and more comprehensive treatises contain introductory sections summarizing the most important principles, which can be good sources for getting an overview. Legal encyclopedias can also serve this purpose.

The overview step is the only one of the five that can be dispensed with alltogether in some research projects. Attorneys with experience in a particular field already have the background to begin research in that area. But for the researcher who is a newcomer, either to legal research generally or to a specific field of law, it is an essential step.

This initial overview has three objects: learning what sorts of law you are looking for, learning the jargon of the area, and learning the "black letter" rules.

a. *Learn What to Look For*

There are many different kinds of legal authority, including decisions, constitutions, statutes, and regulations, both state and federal. It is a rare question that requires extensive research in all of these sources. The overview stage should answer several questions about the sort of law you are looking for: Is the issue governed by state law, federal law, or both? Are there any important statutes that control the area? Does the question raise constitutional issues? Is the area within the regulatory jurisdiction of any administrative agency?

Understanding what authorities are needed is essential for focused, productive research. For a copyright question, for example, it is essential to know that copyrights are governed in the United States by federal law, not by state law. You could spend a good deal of unproductive effort looking for copyright law in the statutes and cases of your state before coming to the realization that you needed to look somewhere else. Worse, you might find the vestiges of the state copyright law that existed before federal law preempted the field, and reach entirely erroneous conclusions about the law.

An overview of copyright law should tell you, for example, that the field is governed almost exclusively by federal statutes and the cases that interpret them. There is little relevant state law. In most situations, there are no significant administrative regulations. There are some important treaties that bear on international copyright practice. Armed with this information, you know where to look for more detailed law.

b. *Learn the Jargon*

Another important function of the overview stage of legal research is learning the language. Each area of the law has "terms of art" that serve as shorthand expressions for relatively complex ideas. To understand appellate practice, for example, you need to know what "certiorari" means, or you will not understand the cases you find. Some of the terms of art you need to learn are not so obvious. In appellate practice again, the phrase "law of the case" stands for a specific legal doctrine. An unprepared novice could easily read a decision that applies the doctrine of "law of the case" without realizing that the phrase is a term of art.

Another reason to become familiar with the language of an area is that its technical terms may be used as index headings in treatises and other sources. Unless you know the language, you may never find what you need in the indexes you consult.

c. *Learn the "Black Letter" Law*

In each area of the law there are broad generalizations that provide structure and reference. It is seldom enough for the researcher to discover these "black letter" principles, but they provide the context within which the rest of the law should be considered. They need to be learned as part of the overview stage in legal research.

It is, for example, a black letter rule of law that an employer is liable for torts committed by an employee while acting in the scope of his or her employment. This rule has innumerable interpretations, extensions, limitations, and exceptions, but none of these will make much sense unless read in the context of the general rule.

3. MAKE AN IN-DEPTH SEARCH FOR LEGAL AUTHORITY

By the time you reach this step you have framed the question and gotten enough background so that you will be able to recognize the relevant authorities when you find them. You are ready to begin searching in earnest.

a. *Case-Finding Tools*

Much of this chapter focuses on the problem of finding case law. This is not because case law is more important than other forms of authority, but because finding it is more difficult and varied. Case-finding tools work by gathering similar cases together. Cases can be gathered in three ways: (1) as references in narrative descriptions of the state of the law; (2) in digests and annotations; and (3) in the results of computer-assisted legal research.

(1) Narrative Descriptions

No matter how unusual or obscure a research issue, chances are that someone has written an in-depth analysis of the applicable law, citing many of the relevant authorities to illustrate or justify that analysis. Narrative descriptions take several forms, including treatises, encyclopedias, law review articles, and cases themselves.

The best narrative description is usually a treatise, written by an expert author familiar with all of the relevant authorities. The author selects the most pertinent authorities, puts them into logical order and perspective, comments on the soundness of their reasoning, notes common problems, identifies majority and minority rules, and projects trends. All these virtues rarely are found in a single treatise. Treatises vary considerably in depth, currency, authoritativeness, and general organizational approach.

Legal encyclopedias are simply broad-ranging treatises that attempt to cover the entire body of American law rather than some smaller subject area. It is usually possible to find a subject treatise that is deeper and more authoritative, and that cites more cases, than the corresponding section of an encyclopedia. Encyclopedias are useful, however, because they present a basic treatment in a standard format of most case law questions. Smaller libraries, which cannot afford to have treatises on every subject, often provide some coverage in any area through an encyclopedia.

Much of the best and most thoughtful narrative legal writing is published in law review articles. These are usually thoroughly researched and copiously footnoted. In contrast to most other narratives, which describe the state of the law without commenting on it, law reviews often delve deeply into issues of social policy and so are very helpful in determining the justice and fairness of legal doctrine.

Finally, each reported decision is itself a narrative description of the state of the law on the points in issue. Cases almost always contain citations to other cases.

(2) Digests and Annotations

Some finding tools gather cases without integrating them into narrative form. Digests and annotations sort cases into various categories and give a one-paragraph summary of each case. It is up to the researcher to mold the cases into a coherent view of the state of the law.

The leading digests are published by the West Publishing Company and use the West Key Number System. Each of the 100,000 topically arranged key numbers can be thought of as a pigeonhole in which a researcher can find summaries of a specific point of law.

Annotated reports function similarly, by summarizing decisions that discuss a key issue raised in the reported case. The various series of *ALR* (*American Law Reports,* published by the Lawyers Co-operative Publishing Company) provide somewhat more detailed abstracts than do most digests, and they incorporate some of the virtues of a treatise by introducing each annotation with a narrative summary of the point of law covered.

Other finding tools contain the same sort of information, but gather the cases together differently. Annotated codes (in addition to giving the texts of statutes) collect cases that interpret each code section. If a section has been interpreted in many cases, the case annotations are subdivided topically. Many looseleaf services include sections that are essentially annotated codes or specialty digests, as well as narrative sections with the characteristics of treatises.

The narrative method has several advantages over the digest/annotation method. Narratives are easier to understand, because they show where each cited cases fits in an overall description of the state of the law. Narratives can be critical as well as descriptive. They can be more closely tailored to the cases they discuss because they are not based on pre-established classifications. Unlike digests or annotations, narratives written by respected authors can themselves be considered persuasive legal authority.

But narratives also have disadvantages. Narratives are selective in the authority they cite and discuss. Many older treatises undertook to include at least a note to every reported case relevant to the discussion, but the body of case law has grown too large for this approach to work in any but the most narrow areas of the law. Narratives tend to cite leading cases, but not necessarily every case that might be relevant to a particular search.

Digests and annotations have the advantage that they can be more comprehensive than narratives. For example, West digests contain at least one abstract for literally every substantive reported case, and the authors of *ALR* annotations go to great lengths to find and summarize all relevant cases.

(3) *Computer–Assisted Legal Research*

A third, very different approach to finding cases is by the use of computer-assisted legal research systems, the most common of which are LEXIS and WESTLAW.

Some computer-assisted research functions are simply automated versions of the manual tools described above. For example, both LEXIS and WESTLAW offer versions of Shepard's citators that perform the same functions as the paper Shepard's but do so faster and more conveniently. WESTLAW can search by key number, allowing the user to perform certain kinds of digest searches more easily than they can be done in the printed volumes.

The primary use of computer-assisted legal research systems, however, is for keyword searching, a technique that has no true equivalent in paper publishing. Keyword searching is different from consulting a digest or annotation in one essential way: the searcher supplies his or her own criteria instead of relying on preexisting annotation topics or digest locations established by an editor. The searcher creates, in effect, a new digest entry for each search question. This new digest entry can be limited by court or jurisdiction, by date, by judge, or in any number of other ways.

The rules the computer uses to decide which cases are retrieved are simple and objective. They work best when the searcher's needs are also objective. For example, a case either was decided in 1989 or it wasn't, and the computer can tell the difference. Computers cannot evaluate cases for retrieval on the basis of more subjective criteria, such as what they are "about."

Computer-assisted legal research assembles lists of cases not by subject, as a human indexer would, but rather by what words or combinations of words they contain. To do effective subject searching by computer, one must be able to anticipate the words that are likely to occur in relevant documents.

Computer-assisted research has three main strengths. First, it can save time. Using LEXIS or WESTLAW is ordinarily much quicker than similar research that relies on printed publications. Second, it is usually very current. It is easier to update an online database than a paper book. Third, it is flexible. The ability to create customized lists of cases is particularly valuable when the manual research tools are not very helpful. For example, because most law books are indexed by legal theory rather than by fact pattern, researchers looking for particular facts can benefit greatly by defining their own search criteria.

Computer-assisted research also has weaknesses. A computer cannot really read and understand cases, so it is not as effective as a human indexer at selecting cases by subject. When a manual tool has gathered cases according to criteria that fit your needs, it usually outperforms a similar keyword search both in finding relevant cases and in excluding the irrelevant. Another major disadvantage is that computer-assisted research is very expensive, although the research time saved can often justify the cost.

Because computer searching is fast, easy and mysterious, it is tempting to place undue reliance on its results. Remember, however, that what comes out is only as reliable as what goes in. If your computer search finds no cases, it doesn't mean that there are none to be found. It may mean that you wrote a poor search, misunderstood the system's rules of syntax, or simply misspelled a word. A novice researcher should *always* verify computer-assisted research results with other approaches.

b. General Search Techniques

How you approach research tools depends on what you know about the search question. Sometimes a topical approach is the best or only method available. When you are aware of a relevant case or statute, it is often better to base research on the authority already known.

(1) Working With a Subject

There are subject indexes for all of the tools discussed in this section, including treatises, encyclopedias, law reviews, annotated codes, digests, and annotations. The key to using any subject index is finding the right index term, or "subject heading", for the material you seek.

Most indexes are based on a controlled vocabulary of index terms. For example, an index might list items concerning children under "children", "juveniles," or "minors", but it will not list some items under each word. Once you find the way by which a particular index refers to children, you will find all of the listings in one place.

Indexes to legal materials are different from the indexes with which most non-lawyers are familiar. In the general literature, index terms tend to be fairly specific, like "Gun control." In a legal index, the same idea is likely to be represented by a stack of index terms headed by a relatively general concept, like "Weapons—Handguns—Registration requirements". Legal indexes are no more difficult to use in the long run, but they can be very frustrating for beginning researchers. When approaching a new research tool for the first time, it often pays to browse through the index to see how general the first-level indexing terms are.

Writing subject searches for the computer is, in a way, the opposite of searching in a conventional subject index. In using an index, you take an idea that could be expressed in a number of ways and try to find the one canonical way it is expressed in the index's controlled vocabulary. In computer searching, you try to imagine all of the different ways an idea could be expressed in the uncontrolled vocabulary of cases. Computer-assisted subject searching works best when there is a relatively close relationship between the idea being researched and a fairly distinctive set of words.

(2) *Working From a Known Case*

When you already know a relevant case or two, you can often avoid subject indexes entirely. The research tools discussed above gather similar cases, so you can find additional cases simply by finding references to a case that you already know is relevant and scanning nearby entries. The mechanics of the case method differ from tool to tool. Here are some of the more common techniques:

West Digest System. Each case reported in West's National Reporter System is preceded by the headnotes that also appear in the various West digests. When you have one relevant case, you can often find similar cases easily. Look at the headnotes that precede the case and choose the ones that correspond to the part of the opinion that makes it relevant. Look in a West digest under the topics and key numbers assigned to those headnotes.

All West digests use the same numbering system, so when you are using the case method you are not restricted to digests that include the known case. For example, if you start with a New Mexico case, you are not restricted to cases that appear in the New Mexico or Pacific digests—you can find federal cases under the same topic and key number in federal digests, and cases from another state in the digests for that state or its region.

If the cases you find this way are not on point, check the topic analysis that appears at the beginning of the topic in the digest. Sometimes the aspect of the headnote that determines its location in the digest is not the aspect that interests you. If this happens, digest research may not be helpful.

Treatises. Most treatises have a table of cases. If your known case is discussed in a treatise, you can find the part of the text that discusses other cases involving similar issues. This technique works best when the known case is a leading case and therefore more likely to be discussed in a treatise.

Shepard's Citations. Citators allow you to tap into millions of hours of expert research that is reflected in the opinions of reported cases. Each case is a miniature treatise on the law under which it is decided. While some cases are much more helpful research tools than others, the body of reported cases is collectively the most exhaustive research tool available.

Each citation in a reported decision links the citing case backwards in time to the cited case, and the cited case forwards in time to the citing case. Tracing the backwards links is easy. The citing case provides a full citation to earlier decisions, and often tells you enough about them so that you can decide which should be read.

Tracing the forward links in a citation chain is more difficult and tedious for two reasons: (1) you have to consult a separate source, the citator, to get the reference, and (2) the citator does not tell very much about the relationship between the two cases. But tracing the forward links is an essential task, because recent cases are often more important than older ones.

The online versions of *Shepard's Citations* on LEXIS and WESTLAW make citation research much easier. The mechanics of Shepardizing by computer are much simpler than those of Shepardizing in paper volumes and pamphlets. On LEXIS or WESTLAW, one can move from the list of citing cases to the texts of those cases themselves, making it much easier to see which citing cases are relevant and worth reading.

Computer-assisted legal research. The names and citations of cases can be searched as keywords in computer-assisted legal research databases. This sort of search uses the computer like a citator to find later cases that mention a known case. The chief advantage of this sort of search is that it can find very recent decisions that have not yet been listed in Shepard's citators.

(3) Working From a Known Statute

An annotated code is almost always the best place to begin research on a statutory question. The code provides the text of the statute, and the annotations provide the first and best guide to related statutes, regulations, and case interpretations.

Some areas of the law are so complicated that a beginner cannot make sense of the statutory text without help. A good example is the Internal Revenue Code. In these areas, the research tool of choice is usually a specialty treatise or looseleaf service devoted to the interpretation of the statute. Most tax practitioners, for example, rely heavily on either CCH's *Standard Federal Tax Reports* or Prentice Hall's *Federal Taxes.* Each of these sets is, in effect, a very thoroughly annotated Internal Revenue Code.

Even when the text of a statute is relatively straightforward, its interpretation and implementation by the courts are frequently the focus of research. In an annotated code, cases that interpret or apply statutes are represented by digest paragraphs following each section. Other cases can also be found by Shepardizing statutes or by using their citations in a computer search, but annotated codes are usually more helpful because they provide summaries of citing cases and because they omit cases that merely mention the statute. Very recent cases can be found by consulting the "Table of Statutes Construed" in the front of recent National Reporter System volumes and advance sheets.

Administrative agencies have the power to make regulations only if it is granted to them by statute, so all regulations have a related statutory authority. Citations to regulations, as well as cases interpreting those regulations, can often be found in the annotations to the authorizing statute. The *Code of Federal Regulations* and many state administrative codes have tables of statutory authority listing regulations by code section.

c. *Putting It All Together: A Strategy for Searching*

Each of the three major case-finding tools has strengths and weaknesses. Narratives are easy to use, but not comprehensive. Digests and annotations are thorough, but not very easy to use. Computer-assisted legal research is fast and flexible, but not always accurate on subject searches.

The best strategy is almost always to use a combination of different search tools and techniques. Approaches will vary from question to question, but this section offers some general guidelines and suggestions.

Begin case-finding research with tools that are fast and easy to use. The first priority in a case-finding problem should be to find a few relevant cases fast. Do not worry too much at this stage about being comprehensive. Having a few cases in hand allows you to use the case approach rather than the subject approach later on.

A treatise is usually the best place to begin. It may already have been useful for earlier research steps of question framing and overview. The narrative explanation will help refine a search question and discuss a few relevant cases with which to start. If you are working in a library that does not have a suitable treatise in the subject area of your question, try using an encyclopedia as a substitute.

Also consider using computer-assisted research early in your search. The computer will seldom turn up everything you can find with manual research, but for many questions you will find a few "seed" cases very easily.

Another source to consider early in your search is the *Index to Annotations* (which covers annotations in *ALR* and *Lawyers' Edition*). A relevant annotation is particularly helpful, because it provides both a narrative introduction and a very thorough digest-like treatment.

Use the links between research tools. Most research tools refer to other tools, particularly those published by the same company. Following these references can lead quickly from one kind of treatment to another. For example, a section of *Corpus Juris Secundum* may refer to relevant West key numbers, and an *American Jurisprudence 2d* footnote may cite a valuable *ALR* annotation.

Use the most difficult and comprehensive tools last. Some research tools are prized for thoroughness rather than ease of use. Some of these should usually be included in your search, but you should generally use them later rather than sooner.

Digests are extremely comprehensive, but they can be difficult to understand early in the research process because they neither mold the cases into a coherent view of the law nor identify leading cases. Once you know the outline of the law and the leading cases, you will use the digest more quickly and efficiently.

The case-finding technique to use last is citation research. It is often the most comprehensive and the most tedious search technique. It belongs at the end of the case-finding stage of research because it naturally includes the two steps yet to be discussed, reading the cases and bringing them up to date.

Use several case-finding techniques. No case finder is perfect. Some research questions lend themselves more to one approach than another, but it is usually wise to use a variety of tools. The shortcomings of one may be overcome by the strengths of another. Knowing how many different tools to use is essentially the same as knowing when to stop doing research, which is discussed later in this chapter.

4. READ AND EVALUATE THE PRIMARY AUTHORITIES

The finding tools you use for your in-depth search for legal authorities are likely to tell you a good deal about the authorities themselves. A digest, for example, contains not only the citation to a decision which appears relevant, but a one-paragraph summary of the particular point of law. Other finding tools provide similar information. But you must not rely on finding tools for accurate statements of the law. The object of legal research is to find legal authorities, not digest paragraphs.

There are two reasons that make it necessary to go to the authorities themselves: (1) the digest paragraph or discussion of an authority does not fully represent its content (or, all too often, is simply wrong), and (2) the authorities themselves can be used as finding tools to locate other authorities.

You must also read the authorities to try to reconcile the conflicts among them. Two cases that have nearly identical digest paragraphs could well have very different facts and holdings. A comparison of two similar cases can show the state of the law much more clearly than either case alone.

5. BRING THE LAW UP TO DATE

The law is constantly changing. When using any research tool, you should ask yourself two questions:

How current is the information I'm getting?

How can it be brought more up to date?

Bringing your research up to date is both a continuous part of the process and a distinct final step. You should try to update each source as you use it. For example, when using an annotated code or a treatise, you naturally check the pocket part at the same time you use the bound volume.

For many sources, an array of available update services varies in currency, ease of use, and cost. Consider, for example, the problem of bringing a federal statute up to date. Both of the commercially-published sets, *USCA* and *USCS,* print the United States Code in bound volumes. Each updates the volumes annually with pocket parts, provides quarterly pamphlets that update the pocket parts, and has a monthly service that prints the latest statutes as public laws before they have been codified. It is possible to bring federal statutes even more up to date, sometimes at considerable expense. In some subject areas, there are looseleaf services that provide copies of new federal statutes within days of enactment. Document delivery services can provide copies of new statutes within hours. Other services track pending legislation, keeping their subscribers up to date on changes in the law before they have even taken place.

How current you need to be for any particular research question depends on several factors. Some subjects in the law are changing faster than others. For example, the law of biotechnology is changing much faster than the law of estates in land. Questions in more rapidly changing areas may merit more scrupulous updating.

Similarly, some sources of the law change faster than others. The United States Constitution changes with glacial slowness—anyone who reads a newspaper ought to be aware of amendments to the Constitution long before they are ratified. In contrast, federal regulations change so quickly that the entire *Code of Federal Regulations* is revised annually, and new regulations are printed daily in the *Federal Register.*

As with any other part of the research process, updating calls for judgment on the part of the researcher. The update process itself is relatively mechanical, so there is some room for fixed rules. Here are some suggested *minimum* standards for updating legal authority:

Constitutions. Do not worry about updating the United States Constitution. Most state constitutions are less stable; update them the same way you do state statutes.

Statutes. Check the most recent annual supplement and any interim pamphlets, scan the annotations, and Shepardize.

Regulations. For federal regulations, consult the most recent *LSA: List of CFR Sections Affected* pamphlet and the *Federal Register.* Updating state regulations is different in every state—follow local practice.

Decisions. Shepardize the decision and look at every case from the same jurisdiction that has any of the following marginal notes:

a	(affirmed)	m	(modified)
c	(criticized)	o	(overruled)
d	(distinguished)	q	(questioned)
D	(dismissed)	r	(reversed)
h	(harmonized)	S	(superseded)
L	(limited)	v	(vacated)

Bear in mind that these are minimum guidelines for updating an authority. For each source it is possible to be more thorough, which is often wise and sometimes essential.

One of the best ways to guard against missing changes in the law is to use *current awareness* services. Attorneys who specialize in a particular field usually try to learn of new developments before the information is needed for any particular client or matter. Law firms with sophisticated specialty practices subscribe to current awareness newsletters that focus on narrowly defined areas of the law. A wide range of such services is available, but they are usually very expensive.

General practitioners often try to stay current on significant developments in a wide range of legal topics. Several legal magazines and newspapers have current awareness summaries that facilitate this. Some lawyers make it a practice to scan every new opinion from the United States Supreme Court and from the highest court in their state.

C. WHEN TO STOP THE SEARCH

A last, essential step in learning how to do research is knowing when to stop. No one rule covers all situations, but some stopping rules make more sense than others. This section considers some of the possible stopping rules that might be adopted.

1. UPON GETTING THE ANSWER

One requirement for ending research is an understanding of what the state of the law is. If you are still uncertain, you are probably not finished. Getting "the answer" to a particular question is a different matter. While some situations are clearly governed by binding precedent or clearly worded statutes, problems that end up in court or as the subject of legal research are usually subject to conflicting interpretations. A single precise answer is not possible. Research is usually not completed, however, until you arrive at *some* answer.

Finding an answer often requires evaluation of several authorities to reconcile differences. It is rarely satisfied by finding just one relevant authority. Legal authorities often conflict, so the existence of an authority that appears to control the question at hand does not preclude the existence of a contrary authority of equal or greater weight. You need to find an answer that seems adequate *and* to conduct enough additional research to be confident that there is no contrary authority.

For some research questions there is no answer, because there are no authorities to be found. Determining that nothing is available has value, because you are in a much better position knowing that there is no authority than being unsure what authority there is. You learn this not by finding the answer, but by making an appropriate research effort and finding no answer. What constitutes an appropriate research effort has to be determined by some other stopping rule.

Despite these uncertainties, with experience you will develop a sense of what constitutes completed research on a question. This is helpful, but also a little dangerous. A novice researcher can often find pertinent authority that the more experienced researcher misses, simply because the experienced researcher did not expect it to exist.

2. AFTER FINDING ALL RELEVANT AUTHORITIES

Finding every relevant authority is an admirable research goal. As with perfection in any other area of human endeavor, however, it is entirely unattainable. The scope of relevance must be determined anew for each research question, but authorities are indexed and classified without this specific focus. For example, two decisions may be assigned very different key numbers by digest editors but both be very relevant to a particular question. Only by reading all published decisions with a particular question in mind would a researcher be able to determine their relevance. Computer-assisted research helps by permitting customized searches, but it will not retrieve cases expressing similar concepts in different terms.

Yet the myth persists that in legal research it is not only possible, but necessary, to find everything there is to find. Lawyers, law professors, and even the authors of legal research texts sometimes hold novices to this impossible standard. Their purpose, usually, is to communicate the fact that legal research requires a great deal of effort and concentration. Do not, however, take the myth of comprehensive research so literally that you make it your stopping rule, since you will never be sure that you have found everything.

3. AFTER LOOKING EVERYWHERE

Once you have thoroughly examined every available resource, you should obviously stop doing research. But in law it is unlikely that you will reach this point. A well-stocked law library furnishes the tools for dozens of different approaches to research questions. It could take weeks to use them all. Most research is complete long before the available resources are exhausted.

While it is not literally possible to look *everywhere*, there are places that must be checked before research is complete. A modified version of this rule is: *Do not stop until you have looked in all the really important places.* Here is a short list of essentials:

(a) Always look at the annotated code—state, federal, or both—and always scan the annotations to the statutes you find;

(b) Always Shepardize any case, statute, or regulation you use; and

(c) Always look at the pocket part (or other supplement) to any book you use that has one.

An experienced researcher may fudge occasionally even on these three. If you are sure, for example, that a question is not statutory, you can skip the annotated code. Most of the time, however, you will need to do all of these and more.

As a novice researcher, if you are not sure that you have looked everywhere you should, *ask.* Ask your boss, or your professor, or a law librarian. They may suggest some resources you have neglected or others you did not even know existed. This is particularly important if you are not finding anything.

4. WHEN THE RESEARCH COST EXCEEDS ITS EXPECTED BENEFIT

Asked how they know when to stop doing research, practicing attorneys would probably say that they stop when they run out of time. Successful lawyers become experts at allocating their time among many necessary tasks, spending just enough time on each. If they do not allocate more time for research, it is because they have decided that the research does not merit more time.

Most lawyers rarely have the luxury of pursuing research questions for intellectual satisfaction. They cannot spend $2,000 doing research for a case worth $1,000, no matter how many or how difficult the research questions. They must stop doing research when the cost of continuing is greater than the return.

Law students must be able to budget their time, but most need not be concerned about other costs such as computer-assisted research charges. Because economic constraints will usually be very important after graduation, however, it is best to learn early the costs and benefits of legal research.

The experienced researcher often has a feel for how valuable it would be to continue searching for new authority. A novice should probably err on the side of doing too much research rather than too little. Extra time spent looking for authority may not turn out to be worthwhile with respect to the immediate research question, but it will provide more experience in the research process and make future legal research more cost-effective.

5. UPON ACHIEVING CLOSURE

"Closure" in a search for legal authority is finding the same authorities over and over. It distinguishes research that is relatively complete from research that is simply ineffective. Finding a relevant case that you have already found elsewhere tells you that you are looking in the right places, and that if there were other relevant cases you should have found them. Not finding relevant cases you already know about may suggest that you are looking in the wrong place.

But you should be wary of "false closure," which can result from using research tools that are closely related to each other. If, for example, West Publishing Company editors do not write a headnote for an important point in a case, that point will not appear in any of West's key number digests. It is also unlikely that it will appear in any of the other West case-finders, because they are based on the same indexing effort that creates the digests. This propagation of error is particularly likely within the offerings of a single publisher, but omissions may also spread to other works which based their analysis of the case on West's headnotes.

Thus, before you stop your search because you have achieved closure, you should give some thought to whether the research tools you have used are independent of each other. While it can be useful to use the links among related publications in, for example, Lawyers Co-op's "Total Client–Service Library," you should be aware that to some extent you are simply getting the same information in different forms. You can be more confident that you have reached true closure if you have used publications from different sources.

The most independent research tool is computer-assisted research. As discussed above, computers are not particularly good at finding cases by subject, but the errors they make are not related to indexing errors made by editors. Thus, even though computer-assisted research will generally not provide as many cases as careful research using other case-finding tools, it routinely produces some that cannot be found any other way.

Tools that appear immediately after a decision is announced are also relatively independent of each other. An editor handling a new case is not influenced by the perspective of some other editor, and so cannot repeat an error. For this reason, West's National Reporter System and some looseleaf case reporting services are quite independent and may treat the same decision in very different ways. On the other hand, many treatise authors rely on West advance sheets to update their publications and therefore tend to be heavily influenced by West's treatment of the case.

Of all the stopping rules, closure seems the most practical and the most satisfactory. Achieving closure does not guarantee that you have found all there is to find, but nothing does. On any large case-finding question, take it for granted that you will never find everything.

D. SUMMARY

Legal research is interesting and rewarding because it is so varied. Each new problem is a challenge to the knowledge and imagination of the researcher. There is no one right way to do research—each person needs to develop a personal style based on his or her own preferences. Those who master a wide variety of research tools can develop a richer and more effective style.

As you search for the law, remember that the question of what the law is cannot be removed from the larger question of what the law should be. Each active citizen tries to wrest from the institutions of government formulations of the law that will help to realize his or her own aspirations for society. These aspirations may be based on different values or visions, and may even be venal and self-serving. The resulting law may not reflect your own concept of justice, but it is from justice that the law takes its structure. Search for the law with passion and conscience, and you will find this structure.

Remember also that in arguing the law you should not rely exclusively on legal authority. It is always permissible and almost always wise to tell the court how the law ought to be, and why the world will be a better place if your view is adopted. If you put into research your sense of the justice of your cause, both your research and the use you make of it will be improved.

Appendix A

STATE LEGAL RESEARCH GUIDES AND BIBLIOGRAPHIES

While state legal research generally follows the patterns discussed in this book, the legal system and bibliographic resources of a particular state may cause specialized problems or may offer shortcuts not available elsewhere. A general treatise such as this cannot fully treat the many special characteristics of legal research in each state. There are, however, an increasing number of guides and manuals available for particular states. Some of these are major, detailed treatments, while many are brief pamphlets prepared for American Association of Law Libraries (AALL) meetings. In addition to the following separately published works, articles in bar journals and law reviews sometimes provide valuable information on research strategies in particular jurisdictions.

Alaska

A. Ruzicka, *Alaska Legal and Law–Related Publications: A Guide for Law Librarians* (AALL, 1984).

Arizona

R. Teenstra, *Survey of Arizona State Legal and Law–Related Documents* (AALL, 1984).

Arkansas

L. Foster, *Arkansas Legal Bibliography: Documents and Selected Commercial Titles* (AALL, 1988).

California

M. Fink, *Research in California Law,* 2d ed. (Dennis, 1964).

D.F. Henke, *California Law Guide,* 2d ed. (Parker & Son, 1976, and 1985 supplement).

K. Ranharter, *The State of California: An Introduction to Its Government Publications and Related Information* (AALL, 1979).

N.J. Young, ed., *Locating the Law: A Handbook for Non–Law Librarians* (Southern California Association of Law Libraries, 1984).

Colorado G. Alexander et al., *Colorado Legal Resources: An Annotated Bibliography* (AALL, 1987).

Connecticut S.R. Bysiewicz, *Sources of Connecticut Law* (Butterworth, 1987).

D.R. Voisinet et al., *Connecticut State Legal Documents: A Selective Bibliography* (AALL, 1985).

District of Columbia C.P. Ahearn et al., *Selected Information Sources for the District of Columbia,* 2d ed. (AALL, 1986).

Florida G.G. Reinertsen & R.L. Brown, *Guide to Florida Legal Research,* 2d ed. (Florida Bar, Continuing Legal Education, 1986).

H.L. French, *Research in Florida Law,* 2d ed. (Oceana, 1965).

C.A. Roehrenbeck, *Florida Legislative Histories: A Practical Guide to Their Preparation and Use* (D & S Publishers, 1986).

Georgia L.F. Chanin, *Reference Guide to Georgia Legal History and Legal Research* (Michie, 1980).

Hawaii R.F. Kahle, *How to Research Constitutional, Legislative and Statutory History in Hawaii* (Hawaii Legislative Reference Bureau, 1986).

Illinois B.J. Davies & F.J. Rooney, *Research in Illinois Law* (Oceana, 1954).

R.F. Jacobs et al., *Illinois Legal Research Sourcebook* (Illinois Institute for Continuing Legal Education, 1977).

C.R. Nyberg et al., *Illinois State Documents: A Selective Annotated Bibliography for Law Librarians* (AALL, 1986).

Indiana L.K. Fariss & K.A. Buckley, *An Introduction to Indiana State Publications for the Law Librarian* (AALL, 1982).

Kansas F. Snyder, *A Guide to Kansas Legal Research* (Kansas Bar Association, 1986).

M.E. Wisnecki, *Kansas State Documents for Law Libraries: Publications Related to Law and State Government* (AALL, 1984).

Kentucky W. Gilmer, Jr., *Guide to Kentucky Legal Research 2d: A State Bibliography* (State Law Library, 1985).

Louisiana W.S. Chiang, *Louisiana Legal Research* (Butterworth, 1985).

C. Corneil & M. Hebert, *Louisiana Legal Documents and Related Publications: A Selected Annotated Bibliography* (AALL, 1984).

K. Wallach, *Louisiana Legal Research Manual* (Louisiana State University Law School, Institute of Continuing Legal Education, 1972).

Maine

W.W. Wells, Jr., *Maine Legal Research Guide* (Tower Publishing, 1989).

Maryland

L.C. Davis, *An Introduction to Maryland State Publications for the Law Librarian* (AALL, 1981).

M.S. Miller, *Ghost Hunting: Finding Legislative Intent in Maryland* (Maryland State Law Library, 1984).

Massachusetts

M. Botsford et al., *Handbook of Legal Research in Massachusetts,* rev. ed. (Massachusetts Continuing Legal Education, 1988).

Guide to Legislative and Government Research (State Library of Massachusetts, 1977).

L. McAuliffe & S.Z. Steinway, *Massachusetts* (AALL, 1985).

Michigan

R.L. Beer, *An Annotated Guide to the Legal Literature of Michigan* (Fitzsimmons Sales, 1973).

S.D. Yoak & M.A. Heinen, *Michigan Legal Documents: An Annotated Bibliography* (AALL, 1982).

Minnesota

M.L. Baum & M.A. Nelson, *Guide to Minnesota State Documents and Selected Law-Related Materials* (AALL, 1986).

A.M. Soderberg & B.L. Golden, *Minnesota Legal Research Guide* (Hein, 1985).

Mississippi

B. Cole, *Mississippi Legal Documents and Related Publications: A Selected Annotated Bibliography* (AALL, 1987).

Missouri

P. Aldrich et al., *A Law Librarian's Introduction to Missouri State Publications* (AALL, 1980).

Nebraska

M.J. Fontent et al., *Nebraska State Documents Bibliography* (AALL, 1988).

P.F. Hill, *Nebraska Legal Research and Reference Manual* (Mason, 1983).

Nevada

K. Henderson, *Nevada State Documents Bibliography, Part I: Legal Publications and Related Material* (AALL, 1984).

New Jersey

C. Allen, *A Guide to New Jersey Legal Bibliography and Legal History* (Rothman, 1984).

P. Axel–Lute, *New Jersey Legal Research Handbook* (New Jersey Institute for Continuing Legal Education, 1985).

C.M. Senezak, *New Jersey State Publications: A Guide for Law Librarians* (AALL, 1984).

New Mexico

A.W. Poldervaart, *Manual for Effective New Mexico Legal Research* (University of New Mexico Press, 1955).

P.D. Wagner, *Guide to New Mexico State Publications* (AALL, 1983).

D. Warden & H.S. Carter, *Basic List of State Legal Documents for the State of New Mexico* (University of New Mexico, School of Law Library, 1978).

New York

R.A. Carter, *Legislative Intent in New York State: Materials, Cases and Annotated Bibliography* (New York State Library, 1981).

R.A. Carter, *New York State Constitution: Sources of Legislative Intent* (Rothman, 1988).

S.L. Dow & K.L. Spencer, *New York Legal Documents: A Selective Annotated Bibliography* (AALL, 1985).

E.M. Gibson, *New York Legal Research Guide* (Hein, 1988).

North Carolina

I.I. Kavass & B.A. Christensen, *Guide to North Carolina Legal Research* (Hein, 1973).

T.M. Steele & D. Tarleton, *Survey of North Carolina State Legal and Law–Related Documents* (AALL, 1988).

North Dakota

For All Intents and Purposes: Essentials in Researching Legislative Histories (North Dakota Legislative Council, 1981).

Ohio

C.A. Corcos, *Ohio State Legal Documents and Related Publications: A Selected, Annotated Bibliography* (AALL, 1986).

D.M. Gold, *A Guide to Legislative History in Ohio* (Ohio Legislative Service Commission, 1985).

Ohio Legal Resources—An Annotated Bibliography and Guide, 2d ed. (Ohio Regional Association of Law Libraries and Ohio Library Association, 1984).

S. Schaefgen & M.K. Putnam, *Ohio Legal Research: Effective Approaches and Techniques* (Professional Education Systems, 1988).

Oklahoma C.A. Corcos, *Oklahoma Legal and Law–Related Documents and Publications: A Selected Bibliography* (AALL, 1983).

Oregon L.A. Buhman et al., *Bibliography of Law Related Oregon Documents* (AALL, 1984).

Pennsylvania J. Fishman, *An Introduction to Pennsylvania State Publications for the Law Librarian* (AALL, 1985).

C.C. Moreland & E.C. Surrency, *Research in Pennsylvania Law,* 2d ed. (Oceana, 1965).

South Carolina R.K. Mills & J.S. Schultz, *South Carolina Legal Research Handbook* (Hein, 1976).

South Dakota D.A. Jorgensen, *South Dakota Legal Documents: A Selective Bibliography* (AALL, 1988).

D.A. Jorgensen, *South Dakota Legal Research Guide* (Hein, 1988).

Tennessee L.L. Laska, *Tennessee Legal Research Handbook* (Hein, 1977).

D.C. Picquet & R.A. Best, *Law and Government Publications of the State of Tennessee* (AALL, 1988).

Texas M. Allison & K. Schlueter, *Texas State Documents for Law Libraries* (AALL, 1983).

K.T. Gruben & J.E. Hambleton, eds., *A Reference Guide to Texas Law and Legal History: Sources and Documentation,* 2d ed. (Butterworth, 1987).

P. Permenter & S.F. Ratliff, *Guide to Texas Legislative History* (Legislative Reference Library, 1986).

Virginia J.D. Eure, ed., *A Guide to Legal Research in Virginia* (Virginia Law Foundation, 1989).

J. Lichtman & J. Stinson, *A Law Librarian's Introduction to Virginia State Publications* (AALL, 1988).

Washington S.F. Burson, *Washington State Law–Related Publications: A Selective Bibliography with Commentary* (AALL, 1984).

Wisconsin R.A. Danner, *Legal Research in Wisconsin* (University of Wisconsin, Extension Law Department, 1980).

W. Knudson, *Wisconsin Legal Research Guide* (University of Wisconsin, Extension Law Department, 1972).

J. Oberla, *An Introduction to Wisconsin State Documents and Law Related Materials* (AALL, 1987).

Wyoming N.S. Greene, *Wyoming State Legal Documents: An Annotated Bibliography* (AALL, 1985).

Appendix B

STATE PRIMARY LEGAL SOURCES[1]

Model:

Court reports: (years generally indicate periods of coverage, not imprint dates)

1. Official state reports first (whether or not discontinued)
2. Regional reporter, and West reprint (state reporter with regional reporter pagination) if any
3. Online databases (in LEXIS, file for specific court)

* indicates current official status

Session laws: (including advance session law services, if any)

Statutory compilation(s): (with publishers of commercial annotated codes)

Administrative code:

Administrative register: (with frequency of publication)

Court rules: (excluding statutory compilations, if other sources available)

ALABAMA

- **Court reports:**

Supreme Court

	Alabama Reports	1840–1976	Ceased with vol. 295
*	Southern Reporter	1886–date	Official since 1976
*	Alabama Reporter (West reprint)	1976–date	
	ALA/ALA (LEXIS)	1965–date	
	AL–CS (WESTLAW)	1945–date	

Court of Civil Appeals and Court of Criminal Appeals (Court of Appeals before 1969)

1. This is an abridged version of Appendix B in *How to Find the Law,* 9th ed. Its coverage of court reports is limited to courts of last resort and intermediate appellate courts, and excludes nominative and miscellaneous reports.

	Alabama Appellate Court Reports	1910–1976	Ceased with vol. 57
*	Southern Reporter	1911–date	Official since 1976
*	Alabama Reporter (West reprint)	1976–date	
	ALA/CIVAPP (LEXIS)	1969–date	
	ALA/CRMAPP (LEXIS)	1969–date	
	ALA/APP (LEXIS)	1965–1969	
	AL–CS (WESTLAW)	1944–date	

- **Session laws:**
  Acts of Alabama
- **Statutory compilations:**
  Code of Alabama 1975 (Michie)
  ALA/CODE or ALCODE (LEXIS)
  AL–ST or AL–ST–ANN (WESTLAW)
- **Administrative code:**
  Alabama Administrative Code
- **Administrative register:**
  Alabama Administrative Monthly
- **Court rules:**
  Alabama Practice: Rules of Civil Procedure Annotated (West)
  Alabama Rules of Court (West)

ALASKA

- **Court reports:**

Supreme Court

*	Pacific Reporter	1960–date
*	Alaska Reporter (West reprint)	1960–date
	ALAS/ALAS (LEXIS)	1965–date
	AK–CS (WESTLAW)	1960–date

Court of Appeals

*	Pacific Reporter	1980–date
*	Alaska Reporter (West reprint)	1980–date
	ALAS/APP (LEXIS)	1980–date
	AK–CS (WESTLAW)	1980–date

- **Session laws:**
  Alaska Session Laws
  Alaska Advance Legislative Service (Michie)
- **Statutory compilations:**
  Alaska Statutes (Michie)
  ALAS/CODE or AKCODE (LEXIS)
  AK–ST or AK–ST–ANN (WESTLAW)
- **Administrative code:**
  Alaska Administrative Code
- **Administrative register:**
  Alaska Administrative Journal (biweekly)
- **Court rules:**
  Alaska Rules of Court Procedure and Administration (Book Pub. Co.)

ARIZONA

• **Court reports:**

Supreme Court

* Arizona Reports 1866–date
Pacific Reporter 1866–date
ARIZ/ARIZ (LEXIS) 1898–date
AZ–CS (WESTLAW) 1885–date

Court of Appeals

Arizona Appeals Reports .... 1965–1976 Ceased with vol. 27
* Arizona Reports 1976–date
Pacific Reporter 1965–date
ARIZ/APP (LEXIS) 1965–date
AZ–CS (WESTLAW) 1965–date

• **Session laws:**
Session Laws of Arizona
Arizona Legislative Service (West)
AZ–LEGIS (WESTLAW)

• **Statutory compilation:**
Arizona Revised Statutes Annotated (West)

• **Administrative code:**
Arizona Administrative Code

• **Administrative register:**
Arizona Administrative Register (monthly)

• **Court rules:**
Arizona Rules of Court (West)
AZ–RULES (WESTLAW)

ARKANSAS

• **Court reports:**

Supreme Court

* Arkansas Reports 1837–date
South Western Reporter 1886–date
Arkansas Cases (West reprint) .. 1886–date
ARK/ARK (LEXIS) 1965–date
AR–CS (WESTLAW) 1945–date

Court of Appeals

* Arkansas Appellate Reports ..... 1981–date Bound with Arkansas Reports
Arkansas Reports 1979–1981
South Western Reporter 1979–date
Arkansas Cases (West reprint) .. 1979–date
ARK/APP (LEXIS) 1979–date
AR–CS (WESTLAW) 1979–date

• **Session laws:**
General Acts of Arkansas
Arkansas Advance Legislative Service (Michie)

- **Statutory compilations:**
  Arkansas Code of 1987 Annotated (Michie)
  ARK/CODE or ARCODE (LEXIS)
  AR–ST or AR–ST–ANN (WESTLAW)
- **Administrative code:**
  ———
- **Administrative register:**
  Arkansas Register (monthly)
- **Court rules:**
  Arkansas Code of 1987 Annotated: Court Rules

CALIFORNIA

- **Court reports:**

Supreme Court

* California Reports

1st series	1850–1934	220 vols.
2d series	1934–1969	71 vols.
3d series	1969–date	
Pacific Reporter	1883–date	
West's California Reporter	1959–date	
CAL/CAL (LEXIS)	1883–date	
CA–CS (WESTLAW)	1883–date	

Court of Appeal (District Court of Appeal before 1966)

* California Appellate Reports

1st series	1905–1934	140 vols.
2d series	1934–1969	276 vols.
3d series	1969–date	
Pacific Reporter	1905–1959	
West's California Reporter	1959–date	
CAL/APP (LEXIS)	1954–date	
CA–CS (WESTLAW)	1955–date	

- **Session laws:**
  Statutes of California
  Advance Legislative Service to Deering's California Codes Annotated
  West's California Legislative Service
  CAL/ALS (LEXIS)
  CA–LEGIS (WESTLAW)
- **Statutory compilations:**
  Deering's California Codes Annotated (Bancroft–Whitney)
  West's Annotated California Codes
  CAL/CODE or CACODE (LEXIS)
  CA–ST or CA–ST–ANN (WESTLAW)
- **Administrative code:**
  California Code of Regulations
- **Administrative register:**
  California Regulatory Notice Register (weekly)
- **Court rules:**
  California Rules of Court (Administrative Office of the Courts)

California Rules of Court (West)
CAL/RULES (LEXIS)

COLORADO

- **Court reports:**

Supreme Court

Colorado Reports	1864–1980	Ceased with vol. 200
* Pacific Reporter	1883–date	Official since 1980
* Colorado Reporter (West reprint)	1883–date	Official since 1980
COLO/COLO (LEXIS)	1864–date	
CO–CS (WESTLAW)	1864–date	

Court of Appeals

Colorado Court of Appeals Reports	1891–1905 1912–1915 1970–1980	Ceased with vol. 44
* Pacific Reporter	1891–1905 1912–1915 1970–date	
* Colorado Reporter (West reprint)	1891–date	
COLO/APP (LEXIS)	1970–date	
CO–CS (WESTLAW)	1970–date	

- **Session laws:**
  Session Laws of Colorado
  New Statutes Service (Colorado Session Reports)
- **Statutory compilation:**
  Colorado Revised Statutes (Bradford)
- **Administrative code:**
  Code of Colorado Regulations
- **Administrative register:**
  Colorado Register (monthly)
- **Court rules:**
  Colorado Civil Rules Annotated (West)
  Colorado Court Rules (Michie)
  Colorado Court Rules (West)

CONNECTICUT

- **Court reports:**

Supreme Court (Supreme Court of Errors before 1965)

* Connecticut Reports	1814–date
Atlantic Reporter	1885–date
Connecticut Reporter (West reprint)	1885–date
CONN/CONN (LEXIS)	1938–date
CT–CS (WESTLAW)	1937–date

Appellate Court

* Connecticut Appellate Reports	1983–date	
Atlantic Reporter	1983–date	
Connecticut Reporter (West reprint)	1983–date	
CONN/APP (LEXIS)	1983–date	
CT–CS (WESTLAW)	1983–date	

- **Session laws:**
  Connecticut Public and Special Acts
  Connecticut Legislative Service (West)
  CONN/ALS (LEXIS)
  CT–LEGIS (WESTLAW)
- **Statutory compilations:**
  General Statutes of Connecticut
  Connecticut General Statutes Annotated (West)
  CONN/CODE or CTCODE (LEXIS)
  CT–ST or CT–ST–ANN (WESTLAW)
- **Administrative code:**
  Regulations of Connecticut State Agencies
- **Administrative register:**
  Connecticut Law Journal (weekly)
- **Court rules:**
  Connecticut Practice: . . . Rules (West)
  Connecticut Practice Book (Commission on Official Legal Publications)
  Connecticut Rules of Court (West)

DELAWARE

- **Court reports:**

Supreme Court

Delaware Reports	1832–1966	Ceased with vol. 59
Delaware Chancery Reports	1814–1968	Ceased with vol. 43
* Atlantic Reporter	1884–date	Official since 1966
* Delaware Reporter (West reprint)	1966–date	
DEL/DEL (LEXIS)	1952–date	
DE–CS (WESTLAW)	1945–date	

- **Session laws:**
  Laws of Delaware
- **Statutory compilations:**
  Delaware Code Annotated (Michie)
  DEL/CODE or DECODE (LEXIS)
  DE–ST or DE–ST–ANN (WESTLAW)
- **Administrative code:**
  ______
- **Administrative register:**
  ______

- **Court rules:**
  16–17 *Delaware Code Annotated*

DISTRICT OF COLUMBIA

- **Court reports:**

Court of Appeals (Municipal Court of Appeals before 1970)

Atlantic Reporter	1943–date	
DC/DCAPP (LEXIS)	1965–date	
DC–CS (WESTLAW)	1945–date	

- **Session laws:**
  District of Columbia Statutes at Large
- **Statutory compilation:**
  District of Columbia Code Annotated (Michie)
- **Administrative code:**
  District of Columbia Municipal Regulations
- **Administrative register:**
  District of Columbia Register (weekly)
- **Court rules:**
  District of Columbia Court Rules Annotated (Michie)

FLORIDA

- **Court reports:**

Supreme Court

Florida Reports	1846–1948	Ceased with vol. 160
Southern Reporter	1886–date	
* Florida Cases (West reprint)	1941–date	Official since 1948
FLA/FLA (LEXIS)	1886–date	
FL–CS (WESTLAW)	1886–date	

District Court of Appeal

Southern Reporter	1957–date	
* Florida Cases (West reprint)	1957–date	
FLA/APP (LEXIS)	1957–date	
FL–CS (WESTLAW)	1957–date	

- **Session laws:**
  Laws of Florida
  West's Florida Session Law Service
  FLA/ALS (LEXIS)
  FL–LEGIS (WESTLAW)
- **Statutory compilations:**
  Florida Statutes
  Harrison's Florida Statutes Annotated
  West's Florida Statutes Annotated
  FLA/CODE or FLCODE (LEXIS)
  FL–ST or FL–ST–ANN (WESTLAW)
- **Administrative code:**
  Florida Administrative Code Annotated

- **Administrative register:**
  Florida Administrative Weekly
- **Court rules:**
  Florida Rules of Court (West)
  Florida Rules of Court Service (D & S Publishers)
  FL–RULES (WESTLAW)

GEORGIA

- **Court reports:**

Supreme Court

*	Georgia Reports	1846–date
	South Eastern Reporter	1887–date
	Georgia Cases (West reprint)	1939–date
	GA/GA (LEXIS)	1955–date
	GA–CS (WESTLAW)	1937–date

Court of Appeals

*	Georgia Appeals Reports	1907–date
	South Eastern Reporter	1907–date
	Georgia Cases (West reprint)	1939–date
	GA/APP (LEXIS)	1955–date
	GA–CS (WESTLAW)	1945–date

- **Session laws:**
  Georgia Laws
- **Statutory compilations:**
  Official Code of Georgia Annotated (Michie)
  Georgia Code Annotated (Harrison)
- **Administrative code:**
  Official Compilation: Rules and Regulations of the State of Georgia
- **Administrative register:**
  ———
- **Court rules:**
  Georgia Court Rules and Procedure (West)
  Georgia Rules of Court (D & S Publishers)
  Georgia Rules of Court Annotated (Michie)

HAWAII

- **Court reports:**

Supreme Court

*	Hawaii Reports	1847–date
	Pacific Reporter	1959–date
	HAW/HAW (LEXIS)	1965–date
	HI–CS (WESTLAW)	1959–date

Intermediate Court of Appeals

*	Hawaii Appellate Reports	1980–date
	Pacific Reporter	1980–date

HAW/APP (LEXIS) 1980–date
HI–CS (WESTLAW) 1980–date

- **Session laws:**
  Session Laws of Hawaii
- **Statutory compilations:**
  Hawaii Revised Statutes
  Hawaii Revised Statutes Annotated (Michie)
- **Administrative code:**
  ———
- **Administrative register:**
  ———
- **Court rules:**
  Hawaii Rules of Court (West)
  Rules of Court (Judiciary of Hawaii)

IDAHO

- **Court reports:**

Supreme Court
* Idaho Reports 1866–date
Pacific Reporter 1881–date
IDA/IDA (LEXIS) 1945–date
ID–CS (WESTLAW) 1945–date

Court of Appeals
* Idaho Reports 1982–date
Pacific Reporter 1982–date
IDA/APP (LEXIS) 1982–date
ID–CS (WESTLAW) 1982–date

- **Session laws:**
  Session Laws of Idaho
- **Statutory compilations:**
  Idaho Code (Michie)
  IDA/CODE or IDCODE (LEXIS)
  ID–ST or ID–ST–ANN (WESTLAW)
- **Administrative code:**
  ———
- **Administrative register:**
  ———
- **Court rules:**
  Idaho Court Rules (Michie)

ILLINOIS

- **Court reports:**

Supreme Court
* Illinois Reports
1st series .... 1819–1954 415 vols.
2d series 1954–date
North Eastern Reporter 1885–date
West's Illinois Decisions 1976–date

ILL/ILL (LEXIS) 1899–date
IL–CS (WESTLAW) 1885–date

Appellate Court

* Illinois Appellate Court Reports

1st series	1877–1954	351 vols.
2d series	1954–1972	133 vols.
3d series	1972–date	
North Eastern Reporter	1936–date	
West's Illinois Decisions	1976–date	
ILL/APP (LEXIS)	1955–date	
IL–CS (WESTLAW)	1945–date	

- **Session laws:**
  Laws of Illinois
  Illinois Legislative Service (West)
  IL–LEGIS (WESTLAW)
- **Statutory compilations:**
  Illinois Revised Statutes
  Smith–Hurd Illinois Annotated Statutes (West)
  IL–ST or IL–ST–ANN (WESTLAW)
  ILL/CODE or ILCODE (LEXIS)
- **Administrative code:**
  Illinois Administrative Code
- **Administrative register:**
  Illinois Register (weekly)
- **Court rules:**
  Illinois Code of Civil Procedure and Rules of Court (West)
  Illinois Courts Rule Book (Law Bulletin Publishing)
  Illinois Rules & Practice Handbook (Pantagraph)
  IL–RULES (WESTLAW)

INDIANA

- **Court reports:**

Supreme Court

Indiana Reports	1848–1981	Ceased with vol. 275
* North Eastern Reporter	1885–date	Official since 1981
* Indiana Cases (West reprint)	1936–date	Official since 1981
IND/IND (LEXIS)	1938–date	
IN–CS (WESTLAW)	1935–date	

Court of Appeals (Appellate Court before 1972)

Indiana Court of Appeals Reports	1890–1979	Ceased with vol. 182
* North Eastern Reporter	1890–date	Official since 1979
* Indiana Cases (West reprint)	1936–date	Official since 1979
IND/APP (LEXIS)	1951–date	
IN–CS (WESTLAW)	1945–date	

- **Session laws:**
  Acts of Indiana
  Advance Legislative Service to Burns Indiana Statutes Annotated

West's Indiana Legislative Service
IN–LEGIS (WESTLAW)

- **Statutory compilations:**
  Indiana Code
  Burns Indiana Statutes Annotated (Michie)
  West's Annotated Indiana Code
  IND/CODE or INCODE (LEXIS)
  IN–STB or IN–STB–ANN (WESTLAW)
- **Administrative code:**
  Indiana Administrative Code
- **Administrative register:**
  Indiana Register (monthly)
- **Court rules:**
  Indiana Practice: Rules of Procedure Annotated (West)
  Indiana Rules of Court (West)

IOWA

- **Court reports:**

Supreme Court

Iowa Reports	1855–1968	Ceased with vol. 261
North Western Reporter	1878–date	
IOWA/CIV and CRIM (LEXIS)	1960–date	
IA–CS (WESTLAW)	1944–date	

Court of Appeals

North Western Reporter	1977–date
IOWA/CIV and CRIM (LEXIS)	1977–date
IA–CS (WESTLAW)	1977–date

- **Session laws:**
  Acts and Joint Resolutions of Iowa
  Iowa Legislative Service (West)
  IA–LEGIS (WESTLAW)
- **Statutory compilations:**
  Code of Iowa
  Iowa Code Annotated (West)
  IOWA/CODE or IACODE (LEXIS)
  IA–ST or IA–ST–ANN (WESTLAW)
- **Administrative code:**
  Iowa Administrative Code
- **Administrative register:**
  Iowa Administrative Bulletin (biweekly)
- **Court rules:**
  Iowa Court Rules (State of Iowa)
  Iowa Rules of Court (West)
  IA–RULES (WESTLAW)

KANSAS

• **Court reports:**

Supreme Court

*	Kansas Reports	1862–date	
	Pacific Reporter	1883–date	
	Kansas Cases (West reprint)	1968–date	
	KAN/KAN (LEXIS)	1963–date	
	KS–CS (WESTLAW)	1945–date	

Court of Appeals

*	Kansas Court of Appeals Reports		
	1st series	1895–1901	10 vols.
	2d series	1977–date	
	Pacific Reporter	1895–1901 1977–date	
	Kansas Cases (West reprint)	1977–date	
	KAN/APP (LEXIS)	1977–date	
	KS–CS (WESTLAW)	1977–date	

• **Session laws:**

Session Laws of Kansas

KAN/ALS (LEXIS)

• **Statutory compilations:**

Kansas Statutes Annotated

Vernon's Kansas Statutes Annotated (West)

KAN/CODE or KSCODE (LEXIS)

• **Administrative code:**

Kansas Administrative Regulations

KAN/KSADMN (LEXIS)

• **Administrative register:**

Kansas Register (weekly)

• **Court rules:**

Kansas Court Rules and Procedure (West)

KAN/RULES (LEXIS)

KENTUCKY

• **Court reports:**

Supreme Court (Court of Appeals before 1976)

	Kentucky Reports	1785–1951	Ceased with vol. 314
*	South Western Reporter	1886–date	Official since 1973
*	Kentucky Decisions (West reprint)	1886–date	Official since 1973
	KY/KY (LEXIS)	1954–date	
	KY–CS (WESTLAW)	1944–date	

Court of Appeals

*	South Western Reporter	1976–date	
*	Kentucky Decisions (West reprint)	1976–date	
	KY/APP (LEXIS)	1976–date	

KY–CS (WESTLAW) 1976–date

- **Session laws:**
  Kentucky Acts
  Kentucky Revised Statutes & Rules Service (Banks–Baldwin)
- **Statutory compilations:**
  Baldwin's Kentucky Revised Statutes Annotated (Banks–Baldwin)
  Kentucky Revised Statutes Annotated (Michie)
  KY/CODE, STAT, KYCODE or KYSTAT (LEXIS)
  KY–ST or KY–ST–ANN (WESTLAW)
- **Administrative code:**
  Kentucky Administrative Regulations Service
- **Administrative register:**
  Kentucky Administrative Register (monthly)
- **Court rules:**
  Kentucky Practice: Rules of Civil Procedure Annotated (West)
  Kentucky Rules Annotated (Michie)
  Kentucky Rules of Court (West)
  KY/RULES (LEXIS)

LOUISIANA

- **Court reports:**

Supreme Court

Louisiana Reports	1809–1972	Ceased with vol. 263
Southern Reporter	1887–date	
Louisiana Cases (West reprint) ..	1966–date	
LA/LA (LEXIS)................	1945–date	
LA–CS (WESTLAW)	1887–date	

Court of Appeal

Southern Reporter	1928–date
Louisiana Cases (West reprint) ..	1966–date
LA/APP (LEXIS)	1965–date
LA–CS (WESTLAW)	1945–date

- **Session laws:**
  Acts, State of Louisiana
  Louisiana Session Law Service (West)
  LA–LEGIS (WESTLAW)
- **Statutory compilations:**
  West's Louisiana Statutes Annotated
  LA–ST or LA–ST–ANN (WESTLAW)
- **Administrative code:**
  Louisiana Administrative Code
- **Administrative register:**
  Louisiana Register (monthly)
- **Court rules:**
  West's Louisiana Rules of Court
  LA–RULES (WESTLAW)

MAINE

- **Court reports:**

Supreme Judicial Court

	Maine Reports	1820–1965	Ceased with vol. 161
*	Atlantic Reporter	1885–date	Official since 1966
*	Maine Reporter (West reprint)	1966–date	
	MAINE/ME (LEXIS)	1965–date	
	ME–CS (WESTLAW)	1945–date	

- **Session laws:**
  Laws of Maine
  Maine Legislative Service (West)
  ME–LEGIS (WESTLAW)
- **Statutory compilation:**
  Maine Revised Statutes Annotated (West)
- **Administrative code:**
  Code of Maine Rules
- **Administrative register:**
  ———
- **Court rules:**
  Maine Rules of Court (West)

MARYLAND

- **Court reports:**

Court of Appeals

*	Maryland Reports	1851–date
	Atlantic Reporter	1885–date
	Maryland Reporter (West reprint)	1942–date
	MD/MD (LEXIS)	1938–date
	MD–CS (WESTLAW)	1938–date

Court of Special Appeals

*	Maryland Appellate Reports	1967–date
	Atlantic Reporter	1967–date
	Maryland Reporter (West reprint)	1967–date
	MD/MDAPP (LEXIS)	1967–date
	MD–CS (WESTLAW)	1967–date

- **Session laws:**
  Laws of Maryland
- **Statutory compilations:**
  Annotated Code of Maryland (Michie)
  MD/CODE or MDCODE (LEXIS)
  MD–ST or MD–ST–ANN (WESTLAW)
- **Administrative code:**
  Code of Maryland Regulations
- **Administrative register:**
  Maryland Register (biweekly)

- **Court rules:**
  Maryland Rules (Michie)

MASSACHUSETTS

- **Court reports:**

Supreme Judicial Court

* Massachusetts Reports 1804–date
  North Eastern Reporter 1884–date
  Massachusetts Decisions
    (West reprint) 1884–date
  MASS/MASS (LEXIS)........... 1950–date
  MA–CS (WESTLAW)............ 1899–date

Appeals Court

* Massachusetts Appeals Court
    Reports 1972–date
  North Eastern Reporter 1972–date
  Massachusetts Decisions
    (West reprint) 1972–date
  MASS/APP (LEXIS) 1972–date
  MA–CS (WESTLAW)............ 1972–date

- **Session laws:**
  Acts and Resolves of Massachusetts
  Massachusetts Advance Legislative Service (Lawyers Co-op)
  Massachusetts Legislative Service (West)
  MA–LEGIS (WESTLAW)
- **Statutory compilations:**
  General Laws of the Commonwealth of Massachusetts
  Annotated Laws of Massachusetts (Lawyers Co-op)
  Massachusetts General Laws Annotated (West)
  MA–ST or MA–ST–ANN (WESTLAW)
- **Administrative code:**
  Code of Massachusetts Regulations
- **Administrative register:**
  Massachusetts Register (biweekly)
- **Court rules:**
  Massachusetts Practice: Rules Practice (West)
  Massachusetts Rules of Court (West)
  The Rules (Lawyers Weekly)

MICHIGAN

- **Court reports:**

Supreme Court

* Michigan Reports............... 1847–date
  North Western Reporter 1879–date
  Michigan Reporter
    (West reprint) 1941–date
  MICH/MICH (LEXIS)........... 1937–date
  MI–CS (WESTLAW) 1899–date

Court of Appeals

* Michigan Appeals Reports	1965–date	
North Western Reporter	1965–date	
Michigan Reporter (West reprint)	1965–date	
MICH/APP (LEXIS)	1965–date	
MI–CS (WESTLAW)	1965–date	

- **Session laws:**
  Public and Local Acts of Michigan
  Michigan Lesgislative Service (West)
  MI–LEGIS (WESTLAW)
- **Statutory compilations:**
  Michigan Compiled Laws
  Michigan Compiled Laws Annotated (West)
  Michigan Statutes Annotated (Callaghan)
- **Administrative code:**
  Michigan Administrative Code
- **Administrative register:**
  Michigan Register (monthly)
- **Court rules:**
  Michigan Court Rules Practice (West)
  Michigan Rules of Court (West)

MINNESOTA

- **Court reports:**

Supreme Court

Minnesota Reports	1851–1977	Ceased with vol. 312
* North Western Reporter	1879–date	Official since 1978
* Minnesota Reporter (West reprint)	1978–date	
MINN/MINN (LEXIS)	1925–date	
MN–CS (WESTLAW)	1898–date	

Court of Appeals

* North Western Reporter	1983–date	
* Minnesota Reporter (West reprint)	1983–date	
MINN/APP (LEXIS)	1983–date	
MN–CS (WESTLAW)	1983–date	

- **Session laws:**
  Laws of Minnesota
  Minnesota Session Law Service (West)
  MN–LEGIS (WESTLAW)
- **Statutory compilations:**
  Minnesota Statutes
  Minnesota Statutes Annotated (West)
  MINN/CODE or MNCODE (LEXIS)
  MN–ST (WESTLAW)

- **Administrative code:**
  Minnesota Rules
- **Administrative register:**
  Minnesota State Register (weekly)
- **Court rules:**
  Minnesota Practice: . . . Rules Annotated (West)
  Minnesota Rules of Court (West)

MISSISSIPPI

- **Court reports:**

Supreme Court

Mississippi Reports	1818–1966	Ceased with vol. 254
* Southern Reporter	1886–date	Official since 1966
* Mississippi Cases (West reprint)	1966–date	
MISS/MISS (LEXIS)	1965–date	
MS–CS (WESTLAW)	1945–date	

- **Session laws:**
  General Laws of Mississippi
- **Statutory compilation:**
  Mississippi Code 1972 Annotated (Harrison/Lawyers Co-op)
- **Administrative code:**
  ———
- **Administrative register:**
  Mississippi Register (monthly)
- **Court rules:**
  Mississippi Rules of Court (West)

MISSOURI

- **Court reports:**

Supreme Court

Missouri Reports	1821–1956	Ceased with vol. 365
* South Western Reporter	1886–date	Official since 1956
* Missouri Decisions (West reprint)	1886–date	Official since 1956
MO/MO (LEXIS)	1945–date	
MO–CS (WESTLAW)	1924–date	

Court of Appeals

Missouri Appeal Reports	1876–1952	Ceased with vol. 241
* South Western Reporter	1902–date	Official since 1952
* Missouri Decisions (West reprint)	1902–date	Official since 1952
MO/APP (LEXIS)	1945–date	
MO–CS (WESTLAW)	1944–date	

- **Session laws:**
  Laws of Missouri
  Vernon's Missouri Legislative Service (West)
  MO–LEGIS (WESTLAW)

- **Statutory compilations:**
  Missouri Revised Statutes
  Vernon's Annotated Missouri Statutes (West)
  MO/CODE or MOCODE (LEXIS)
  MO–ST and MO–ST–SUPP (WESTLAW)
- **Administrative code:**
  Missouri Code of State Regulations
- **Administrative register:**
  Missouri Register (monthly)
- **Court rules:**
  Missouri Rules of Court (West)
  Vernon's Annotated Missouri Rules (West)
  MO/RULES (LEXIS)

MONTANA

- **Court reports:**

Supreme Court

* Montana Reports 1868–date
Pacific Reporter 1882–date
MONT/MONT (LEXIS) 1965–date
MT–CS (WESTLAW) 1945–date

- **Session laws:**
  Laws of Montana
- **Statutory compilations:**
  Montana Code Annotated
  MONT/CODE or MTCODE (LEXIS)
- **Administrative code:**
  Administrative Rules of Montana
- **Administrative register:**
  Montana Administrative Register (biweekly)
- **Court rules:**
  Montana Rules of Court (West)

NEBRASKA

- **Court reports:**

Supreme Court

* Nebraska Reports............... 1860–date
North Western Reporter 1879–date
NEB/NEB (LEXIS) 1965–date
NE–CS (WESTLAW) 1945–date

- **Session laws:**
  Laws of Nebraska
- **Statutory compilations:**
  Revised Statutes of Nebraska
  NEB/CODE or NECODE (LEXIS)
- **Administrative code:**
  Nebraska Administrative Code

- **Administrative register:**

———

- **Court rules:**
Nebraska Court Rules and Procedure (West)

NEVADA

- **Court reports:**

Supreme Court

* Nevada Reports 1865–date
Pacific Reporter 1882–date
NEV/NEV (LEXIS) 1965–date
NV–CS (WESTLAW) 1945–date

- **Session laws:**
Statutes of Nevada
- **Statutory compilations:**
Nevada Revised Statutes
Nevada Revised Statutes Annotated (Michie)
NEV/CODE or NVCODE (LEXIS)
NV–ST or NV–ST–ANN (WESTLAW)
- **Administrative code:**
Nevada Administrative Code
- **Administrative register:**

———

- **Court rules:**
Nevada Revised Statutes Annotated: Court Rules Annotated

NEW HAMPSHIRE

- **Court reports:**

Supreme Court

* New Hampshire Reports 1816–date
Atlantic Reporter 1886–date
NH/NH (LEXIS)................ 1965–date
NH–CS (WESTLAW)............ 1945–date

- **Session laws:**
Laws of New Hampshire
- **Statutory compilation:**
New Hampshire Revised Statutes Annotated (Equity)
- **Administrative code:**
New Hampshire Code of Administrative Rules Annotated
- **Administrative register:**
New Hampshire Rulemaking Register (monthly)
- **Court rules:**
New Hampshire Court Rules Annotated (Equity)

NEW JERSEY

- **Court reports:**

Supreme Court (Court of Errors and Appeals before 1948)

New Jersey Law Reports .... 1790–1948 137 vols.

New Jersey Equity Reports ..... 1830–1948 142 vols.
* New Jersey Reports 1948–date
Atlantic Reporter 1885–date
NJ/NJ (LEXIS) 1948–date
NJ–CS (WESTLAW) 1899–date

Superior Court

* New Jersey Superior Court Reports 1948–date
Atlantic Reporter 1885–date
NJ/SUPER (LEXIS) 1948–date
NJ–CS (WESTLAW) 1899–date

- **Session laws:**
  Laws of New Jersey
  New Jersey Session Law Service (West)
  NJ–LEGIS (WESTLAW)
- **Statutory compilation:**
  New Jersey Statutes Annotated (West)
  NJ–ST (WESTLAW)
- **Administrative code:**
  New Jersey Administrative Code
- **Administrative register:**
  New Jersey Register (biweekly)
- **Court rules:**
  Current Rules Governing the Courts of the State of New Jersey (Gann)
  New Jersey Practice: Court Rules Annotated (West)
  Rules Governing the Courts of the State of New Jersey (West)

NEW MEXICO

- **Court reports:**

Supreme Court

* New Mexico Reports 1852–date
Pacific Reporter 1883–date
NM/NM (LEXIS) 1965–date
NM–CS (WESTLAW)............ 1945–date

Court of Appeal

* New Mexico Reports 1966–date
Pacific Reporter 1966–date
NM/APP (LEXIS) 1966–date
NM–CS (WESTLAW)............ 1966–date

- **Session laws:**
  Laws of New Mexico
  New Mexico Advance Legislative Service (Michie)
- **Statutory compilations:**
  New Mexico Statutes Annotated (Michie)
  NM/CODE or NMCODE (LEXIS)
  NM–ST or NM–ST–ANN (WESTLAW)

• **Administrative code:**

———

• **Administrative register:**

———

• **Court rules:**
New Mexico Statutes Annotated: Judicial Volumes

NEW YORK

• **Court reports:**
Court of Appeals
* New York Reports

1st series	1847–1956	309 vols.
2d series	1956–date	
North Eastern Reporter	1885–date	
New York Supplement	1847–date	
NY/NY (LEXIS)	1884–date	
NY–CS (WESTLAW)	1885–date	

Supreme Court, Appellate Division
* Appellate Division Reports

1st series	1896–1956	286 vols.
2d series	1956–date	
New York Supplement	1896–date	
NY/APPDIV (LEXIS)	1919–date	
NY–CS (WESTLAW)	1918–date	

• **Session laws:**
Laws of New York
McKinney's Session Laws of New York and *McKinney's Session Law News of New York* (West)
New York Consolidated Laws Service Session Laws and *Advance Legislative Service for the New York Consolidated Law Service*
NY–LEGIS (WESTLAW)

• **Statutory compilations:**
Gould's Consolidated Laws of New York
Michie's New York Consolidated Laws
McKinney's Consolidated Laws of New York Annotated (West)
New York Consolidated Laws Service (Lawyers Co-op)
NY/CODE (LEXIS)
NY–ST or NY–ST–ANN (WESTLAW)

• **Administrative code:**
Official Compilation of Codes, Rules and Regulations of the State of New York

• **Administrative register:**
New York State Register (weekly)

• **Court rules:**
McKinney's New York Rules of Court (West)
22 *Official Compilation of Codes, Rules and Regulations of the State of New York*

NORTH CAROLINA

- **Court reports:**

Supreme Court

*	North Carolina Reports	1778–date
	South Eastern Reporter	1887–date
	North Carolina Reporter (West reprint)	1939–date
	NC/NC (LEXIS)	1965–date
	NC–CS (WESTLAW)	1945–date

Court of Appeals

*	North Carolina Court of Appeals Reports	1968–date
	South Eastern Reporter	1968–date
	North Carolina Reporter (West reprint)	1968–date
	NC/APP (LEXIS)	1968–date
	NC–CS (WESTLAW)	1968–date

- **Session laws:**

Session Laws of North Carolina

Advance Legislative Service to the General Statutes of North Carolina

- **Statutory Compilations:**

General Statutes of North Carolina (Michie)

NC/CODE or NCCODE (LEXIS)

NC–ST or NC–ST–ANN (WESTLAW)

- **Administrative code:**

North Carolina Administrative Code

- **Administrative register:**

North Carolina Register (monthly)

- **Court rules:**

Annotated Rules of North Carolina (Michie)

North Carolina Rules of Court (West)

NORTH DAKOTA

- **Court reports:**

Supreme Court

	North Dakota Reports	1890–1953	Ceased with vol. 79
*	North Western Reporter	1890–date	Official since 1953
	ND/ND (LEXIS)	1965–date	
	ND–CS (WESTLAW)	1945–date	

Court of Appeals

*	North Western Reporter	1987–date
	ND/APP (LEXIS)	1987–date
	ND–CS (WESTLAW)	1987–date

- **Session laws:**

Laws of North Dakota

- **Statutory compilation:**
  North Dakota Century Code (Michie)
- **Administrative code**
  North Dakota Administrative Code
- **Administrative register:**
  ____
- **Court rules:**
  North Dakota Court Rules (West)

OHIO

- **Court reports:**

Supreme Court

Ohio Reports	1821–1851	20 vols.
* Ohio State Reports		
1st series	1852–1964	177 vols.
2d series	1964–1982	70 vols.
3d series	1982–date	Bound with Ohio App.3d and Ohio Misc.2d as *Ohio Official Reports*
North Eastern Reporter	1885–date	
Ohio Cases (West reprint)	1933–date	
OHIO/OHIO and OSUP (LEXIS)	1821–date	
OH–CS (WESTLAW)	1821–date	

Court of Appeals

* Ohio Appellate Reports		
1st series	1913–1965	120 vols.
2d series	1965–1982	70 vols.
3d series	1982–date	
North Eastern Reporter	1927–date	
Ohio Cases (West reprint)	1943–date	
OHIO/APP and OAPP (LEXIS)	1913–date	
OH–CS (WESTLAW)	1925–date	

- **Session laws:**
  Laws of Ohio
  Baldwin's Ohio Legislative Service
  Page's Ohio Revised Code: Legislative Bulletin
  OHIO/ALS (LEXIS)
  OH–LEGIS (WESTLAW)
- **Statutory compilations:**
  Baldwin's Ohio Revised Code Annotated (Banks–Baldwin)
  Page's Ohio Revised Code Annotated (Anderson)
  OHIO/CODE or OHCODE (LEXIS)
  OH–ST or OH–ST–ANN (WESTLAW)
- **Administrative code:**
  Ohio Administrative Code
  OHIO/ADMN (LEXIS)

- **Administrative register:**
  Ohio Monthly Record
- **Court rules:**
  Ohio Practice: Rules of Civil Procedure Annotated (West)
  Ohio Rules of Court (West)
  Rules Governing the Courts of Ohio (Anderson)
  OHIO/RULES (LEXIS)

OKLAHOMA

- **Court reports:**

Supreme Court

Oklahoma Reports	1890–1953	Ceased with vol. 208
* Pacific Reporter	1890–date	Official since 1953
* Oklahoma Decisions (West reprint)	1931–date	Official since 1953
OKLA/OKLA (LEXIS)	1965–date	
OK–CS (WESTLAW)	1945–date	

Court of Criminal Appeals (Criminal Court of Appeals before 1959)

Oklahoma Criminal Reports	1908–1953	Ceased with vol. 97
* Pacific Reporter	1908–date	Official since 1953
* Oklahoma Decisions (West reprint)	1931–date	Official since 1953
OKLA/CRMAPP (LEXIS)	1965–date	
OK–CS (WESTLAW)	1945–date	

Court of Appeals

* Pacific Reporter	1969–date
* Oklahoma Decisions (West reprint)	1969–date
OKLA/CIVAPP (LEXIS)	1969–date
OK–CS (WESTLAW)	1969–date

- **Session laws:**
  Oklahoma Sessions Laws
  Oklahoma Session Law Service (West)
  OK–LEGIS (WESTLAW)
- **Statutory compilations:**
  Oklahoma Statutes
  Oklahoma Statutes Annotated (West)
  OK–ST or OK–ST–ANN (WESTLAW)
- **Administrative code:**

  ———
- **Administrative register:**
  Oklahoma Register (monthly)
- **Court rules:**
  Oklahoma Court Rules and Procedure (West)

OREGON

- **Court reports:**

Supreme Court

* Oregon Reports 1853–date
Pacific Reporter 1883–date
Oregon Cases (West reprint) 1967–date
ORE/ORE (LEXIS) 1965–date
OR–CS (WESTLAW) 1945–date

Court of Appeals

* Oregon Reports, Court of Appeals 1969–date
Pacific Reporter 1969–date
Oregon Decisions (West reprint) . . 1969–date
ORE/APP (LEXIS) 1969–date
OR–CS (WESTLAW) 1969–date

- **Session laws:**
  Oregon Laws
- **Statutory compilations:**
  Oregon Revised Statutes
  Oregon Revised Statutes Annotated (Butterworth)
  ORE/CODE (LEXIS)
- **Administrative code:**
  Oregon Administrative Rules Compilation
- **Administrative register:**
  Oregon Administrative Rules Bulletin (biweekly)
- **Court rules:**
  Oregon Rules of Civil Procedure Annotated (Butterworth)
  Oregon Rules of Court (West)

PENNSYLVANIA

- **Court reports:**

Supreme Court

* Pennsylvania State Reports 1845–date
Atlantic Reporter 1885–date
Pennsylvania Reporter (West) . . . 1939–date
PA/PA (LEXIS) 1930–date
PA–CS (WESTLAW) 1885–date

Superior Court

* Pennsylvania Superior Court Reports 1895–date
Atlantic Reporter 1931–date
Pennsylvania Reporter (West) . . . 1939–date
PA/SUPER (LEXIS) 1955–date
PA–CS (WESTLAW) 1944–date

- **Session laws:**
  Laws of Pennsylvania
  Purdon's Pennsylvania Legislative Service (Bisel/West)

PA–LEGIS (WESTLAW)

- **Statutory compilations:**
  Pennsylvania Consolidated Statutes
  Purdon's Pennsylvania Statutes and Pennsylvania Consolidated Statutes Annotated (Bisel/West)
- **Administrative code:**
  Pennsylvania Code
- **Administrative register:**
  Pennsylvania Bulletin (weekly)
- **Court rules:**
  Pennsylvania Code, titles 201–246
  Pennsylvania Rules of Court (West)
  PA–RULES (WESTLAW)

RHODE ISLAND

- **Court reports:**

Supreme Court

Rhode Island Reports	1828–1980	Ceased with vol. 122
Atlantic Reporter	1885–date	
Rhode Island Reporter (West)	1980–date	
RI/RI (LEXIS)	1965–date	
RI–CS (WESTLAW)	1945–date	

- **Session laws:**
  Public Laws of Rhode Island
  Rhode Island Acts and Resolves
- **Statutory compilations:**
  General Laws of Rhode Island 1956 (Michie)
  RI/CODE or RICODE (LEXIS)
  RI–ST or RI–ST–ANN (WESTLAW)
- **Administrative code:**

  ———
- **Administrative register:**

  ———
- **Court rules:**
  Rhode Island Court Rules Annotated (Michie)

SOUTH CAROLINA

- **Court reports:**

Supreme Court

* South Carolina Reports	1868–date
South Eastern Reporter	1886–date
SC/SC (LEXIS)	1965–date
SC–CS (WESTLAW)	1945–date

Court of Appeals

* South Carolina Reports	1983–date
South Eastern Reporter	1983–date
SC/APP (LEXIS)	1983–date
SC–CS (WESTLAW)	1983–date

- **Session laws:**
  Acts and Joint Resolutions of South Carolina
- **Statutory compilation:**
  Code of Laws of South Carolina 1976 Annotated (Lawyers Co-op)
- **Administrative code:**
  Code of Laws of South Carolina 1976 Annotated: Code of Regulations
- **Administrative register:**
  South Carolina State Register
- **Court rules:**
  South Carolina Rules of Court (West)

SOUTH DAKOTA

- **Court reports:**

Supreme Court

	South Dakota Reports	1890–1976	Ceased with vol. 90
*	North Western Reporter	1890–date	Official since 1976
	SD/SD (LEXIS)	1965–date	
	SD–CS (WESTLAW)	1945–date	

- **Session laws:**
  Laws of South Dakota
- **Statutory compilation:**
  South Dakota Codified Laws (Michie)
  SD–ST or SD–ST–ANN (WESTLAW)
- **Administrative code:**
  Administrative Rules of South Dakota
- **Administrative register:**
  South Dakota Register (weekly)
- **Court rules:**
  Various sections of *South Dakota Codified Laws*

TENNESSEE

- **Court reports:**

Supreme Court

	Tennessee Reports	1791–1972	Ceased with vol. 225
*	South Western Reporter	1886–date	Official since 1972
*	Tennessee Decisions (West reprint)	1886–date	Official since 1972
	TENN/TENN (LEXIS)	1965–date	
	TN–CS (WESTLAW)	1945–date	

Court of Appeals

	Tennessee Appeals Reports	1925–1971	Ceased with vol. 63
*	South Western Reporter	1932–date	Official since 1972
*	Tennessee Decisions (West reprint)	1932–date	Official since 1972
	TENN/APP (LEXIS)	1965–date	
	TN–CS (WESTLAW)	1945–date	

Court of Criminal Appeals

Tennessee Criminal Appeals Reports .... 1967–1971 Ceased with vol. 4

* South Western Reporter .... 1967–date Official since 1972

* Tennessee Decisions (West reprint) .... 1967–date Official since 1972

TENN/CRMAPP (LEXIS) 1967–date

TN–CS (WESTLAW) 1967–date

- **Session laws:**

Tennessee Public Acts

Tennessee Advance Legislative Service (Michie)

- **Statutory compilations:**

Tennessee Code Annotated (Michie)

TENN/CODE or TNCODE (LEXIS)

TN–ST or TN–ST–ANN (WESTLAW)

- **Administrative code:**

Official Compilation: Rules and Regulations of the State of Tennessee

- **Administrative register:**

Tennessee Administrative Register (monthly)

- **Court rules:**

Tennessee Court Rules Annotated (Michie)

Tennessee Practice: Rules of Civil Procedure Annotated (West)

Tennessee Rules of Court (West)

TEXAS

- **Court reports:**

Supreme Court

Texas Reports .... 1846–1962 Ceased with vol. 163

South Western Reporter 1886–date

Texas Cases (West reprint) 1886–date

TEX/TEX (LEXIS) 1886–date

TX–CS (WESTLAW) 1886–date

Court of Criminal Appeals

Texas Criminal Reports .... 1892–1963 Ceased with vol. 172

South Western Reporter 1892–date

Texas Cases (West reprint) 1892–date

TEX/CRMAPP (LEXIS) 1948–date

TX–CS (WESTLAW) 1944–date

Court of Appeals (Court of Civil Appeals before 1981)

Texas Civil Appeals Reports .... 1892–1911 Ceased with vol. 63

South Western Reporter 1892–date

Texas Cases (West reprint) 1892–date

TEX/APP (LEXIS) 1949–date

TX–CS (WESTLAW) 1944–date

- **Session laws:**

General and Special Laws of Texas

Vernon's Texas Session Law Service (West)

TX-LEGIS (WESTLAW)

- **Statutory compilations:**
  Vernon's Texas Statutes and Codes Annotated (West)
  TEX/CODE or TXCODE (LEXIS)
  TX-ST or TX-ST-ANN (WESTLAW)
- **Administrative code:**
  Official Texas Administrative Code
  TX-AD (WESTLAW)
- **Administrative register:**
  Texas Register (twice weekly)
- **Court rules:**
  Texas Rules of Civil Procedure (Butterworth)
  Texas Rules of Court (West)
  Vernon's Texas Rules Annotated (West)
  TX-RULES (WESTLAW)

UTAH

- **Court reports:**

Supreme Court

	Utah Reports		
	1st series	1855–1952	123 vols.
	2d series	1953–1974	Ceased with vol. 30
*	Pacific Reporter	1881–date	Official since 1974
*	Utah Reporter (West reprint)	1974–date	
	UTAH/UTAH (LEXIS)	1965–date	
	UT–CS (WESTLAW)	1945–date	

Court of Appeals

*	Pacific Reporter	1987–date	
*	Utah Reporter (West reprint)	1987–date	
	UTAH/APP (LEXIS)	1987–date	
	UT–CS (WESTLAW)	1987–date	

- **Session laws:**
  Laws of Utah
- **Statutory compilation:**
  Utah Code Unannotated (Michie)
  Utah Code Annotated (Michie)
- **Administrative code:**
  Utah Administrative Code
- **Administrative register:**
  Utah State Bulletin (biweekly)
- **Court rules:**
  Utah Court Rules Annotated (Michie)

VERMONT

- **Court reports:**

Supreme Court

*	Vermont Reports	1826–date
	Atlantic Reporter	1885–date

VT/VT (LEXIS) 1965–date
VT–CS (WESTLAW) 1945–date

- **Session laws:**
  Laws of Vermont
- **Statutory compilation:**
  Vermont Statutes Annotated (Equity)
- **Administrative code:**
  Vermont Administrative Code
- **Administrative register:**
  ———
- **Court rules:**
  Vermont Court Rules Annotated (Equity)

VIRGINIA

- **Court reports:**

Supreme Court (Supreme Court of Appeals before 1971)
* Virginia Reports 1790–date
South Eastern Reporter 1887–date
VA/VA (LEXIS) 1925–date
VA–CS (WESTLAW) 1925–date
Court of Appeals
* Virginia Court of Appeals Reports 1985–date
South Eastern Reporter 1985–date
VA/APP (LEXIS) 1985–date
VA–CS (WESTLAW) 1985–date

- **Session laws:**
  Acts of Assembly of Virginia
- **Statutory compilations:**
  Code of Virginia 1950 Annotated (Michie)
  VA/CODE or VACODE (LEXIS)
  VA–ST or VA–ST–ANN (WESTLAW)
- **Administrative code:**
  ———
- **Administrative register:**
  Virginia Register of Regulations (biweekly)
- **Court rules:**
  21B *Michie's Jurisprudence of Virginia and West Virginia*
  Virginia Rules Annotated (Michie)

WASHINGTON

- **Court reports:**

Supreme Court
* Washington Reports
1st series .... 1889–1939 200 vols.
2d series 1939–date
Pacific Reporter 1880–date
WASH/WASH (LEXIS) 1938–date

WA–CS (WESTLAW)............ 1899–date

Court of Appeals

* Washington Appellate Reports .. 1969–date

Pacific Reporter 1969–date

WASH/APP (LEXIS)............ 1969–date

WA–CS (WESTLAW)............ 1969–date

- **Session laws:**

  Laws of Washington

  West's Washington Legislative Service

  WA–LEGIS (WESTLAW)

- **Statutory compilations:**

  Revised Code of Washington

  West's Revised Code of Washington Annotated

  WASH/CODE or WACODE (LEXIS)

- **Administrative code:**

  Washington Administrative Code

- **Administrative register:**

  Washington State Register (biweekly)

- **Court rules:**

  Official Rules of Court (State Law Reports Office)

  Washington Court Rules Annotated (Bancroft–Whitney)

  Washington Practice: Rules Practice (West)

  Washington Rules of Court (West)

WEST VIRGINIA

- **Court reports:**

Supreme Court of Appeals

* West Virginia Reports 1864–date

South Eastern Reporter......... 1886–date

WVA/WVA (LEXIS) 1965–date

WV–CS (WESTLAW) 1945–date

- **Session laws:**

  Acts of the Legislature of West Virginia

- **Statutory compilations:**

  West Virginia Code (Michie)

  WVA/CODE or WVCODE (LEXIS)

  WV–ST or WV–ST–ANN (WESTLAW)

- **Administrative code:**

  West Virginia Code of State Rules

- **Administrative register:**

  West Virginia State Register (weekly)

- **Court rules:**

  21B *Michie's Jurisprudence of Virginia and West Virginia*

WISCONSIN

- **Court reports:**

Supreme Court

* Wisconsin Reports		
1st series	1853–1957	275 vols.
2d series	1957–date	
North Western Reporter	1879–date	
* Wisconsin Reporter (West reprint)	1941–date	Co-official since 1975
WISC/WISC (LEXIS)	1964–date	
WI–CS (WESTLAW)	1945–date	

Court of Appeals

* Wisconsin Reports	1978–date	
North Western Reporter	1978–date	
* Wisconsin Reporter (West reprint)	1978–date	
WISC/APP (LEXIS)	1978–date	
WI–CS (WESTLAW)	1978–date	

- **Session laws:**
  Laws of Wisconsin
  West's Wisconsin Legislative Service
  WISC/ALS (LEXIS)
  WI–LEGIS (WESTLAW)
- **Statutory compilations:**
  Wisconsin Statutes
  West's Wisconsin Statutes Annotated
  WISC/CODE or WICODE (LEXIS)
- **Administrative code:**
  Wisconsin Administrative Code
- **Administrative register:**
  Wisconsin Administrative Register (biweekly)
- **Court rules:**
  Wisconsin Court Rules and Procedure (West)
  WI–RULES (WESTLAW)

WYOMING

- **Court reports:**

Supreme Court

Wyoming Reports	1870–1959	Ceased with vol. 80
* Pacific Reporter	1883–date	Official since 1959
* Wyoming Reporter (West reprint)	1959–date	
WYO/WYO (LEXIS)	1965–date	
WY–CS (WESTLAW)	1945–date	

- **Session laws:**
  Session Laws of Wyoming

- **Statutory compilations:**
  Wyoming Statutes Annotated (Michie)
  WYO/CODE or WYCODE (LEXIS)
- **Administrative code:**
  ______
- **Administrative register:**
  ______
- **Court rules:**
  Wyoming Court Rules Annotated (Michie)

Appendix C

COVERAGE OF WEST REGIONAL REPORTERS

Atlantic Reporter (1886 to date): Includes decisions beginning with the designated volume of the following major state reports: 53 Connecticut, 1 Connecticut Appellate, 19 Connecticut Supplement, 12 Delaware (7 Houston), 6 Delaware Chancery, 77 Maine, 63 Maryland, 1 Maryland Appellate, 63 New Hampshire, 47 New Jersey Law, 40 New Jersey Equity, 1 New Jersey, 1 New Jersey Superior, 108 Pennsylvania State, 102 Pennsylvania Superior, 1 Pennsylvania Commonwealth, 15 Rhode Island, 58 Vermont

California Reporter (1960 to date): 53 California 2d, 176 California Appellate 2d

New York Supplement (1888 to date): 1 New York (1 Comstock) (reprints without N.Y.S. pagination until 1 New York 2d), 1 Appellate Division, 1 Miscellaneous, and many other now discontinued lower court reporters

North Eastern Reporter (1885 to date): 112 Illinois, 284 Illinois Appellate, 102 Indiana, 1 Indiana Appellate, 139 Massachusetts, 1 Massachusetts Appeals, 99 New York, 43 Ohio State, 20 Ohio Appellate, 1 Ohio Miscellaneous

North Western Reporter (1879 to date): 1 Dakota, 51 Iowa, 41 Michigan, 1 Michigan Appeals, 26 Minnesota, 8 Nebraska, 1 North Dakota, 1 South Dakota, 46 Wisconsin

Pacific Reporter (1884 to date): 1 Arizona, 1 Arizona Appeals, 64 California, 1 California Appellate, 7 Colorado, 1 Colorado Appeals, 44 Hawaii, 1 Hawaii Appellate, 2 Idaho, 30 Kansas, 1 Kansas Appeals, 4 Montana, 17 Nevada, 3 New Mexico, 1 Oklahoma, 1 Oklahoma Criminal, 11 Oregon, 1 Oregon Appeals, 3 Utah, 2 Washington Territory, 1 Washington, 1 Washington Appellate, 3 Wyoming

South Eastern Reporter (1887 to date): 77 Georgia, 1 Georgia Appeals, 96 North Carolina, 1 North Carolina Appeals, 25 South Carolina, 82 Virginia, 1 Virginia Appeals, 29 West Virginia

South Western Reporter (1887 to date): 47 Arkansas, 1 Arkansas Appellate, 1 Indian Territory, 84 Kentucky, 8 Kentucky Law Reporter, 89 Missouri, 93 Missouri Appeals, 85 Tennessee, 16 Tennessee Appeals, 1 Tennessee Criminal Appeals, 66 Texas, 21 Texas Criminal Appeals, 1 Texas Civil Appeals

Southern Reporter (1887 to date): 80 Alabama, 1 Alabama Appellate, 22 Florida, 104 Louisiana, 39 Louisiana Annual, 9 Louisiana Appeals, 64 Mississippi

*

Appendix D

SOURCES OF FEDERAL REGULATORY AGENCY RULES, REGULATIONS AND ADJUDICATIONS [1]

---

1. Prepared by Terry L. Swanlund, Reference Librarian, Harvard Law School Library.

AGENCY	RULES AND REGULATIONS		ADJUDICATIONS, INTERPRETATIONS AND OPINIONS	
	Official	**Commercial** *	**Official**	**Commercial**
Agriculture, Department of	7, 9, 36, 48 CFR various parts		*Agriculture Decisions*	
Commodity Futures Trading Commission	17 CFR Parts 1–199	*Commodity Futures Law Reports* (CCH); *Securities Regulation and Law Report* (BNA) [L,W]; FEDSEC/CFR (LEXIS); FSEC–CFR (WESTLAW)	Available for inspection at CFTC offices, Washington, D.C.	*CFTC Administrative Reporter* (WSB); *Commodity Futures Law Reports* (CCH); FEDSEC/CFTC (LEXIS); FSEC–CFTC (WESTLAW)
Comptroller of the Currency (Department of the Treasury)	12 CFR Parts 1–199	*Federal Banking Law Reports* (CCH); BANKNG/REGS (LEXIS); FFIN–CFR (WESTLAW)	Office of the Comptroller of the Currency Interpretive Letters in *OCC Quarterly Journal* [L, W] (selected)	*Federal Banking Law Reports* (CCH); BANKNG/OCCIL (LEXIS); FFIN–OCCIL (WESTLAW)
Consumer Product Safety Commission	16 CFR Parts 1000–1799	*Consumer Product Safety Guide* (CCH); *Product Safety & Liability Reporter* (BNA); Reams & Ferguson, *Federal Consumer Protection: Laws, Rules and Regulations* (Oceana)	Advisory Opinions available for inspection at CPSC Public Reference Room, Washington, D.C.	*Consumer Product Safety Guide* (CCH) (digests)
Energy, Department of (DOE)	10 CFR Parts 200–1099	*Federal Energy Guidelines: Energy Management* (DOE/CCH); ENERGY/CFR (LEXIS); FEN–CFR	Economic Regulatory Administration Opinions and Orders and Office of Hearings and Appeals	

		(WESTLAW)	Decisions and Orders in *Federal Energy Guidelines: Energy Management* (DOE/CCH)	
Environmental Protection Agency	40 CFR Parts 1–762	*Chemical Regulation Reporter* (BNA) [L, W]; *Environment Reporter* (BNA) [L, W]; *Environmental Law Reporter* (ELI) [L, W]; ENVIRN/CFR (LEXIS); FENV–CFR (WESTLAW)	General Counsel Memoranda obtainable from EPA Library (Public Information Reference Unit), Washington, D.C.	FENV–GCM (WESTLAW)
Equal Employment Opportunity Commission	29 CFR Parts 1600–1612	*Employment Practices Guide* (CCH); LABOR/CFR (LEXIS); FLB–CFR (WESTLAW)	*Equal Employment Opportunity Commission Decisions—Federal Sector*	*Employment Practices Guide* (CCH); *Fair Employment Practices* (BNA); FLB–EEOC (WESTLAW)
Federal Aviation Administration (Department of Transportation)	14 CFR Parts 1–199	*Aviation Law Reports* (CCH) (selected)		
Federal Communications Commission	47 CFR Parts 0–199	*FCC Rulemaking Reporter* (CCH); *Radio Regulation* (Pike & Fischer); FEDCOM/CFR (LEXIS); FCOM–CFR (WESTLAW)	*Federal Communications Commission Record*	*Radio Regulation* (Pike & Fischer); FEDCOM/FCC (LEXIS); FCOM–FCC (WESTLAW)

* The latest edition of the entire CFR is available online in GENFED/CFR (LEXIS) and CFR (WESTLAW).

L,W. Publication available online in LEXIS (L) and/or WESTLAW (W).

AGENCY	RULES AND REGULATIONS		ADJUDICATIONS, INTERPRETATIONS AND OPINIONS	
	Official	**Commercial** *	**Official**	**Commercial**
Federal Deposit Insurance Corporation	12 CFR Parts 300–353	*Federal Banking Law Reports* (CCH); BANKNG/REGS (LEXIS); FFIN–CFR (WESTLAW)	FDIC Enforcement Decisions and FDIC Interpretive Letters (selectively released)	*FDIC Enforcement Decisions* (PH); BANKNG/FDICED and FDICIL (LEXIS)
Federal Election Commission	11 CFR Parts 1–9099	*Federal Election Campaign Financing Guide* (CCH)	Advisory Opinions—full text available from Public Records Office, FEC, digests in *Federal Election Commission Record*	*Federal Election Campaign Financing Guide* (CCH)
Federal Energy Regulatory Commission (Department of Energy)	18 CFR Parts 1–399	*Federal Energy Guidelines: FERC Statutes & Regulations* (FERC/CCH); *Utilities Law Reports* (CCH); ENERGY/CFR (LEXIS); FEN–CFR (WESTLAW)	*Federal Energy Guidelines: FERC Reports*	*Utilities Law Reports* (CCH); ENERGY/FERC (LEXIS); FEN–FERC and FEN–FERCGC (WESTLAW)
Federal Home Loan Bank Board	12 CFR Parts 500–589	*BNA's Banking Report* [L, W]; *Federal Banking Law Reports* (CCH); BANKNG/REGS (LEXIS); FFIN–CFR (WESTLAW)	General Counsel Opinions (no official publication)	*Federal Banking Law Reports* (CCH); BANKNG/FHLBB (LEXIS); FFIN–FHLBB (WESTLAW)
Federal Labor Relations Authority	5 CFR Parts 2411–2430	*Federal Labor Relations Reporter* (LRP); FLB–CFR (WESTLAW)	*Decisions of the Federal Labor Relations Authority*	*Federal Labor Relations Reporter* (LRP); *Government Employee Relations Report* (BNA) (digests); LABOR/FLRA (LEXIS); FLB–FLRA and

				FLB–FLRAAJ (WESTLAW)
Federal Reserve System Board of Governors	12 CFR Parts 220–269b	*Federal Banking Law Reports* (CCH); BANKNG/REGS (LEXIS)	CFR; *Federal Reserve Bulletin; Federal Reserve Regulatory Service*	*Federal Banking Law Reports* (CCH)
Federal Service Impasses Panel (Federal Labor Relations Authority)	5 CFR Parts 2470–2472	FLB–CFR (WESTLAW)	Federal Service Impasses Panel Releases	LABOR/FSIP (LEXIS); FLB–FSIP (WESTLAW)
Federal Trade Commission	16 CFR Parts 0–999	*Trade Regulation Reports* (CCH); TRADE/CFR (LEXIS); FABR–CFR (WESTLAW)	*Federal Trade Commission Decisions*	*Trade Regulation Reports* (CCH); TRADE/FTC (LEXIS); FABR–FTC (WESTLAW)
Food and Drug Administration (Department of Health and Human Services)	21 CFR Parts 1–1299	*Food Drug Cosmetic Law Reports* (CCH) (selected); *Medical Devices Reporter* (CCH) (selected)	FDA Orders in *Federal Register*	*Food Drug Cosmetic Law Reports* (CCH) (selected FDA orders); *Medical Devices Reporter* (CCH) (summaries of selected FDA regulatory letters)
Health Care Financing Administration (Department of Health and Human Services)	42 CFR Parts 400–498	*Medicare and Medicaid Guide* (CCH)		
Immigration and Naturalization Service, Board of Immigration Appeals (Department of Justice)	8 CFR Parts 1–499	*Federal Immigration Law Reporter* (WSB); *Immigration Law and Procedure Reporter* (Bender); *Interpreter*	*Administrative Decisions under Immigration and Nationality Laws of the United States*	*Federal Immigration Law Reporter* (WSB) (summaries and selected full texts); *Immigration Law and Procedure*

* The latest edition of the entire CFR is available online in GENFED/CFR (LEXIS) and CFR (WESTLAW).

L,W. Publication available online in LEXIS (L) and/or WESTLAW (W).

AGENCY	RULES AND REGULATIONS		ADJUDICATIONS, INTERPRETATIONS AND OPINIONS	
	Official	**Commercial** *	**Official**	**Commercial**
		Releases (Fed.Pub.) (selected); FIM–CFR (WESTLAW)		*Reporter* (Bender) (selected full texts); *Hein's Interim Decisions Service; Interpreter Releases* (Fed. Pub.) (selected digests)
Interior Board of Indian Appeals (Department of the Interior)	43 CFR Part 4.310–4.340		*Decisions of the Interior Board of Indian Appeals*	*Indian Law Reporter* (headnotes and selected full texts); IBIA (WESTLAW)
Interior, Department of	25, 41, 43, 48 CFR various parts		*Decisions of the Department of the Interior*	
Internal Revenue Service (Department of the Treasury)	26 CFR Parts 1–602	*Federal Tax Coordinator (RIA)* [L]; *Federal Taxes* (PH); *Standard Federal Tax Reports* (CCH); FEDTAX/TXLAWS, OMNI and REGS (LEXIS); FTX–CFR (WESTLAW)	Actions on Decisions; General Counsel Memoranda; Private Letter Rulings; Revenue Rulings (in *Internal Revenue Bulletin/ Cumulative Bulletin* [L, W]); Technical Advice Memoranda; Technical Memoranda	*IRS Letter Rulings Reports* (CCH); *IRS Positions* (CCH) (AODs, GCMs and TMs); *Pension Reporter* (BNA) [L, W] (selected GCMs, PLRs and TAMs); FEDTAX (LEXIS) (all documents); FTX (WESTLAW) (all documents)
International Trade Commission	19 CFR Parts 200–212	*International Trade Reporter (BNA)* [L, W]	U.S. International Trade Commission Investigations	*United States Patents Quarterly* (BNA) (selected full texts); ITRADE/ITC (LEXIS); FINT–ITC (WESTLAW)

Interstate Commerce Commission	49 CFR Parts 1000–1332	*Federal Carriers Reports* (CCH); TRANS/CFR (LEXIS)	*Interstate Commerce Commission Reports*	*Federal Carriers Reports* (CCH) (digests and selected full texts); TRANS/ICC (LEXIS)
Justice, Department of	28 CFR Parts 0–71		*Opinions of the Attorney General of the United States; Opinions of the Office of Legal Counsel of the U.S. Department of Justice;* Antitrust Division Business Review Letters	GENFED/USAG (LEXIS) (Attorney General Opinions); USAG (Attorney General and OLC Opinions) and FABR–BRL (Business Review Letters) (WESTLAW)
Labor Department Office of Administrative Law Judges	29 CFR Part 18	LABOR/CFR (LEXIS); FLB–CFR (WESTLAW)	*Decisions of the Office of Administrative Law Judges and Office of Administrative Appeals*	
Merit Systems Protection Board	5 CFR Parts 1200–1261	*Federal Merit Systems Reporter* (LRP); FLB–CFR (WESTLAW)	*Decisions of the United States Merit Systems Protection Board*	*Federal Merit Systems Reporter* (LRP); *U.S. Merit Systems Protection Board Reporter* (West); LABOR/MSPB (LEXIS); FLB–MSPB and FLB–MSPBG (WESTLAW)
Mine Safety and Health Administration	30 CFR Parts 1–199	*Employment Safety and Health Guide* (CCH)	*Federal Mine Safety and Health Review*	*Employment Safety and Health Guide* (CCH);

* The latest edition of the entire CFR is available online in GENFED/CFR (LEXIS) and CFR (WESTLAW).

L,W. Publication available online in LEXIS (L) and/or WESTLAW (W).

AGENCY	RULES AND REGULATIONS		ADJUDICATIONS, INTERPRETATIONS AND OPINIONS	
	Official	**Commercial ***	**Official**	**Commercial**
(Department of Labor) and Federal Mine Safety and Health Review Commission	29 CFR Parts 2700–2706	(selected); *Mine Safety and Health Reporter* (BNA)	*Commission Decisions*	*Mine Safety and Health Reporter* (BNA)
National Labor Relations Board	29 CFR Parts 100–103	*Labor Law Reports* (CCH); *Labor Relations Reporter: Labor Relations Expediter* (BNA); FLB–CFR (WESTLAW)	*Decisions and Orders of the National Labor Relations Board*	*Labor Law Reports* (CCH); *Labor Relations Reference Manual* (BNA) (digests and full texts); LABOR/NLRB (LEXIS); FLB–NLRB (WESTLAW)
National Transportation Safety Board	49 CFR Parts 800–850	*Aviation Law Reports* (CCH); TRANS/CFR (LEXIS)	*National Transportation Safety Board Decisions*	*Aviation Law Reports* (CCH) (selected); TRANS/NTSB (LEXIS); FTRAN–NTSB (WESTLAW)
Nuclear Regulatory Commission	10 CFR Parts 0–199	*Nuclear Regulation Reports* (CCH); ENERGY/CFR (LEXIS); FEN–CFR (WESTLAW)	*Nuclear Regulatory Commission Issuances*	*Nuclear Regulation Reports* (CCH); ENERGY/NRC (LEXIS); FEN–NRC (issuances) and FEN–NRCEA (summaries and records of NRC Office of Enforcement Actions) (WESTLAW)
Occupational Safety and Health Administration (Department of Labor) and Occupational Safety and Health Review	29 CFR Parts 1900–1990 29 CFR Parts 2200–	*Employment Safety and Health Guide* (CCH); *Noise Regulation Reporter* (BNA) (selected); *Occupational Safety &*	*Occupational Safety and Health Review Commission Reports*	*Occupational Safety & Health Cases* (BNA); *Occupational Safety and Health Decisions* (CCH) LABOR/OSHRC (LEXIS);

Commission	2400	*Health Reporter* (BNA); LABOR/CFR (LEXIS); FLB–CFR (WESTLAW)		FLB–OSRC (WESTLAW)
Patent and Trademark Office (Department of Commerce)	37 CFR Parts 1–150	PATCOP/CFR (LEXIS); FIP–CFR (WESTLAW)	Decisions of the Commissioner of Patents and Trademarks; Decisions of the Board of Patent Appeals and Interferences; Trademark Trial and Appeal Board Decisions	*United States Patents Quarterly* (BNA); PATCOP/PTO, COMMR, PATAPP and TTAB (LEXIS); FIP–PTO (WESTLAW)
Pension and Welfare Benefits Administration (Department of Labor)	29 CFR Parts 2509–2580	*Pension Plan Guide* (CCH); LABOR/CFR (LEXIS); FLB–CFR (WESTLAW)	Pension and Welfare Benefits Administration (ERISA) Opinion Letters	*Pension Plan Guide* (CCH) (selected summaries); LABOR/ERISA and FEDTAX/ERISA (LEXIS); FLB–ERISA (WESTLAW)
Pension Benefit Guaranty Corporation	29 CFR Parts 2601–2677	*Pension Plan Guide* (CCH); LABOR/CFR (LEXIS); FLB–CFR (WESTLAW)	*Pension Benefit Guaranty Corporation Opinion Letters*	*Pension Plan Guide* (CCH) (selected summaries); LABOR/PBGC and FEDTAX/PBGC (LEXIS); FLB–PBGC (WESTLAW)
Securities and Exchange Commission	17 CFR Parts 200–301	*Federal Securities Law Reports (CCH); Federal Securities Laws* (CCH); *Securities Regulation* (PH); FEDSEC/CFR (LEXIS); FSEC–CFR (WESTLAW)	*SEC Docket* (SEC/CCH) W (formerly *Securities and Exchange Commission Decisions and Reports)*; Interpretive Releases (in *Federal Register*); No–	*Federal Securities Law Reports* (CCH) (Adjudicative Decisions, Interpretive Releases, selected No–Action Letters); *Securities*

* The latest edition of the entire CFR is available online in GENFED/CFR (LEXIS) and CFR (WESTLAW).

L,W. Publication available online in LEXIS (L) and/or WESTLAW (W).

AGENCY	RULES AND REGULATIONS		ADJUDICATIONS, INTERPRETATIONS AND OPINIONS	
	Official	Commercial *	Official	Commercial
			Action Letters	*Regulation* (PH) (Adjudicative Decisions, selected full texts or digests; No–Action Letters, selected summaries); FEDSEC/SECREL and NOACT (LEXIS); FSEC–DKT, FSEC–DEC, FSEC–IR, and FSEC–NAL (WESTLAW)
Small Business Administration	13 CFR Parts 101–144	FGC–CFR (WESTLAW)	SBA Office of Hearings and Appeals Decisions (SBA Public Files)	FGC–SBA (WESTLAW)
Social Security Administration (Department of Health and Human Services)	20 CFR Parts 400–499	*Medicare and Medicaid Guide* (CCH); *Unemployment Insurance Reports* (CCH); *West's Social Security Reporting Service: Regulations*; LABOR/CFR (LEXIS); FLB–CFR (WESTLAW)	*Social Security Rulings*	*Unemployment Insurance Reports* (CCH) (selected summaries); *West's Social Security Reporting Service: Rulings*

* The latest edition of the entire CFR is available online in GENFED/CFR (LEXIS) and CFR (WESTLAW).

L,W. Publication available online in LEXIS (L) and/or WESTLAW (W).

Appendix E

SUBJECT GUIDE TO SELECTED LOOSELEAF SERVICES

Abbreviation	*Publisher*
BNA	Bureau of National Affairs, Inc.
Bender	Matthew Bender & Co.
CCH	Commerce Clearing House, Inc.
FPAS	Federal Programs Advisory Service
FT	Foreign Tax Law Publishers, Inc.
Hawkins	Hawkins Publishing Co.
IBFD	International Bureau of Fiscal Documentation
LCP	Lawyers Co-operative Publishing Co.
L–M	Legal–Medical Studies, Inc.
PH	Prentice Hall Information Services
P & F	Pike & Fischer, Inc.
RIA	Research Institute of America, Inc.
Stephens	Mark A. Stephens, Ltd.
Thompson	Thompson Publishing Group
UPA	University Publications of America
WG & L	Warren, Gorham & Lamont, Inc.
WSB	Washington Service Bureau, Inc.

Accounting

Accountancy Law Reports (CCH)

Cost Accounting Standards Guide (CCH)

Federal Audit Guides (CCH)

Admiralty

Benefits Review Board Service: Longshore Reporter (Bender)
Federal Maritime Commission Service (Hawkins)
Marine Operations Reporter (Marine Advisory Services, Inc.)
Shipping Regulation (P & F)

Advertising

Advertising Compliance Service (Greenwood Press)
National Insurance Advertising Regulation Service (NIARS Corp.)

Affirmative action, see Employment practices

Alcoholic beverages

Liquor Control Law Reports (CCH)

American Indians, see Native Americans

Antitrust, see Trade regulation

Attorneys, see Lawyers and legal ethics

Aviation

Aviation Law Reports (CCH)
Aviation Regulatory Digest Service (Hawkins)

Banking

BNA's Banking Report (BNA)
Control of Banking (PH)
Federal Banking Law Reports (CCH)

Bankruptcy

Bankruptcy Law Reports (CCH)
Bankruptcy Service, Lawyers Edition (LCP)

Carriers

Federal Carriers Reports (CCH)
Motor Carrier–Freight Forwarder Service (Hawkins)
Rail Carrier Service (Hawkins)
State Motor Carrier Guide (CCH)

Charities and foundations

Charitable Giving and Solicitation (PH)
Exempt Organizations Reports (CCH)
Tax–Exempt Organizations (PH)

Chemical and toxic substances, see Environment

Commercial law

Business Strategies (CCH)
Canadian Commercial Law Guide (CCH)
Consumer and Commercial Credit (PH)
Consumer Credit Guide (CCH)
RICO Business Disputes Guide (CCH)
Secured Transactions Guide (CCH)

Communications

Media Law Reporter (BNA)
Radio Regulation (P & F)

Compensation and benefits. See also Employment practices; Labor relations; Pensions and profit sharing

Canadian Employment Benefits and Pension Guide (CCH)
Compensation (BNA)
Employee Benefits Cases (BNA)
Employee Benefits Compliance Coordinator (RIA)
Executive Compensation (PH)
Executive Compensation & Taxation Coordinator (RIA)
Fringe Benefits Tax Guide (CCH)
Payroll Guide (PH)
Payroll Management Guide (CCH)
Wages and Hours (BNA)
Wage–Hour Guide (PH)

Consumer products, see Products liability and safety

Copyright, see Intellectual property

Corporations

Business Franchise Guide (CCH)
Canada Corporations Law Reports (CCH)
Closely Held Business (PH)
Corporate Acquisitions, Mergers and Divestitures (PH)
Corporate Capital Transactions Coordinator (RIA)
Corporate Practice Series (BNA)
Corporate Secretary's Guide (CCH)
Corporation (PH)
Professional Corporations Handbook (CCH)

Tax Service for Corporate Acquisitions and Dispositions of Businesses (Stephens)

Criminal law

Criminal Law Reporter (BNA)

Education

Education for the Handicapped Law Report (CRR Publishing Co.)

Elections

Federal Election Campaign Financing Guide (CCH)

Employment practices

Affirmative Action Compliance Manual for Federal Contractors (BNA)

Employment Practices Guide (CCH)

Employers' Immigration Compliance Guide (Bender)

Fair Employment Practices (BNA)

Fair Labor Standards Handbook for States, Local Governments and Schools (Thompson)

Termination of Employment (PH)

Energy

Energy Management and Federal Energy Guidelines (CCH)

Energy Resources Tax Reports (CCH)

Energy Users Report (BNA)

Federal Taxes: Oil and Gas/Natural Resources (PH)

Natural Gas Policy Act Information Service (FPAS)

Natural Gas Transportation Information Service (FPAS)

Nuclear Regulation Reports (CCH)

Oil & Gas Reporter (Bender)

Utilities Law Reports (CCH)

Environment

Chemical Regulation Reporter (BNA)

Environment Reporter (BNA)

Environmental Law Reporter (Environmental Law Institute)

International Environment Reporter (BNA)

Noise Regulation Reporter (BNA)

Pollution Control Guide (CCH)

Toxics Law Reporter (BNA)

Estate and financial planning. See also Taxation, estate and gift

Canadian Estate Planning and Administration Reporter (CCH)
Estate Planning: Wills, Estates, Trusts (PH)
Estate Planning & Taxation Coordinator (RIA)
Financial and Estate Planning (CCH)
Financial Planning (PH)
Life Insurance Planning (PH)
Successful Estate Planning: Ideas & Methods (PH)

Family law

Canadian Family Law Guide (CCH)
Divorce Taxation (PH)
Family Law Reporter (BNA)
Family Law Tax Guide (CCH)
Reporter on Human Reproduction and the Law (L–M)

Food and drug

Food Drug Cosmetic Law Reports (CCH)

Foundations, see Charities and foundations

Government contracts

Federal Contracts Report (BNA)
Government Contracts Reports (CCH)

Government information

Access Reports/Freedom of Information (Monitor Publishing Co.)
Ethics in Government Reporter (WSB)

Handicapped

Education for the Handicapped Law Report (CRR Publishing Co.)
Handicapped Requirements Handbook (Thompson)

Housing

Equal Opportunity in Housing (PH)
Housing and Development Reporter (WG & L)

Immigration

Employers' Immigration Compliance Guide (Bender)
Federal Immigration Law Reporter (WSB)
Immigration Law and Procedure Reporter (Bender)
Immigration Law Service (LCP)

Insurance. See also Workers' compensation

Automobile Law Reports (CCH)

Canadian Insurance Law Reports (CCH)

Insurance Law Reports—Fire and Casualty (CCH)

Insurance Law Reports—Life, Health & Accident (CCH)

Insurance Guide (PH)

Life Insurance Planning (PH)

Intellectual property

Copyright Law Reports (CCH)

Patent, Trademark & Copyright Journal (BNA)

United States Patents Quarterly (BNA)

International trade. See also Taxation, international and foreign

Commercial Laws of the World (FT)

Common Market Reports (CCH)

Foreign Tax and Trade Briefs (Bender)

International Trade Reporter (BNA)

Labor relations. See also Compensation and benefits; Employment practices; Occupational safety and health; Personnel management

Canadian Labour Law Reports (CCH)

Collective Bargaining: Negotiations and Contracts (BNA)

Constructive Labor Report (BNA)

Employment Coordinator (RIA)

Federal Regulation of Employment Service (LCP)

Government Employee Relations Report (BNA)

Industrial Relations Guide (PH)

Labor Arbitration Awards (CCH)

Labor Arbitration Reports (BNA)

Labor Law Reports (CCH)

Labor Relations Guide (PH)

Labor Relations Week (BNA)

Labor Relations Reporter (BNA)

Public Employee Bargaining (CCH)

Union Labor Report (BNA)

Lawyers and legal ethics

ABA/BNA Lawyer's Manual on Professional Conduct (BNA)

Ethics in Government Reporter (WSB)

National Reporter on Legal Ethics and Professional Responsibility (UPA)

Reporter on the Legal Profession (L–M)

Legislation

Congressional Index (CCH)

State Legislative Reporting Service (CCH) (for each state)

Maritime law, see Admiralty

Medicine. See also Food and drug

AIDS Law & Litigation Reporter (University Publishing Group)

BioLaw (UPA)

Hospital Cost Management (PH)

Medical Devices Reporter (CCH)

Medicare and Medicaid Guide (CCH)

Military law

Military Law Reporter (Public Law Education Institute)

Motor carriers, see Carriers

Native Americans

Indian Law Reporter (American Indian Lawyer Training Program, Inc.)

Occupational safety and health

Canadian Employment Safety and Health Guide (CCH)

Employment Safety and Health Guide (CCH)

Job Safety and Health Reporter (Business Publishers, Inc.)

Labor Relations Guide with OSHA (PH)

Mine Safety and Health Reporter (BNA)

Occupational Safety & Health Reporter (BNA)

Partnerships and S corporations

Partnership & S Corporation Coordinator (RIA)

Partnership Tax Reporter (CCH)

S Corporations (PH)

S Corporations Guide (CCH)

Tax Service for "S" Corporations and their Shareholders (Stephens)

Patents, see Intellectual property

Pensions and profit sharing. See also Compensation and benefits

Canadian Employment Benefits and Pension Guide (CCH)
ERISA Update (WSB)
Individual Retirement Plans Guide (CCH)
Pension and Profit Sharing (PH)
Pension Coordinator (RIA)
Pension Plan Guide (CCH)
Pension Reporter (BNA)
Tax Service for Employee Retirement Plans (Stephens)

Personnel management

Employment and Training Reporter (BNA)
Employment Testing (UPA)
Human Resources Management (CCH)
Human Resources Management Reporter (WG & L)
Personnel Management (BNA)
Personnel Management (PH)
Public Personnel Administration (PH)

Products liability and safety

Canadian Product Safety Guide (CCH)
Consumer Product Safety Guide (CCH)
Product Safety & Liability Reporter (BNA)
Products Liability Reports (CCH)
Tobacco Products Litigation Reporter (TPLR Inc.)
Toxics Law Reporter (BNA)

Public utilities, see Energy

Rail carriers, see Carriers

Real estate

Property Taxes (PH)
Real Estate Coordinator (RIA)
Real Estate Guide (PH)
Real Estate Investment Planning (PH)
Real Estate Taxation (Thompson)

S corporations, see Partnerships and S corporations

Securities

Blue Sky Law Reports (CCH)
CFTC Administrative Reporter (WSB)
Canadian Securities Law Reports (CCH)
Capital Adjustments (PH)
Capital Changes Reporter (CCH)
Commodity Futures Law Reports (CCH)
Executive Disclosure Guide (CCH)
Federal Securities Law Reports (CCH)
Mutual Funds Guide (CCH)
New York Stock Exchange Guide (CCH)[1]
SEC Compliance (PH)
Securities Regulation and Law Report (BNA)
Securities Regulation (PH)
Stock Transfer Guide (CCH)

Social security

Social Security Law and Practice (LCP)
Unemployment Insurance Reports (CCH)

Supreme Court of the United States

U.S. Supreme Court Bulletin (CCH)
United States Law Week (BNA)

Taxation (general)

Federal Tax Coordinator 2d (RIA)
Federal Taxes (PH)
Standard Federal Tax Reports (CCH)
Tax Ideas (PH)
Tax Management (BNA)
Tax Notes (Tax Analysts)
U.S. Tax Week (Bender)

Taxation, estate and gift. See also Estate and financial planning

Estate Planning & Taxation Coordinator (RIA)
Federal Estate and Gift Tax Reports (CCH)
Federal Taxes: Estate & Gift Taxes (PH)

1. CCH also publishes guides for the following exchanges: American Stock; Boston Stock; Chicago Board Options; Coffee, Sugar and Cocoa; Midwest Stock; New York Futures; New York Mercantile; Pacific Stock; and Philadelphia Stock.

Inheritance, Estate and Gift Tax Reports (CCH)

State Inheritance Taxes (PH)

Taxation, excise

Federal Taxes: Excise Taxes (PH)

Federal Excise Tax Reports (CCH)

Taxation, international and foreign. See also International trade

African Tax Systems (IBFD)

Australian Federal Tax Reports (CCH)

British Tax Guide (CCH)

Canadian Sales Tax Reports (CCH)

Canadian Tax Reports (CCH)

Foreign Tax and Trade Briefs (Bender)

Guides to European Taxation (IBFD)

- Taxation of Patent Royalties, Dividends, Interest in Europe
- Taxation of Companies in Europe
- Taxation of Private Investment Income
- Value Added Taxation in Europe
- Taxation in European Socialist Countries

Tax Laws of the World (FT)

Tax Treaties (CCH)

Tax Treaties (PH)

Taxation in Latin America (IBFD)

Taxes and Investment in Asia and the Pacific (IBFD)

Taxes and Investment in the Middle East (IBFD)

U.S. Taxation of International Operations (PH)

Taxation, state

All–State Sales Tax Reports (CCH)

All States Tax Guide (PH)

Multistate Corporate Income Tax Guide (CCH)

Property Taxes (PH) (for each state)

Sales Taxes (PH)

State and Local Taxes (PH) (for each state)

State Income Taxes (PH) (for each state)

State Tax Guide (CCH)

State Tax Reports (CCH) (for each state)

Telecommunication, see Communications

Trade regulation

Antitrust & Trade Regulation Report (BNA)

Australian Trade Practices Reports (CCH)

Trade Regulation Reports (CCH)

Unemployment insurance, see Social security

Urban development, see Housing

Utilities, see Energy

Workers' compensation

Benefits Review Board Service: Longshore Reporter (Bender)

Black Lung Reporter (Bender)

Workers' Compensation Law Reports (CCH)

*

Name Index

References are to pages

Title Index

References are to pages

Boldface references are to illustrations

Boldface references are to illustrations

Boldface references are to illustrations

Boldface references are to illustrations

Boldface references are to illustrations

Boldface references are to illustrations

Boldface references are to illustrations

Boldface references are to illustrations

Subject Index

References are to pages

Boldface references are to illustrations

Boldface references are to illustrations

Boldface references are to illustrations

Boldface references are to illustrations

Boldface references are to illustrations

Boldface references are to illustrations

Boldface references are to illustrations

†